RENEWALS 458-4574

DATE DUE   2440

FEB 13		
APR - 3	OCT 06	
APR 13	NOV 23	
APR 2 6	MAR 5 -	
AUG 0 6	MAR 19	
	OCT 04 2006	
NOV 3 0	SEP 10 2006	
	DEC 02 2006	
OCT 09		
APR 14		
MAY 13		
SEP 16		
APR 25		

Serial Murder

The International Library of Criminology, Criminal Justice and Penology
Series Editors: Gerald Mars and David Nelken

Titles in the Series:

Serial Murder

Modern Scientific Perspectives

Edited by

Elliott Leyton

The Hebrew University of Jerusalem

With the assistance of

Linda Chafe

Memorial University of Newfoundland

Ashgate

DARTMOUTH

Aldershot • Burlington USA • Singapore • Sydney

Published by
Dartmouth Publishing Company Limited
Ashgate Publishing Limited
Gower House
Croft Road
Aldershot
Hants GU11 3HR
England

Ashgate Publishing Company
131 Main Street
Burlington
Vermont 05401
USA

Ashgate website: http://www.ashgate.com

British Library Cataloguing in Publication Data
Serial murder : modern scientific perspectives. – (The
  international library of criminology, criminal justice and
  penology)
  1. Serial murder 2. Serial murderers – Psychology
  I. Leyton, Elliott, 1939–   II. Chafe, Linda
  364.1'523

Library of Congress Catalog Card Number: 99-65075

ISBN 1 84014 452 1

Printed by WBC Book Manufacturers, Bridgend

Contents

PART IV   PSYCHIATRIC DIAGNOSIS AND THE LAW

PART V   PSYCHOLOGICAL PERSPECTIVES

PART VI   GENDER ISSUES

PART VII   POLICING CONCERNS

Acknowledgements

The editor and publishers wish to thank the following for permission to use copyright material.

American Academy of Psychiatry and the Law for the essay: Park Elliott Dietz, Robert R. Hazelwood and Janet Warren (1990), 'The Sexually Sadistic Criminal and His Offenses', *Bulletin of the American Academy of Psychiatry and Law*, **18**, pp. 163–78. Copyright © 1990 American Academy of Psychiatry and the Law. Reprinted with permission.

American Psychiatric Association for the essays: Seymour Halleck (1965), 'American Psychiatry and the Criminal: A Historical Review', *American Journal of Psychiatry*, **121**, (Supplement 9), pp. i–xxi. Copyright © 1965 American Psychiatric Association. Reprinted by permission; Foster Kennedy, Harry R. Hoffman and William H. Haines (1947), 'A Study of William Heirens', *American Journal of Psychiatry*, **104**, pp. 113–21. Copyright © 1947 American Psychiatric Association. Reprinted by permission; Robert K. Ressler, Ann Wolbert Burgess and John E. Douglas (1983), 'Rape and Rape-Murder: One Offender and Twelve Victims', *American Journal of Psychiatry*, **140**, pp. 36–40. Copyright © 1983 American Psychiatric Association. Reprinted by permission; Robert Alan Prentky, Ann Wolbert Burgess, Frances Rokous, Austin Lee, Carol Hartman, Robert Ressler and John Douglas (1989), 'The Presumptive Role of Fantasy in Serial Sexual Homicide', *American Journal of Psychiatry*, **146**, pp. 887–91. Copyright © 1989 American Psychiatric Association. Reprinted by permission.

ASTM for the essay: Park Elliott Dietz, Bruce Harry and Robert R. Hazelwood (1986), 'Detective Magazines: Pornography for the Sexual Sadist?', *Journal of Forensic Sciences*, **31**, pp. 197–211. Copyright © American Society for Testing and Materials, 100 Bar Harbor Drive, West Conshohocken, PA 19428.

Canadian Scholars' Press, Inc. for the essays: R.S. Ratner (1996), 'Ideological Homicide', in Thomas O'Reilly-Fleming (ed.), *Serial and Mass Murder: Theory, Research and Policy*, Toronto: Canadian Scholars' Press, pp. 123–32; Candice Skrapec (1996), 'The Sexual Component of Serial Murder', in Thomas O'Reilly-Fleming (ed.), *Serial and Mass Murder: Theory, Research and Policy*, Toronto: Canadian Scholars' Press, pp. 155–79.

Criminal Justice Review for the essay: Philip Jenkins (1992), 'A Murder "Wave"? Trends in American Serial Homicide 1940–1990', *Criminal Justice Review*, **17**, pp. 1–19. Copyright © 1992 Criminal Justice Review & College of Public and Urban Affairs.

Elsevier Science for the essay: Philip Jenkins (1988), 'Serial Murder in England 1940–1985', *Journal of Criminal Justice*, **16**, pp. 1–15. Copyright © 1988 Pergamon Press Plc. Reprinted with permission from Elsevier Science.

Whurr Publishers Limited for the essay: David M. Gresswell and Clive R. Hollin (1992), 'Towards a New Methodology for Making Sense of Case Material: An Illustrative Case Involving Attempted Multiple Murder', *Criminal Behaviour and Mental Health*, **2**, pp. 329–41. Copyright © 1992 Whurr Publishers Ltd.

John Wiley & Sons, Inc. for the essay: Michael J. Herkov and Monica Biernat (1997), 'Assessment of PTSD Symptoms in a Community Exposed to Serial Murder', *Journal of Clinical Psychology*, **53**, pp. 809–15. Copyright © 1997 John Wiley & Sons, Inc.

Series Preface

The International Library of Criminology, Criminal Justice and Penology, represents an important publishing initiative to bring together the most significant journal essays in contemporary criminology, criminal justice and penology. The series makes available to researchers, teachers and students an extensive range of essays which are indispensable for obtaining an overview of the latest theories and findings in this fast changing subject.

This series consists of volumes dealing with criminological schools and theories as well as with approaches to particular areas of crime, criminal justice and penology. Each volume is edited by a recognised authority who has selected twenty or so of the best journal articles in the field of their special competence and provided an informative introduction giving a summary of the field and the relevance of the articles chosen. The original pagination is retained for ease of reference.

The difficulties of keeping on top of the steadily growing literature in criminology are complicated by the many disciplines from which its theories and findings are drawn (sociology, law, sociology of law, psychology, psychiatry, philosophy and economics are the most obvious). The development of new specialisms with their own journals (policing, victimology, mediation) as well as the debates between rival schools of thought (feminist criminology, left realism, critical criminology, abolitionism etc.) make necessary overviews that offer syntheses of the state of the art. These problems are addressed by the INTERNATIONAL LIBRARY in making available for research and teaching the key essays from specialist journals.

GERALD MARS
Professor in Applied Anthropology, University of Bradford
School of Management

DAVID NELKEN
Distinguished Research Professor, Cardiff Law Schoool,
University of Wales, Cardiff

Introduction
Current Issues in the Study of Serial Murder

John-Paul Sartre cut to the bone in 'Herostratus', his prescient description of the inner life of a serial killer first translated into English in 1941, 50 years before the study of serial murder became a legitimate academic subdiscipline. In the essay that opens this volume, Sartre outlined many of the killers' traits that would only later come to be widely understood by modern scholarship – the self-absorption, the anger and desire for revenge for real or imagined slights, the pleasure in the suffering of others, the need to demonstrate their 'superiority' by taunting the authorities, the urge for lasting celebrity, and the peculiar mixture of reality and fantasy in their lives. Yet Sartre's work was foreshadowed by even earlier commentators, including the prodigal William Bolitho who challenged orthodox psychiatry as long ago as 1926 when he noted that such multiple killers were no 'deranged automata': indeed, he wrote, they were 'the worst men, not madmen' (Bolitho, 1926: 7–8).

These were but the distinguished predecessors of a field of inquiry that between the Second World War and the mid-1980s would come to be dominated almost entirely by psychiatry (as expressed most magisterially in Lunde's classic 1979 volume, *Murder and Madness*). Suddenly in the mid-1980s there was a creative explosion in criminal justice studies, and seemingly out of nowhere (yet echoing the public fear that was widespread at the time) came a series of major books in a single decade: Levin and Fox's *Mass Murder* in 1985, Leyton's *Compulsive Killers* in 1986 (entitled *Hunting Humans* in its various British and Canadian editions), Cameron and Frazer's *The Lust To Kill* in 1987, Holmes and DeBurger's *Serial Murder* in 1988, Egger's *Serial Murder* in 1990, Hickey's *Serial Murderers and Their Victims* in 1991, Black's *The Aesthetics of Murder* in 1991, Jenkins' *Using Murder* and Canter's *Criminal Shadows* in 1994. Since then, the field has continued to expand, with many significant essays from various social and psychological perspectives that are reprinted in this volume, as well as books such as Giannangelo's *The Psychopathology of Serial Murder* in 1996, Egger's *The Killers Among Us* in 1998, Duclos' *The Werewolf Complex*, translated into English in 1998 and Skrapec's dissertation, *Serial Murder: Motive and Meaning* in 1997.

This work has, on the whole, been relatively free of the smothering ideological rigidity, factionalization and discourtesy that characterize so much of modern criminology. Merton (1972: 9 ff.) described this unfortunate and anti-scientific process as one in which feuding factions coalesce around a single perspective: each faction 'develops highly selective perceptions of what is going on in the other'; grows 'less and less motivated to examine the ideas of the other'; and devotes its time to scanning the other's 'writings just enough to find ammunition for new fusillades'. In such an antagonistic milieu, character assassination often takes priority over collegial and scientific debate: this prompted Downes and Rock (1988: 1–2) to complain that such 'factious, partisan, and combative' writing leaves the defenceless reader ('bombarded by magisterial claims and criticisms') 'giddy, defeated, or prematurely committed'.

For the most part, the study of serial murder has avoided this empty and self-destructive behaviour, and senior scholars with profound differences tend merely to ignore one another's writings as if willing them not to have happened. Yet, at its worst, the field shares some of the extravagant flaws of criminology, sometimes making absurd claims and shoplifting ideas more or less at will. Among the premier claims-makers, for example, are those – both police and academics – who insist that they and they alone were the 'first' to recognize the phenomenon, or even the first to use the term 'serial murder'. However, there is nothing new in the use of the term: writing over 60 years ago, H. Russell Wakefield spoke of the French multiple murderer, Landru, 'as the arch-type of serial butchers', and described his motivation with impressive modernity:

> Landru's consistent failure to succeed in his chosen career, the realisation that that failure was invariably due to the venom of his dupes, the knowledge that the horrors of life-long exile would be the consequence of one more failure, turned Landru into a serial-murderer. (Wakefield, 1936: 17–19)

Also rampant in the field is the unscholarly and discourteous practice of 'borrowing' ideas and redeploying them as one's own without pausing to acknowledge their source. This defect is especially (but by no means exclusively) to be found in the less widely read journals, where the professional need for publication and the personal need for status sometimes results in claims that an old and well published idea is the author's unique invention. Such dispiriting matters aside, the field is otherwise alive and vigorous and has made real advances since the mid-1980s.

Definitions

In their initial classificatory scheme, Levin and Fox (1985) preferred the use of the general term, mass murder, to refer to all forms of interpersonal multiple killing – including serial, mass and familicidal homicides. A few years later, however, at an international conference on serial murder at the University of Windsor, they publicly capitulated to what had, by then, become common usage – formalizing the distinctions between serial (killing over time), mass (killing in one brief explosion), and familicidal (the mass killing of family members) murders. In 1986 Leyton unnecessarily restricted his own definition by *motive*, confining himself to those who killed only for personal satisfaction, to the kind of 'joy murders' the Germans called *Lustmord*.

In 1991 Hickey expanded this narrow definition of serial murder into what is now most widely accepted: it includes anyone who kills in sequence over time, *regardless of motive* – that is, simply 'all offenders who through premeditation killed three or more victims over a period of days, weeks, months, or years' (Hickey, 1991: 7). Hickey's definition has many advantages, not least of which is its flexibility and its consequent ability to incorporate many female serial killers (who are more likely to kill for financial gain than for obvious sexual gratification). However, opinions still differ on the minimum number of victims: some accept as little as two (understanding, like Canter, that the number of many serial killers' victims are reduced if they are speedily arrested), others insisting on at least five, with the majority of scholars settling on a minimum of two victims. Egger's recent definition is perhaps the most comprehensive: for him, the defining qualities of serial murder are simply when 'one or more individuals (in many cases, males) commit(s) a second murder'. He adds that: 'there is generally no prior relationship between victim and attacker'; that the following murders may have no relation in time or place to the initial murder; that 'the motive is not for material gain [but rather] the murderer's desire to have power or dominance over his victims'; and that 'victims may have symbolic value for the murderer and/or are perceived to be prestigeless and in most instances are unable to defend themselves or alert others to their plight'. Egger further maintains that such victims are typically 'vagrants, the homeless, prostitutes, migrant workers, homosexuals, missing children, single women (out by themselves), elderly women, college students, and hospital patients' (Egger, 1998: 5–6).

The Great Debates

Socio-historical Analysis

Perhaps the central problem in a longitudinal analysis of serial murder's origins is the quality and depth of pre-twentieth-century data. Although certain nations – primarily England, France and Japan – have had well developed bureaucracies collecting social data for many centuries, they are relatively unusual and, even there, we cannot be certain about the reliability of the data – although the historian Capp insists that 'mass murder was unlikely to escape detection' in Britain (Capp, 1996: 22).

What we do seem to know is that while there may have been a large number of multiple murders perpetrated primarily for economic gain (such as the infamous Sawney Bean family which preyed on travellers in fifteenth-century Scotland: cf. Leyton, 1986: 269), there had been very few substantiated cases of what the Germans call *Lustmord* (joy murder) until the close of the eighteenth century. In his commentary on seventeenth-century England, for example, Capp emphasizes that the multiple murder cases 'do not correspond exactly to modern equivalents', and 'none appears to have been motivated by perverted sexual drives' (Capp, 1996: 26). Indeed, the two best known archaic cases are both European paedophilic aristocrats from the fifteenth century: the French Baron Gilles de Rais – one of the wealthiest men in the world and a companion-at-arms with Joan of Arc – is believed to have tortured, raped and murdered hundreds of peasant boys; while the Hungarian Countess Elizabeth Bathory is believed to have tortured, murdered and drunk the blood of several hundred girls and young women (Hickey, 1991: 23). Nevertheless, some doubt has recently been cast on the authenticity of even these cases and it is not clear, for example, if de Rais' confession – which was extorted under torture – is valid.

In any case, only one commentator has so far constructed a sociohistorical theory of the development of *Lustmord*-style serial murder. Leyton's *Hunting Humans* (1986: 269) argued that it was the most threatened class in each historical epoch that produced serial killers; 'the pre-industrial multiple killer was an aristocrat who preyed on "his" [increasingly rebellious] peasants; that the industrial era produced a new kind of killer, most commonly a new bourgeois (doctors, clerks, teachers, functionaries of the emerging industrial order) who preyed upon prostitutes, homeless boys, and housemaids [who defied the emerging puritanical ethos]; and that in the mature industrial era, he is most often a failed bourgeois' who stalks both prostitutes and middle-class victims such as university women. Jenkins, writing in the journal *Crime, Law and Social Change*, acknowledges Leyton's attempt to explain the increase in modern multiple murder 'in terms of the dehumanization and alienation attendant upon modern mass society', but described the project as 'perhaps excessively' ambitious. Certainly the very paucity of available data on this period so far mitigates against any reliable confirmation or rejection of this approach.

Gender-based Criticism

The essential argument of radical feminist thought has been an extravagant one, that serial murder is little more than a male-approved 'systematic execution of women', all part of a misogynistic 'worldwide conspiracy for the mass extermination of women' (T. McKenzie, pers comm). The central case was made by Cameron and Frazer in their influential volume *The Lust To Kill: A Feminist Investigation of Sexual Murder*. Here they argued that male-dominated science has consciously and inaccurately portrayed the sex murderer as somehow defective, as 'deviant from male sexuality' (that is, as biologically or psychologically deficient, say, or warped by a violent culture) when, in fact, such killers were male heroes 'at the centre of literary and philosophical celebration'. Arguing from an ideological rather than empirical base, it seemed apparent to Cameron and Frazer that male violence was the mere acting out of the iron 'law of misogyny', in which women were seen as mere objects to be consumed by men. Thus not only did they argue that sex murderers were *always* male and that 'there has never been a female Peter Sutcliffe' (the 'Yorkshire Ripper'), but they also claimed that sexual murder was the *essence of maleness* and masculinity, and that the murder of women for sexual pleasure was the natural expression of male identity (Cameron and Frazer, 1987: 1, 166–68).

These provocative claims were severely tested by Hickey's (1991) data which demonstrated that, far from being non-existent, females constituted some 17 per cent of serial killers. Moreover, Hickey noted that the idea of serial murder as a 'war on women' did not repay close scrutiny since a very substantial minority of the victims were men: while more than one-third of male serial killers preyed exclusively on women, just under a half killed both males and females, and a fifth killed only males (Hickey, 1991: 143). He did find that the *motives* of female serial killers seemed much more likely to involve material or social gain (women murdering family members, in order, for example, to collect life insurance) than the crude sexuality of male killers: still, the more subtle nature of female sexuality makes it more difficult to confirm even this assertion (ibid., 107ff.). This theme of female sexuality was taken up by Candice Skrapec in the 1996 essay reprinted as Chapter 26 of this volume: she asked us to consider the possibility that, since a significant minority of serial killers was female, a deformed sexuality might not be entirely a masculine preserve. She went on to emphasize that if male perversions 'tend to be more overtly sexual', female sexual perversions 'are manifestly more subtle' than those of the male, and involve 'symbolic acts centred on emotional dramas of abandonment, separation and loss'. Moreover, she adds, 'these differences serve to mask the more substantive underlying [and unexplored] similarities between male and female multiple murderers (this volume: 528).

In *Using Murder*, Jenkins explained the fundamentally *political* nature of radical feminist theory, noting that it 'places the blame for the offense firmly on masculine characteristics' and 'the structure of a male-dominated society', thereby transforming the fear of serial murder into an 'ideological weapon' against patriarchal society (Jenkins, 1994: 143–44). He observed that far from patriarchal society constituting a kind of unilateral war on women, white women, for example, were only one-third as likely as men to fall victim to a homicide. Nevertheless, Jenkins concluded that if the feminist case on serial murder was lacking in 'scholarly merit', the theories have still played an important social role in sensitizing the public to the very real oppression of women in patriarchal societies (ibid., 156–57). Julie Cluff and her colleagues (Chapter 27) expanded on this case in their essay reprinted in this volume, and noted that any 'improvement' in the quality of radical feminist analysis must begin with the serious examination of the female serial killer (this volume: 547–48).

Statistical Frequency

One of the great debates in serial murder studies concerns the actual frequency of occurrence of such killers, and the number of victims they might claim worldwide. Scholarly opinion has been sharply divided on the questions of whether such killers are in fact statistically rare and whether or not some countries – such as the USA or the UK – produce disproportionately large numbers of these offenders. It is true that the greatest number of *reported* cases come from the USA, but it is by no means clear if this is a function of their much higher overall homicide rate, their very large population or the existence of a journalism industry devoted to publicizing such murders. Indeed, Egger's earlier comments still apply: the actual extent and the prevalence of serial murder 'is as yet unknown' (Egger, 1990: 29). Moreover, in the continuing absence of truly reliable international data, precisely how countries' rates compare with each other remains unresolved, and our ability to construct meaningful explanations is correspondingly impaired.

The earliest commentators in the mid-1980s speculated that the number of serial killers was very high. Levin and Fox initially hypothesized that the US figures had been 'grossly underestimated' and suggested that 'many of the more than five thousand unsolved homicides' in the USA each year might be the work of 'a few very effective killers' (Levin and Fox, 1985: 186). In a similar vein, Leyton (1986) claimed there had been a 'remarkable increase' in US multiple murders since the mid-1960s, and Holmes and DeBurger (1988) guessed that between 3500 and 5000 people might be murdered by serial killers each year in the USA alone. Hickey, whose data have proved to be the most reliable to date, showed that between 1795 and 1988, 34 women and 169 men in the USA were responsible for approximately 2000 homicides. He also noted a 'ten-fold increase in the number of cases during the past 20 years in comparison to the previous 174 years' and suggested that '35–100 [killers] may be active in a given year (Hickey, 1991: 75, 18–19). In 1996, Canter *et al.* (Chapter 11) published their preliminary analysis of the 'Missen Corpus' which is certainly the most ambitious international survey to date: their data from more than 30 countries elicited 3532 serial killers between 1860 and the present, and showed an increase in the production of serial killers in the fourth quarter of the twentieth century that paralleled the overall increase in homicide rates that took place in that same period. The majority (2617) of these killers came from the USA, but Canter and his colleagues identified 164 in the UK, 144 in France, and 165 in Germany – and they estimated that as many as five serial killers were 'active' each year in the three European nations (this volume: 212–13).

This estimate conflicts fundamentally with Greswell and Hollin's review (reprinted as Chapter 12 of this volume), which found 'little empirical support' for the idea of such a dramatic postwar increase, at least in Britain (this volume: 228). It also conflicts with Jenkins' more complex argument: Jenkins found serial murder to occur occasionally in England and Wales between 1880 and 1990 and to be 'common' between 1919 and the 1940s in many industrial nations such as France and Germany. In the USA, the history of serial murder fell into three periods: a rather high rate until 1940, when there were at least 24 'extreme' serial killers who murdered a minimum of ten; 'a time of relative tranquility in the mid-century'; and a renewed 'murder wave' that has continued from the mid-1960s to the present. Thus the increase of serial killing since 1965 in the USA was not 'a wholly new phenomenon', but rather 'a return to earlier historical patterns' (Jenkins, 1994: 40, 49, 53). Moreover, Jenkins argues, even the idea of American 'uniqueness' may be exaggerated: the total number of serial killers may be higher in the USA simply because the overall homicide rate is so much higher, and in both the USA and the UK the *proportion* of all murders that are serial murders hovers around 1 per cent. He even goes so far as to speculate that tighter libel laws in the UK make it more difficult for the media to attribute additional murders to killers who have been convicted 'only' of one or two, and that official British statistics might therefore arbitrarily record fewer serial killers than actually exist.

Egger was clearly right: scholarship has so far provided 'no decisive answers', and the issue remains quite unresolved (Egger, 1998: 59–60). This in turn raises the profound ethical challenge noted by Kiger: without truly reliable international statistics we not only 'will be unable to develop informed typologies, theories and policy decisions', but we also 'run the risk of creating a social problem, the magnitude of which may be greatly exaggerated' (Kiger, 1990: 36).

Psychiatric Origins of the Impulse

Another central debate in the field concerns the psychiatric sciences' common claim that these killers were victims of a (usually vaguely defined) mental illness. In response to this, the social sciences tended to argue that the killers' motives were 'neither insane nor random but buried deeply in the social order, part of a continuously evolving social process' (Leyton, 1989: 329–30). Levin and Fox also severely criticized what they called 'the psychiatric mistake': they argued that psychiatric analyses were bedevilled by unwarranted generalizations and that their validity was restricted to an unrepresentative handful of cases. Moreover, the psychiatric focus on the indicators of troubled childhoods tended to produce mere lists of symptoms – such as bedwetting, fire-setting, and cruelty to animals – rather than generate explanatory discussions of cause (Levin and Fox, 1985: 24, 26–27, 31). Yet much of this argument verges on the semantic, and most psychiatrists and psychologists have recently shifted their attention away from mental illness and the essentially *legal* category of 'insanity', aware, as they often are, of the criticism (amply illustrated by the three essays on the 'Hillside Strangler' case reprinted as Chapters 19, 20 and 21 of this volume) by distinguished psychiatrist Willard Gaylin that psychiatric diagnoses can be 'trivial, ephemeral, descriptive, and meaningless' (Gaylin, 1983: 249).

The landmark in psychiatric studies of serial murder remains Lunde's 1975 classic, *Murder and Madness*, which concludes that such killers 'are almost always insane'. Lunde hypothesized that many of these killers are the victims of a hostile paranoid schizophrenia characterized by hallucinations, 'delusions of grandiosity or persecution, [and] bizarre religious ideas' and caused by a combination of 'genetic, metabolic, and psychological' factors. Lunde thought many of the others were sexual sadists who, early in life, fused their 'sexual and violent aggressive impulses', and who therefore could only achieve sexual fulfilment through 'torture and/or killing and mutilation' (Lunde, 1975: 48–56).

Orthodox psychiatry continues to produce provocative but inconclusive case studies. Abrahamsen, for example, suggests that the 'Son of Sam' was the victim of a 'death wish' which he turned 'directly against others' by killing, and 'indirectly against himself' by allegedly ensuring that he would be captured and punished. He postulates that the 'Son of Sam's' rage developed after discovering that he had been rejected by his natural parents and put out for adoption: his vengeful killing spree, according to the psychiatrist's psychoanalytic analysis, 'was rooted in his fantasies about killing his mother and half sister' (Abrahamsen, 1985: 201, 205).

Perhaps the most widely promulgated concept today is that of *psychopathy* (sometimes called sociopathy, or antisocial personality disorder), which describes a remorseless and unfeeling personality that cannot respond to the humanity in other people. Hare and his colleagues, among others, have written extensively of the 'common core of attributes' of psychopathy. These include 'pathological lying', 'impulsivity', 'a lack of remorse, guilt and shame; [and an] inability to experience empathy or concern for others' (Hare, nd: 95–96). The ancient nature–nurture controversy continually resurfaces around this notion of psychopathy, some scholars arguing that such personalities are 'born that way', and others insisting that the disorder is created – most commonly by severe abuse in childhood.

Giannangelo's 1996 volume, *The Psychopathology of Serial Murder*, tries to take a balanced approach and suggests that a history of 'physical, sexual, or mental abuse' may be the most important trait shared by serial killers. As a result of their alleged abuse in childhood (despite its plausibility to the modern mind, no firm data have yet established this hypothesis), serial killers have developed 'a pervasive lost sense of self and intimacy, an inadequacy of identity, [and a] feeling of no control'. These deficits manifest themselves in what may be 'the ultimate act of control' – the termination of the lives of many people. Attempting to straddle the various psychological and sociological perspectives, he describes serial killers as entering childhood with physiological anomalies that may be congenital or trauma-induced, experiencing a childhood filled with severe abuse, and as being driven to display, quite early on, various antisocial and/or criminal behaviours. Moreover, while offering evidence of pervasive sexual deviance, their internal life seems to be rooted in a state of fantasy (Giannangelo, 1996: 19, 48, 53).

Nevertheless, the problem remains that, if the concept of psychopathy accurately *lists* many of the personality characteristics associated with serial murderers, it does not explain why so many who have these qualities do not kill. Indeed, psychiatrist J. Reid Meloy posits that such a diagnosis is 'too descriptive, inclusive, criminally based, and socioeconomically skewed to be of much clinical or research use' (Meloy, 1988: 6). Psychologist David Canter also considers 'psychopath and sociopath' to be 'curious terms that imply a medical, pathogenic origin yet in fact describe someone for whom no obvious organic or psychotic diagnosis can be made' (Canter, 1994: 263). Egger concludes that the impossibility of predicting whether a psychopath will become a remorseless killer or a corporate executive merely reminds us 'that we in fact don't know why these people act as they do' (Egger, 1998: 28).

Social Perspectives

Social scientists have argued that the origin of the impulse to kill comes not from a mental illness, but from a socially constructed identity. Levin and Fox wrote that those who come to serial murder feel rejected, abused and marginalized by their familial and social experiences, and their murder sprees are designed somehow to cure their sense of impotence through 'controlling, manipulating, or eliminating' others. In addition, such personalities 'have failed to internalize a moral code for the treatment of others': thus they are not victims of some hypothetical mental illness, but remorseless men 'incapable of experiencing normal amounts of love and empathy' (Levin and Fox, 1985: 60–61, 63–64).

Leyton (1986) reasoned in political terms that multiple murders aimed at more than just the gratification of sexual and psychosymbolic appetites. Rather, their sprees are a kind of deformed social protest – 'deformed', because they punish the innocent, not the guilty and because their protest is on behalf of themselves, not others. A parallel argument here is his *cultural* one: like African witches, whose social function is to underline the realms of perceived Good and Evil, the serial killer reverses all social values to make 'a demonstration to the authorities' (as one killer put it) in a manner that he thinks will force them somehow to authenticate his legitimacy. Moreover, the essence of modern industrial civilization is that it dehumanizes people-as-objects and legitimizes violence as an acceptable response to frustration, allowing the killer to 'grasp the "manly" identity of pirate and avenger' (Leyton, 1986: 261, 28).

Hickey's (1991) *trauma-control model* was among the first to mount a sustained argument that serial killers are the product of severe childhood trauma, which include 'unstable home life, death of parents, divorce, corporal punishments, sexual abuse' and other disfiguring events. Thus the abused child 'feels a deep sense of anxiety, mistrust and confusion'. Many victims of child abuse search for, and find, healthy ways of treating their wounds, but those who might become serial killers never learn to cope with these trauma. They begin to act out their rage in an antisocial manner, assaulting animals, objects and people as a way of regaining the internal equilibrium that has been taken from them by those in authority (Hickey, 1991: 65–67).

Curiously, the obviously *sexual* motivation underlying serial murder remains largely unanalysed, and it was not until Skrapec's 1996 essay (see Chapter 26) that we were reminded that serial killing is about sex as much as it is about murder. Initially, perhaps, a killer attacks symbols 'of something that arouses tremendous hatred (or conflict) within him', Skrapec writes. Yet during the murder 'he did, nonetheless, experience the arousal', and this flush of sexual pleasure (rather than killing symbols of what is hated) may become a primary factor in any repetition of such acts (this volume: 528).

Typologies

While some scholars may share the privately expressed opinion of the late Professor Sir Edmund Leach that the construction of typologies is but a glorified version of butterfly collecting, the majority of those working in the area of serial murder feel that it is a necessary and important first step. Holmes and DeBurger are among the most widely accepted commentators on the types of serial murder: for them, poverty, poor neighbourhoods, unstable families and a subculture of violence cannot be the cause of serial murder since few who are exposed to such social stresses become serial killers. Thus they reject purely 'social' explanations in favour of what they call psychological variables. Their classificatory schema includes the *Visionary Type*, who responds to '"voices" or "visions" that demand that a person or category of persons be destroyed'; the *Mission-Oriented Type* who typically sees himself as 'on a "mission" to rid the world of a category of people' he despises (such as prostitutes); the *Hedonistic Type* who murders for thrills, seeking only 'pleasure or a sense of well-being'; and the *Power/Control-Oriented Type*, whose primary satisfaction comes from his complete domination over the life and death of the victim (Holmes and DeBurger, 1988: 56–59).

   Gresswell and Hollin (Chapter 12) are among those who have been critical of Holmes' and DeBurger's categories. The types' lack of mutual exclusivity makes it difficult to distinguish clearly one from another (for example, the visionary type can be distinguished from the missionary type only on the basis of the former's alleged insanity). Second, the categories are neither exhaustive nor consistent: for example, they exclude contract killers because their motivation is deemed financial and therefore 'extrinsic', while they include such practical (and therefore 'extrinsic') motives as killing for insurance or to eliminate the witness to a sexual assault. Finally, the typology does not account for killers whose motivations may change over time (perhaps changing from a primarily murderous urge to an urge to mutilate, for example, or to guaranteeing celebrity through extensive coverage in the media). Their essay calls for a more flexible typological system that would clearly 'recognize that there is a process to multiple murder' (this volume: 227).

Consensus

Despite the divergence of theoretical positions, there are a number of significant observations that are widely shared. Indeed, a real consensus exists that serial killers are damaged and limited persons, incapable of interacting as equals with others, who see their victims as somehow representing a category of person that has foiled their ambitions or ruined their lives: thus, to them, their killing spree is a form of sexualized vengeance. Whatever the reason may be – a childhood retreat from abuse, total self-absorption, or some congenital incapacity – these killers remain 'morally immune' from their killings and at best indifferent to the havoc they wreak. The latest work to emerge from the subdiscipline explores several fundamental dimensions of the killers' aetiology, motivation and thought.

   David Canter's *Criminal Shadows* explored the 'secret' inner life of serial killers in order to elucidate how they themselves can deal with their own remorseless use and abuse of other people. Focusing on the 'discernible structure' of the killers' inner lives, Canter examines the use of internal *narratives*, or autobiographies, which these killers tell themselves in the process of constructing their own identities. If everyone develops a storyline to describe his or her own life, and if this autobiography leans heavily on the civilization in which the teller lives, the narrative of the average person is nevertheless usually a 'public story of successes and failures', of family, friends and career. A serial killer has also developed a story of his life, but in his narrative all other characters are considered as consumable objects – not as persons. In other words, the personal narratives of violent offenders distort the 'themes of intimacy and appropriate use of power', deny empathy and self-respect, and consistently portray others as less than human. This means that their victims can become mere 'objects of anger or desire, vehicles to satisfy the perpetrator, possessions that are jealously guarded, targets for him to act upon'. Such an autobiography inhibits the ability of any personality to feel compassion for others, or to maintain a personal sense of self-respect (Canter, 1994: 205, 232, 240–41, 285).

In a parallel vein, Candice Skrapec's doctoral dissertation focused on the subjective experiences of five incarcerated serial murderers, and examined the 'personal construction of meaning regarding himself and his experiences' of each to reveal three 'dominant themes'. Each of these themes has been commented on by other writers (see also Leyton, 1986; Cameron and Frazer, 1987; Hickey, 1991; Canter, 1994; Ratner, Chapter 8, this volume), but are here brought together in one sustained analysis: first, a remarkable sense of 'entitlement', a sense so strong that the killers actually perceive themselves as victims, not victimizers; second, a sense of 'empowerment' that is derived from the 'total control and possession of victims'; and, third, a 'perverse quest for vitality' in their lives (Skrapec, 1997: iv). Skrapec notes that while most people wish for entitlement, empowerment and vitality in their own lives, 'these same forces are exaggerated and distorted' in serial killers. She notes that all five of the killers in her study 'experienced themselves as unloved (yet believed they were lovable) and felt rage at being powerless to get what they needed'. Moreover, 'the anger each felt at having been denied love or recognition motivated him to punish, to kill, those who had diminished him'. The killer – feeling powerless – is empowered by his total control over his victim and experiences it 'as a kind of transcendance – from helpless victim to omnipotent killer'. Finally, the subjects' obsession with death drives them to engage in high-risk behaviour, to 'feel they were alive by virtue of "being somebody"', thereby defeating death through their own experience of vitality. From the killer's point of view, then, he alters himself from 'reactive object to proactive agent – victim becoming victimizer', and what appears to others to be an offensive behaviour is to them a defensive one, as the killing becomes 'a matter of controlling the threat, controlling the source of power that threatens' him (Skrapec, 1997: 193–96). Skrapec concludes with a statement that concisely expresses the modern view that serial killing:

> . . . is more than the mere product of a particular psychopathology in which the individual is so lacking in moral faculty that, like the psychopath, he can without hesitation satisfy personal desires at the expense of the well-being of others. The narratives from all five subjects suggest instead that serial murder is more fundamentally a pathology of self process . . . [and that] pathology relates to how he develops boundaries for himself in his struggle to experience himself as someone of consequence . . . . The important fact that the majority of serial murders in the United States are perpetrated by white males may be explained by an entitlement to social esteem and personal gratification that they may feel is their due – solely by virtue of being white and male in this society – so that when an individual (white male) is denied he feels justified in punishing those who would withhold that which he feels is his basic entitlement. (Skrapec, 1997: 196–97)

Yet what is perhaps the most incisive statement of all comes from R.S. Ratner, a sociologist whose brief excursion into this field is reprinted as Chapter 8 in this collection. In 'Ideological Homicide', he offers a sweeping interpretation of serial murder that brings us closest to an understanding of the *social* origins of psychopathy. Ratner notes that historical periods of economic instability – periods of either rising or declining affluence – are also usually times when cultural controls begin to crumble, and he observes that the two waves of multiple murder in the USA (1910–30 and 1970–96) were also periods of 'massive economic destabilization'. During such periods of social upheaval, of sudden hardship *or* affluence, 'cultural codes harmonizing class goals and individual aspirations are no longer efficiently transmitted through weakened family units'. Vulnerable individuals then become more likely to seek solutions to their predicaments through a fantasy of vengeance that is 'bereft of scruples' (this volume: 166).

Thus Ratner's hypothesized socioeconomic trajectory for the lives of serial killers is as follows: general economic destabilization and cultural collapse increase the societal tension that results from social inequality; this in turn tends to destabilize all interpersonal relations, especially for the children of 'dysfunctioning families, who suffer flagrant abuse and neglect'. This abuse 'is partially eroticized by the child as the only available means of rationalizing maltreatment and maintaining some form of necessary emotional contact'. Moreover, because the abuse and pain cannot be comprehended by the victim, they must be 'anaesthetized' if the pain is to be reduced: but the resulting 'deadening of emotion' is precisely what produces sociopathy in the child. Even when the pain is thus deadened and compartmentalized, it does not disappear, and inevitably it will later be expressed: 'scripted eroticized violence' becomes the fantasy through which the powerlessness of the child is 'symbolically neutralized and avenged'. In the ultimate orgy of serial murder, Ratner concludes, victims are ritually captured, possessed, defiled, and disposed of, affording the killer 'brief vengeance against the rejecting family/society' (this volume: 165–67).

Future Research

The field has been severely constrained – almost strangled – by the absence of reliable data (whether historical, national or international), but this is a problem that is shared by students of all dimensions of violence (from domestic violence to mass murder). A further complication is that every developed nation defines homicide rather differently (for example some include attempted murder in their statistics and some include negligent homicide in vehicle accidents) so that even crude rates are not invariably comparable. Moreover, developing nations hardly keep accurate records at all, and the chance of such a country linking what many would assume to be isolated killings is very low. If the field is to reach maturity, it must have a truly reliable international database, although this would require an enormous multinational cooperative effort that is unlikely to emerge. Nevertheless, until this is accomplished, we will have no realistic grasp of the scale of the phenomenon that so engages our attention.

A second and fundamental unresolved question remains whether serial killers themselves have been, in fact, the victims of savage child abuse. The earliest commentators, especially Leyton (1986) and Levin and Fox (1985), found no substantive evidence that serial killers were more abused than other criminals or, for that matter, other non-criminals. Yet later research (discussed especially by Hickey, 1991, Ressler *et al.*, 1988, and Ratner, Chapter 8, this volume) has, without much in the way of solid statistical verification, insisted that child abuse is *the significant and recurring* factor in the personal history of these killers. Whether such claims are legitimate, or mere attempts by their imprisoned informants to exonerate themselves from responsibility, will require sustained and long-term study and, possibly, the development of new techniques for the verification of claims. However, even if the killers do prove to come from savagely abusive families, the longstanding sociological question is still begged: why do some victims of abuse react by committing their own atrocities while most resolve their rage in alternative ways – such as through alcoholism, drug addiction or the excesses of religious or political fundamentalism?

A third and equally significant question remains the still unknown role of biological/chemical/ hormonal imbalances in the construction of the murderous personality. Despite many provocative claims, and despite the promising preliminary results of some serotonin studies (see, for example, M. Leyton *et al.*, 1977), no conclusive evidence has yet been assembled.

References

Abrahamsen, David (1985), *Confessions of Son of Sam*, New York: Columbia University Press.

Black, Joel (1991), *The Aesthetics of Murder: A Study in Romantic Literature and Contemporary Culture*, Baltimore: The Johns Hopkins University Press.

Bolitho, William (1926), *Murder For Profit*, New York: Garden City.

Cameron, Deborah and Frazer, Elizabeth (1987), *The Lust to Kill: A Feminist Investigation of Sexual Murder*, New York: New York University Press.

Canter, David (1994), *Criminal Shadows: Inside the Mind of the Serial Killer*, London: HarperCollins.

Canter, David, Missen, Christopher and Hodge, Samantha (1996), 'Are Serial Killers Special?', *Policing Today*, April, pp. 22–28.

Capp, Bernard (1996), 'Serial Killers in 17th-Century England', *History Today*, **46**, pp. 21–26.

Cluff, Julie, Hunter, Allison and Hinch, Ronald (1997), 'Feminist Perspectives on Serial Murder: A Critical Analysis', *Homicide Studies*, **1**(3), pp. 291–308.

Downes, David and Rock, Paul (1988), *Understanding Deviance: A Guide to the Sociology of Crime and Rule Breaking*, Oxford: Clarendon Press.

Duclos, Denis (1998), *The Werewolf Complex: America's Fascination with Violence*, Oxford: Berg (Oxford International).

Egger, Steven A. (ed.) (1990), *Serial Murder: An Elusive Phenomenon*, New York: Praeger.

Egger, Steven A. (1998), *The Killers Among Us: An Examination of Serial Murder and its Investigation*, Upper Saddle River, NJ: Prentice Hall.

Gaylin, Willard (1983), *The Killing of Bonnie Garland: A Question of Justice*, New York: Penguin.

Giannangelo, Stephen J. (1996), *The Psychopathology of Serial Murder: A Theory of Violence*, Westport, CT: Praeger.

Gresswell, David M. and Hollin, Clive R. (1994), 'Multiple Murder: A Review', *British Journal of Criminology*, **34**, pp. 1–14.

Hare, Robert D. (nd), 'Psychopathy and Crime', in Laura Otten (ed.), *Colloquium on Correlates of Crime and the Determinants of Criminal Behavior*, Mitre.

Hickey, Eric W. (1991), *Serial Murderers and Their Victims*, Pacific Grove, CA: Brooks/Cole.

Holmes, Ronald M. and DeBurger, James (1988), *Serial Murder*, Beverly Hills, CA: Sage.

Jenkins, Philip (1994), *Using Murder: The Social Construction of Serial Homicide*, New York: Aldine de Gruyter.

Jenkins, Philip (1996), 'Review of *Men of Blood: Murder in Modern England*', *Crime, Law & Social Change*, **25**(1), pp. 102–4.

Kiger, Kenna (1990), 'The Darker Figure of Crime: The Serial Murder Enigma', in Steven A. Egger (ed.), *Serial Murder: An Elusive Phenomenon*, New York: Praeger.

Levin, Jack and Fox, James Alan (1985), *Mass Murder: America's Growing Menace*, New York: Plenum.

Leyton, Elliott (1986), *Compulsive Killers: The Story of Modern Multiple Murder*, New York: New York University Press. Published simultaneously in Canada as *Hunting Humans: The Rise of the Modern Multiple Murderer*, Toronto: McClelland & Stewart. Revised edition published 1989, London: Penguin Books.

Leyton, Marco, Diksic, M., Young, S.N., Okazawa, H., Nishizawa, S., Paris, J., Mzengeza, S. and Benkelfat, C. (1997), 'PET Study of Brain 5HT Synthesis in Borderline Personality Disorder', *Biological Psychiatry* (Abstract) **41**(7S), p. 17S.

Lunde, Donald T. (1975), *Murder and Madness*, New York: W.W. Norton.

Meloy, J. Reid (1988), *The Psychopathic Mind: Origins, Dynamics, and Treatment*, Northvale, NJ: Jason Aronson.

Merton, Robert K. (1972), 'Insiders and Outsiders: A Chapter in the Sociology of Knowledge', *American Journal of Sociology*, **78**, pp. 9–47.

O'Reilly-Fleming, Thomas (ed.) (1996), *Serial and Mass Murder: Theory, Research and Policy*, Toronto: Canadian Scholars' Press.

Ratner, R.S. (1996), 'Ideological Homicide', in Thomas O'Reilly-Fleming (ed., 1996).

Ressler, Robert K., Burgess, Ann W. and Douglas, John E. (1988), *Sexual Homicide: Patterns and Motives*, Lexington, MA: Lexington Books.

Skrapec, Candice (1996), 'The Sexual Component of Serial Murder', in Thomas O'Reilly-Fleming (ed., 1996).

Skrapec, Candice (1997), *Serial Murder: Motive and Meaning*, PhD dissertation in Criminal Justice, City University of New York.

Wakefield, H. Russell (1936), 'Landru: A Real Life Bluebeard', in J.M. Parrish and John R. Crossland (eds), *The Fifty Most Amazing Crimes of the Last 100 Years*, London: Odhams.

Part I
Cultural Overview

[1]

HEROSTRATUS

by JEAN-PAUL SARTRE

PEOPLE should be seen from above. I used to put out the light and stand at the window: they didn't even suspect that they could be observed from on top. They take pains with the front, sometimes with the rear, but all their effects are designed for an audience five feet eight. Who ever thought about the shape of a bowler hat seen from the sixth floor? They fail to protect their shoulders and their skulls with bright colors and gaudy materials, they don't know how to combat that great enemy of the Human: the downward perspective. I would lean out, and begin to laugh: where was their famous "upright carriage" that they were so proud of: they were squashed against the sidewalk and two long half-crawling legs came out from under their shoulders.

A sixth floor balcony: that's where I should have spent my whole life. Moral advantages have to be bolstered up with material symbols, or they collapse. Now what is, precisely, my advantage over people? An advantage of position, nothing else: I have raised myself above the human element in me, and I contemplate it. It's why I used to love the towers of Notre-Dame, the platforms of the Eiffel Tower, Sacré-Coeur, my sixth floor place on the Rue Delambre. They are fine symbols.

Sometimes I had to go down into the streets. To go to the office, for instance. I was smothered. When you are on a level with people it is much harder to think of them as ants: they *touch*. Once I saw a dead man in the street. They turned him over, he was bleeding. I saw his eyes open and his crooked look and all that blood. I said to myself: "It's nothing, it's no more moving than a fresh picture. They have daubed his nose with red, that's all." But I felt a nasty softness coming over my legs and the back of my neck, I fainted. They took me into a drugstore, clapped me on the shoulders and made me drink alcohol. I could have killed them.

I knew they were my enemies but they didn't know. They were full of mutual love, they pressed against one another; they would have liked to give me a punch here and there too, because they thought I was their fellow-being. But if they had been able to guess the tiniest particle of the truth they would have beaten me. As, later, they did. When they had got hold of me and knew *who* I was, they let me have it, they played on me for two hours, in the police station, slapped me and struck me, twisted my arms, tore off my trousers, and to finish off they threw my glasses on the ground and while I looked for them on all fours they kicked me from behind, laughing. I always knew they would end up by beating me: I am not strong and I can't defend myself. Some of them had been lying in wait for me for a long time: the big ones. They jostled me in the street, for a laugh, just to see what I would do. I said nothing. I pretended not to understand. And still they got me. I was afraid of them: it was a presentiment. But naturally there were more serious reasons for my hate.

From that point of view, everything went much better from the day when I bought a revolver. It makes you feel strong to carry so diligently on your person one of those things that can explode and make noise. I used to take it on Sundays, simply put it in my trousers pocket and go for a walk— usually on the Boulevards. I would feel it pulling at my trousers like a crab, I felt the cold of it against my thigh. But gradually it got warm from rubbing my body. I slipped my hand into my pocket and I felt the *thing*. Once in a while I went into a urinal—even there I was careful because one often has neighbors—I took out my revolver, weighed it, looked at its black checkered butt and its black trigger like a half closed eyelid. The others, the ones outside who saw my spread legs and the bottoms of my trousers, thought I was urinating. But I never do that in urinals.

One evening it occurred to me to fire at people. It was a Saturday night, I had gone out to look for Lea, a blonde who keeps watch in front of a hotel on the Rue Montparnasse. I have never had intimate relations with a woman: I would have felt robbed. I ask nothing from anyone, but I don't want to give anything either. Or else I would have needed a cold and pious woman who would have submitted to me with disgust. The first Saturday of every month I went with Lea to a room in the Hotel Duquesne. She undressed and I watched without touching her: sometimes I had time to get home for the effect. That evening I didn't find her at her post. I waited a minute, and as she didn't show up I gathered she must have the grippe. It was the beginning of January and very cold. I was broken-hearted: I have imagination, and I had worked up a vivid picture of the pleasure I meant to get from that evening. There was still of course, in the Rue d'Odessa, the dark-haired one that I had often noticed, somewhat past her prime but firm and plump: I don't mind aging women: with their clothes off they look more naked than the others. But she wasn't up on my conventions, and I was a little shy of exposing that to her out of the blue. And then I distrust new acquaintances: that sort of woman is quite capable of hiding a ruffian behind the door, and when it's over the guy jumps out and takes your money. Lucky if he doesn't beat you up. Nevertheless, I felt peculiarly bold that evening, I decided to go back to my place for the revolver and try my luck.

When I went up to the woman, a quarter of an hour later, the weapon was in my pocket and I was over my fear. From close to me she seemed more wretched than anything else. She looked like my neighbor across the way, the adjutant's wife, and I was glad because for a long time I had wanted to see that one stripped. She used to dress with the window open, when the adjutant was out, and I often stood behind my curtain to catch her. But she dressed at the other end of the room.

There was only one room left in the Hotel Stella, on the fourth floor. We went up. The woman was rather heavy and kept stopping to puff. I was perfectly at ease: I have a hard body, in spite of my stomach, and it takes more than four flights to put me out of breath. On the landing of the fourth floor she stopped, breathing very hard, and put her right hand on her heart. In her left hand she held the key of the room.

"It's a long way up," she said with an attempt to smile. I took the key from her without answering and opened the door. I had the revolver in my left hand, pointed straight ahead of me through the pocket, and I didn't let go of it until I had turned the switch. The room was empty. On the washstand they had put a little cake of green soap. I smiled: in my case bidets and little cakes of soap are aside from the point. The woman was still puffing behind me, and that excited me. I turned around; she stretched her lips toward me. I pushed her away.

"Take off your clothes," I said.

I sat down comfortably in an upholstered chair. Those are the times when I'm sorry I don't smoke. The woman took off her dress and then paused, giving me a suspicious look.

"What's your name?" I asked her, settling back.

"Renée."

"Well, Renée, hurry up, I'm waiting."

"You're not undressing."

"Go on, go on," I said, "don't worry about me."

She let her pants fall to her feet, then picked them up and laid them carefully on her dress with her brassiere.

"O, monkey business. Lazy, are you, honey?" she asked me.

At the same time she took a step toward me and leaning on the arm of my chair she tried clumsily to caress me, but I pushed her rudely away.

"None of that," I said.

She looked at me, surprised.

"But what do you want me to do?"

"Nothing. Walk, just walk up and down, that's all."

She began to walk around, awkwardly. Nothing annoys women more than walking naked. They are not used to putting their heels down flat. The tart arched her back and let her arms hang. I was in heaven: there I was, seated quietly in an arm-chair, dressed to the neck, I had even kept on my gloves, and this full-blown lady was naked at my command and pivoting around me.

She turned her head toward me, and to keep up appearances, smiled coyly:

"Do you like my looks? Getting an eyeful?"

"Don't worry about that."

"Listen," she said in sudden indignation, "do you expect me to keep walking like this much longer?"

"Sit down."

She sat down on the bed and we looked at each other silently. She had the flesh of a whore. The clatter of an alarm clock came from the other side of the wall. Suddenly I began to laugh until the tears came to my eyes. I said to her simply:

"Do you realize?"

And I burst out laughing again.

She looked at me in amazement and then blushed violently. "Pig," she said with her teeth clenched.

But I laughed even harder, and she jumped up and took her brassiere from the chair.

"Hey," I said, "it's not over. I'll give you fifty francs later, but I want my money's worth."

She picked up her pants nervously.

"I'm tired of this, see? I don't know what you want. And

if you got me up here to make fun of me. . ."

Then I took out my revolver and showed it to her. She gave me a serious look and dropped her pants without a word.

"Move," I said. "Walk around."

She walked five more minutes. Then I had her perform with my cane. At last I got up and offered her a fifty franc note. She took it.

"Goodbye," I added, "I haven't tired you much for the price."

I went out, leaving her naked in the middle of the room. her brassiere in one hand and the fifty franc note in the other. I didn't regret the money: I had bewildered her, and it's not so easy to startle a whore. I thought on my way downstairs: "That's what I'd like, to startle them all." I was as happy as a child. I had carried off the green soap and when I got home I rubbed it a long time under the hot water until it was only a slim pellet between my fingers, like a mint candy that had been sucked a long time.

But in the night I woke with a start and I saw her face, the eyes she made when I showed her my weapon, and her fat stomach jumping at every step. "What a fool I was," I said to myself. And I felt bitter remorse: I should have shot while I was there, punctured that stomach like a cullender. That night and for three nights following I dreamed of six little red holes grouped in a circle around the navel.

After that I never went out without my revolver. I watched peoples' backs and imagined, from the way they walked, how they would fall if I opened up on them. Sundays I took to going and standing outside the Chatelet at the close of the classical concerts. Around six o'clock I heard bells ringing and then the ushers came to hook back the glass doors. It was the beginning: the crowd came out slowly; people walked with a flowing step, eyes still dreamy, heart still full of gentle feelings. Many looked around with astonishment: the street must have seemed to them all blue. Then they smiled mysteriously: they were passing from one world to another. I was waiting for them in the other. I had slipped my right hand in my pocket and I was pressing the butt of my weapon with all my strength. After a minute I *saw* myself shooting at them. I toppled them over like pipes, they fell on top of each other and the survivors, panic-stricken, streamed back into the theatre breaking the panes of the doors. It was a very nerve-wracking game: my fingers trembled at the end and I had to go and drink a cognac at Dreher's to recuperate.

I wouldn't have killed the women. I would have shot at their loins. Or at their calves, to make them dance.

I had not yet come to any decision. But I determined to act as if it were all decided. I began by settling incidental details. I went to practice in a shooting gallery, at the fair at Denfert-Rochereau. I didn't do any too well, but people offer a big target, especially at point-blank. Then I took care of the publicity. I chose a day when all my colleagues were together at the office. A Monday morning. I was very friendly with them, on principle, even though I couldn't bear to shake their hands. They took off their gloves to say goodmorning, they had an obscene way of undressing their hand, pulling the glove down and letting it slip slowly the length of their fingers, exposing the fat and crumpled nakedness of the palm. I always kept my gloves on.

Nothing much happens Monday morning. The stenographer from the wholesale house had just brought us the receipts. Lemercier joked pleasantly with her and when she had left they had a bored and proficient discussion of her charms. Then they talked about Lindbergh. They were very fond of Lindbergh. I said:

"What I like is black heroes."

"Negroes?" Massé asked.

"No, black, the way you say Black Magic. Lindbergh is a white hero. He doesn't interest me."

"If you think it's easy to cross the Atlantic," Bouxin said sourly.

I explained to them my conception of the black hero.

"An anarchist," Lemercier concluded.

"No," I said softly, "anarchists love people in their way."

"Then you mean a madman."

But Massé who had done some reading interrupted at that point:

"I know your man," he said to me. " His name was Herostratus. He wanted to be famous, and all he could think of was to burn the Temple of Ephesus, one of the seven wonders of the world."

"And what was the name of the architect of that temple?"

"I don't remember," he admitted. "I don't believe his name is even known."

"Really? And you remember the name of Herostratus? You see his figuring was pretty good."

The conversation ended there, but my mind was at peace: they would remember when the time came. For me, who had never before heard of Herostratus, the story was heartening. He had been dead for over two thousand years, and his act was still shining, like a black diamond. I began to believe that my fate would be short and tragic. It frightened me at first but I got used to it. If you take it in a certain way it is ghastly, but from another angle it gives the passing moment considerable strength and beauty. When I went down into the street again I felt a strange power in my body. I had my revolver on me, that thing that bursts and makes a noise. But my assurance was now derived not from that but from myself: I was a being made of the stuff of revolvers, explosives and bombs. I too, some day, at the end of my gloomy life, I would explode and light up the world with a brief and violent flame like a magnesium flare. During that period I had the same dream several nights. I was an anarchist, I had planted myself on the Czar's route with a grenade. At the appointed time the procession passed, the bomb exploded, and we popped into the air, I, the Czar and three officers bedecked with gold, before the eyes of the crowd.

I let whole weeks go by now without showing myself at the office. I took walks on the boulevards, in the midst of my future victims, or else I shut myself up in my room and made plans. I was fired at the beginning of October. After that I spent my time draughting the following letter, of which I made a hundred and two copies:

"Dear Sir:

You are famous and your works are published in editions of thirty thousand. I will tell you why: it is because you love people. You have humanism in your blood: a fine stroke of luck. In company, you blossom; as soon as you see one of your fellow-beings, even without knowing him, you feel sympathy. You have a taste for his body, for the way it is jointed, for his legs that open and close at will, above all for his hands: you are glad that he has five fingers on each hand and that he can touch the other fingers with his thumb. You are delighted when your neighbor picks up a cup from the table, because he has a way of picking up that is strictly human and that you have often described in your works, less supple, less quick than a monkey's way, but so much more intelligent. You also love man's flesh, his gait like that of a wounded man learning again, his air of re-inventing his walk at every step, and the famous look in his eye that wild animals cannot face. It has therefore been easy for you to find the proper tone for speaking to man about himself: a tone chaste but passionate. People cannot wait to devour your books, they read them in a big chair, they think of the great unhappy and unobtrusive love that you bear them and it consoles them for many things, for being ugly, for being cowards, for being betrayed, for not getting a raise on the first of the year. And they like to say of your latest novel: it is a good deed.

"You would be curious to know, I presume, what a man is like who has no love of people. Well, that man is I, and I love them so little that I am shortly going to kill half a dozen of them: you may ask: why *only* half a dozen? Because there are only six cartridges in my revolver. Monstrous, isn't it? And besides, so absolutely unwise! But I tell you that I *cannot* love them. I very well understand your feelings. But what attracts you in them is to me revolting. I too have seen men chewing decorously and with a pertinent look in their eye while their left hand thumbed through an economic journal. Is it my fault if I would rather attend the feeding of seals? Man can use his face for nothing without its becoming a game of physiognomy. When he chews with his mouth shut the corners of his mouth rise and fall as if he were ceaselessly alternating between peace and a weepy surprise. You like that, I know, you call it the ever-presence of the Spirit. But it sickens me: I don't know why; I was born that way.

"If there were between us only a difference of taste I would not trouble you. But everything is run as if you were blessed and I not. I am free to like or dislike lobster American-style, but if I dislike people I am a wretch and there is no room for me under the sun. They have swallowed up the meaning of life. I hope I am making myself clear. For thirty-three years now I have been hurling myself at closed doors over which is written: "Only humanists may enter here." Everything that I have undertaken I have had to give up; I had to choose: either it was an absurd and foredoomed attempt, or sooner or later it must be to their benefit. I was not able to detach from myself, to formulate the thoughts that were not especially directed to them: they remained in me like slight organic movements. Even the tools I used I felt belonged to them; words for instances: I wanted words of *my own*. But the ones at my disposal have trailed through any number of minds; they become grouped in my head all by themselves because of habits acquired in others, and it is not without repugnance that I employ them in writing to you. But it is for the last time. I say to you: one must love people, or the very most one is permitted is to shuffle along. Well, I don't want to shuffle. I will take my revolver presently, I will go into the street and I will see if one can't achieve something *against* them. Goodbye dear sir, it may be you that I will meet. In that case you will never know with what joy I will blow out your brains. If not—which is more likely—read tomorrow's papers. You will learn there that an individual named Paul Hilbert in an attack of madness shot down five passers-by on the Boulevard Edgar-Quinet. No one knows better than you what the prose of the great dailies is worth. You will therefore understand that I am far from "mad." I am on the contrary quite calm and I beg you to accept, dear sir, the assurance of my most distinguished sentiments.

Paul Hilbert"

I put the hundred and two letters in a hundred and two envelopes and wrote on the envelopes the addresses of a hundred and two French writers. I then placed the lot in my drawer with six booklets of stamps.

In the following two weeks I went out very little, I let my crime slowly take hold of me. In the mirror, where I looked at myself occasionally, I was pleased to notice the changes in my face. The eyes had grown, they ate up the entire face. They were black and soft behind the glasses and I made them roll like planets. Beautiful artist's and murderer's eyes. But I expected to change far more deeply still when the massacre was done. I once saw the pictures of those two handsome servant girls who killed and looted their mistresses. I saw the photographs of *before* and *after*. *Before*, the faces hovered like modest flowers over piqué collars. They breathed hygiene and delicious honesty. A discreet iron had waved their hair likewise. And even more reassuring than their curled hair. their collars and their look of paying a visit to the photographer, was their resemblance as sisters, their so worthy resemblance which brought straight to the foreground the ties of blood and the natural roots of the family group. *After,* their faces blazed like fires. Their necks were bare in preparation for the knife. Lines all over, dreadful lines of fear and hatred, folds, holes in the flesh as if a beast had clawed its way around their faces. And the eyes, those great black bottomless eyes—like mine. Nevertheless, the resemblance was gone. Each bore in her own way the memory of their common crime. I said to myself, "If a transgression that was largely a matter of chance can so transform those orphan-

like faces, what may I not hope for from a crime utterly conceived and organized by myself." It would seize upon me,
lay waste my too human ugliness . . . a crime cuts in two the
life of the man who has committed it. There must be moments when one longs to go back, but it is there, behind you,
a sparkling mineral, blocking your way. I asked only an hour
to enjoy mine, to feel its overwhelming weight. I would fix
everything to have that hour for myself: I decided to carry
out the deed at the end of the Rue d'Odessa. In the general
consternation I would flee, leaving them to pick up their dead.
I would run, cross the Boulevard Edgar-Quinet and turn
quickly into the Rue Delambre. It would take me only thirty
seconds to reach the building I lived in. At that moment my
pursuers would still be on the Boulevard Edgar-Quinet, they
would lose my track and take at least an hour to find it again.
I would wait for them at home and when I heard them knocking at my room I would re-load my revolver and shoot myself
in the mouth.

I lived more grandly; I had made an agreement with a
restaurant on the Rue Vavin and they sent me nice little dishes
morning and night. The delivery man rang, I didn't answer,
after waiting a few minutes I opened the door a crack and
saw full steaming plates in a long basket on the floor.

At six o'clock in the evening on the 27th of October I had
seventeen and a half francs left. I took my revolver and the
package of letters, I went down. I was careful not to shut the
door, so I could come back faster when the thing was done.
I felt badly, my hands were cold and my head heavy, my eyes
itched. I looked at the shops, the Hotel des Écoles, the stationery where I buy my pencils, and I didn't recognize them.
I said to myself: "What street is this?" Boulevard Montpar-
nasse was full of people. They jostled me, pushed me, knocked
me with their elbows and shoulders. I let myself be tossed
about, I hadn't the strength to pick my way between them. I
saw myself suddenly at the center of that crowd, horribly
alone and small. How they could have hurt me if they had
wanted to! I was afraid on account of the weapon in my
pocket. It seemed to me they were going to guess that it was
there. They would look at me with their hard eyes, they
would say: "Oh, but . . . but . . ." with happy indignation,
harpooning me with their human paws. Lynched! They
would throw me over their heads and I would fall back in their
arms like a puppet. It seemed wiser to postpone the execution
of my plan to the next day. I had dinner at the Coupole for

sixteen francs ninety. That left me seventy centimes which I threw in the gutter.

I stayed three days in my room, without eating, without sleeping. I had closed the shutters and I dared neither to go near the window nor to turn on the light. On Monday some-one buzzed at my door. I held my breath and waited. A min-ute later they rang again. I tiptoed to the door and peeked through the key-hole. All I saw was a piece of black material and a button. The man rang again and then went away: I don't know who it was. During the night I had cool visions, palms, running water, a violet sky over a cupola. I was not thirsty because every hour I drank from the tap in the sink. But I was hungry. I saw the dark-haired prostitute again too. It was in a castle I had had built on the Causses Noires, fifty miles from the nearest village. She was naked and alone with me. Under the threat of my revolver I made her kneel and run on all fours; then I tied her to a pillar, and after giving her a long explanation of what I was going to do I riddled her with bullets. These images upset me so that I had to satisfy myself. Afterwards I lay motionless in the dark, my head absolutely empty. The furniture began to creak. It was five o'clock in the morning. I would have given anything to leave my room but I couldn't go out because of the people walking in the streets.

Day came. I was no longer aware of hunger, but I began to sweat: I soaked my shirt. Outside the sun was shining. Then I thought: "He is cowering in a closed room, in the dark. For three days He has neither eaten nor slept. They rang and He didn't answer. Pretty soon He will go into the street and He will kill." I was afraid of myself. At six o'clock in the evening my hunger came back. I was furiously angry. I hit the furniture a while, then turned on the elec-tricity in the rooms, the kitchen, the closets. I began to sing my head off, I washed my hands and went out. It took me two full minutes to put all my letters in the post-box. I stuck them in in packages of ten. I must have rumpled several of the envelopes. Then I went down the Boulevard Montpar-nasse to the Rue d'Odessa. I paused before the window of a haberdashery, and seeing my face there I thought: "It will be tonight."

I planted myself at the end of the Rue d'Odessa, not far from a streetlight, and waited. Two women passed. They were arm in arm, the blonde saying:

"They had hangings over all the windows and the nobles from around there got parts as extras."

"Are they broke?" the other asked.

"You don't have to be broke to want to make five hundred francs a day."

The dark-haired one was dazzled. "Five hundred francs!" She added, passing near me: "And then I suppose it was fun for them to wear the costumes of their ancestors."

They moved away. I was cold but sweating copiously. A minute later I saw three men coming; I let them pass; I needed six. The one on the left looked at me and clicked his tongue. I turned my eyes away.

At five after seven two groups close to each other emerged from the Boulevard Edgar-Quinet. There was a man and a woman with two children. Behind them came three old women. I took a step forward. The woman looked angry and was shaking the little boy by the arm. The man said in a drawling voice:

"He's lousy, too."

My heart was beating so hard that it hurt my arms. I stepped forward and stood in front of them, motionless. My fingers, in my pocket, were all soft around the trigger.

"Excuse me," the man said as he bumped into me.

I remembered that I had closed the apartment door and that annoyed me: I would have to waste valuable time getting it open. The people moved away. I turned around and followed them mechanically. But I didn't want to shoot them any more. They got lost in the crowd on the boulevard. I leaned against the wall. I heard eight o'clock strike, and nine. I kept saying to myself: "Why kill people who are already *dead*," and I felt like laughing. A dog came and sniffed at my feet.

When the fat man went past me I came to with a start and fell in step with him. I saw the fold of his red neck between his hat and the collar of his overcoat. He waddled a little and breathed hard, he looked husky. I got out the revolver: it was bright and cold, it disgusted me, I didn't remember very well what I was supposed to do with it. I kept looking first at that and then at the man's neck. The fold in the neck smiled at me, like a smiling and bitter mouth. I wondered if I wasn't going to throw my revolver down a sewer.

Suddenly the man turned around and gave me an irritated look. I took a step back.

"I wanted to . . . ask you . . ."

He didn't seem to listen, he was looking at my hands. I finished laboriously.

"Could you tell me how to get to the Rue de la Gaité?"

His face was fat and his lips were trembling. He said nothing, he reached out his hand. I withdrew farther and said:

"I would like . . ."

At that moment I *knew* that I was going to scream. I didn't want to: I fired three bullets into his stomach. He fell idiotically on his knees and his head rolled over on his left shoulder.

"Bastard," I said to him, "God damn bastard!"

I fled. I heard him coughing. I also heard shouts and running behind me. Someone asked: "What's the matter? Is there a fight?" and right after came the cry: "Stop the murderer: Stop the murderer!" I didn't think these shouts concerned me. But they sounded sinister, like the siren of the fire-engines when I was a child. Sinister and slightly ridiculous. I ran with all my strength.

Only I had made an unforgivable mistake: instead of going back up the Rue d'Odessa toward the Boulevard Edgar-Quinet, *I was going down toward the Boulevard Montparnasse.* By the time I realized it, it was too late: I was already right in the middle of the crowd, faces turned toward me in astonishment (I remember one of a woman who had on a lot of powder and a green hat with a plume) and I heard the fools from the Rue d'Odessa crying murderer behind me. A hand came down on my shoulder. Then I lost my head: I didn't want to die stifled by that crowd. I fired two more shots. People began to squawk and scattered. I ran into a café. The customers rose as I passed but didn't try to stop me, I crossed the whole length of the café and locked myself into the lavatory. There was one bullet left in my revolver.

A minute passed. I was out of breath and panting. Everything was extraordinarily still, as if people had stopped talking on purpose. I raised my weapon to the level of my eyes and saw its little round black hole: that was where the bullet would come out; the powder would burn my face. I let my arm drop and waited. A minute later they approached stealthily; there must be a whole gang, judging by the rustling of feet on the floor. They whispered a little and then were silent. I was still puffing and I thought they could hear me puff through the partition. Someone came forward slowly and shook the door handle. He must have plastered himself against the wall on the side, to avoid my bullets. Just the same I felt like firing—but the last bullet was for me.

"What are they waiting for?" I wondered. If they threw themselves at the door and battered it in *right away* I wouldn't have time to kill myself and they would take me alive. But they didn't hurry, they left me plenty of time to die. The swine, they were scared.

After a while a voice was raised.

"Come on, open up, you won't be hurt."

Silence, and then the same voice again:

"You know you can't get away."

I didn't answer, I was still panting. To get up my courage to fire I told myself: "If they get me they'll beat me, they'll break my teeth, maybe squash an eye." I wished I knew whether the fat man was dead. Perhaps I had only wounded him . . . and perhaps the two other bullets hadn't struck anyone . . . Were they getting ready for something, were they dragging something heavy across the floor? I hurried to put the butt of my weapon in my mouth and I bit it hard. But I couldn't fire, couldn't even put my finger on the trigger. Everything was still again.

Then I threw down the revolver and opened the door for them.

(Translated by Eleanor Clark)

JOHN LANDLESS LEADS THE CARAVAN

Have I a hundred years since or
A hundred thousand tramped these wastes
With a track more vulnerable
Than fire of a sun that hastes?

My camel leads the caravan
Through centuries of rusted sand
To find as might any profane wind
The key to the oblivion land

[2]

Son of Cain or Son of Sam? The Monster as Serial Killer in *Beowulf*

Brian Meehan

The monster Grendel's final assault on the meadhall is often called the most terrifying scene in *Beowulf*. Three separate passages describe the killer striding from the moors toward Heorot. In each he grows closer and larger, until finally, his eyes burning in the darkness, he bursts into the room where the warriors sleep and where Beowulf — and we — await him. A critic has called the effect of these passages cinematic; visual details are precisely rendered as a long shot progressively becomes a close up (*Beowulf* 306). But if this scene chills us, there may be another reason, one that has less to do with precision of art than with its ambiguity. Throughout the telling of the Grendel story, the poet makes it difficult for us to name precisely the terror that is coming and to distance ourselves from it. Sometimes Grendel is called a fiend and sometimes a man; sometimes a monster and sometimes a warrior. At times he kills with claws, at other times with hands. Perhaps we are meant also to wonder in that dark room whether those fierce eyes are inhuman or human. Perhaps we stand closer than we think to this creature whom the poet calls "bereft of joys" and who lives only to kill. Should he be one of us, then of course our terror is greater and this dark poem, darker.

If thoughts like these unnerve us, there are critics anxious to put us at ease. The introduction to *Beowulf* in a major college anthology assures us that we "can safely assume" that Grendel is only a "fabulous [monster] of the night" (Kermode 1, 23). This solicitude is charming, though we may hear in it the briefest of hints that if we cannot assume so we may not be entirely safe. W. P. Ker, in his classic study *Epic and Romance*, finds "nothing particularly interesting" in Beowulf's struggle against Grendel (165). The monster is nothing more than a common folk motif on yet another rampage, as if Grendel is less to be feared because there are many of him instead of one. Indeed, quite understandably, in such ways is Beowulf often read: as an epic and artifact of the dark ages, its ethic the mores of Anglo-Saxon warrior culture, its monsters the products of Germanic and Biblical mythology. But I wish to examine the possibility that the raging hatred and repulsive crimes of Grendel may owe less to fiction than we think. The Grendel episode may represent the articulation of a horror so real and so much in need of the language of psychopathology to define it that it could be expressed by myth alone, the only clinical language available to poets of the dark ages. For if Grendel terrifies us, it is because both we and the poet know that his murders flow not from conventions of folklore but from the state of his mind. And we recognize in the profound hatred of that mind something that is not bestial but dysfunctionally human, and thus still with us. This paper will argue that the *Beowulf* poet intended to portray the kind of terror caused by serial murder for the following reasons, each one progressively more compelling than the other: because of the way Grendel acts, because of the way he thinks, because of the way he is represented in folklore, and because of the way he is transformed by myth.

The easiest part of this task, though the least convincing, is to identify the traits Grendel shares with modern serial killers. Consider the following examples: His mind is twisted by envy and

Department of English, Salem College, Winston-Salem, NC 27108

Connecticut Review Fall 1994   *Meehan*

hatred, "crazed with evil anger." He is profoundly anhedonic and depressive — "deprived of joys" (*Beowulf* 91). "He [grieves] not at all for his wicked deeds," and is therefore sociopathic. He is isolated from humanity, anomalous, "one against many" (57). His murders spring from fantasies in which he nurses his anger and plans his crimes. He is called a "moor stalker" and "a dark walker" because he prowls a particular territory, stalks his victims, peers into their rooms at night, and ambushes them when they are vulnerable (55;89). Evading capture, he is never satisfied and kills repeatedly for "the space of twelve winters" (57). He prefers a certain type of victim: warriors who, unlike him, are as happily bonded with their society as the sorority women Ted Bundy bludgeoned to death. And strangely, although these men are strong, they still share a characteristic with victims of modern serial killers. Like trusting coeds, like prostitutes who enter strangers' cars, these warriors have a weakness, a vulnerability the murderer exploits. Every night they drink themselves insensible and when Grendel comes they lie as passive before him as any dozing victim of Richard Ramiriz or young male handcuffed by Wayne Gacy. Further, Grendel murders for the sake of murder; he is "at feud with God," a feud which cannot be stopped by the paying of wergild, the Anglo-Saxon technique for curbing the murder rate (95). When he murders, he enjoys inflicting humiliation and pain, violating the human body by gutting and eating it; like Jeffrey Dahmer and his brother-in-fiction Hannibal Lector, he likes a good bit of flesh, but prefers blood to Amarone. Grendel keeps trophies, taking "plunder" back to his lair (57). Finally, like Albert DeSalvo, he has a bizarre reverence for the people he kills and the places where he kills them. He wanders in Heorot, in a kind of daze, wanting something in that place he can never have, figuratively or literally: the "gift-throne," the king's treasure, the symbol of bonding among the warriors he kills.

These similarities are undeniable but perhaps coincidental. If we focus on the motivation of Grendel, the possibility that he represents the most terrible of murderers becomes stronger. He is angry, depressed, and paranoid; he lives on the fringes of normal society. Spying on the warriors at night, he especially hates the symbolic ring-giving, as well as the joyful sounds of community, the music of the harp, and the alliterative Anglo-Saxon poetic line, itself created by a kind of bonding. For these reasons (and no others) he enters the hall in a murderous rage, smashing as many bodies as he can. Purely by chance, the scene recalls Ted Bundy's assault on the Chi Omega sorority house after he drank in a college bar and watched students dance, a healthy ritual of joy from which we know he felt forever exiled. His rage grew at last uncontrollable and savage. Out of the darkness he entered the sorority house, a place where women bond, and where, like Grendel, he smashed skulls and savaged bodies with his teeth.

It may not be pure chance, however, that Grendel's state of mind mirrors that of modern serial killers as described by those who study them, seeking clues to the etiology of this pathological condition. Eric Hickey, for example, reports that "the underlying pathology of serial killers typically is frustration, anger, hostility, feelings of inadequacy, and low self-esteem," and he concludes that "these feelings may be manifested in many ways, but the source or underlying pathology appears as a common denominator" (51). Statistically the most common form of childhood trauma among serial killers is not physical or sexual abuse, but early rejection and other problems more related to bonding and social class than to witnessing or being the object of unusual violence (Hickey 154). Elliott Leyton in his thoughtful book on the causes of multiple murder argues that "serial and mass murderers are overwhelmed with a profound sense of alienation and frustration stemming from their feelings that . . . no matter what they might do, they could not achieve the place in society to which they aspired." And even though Leyton argues that serial murder is a very late development of our culture, springing from growing tensions of class division, the cultural divisions he claims produce

Connecticut Review Fall 1994 *Meehan*

serial murderers actually parallel closely the strong class structure of Anglo-Saxon society which Grendel attacks. For Leyton, modern serial murderers "are among the most *class conscious* people in America. . . . their truncated sense of self and identity . . . pushes them toward finding their identity and their personal fulfillment in the killings." He points out what we have already noted is true of Grendel: "Typically, their victims are drawn from a single social type or category . . . members . . . of a specific social class, most often one or two narrow social bands above the killer." These murderers "select members of that social class whom they find beautiful" (30). In this context it is interesting to recall that Grendel is called an "evil warrior." Those whom he resents are indeed like him, for they too kill serially in feuds. And it is their beauty — of body, of poetry, of friendship — that he hates.

Still, as Professor Ker rightly reminds us, Grendel is a monster, a creature of folklore, a common and appropriately labeled folk motif, a fact this essay cannot ignore. Is there something about the way this poet shapes what he inherits from Germanic and Scandinavian folklore that might reveal to us, not simply characteristics Grendel shares with our kind of murderer, but that an emphasis on Grendel's humanity as he murders was in fact the intention of the poet?

We of course still call savage killers monsters, but no form of this latinate word appears in *Beowulf*. The class of monster from which Grendel springs is that of the Germanic *eotenas*, man-eating giants, and *orc-neas*, walking dead men, very irritable zombies who attack the living in folktales and sagas, and who walk among us still in George Romero films. Also, as we would expect from a Christian poet, Grendel is called "a fiend from hell," another appelation which suggests that his evil is not of this world. But the way this poet uses language should keep us from making too easy assumptions about how unlike us Grendel may be. When it suits the poet, for example, the phrase "fiend from hell" is applied to human beings who carry on feuds. Moreover, the Grendel of the poem is far more complex than his humble folkloric origins suggest, for the language of the poem is rich and often intentionally ambiguous. At times, the presumption that Grendel is more a creature of the night than one of us can justify less than precise translations as when the Old English word *handa* meaning *hands* is translated as *claws* (*Beowulf* 92). As in *Paradise Lost* or *Finnegan's Wake*, there are thematic puns. Studying the original, one is surprised at the number of times Grendel is called a man; the poet, in fact, at various points uses virtually every Anglo-Saxon synonym for man to do so. But when the poet uses the ancestor of our word *man*, he puns, for in Anglo-Saxon, *mán* with a long *á* meant evil, with a short *a*, man. Thus when Grendel is called a *mán-scatha* or *evil harmer*, the compound is rich with several other meanings, one of which is that he is a man who harms others (*Beowulf* 307). Such elaborate craft we expect from a scop. Rather like Joyce, this poet brings several realities at once into the space of a single word. Thus the poet builds one of the bridges by which Grendel passes from the world of folklore to that of fact. As one translator has noted, "Grendel is often called 'man' or 'warrior'; he lives exiled from the joys of men; and the poet treats him ironically as a hapless retainer" (*Beowulf* 307). Thus Grendel is a man because the poet at times intends him to be one; and the man he is resembles the criminal personality we are discussing.

There is also a natural affinity between folklore and savage crime, and perhaps more importantly, between traditional images of folklore and the narcissism of real murderers. Serial murder is so innately horrible and so apparently inexplicable that the criminals who commit it have been associated with supernatural forces. Hickey has noted that "some of the early European serial killers who were thought to have been vampires or other 'creatures of the night' in reality were nothing more than depraved murderers." Thus Gilles de Rais, who drank the blood of murdered

Connecticut Review Fall 1994   *Meehan*

children in fifteenth century France, was thought a vampire (23). The culture's intention in so doing is not to fictionalize the crime, but to lessen the threat such irrationality poses to a belief in an ordered world. In a universe of angels, devils, and human beings, all overseen by an omnipotent god, vampires are far less disturbing than a real Ted Bundy.

Of more importance, however, particularly as we approach the mythic dimension of *Beowulf*, is the serial murderer's eagerness to play at creating metaphor by reciprocating his culture's desire for bestial and satanic comparisons that will convey the inhumanity of the crime, an eagerness shared by the media. David Berkowitz, before he invented the possibly disingenuous name "Son of Sam," signed his first note, "Mr. Monster." The *Los Angeles Times* helped to turn Richard Ramiriz into "The Night Stalker." Ramiriz, like Berkowitz, took his supernatural role seriously and, when caught, issued ominous satanic bulletins in courtroom appearances. Hickey quotes a poem composed by a murderer about his impulse to kill that sounds quite like something Grendel might say if he had ever addressed us in the first person: "Like a beast I overcome him / ... utterly destroy him / And I cut out his heart and eat it / And I guzzle his blood like nectar" (53-54). If imaginary monsters come to us from folklore, real murderers travel in the other direction. And if Berkowitz can find a mirror in metaphors of folklore, why not any killer in any period? In a primitive society, a story-teller's frightening tale of a monster's violence, full of bestial images, might well seem a plan of action to the one among them who, for whatever reason of genetics or nurture, is predisposed toward the same savage violence.

And thus it is precisely in the area of symbol and metaphor that we see an affinity between the mind of a serial murderer and the mind of a poet. Each is unusually sensitive to the metaphors that convey unspeakable violence, and each believes passionately that literal truth must lie at the heart of figures of speech. In terms of imagination, murderer and poet may be more closely allied than is the poet with his merely ordinary audience. And nowhere is this strange alliance more important than on the level of myth. For serial murderers crave a mythic significance at least as much as poets wish to give it to them. For this reason, before the invention of clinical terms of psychiatry, the language of myth was the only language adequate to convey the nature and imagination of such a bizarre criminal mind.

Myths are rooted in action as much as imagination; they remain only if they are acted out, literally or ceremonially. Myth by its very nature is fed by the world of actuality. When Milton in *Paradise Lost* created his Satan, so important to the later development of the eighteenth century sublime, with its love of the vast, the terrifying, and the deadly, he gave him not only a standard issue human mind, but also modeled him in part on Charles II. It seems unlikely that Charles could have fathered the sublime by himself; he had to be transformed, by mythic exaggeration, into an archetype. Thus it is that we in our century are able to see in that Restoration Satan the narcissism, the disordered urges, the self-destructiveness of a mind like that of Hitler or of Stalin. Milton was no prophet; he simply understood the tyrannical mind, a continually recurring pathology. And because myths are manifested in human behavior, they are always in a state of becoming.

In primitive cultures, as Mircea Eliade has pointed out, myth precedes objective history and "just as modern man considers himself to be constituted by History, the man of the archaic societies declares that he is the result of a certain number of mythical events" (12). This does not mean, however, that primitive societies accept all their stories as true; Eliade points out that they "carefully distinguish myths — 'true stories' — from fables or tales, which they call 'false stories.'" Now "'true stories' . . . include . . . those which deal with the beginnings of the world," and the reason "creation stories are real" is that they account for what undeniably exists (8). Therefore, "the cosmogonic myth is 'true' because the existence of the world is there to prove it" (6). Myths, more than folklore, explain what we actually see happening around us.

Beowulf, of course, is a poem of a primitive tribal culture which had in its store of wisdom precisely the sorts of tales and myths of which Eliade speaks. And very early in this poem, in one of its most famous passages, a poet recites the creation hymn, which in a few joyful lines retells the cosmogonic myth of Anglo-Saxon Christian culture. It lifts the gloom of the poem, but only briefly. For it is at precisely this point that the murderer Grendel first appears, wishing to reverse creation and to kill those whose hymn it is:

> [The Almighty] victory creative,   set out the brightness
> of sun and moon   as lamps for earth-dwellers,
> adorned the green fields,   the earth, with branches,
> shoots, and green leaves;   and life He created,
> in each of the species   which live and move.
> Thus the brave warriors   lived in hall-joys,
> blissfully prospering   until a certain one
> began to do evil ...
> That murderous spirit   was named Grendel,
> huge moor-stalker   who held the wasteland,
> fens and marshes;   unblessed, unhappy . . . (*Beowulf* 55)

By introducing Grendel when he does, the poet attaches him for all time to the creation myth, a sign perhaps that he thought a mind such as Grendel's to be as real as the earth and the sun and, like those other realities, in need of explanation.

If Eliade's observations about primitive cultures are correct, this passage best reveals the poet's intention in characterizing the crimes of Grendel, and a number of important consequences flow from it. First, as Tolkien noted long ago, if Grendel is a kinsman of Cain, he is also a kinsman of Adam (89); he is as human, therefore, as he is monstrous. In his very first appearance in the poem, therefore, he ceases to be a fiction drawn from folklore and becomes, for the poet, a fact of Christian myth. And, surprisingly, when the poet so transforms him, he reverses the chronology of Genesis. Grendel the murderer is named before Cain, the original of murderers. Why? Is the threat represented by Grendel the murderer so immediate and his kind of murder so much worse than Cain's that the culture demands a new archetype? Is a revision of the cosmogonic myth necessary to account for a new reality — the murder not of one brother but of many strangers?

We modern readers think of both Cain and Grendel as equally legendary. The poet of course could not have thought that. The allusions to Cain in the poem are meant not only to be rhetorically effective and theologically orthodox, but also psychologically analytical and thus of practical importance, rather like Freud's appeal to the myth of Narcissus, or Jung's insistence that we see our ordinary selves in terms of archetypes. The poet invokes Cain to make Grendel's murders as real as possible and also to account for the dysfunction of his very human mind. For, as Eliade points out, "Judeo-Christianity put the stamp of falsehood and 'illusion' on whatever was not justified or validated by the two Testaments" (2). Grendel, to be actual, must cease to be a creature of the night and become a creature of the sixth day of creation. And thus when Hrothgar the king, desperate to be rid of the horror of Grendel, prays to the old pagan gods, the poet considers him foolish; the old gods are fictions; they cannot defeat a murderer as real as Grendel.

5

Connecticut Review Fall 1994   *Meehan*

In his famous chronicle of the early Middle Ages, *The History of the Franks*, Gregory of Tours recounts the murder of his brother Peter, who was speared by an assassin. He says of the murderer, "Because of the crime which he had committed, he became a wanderer, with no fixed place of abode . . . the innocent blood which he had shed cried unto God from the ground" (Gregory of Tours 261). This murder occurred in a European street in 574 AD, but the language is straight from Genesis, and so inevitably echoes descriptions of Grendel, the exile, composed centuries later. Gregory did not wish to impart a sense of antiquity to his brother's murder, but to heighten its reality. The murderer of Peter is a contemporary but he is also Cain; the real murderer and his archetype forever share the same language and fate. Thus Gregory gives the myth new life because he has witnessed its reenactment.

Finally, as was the case with folklore, a terrifying attraction exists between the imagination of the serial killer and the ceremonies and language of myth. And, as a corollary of this, there is a necessary correspondence between the mind of this murderer and the mind of the poet who must represent him. It is on the field of myth that poet and murderer meet to do battle over their fundamentally opposed visions of the world, the murderer assaulting, the poet defending the frontier between life and death. To tell truly the extreme perversity and pathology of Grendel's human mind, the poet must represent him in mythic terms. For, like Grendel, serial killers attack creation itself; their purpose is to annihilate, to commit not a murder, but ultimate murder. Their crimes are as symbolic as they are literal, and not infrequently they parody their culture's central myths and rituals. It was Ted Bundy who said he wished "to master life and death" (qtd. in Leyton 107), assigning himself the epic task of heroes from Gilgamesh to Christ. And the real horror of murderers assuming mythic roles lies in the fact that they are such terrifying literalists. The thrill for them comes from actualizing the symbol. Consider Jeffrey Dahmer's plan for an altar of bones on which to worship, like the Grail, the remains of those he has sacrificed (Masters qtd. in Highsmith 5). Consider Edmund Kemper, whose first victim became a sort of patron saint of his murderous career, and the ravine where he threw her a place of pilgrimage. Consider Berkowitz's messianic obedience to Sam; Ramiriz's Faustian service to the powers of darkness; DeSalvo's parody of religious holidays when he leaves a Happy New Year card propped against the toe of his hideously postured last victim. All of these in a sense wish to master life and death, to shatter the barriers of the physical world in ways we dare to do only symbolically. Communion becomes cannibalism; beatific union, necrophilia; the ineffable, the unspeakable. Through his sacrificial victims, the serial killer gains entry at last to the land of the dead, where, in the hatred that passes all understanding, he finds the joyless stasis he seeks, and where, a walking dead man, he remakes others in his own image. It is the murderer's pathology that makes him undertake this morbid journey to his own underworld, and the poet's imagination has no choice but to follow where the murderer goes and to describe the visions they both see.

We have of course found clinical terms for these crimes and scientific explanations. But our language will never abandon the old metaphors and myths. They belong to the murderers who are driven to act them out, and to the writers who seek figures to express the unspeakable. Because of the mind of its writer, because of the mind of its murderer, *Beowulf*, like all enduring literature, is contemporary.

Works Cited

Beowulf: A Dual Language Edition. Trans. Howell D. Chickering, Jr. New York: Anchor, 1977.

Eliade, Mircea. *Myth and Reality.* Trans. Willard R. Trask. New York: Harper Colophon, 1963.

Gregory of Tours. *The History of the Franks.* Trans. Lewis Thrope. New York: Penguin, 1979.

Hickey, Eric W. *Serial Murderers and their Victims.* Pacific Grove, California: Brooks/Cole, 1991.

Highsmith, Patricia. "From Fridge to Cooler: Exploring the Psychology of a Serial Killer." Rev. of *The Shrine of Jeffrey Dahmer*, by Brian Masters, and *Jeffrey Dahmer*, by Joel Norris. TLS. 16 April 1993: 5-6.

Ker, W. P. *Epic and Romance: Essays on Medieval Literature.* New York: Dover, 1957.

Kermode, Hollander, et al, eds. *The Oxford Anthology of English Literature.* 2 vols. New York: Oxford: Oxford UP, 1973.

Leyton, Elliott. *Compulsive Killers: the Story of Modern Multiple Murder.* New York: Washington Mews Books; NYUP, 1986.

Tolkien, J. R. R. *"Beowulf: The Monsters and the Critics." An Anthology of Beowulf Criticism.* Ed. Lewis E. Nicholson. Notre Dame, Indiana: Notre Dame, 1963.

[3]

TOWARDS AN HISTORICAL SOCIOLOGY OF MULTIPLE MURDER

Other sinnes onley speake;
Murther shreikes out.

THE DUCHESS OF MALFI

This book has explicated the texts left by half a dozen killers of our time. It has not focused on these murderers because their thoughts or acts are of any merit, but because it is only through a detailed examination of their careers that we can hope to understand the origin and meaning of their activities. We have taken as our starting point the observation of Robert Darnton that it is precisely 'when we run into something that seems unthinkable to us [that] we may have hit upon a valid point of entry into an alien mentality'. Having done this, we will now try to marry the great historical and anthropological enterprises. In doing so, we will 'have puzzled through to the native's point of view' and mounted an explanation of the inexplicable. So far we have tried to reveal the immediate motives behind the killers' acts: now our task is to transcend the immediate, to suggest that these motives are neither insane nor random but buried deeply in the

Hunting Humans

social order, part of a continuously evolving social process.[1]

The murderer of strangers has probably always been among us. However much we may wish to dismiss him as a freak, an aberration, or an accident, his tastes and desires are part of the human repertoire, the human experience, and the human capability. Nor must we dismiss him and his behaviour as meaningless, for mankind is a gregarious and social species, and anything its members do has some social meaning. But wherein lies the origin of the social process we have now described, that sequence of events which so deforms a man that he comes to think of himself as a kind of automaton, a 'robot' going through the motions of social life without any hope that future events might make his life endurable? The killers customarily explain themselves in conventional ideas borrowed from the wider culture, as did the torturer and multiple murderer Joseph Kallinger in his autobiographical poem, 'The Unicorn in the Garden'.[2]

> *When I was a little boy,*
> *My adoptive parents,*
> *Anna and Stephen,*
> *Killed the unicorn in my garden*
>
> *Exiled from the street,*
> *Isolated from other children,*
> *I lived among shoes and knives and hammers.*
> *Unknown, unwanted, unloved,*
> *I learned to shape soles, replace heels, drive nails.*
> *My own soul was hidden from me by the shop's*
> *Dead world.*
> *A robot to their will,*
> *I died with the unicorn in my garden.*

Yet this self-pitying interpretation leaves unanswered so many questions. If his own adoptive parents were so insensitive to his needs, why was he dramatically more so when he tortured and murdered his own

An Overview

small son? If his childhood was so difficult, was his adulthood (he had a bearable occupation, in which he was very highly regarded, and a loving wife and family, who seemed devoted to him) provocative of anything resembling his gruesome acts? I think not. It is therefore incumbent upon us to look much more deeply into the historical process and its impact upon the lives of individuals, if we are ever to have anything resembling a clear understanding of these men.

Before we do so, let us be clear about the manner of beast we have been discussing, and how he stands in relation to other 'criminal' species. He is not quite like the majority, whose thefts of *property* garner a combination of financial profit and 'the intoxicating pleasure of intensive activity'. Such property offences attract bank robbers, political commissars, and corporate executives, not the men of whom we speak (who reap neither wealth nor security from their crimes). Neither is the multiple murderer quite like those who commit crimes against the *person* (be it rape, assault, or even homicide), for these offences tend to be little more that a demonstration of individual power and a cathartic release of rage.

Our multiple murderers transcend mere catharsis and temporary gratification: their aim is a more ambitious one, a kind of sustained sub-political campaign directed towards 'the timelessness of oppression and the order of power'. But their protest is not on behalf of others, only themselves; their anguish is trivial, not profound; and they punish the innocent, not the guilty. It is thus only an extreme version of other nihilistic crimes, in which the killer typically reverses all social values as his only way of making 'a demonstration to the authorities' in a manner so forceful that they must consider it. Since all he is protesting is his lack of a crisp identity and his refusal to tolerate the position society has allocated him, it is less than tragic – even ironic, but intellectually

331

Hunting Humans

unacceptable – that what Peter and Favret call a
'clumsy psychiatry' tries to declare him insane and
suggest that

the native's speech had no weight, was not even an
effect of monstrosity; such criminals were only disturbed
children who played with corpses as they played with
words. The resentment they displayed had no reason
for its existence; it was merely a product of their
imagination.[3]

There is one problem that remains undiscussed
and it is central to any biographical enterprise: if we
can analyse the mass of humanity in sociological
terms, how can we hope to do so with individuals?
According to the late historical sociologist Philip
Abrams, 'The problem of accounting sociologically
for the individual in particular is really only a more
precise version of the problem of accounting for
individuals in general.' Analysed in historical terms,
'Lenin and Luther, the Sun King and Shakespeare no
more elude or defy sociological explanation than do
Russian proletarians in 1900.' Abrams insists, and
our data force us largely to concur, that 'becoming a
deviant is not a matter of personal or social pathology, social disorganization, deprivation, broken
homes, viciousness, bad company or chance but of *a
negotiated passage to a possible identity* [my italic]', in
which the individual can only be understood as
'creatively seizing opportunities for personal self-
definition' – as did all our multiple murderers.

Individuals *are* their biographies. And in so far as a
biography is fully and honestly recorded what it reveals
is some historically located history of self-construction –
a moral career in fact. The setting of the biography is
this or that historically given system of probabilities or
life chances. The biography realizes some life chances
within that system and perforce abandons others.

The point, then, is that to understand an exceptional
individual, we must observe 'the meshing of life-
history and social history in a singular fate'; which is

An Overview

to say that we must look at the social system's matrix of choices and opportunities, rewards and punishments, in terms of which each individual calculates his future. Later in this chapter, we will suggest that nowhere more than in modern America is an individual likely to negotiate the identity of a multiple murderer.[4]

Yet the problem remains that while many people are subject to the same tainted origins and thwarted ambitions, only a tiny minority of them become killers. Why then do most of them refuse to do so? There are no data that would allow us to address the problem in any scientific fashion, no control group of biographies of individuals who have been diverted from the formative process at different stages. Yet it seems most likely that such people (the vast majority) are touched, however superficially, by some person or institution that renders their lives bearable – offering the common life of 'quiet desperation' in place of the massive refusal of self and life that characterizes our killers. We can only posit that somewhere in the journey from institutionalized or illegitimate child to lofty but thwarted ambition, some family member, a lover, a job, or group membership (or the hope of any of these) offers most people a taste of fulfilment and interrupts their passage to murderous identities.

THE LITERATURE

For crimes against persons (murder, rape, assault) we have no theory as to the value of such offences, and hence no theory as to what would affect the returns from such crimes.
RALPH ANDREANO AND JOHN SIEGFRIED[5]

Homicide

The poverty of conventional explanation is nowhere better represented than in the above quotation from

333

Hunting Humans

a group of economists who confess to being bewildered by a crime which offers no economic return. The other social sciences have fared rather better in their attempts to deal with homicide, at least in its 'normal' manifestations. We have already demonstrated that, at least in theory, single and multiple murder are quite different phenomena, with profoundly different characteristics. The psychiatrist Lunde has made it clear that 'the most important single contrast between mass murderers and murderers of a single person is a difference in their relationships to the victims', the former killing strangers, the latter killing intimates. This curious phenomenon of the murder of strangers is extremely rare in so-called 'primitive' societies, a fact which social scientist Stuart Palmer corroborates with anthropological data showing that 'in the vast majority of non-literate societies analyzed, forty-one out of forty-four homicidal victims and offenders are rarely if ever strangers'. It is in our own tradition, buried both in our historical past and in our industrial present, that stranger-murder has been a major homicidal theme. In criminologist Wolfgang's classic study of 550 homicides in 1958 in Philadelphia, 12.2 per cent of the killings were between strangers; and the FBI report that 15.5 per cent of the 22,516 murders committed in the US in 1981 were between strangers.[6]

The perpetrators of the types of murder are also profoundly different. Virtually all social analysts agree that single murder is primarily the province of the truly disenfranchised. 'It is the oppressed who are the homicidal,' writes Palmer. 'The poor, the uneducated, those without legitimate opportunities, respond to their institutionalized oppression with outward explosions of aggression.' This notion of exactly who the oppressed are has been much refined in the current debate on whether it is absolute

An Overview

poverty or relative inequality (or subcultural variation) which actually accounts for homicides. Nevertheless, Williams's tentative conclusion in the
sociological journals remains that 'racial economic
inequality is a major source of criminal violence in
the United States', and that 'poverty, in addition to
racial inequality, also provides "fertile soil for criminal violence"'. It is obvious that our multiple murderers are drawn from very different social niches,
for they are rarely from the ranks of the truly
oppressed; they are rarely women, and almost never
black. Indeed, they are generally white and gainfully
employed, and, sometimes, have reasonable expectations of 'brilliant' futures. They are not at all the
same men who kill an intimate in a moment of rage
or venality; nor are their generally spontaneous acts
part of any organized and meaningful campaign.
Lunde was quite right then to berate the scholars of
homicide for their 'tendency to assume that the single
fact of having committed a murder is a sufficient
basis for identifying a class of people, murderers'
who are essentially the same, for nothing could be
further from the truth.[7]

There are perspectives on homicide other than the
purely sociological, but they tend to be mired in
irrelevancy or based on mechanisms that do not
exist. Perhaps the most popular of these has been the
pseudo-biological school, which has held a certain sway
since the nineteenth-century criminologist Lombroso
began measuring the foreheads of Italian criminals
and the twentieth-century criminologists, the
Gluecks, assessed the testicles of American delinquents – all searching for the 'criminal physical type'.
This tradition tends to fixate on such unfathomable
matters as the purported brain temperatures of murderers, and has long ago been revealed as ideology
masquerading as science. The 'discovery' of the
XYY chromosomes is perhaps the best known
example of this nonsense: many unsubstantiated

335

Hunting Humans

claims have been made that the possession of this
chromosome inclines the victim towards violence
(including falsely attributing such XYY chromosomes to Richard Speck, the Chicago nurse-
murderer). These notions persist in the popular culture despite the fact that later studies have established
that only a small proportion of violent offenders
actually have XYY chromosomes. Furthermore, the
imprisoned offenders who did have the XYY chromosomes were actually *less* likely to have committed
violent crimes than those with 'normal' chromosomes. Indeed, the only reasonable conclusion that
has come out of the biological approach is sociobiol-
ogist Edward O. Wilson's observation that there is
no evidence whatever for any universal aggressive
instinct (as had been posited by ethologists such as
Lorenz and Ardrey), and that human 'behaviour
patterns do not conform to any general innate restric-
tions'. Sadly for the scientific enterprise, most 'socio-
biologists' – even ones as literate as Melvin Konner –
simply ignore the reality that human evolution's
super-development of the cortex (or thinking, conscious part of the brain) has overridden any instinc-
tive or genetically coded behaviours among humans.
Similarly, they ignore the reality that if human behaviour were genetically determined, it would be everywhere the same instead of ranging from the gentility
of the 'primitive' Fore peoples of New Guinea to the
violence of South America's Yanomamo.[8]

The *psychological* tradition also looks for the cause
of aggression within the individual, but finds it
buried in the psyche rather than in the chromosome.
Here, the assumption which runs throughout the
literature is that anyone who murders must be suffering from some form of psychopathology, a dubious
assumption indeed when working-class culture so
obviously venerates violent display as an intrinsic
manifestation of manhood. The psychologists and
psychiatrists differ as to where they find the cause of

An Overview

this disorder. The psychiatrist Abrahamsen points to 'persistent internal conflict between the environment around them and the word within them – the world of infantile sexual and life-preserving drives', a conflict which is caused by some traumatic experience in early childhood (before the child is two!). The psychologist Megargee hypothesizes that the violent criminal virtually always 'has' one of two types of personalities, either 'undercontrolled' or 'overcontrolled', which leaves the critic marvelling at how many walk the tightrope between the two. Still, two of America's most gifted psychiatrists refute their profession's stance. Lunde notes that 'the incidence of psychosis among murderers is no greater than the incidence of psychosis in the total population'; and Willard Gaylin readily admits that psychiatry occupies a 'primitive position' regarding 'the nature of the cause of the disease'. My criticism here is not that psychology and psychiatry have nothing to contribute to the study of murder, for they certainly do; but rather that they, no more than pseudo-biology, cannot account for variations in homicide rates over time or between societies. Their special gift in fact is not at all to account for cause – for that lies within tensions generated in the social order – but to analyse the process in which the individual psyche accommodates itself to its environment.[9]

Multiple Murder

If the literature on homicide has a certain richness about it, curiously, no such assessment can be made about the subject of our inquiry. Multiple murder has attracted very little specialized attention and should the reader glance through four books, he will have mastered the number which have devoted themselves exclusively to the phenomenon. Even those four are primarily descriptive, not analytic.

Hunting Humans

The first is still the best; but it (criminologist Bolitho's *Murder for Profit*) concerns itself only with the
mendacious economic form that we ignore here –
killing for profit. However, Bolitho's comments,
now over half a century old, repay close examination. He noted then what those who followed him
overlooked, that the killers were no 'deranged automata' and that they were 'the worst men, not
madmen'.

If they very commonly construct for themselves a life-
romance, a personal myth in which they are the mal-
treated hero, which secret is the key of their life, in such
comforting daydreams many an honest man has
drugged himself against despair.

He observed that many of them thought of themselves as being in a kind of 'social war, in which his
hand is against society, and all is fair', but he
understood that this is a common way of thinking
among any 'men in an unsheltered corner of this
competitive world'. He concluded with a remarkably
sophisticated recognition of the complicity of the
modern nation-state in the creation of these multiple
murderers, remarking of the Fritz Haarmann case in
Germany between the wars, 'The state had used all
its best tools upon him: church, prison, army,
school, family, asylum – it can hardly disclaim direct
responsibility from the result.'[10]
    What might have been the beginning of a rich
tradition of inquiry soon dissolved. In 1928, two
years after the publication of Bolitho's book, criminologist Guy Logan published his *Masters of Crime*
which purported to be a study of multiple murder.
In fact, however, it was merely unanalysed case
material, and the subject lay unstudied for another
thirty years. Then two books appeared in 1958.
Criminologist Grierson Dickson's *Murder by Numbers*
focused on what today we would call serial murderers, and argued that their motives were either 'profit'

338

An Overview

or 'perversion'. Regrettably, his work is purely descriptive, and he has no explanation for the phenomenon, merely noting in passing the 'unfortunate origins' of the killers and that 'parental influence was either absent or hostile'. He did, however, observe one of the striking qualities of the killers, the fact that 'lack of economic security does not seem a factor to be considered, as few of our subjects came from really poverty-stricken homes'; and he registered the conclusion that 'not one of our perverts could have had that feeling, so comforting to a youngster, that he was a normal boy among other normal boys . . . [for] all of our perverts felt themselves to be set apart from their fellows, mostly by a sense of shame or inferiority'. Still, he does not tell us *why* this should be so.[11]

In that same year, crime writer Philip Lindsay published *The Mainspring of Murder*, which again rehashed the classical cases without venturing into much explanation. Yet Lindsay came the closest, despite the fact that he devoted only a few paragraphs to his attempt. 'Mass Murder,' Lindsay wrote, 'is largely a modern phenomenon.'

It begins its great career in the late eighteenth century, growing stronger during the nineteenth century until it arrives in full red horror in the twentieth century. Why? One point which cannot be avoided is its link with industrialism. With the dying of a pastoral England and the growth of industry with wretched communities gathered in towns and cities, the spirit of hatred grew to fury and the lost ones struck at a world they distrusted and feared.

Having glimpsed the key to the puzzle, he passes on, whining evermore about the advance of socialism and the collapse of individuality in modern society. Still, he also noted the strange paradox that it did not seem to be economic insecurity (which has always been with us), but personal and spiritual insecurity

339

Hunting Humans

that formed the breeding ground for the modern
multiple murderer.[12]

The only contemporary authority is Donald
Lunde, whose *Murder and Madness* largely concerns
itself with multiple murderers who are, in contrast
to single murderers, he says, '*almost always insane*'.
To Lunde, the killers are either victims of a paranoid
schizophrenia – 'a psychosis characterized by hallucinations ("hearing voices" in most cases), delusions
of grandiosity or persecution, bizarre religious ideas
(often highly personalized), and a suspicious, hostile,
aggressive manner' – or they are victims of sexual
sadism, 'a deviation characterized by torture and/or
killing and mutilation of other persons in order to
achieve sexual gratification'. Regrettably for this
theory, however, none of our multiple murderers in
this volume was reliably diagnosed as a victim of *any*
serious mental disorder.[13]

Lunde's second point, which also is contradicted
by all our data, is that while 'we do not *know* the
precise causes of these psychotic mentalities', we do
know that they 'are *not a product of the times*. Other
countries and other centuries have produced sex
murderers similar to those I have described from
recent US history.' Lunde takes great pains to lodge
the cause of these behaviours in the psyches of the
killer, arguing that for 'rare individuals, for reasons
that are not well understood, sexual and violent
aggressive impulses merge early in the child's development, ultimately finding expression in violent
sexual assault'. Very much in a Freudian vein, he
dwells on the sexual pleasure the killer sometimes
receives from the murder and mutilation of his
victims, reflecting on their rich fantasy lives in which
'they imagine sadistic scenes and derive great pleasure from this activity'. Lunde's gifts are considerable,
but his imprisonment within traditional psychiatry
makes it impossible for him to transcend the non-
explanation and mere categorization of his art. For

An Overview

an *explanation*, we must turn to the forces that create, shape, and deform individuals in a modern stratified society.*[14]

THE HISTORICAL METAMORPHOSES

We are encountering more and more . . . (of those who) have turned the life instinct on its head: Meaning for them can only come from acts of destruction.
ROGER KRAMER AND IRA WEINER[15]

Multiple murderers are not 'insane' and they are very much products of their time. Far from being a randomly occurring freakish event, the arrival of the multiple murderer is dictated by specific stresses and alterations in the human community. Moreover, far from being deluded, he is in many senses an embodiment of the central themes in his civilization as well as a reflection of that civilization's critical tensions. He is thus a creature and a creation of his age. As such, we would expect him to change his character over time, and all the evidence suggests that that is precisely what he does. In what follows, I shall show that the pre-industrial multiple killer was an aristocrat who preyed on his peasants; that the industrial era produced a new kind of killer, most commonly a new bourgeois who preyed upon prostitutes, homeless boys, and housemaids; and that in the mature industrial era, he is most often a failed bourgeois

* If there is virtually no social theory of multiple murderers, there is a great deal of purely descriptive case material. See, for example, Hilde Bruch, 'Mass Murder: The Wagner Case'; Robert Hazelwood and John Douglas, 'The Lust Murderer; Robert Brittain, 'The Sadistic Murderer'; Allen Bartholomew, K. L. Milte, and F. Galbally, 'Sexual Murder: Psychopathology and Psychiatric Jurisprudential Considerations'; James Calvin and John MacDonald, 'Psychiatric Study of a Mass Murderer'; Marvin Kahn, 'Psychological Test Study of a Mass Murderer'; as well as M. Foucault, *I, Pierre Rivière . . .*, and Donald Lunde and Jefferson Morgan, *The Die Song*.

341

Hunting Humans

who stalks university women and other middle-class
figures. Thus for each historical epoch, both the
social origins of the killers and the social characteristics of their victims are highly predictable: they are
thus very much men of their time.

The Pre-industrial Multiple Murderer

Our evidence is not what we might wish, but we
must take what is available, and the overwhelming
weight of that suggests that multiple murder for its
own sake was very rare in the archaic order of the
pre-industrial era. Indeed, the famous multiple murderers of that era killed for profit – as was the case
with Sawney Bean in fifteenth-century Scotland who
murdered to steal the possessions of passers-by and
eat their bodies; so too with Madame de Brinvilliers
in seventeenth-century France who murdered her
family to inherit their wealth; and with Catherine
Montvoisin, also in seventeenth-century France,
who arranged (for payment) the elimination of
hundreds of infants. The only name that emerges
from this era as indisputably one of our subjects of
inquiry is an aristocrat of great wealth and
achievement.[16]

The Baron Gilles de Rais was born in 1404 into
one of the greatest fortunes of France. During the
last eight years of his life, retired to his great estates,
he murdered somewhere between 141 and 800 children, mostly boys. He would take the local children
to his castle and, after raping them in one manner or
another, would torture and kill them. His accomplice
Griart told the court in 1440 that 'the said Gilles, the
accused, exercised his lust once or twice on the
children. That done, the said Gilles killed them
sometimes with his own hand or had them killed.'
As to the manner in which the children were killed,
Griart remembered: 'sometimes they were decapi-
tated, and dismembered; sometimes he [Gilles] cut

342

An Overview

their throats, leaving the head attached to the body; sometimes he broke their necks with a stick; sometimes he cut a vein in their throats or some other part of their necks, so that the blood of the said children flowed'. 'As the children were dying,' wrote his biographer, Leonard Wolf, 'Gilles, the artist of terror, the skilled Latinist who read Saint Augustine; Gilles, the devoted companion of Jeanne d'Arc, squatted on the bellies of the children, studying their languishing faces, breathing in their dying sighs.'[17]

When the court interrogators asked him who had induced him to do his crimes and taught him how to do the killings, the Baron replied: 'I did and perpetrated them following [the dictates] of my imagination and my thought, without the advice of anyone, and according to my own judgement and entirely for my own pleasure and physical delight, and for no other intention or end.' Under threat of being put to the torture, he confessed, 'for my ardour and my sensual delectation I took and caused to be taken a great number of children – how many I cannot say precisely, children whom I killed and caused to be killed; with them, I committed the vice and the sin of sodomy . . . and . . . I emitted spermatic semen in the most culpable fashion on the belly of . . . the children, as well before as after their deaths, and also while they were dying. I, alone, or with the help of my accomplices, Gilles de Sillé, Roger de Bricqueville, Henriet [Griart], Etienne Corrilaut [Poitou], Rossignol and Petit Robin, have inflicted various kinds and manners of torture on these children. Sometimes I beheaded them with daggers, with poignards, with knives; sometimes I beat them violently on the head with a stick or with other contusive instruments . . . sometimes I suspended them in my room from a pole or by a hook and cords and strangled them; and when they were languishing, I committed with them the vice of sodomy . . . When the children were dead, I embraced them, and I gazed

343

Hunting Humans

at those which had the most beautiful heads and the loveliest members, and I caused their bodies to be cruelly opened and took delight in viewing their interior organs; and very often, as the children were dying, I sat on their bellies and was delighted to see them dying in that fashion and laughed about it with . . . Corrilaut and Henriet, after which I caused [the children] to be burned and converted their cadavres into dust.'[18]

In a manner that will be unfamiliar only to those who have not read the other confessions in this book, the Baron interrupted his homicidal memoir to lecture the grieving parents on how to raise children. But first, during the reading in open court of his crimes, surrounded by the families of his victims (peasants all), he allowed himself to express outrage at the lowly estate of those who were acting as his judges. Hearing the bishop and the vicar of the inquisition name his acts in front of the peasant parents, he shouted: 'Simoniacs, ribalds, I'd rather be hanged by the neck than reply to the likes of such clerics and such judges. It is not to be borne . . . to appear before such as you.' Turning to the Bishop Malestroit, he sneered, 'I'll do nothing for you as Bishop of Nantes.'[19]

Following threats of excommunication and torture, he capitulated. 'From the time of my youth I have committed many great crimes,' he told the court, 'against God and the Ten Commandments, crimes still worse than those of which I stand accused. And I have offended our Saviour as a consequence of bad upbringing in childhood, when I was left uncontrolled to do whatever I pleased [and especially] to take pleasure in illicit acts.' Once more reminiscent of the killers of later centuries, he begged his judges to publish his confessions, and do so in 'the vulgar tongue' so that the peasants would know of what he had done. What was the moral he wished to point out to his audience? 'When I was a child, I

344

An Overview

had always a delicate nature, and did for my own pleasure and according to my own will whatever evil I pleased. To all [of you who are] fathers and mothers, friends and relatives of young people and children, lovingly I beg and pray you to train them in good morals, [teach] them to follow good examples and good doctrines; and instruct them and punish them, lest they fall into the same trap in which I myself have fallen.' The Baron was hanged and burned on 26 October 1440.[20]

Why should the classic case of pre-industrial multiple murder be a wealthy and powerful aristocrat? And why has this class vanished from participation in modern multiple murder? What was happening in the second quarter of the fifteenth century to put special stress upon the ancient landed aristocracy? The world into which Gilles de Rais was born had existed for centuries: it was essentially a two-class social universe, a vast mass of peasants and a tiny collection of 'noble' overlords, who expropriated the surplus of the former. These were hard times for humanity – and especially the peasants – for plague, famine, and war were frequent and devastating. There were, however, some compensations. The peasants' transfer of their surplus to their rulers was balanced by the provision of minimal security for the cultivators, who were given rights of use of the land in perpetuity. A social correlate of this relative economic security was the humanizing personalization of social relationships. The historian Peter Laslett has written that although exploitation was endemic to the system, 'everyone belonged to a group, a family group', and 'everyone had his or her circle of affection: every relationship could be seen as a love-relationship'. This is not to say that 'love' was the rule, or even the norm, in human encounters, but rather that human relationships were personalized and on a human scale: whether the relationship was full of warmth or riddled with conflict, it was a

345

Hunting Humans

relationship between human beings. Institutional
relationships and life were virtually unknown; and if
groups of men and women occasionally worked
together in rural life, they did so as households
cooperating with one another for mutual goals. This
personal world of the peasant did not encourage the
growth of our multiple murderers.[21]

What was happening to the landed aristocracy? It
was in a state of *crisis*, assaulted on all sides by
peasantry and merchants. For historian Immanuel
Wallerstein, the crisis of feudalism began between
the thirteenth and fifteenth centuries. What provoked
this crisis was that 'the optimal degree of productiv-
ity has been passed' in the archaic feudal system, and
'the economic squeeze was leading to a generalized
seignior-peasant class war, as well as ruinous fights
within the seignioral classes'. Moreover, the peasantry had begun to protest its condition, and peasant
revolts became 'widespread in western Europe from
the thirteenth century to the fifteenth century'; peasant republics were declared in Frisia in the twelfth
and thirteenth centuries and in Switzerland in the
thirteenth century; French peasants rebelled in 1358
as they did in Italy and Flanders at the turn of the
fourteenth century.[22]

Critical to our purpose, the fifteenth century – the
time of the Baron Gilles de Rais – was the era in
which the established order strove to reassert itself,
often through the savage repression of political and
religious peasant rebellions. This was the century,
Wallerstein wrote, that 'saw the advent of the great
restorers of internal order in western Europe: Louis
XI in France, Henry VII in England, and Ferdinand
of Aragon and Isabella of Castile in Spain. The major
mechanisms at their disposal in this task, as for their
less successful predecessors, were financial: by means
of the arduous creation of a bureaucracy (civil and
armed) strong enough to tax and thus to finance a
still stronger bureaucratic structure.' It can be no

346

An Overview

coincidence that the only pre-industrial multiple murderer, who killed purely for its own sake and of whom we have reliable record, was a member of that threatened established order. Neither does it require an impossible stretch of the imagination to speculate that the manner in which the Baron (accustomed to giving free rein to all his emotional impulses) tortured and killed the children of the peasantry was a personalized expression of the sweeping repressive thrust of his class, and a sexual metaphor in which he tested and enforced his terrible powers. Thus his indulgence of his violent sexual fantasy was an embroidery upon the central political event of his era – the subordination of the rebellious peasantry and the restoration of the absolute powers of the old nobility. What better way to deal with this threatened domination than through the idle torture and murder – as if they were nothing – of the class which dared stake a claim to equality? Three centuries later, with the bourgeoisie ascendant, another noble, the Marquis de Sade, would be relegated to harmless fantasizing and scribbling – for his class was already redundant: de Rais and his *confrères* had lost their struggle.[23]

The Industrial Era

Towards the end of the eighteenth century, there began that profound upheaval of all economic and social relations that we call the industrial revolution. It created entirely new social classes, raising some to prominence and dominance, and displacing others. 'The key figure of the eighteenth century,' the gifted historian Robert Darnton wrote, was 'the owner of the modes of production, a certain variety of Economic man with his own way of life and his own ideology.' This new man was the bourgeois: he 'acquired class-consciousness and revolted [against

347

Hunting Humans

the old aristocracy], leading a popular front of peasants and artisans'. The political culture necessary for
the fusion of 'this striking force' was designed to
allow the bourgeoisie 'to saturate the common
people with its own ideas of liberty (especially free
trade) and equality (especially the destruction of
aristocratic privilege)'. By the nineteenth century,
the series of mechanical inventions made possible a
new economic order dominated by machine production. The new bourgeoisie which owned this
machinery gained control of the emerging industrial
states and relegated the old aristocracy to the sidelines
of history (or joined with them through marriage).
But it was neither from the ranks of the old aristocracy – nor the triumphant new bourgeoisie – that the
leaders of the *homicidal revolution* would be drawn:
there are no Wedgwoods or Rockefellers among the
multiple murderers of the time. This should not be
surprising, for unthreatened classes do not produce
them.

Throughout the industrializing world, traditional
communal life and activity was snuffed out. In
Laslett's terms,

the removal of the economic functions from the patriarchal family at the point of industrialization created a
mass society. It turned the people who worked into a
mass of undifferentiated equals, working in a factory or
scattered between the factories, the mines and the
offices, bereft for ever of the feeling that work was a
family affair, done within the household.

The new industrial order, Wolf wrote, 'cut through
the integument of custom, severing people from
their accustomed social matrix in order to transform
them into economic actors, independent of prior
social commitments to kin and neighbours'.

This liberation from accustomed social ties and the
separation which it entailed constituted the historical
experience which Karl Marx would describe in terms of

348

An Overview

'alienation'. The alienation of men . . . from themselves
to the extent to which they now had to look upon their
own capabilities as marketable commodities; their alienation from their fellow men who had become actual or
potential competitors in the market.

The capitalism of the late eighteenth and nineteenth
centuries was thus an extraordinarily *radical* force;
and its capture of the emerging industrial system left
the new worker naked and exposed. At the same
time, Europe and America altered its living arrangements in order to supply the workers for the new
factory system: vast and anonymous cities were
created. Wolf provides British data to illustrate this
clustering of populations in urban areas. In 1600,
only 1.6 per cent of the population in England and
Wales lived in cities of 100,000 or more; but the
figures through the nineteenth century document the
flight from the land. By 1801, one-tenth of the
population was living in cities, a proportion which
doubled by 1840 and doubled again by the end of the
century: by 1900, Britain was an urban society. To
this depersonalized new world – in which the worker
lost even that tattered blanket of protection of kin
and community, and instead toiled in vast factories
and took rooms in anonymous boarding houses –
was added a further humiliation. The new bourgeois
ideology penalized the losers, the unemployed or the
under-employed, for the new cultural system trans-
muted 'the distinction between the classes into distinctions of virtue and merit'.[24]
  Such conditions of poverty and humiliation, insecurity and inequality, entailed many social costs,
among the most notable of which was the creation
of new types of murderers. Wilson complains that
murder in the pre-industrial era had been essentially
dull, springing generally 'out of poverty and misery':
such murders 'do not really involve much human
choice – much good or evil'. The nineteenth and

Hunting Humans

early twentieth centuries would be much more oblig-
ing, for 'with a few interesting exceptions, all the
"great" murder cases of the nineteenth century –
Lizzie Borden, Charles Bravo, Dr Pritchard, Professor Webster – concerned the socially comfortable
classes. Not the extremely rich or the aristocracy . . .
but the middle classes.' Indeed, one is driven to note
the number of professional, especially medical, titles
attached to their names – Dr William Palmer, Dr
Thomas Cream, Dr Marvel Petiot, and many
others.[25]

Of those multiple murderers who were killing
apparently for its own sake, two homicidal themes
emerged. The major theme was one in which
middle-class functionaries – doctors, teachers, pro-
fessors, civil servants, who belonged to the class
created to serve the new triumphant bourgeoisie –
preyed on members of the lower orders, especially
prostitutes and housemaids. If the prevailing 'need'
of the era's economic formations was to discipline
the lower orders into accepting the timetable of the
machine and industrial employment, then this form
of homicide can be usefully seen as the means by
which these new members of a new middle class
took the prevailing ethos to its logical conclusion. In
killing the failures and the unruly renegades from the
system, and doing so with such obvious pleasure,
they acted as enforcers of the new moral order. We
will never know the identity of 'Jack the Ripper',
who terrorized the prostitutes of London by disembowelling them with surgical precision; but we do
know that Dr Thomas Cream began to poison
prostitutes in London in 1891, offering them drinks
from his toxic bottle, and sending taunting letters to
the police.

By the third quarter of the nineteenth century,
they began to appear everywhere in the Western
world, but most especially in the advanced industrializing nations of England, France, Germany, and

An Overview

the United States. By the early twentieth century, it had become a common art form. Few cases have left us with much detail to analyse, although we do have their gory crimes and brief confessions. Between 1920 and 1925, Grossman, Denke, Haarmann, and Kurten were all killing in Germany. In Hungary in 1931, Sylvestre Matuschka blew up a train, killing twenty-five and maiming 120 others. At first he explained, 'I wrecked trains because I like to see people die. I like to hear them scream. I like to see them suffer'; but later he struck a curiously modern note by blaming his action on a demon spirit named Leo. In France, during the 1860s, Joseph Philippe strangled and cut the throats of prostitutes; and many more followed his path. In the 1920s, Earle Nelson raped and killed at least twenty boarding-house landladies, strangling in an arc from San Francisco to Winnipeg. In Chicago, Herman Mudgett (alias Dr H. H. Holmes), a medical student who had abandoned his studies when he had run out of funds, killed dozens of young women in his 'castle'. Among his last words before he was hanged in 1896 was a curious confession: 'I have commenced to assume the form and features of the Evil One himself.' Hamilton Fish, the son of a Potomac River boat captain and a deeply religious man who wished to be a minister, began a serial-murder career that spanned decades, torturing and murdering at least a dozen children, primarily from the working classes. His last child-victim was young Grace Budd: after he killed her, he wrote to her mother: 'On Sunday June the 3 – 1928 I called on you at 406 W 15th St. Brought you pot cheese – strawberries. We had lunch. Grace sat in my lap and kissed me. I made up my mind to eat her. On the pretence of taking her to a party. You said Yes she could go. I took her to an empty house in Westchester I had already picked out . . . How she did kick – bite and scratch. I choked her to death, then cut her in small pieces so I could take my meat

351

Hunting Humans

to my rooms, Cook and eat it. How sweet and
tender her little ass was roasted in the oven. It took
me nine days to eat her entire body. I did *not* fuck
her tho I could of had I wished. She died a *virgin*.'[26]

The Major Theme: Petit Bourgeois Sensibilities

The major homicidal theme of this era was one in
which newly middle-class persons (with all the in-
securities such *arriviste* status entails) disciplined the
lower orders who threatened their morbid sensitivity
to their class position, or who behaved without the
appropriate 'refinement' required by the new era.
Perhaps the best illustration of these points was
contained in the Wagner case of 1913. He was one of
ten children of an alcoholic and braggart peasant
father who died when he (Wagner) was two years
old, leaving drinking debts of such magnitude that
the homestead had to be sold. His mother's second
marriage ended in divorce when he was seven,
reportedly because of her promiscuity. Even as a
child, 'he was known in the village as "the widow's
boy",' the psychiatrist Bruch recorded, 'and suffered
from depressions, suicidal thoughts, and nightmares'. Somehow Wagner obtained an education and
qualified as a schoolteacher; but he never recovered
from the hypersensitivity that such a rapid rise in the
social hierarchy can create.

During the night of September 4, 1913, the citizens of
Mühlhausen . . . were awakened by several large fires.
As they ran into the street, they were met by a man, his
face covered by a black veil, who was armed with two
pistols. He shot with great accuracy and killed eight
men and one girl immediately; twelve more were
severely injured. Then his two pistols ran out of ammunition, and he was overpowered and beaten down with
such violence that he was left for dead; however, he
was only unconscious. He had 198 more bullets in his

352

An Overview

possession. The innkeeper identified the murderer as his thirty-nine-year-old brother-in-law, who had been a schoolteacher in this village more than ten years earlier.

Wagner confessed that during the preceding night he had quietly killed his wife and four children . . . He also confessed that he had come to Mühlhausen to take revenge on the male inhabitants for their scorn and disdain for him. However, even while lying severely wounded and exposed to the hatred of the attacked people, he noticed that no one employed the term of abuse that would refer to his sexual sins, which he felt had been the cause of all the persecution, ridicule, and condemnation.

Wagner's life was spared when it was recognized, during the pre-trial examination, that he was mentally ill. He was committed to an insane asylum, where he spent the rest of his life, twenty-five years.

During the preceding week [before the killings] he had written a series of letters which were not mailed until September 4 . . . one which contained a complete confession of all his crimes. It was addressed to the largest newspaper in Stuttgart and was to be used as an editorial . . . Wagner had planned to return to his brother's house the following night with the intent of killing him and his family and of burning down his house as well as the house in which he had been born. As a final step he had planned to proceed to the royal castle in Ludwigsburg, overpower the guards, set fire to the castle, and die in the flames or jump off its walls, thereby terminating his own life.

He was vituperative in expressing his hatred against Professor Gaupp, in whom he had confided the motives for his deed and who had then expressed the opinion that he was mentally sick and therefore not responsible . . . 'If I am insane, then a madman has been teaching all these years.'

[Former associates] described him as an admirable citizen, dignified, somewhat quiet . . . Only a few had noted a certain amount of standoffishness and affectation. All commented on the fact that in a region in which

353

Hunting Humans

a heavy dialect was spoken by educated and uneducated alike, he insisted on using high German, even in his private life.

This fateful chain of events had its beginning, according to his self-accusation, with one or more sodomistic acts in the late summer of 1901, when he was twenty-seven years old . . . Of decisive importance was the fact that his sexual urges and acts stood in irreconcilable contrast to his high moral standards and ethical concepts. His deep sense of guilt never diminished . . . he soon began to make certain 'observations' and to 'hear' certain slanderous remarks, which led to the unshakeable conviction that his 'crime' was known. He felt himself continuously observed, mocked, and ridiculed, and lived in constant dread of arrest. He was determined not to suffer this public shame and humiliation, and therefore he always carried a loaded pistol . . . he began an affair with the innkeeper's daughter . . . His future wife gave birth to a girl in the summer of 1903 and he married her (with many inner misgivings) in December 1903. He felt that he no longer loved her and that she was intellectually not his equal; he considered her more a servant than a wife . . . She objected to his spending money and time on his literary interests. There were five children . . . He was unhappy about the birth of each child and felt confined by the financial hardship of a large family subsisting on the meager income of a village schoolteacher.

Gradually he began also to make 'observations' in Radel stetten [the village in which he had taken a new position] and felt convinced that the people of Mühlhausen had communicated their 'knowledge' to the people at his new location. He could notice it because of certain insinuations and the occasional arrogance which some allegedly showed against him. He felt caught in the old dilemma: there was never a direct statement, but he 'heard' pointed remarks containing hints. He knew if he reacted he would be publicly humiliated . . . Gradually the conviction ripened that there was only one way out. He must kill himself and his children, *out of pity* to save them from a future of being the target of contempt and

354

An Overview

evil slander and *to take revenge* on the people of Mühlhausen who had forced him to this horrible deed . . .
Since the men of Mühlhausen had started and spread
the slander, they had to die. In a life that as a whole had
been a series of depressing and frustrating disappoint-
ments, he was grateful that it had been given to him to
avenge his terrible torture and suffering. He was disap-
pointed to learn that he had killed only nine people
[plus his own family].

Even in 1938, when he knew that death from advanced
tuberculosis was imminent, he still felt that he had been
justified in his action – that even if he had killed all of
them it would not have balanced the suffering that had
been inflicted on him . . . the people of Mühlhausen
had made it impossible for him to lead a decent life of
work and orderliness and to gain recognition as a
literary figure and great dramatist . . . Since his student
days literature had been his great love and avocation.
He craved literary success, not only during the frugal
days . . . His profession of schoolteacher was not satisfactory to him. He considered himself in all seriousness
as one of the greatest dramatists of his time and spoke
with condescension of those whose works were
performed.*

I have quoted Bruch at great length because in many
important respects the Wagner case can be treated as
the text for the purple explosion of middle-class
multiple murder in the nineteenth and early twentieth centuries. What were the central themes in the
memoir of this tormented man? Were his delusions
of persecution merely bizarre psychic accident, or
did they reflect some of the central fractures in the
social order of his time?

Let us re-examine his life and his confessions. The
son of a drunken peasant and a 'promiscuous'
mother, his childhood must have been cursed with
the demeaning insults of his fellows. Yet he rose

* 'Mass Murder: The Wagner Case', by Hilde Bruch, *American
Journal of Psychiatry*, vol. 124, pp. 693–8, 1967.

Hunting Humans

from this crushing poverty and abasement to a modest position in the marginal middle classes as the village schoolteacher. But his ambitions were loftier still, for he regarded himself as a literary genius and he hungered for the recognition such status would bring. Being young, he contracted a sexual relationship with the innkeeper's daughter and impregnated her. The rigid demands of his time and his class meant that he had to marry her. This threatened his hard-won status, for an innkeeper's daughter was socially beneath him: moreover, she did not understand his middle-class (which is to say literary) pretensions or the expenses they entailed. Soon he had ceased to 'love' her, and began treating her as 'more a servant than a wife'.[27]

The new industrial order created a host of new 'professions', marginal middle-class occupations with a certain status which the clever sons of peasants might fill. Yet few things are so corrosive to the individual as rapid social mobility: he is no longer in the world that he knows; he does not know quite how to behave, nor how much leeway the public will allow him in the performance of his role. All he knows is that the penalty for failure is disgrace and an unceremonious return to the ugly status from which he has escaped: hence the common quality of a defensive status hysteria – which manifests itself as a kind of extreme personal insecurity – that is found so often among those who have risen or fallen dramatically in the social hierarchy. For Wagner, this fearful anxiety focused on the possibility that his brief pre-marital homosexual affair might be discovered: it was not his 'high moral standards' that made it impossible for him to cope with this memory, but his high social aspirations which would all collapse if he were unmasked as a sodomist. More and more his fear expressed itself in odd ways – most especially in his strange affectations of speaking and dressing over-formally and inappropriately (inappropriately

An Overview

to whom? To those who understand precisely the
demands of middle-class status). Might the neighbours know of his shame? He must watch their every
gesture and hear their every word, looking for signs
that they would unmask him. His morbid sensibility
– only an intense version of the compulsive rigidity
of his new class – began to dwell upon, then become
obsessed with, this fear of exposure until he was
interpreting all the behaviour of his fellow villagers
in these terms. They knew, they sensed, they felt.
Real or fancied insults and slights were converted
immediately into 'knowledge' of his guilt. Yet he
could not react: he could not charge them with
tormenting him for if he did so, 'he would be
publicly humiliated'. Therein lay the seed of his
terrible crimes: the only way to avoid the impossible
abasement of himself and his family, and claim
revenge, was to kill them all.

But why burn down his house and that of the
royal family? Nothing could have been more appropriate; for in this double and incendiary act he would
destroy all evidence of his humble origins and erase
his lowly past, while obliterating the seat and symbol
of the entire social order – the royal castle – that
orchestrated his anguish. This was not so much
delusional madness as the response of a tormented
person driven by an unrelenting fear; he knew that
its origins lay in the social order, and he sensed that
only such a murderous campaign could justify his
existence and bury his shame. Small wonder then
that he was so affronted when the psychiatrists and
court declared him insane, for he knew he was
struggling with something that was very real. 'If I
am insane, then a madman has been teaching all these
years,' he cried. He knew that he had spared himself
any further torment and avenged himself on his
oppressors; and ensured that they understood his
mission by announcing it to the public in an editorial
in the largest newspaper in Stuttgart. No case better

357

Hunting Humans

represents the timorous nature of the new petite
bourgeoisie than Wagner, disciplining the social
inferiors who threatened his position.

The Minor Theme: Proletarian Rebellion

The second major homicidal theme that emerged in
the burgeoning industrial era was one in which the
lower orders engaged in a kind of sub-political
rebellion that expressed their rage at their exclusion
from the social order. Their confessions remain
scanty so we must piece together what we can: still,
there is enough to suggest a great deal. If the killer
Panzram gives us chapter and verse, his contemporary, Peter Kurten, from the Germany of the 1920s
raises many questions. Kurten murdered two boys
when he himself was only nine years old; then as an
adult, he murdered several dozen men and women,
boys and girls, by knifing, by strangling, and by
hammering. When he was finally captured, the forty-
seven-year-old married factory labourer (whose
father had been jailed for abusing him and raping his
sister) insisted, 'I derived no sexual satisfaction from
what I did. My motives were principally to arouse
excitement and indignation in the population.
Through setting fire to the body I thought I would
increase the rage.' But why did he desire to so
antagonize his fellows? The authorities rooted
through his past and discovered that as a youth he
had spent much time in the Chamber of Horrors, a
waxwork exhibition in Kölnerstrasse. A childhood
friend recalled that he always gravitated towards the
wax figures of murderers. Kurten once said to him,
'I am going to be somebody famous like those men
one of these days.' After his arrest, he spoke of his
younger days in prison for the murder of the two
children: 'In prison, I began to think about revenging
myself on society. I did myself a great deal of damage
through reading blood-and-thunder stories, for

An Overview

instance I read the tale of "Jack the Ripper" several
times. When I came to think over what I had read,
when I was in prison, I thought what pleasure it
would give me to do things of that kind once I got
out again.' But why should he need such terrible
revenge; and why take it out on the innocent?[28]

For a full explanation of this metaphor we must
turn to the American Carl Panzram,* one of a small
proportion of our murderers who come from anything resembling a truly oppressed segment of society. He was imprisoned first in 1903, when he was
eleven, for breaking into a neighbour's home: for
that he was subjected to the sexual and physical
brutality of a reform-school staff. He did not begin
his twenty-year career in multiple murder until he
had experienced years of unspeakable torture (which
he documented and catalogued in his journal) and
sexual assault in the nation's prison system. He raped
and murdered sailors, 'natives', little boys, whom-
ever he could get his hands on; he destroyed property
wherever and whenever he could; and he hatched far
more ambitious schemes, which came to naught:
poisoning a town, blowing up a passenger train and,
he hoped, staging a political incident that might
spark a war between Britain and the United States.
'In my lifetime,' Panzram wrote as he sat in prison
eagerly awaiting his execution, 'I have murdered
twenty-one human beings, I have committed thousands of burglaries, robberies, larcenies, arsons and
last but not least I have committed sodomy on more
than 1,000 male human beings. For all of these things
I am not the least bit sorry. I have no conscience so
that does not worry me. I don't believe in man, God
nor Devil. I hate the whole damned race including
myself.'

He concluded, 'We do each other as we are done

* See Gaddis and Long's fine book, *Killer*, for Panzram's
journal.

Hunting Humans

by. I have done as I was taught to do. I am no
different from any other. You taught me how to live
my life, and I have lived as you taught me. I have no
desire whatever to reform myself. My only desire is
to reform people who try to reform me. And I
believe that the only way to reform people is to kill
'em.' He wrote his journal/manifesto, he said, 'so
that I can explain my side of it even though no one
ever hears or reads of it except one man. But one
man or a million makes no difference to me. When I
am through I am all through, and that settles it with
me . . . If you or anyone else will take the trouble
and have the intelligence or patience to follow and
examine every one of my crimes, you will find that
I have consistently followed one idea through all my
life. I preyed upon the weak, the harmless and the
unsuspecting. This lesson I was taught by others:
might makes right.'[29]

Panzram traced the origin of his commitment to
revenge against all humanity to the torture sessions
he endured in the 'reform school'. 'At that time I
was just learning to think for myself. Everything I
seemed to do was wrong. I first began to think that
I was being unjustly imposed upon. Then I began to
hate those who abused me. Then I began to think
that I would have my revenge just as soon and as
often as I could injure someone else. Anyone at all
would do. If I couldn't injure those who injured me,
then I would injure someone else.' 'When I got out
of there I knew all about Jesus and the Bible – so
much so that I knew it was all a lot of hot air. But
that wasn't all I knew. I had been taught by Chris-
tians how to be a hypocrite and I had learned more
about stealing, lying, hating, burning and killing. I
had learned that a boy's penis could be used for
something besides to urinate with and that a rectum
could be used for other purposes than crepitating.
Oh yes, I had learned a hell of a lot from my expert
instructors furnished to me free of charge by society

360

An Overview

in general and the State of Minnesota in particular. From the treatment I received while there and the lessons I learned from it, I had fully decided when I left there just how I would live my life. I made up my mind that I would rob, burn, destroy, and kill everywhere I went and everybody I could as long as I lived. That's the way I was reformed in the Minnesota State Training School. That's the reason why.'[30]

Despite his protestations, his resolution did not harden completely until he had been tortured beyond all endurance at the various penitentiaries – for the crime of refusing to bow to authority. Yet once his philosophy had been formed and his life committed to it, there was no turning back until he sickened of life entirely and capitulated to the authorities, demanding his own execution. In his final days in prison, he was well treated: 'If in the beginning,' he wrote, 'I had been treated as I am now, then there wouldn't have been quite so many people in this world that have been robbed, raped, and killed, and perhaps also very probably I wouldn't be where I am today.' 'Why am I what I am? I'll tell you why. I did not make myself what I am. Others had the making of me.' Still, he rejected all thoughts of 'rehabilitation'. 'I could not reform if I wanted to. It has taken me all my life so far, thirty-eight years of it, for me to reach my present state of mind . . . My philosophy of life is such that very few people ever get, and it is so deeply ingrained and burned into me that I don't believe I could ever change my beliefs. The things I have had done to me by others and the things I have done to them can never be forgotten or forgiven either by me or others. I can't forget and I won't forgive. I couldn't if I wanted to. The law is in the same fix . . . If the law won't kill me, I shall kill myself. I fully realize that I am not fit to live among people in a civilized community. I have no desire to do so.'[31]

361

Hunting Humans

When anti-capital-punishment groups tried to
block his execution, Panzram entered into a kind of
conspiracy with federal officials to obtain his own
death. Musing alone in his cell, he wrote: 'Wherever
I go, there is sure to be bad luck and hard times for
somebody and sometimes for everybody. I am old
bad-luck himself . . . I had a lot of different people
ask me at different times who I was and what good I
was. My answers were all the same. "I am the fellow
who goes around doing people good." Asked what
good I had ever done anyone: Again my answers
were the same to all. "I put people out of their
misery." They didn't know that I was telling them
the truth. I have put a lot of people out of their
misery and now I am looking for someone to put me
out of mine. I am too damned mean to live.' 'I intend
to leave this world as I have lived in it. I expect to be
a rebel right up to my last moment on earth. With
my last breath I intend to curse the world and all
mankind. I intend to spit in the warden's eye or
whoever places the rope around my neck when I am
standing on the scaffold . . . That will be all the
thanks they'll get from me.'[32]
    The day before his execution, he promised visiting
journalists that he would 'prance up those thirteen
steps like a blooded stallion', and he asked the guard
to ensure that the scaffold was 'strong enough to
hold me'. Robert Stroud, later to become famous as
the 'birdman of Alcatraz', was in an adjoining cell
during Panzram's last night of life: 'All night long
that last night,' Stroud remembered, 'he walked the
floor of his cell, singing a pornographic little song
that he had composed himself . . . the principal
theme was "Oh, how I love my roundeye!"' When
Panzram's cell door opened just before 6 a.m. and he
saw two men in clerical garb, he roared: 'Are there
any Bible-backed cocksuckers in here? Get 'em out.
I don't mind being hanged, but I don't need any
Bible-backed hypocrites around me. Run 'em out,

362

An Overview

Warden.' When Panzram finally emerged from his cell, his biographers Gaddis and Long recorded, he 'was almost running ahead, half dragging his taller escorts'. Panzram stared straight ahead at the rope, pausing only at the foot of the gallows to notice his audience. He paused for a moment and spat, then returned his gaze to the rope. 'Everyone's nostrils inhaled the sweet smell of new oak and hemp. He hurried up the gallows, as toward a gate.'[33]

THE MODERN ERA

This is the American Dream . . . in America, anything is possible if you work for it.
VICE-PRESIDENTIAL CANDIDATE, 1984

After the Second World War, the industrial economics – both East and West – moved into an era of unprecedented expansion and prosperity. With the growth of the industrial sector came a parallel development of social-service agencies – running the gamut from education to medicine to welfare. This remarkable growth in both the corporate and social sectors created two post-war decades in which individuals with even the most marginal of qualifications and abilities could enter occupations which offered a measure of dignity and recompense. As might be expected, these were quiet years for multiple murder as the population scrambled to better itself.

The explosion in the rate of production of these most modern of killers began in the late 1960s, and it continued in an almost exponential path for the following twenty years. This directly paralleled, and may well have owed its initial impetus to, the *closure* that was taking place in the American economy. From the late 1960s onward, the myriad middle-class positions that had been created since the Second World War began to be filled, or reduced in number. Inexorably, more and more socially ambitious, but

363

Hunting Humans

untalented (or unconnected) young men must have
found it difficult to achieve their goals of 'successful'
careers. A proportion of these men – we can never
know how large – began to fantasize about revenge;
and a tiny, but ever-increasing, percentage of them
began to react to the frustration of their blocked
social mobility by transforming their fantasies into a
vengeful reality.

All this took place in a *cultural* milieu which for
more than a century and a half had glorified violence
as an appropriate and manly response to frustration,
a cultural motif without parallel in the Western
industrial world. *The History of Violence in America*
documented the public response to a robbery in
which a young girl had been shot in the leg: the
Kansas City *Times* called the robbery 'so diabolically
daring and so utterly in contempt of fear that we are
bound to admire it and revere its perpetrators'. A
few days later, the same newspaper commented:

It was as though three bandits had come to us from
storied Odenwald, with the halo of medieval chivalry
upon their garments and shown us how the things were
done that poets sing of. Nowhere else in the United
States or in the civilized world, probably, could this
thing have been done.

No single quality of American culture is so distinctive as its continued assertion of the nobility and
beauty of violence – a notion and a mythology
propagated with excitement and craft in all popular
cultural forms, including films, television, and print.
This cultural predilection must have been immeasur-
ably enhanced by the television coverage of the
Vietnam War, which brought real bloodletting and
killing into every American living-room, and rendered death sacred no more. Encouraged thus to act
out their fantasies, our killers would come to find
that their murderous acts would serve both to validate and to relieve their grievances.[34]

364

An Overview

Moreover, the *character* of both killers and victims underwent a further transformation. The social origins of the killers continued to fall: gone were the aristocrats of the fifteenth century, and the doctors and teachers of the nineteenth century. Now the killers were drawn from the ranks of the upper-working and lower-middle classes: they were security guards, computer operators, postal clerks, and construction workers. Conversely, the social origins of the victims continued to pursue an opposite path: where they had been peasants in the fifteenth century, housemaids and prostitutes in the nineteenth century, now they were more likely to be drawn from the middle-class neighbourhoods: university students, aspiring models, and pedestrians in middle-class shopping malls. Both killer and victim had altered their form because the nature of the homicidal protest had changed most radically: it was no longer the threatened aristocrat testing the limits of his power; no longer the morbidly insecure new bourgeois checking the threat to his hard-won status; now it was an excluded individual wreaking vengeance on the symbol and source of his excommunication. These killers were almost never drawn from the ranks of the truly oppressed: there are few women, blacks, or native Americans in our files. The truly oppressed have no expectations that a bitter-tasting reality might poison.

Table 1 shows the remarkable increase in the frequency of multiple murder in this century. It is still a most useful guide, even if its construction is bedevilled by the statistical problems that overwhelm any student of multiple murder. It may well underestimate the total number of killers in each decade, but it is a revealing indication of the relative frequency of multiple murder. Regardless of any defects the table may have, the pattern is clear. There was essentially no change in the rate of production of multiple murderers until the 1960s, for the decades

Hunting Humans

between the 1920s and the 1950s produced only one or two apiece. In the 1960s, this jumped to six cases during the decade, for an average of one new killer every twenty months. By the 1970s, this had jumped to seventeen new cases, for an average of one new killer appearing every seven months. During the first four years of the 1980s,* the total had leapt to twenty-five, for an average rate of production of one new killer every 1.8 months.

─────────── *Table 1* ───────────

Recorded instances of multiple murderers in the United States, 1920–84; figure in parentheses is the number of victims with which the alleged killer is implicated.

1920s Earl Nelson (18–26); Carl Panzram (21)

1930s Albert Fish (8–15)

1940s Jarvis Catoe (7); Howard Unruh (13); William Heirens (3)

1950s Charles Starkweather (11)

1960s Melvin Rees (9); Albert DeSalvo (13); Richard Speck (8); Charles Whitman (16); Jerome Brudos (4 +); Antone Costa (*circa* 20)†

1970s John Freeman (7); Dean Corll (27 +); Edmund Kemper III (10); Herbert Mullin (13); Harvey Carignan (5 +); Paul Knowles (18 +); Calvin Jackson (9); James Ruppert (11); Vaughn Greenwood (9–11); Edward Allaway (7); John Wayne Gacy (30 +); Mark Essex (10); David Berkowitz (6); Theodore Bundy (22 +); Kenneth Bianchi and Angelo Buono (10); Juan Corona (25 +)

* To 30 September 1984.
† Only one source assigns so many victims to Costa.

An Overview

1980– Henry Lee Lucas (150 +);* James Huberty
1984 (21); Arthur Bishop (5 +); Randall Woodfield
(4 +); Gerald Stano (41 +); 'Green River'
killer (20 +); Alton Coleman (7); Christopher
Wilder (8); Robert Hanse (17); Michael Silka
(9); Louis Hastings (6); Charles Meach (4);
Robert Diaz (12); Wayne Williams (28 +);
San Rafael 'Trailside Slayer' (8); Douglas
Daniel Clark (6); Coral Eugene Watts (22);
Randy Steven Kraft (14); Frederick Wyman
Hodge (12); Larry Eyler (19); William Bonin
(10 +); Joseph G. Christopher (7); Donald
Miller (4); Stephen Morin (4 +); Michael Ross
(6 +)

Sources: John Godwin, *Murder USA*, the work of
Ann Rule and Andy Stack; and press clippings.
Note: While the figures give a reasonable indication
of the relative incidence of multiple murder between
decades, it should be assumed that each list is profoundly incomplete.

The number of victims also experienced a parallel
increase. During the 1920s, when thirty-nine people
were killed, the average number of murders was
0.325 per month. In the 1930s, with only eight
killings, the figure dropped to 0.06 per month.
During the 1940s, with a minimum of twenty murdered, this average figure rose slightly to 0.16 per
month; and in the 1950s, with eleven killings, the
average was 0.09 victims per month. The number of
victims began to accelerate during the 1960s: the total
of seventy represented a rate of 0.58 per month.
During the 1970s, 219 were murdered, a trebling of
the rate to 1.83 per month; and during the first four
years of the 1980s, the 444 victims represent another
quadrupling of the rate, to 9.25 per month, a frequency of victimization *one hundred times* that of the
1950s.

* This claim is very much in doubt.

367

Hunting Humans

Was this a consequence only of the predatory nature of capitalism? The evidence does not warrant such a conclusion. The structures of humiliation and deprivation coalesce around *any* stratified and hierarchical industrial system, whether it be capitalist or communist; and neither system appears to hold any monopoly on alienation and exclusion, dehumanization and depersonalization. We would thus expect the communist bloc states also to produce multiple murderers – but in varying numbers, according to the degree with which their respective cultures glorify and venerate violence. We cannot confirm these speculations with any precision since communist bloc states restrict the flow of information to their citizens. Nevertheless, distinguished *émigré* writer Valery Chalidze's recent review of Soviet crime makes it clear that multiple murder is by no means unknown in the USSR. In the early 1960s, Chalidze wrote, one man 'became well known to the Moscow public' for murdering children in their own apartments: curiously, the official explanation given for his behaviour was precisely the same as any Western psychiatrist or court might offer – 'his crimes appeared to be the acts of a maniac, and the general belief was that his motives were sexual'. Although the Soviet press did not report the matter, Chalidze suggested that such multiple murders 'are fairly common', although nothing like the American rate.[35]

A similar explosion occurred in Poland in 1962, while the communist regime was preparing to celebrate its twentieth anniversary in power. Lucian Staniak, a twenty-six-year-old translator for the official Polish publishing house wrote anonymously to the state newspaper: 'There is no happiness without tears, no life without death. Beware! I am going to make you cry.' With this typically public flourish, he announced a wave of killings that shocked the state. He first killed on the day commemorating the liberation period: a day replete with meaning for the *apparatchik* apprentice killer. His victim was a seventeen-year-old student, her body left naked, raped, and mutilated. The following day he sent another letter to the newspaper, announcing, 'I picked a juicy flower in Olsztyn and I shall do it again somewhere else, for there is no holiday without a funeral.'[36]

It took him several months, but then he stole a sixteen-year-old girl who had been chosen to lead a parade of students in another rally. Her body was found the day after the parade in a factory basement opposite her home: she had been raped, and a spike had been thrust into her genitals. A third letter to the newspaper told police where to find the body. On All Saints' Day, he killed again: a young blonde hotel receptionist whom he raped and mutilated with a screwdriver. The following day he dispatched a letter: 'Only tears of sorrow can wash out the stain of shame; only pangs of suffering can blot out the fires of lust.' On May Day of 1966, he took a seventeen-year-old, raping and disembowelling her. Her father, crime writer Colin Wilson recorded, 'found her lying in the typical rape position, with her entrails forming an abstract pattern over her thighs, in a tool-shed behind the house'. As Warsaw's homicide team began assembling data on fourteen other similar murders, police boarded a train on Christmas Eve of 1966 to find the mutilated body of a young woman, her abdomen and thighs slashed. Another letter to the newspaper merely said, 'I have done it again.'[37]

Staniak was ultimately arrested: he was a member of the liberal Arts Lovers Club, and a painter. One of his paintings, entitled 'The Circle of Life', depicted a cow eating a flower, a wolf eating the cow, a hunter shooting the wolf, a woman driving her car over the hunter, and an unspecified force leaving the woman lying in a field with her stomach ripped open, flowers sprouting from her body. After his arrest, Staniak confessed to a total of twenty such

369

Hunting Humans

murders. He 'explained' that he did them because when he was a young man, his parents and sister had been hit by a car driven by a Polish Air Force pilot's wife – who resembled the young blonde women he had killed. His explanation is curiously familiar to us, for it possesses that distinctive mixture of bizarre pseudo-rationality and apparent insanity that multiple murderers customarily deliver to us and to the authorities. We do not know enough about his life to speak with any certainty about what created him: we can only note how similar in feel and texture the case is to our own.[38]

Regardless of the question of national affiliation – an almost insurmountable one, given the problem of restricted information – is there anything special in the social backgrounds of North American multiple murderers to distinguish them from the remaining mass of humanity (who are of course also subject to the impersonal and depersonalizing forces of the modern industrial state)? Table 2 summarizes the social histories of twenty-three North American multiple murderers for whom such data are available: it shows clearly that they *are* a very distinctive group. Overwhelmingly, they come from that 12 to 20 per cent of the population of a modern nation-state who possess one of four social characteristics indicative of considerable press-. ure within the natal family: adopted, illegitimate, institutionalized in childhood or adolescence, or with mothers who have married three or more times. What is there about these characteristics that might propel a man towards a career in murder?

—————————— *Table 2* ——————————

North American multiple murderers whose social origins are known.

Joseph Kallinger	Adopted
John Bianchi	Adopted
Earle Nelson	Adopted

An Overview

David Berkowitz	Adopted, illegitimate
Theodore Bundy	Illegitimate
Harvey Carignan	Illegitimate, institutionalized (juvenile home)
Albert Fish	Institutionalized (orphanage)
Edmund Kemper III	Institutionalized (mental hospital)
Jerome Brudos	Institutionalized (mental hospital)
Clifford Olson	Institutionalized (juvenile home)
Albert DeSalvo	Institutionalized (juvenile home)
William Bonin	Institutionalized (juvenile home)
Richard Speck	Institutionalized (juvenile home)
Robert Irwin	Institutionalized (juvenile home)
William Heirens	Institutionalized (juvenile home)
Robert Carr III	Institutionalized (juvenile home)
Carl Panzram	Institutionalized (juvenile home)
Dean Corll	Mother thrice married
'Norman Collins'	Mother thrice married
Antone Costa	Conventional
Charles Starkweather	Conventional (mass murderer)
Mark Essex	Conventional (mass murderer)
Randall Woodfield	Conventional
James Huberty	Conventional (mass murderer)

Sources: Damore (1981); Klausner (1981); Miller (1978); Olsen (1974); Angelella (1981); Keyes (1976); Stack (1983a, 1983b, 1984); Schreiber (1983); Lunde and Morgan (1980); Tanay (1976); Frank (1967); Allen (1976); Cheney (1976); Rule (1980); Schwarz (1981); Gaddis and Long (1970); Buchanan (1979); Hernon (1978); Freeman (1955); Altman and Ziporyn (1967); and various press clippings. It is, of course, highly regrettable that so few records of this nature are available on modern multiple murderers.

The simple fact of human social life is that in order for individuals to behave 'normally', they must grow up feeling that they have some place in the social order – which is to say a coherent and socially constructed identity. Unfortunately, individuals who bear the social characteristics listed above often come to feel excluded from the social order – a separation

371

Hunting Humans

I have often heard in 'training schools', where juveniles refer to civilians as 'humans' – and such exclusion can exact a fearful price. But many people who bear these social characteristics grow into a mature and balanced adulthood: why should some fail to do so? Several other factors are necessary in the biography before a multiple murderer can be produced. He must also be inculcated with an ambition – or a 'dream' – which either circumstances rob from him (as when DeSalvo's wife, Irmgard, 'refused' him admission to the lower-middle class), or which he cannot feel at ease in living (as when Bundy spurned his long-sought socialite fiancée). He is never Durkheim's contented man, who:

vaguely realizes the extreme limit set to his ambitions and aspires to nothing beyond . . . he feels that it is not well to ask more. Thus, an end and goal are set to the passions . . . This relative limitation and the moderation it involves, make men contented with their lot while stimulating them moderately to improve it; and this average contentment causes the feeling of calm, active happiness, the pleasure in existing and living which characterizes health for societies as well as for individuals.

It is in this light that we must interpret and understand the fierce social ambition of so many of our multiple murderers – and the feeling of being a robot that torments so many of them as they pursue their goals.[39]

Finally, for the production of multiple murderers to reach the unprecedented levels that it has in the America of the 1970s and 1980s, we require the existence of *cultural forms* that can mediate between killer and victim in a special sense – ridding the potential victims of any humanity, and the potential killer of any responsibility. Both sociologists Christopher Lasch and Barbara Ehrenreich have argued most persuasively that we have developed these forms with no little refinement. Lasch devoted a

An Overview

volume to delineating the nature of this 'culture of competitive individualism' which carries 'the logic of individualism to the extreme of a war of all against all, the pursuit of happiness to the dead end of a narcissistic preoccupation with the self'. Ehrenreich dwelt upon the sources of this ideology which so encouraged the severing of responsibility between people. She saw its roots in the developing post-war male culture of 'escape – literal escape from the bondage of breadwinning'. Here, men were urged to take part in the superficial excitement of 'the night-mare anomie of the pop psychologists' vision: a world where other people are objects of consumption, or the chance encounters of a "self" propelled by impulse alone'.[40]

Thus the freedom for which mankind had struggled over the centuries proved to be a two-edged sword. The freedom from the suffocation of family and community, the freedom from systems of religious thought, the freedom to explore one's self, all entailed heavy penalties to society – not the least of which was the rate of multiple murder. These tendencies are much intensified in America, perhaps the only industrial nation on earth to take the idea of freedom to its bitter logical conclusion. A major by-product of this literal interpretation of freedom is that all systems of value come to be seen as possessing equal legitimacy: therefore, in this ultimate vulgarization of the doctrine of cultural relativity, murder as a response to mundane frustration takes on a culturally programmed and culturally validated appearance.

Moreover, whether the industrial system was socialist or capitalist, its members were forced to look upon themselves and others as marketable commodities. It can hardly be surprising, then, that some fevered souls, feeling like automatons, might choose to coalesce their fuzzy identity in a series of fearful acts. Their ambitions crushed, some would lash out

373

Hunting Humans

in protest at objects (most often sexual) which they had been taught to see as essentially insignificant. Now the question asked by the killer Bundy seems less inappropriate: 'What's one less person on the face of the earth, anyway?'

Each of our case studies reveals that at a certain point in his life, the future killer experiences a kind of internal *social* crisis, when he realizes that he cannot be what he wishes to be – cannot live his version of the American dream. When these killers reach that existential divide, the seed is planted for a vengeance spree. Sometimes their motives are entirely conscious (as with Essex, Bundy, and Panzram); while with others (like Berkowitz and DeSalvo), they are only dimly understood. In either case, it is unrealizable ambition that motivates them, as they launch a kind of sub-political and personal assault on society, aiming always at the class or group they feel oppresses or excludes them. Some require minimal justification for their acts, obtaining temporary relief from their rage through the killings and then 'forgetting' or compartmentalizing their memories, as when DeSalvo remarked: 'I was there, it was done, and yet if you talked to me an hour later, or half-hour later, it didn't mean nothing.' Still others construct elaborate intellectual (Panzram) or spiritual (Berkowitz's demons) rationalizations to explain and justify their killings. Only a few (such as Joseph Kallinger, and California's Herbert Mullins, who murdered to 'stop earthquakes') detach themselves so much from conventional reality that they construct their own universes, thereby entering that state the psychiatrists call madness.

Yet what they are *all* orchestrating is a kind of social levelling, in which they rewrite the universe to incorporate themselves: no one expressed this more clearly than Starkweather when he said: 'dead people are all on the same level'. They are all

374

An Overview

engaged in the same process, punishing the innocent, and in doing so they re-create the dehumanized industrial system in a form that gives
themselves a central position. One hundred eyes for
an eye: it is by no means the first time in human
history that retaliating men have grossly exceeded
the degree of the original insult.

Neither do they form their missions in a private
vacuum, bereft of all advice, for the larger culture
encodes in them a respect for violent display – a
central theme in the media messages beamed at the
working class – and the ready availability of stimulating materials in books and magazines, films and
videotapes, teaches them to link their lust with
violence. If we were charged with the responsibility
for designing a society in which all structural and
cultural mechanisms leaned towards the creation of
the killers of strangers, we could do no better than
to present the purchaser with the shape of modern
America, for the angry and the troubled can reach
into the dominant culture to seize a *socially validated
violent identity*. If the negotiation of the identity of a
violent culture hero yields the killer little admiration
or love, the absence of these qualities will be more
than compensated for by the public respect and
media attention he will surely receive. In this special
sense, homicidal values and behaviours are in perfect
harmony with the dominant culture.

The Negotiation of Murderous Identity

The twilight of the human race on this planet may
well have been the thirty or forty thousand years
our ancestors dwelt in relatively egalitarian (one
assumes) hunting and gathering societies. In such
non-stratified societies, there was little specialization
of labour, little production of surplus, and few
opportunities for aggressive and ambitious individuals to overcome the reluctance of their fellows to

375

Hunting Humans

submit to any expropriation of the social commodities for which human beings compete – power,
prestige, and wealth. However, something like
10,000 years ago all our ancestors began to make
the shift from hunting and gathering to agriculture
and pastoralism – new forms of economy that
captured a larger amount of energy for each hour of
work. When eight could thus do the work to feed
ten, the stage was set for the production of a surplus
and the expropriation of that surplus by an emerging class of élites. And so the form and structure of
society was entirely rewritten: now rank and hierarchy, not mutual obligation, began to emerge as
the organizing principles of human society. That
development provided the framework for the
growth over the millennia of social classes: clusters
of individuals with mutual interests who stood in
opposition to individuals of other social classes.
Over time, new classes emerged and struggled for
ascendancy, as did the bourgeoisie in the nineteenth
century. Thus some groups are more threatened
than others in different periods of history. It is
precisely at the point in time when a single class is
most threatened (when its rights are challenged by
another class, its legitimacy questioned by a discon-
tented proletariat, or its new-found status impre-
cisely defined) that we can expect to find some
members of that class beginning to fantasize about
killing members of another class.

   Thus the multiple murderer does not appear at
random through history. He appears at special points
in social evolution, during periods of particular tension. Durkheim's thoughts on destruction (although
he was concerned with self-destruction) are central
here. Despite the glories of humanity, it remains a
fragile species. Its equilibrium is in such a delicate
state of balance that any crisis (financial, industrial,
or social) in the larger system disorientates the individuals in that system. It matters not whether they

An Overview

are crises of prosperity or of poverty: it merely matters that individuals' expectations are profoundly shaken.

Every disturbance of equilibrium, even though it achieves greater comfort and a heightening of general vitality, is an impulse to voluntary death. Whenever serious readjustments take place in the social order, whether or not due to a sudden growth or to an unexpected catastrophe, men are more inclined to self-destruction.

In the archaic, pre-industrial period, it was the old and 'noble' landed aristocracy which was most threatened by the rebellious peasantry and the rising mercantile classes. It makes a certain terrible sense that it was among this threatened class that fantasies of disordered self-indulgent sexuality might turn to the torture and murder of the lower orders. During the industrial revolution of the late eighteenth and nineteenth centuries, while the aristocracy retired to its estates to lick its wounds and the rising bourgeoisie revelled in its ascendancy, it was the new marginal middle classes – men like Wagner and Dr Cream – who, insecure in their unaccustomed roles, would grow obsessed with a sense of possible exposure and failure. During that period, it would primarily be doctors, government clerks, and schoolteachers who might discipline those of the lower orders – who perhaps whispered about past errors exposing class origins or who flaunted their indifference.[41]

In the early twentieth century, a new homicidal theme emerged. Proletarian revolt became a minor expression, in which those (like Panzram) who glimpsed their utter exclusion, who felt their torture at the hands of the bourgeois institutions constructed for their 'rehabilitation', wreaked a similar havoc. These proletarians would continue into the

377

Hunting Humans

modern era, but they would always be a minor
theme: their class would find alternative forms of
protest, either in direct political action, or in smothering their claims in drugs and alcohol, or just as
commonly in theft. Murder for its own sake had
relatively little appeal to a class with such immediate
problems.

The major homicidal form of the modern era is
the man who straddles the border between the upper-
working class and the lower-middle class. Occasionally, as with Robert Hansen in Alaska or cousins
Kenneth Bianchi and Angelo Buono in Los Angeles
(the 'Hillside Stranglers'), they continue a metaphor
from the earlier era and discipline unruly prostitutes
and runaways. More commonly, however, they
punish those above them in the system – preying on
unambiguously middle-class figures such as university women.

All stratified industrial nation-states, regardless of
their professed ideologies, transform their members
into either winners or losers. By the mid-1960s,
however, the increasing closure of middle-class positions meant there would be many more losers, many
more who were alienated and despairing. Moreover,
as these positions were closing, other social forces
within society continued their transformation of
neighbours into strangers: the constriction of the
extended family, the expansion of the anonymous
city and suburb, the geographic mobility of individual familial units, and the disintegration of marriage
and parenthood, all made it progressively easier for
the potential killer to overcome his scruples. The
murder and mutilation of such enemy-strangers is
but the abuse of a commodity. Thus we find the
source of our new multiple murderer primarily
among the ambitious who failed – or who believed
they would fail – and who seek another form of
success in the universal celebrity and attention they
will receive through their extravagant homicides. In
the performance of this task they are aided

378

An Overview

immensely by the extraordinary *tolerance* the social system offers their activities, providing only paltry resources for the monitoring and apprehension of potential killers.★

Whether they kill all at once in a bloody hour or day, or whether they kill over an extended period, whether their motives appear to be 'sexual' or 'psychotic', the objects of our study are all much of a kind. They all decide independently to construct a programme of killing many strangers. On the surface of things they appear to be doing it for the thrill of sexual excitement or the intoxication of conquest; but the truth is they do it to relieve a burning grudge engendered by their failed ambition and to become a kind of cultural hero. Some are so finished with life that they wish to die when they have discharged their brief task: they come to be called 'mass murderers', and they leave it up to a bewildered public to decipher their message. Others wish to live and tell their stories and bask in their fame: they usually come to be called 'serial murderers'.

The tragedy and irony is that what has produced this abomination is the achievement of the freedom for which mankind has struggled for centuries – freedom to explore one's self without reference to rigid systems of thought. That freedom exacts a terrible price, for it releases humans too much from their social contract. Under such conditions, those whose ambitions are denied (and there are more of these each year since the 1960s when closure first occurred) in a culture which so glamorizes and rewards violence, find a solution to all their problems in that purple explosion. As many more come to feel

---

★ 'Tolerance' may sound merely provocative; but compare the tiny and short-term resources allocated to hunting multiple murderers with the huge sums allocated by the state for the monitoring of political dissidents (the FBI ran 300 major operations in 1983, and its budget for undercover work alone in 1984 was $12.5 million). Nothing comparable is given to the police.[42]

Hunting Humans

excluded in this time of industrial and social crisis, we can expect many more to follow the path of the University of Chicago undergraduate, William Heirens, who searched for something – he knew not what – in the dissected entrails of a kidnapped child, and wrote in lipstick upon the walls of another victim's apartment:

FOR HEAVENS SAKE CATCH ME
BEFORE I KILL MORE I CANNOT
CONTROL MYSELF.[43]

NOTES
———•———

N.B. In the interests of readability and the avoidance of notation clutter, the numbering of sources has been limited to one numeral per paragraph within the body text of this book. References to sources noted below beside each numeral are listed in their order of appearance within each respective paragraph of the body text. Ed.

1 Darnton 1984: 262.
2 Joseph Kallinger, in F. R. Schreiber 1983: 410–11.
3 Cusson 1983: 47; and Peter and Favret 1975: 186, 198.
4 Abrams 1982: 267, 273–4, 280, 297.
5 Andreano and Siegfried 1980: 14.
6 Lunde 1979: 48; Palmer 1972: 40; Wolfgang 1975: 207; and FBI 1982: 11.
7 Palmer 1972: 40; cf. Williams 1984, Blau and Blau 1982, Flango and Sherbenou 1976, Gastil 1971, Loftin and Hill 1974, Messner 1982, 1983, Smith and Parker 1980, who are among the major contributors to the debate; Williams 1984: 288–9; cf. Rule 1980; Stark 1984; and Lunde 1979: 98.
8 Cf. Calvert-Boyanowsky and Boyanowsky 1981; for a fascinating discussion of this, see Fox 1971. A solid, if polemical, critique of sociobiology can be found in Lewontin, Rose, and Kamin 1984; Wilson (Edward) 1980; Konner 1982; and Montague 1978.
9 Abrahamsen 1973: 9–10; Megargee 1966; Lunde 1979: 93; and Gaylin 1983: 274.
10 Bolitho 1926, 7, 8, 274, 294.
11 Dickson 1958: 203–204.
12 Lindsay 1958: 194.
13 Lunde 1979: 48.
14 ibid, 49, 59, 53.
15 Kramer and Weiner 1983: 73.
16 Wilson (Colin) 1969: 29ff. See also Dickson 1958.
17 Griart, in Wolf (Leonard) 1980: 145.
18 de Rais, in ibid, 202, 205.
19 de Rais, in ibid, 194.
20 de Rais, in ibid, 204–205.

Hunting Humans

21 Wolf (Eric) 1969: 279; and Laslett 1984: 5, 7ff.
22 ibid, 24.
23 ibid, 29.
24 Darnton 1984: 109–10; Laslett 1984: 18; Wolf (Eric) 1969: 279–80; and Wolf (Eric) 1982: 360, 389–90.
25 Wilson (Colin) 1969: 89–90.
26 Quoted in Lucas 1974: 5–6; Logan 1928: 66ff; quoted in Miller 1978: 156; and Hamilton Fish, quoted in Angelella 1979: 150.
27 Bruch 1967: 697, 693–7.
28 Peter Kurten, in Dickinson 1958: 135, 137.
29 Carl Panzram, in Gaddis and Long 1970: 11–12.
30 Panzram, in ibid, 28, 31–2.
31 Panzram, in ibid, 238, 165, 251–2.
32 Panzram, in ibid, 213–14, 308–309.
33 Panzram, in ibid, 323; quoted in ibid, 325; Panzram, in ibid, 325–6; and Gaddis and Long 1970: 326–7.
34 Frantz, in Graham and Gurr (eds.) 1969: 128.
35 Chalidze 1977: 107.
36 Staniak, in Wilson (Colin) 1969: 250, 251.
37 Staniak, in ibid, 252; Wilson (Colin) 1969: 252–3; and Staniak, in ibid, 253.
38 ibid, 254–5.
39 Durkheim 1961: 919.
40 Lasch 1979: 21; and Ehrenreich 1983: 51, 182.
41 Durkheim 1961: 918.
42 Nat Hentoff, in the *Manchester Guardian Weekly*, 8 July 1984.
43 Heirens, in Freeman 1955: 23.

REFERENCES

ABRAHAMSEN, DAVID
1973   *The Murdering Mind.* New York: Harper and Row.
1983   'Confessions of Son of Sam'. *Penthouse* 15: 58–194.
ABRAMS, PHILIP
1982   *Historical Sociology.* Ithaca: Cornell University Press.
ALLEN, WILLIAM
1976   *Starkweather: The Story of a Mass Murderer.* Boston: Houghton Mifflin.
ALTMAN, JACK and MARVIN ZIPORYN
1967   *Born to Raise Hell: The Untold Story of Richard Speck.* New York: Grove Press.
AMNESTY INTERNATIONAL
1983   *Political Killings by Governments.* London: Amnesty International Publications.
ANDREANO, RALPH and JOHN J. SIEGFRIED (eds.)
1980   *The Economics of Crime.* New York: John Wiley.
ANGELELLA, MICHAEL
1979   *Trail of Blood: A True Story.* New York: New American Library.
BANKS, HAROLD K.
1967   *The Strangler! The Story of the Terror in Boston.* New York: Avon.
BARTHOLOMEW, ALLEN A., K. L. MILTE, and F. GALBALLY
1975   'Sexual murder: Psychopathology and Psychiatric Jurisprudential Considerations'. *Australian and New Zealand Journal of Criminology* 8: 143–152.
BEAVER, NINETTE, B. K. RIPLEY, and PATRICK TRESE
1974   *Caril.* New York: J. B. Lippincott.
BERKOWITZ, DAVID
1981   'Prison Diary'. In Klausner 1981.

Hunting Humans

BLAU, JUDITH R. and PETER M. BLAU
1982   'The Cost of Inequality: Metropolitan Structure and Violent Crime'. *American Sociological Review* 47: 114–29.
BOLITHO, WILLIAM
1926   *Murder for Profit.* New York: Garden City.
BRITTAIN, ROBERT P.
1970   'The Sadistic Murderer'. *Medicine, Science and the Law* 10: 198–207.
BRUCH, HILDE
1967   'Mass Murder: the Wagner Case'. *American Journal of Psychiatry* 124: 693–8.
BRUSSEL, JAMES A.
1968   *Casebook of a Crime Psychiatrist.* New York: Dell.
BUCHANAN, EDNA
1979   *Carr: Five Years of Rape and Murder.* New York: E. P. Dutton.
CALVERT-BOYANOWSKY, JOCELYN, EHOR O. BOYANOWSKY, *et al*.
1981   'Patterns of Passion: Temperature and Human Emotion'. In D. Krebs (ed.), *Readings in Social Psychology: Contemporary Perspectives.* New York: Harper and Row.
CAPOTE, TRUMAN
1965   *In Cold Blood.* New York: New American Library.
CARPOZI, GEORGE JR
1977   *Son of Sam: The .44 Caliber Killer.* New York: Manor Books.
CHALIDZE, VALERY
1977   *Criminal Russia: Essays on Crime in the Soviet Union.* New York: Random House.
CHENEY, MARGARET
1976   *The Co-ed Killer.* New York: Walker.
CUSSON, MAURICE
1983   *Why Delinquency?* Toronto: University of Toronto Press.
DAMORE, LEO
1981   *In His Garden: The Anatomy of a Murderer.* New York: Arbor House.
DARNTON, ROBERT
1984   *The Great Cat Massacre: And Other Episodes in French Cultural History.* New York: Basic Books.

References

DURKHEIM, EMILE
1961 'Anomic Suicide'. In Talcott Parsons, Edward Shils, Kasper D. Naegele, and Jesse R. Pitts (eds.), *Theories of Society: Foundations of Modern Sociological Theory*. New York: Free Press.

EHRENREICH, BARBARA
1983 *The Hearts of Men: American Dreams and the Flight from Commitment*. New York: Anchor.

FEDERAL BUREAU OF INVESTIGATION
1982 *Crime in the United States*. Uniform Crime Reports. Washington, DC: US Government Printing Office.

FLANGO, VICTOR E. and EDGAR L. SHERBENOU
1976 'Poverty, Urbanization, and Crime'. *Criminology* 14: 331–46.

FOUCAULT, MICHEL (ed.)
1975 *I, Pierre Rivière, Having Slaughtered My Mother, My Sister, and My Brother . . . A Case of Parricide in the 19th Century*. New York: Pantheon.

FOX, RICHARD G.
1971 'The XYY Offender: A Modern Myth?' *Journal of Criminal Law, Criminology and Police Science* 62.

FRANK, GEROLD
1967 *The Boston Strangler*. New York: New American Library.

FRANTZ, JOE B.
1969 'The Frontier Tradition: An Invitation to Violence'. In Graham and Gurr 1969.

FREEMAN, LUCY
1955 *'Before I Kill More . . .'* New York: Crown.

FROMM, ERICH
1975 *The Anatomy of Human Destructiveness*. New York: Harper and Row.

GADDIS, THOMAS E. and JAMES O. LONG
1970 *Killer: A Journal of Murder*. New York: Macmillan.

GALVIN, JAMES A. V. and JOHN M. MACDONALD
1959 'Psychiatric Study of a Mass Murderer'. *American Journal of Psychiatry* 115: 1057–61.

Hunting Humans

GARELIK, GLENN and GINA MARANTO
1984   'Multiple Murderers'. *Discover* 5: 26–9.
GASTIL, R. P.
1971   'Homicide and a Regional Culture of Violence'.
American Sociological Review 36: 412–27.
GAYLIN, WILLARD
1983   *The Killing of Bonnie Garland: A Question of Justice.*
New York: Penguin.
GODWIN, JOHN
1979   *Murder USA: The Ways We Kill Each Other.* New
York: Ballantine.
GRAHAM, H. D. and T. R. GURR (eds.)
1969   *The History of Violence in America: Historical and
Comparative Perspectives.* A report submitted to the
National Commission on the Causes and Prevention of
Violence. New York: Praeger.
GRIER, WILLIAM and PRICE COBBS
1968   *Black Rage.* New York: Basic Books.
**HANDELMAN, DON and ELLIOTT
LEYTON**
1978   *Bureaucracy and World View: Studies in the Logic of
Official Interpretation.* St John's Nfld: Studies No. 22,
Institute of Social and Economic Research, Memorial
University.
**HAZELWOOD, ROBERT R. and JOHN E.
DOUGLAS**
1980   'The Lust Murderer'. *FBI Law Enforcement Bulletin,*
April.
HERNON, PETER
1978   *A Terrible Thunder: The Story of the New Orleans
Sniper.* New York: Doubleday.
HOBSBAWM, E. J.
1969   *Bandits.* Harmondsworth: Penguin.
HOWARD, CLARK
1980   *Zebra.* New York: Berkley.
KAHN, MARVIN W.
1960   'Psychological Test Study of a Mass Murderer'.
Journal of Protective Techniques 24: 147–60.

References

KENDALL, ELIZABETH
1981   *The Phantom Prince: My Life With Ted Bundy.* Seattle: Madrona.

KENNEDY, FOSTER, HARRY R.
HOFFMAN, and WILLIAM H. HAINES
1947   'A Study of William Heirens'. *American Journal of Psychiatry* 104.

KEYES, DANIEL
1981   *The Minds of Billy Milligan.* New York: Random House.

KEYES, EDWARD
1976   *The Michigan Murders.* New York: Pocket Books.

KLAUSNER, LAWRENCE D.
1981   *Son of Sam.* New York: McGraw-Hill.

KRAMER, ROGER and IRA WEINER
1983   'Psychiatry on the Borderline'. *Psychology Today* 17: 70–73.

KONNER, MELVIN
1982   *The Tangled Wing: Biological Constraints on the Human Spirit.* New York: Holt, Rinehart, and Winston.

LARSEN, RICHARD W.
1980   *Bundy: The Deliberate Stranger.* Englewood Cliffs: Prentice-Hall.

LASCH, CHRISTOPHER
1979   *The Culture of Narcissism: American Life in an Age of Diminishing Expectations.* New York: Warner.

LASLETT, PETER
1984   *The World We Have Lost: England before the Industrial Age.* Third edition. New York: Charles Scribner's Sons.

LEVINE, RICHARD
1982   *Bad Blood: A Family Murder in Marin County.* New York: Random House.

LEWONTIN, R. C., STEVEN ROSE, and
LEON J. KAMIN
1984   *Not In Our Genes: Biology, Ideology, and Human Nature.* New York: Pantheon.

LEYTON, ELLIOTT
1965   'Composite Descent Groups in Canada'. *Man* LXV (98).

Hunting Humans

1966 'Conscious Models and Dispute Regulation in an Ulster Village'. *Man (NS)* 1: 534–42.

1970 'Spheres of Inheritance in Aughnaboy'. *American Anthropologist* 72: 1378–88.

1974a 'Opposition and Integration in Ulster'. *Man (NS)* 9: 185–98.

1974b (ed.) *The Compact: Selected Dimensions of Friendship.* St John's, Nfld: Papers No. 3, Institute of Social and Economic Research.

1975a *The One Blood: Kinship and Class in an Irish Village.* St John's, Nfld: Studies No. 15, Institute of Social and Economic Research.

1975b *Dying Hard: The Ravages of Industrial Carnage.* Toronto: McClelland and Stewart.

1978 'The Bureaucratization of Anguish: The Workmen's Compensation Board in an Industrial Disaster'. In Handelman and Leyton 1978.

1979 *The Myth of Delinquency: An Anatomy of Juvenile Nihilism.* Toronto: McClelland and Stewart.

1983 'A Social Profile of Sexual Mass Murderers'. In Thomas Fleming and L. A. Visano (eds.), *Deviant Designations: Crime, Law and Deviance in Canada.* Toronto: Butterworths.

LINDSAY, PHILIP

1958 *The Mainspring of Murder.* London: John Long.

LISNERS, JOHN

1983 *House of Horrors.* London: Corgi.

LOFTIN, COLIN and ROBERT H. HILL

1974 'Regional subculture and homicide'. *American Sociological Review* 39: 714–24.

LOGAN, GUY B. H.

1928 *Masters of Crime: Studies of Multiple Murderers.* London: Stanley Paul.

LUCAS, NORMAN

1974 *The Sex Killers.* London: W. H. Allen.

LUNDE, DONALD T.

1979 *Murder and Madness.* New York: W. W. Norton.

LUNDE, DONALD T. and JEFFERSON MORGAN

1980 *The Die Song: A Journey into the Mind of a Mass Murderer.* New York: W. W. Norton.

References

MAILER, NORMAN
1980   *The Executioner's Song*. New York: Warner.
MEGARGEE, E. I.
1966   'Undercontrolled and Overcontrolled Personality Types in Extreme and Social Aggression'. *Psychological Monographs* 80.
MESSNER, STEVEN F.
1982   'Poverty, Inequality, and the Urban Homicide Rate'. *Criminology* 20: 103–14.
1983   'Regional and Racial Effects on the Urban Homicide Rate: The Subculture of Violence Revisited'. *American Journal of Sociology* 88: 997–1007.
MICHAUD, STEPHEN C. and HUGH AYNESWORTH
1983   *The Only Living Witness*. New York: Simon and Schuster.
MILLER, ORLO
1978   *Twenty Mortal Murders: Bizarre Murder Cases From Canada's Past*. Toronto: Macmillan.
MONTAGU, ASHLEY (ed.)
1978   *Learning Non-aggression: The Experience of Non-literate Societies*. Oxford: Oxford University Press.
OSLON, JACK
1974   *The Man with the Candy: The Story of the Houston Mass Murders*. New York: Simon and Schuster.
OLSON, CLIFFORD
1984   Unpublished letters.
PALMER, STUART
1972   *The Violent Society*. New Haven: College and University Press.
PANZRAM, CARL
1970   'Journal'. In Gaddis and Long 1970.
PARKIN, FRANK
1979   *Marxism and Class Theory: A Bourgeois Critique*. New York: Columbia University Press.
PETER, JEAN-PIERRE and JEANNE FAVRET
1975   'The Animal, the Madman, and Death'. In Foucault 1975.

Hunting Humans

RAE, GEORGE W.
1967 *Confessions of the Boston Strangler*. New York: Pyramid.

REINHARDT, JAMES M.
1960 *The Murderous Trail of Charles Starkweather*. Springfield, Ill.: C. C. Thomas.

RULE, ANN
1980 *The Stranger Beside Me*. New York: New American Library.

SCHREIBER, F. R.
1983 *The Shoemaker: The Anatomy of a Psychotic*. New York: Simon and Schuster.

SCHWARZ, TED
1981 *The Hillside Strangler: A Murderer's Mind*. New York: Doubleday.

SMITH, M. DWAYNE and ROBERT NASH PARKER
1980 'Types of Homicide and Variation in Regional Rates'. *Social Forces* 59: 136–47.

STACK, ANDY
1983a *Lust Killer*. New York: New American Library.
1983b *The Want-ad Killer*. New York: New American Library.
1984 *The I-5 Killer*. New York: New American Library.

STARKWEATHER, CHARLES
1959 'Rebellion'. *Parade* 4: 10–14.

TANAY, EMANUEL
1976 *The Murderers*. Indianapolis: Bobbs-Merrill.

TANNENBAUM, ROBERT and PHILIP ROSENBERG
1979 *Badge of the Assassin*. New York: Fawcett Crest.

THOMPSON, THOMAS
1979 *Serpentine*. New York: Dell.

TOBIAS, RONALD
1981 *They Shoot to Kill: A Psycho-survey of Criminal Sniping*. Boulder: Paladin.

WALLERSTEIN, IMMANUEL
1974 *The Modern World System I: Capitalist Agriculture and the Origins of the European World-Economy in the Sixteenth Century*. New York: Academic Press.

References

WEST, DONALD
1974 *Sacrifice Unto Me*. New York: Pyramid.

WILLIAMS, KIRK R.
1984 'Economic Sources of Homicide: Reestimating the Effects of Poverty and Inequality.' *American Sociological Review* 49: 283–9.

WILSON, COLIN
1969 *A Casebook of Murder*. London: Leslie Frewin.

WILSON, EDWARD O.
1980 *Sociobiology*. Abridged edition. Cambridge, Mass.: Harvard University Press.

WILSON, PETER J.
1974 *Oscar: An Inquiry into the Nature of Sanity*. New York: Random House.

WILLEFORD, CHARLES
1980 *Off the Wall*. Montclair, NJ: Pegasus Rex Press.

WINN, STEVEN and DAVID MERRILL
1980 *Ted Bundy: The Killer Next Door*. New York: Bantam.

WOLF, ERIC
1973 *Peasant Wars of the Twentieth Century*. New York: Harper Torchbooks.
1982 *Europe and the People without History*: Berkeley: University of California Press.

WOLF, LEONARD
1980 *Bluebeard: The Life and Crimes of Gilles de Rais*. New York: Potter.

WOLFGANG, MARVIN E.
1975 *Patterns in Criminal Homicide*. Montclair, NJ: Patterson Smith.

Part II
Origins of the Impulse

[4]

A Study of Serial Murder

Constance McKenzie

Abstract: *In the past the focus in studying the serial murderer has been on descriptions of the heinous crimes, profiling, and other law enforcement issues. Through analysis of childhood, adulthood experiences, and personality traits, some tentative factors emerge that set the process in motion for the later emergence of this remarkably antisocial behavior.*

INTRODUCTION

The purpose of this article is to examine some of the case studies and the professional research available on the serial murderer in an effort to ascertain whether there are some dynamic links between them. Several researchers, especially Ressler, Burgess, and Douglas (1988), Norris (1988), Levin and Fox (1985), and Wilson and Seaman (1990), offer empirical data that link these people behaviorally. However, most have only hinted at the possibility that certain factors in the childhood environment act as an "incubator" to enhance and exaggerate childhood behaviors and basic personality tendencies so that when adulthood is reached, in the presence of specific disinhibitors, these already exaggerated tendencies run amok.

METHODOLOGY

From the outset there has been much confusion concerning the definition of serial murder. To muddy the issue authors use several terms interchangeably: lust murder, serial murder, mass murder, sexual homicide, multicide, multiple murder. In this study we are concerned with serial murder of a sexual nature. Serial murder, not to be confused with mass murder (Busch & Cavanaugh, 1986; Leyton, 1986), is now generally defined as: one-on-one murder, repetitive, involving a stranger, with a motive known only to the murderer (Egger, 1990; Holmes & DeBurger, 1987; Ressler et al., 1987). The nature of serial murder becomes sexual when the evidence includes: "victim attire or lack of attire; exposure of the sexual parts of the victim's body; sexual positioning of the victim's body; insertion of foreign objects into the victim's body cavities; evidence of sexual intercourse (oral, anal, vaginal); and evidence of substitute sexual activity, interest, or sadistic fantasy" (Ressler et al., 1988).

A checklist was constructed from 20 cases, journalistic and empirical presentations, and various theoretical perspectives. Traditional familial demographics were not addressed in this research. This list includes

Special thanks to Dr. James Wulach, Professor, John Jay College, for his encouragement.

International Journal of Offender Therapy and Comparative Criminology, 39(1), 1995 personality variables and factors focused on by other theorists: "head trauma" as a causative factor (Norris, 1988); MacDonald triad of enuresis, firesetting, and cruelty to animals (MacDonald, 1963); and early introduction to pornography (Ressler et al., 1987); the traits of "zero state" and grandiosity (Yochelson & Samenow, 1976); and, finally, dissociation (Egger, 1990; Kirschner, 1992; Lifton, 1985; Sears, 1991; Watkins, 1984).

The 28 personality variables were then organized into four categories (see Appendix for explanation of terms): Childhood Environmental Incubator, Childhood Dysfunctional Indicators, Adult Floodgate Disinhibitors, and Adulthood Dysfunctional Contributors. (Dysfunction is defined as a problem located within the individual that cannot be remedied by providing some new type of environment or learning; Wakefield, 1993). The three reappearing practices of and experiences within the family unit were grouped within the Childhood Environmental Incubator (a protected and controlled environment). The eight childhood personality and behavioral traits were grouped within the Childhood Dysfunctional Indicators (see Ressler et al., 1988, for a similar grouping). Alcohol/substance abuse and pornography, parts of sex offender theory that open the "floodgates of inhibitions" (Schwartz, 1988), comprise the category of Adult Floodgate Disinhibitors. Finally, 15 adult traits and behaviors comprised the fourth category of Adult Dysfunctional Contributors.

The 20 cases include: Ted Bundy (Levin & Fox, 1985; Leyton, 1986; Michaud & Aynesworth, 1983; Sears, 1987; Wilson & Seaman, 1990); John Wayne Gacy (Cahill, 1986; Keppel, 1989; Levin & Fox, 1985; Sears, 1991); Edmond Kemperer (Levin & Fox, 1985; Leyton, 1986; Sears, 1987; Wilson & Seaman, 1990); Charles Manson (Levin & Fox, 1985; Norris, 1988; Wilson & Seaman, 1990); Bobby Joe Long (Norris, 1988); Leonard Lake (Norris, 1988; Wilson & Seaman, 1990); Henry Lee Lucas (Levin & Fox, 1985; Norris, 1988; Sears, 1987); Albert DeSalvo (Levin & Fox, 1985; Leyton, 1988; Sears, 1987; Wilson & Seaman, 1990); David Spence (Stowers, 1986); Kenneth Bianchi (O'Brien, 1985; Wilson & Seaman, 1990); Angelo Buono (Levin & Fox, 1985; O'Brien, 1985; Wilson & Seaman, 1990); Delforth (Newspaper and television news reports); H. Glatman (Wilson & Seaman, 1990); Gerald Galego (Biondi & Hecox, 1988); Jeffrey Dahmer (Davis, 1991); Larry Eyler (Kolarik, 1990); Dayton Leroy Rogers (King, 1992); Russian Andrei Chikatilo (Conradi, 1992); Harvey Louis Carignan (Rule, 1983); Randall Woodfield (Rule, 1984).

RESULTS

The findings of the present study are tabulated in Table 1. The Ressler et al. (1988) findings are presented for comparison and validation. Those characteristics that are "starred" were found to be significantly different at

TABLE 1

ENVIRONMENTAL INCUBATOR

Characteristics	% Pres. Study	% Ressler
1. Alcoholic Family Dysfunction (P = 12; R = 29)	75%	69%
2. Lack of consis. par. limit set (P = 15; R = 31)	93%	74
3. Freq. observ. of vio. in home (P = 15; R = 26)	80%	74

CHILDHOOD DYSFUNCTIONAL INDICATORS

Characteristics	% Pres. Study (P = 16)	% Ressler
a. intro. to porn prior to age 12	18.8%	N/A
b. isolated (R = 28)	43.8	71%
c.* firesetting (R = 25)	6	56
d. enuresis (R = 22)	50	68
e.* petty stealing (R = 27)	25	56
f. arrests	43.8	N/A
g. immature/late sexual dev.	37.5	N/A
h. cruelty to animals (R = 28)	25	36

FLOODGATE DISINHIBITORS

Characteristics	% Pres. Study (N = 18)	% Ressler
I. Alcohol/Drug Abuse	72.2%	N/A
II. Pornography Addiction (R = 31)	83.3	81

ADULTHOOD DYSFUNCTIONAL CONTRIBUTORS

Characteristics	% Pres. Study (N = 20)	% Ressler (N = 36)
A. Isolated (R = 26)	55%	73%
B. Feeling of Powerlessness	80	N/A
C. Zero State	85	N/A
D. Need to be correct/right	30	N/A
E. Feeling of duality	30	N/A
F.* Fetishism (R = 29)	15	72
G. Necrophilia	20	N/A
H. Impulsive temper (R = 27)	40	48
I. Compulsive	75	N/A
J. Hatred of Women	35	N/A
K. Love/adoration of women	35	N/A
L. Homosexuality	10	N/A
M. Contempt for mankind	25	N/A
N. Hypersexuality	15	N/A
O. Brain Damage (R = 26)	20	19

*indicate significance at .05 level; P = N in present study; R = n of Ressler study

6   International Journal of Offender Therapy and Comparative Criminology

the .05 level. This difference may be due to definitions and/or more accurate data that is available to the F.B.I. For example, in relationship to more accurate data, the Ressler (1988) study had facts about school behavior and a wide amount of demographic information.

Where data is available, all three characteristics of the Childhood Environmental Incubator are found in 75% or more of the families of the serial murderers. Furthermore, the most frequently occurring characteristic is that of inconsistent parenting and limit setting (93%). These findings are somewhat supported by Ressler et al. (1988). From the MacDonald triad only the characteristic of enuresis occurs 50% of the time. Finally, all the findings in the grouping of Childhood Dysfunctional Indicators appear to be somewhat lower than the findings of Ressler et al. (1988). This may be due to the fact that more accurate data is available to the F.B.I. Both characteristics of the Floodgate Disinhibitors are above 72%, with Pornography Addiction at 83.3%. Both findings are supported by the figures in sex offender research (Schwartz, 1988). Within the Adulthood Dysfunctional Contributors, there were three traits that reach beyond 75%: feeling of powerlessness (80%) with its accompanying trait of zero state (85%), and compulsiveness (75%). Of 12 other traits only isolation (55%) reaches 50%. This author believes that, depending upon the definition, isolation could reach a higher incidence equal to that of Ressler et al. (1988).

The present study, therefore, can be understood either to give additional weight to or challenge other certain findings. The results of the present study demonstrate that alcohol/substance abuse provide a way for the individual to escape the psychological pain resulting from the long-term effects of poor parenting and violence as a way of life. Although Ressler et al. (1988) have tended to focus on violent fantasy life rather than the contributive effects of sadomasochistic pornography addiction of the present study, it would seem that a correlation between the two findings exists and a similar connection between feeling of powerlessness and the zero state reinforces Yochelson's and Samenow's (1976) theory.

However, the findings challenge other authors. First, the incidence of brain injury/trauma was exceedingly low (20%, $N = 4$), thus providing an additional challenge (Levin & Fox, 1985) to Norris' questionable "research." The predictability of the MacDonald triad is once again challenged, as Levin and Fox previously have done (1985). Finally, the issue of dissociation, as presently understood as a feeling of duality, is questioned. This outcome may be a result of missing data or a lack of clear understanding or focus by journalistic authors in this area. What part dissociation plays in life in general, if any, is still not fully understood, and, as Egger has pointed out (1990), more research in this area needs to be done.

AN ATTEMPTED HYPOTHETICAL EXPLANATION

The present study offers a constellation of characteristics and environmental influences in childhood that allows other patterns to emerge in adulthood. Most authorities agree that the early years of life set the stage for the adult years (Warren & Hindelang, 1979). Aichorn (Warren & Hindelang, 1979) has asserted that early problems lead to poor impulse control and Friedlander (Warren & Hindelang, 1979) hold that faulty development leads to an antisocial personality problem of dealing with reality (Warren & Hindelang, 1979). Stern (1985), in his theory of the multiple selves of early childhood, has stated that intense affect-related experiences, such as abuse, can contribute to the lack of integration of experiences, which may result in the splitting of the good and bad selves. This in turn can become state-dependent so that certain conditions have to exist for the infant/child, and ultimately the adult, to reexperience it. DeMause (1990) has suggested that the healthy caregiver/parent becomes the receptacle for the infant's dangerous emotions, assisting the infant to become calm and less threatened by the world. On the other hand, where there is poor parenting (i.e. inconsistency, screaming, brutality), this lack of continuity and the intensity of such experiences undermines the organizational ability of the child (Stern, 1985) as well as, in Eriksonian terms, prohibiting the necessary trust bond to form between parent and child.

The family dysfunction prompted by alcoholism is difficult to dispute. Yet we know that a serial murderer does not emerge from every alcoholically dysfunctional family. What then is the difference? Ressler's data has demonstrated a high incidence of voyeurism, compulsive autoerotic practices, and daydreaming during childhood for several murderers. This arises, perhaps, as a result of tremendous childhood isolation and may be a type of compensation for the lack of positive interpersonal contact. Lacking guidance and reality testing, the potential seeds of thinking errors are deposited. The environmental incubator (an isolated and protected environment) is thus set in motion. Gross thinking errors, for example that women enjoy being brutalized (a message frequently implied in pornographic materials), plus the only way to be happy is to be intoxicated, become repeatedly reinforced through observation of the family interaction and pornography. For some individuals isolation increases frustration with attempts at relief through compulsive autoerotic practices, and other ritualistic, habitual behaviors. Yet this does not fill the void nor does this make the practitioner feel secure. Among the many results is that of ever-increasing frustration. When this individual enters adulthood lacking healthy patterns, he quickly succumbs to circular patterns of heavy substance abuse to relieve the psychological pain coupled with pornography in an attempt to relieve the frustration. Yet the result is increased frustration. Although many serial murderers have had relationships of long duration, they appear to have a hidden or compartmentalized self that thwarts all attempts to find satisfaction. Doubtless the substance abuse reduces the fragmented impulse control that exists. The line between reality and daydreaming are blurred in an intoxicated state and the individual finally puts into action what he believes will make him "happy" only to discover it is short-lived. As Sears (1991) has pointed out, the serial murderer follows a similar pattern to the catathymic crisis described by Revitch & Schlisinger (1989). The difference, for the serial murderer, is that the process is incomplete, and needs to be continually replayed due to a lack of satisfaction. Therefore each murder increases the frustration and "drives" the murderer to commit another murder. Frequently, as the murders increase so does the nature of the brutality. As in the catathymic crisis the relief is only transient because the individual has to return to the cycle of isolation coupled with addictions.

SUGGESTIONS FOR FURTHER RESEARCH

Although considerable attention has been focused on the serial murderer in recent years, much is required for a responsible and tested hypothesis. First, there is a lack of controlled studies. There is essential that there be a standardization of terms and interviewing and testing procedures. Although journalistic cases give tremendous amounts of information, there are definite limitations in an effort to employ this material as a data base. Such data assist in an exploratory study, as the present article, but personal interviews are required to both validate and expand the data base. Although the Ressler et al. (1988) study was a groundbreaking one, it too has limitations. As the present author views it, the purpose is not to contribute to the understanding of the serial murderer but its primary goal is to increase law enforcement personnel's knowledge concerning the crime scene and even to expedite the investigation. In fact even the journalistic approach to cases is focused more on the investigative process; the individual becomes somewhat incidental. On the other hand, the core of the present study is to contribute greater understanding of the murderer for the purpose of future prevention.

Assistance towards the proposal goal would be furthered by a comprehensive questionnaire covering items addressed neither by this study nor by the Ressler. It would be interesting to know how the various items correlate with each other (something neither studies provided) and then with data from intelligence testing, the MMPI, the Hare Checklist of Psychopathy, a measurement of dissociation, and testing for "pathological alcohol reaction" (Maletsky, 1975; Moyer, 1987). Finally it is not sufficient to study such a special category without comparisons with other groups. As Levin and Fox (1985) suggest, a study comparing this group with those convicted of economic homicide, as well as with a sample of the average person, is required. Moreover, important differentiating characteristics might emerge from a comparative study of serial murderers, child abusers, and sex offenders, specifically pedophiles and rapists.

APPENDIX

ENVIRONMENTAL INCUBATOR

1. Alcoholic Family Dysfunction: through control "stifles the emotional, and sometimes physical growth of its members" (Kritsberg, 1988, p. 29).
2. Lack of consistent parental limit setting: periodic excessively harsh discipline (beating, stabbing, burning, starving) and/or isolating (abandonment for hours or days).
3. Frequent observation of violence in the home: watching physical or sexual abuse of one or more family members at least monthly.

CHILDHOOD DYSFUNCTIONAL INDICATORS

b. Isolated: being left alone for hours at least a couple of times weekly.
d. Enuresis: after the age of six, wetting the bed monthly.
f. Arrests: being charged with an offense prior to age 16.

FLOODGATE DISINHIBITORS

I. Alcohol/Drug Abuse: drinking or taking drugs to intoxication and always before killing.
II. Pornography Addiction: the watching of increasingly sado-masochistic pornography at least weekly and always within a week of killing.

ADULTHOOD DYSFUNCTIONAL CONTRIBUTORS

A. Isolated (as an adult): difficulty in maintaining peer relations.
B. Feelings of Powerlessness: inability to take charge of one's life demonstrated by failing grades in school and repeated unemployment.
C. Zero State: belief "that the entire world sees him as a nothing and that his existence is permanently futile" (Yochelson & Samenow, 1976, p. 279).
H. Impulsive temper: low frustration threshold coupled with responding irrationally to an event with excessive anger, which increases rather than diminishes (Yochelson & Samenow, 1977).
I. Compulsive: a ritualistic approach to various aspects of life.

10   International Journal of Offender Therapy and Comparative Criminology

REFERENCES

Biondi, R., & Hecox, W. (1988). *All his father's sins.* Rocklin, CA: Prima.

Busch, K. A., & Cavanaugh, J.L. (1986). The study of multiple murder. *Journal of Interpersonal Violence, 1*(1), 5–23.

Conradi, P. (1992). *The Red Ripper.* New York: Dell Book.

Davis, D. (1991). *The Milwaukee murders.* New York: St. Martin's.

DeMause, L. (1990). The history of child assault. *The Journal of Psychohistory, 18*(1), 1–29.

Egger, S. (1991). *Serial murder: An elusive phenomenon.* New York: Praeger.

Holmes, R., & DeBurger, J. (1988). *Serial murder.* Beverly Hills, CA: Sage.

Keppel, R. (1989). *Serial murder: Future implications for police investigations.* Cincinnati, OH: Anderson.

King, G. C. (1992). *Blood Lust.* New York: Onyx Books.

Kirschner, D. (1992). Understanding adoptees who kill: Dissociation, patricide, and the psychodynamics of adoption. *International Journal of Offender Therapy and Comparative Criminology, 36*(4), 323–333.

Kolarik, G. (1992). *Freed to Kill.* New York: Avon Books.

Kritsberg, W. (1988). *The adult children of alcoholics syndrome.* New York: Bantam Books.

Levin, J., & Fox, J. A. (1985). *Mass murder.* New York: Plenum Press.

Leyton, E. (1986). *Hunting humans.* New York: Simon & Schuster.

MacDonald, J. M. (1963). The threat to kill. *American Journal of Psychiatry, 12,* 125–130.

Maletsky, B.M. (1975). The diagnosis of pathological intoxication. *Journal of Studies on Alcohol, 37,* 1215–1228.

Michaud, S. G.; Aynesworth, H. (1983). *The Only Living Witness.* New York: Signet Books.

Moyer, K. E. (1987). *Violence and aggression.* New York: Paragon House.

Norris, J. (1988). *Serial killers: The growing menace.* New York: Doubleday.

O'Brien, D. (1985). *Two of a kind: The hillside stranglers.* New York: Signet.

Ressler, R., Burgess, A., & Douglas, J. (1987). *Sexual homicide: Patterns and motives.* Lexington, MA: Lexington.

Revitch, E.; Schlesinger, L. B. (1989). *Sex Murder and Sex Aggression.* Springfield, Illinois: Charles C. Thomas.

Rule, A. (1983). *The Want-Ad Killer.* New York: Signet Books.

Schwartz, B. K. (Ed.) (1988). *A Practitioner's Guide to Treating the Incarcerated Male Sex Offender.* Washington, D.C.: U. S. Department of Justice.

Sears, D. (1991). *To kill again.* Wilmington, DE: S R Books.

Stern, D. N. (1985). *The interpersonal world of the infant.* New York: Basic Books, Inc.

Stowers, C. (1986). *Careless whispers: The Wako Lake murders.* New York: Simon & Schuster.

Wakefield, J. C. (1993). Limits of operationalization: A critique of Spitzer and Endicott's 1978 proposed criteria for mental disorder. *Journal of Abnormal Psychology, 102*(1), 160–172.

Warren, M., & Hindelang, M. (1979). Current explanations of offender behavior. In *The Psychology of Crime and Criminal Justice* (1st ed.). New York: Holt, Rinehart & Winston.

Watkins, J. G. (1984). "The Bianchi (L. A. Hillside Strangler) Case: Sociopath or Multiple Personality?," *The International Journal of Clinical and Experimental Hypnosis,* XXXII(2), 67–101.

Wilson, C., & Seaman, D. (1990). *The serial killers.* New York: Carol Publishing Group.

Yochelson, S., & Samenow, S. (1976). *The criminal personality.* New York: Jason Aronson.

Constance McKenzie, M.Ed.
40 Dongan Street
Staten Island, NY 10310
U.S.A.

[5]

Serial Murderers:
Early Proposed Developmental
Model and Typology

Nancy L. Ansevics
Harold E. Doweiko

ABSTRACT. It has been reported that the incidence of serial murder has increased by approximately 400% in the past 15 years (Leyton, 1986). Yet, in spite of the amount of attention in the popular press that the serial murderer commands, clinicians are limited in both the psychological definition of serial murder, and the clinical understanding of such individuals.

In reviewing various investigative popular books and reported documents addressing 11 different serial murderers, the authors looked for and found developmental themes that suggest common developmental characteristics for these individuals during childhood and adolescence. It is the purpose of this paper to review these findings, and to advance a preliminary conceptual framework within which professionals might: (1) become alerted to such characteristics in childhood and adolescence and, (2) through early treatment, possibly decrease a potential for dangerousness in later years.

"What is at issue is the continuing unwillingness on the parts of our court to recognize that an opinion does not become a fact merely because it is held by a doctor . . . there can be no expert testimony where there is no settled body of knowledge." (Meyer 1982, p. 302)

Nancy L. Ansevics, EdD, is Program Planning Director, Department of Superintendent, St. Joseph State Hospital, St. Joseph, MO 64506.

Harold E. Doweiko, EdD, is a Licensed Psychologist on the staff of St. Olaf Mental Health and Treatment Center, Austin, MN 55912-2998.

Special recognition is given to Diane Hargrave for her contributions in both assisting in collation of data and editing this study.

This paper represents the joint efforts of both authors; name order denotes neither junior nor senior authorship.

The importance of childhood on later adult development in both animals and humans has been well documented (Kolb and Brodie, 1982; McElroy, 1978). Chamove, Rosenblum and Harlow (1973) observed infant rhesus monkeys raised together, without a mother figure, and compared their behavior with other rhesus monkeys raised with their mothers. It was found that mothers (with infants) would normally begin to reject the infant's clinging behavior at about 3 months of age. By doing so, the mother seemed to encourage the infant to start to explore the environment, rather than to encourage further dependency. At the same time, those monkeys raised in the absence of mothering demonstrated disturbed attachment behaviors. This study suggests importance of a consistent parent figure (mother in this case) in the development of security that encourages social belonging.

At the other extreme, McElroy's (1978) primate research has suggested that when mother-infant attachments are too intense, which is to say that if dependency is continued for too long a period of time, both sexual and social development may be inhibited. These findings, in McElroy's words, ". . . seem to be analogous to fixations observed in some human studies" (p. 58). Primate studies thus suggest that serious disruption of normal mother-infant relationship patterns can occur, either in the direction of too close an attachment or too distant a mother-infant relationship. Both behaviors are consequent to dependency which is fostered and abandonment which is forced. Neither lend themselves to healthy development.

Bowlby (1980) has explored the impact of selected childhood experiences on subsequent growth and development, including the impact of loss on the human child. Bowlby (1980) postulates that during healthy development the child develops affectional bonds with the parents, a process known as "attachment behavior" (p. 39). This attachment behavior is achieved through consistency in parental-child interactions. As Bowlby (1978, 1980) notes, however, the parents might engage in inconsistent parenting for a number of different reasons. It is even possible that one or perhaps even both parents might leave the child's environment through illness, marital separation, divorce, death, or abandonment. Bowlby (1980) goes on to suggest that:

. . . neurotic and psychotic character might in some cases be the result of mourning processes evoked during childhood having taken an unfavorable course and thereby left the person prone to respond to later losses in a pathological way. (p. 34)

The impact of the parental/child relationship on subsequent growth and development is such that according to Bowlby (1980):

. . . there is a strong causal relationship between an individual's experiences with his parents and his later capacity to make affectional bonds and that certain common variations in that capacity, manifesting themselves in marital problems, in difficulties with children, as well as neurotic symptoms and personality disorders, can be attributed to certain common variations in the ways that parents perform their roles. (p. 10)

In his exploration of their perception of stressful events, Yamamoto, (1979) found that elementary school children rated the loss of a parent as significantly stressful. Further support might be found in the study by Flaherty and Richman (1986) who attempted to understand the role of social support systems on adult psychopathology in humans. It was concluded by Flaherty and Richman (1986) that the quality of the adult's interpersonal relationships is derived from earlier childhood attachment experiences.

Achenbach (1982) identified several different subgroupings of children that were considered to be "at risk" for the development of later psychopathology. It was noted by Achenbach (1982) that the ". . . quality of the psychosocial environment seems critical for many aspects of adaptive development" (p. 640). Among the more significant psychosocial environmental factors that might impact on subsequent growth and development were physical abuse, sexual abuse, neglect, the loss of a parent through death or divorce, and discrepancies between psychological and biological parenthood. This latter condition for example could evolve when children are placed in foster homes for extended periods of time, only to be subsequently reunited with their biological parents, according to Achenbach (1982). Kaufman (1985) noted that "the child's inner well-being is most notably a function of the maternal or parental climate" (p. 16).

Bryer, Nelson, Baker-Miller, and Krol (1987) addressed the issue of sexual or physical abuse in childhood as a possible mediating factor in psychiatric illness, and concluded that "the more severely disturbed patients were, the more likely they were to have been abused in childhood" (p. 1429). This position was supported by Burgess, Hartmand and McCormack (1987). Anderson (1978), in working with adolescents who presented a history of criminal behavior, noted the ". . . persistence into adolescence of a binding tie with mother which seemed to affect strongly, if not preclude, separation and socialization" (p. 378). The clinical picture was: ". . . one of impulsive dominated interaction with others in the home and outside the home" in which the parents would report ". . . periods of superficially compliant behavior interrupted by outbursts of aggressive behavior" (p. 378). Anderson (1978) concluded that although the boys that he worked with had a history of antisocial behaviors, the best diagnostic category for the majority of these boys was that of a borderline personality disorder.

Eight different symptoms of borderline adolescents were found by the Anderson study (1978), including (1) anger directed at a variety of targets, including parents, (2) depression marked by isolation, loneliness, helplessness, but without significant guilt, (3) anxiety, as expressed by the individual's body language, (4) anhedonia, (5) impulsive behavior, (6) lack of empathy in interpersonal relations, (7) brief psychotic episodes with paranoid trends and depersonalization, but without evidence of a thought disorder, and, (8) self-glorifying fantasies (Anderson, 1978).

Anderson's (1978) work revealed that the "emotional unavailability or absence of the fathers after age four and particularly in early adolescence" (p. 378) played a significant role in the evolution of delinquency in nonpsychotic adolescent boys while the emotional unavailability of the mother seemed to have no significant impact on later delinquency in boys.

Indeed, one characteristic that separates the borderline from other more dysfunctional personality patterns according to Millon (1981) is the history of ". . . periodic but reversible psychotic episodes" (p. 329, italics in original) which might be characterized as "psychotic eruptions" . . . "characterized by the loss of reality contact and by both cognitive and emotional dyscontrol" (p. 329).

Millon goes on to point out that for the borderline personality ". . . once these intense feelings are discharged, these patients regain a modicum of psychic balance — until such time as their tensions again mount beyond manageable portions'' (p. 329). Such patients ''. . . experience transient periods in which bizarre behaviors, irrational impulses, and delusional thoughts are exhibited'' (p. 334).

The episodic dyscontrol syndrome behavior expressed itself in a displacement of anger in those sexual offenders examined as it did in adolescent history of serial murderers. The specific characteristics of the victim are of little importance in Prentky and Knight's (1986) opinion. Rather, what is important is that there is a woman available who could serve as a target of the displaced aggression. In contrast to this impulsive behavior was the ''offense-related impulsivity'' (p. 158), which was strongest in those rapists whose behavior was more sexual than a reflection of anger. Such offense-related impulsivity involved a high degree of planning that served as ''. . . the fulfillment of an elaborate preoffense fantasy that is motivated by the need to compensate for felt sexual inadequacies'' (p. 158). Again, this form of impulsivity is regularly described in the self-defined ''compulsion'' of the reviewed serial murderer's profiles.

In reviewing the characteristics of the borderline personality, Millon (1981) noted that the borderline might be viewed as:

> ''. . . showing intense affect, either hostile or depressed; an absence of flatness or pleasure, but frequent depersonalization; a background of episodic and impulsive behavior . . . identity disturbances that are often cloaked by superficial identifications; brief psychotic episodes; and interpersonal relationships that vacillate between superficiality, dependency and manipulativeness.'' (p. 347)

These latter points are of some importance to the present study. For although there is some similarity between the early environments of serial murderers, and the early environment of the antisocial personality disorder as described by the authors (Ansevics & Doweiko, 1983; Doweiko & Ansevics, 1985; Ansevics, 1986), serial murderers seem to have limited similarities to the antisocial personality in adolescent and preadolescent periods, particularly at the level of socialized conformity.

Prentky and Knight (1986) explored the issue of impulsivity, and found subtle differences between the form of impulsive behavior demonstrated by antisocial personalities, and sexual offenders. The authors termed the impulsivity that is a hallmark of the antisocial personality psychopathy, as opposed to the episodic dyscontrol syndrome found in sexual offenders. This latter condition was, seen as a reflection of the suppression of impulses to aggress, which surfaced in "spontaneous and unpredictable expressions of violence" (Prentky and Knight, 1986, p. 143).

There seems to be a subtle, but very real, difference between the impulsive actions of the antisocial personality, and sexual offenders (Prentky & Knight, 1986); with the degree of planning serving to highlight the role of self-glorifying fantasy (Prentky, R., Burgess, A. et al., 1989); and the need to compensate for perceived sexual inadequacies. The most impulsive of sexual offenses seemed to reflect the need to displace anger on to a target (MacCulloch et al., 1983), usually the most available woman, with the release of anger serving to help the individual avoid or reduce internal and external stress (Ressler et al., 1986/Ressler et al., 1988).

Harrington (1972) explored the differences between the sociopath, perhaps better known as the "antisocial personality," and the "sexual psychopath." This latter classification is composed of individuals who engage in almost compulsive sexual assaults, and who seem to channel their aggression through repetitive sexual assaults. There are strong similarities between what Harrington (1972) has classified as the "sexual psychopath," and the individual who in Prentky and Knight's (1986) paper demonstrated "offense-related impulsivity" in order to compensate for perceived inadequacies. For such individuals, the assault seems to be an attempt to meet an internal need, namely to overcome feelings of some form of inadequacy.

Kaufman (1989) extends this concept, noting that the "sexual psychopath is shame-based," and that their "acts are acts of power and revenge, born of impotence and fueled by shame." By defeating and humiliating (or killing) the victim, "the perpetrator momentarily becomes freed of shame." Kaufman adds that in an "abuse syndrome, intense shame (humiliation) is the predominant affect and is accompanied by fear, distress (crying, sadness) and rage." In the midst of viewing abuse or experiencing their own abuse, the victim (soon perpetrator) feels to blame – an inevitable result of shame.

Thus, a consistent theme of research involving both primates and humans is that, if there is a serious disruption in the quality of parent-child interactions; there is the potential for lifelong disruption of normal social/sexual growth. The role of the mother seems to be most significant in very early life, while in 4 years to preadolescent/adolescent years the role of the father seems most significant. The child might experience loss of one or both parents, observe or experience physical and/or sexual abuse, or the nuclear family might be disruptive in any of a number of different ways. The impact of any of these conditions upon subsequent growth and development seems to be a disturbance in the individual's later ability to form mature interpersonal relationships.

Physical/sexual abuse during childhood seems to be significantly correlated with a history of being an abuser in later years (Ressler et al., 1986), with the longer the period of abuse suffered as a child being correlated with the frequency and violence of the abuse demonstrated by that child later in adulthood (Ressler et al., 1986). For some, there may be a compulsive displacement of shame/anger on to others, especially upon women, which serves to relieve internal pressure.

On the other hand, the original violation scene (Kaufman 1989, p. 125) may replay itself in consciousness/sexual perversions/night terrors/or hover at the periphery of awareness. If, instead, the scene is banished from awareness, disowned or denied by significant others, the self emerges frozen into adulthood, statue like. The former victim or viewer who may be haunted by scenes of actual torment as a child, begins to use sadistic fantasy in adolescence to objectify and control the torment, and become driven to reenact them; this time in the role of the tormentor, thus reversing roles. This would result in momentarily being freed from the shame born of impotence.

SUMMARY AND CONCLUSIONS

Overall, there seems to be significant evidence that serial murderers represent a subtype not of the antisocial personality disorder, but rather of the borderline personality disorder. Each of the eleven serial murderers studied in this retrospective analysis suffered a significant loss at about the age of five. Nine of the eleven serial murderers studied grew up in an environment where there was violence in the family. Six of the eleven came from families that were seriously disturbed in one way or another, while all eleven might be characterized as having an overly close attachment to their mother. All mothers were dominant in the family. All fathers were either physically or emotionally absent from the sons during preteenage years and teenage years. All sons were "favorite" children of the mothers.

During adolescence, each of the eleven serial murderers reviewed appeared to achieve a tenuous adjustment to society, at least at first glance. However, nine of the eleven serial murderers included in this study had a history of sadistic/violent fantasies during adolescence. Nine of eleven had a history of exhibitionism, cross-dressing, and/or developed sexual fetishes. All eleven had a history of petty theft during adolescence. None of the eleven serial murderers studied dated while in high school, nor did any of the eleven serial murderers have their first sexual experience until after high school. All were puritanical about sexual encounters and saw females within the "Madonna"/whore dichotomy. All wrote melodramatic poetry about "love," which they continued to write into adulthood.

As a group, the serial murderer might be classified as being of above-average intelligence, and nine of the eleven serial murderers studied had no history of chemical abuse. Nine individuals had been social users of alcohol, while one individual appeared to go through a phase of drug abuse in the military. Following rejection at the hands of their first, and only, significant lover in adulthood, ten of the eleven serial murderers seemed to have decompensated, and to have experienced a great deal of rage directed against women. Each of the eleven serial murderers studied seems to have utilized violent pornography, and ten had a reported history of rape prior to starting their murderous activities.

For these individuals, the act of murder would seem to reflect a "working through" process, or an attempt on the part of the individual to achieve some measure of adjustment to internal (possibly shame) and external (possibly stress) adaptive demands.

There are strong similarities to the manner in which violence is expressed for the serial murderer, and that commonly seen in the more traditional borderline personality disorder. It is the hypothesis of the authors of this paper that this violence also serves the same function for both groups of people. There is a murderer-specific pattern for victim characteristics, and the murder seems to be an act of aggression/control directed against a specific characteristic victim, through the use of a murderer-specific aggressive pattern.

It is the perspective of the authors that the manipulativeness seen in serial murderers reflects not an antisocial manipulativeness, but rather the manipulative tendency seen in the borderline personality disorder. The superficial adjustment to society would also seem to be more characteristic of the borderline, than of the antisocial personality, especially in that the serial murderer seems to suffer from the same brief reactive compulsive pseudo-psychotic episodes characteristic of the borderline personality disorder. Thus, it is the contention of the authors that the serial murderer reflects a form of borderline personality disorder, rather than the antisocial personality, as commonly considered.

A retrograde reconstruction of clinical, social and criminal justice information presented in documents and literature for eleven known serial murderers reveals a developmental pattern that is both similar to, and different from, profiles offered in the literature on serial murderers (Ressner et al., 1986; Hales et al., 1987). Antisocials evidence preliminary developmental deficits during early childhood, in childhood, and during adolescence (Doweiko and Ansevics, 1985). Serial murderers appear to have primary deficit at early childhood and pre-adolescence.

Clinicians are alerted to the observed progressive model of common behaviors found in serial murderers' developmental histories (Figure 1) in the hopes that early intervention during childhood or adolescence may decrease the event of serial murder.

Further, it is the contention of the authors that the serial murderer (Figure 2) reflects a variation of the borderline personality disorder, and should be treated as such rather than as an antisocial personality disorder, for reasons that are explored in detail in this paper.

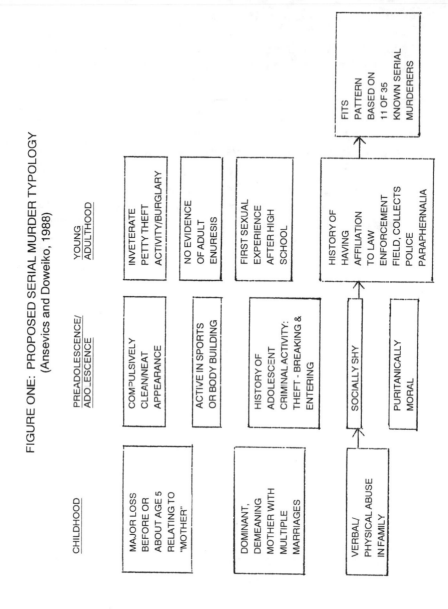

FIGURE ONE: PROPOSED SERIAL MURDER TYPOLOGY
(Ansevics and Doweiko, 1988)

CHILDHOOD	PREADOLESCENCE/ ADOLESCENCE	YOUNG ADULTHOOD
MAJOR LOSS BEFORE OR ABOUT AGE 5 RELATING TO "MOTHER"	COMPULSIVELY CLEAN/NEAT APPEARANCE	INVETERATE PETTY THEFT ACTIVITY/BURGLARY
	ACTIVE IN SPORTS OR BODY BUILDING	NO EVIDENCE OF ADULT ENURESIS
DOMINANT, DEMEANING MOTHER WITH MULTIPLE MARRIAGES	HISTORY OF ADOLESCENT CRIMINAL ACTIVITY: THEFT - BREAKING & ENTERING	FIRST SEXUAL EXPERIENCE AFTER HIGH SCHOOL
VERBAL/ PHYSICAL ABUSE IN FAMILY	SOCIALLY SHY	HISTORY OF HAVING AFFILIATION TO LAW ENFORCEMENT FIELD, COLLECTS POLICE PARAPHERNALIA
	PURITANICALLY MORAL	

FITS PATTERN BASED ON 11 OF 35 KNOWN SERIAL MURDERERS

116

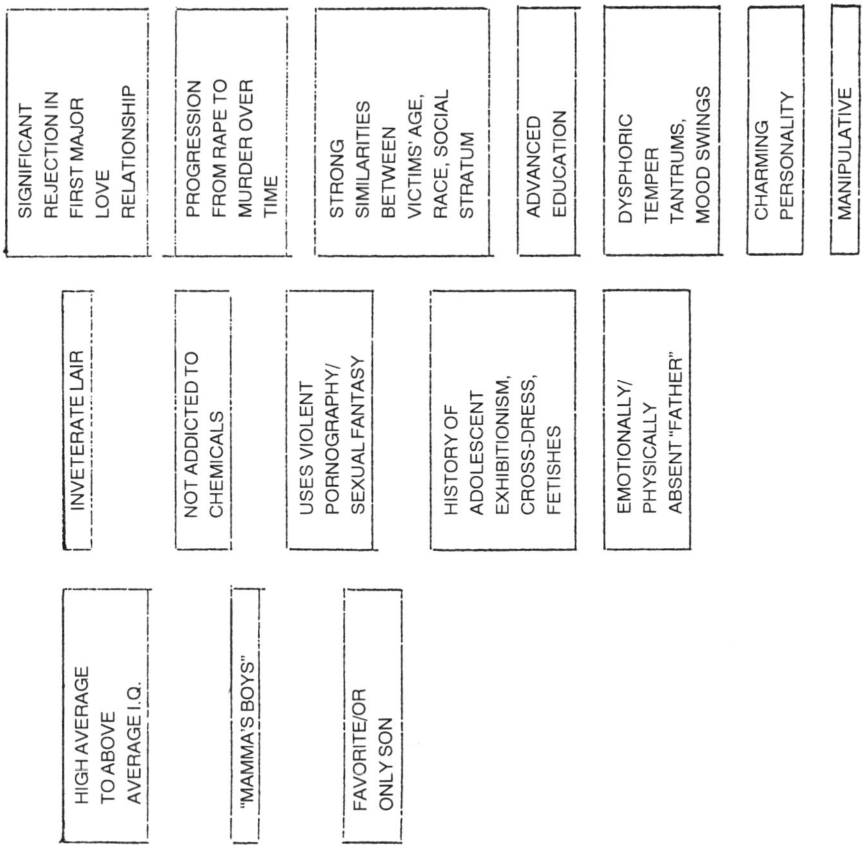

SIGNIFICANT REJECTION IN FIRST MAJOR LOVE RELATIONSHIP

PROGRESSION FROM RAPE TO MURDER OVER TIME

STRONG SIMILARITIES BETWEEN VICTIMS' AGE, RACE, SOCIAL STRATUM

ADVANCED EDUCATION

DYSPHORIC TEMPER TANTRUMS, MOOD SWINGS

CHARMING PERSONALITY

MANIPULATIVE

INVETERATE LAIR

NOT ADDICTED TO CHEMICALS

USES VIOLENT PORNOGRAPHY/ SEXUAL FANTASY

HISTORY OF ADOLESCENT EXHIBITIONISM, CROSS-DRESS, FETISHES

EMOTIONALLY/ PHYSICALLY ABSENT "FATHER"

HIGH AVERAGE TO ABOVE AVERAGE I.Q.

"MAMMA'S BOYS"

FAVORITE/OR ONLY SON

117

FIGURE TWO:
PERCENTAGES OF CHARACTERISTICS FOR
SERIAL MURDERES REVIEWED

Age at onset   24.7 years

Education   13.45 years

Religion   64% Roman Catholic
                    36% Born Again Christian

Marital Status   73% single
                    (36% single and living with someone)
                    27% married
                    (63% had live-in person)

Average IQ   116.73
                    (Bright normal - 84%)
                    1 SD above average (mean)

Drug Abuse History 82% no substance abuse history
                    73% used drugs and/or alcohol before
                    commission of murder

Average height of serial murderer	71 inches
Police affiliation or paraphrenalia	91%
Family violence history	82%
Sexual abuse history	9%
Used violent pornography	73%
Adolescent sexual acting-out history without treatment	91%
Sexual fetish	100%

119

REFERENCES

Abramhamsen, D. 1975. *The Murdering Mind*. New York: Harper & Row, Publishers.

Achenbach, T.M. 1982. *Developmental Psychopathology* (2nd ed). New York: John Wiley & Sons, Inc.

American Psychiatric Association. DSM III, 1980.

Anderson, R. 1978. Thought on fathering: Its relationship to the borderline condition in adolescence and to transitional phenomena (in) *Adolescent Psychiatry* (Feinstein and Giovacchini, eds), Chicago: University of Chicago Press.

Ansevics, N.L., & Doweiko, H.E. 1983. A conceptual framework for intervention with the antisocial personality. *Psychotherapy in Private Practice, 1* (3), 43-52.

Ansevics, N.L. 1986. *The Cognitive-Developmental Status of the Adult Male Anti-Social Personality: An Assessment Instrument*. University Microfilms, Inc. Harvard Press.

Ansevics, N.L. and Doweiko, H. 1988. *Serial Murder: Typology*. Paper presented at APA Mid-winter Conference, Scottsdale, AZ.

Bowlby, J. 1978. Attachment theory and its therapeutic implications. In: *Adolescent Psychiatry* (Vol. VI). (Feinstein, S.C., Giovacchini, P.O., editors). Chicago: University of Chicago Press.

Bowlby, J. 1980. *Loss*. New York: Basic Books, Inc.

Brussel, J. 1970. *Casebook of a Crime Psychiatrist*. New York: Dell Publishing Co.

Bryer, J.B., Nelson, B.A., Baker-Miller, J., Krol, P.A. 1987. Childhood sexual and physical abuse as factors in adult psychiatric illness. *American Journal of Psychiatry*, 144, 1426-1430.

Carpozi, G. 1977. *Son of Sam: The .44 Caliber Killer*. New York: Manor Books, Inc.

Chamove, A.S., Rosenblum, L.A., and Harlow, H.F. 1973. Monkeys raised only with peers: A Pilot study. *Animal Behavior, 21*, 216-235.

Cross, R. 1981. *The Yorkshire Ripper*. New York: Dell Publishing Co.

Damore, L. 1982. *The Anatomy of a Murderer: In His Garden*. New York: Berkley Books.

Doweiko, H.E., and Ansevics, N.L. 1985. Antisocial personality "burnout" and adult developmental theory: Implications for psychotherapy. *Psychotherapy in Private Practice, 3* (2), 59-63.

Engel, G. 1961. Is grief a disease? *Psychosomatic Medicine*, 23, 18-22.

Flaherty, J.A., & Richman, J.A. 1986. Effects of childhood relationships on the adult's capacity to form social supports. *American Journal of Psychiatry, 143*, 7, 851-855.

Frank, G. 1967. *The Boston Strangler*. New York: New American Library.

Freeman, L. 1976. *Before I Kill More*. New York: Simon and Schuster.

Groth, A.N. 1979. *Men Who Rape, The Psychology of the Offender*. New York: Plenum Press.

Hales, R. & Frances, A. (eds.). 1987. Serial Murder in *American Psychiatric Association Annual Review/Vol. 6*, American Psychiatric Press, pp. 484-485.

Harrington, A. 1972. *Psychopaths*. New York: Simon & Schuster.

Keyes, E. 1976. *The Michigan Murders*. New York: Simon & Schuster.

Knight, R. & Prentky, R. 1987. The developmental antecedents and adult adaptations of rapist subtypes, *Journal of Criminal Justice and Behavior*, Vol. 14, No. 4, Dec.

Kolb, L.C., & Brodie, H.K.H. 1982. *Modern Clinical Psychiatry* (10th ed). Philadelphia, PA: W.B. Saunders Co.

Larsen, R. 1986. *Bundy: The Deliberate Stranger*. New York: Prentice-Hall, Inc.

Leaff, L.A. 1978. The antisocial personality: Psychodynamic implications. *The Psychopath* (W.H. Reid, editor). New York: Brunner-Mazel.

Leyton, E. 1986. *Compulsive Killers: The story of modern multiple murder*. New York: New York University Press.

McElroy, E. 1978. Maternal deprivation and other developmental studies. In, *Basic Psychopathology*, (Balis, G.U. Editor in Chief). Boston: Butterworth Publishers, Inc.

Meyer, P. 1982. *The Yale Murder*. Harper & Row, New York, 302.

Millon, T. 1981. *Disorders of Personality*. New York: John Wiley & Sons.

Nolan, J.R., & Connolly, M.J. 1979. *Black's Law Dictionary* (5th ed). St. Paul, MN: West Publishing Co.

O'Brien, D. 1985. *Two of a Kind: The Hillside Stranglers*. New York: New American Library.

Palmer, S. 1962. *The Psychology of Murder*. New York: Thomas Y. Crowell Co.

Piaget, J. 1970. Piaget's theory. In P. Mussen (Ed.) *Carmichael's manual of child psychology*, 3rd Edition. New York: John Wiley & Sons.

Prentky, R.A., & Knight, R.A. 1986. Impulsivity in the lifestyle and criminal behavior of sexual offenders. *Criminal Justice and Behavior*, *13*, 141-164.

Prentky, R.A., Burgess, A.W., Rokous, F., Lee, A., Hartman, C., Ressler, R., Douglas, J. 1989. The Presumptive Role of Fantasy in Serial Sexual Homicide. *American Journal of Psychiatry* 146:887-891, July.

Ressler, R., Burgess, A., Hartman, C. & D'Agostino, R. 1986. Sexual Killers and Their Victims, *J. of Interpersonal Violence*, Vol. 1, No. 3, Sept. pp. 288-308.

Ressler, R., Burgess, A., Hartman, C., Douglas, J., McCormack, A. 1986. Murderers Who Rape and Mutilate. *Journal of Interpersonal Violence*, Vol. 1, No. 3, Sept. pp. 273-287.

Ressler, R., Burgess, A., Douglas, J. 1988. *Sexual Homicide: Patterns and Motives*. Lexington, Massachusetts/Toronto, Canada: D. C. Heath and Company.

Rule, A. 1981. *The Stranger Beside Me*. New York: New American Library.

Schwartz, T. 1982. *The Hillside Strangler: A Murderer's Mind*. New York: Doubleday & Co.

122   *PSYCHOTHERAPY IN PRIVATE PRACTICE*

Stack, A. 1983. *Lust Killer*. New York: New American Library.
Stack, A. 1984. *The I-5 Killer*. New York: New American Library.
Winn, S., & Merrill, D. 1979. *Ted Bundy: The Killer Next Door*. New York: Bantam Books.
Yamamoto, K. 1979. Children's ratings of the stressfulness of experience. *Developmental Psychology, 15*, 581-582.

[6]

Park Elliott Dietz,[1] *M.D., M.P.H., Ph.D.; Bruce Harry,*[2] *M.D.; and
Robert R. Hazelwood,*[3] *M.S.*

Detective Magazines: Pornography
for the Sexual Sadist?

REFERENCE: Dietz, P. E., Harry, B., Hazelwood, R. R., **"Detective Magazines: Pornography
for the Sexual Sadist?"** *Journal of Forensic Sciences*, JFSCA, Vol. 31, No. 1, Jan. 1986, pp.
197–211.

ABSTRACT: The origins of detective magazines can be traced to 17th and 18th century crime
pamphlets and to 19th century periodicals that Lombroso called "really criminal newspapers." Content analysis of current detective magazines shows that their covers juxtapose erotic images with
images of violence, bondage, and domination; that their articles provide lurid descriptions of murder, rape, and torture; and that they publish advertisements for weapons, burglary and car theft
tools, false identification, and sexual aids. Six case histories of sexual sadists illustrate the use of
these magazines as a source of fantasy material. We postulate that detective magazines may contribute to the development of sexual sadism, facilitate sadistic fantasies, and serve as training
manuals and equipment catalogs for criminals. We recommend that detective magazines be considered during policy debates about media violence and pornography.

KEYWORDS: psychiatry, criminal sex offenses, deviant sexual behavior, detective magazines,
sexual sadism, pornography, criminal behavior, sexual homicide

A class of popular periodicals known as "detective magazines" has apparently eluded the
attention of researchers and commentators concerned with media violence and pornography.
These magazines provide factual accounts of crimes and criminals, and are thereby distinguished from mystery fiction. They rarely contain photographs of nudes, and are thereby
distinguished from those publications that most individuals casually refer to as erotic, pornographic, or obscene.

In this paper, we review the historical roots of these detective magazines, report data on the
content of current detective magazines, present six case histories in which detective magazines
were a source of fantasy material, and discuss the possible psychiatric and criminologic significance of detective magazines.

We postulate that detective magazines serve as pornography for sexual sadists. The works of
the Marquis de Sade and his literary disciples, though known outside the literati, are too

An earlier version of this paper was presented by the authors in a panel entitled "Bloody Instructions:
Intolerable Crimes in Mass Market Magazines" at the Annual Meeting of the American Academy of
Psychiatry and the Law, New York, NY, 24 Oct. 1982. Received for publication 6 May 1985; accepted for
publication 31 July 1985.
[1]Associate professor of law and of behavioral medicine and psychiatry and medical director, Institute
of Law, Psychiatry and Public Policy, University of Virginia Schools of Law and Medicine, Charlottesville, VA.
[2]Assistant professor of psychiatry and adjunct assistant professor of law, University of Missouri–
Columbia, Columbia, MO.
[3]Supervisory special agent and instructor, Behavioral Science Unit, FBI Academy, Quantico, VA.

198   JOURNAL OF FORENSIC SCIENCES

erudite and too remote in setting from everyday life to appeal to the sexual sadist of average intelligence and educational level. In contrast, detective magazines depict and describe sadistic acts in familiar settings, using the imagery and language of tabloid newspapers. This class of periodicals receives little commentary in comparison with those that are considered obscene or pornographic on the basis of their explicit use of erotic imagery. Detective magazines characteristically pair violent and sadistic images with erotic images, yet are more accessible for purchase by young persons than are magazines that depict naked bodies.

The Origins and Readership of Detective Magazines

Periodicals reporting crime are thought to have originated in 17th century England [*1*]. Crime pamphlets and related publications appeared at a time when oral renditions of crime were still provided by street merchants for a fee. Around 1864, Mayhew described "death hunters" and "running patterers" who were paid to shout out stories of crimes [*2*]. Death hunters went to the scenes of murders and reported on the details of the killings; running patterers fabricated or embellished the stories of infamous crimes. Mayhew also described "caravan shows," a form of "peep show" in which carts containing a miniature stage, curtains, and scenery were used by puppeteers to reenact infamous murders [*3*].

Crime pamphlets flourished throughout 18th century England and appeared in America during the last half of that century. By the middle of the 19th century, as British and American journalists embraced sensationalism [*4*], the chaotic relationship between crime and law enforcement [*5*] found its natural literary outlet. Gradually, newspapers and crime magazines began to replace other forms of information about crime.

The first financially successful American crime magazine was *The National Police Gazette*, which appeared in 1845 [*6*]. This magazine was highly celebrated, and at least 22 related magazines followed in its wake [*7-9*]. The *Gazette* survived well into the 20th century. We examined all issues of the *National Police Gazette* from its first year of publication. Initially, it featured stories of actual crimes and made modest use of woodcut illustrations. There were many advertisements for home remedies, sexual enhancement and augmentation preparations, trusses, clothing, hats, boots, jewelry, guns, and "cheap" books. By the late 19th century, the *Gazette* was printed on pink paper and had detailed illustrations of shootings, stabbings, hangings, and debauchery, as well as graphic descriptions of bareknuckle boxing, wrestling, and cockfights. Advertisements offered revealing photographs of women; treatments for venereal diseases, impotence, and "self abuse"; and the services of lawyers and detectives. The *Gazette* was "for some years the most widely circulated of weekly journals" [*10*].

The *Gazette's* decline began around 1920, and "modern" detective magazines appeared by 1924. They were quickly assessed as having virtually no cultural value [*11,12*], and they proliferated. More than 20 are currently published on a regular basis. Four detective magazines for which data were available had a combined monthly circulation of 996 000 issues in about 1980 [*13*].

Otto examined eleven detective magazines as part of a larger study of newsstand magazines in the 1960s and found that they offered the most sexual and nonsexual violence of all general circulation magazines, even though his data excluded advertisements and covers [*14*]. Reporting on the content of two detective magazines, Lyle noted that "the stories in general are fairly explicit in describing what kind of violence was committed, how it was done, and to what effect" [*15*]. Beattie studied one issue each of *Official Detective* and *True Detective* as part of his study of mass market magazines and concluded that detective magazines were among those with the most violent content [*16*].

The readership of detective magazines has not been identified. Lazarsfeld and Wyant included 1 detective magazine in their study of reading habits in 90 American cities [*17*], but their statistical analysis excluded the genre. Freidman and Johnson surveyed media use among "aggressive" and "nonaggressive" eighth and ninth grade boys, 20% of whom read "crime and detective magazines"; differences between the two groups in amount and type of magazine reading were not significant [*18*]. In contrast, Lyle and Hoffman reported that 9% of a sample of sixth grade boys and girls, and 6 and 7%, respectively, of a sample of tenth grade boys and girls, preferred to read "detective/mystery" magazines [*19*]. Whether these data refer to such magazines as *Alfred Hitchcock's Mystery Magazine* and *Ellery Queen's Mystery Magazine* or to the detective magazines considered here is not known. Thus, there is no audience whose rate of use of detective magazines is known.

The Content of Detective Magazines

Detective magazines are readily available at newsstands, drugstores, supermarkets, convenience stores, and elsewhere. One copy of each detective magazine issue available on a single day at ten suburban Boston stores was purchased and studied in detail. The mean purchase price was $1.11; the range was from $0.95 to $2.50. These magazines generally were displayed along with women's, "confession," and children's magazines, usually adjacent to adventure and gun magazines, and always on a different rack from espoused erotic men's magazines. We have subsequently confirmed these observations regarding display patterns in stores in Charlottesville, VA; Chicago, IL; Columbia, MO; Houston, TX; Kansas City, MO; Los Angeles, CA; New York, NY; St. Louis, MO; Washington, DC; Toronto, Ontario, Canada; and Melbourne, Victoria, Australia.

Nineteen detective magazine issues, representing eighteen different titles from six publishers, were studied. They were: *Detective Cases, Detective Diary, Detective Dragnet, Detective Files, Detective World, Front Page Detective, Guilty! The Best from True Detective, Headquarters Detective, Homicide Detective, Inside Detective, Master Detective, Offical Detective Stories, Police Detective* (two issues), *Real Detective, Startling Detective, True Detective, True Police Cases,* and *True Police Yearbook.*

We analyzed several aspects of the content of these 19 issues. First, we analyzed the violent and sexual imagery in photographs used for front covers, article illustrations, and commercial advertisements. Second, we analyzed the words expressive of violence and sexuality used in the titles of articles promoted on the front covers and listed in the tables of contents. Third, we analyzed the textual content of articles for descriptions of violent and sexual behavior. For this third purpose, a stratified, random sample of 38 articles was selected (2 articles randomly selected from the signed articles in each issue). The results of these content analyses are presented in the following sections.

Illustrations

The covers of the 19 magazines bore 21 photographs. The most common image on front covers was that of a woman in an inferior or submissive position. Seventy-six percent of the cover photographs showed domination and submission imagery. Men dominated women in 71% of cover pictures, while women dominated men in 5%. Some pictures showed a woman alone in a submissive or subjugated position. Bondage was depicted in 38% of the cover pictures, and all of the bound subjects were women. Ropes, chains, handcuffs, and cloth were used to achieve this bondage with equal frequency. In order of decreasing frequency, other repetitive cover imagery included violent struggles, brassieres, guns, accentuated breasts, strangulation, corpses, blood, and knives or other cutting instruments. Table 1 shows the percentages of each type of image in covers, articles, and advertisements.

In contrast to the cover photographs, the illustrations accompanying articles most often pictured buildings or other settings and conventionally dressed people. Law enforcement personnel were often shown processing a crime scene or working at a desk; they were always men. Violent and erotic imagery was much less prevalent in article photographs than in cover photographs. Where it did occur, the most prevalent form was domination and submission imagery.

200   JOURNAL OF FORENSIC SCIENCES

TABLE 1—*Percentages of photographs depicting particular types of images in detective magazine covers, articles, and advertisements.*

Images	Covers (N = 19)	Articles (N = 891)	Advertisements (N = 926)
Bondage and domination imagery			
bondage	38	5	0.1
domination	76	36	0
Struggles			
strangulation	14	0.6	0
other violent struggles	29	2	3
Weapons			
guns	29	4	6
knives or other cutting instruments	14	0.7	2
blunt instruments	5	0.8	2
bombs	5	0.1	0
saws	5	0	3
other weapons[a]	0	1.5	0.1
Sadistic imagery			
corpses	14	3	0
blood	14	1	0
mutilation/slashing	0	0.3	0
Body parts			
breasts accentuated	24	1	3
buttocks accentuated	5	0.2	2
genitals	0	0	2
Clothing			
brassiere	29	1	3
negligee	5	2	0
panties	0	2	4
other "erotic" clothing[b]	0	1.5	3.1
Sexual behaviors			
intercourse[c]	0	0.1	3.2
masturbation	0	0	1
crossdressing	0	0.2	0.1

[a]Includes fire, whips, gas chambers, gallows, and brass knuckles.
[b]Includes stockings, garters, hoods, exaggerated shoes and boots, and constrictive waist garments.
[c]Includes heterosexual and homosexual genital intercourse, fellatio, cunnilingus, and anal intercourse.

Men dominated women in 5% of the article pictures, and women dominated men in less than 1%. Individuals were most often bound with ropes or handcuffs, less commonly with leather, chains, or cloth.

In illustrated, commercial advertisements (that is, excluding classified advertisements), potential weapons such as guns, knives, blunt instruments, or saws were depicted slightly more often than body adornments such as panties, brassieres, or stockings. The guns, knives, and blunt instruments were for sale. The saws appeared in advertisements offering instruction in sharpening saws. Undergarments most often appeared in the illustrations of advertisements for other merchandise.

Seventy-three advertisements in our sample promoted enhancement of sexual control, appeal, or function. Detective or law enforcement training was advertised in 68. Fifty-nine promoted "official" photographic identification cards, police badges, or other means of certifying identity. Mind control techniques were offered in 35 advertisements. Female wrestlers were depicted in 18, and male wrestlers in 9. Most issues had advertisements for mail-order brides, lonely hearts clubs, "locksmith training," and equipment for picking locks, opening car doors, duplicating keys, and building handgun silencers.

Titles and Text

The titles of articles are similar in construction and terminology among detective magazines. Compare, for example, the titles from two magazines published two years apart by two different publishers: "A TRUNK-FULL OF FLESH"; "CANADA'S NUMBER 1 MURDER MYSTERY"; "MURDER BY FREIGHT TRAIN"; "ANNA TOOK THE BLADE 90 TIMES!"; "SEX COP'S DEATH CHAMBER"; "IT TAKES A COP"; "OLD FRIEND-SHIPS DIE EASY WITH A .38"; "PORTLAND'S BLOODY SUMMER"; and "TOR-TURE-SLAYER OF EL TORO" (*Startling Detective*, Vol. 73, No. 3, May 1983, published by Globe Communications Corp.); "SATANIST SMILED AS HE SNUFFED THE SNITCH!"; "ROAST A FAMILY OF SIX!"; "BULLET BARRAGE KO'D THE BOXING REF!"; "WHO LEFT THE NAKED MAN'S HEAD SOAKED IN GORE?"; "THE HOLY VAM-PIRE DRANK HIS VICTIM'S BLOOD!"; "WHO BLEW THE BICKERING COUPLE AWAY?"; "WEIRD FETISHES OF WASHINGTON'S RAPE-SLAYER!"; " 'HE WAS PLAYING HERO, SO I SHOT THE S.O.B.!' "; "ORDEAL OF THE KIDNAPPED GIRL IN THE PIT!"; and "LETHAL LESSON: NEVER MESS WITH A MARRIED MAN!" (*Front Page Detective*, Vol. 48, No. 5, May 1985, published by RGH Publishing Corp.).

The magazine covers gave the titles of 77 of the 186 articles listed in the tables of contents. Table 2 shows the percentages of words about particular themes on the covers and in article titles. Words describing various forms of killing were most prevalent and included "kill," "murder," "execute," "slay," and "hit-man." Roles described included "stranger," "lover," "victim," "bride," "dame," "whore," "slut," "gigolo," and "mistress." Descriptors of mental states and traits included "crazy," "mad," "maniac," "greed," "treachery," "lust," and "hang-ups." Death-related words included "dead," "body," "corpse," "graveyard," "ceme-tery," "coffin," and "bloodthirsty." While law enforcement words such as "detective," "po-lice," "crime," "case," and "cop" appeared in the names of every magazine, they were less commonly used in article titles. Sexual terms such as "rape," "gay," "drag," and "sex" made up the next most prevalent category. As can be seen in Table 2, the rank order of themes identi-fied in article titles in the tables of contents was nearly identical to that for articles listed on covers.

In the 38 articles sampled for analysis, there were 40 killings. Fifteen involved torture, and the other twenty-five were less protracted murders of helpless victims. There were 44 episodes

TABLE 2—*Percentages of detective magazine article titles mentioning particular themes.*

Theme	On Cover ($N = 77$)	In Table of Contents ($N = 186$)
Killing	38	32
Roles	36	24
Mental state	34	16
Death	30	15
Law enforcement	25	10
Sex	19	14
Strangulation	9	5
Weapons	9	5
Mutilation	6	4
Relentless pursuit	6	3
Secret location	5	3
Life	3	2

202 JOURNAL OF FORENSIC SCIENCES

of sexual violence (including 13 sexual mutilations), 14 robberies, and 3 burglaries. The incidents described included 50 shootings, 40 stabbings, 14 strangulations, 10 episodes of being bound and gagged, 7 bludgeonings, 3 burnings, 1 poisoning, and 1 electrocution.

Personal characteristics of victims and perpetrators were usually specified, adding to the credibility of the articles. Forty-seven perpetrators acted against ninety-eight victims. The offenders included 43 males and 4 females; the victims were 42 males and 56 females. When age was mentioned, offenders were usually between 15 and 35, while their victims were usually either 15 to 25 years old, or older than 46. Of the cases identifying race, 12 of 35 offenders and 4 of 44 victims were black. Twenty perpetrators were described as having been previously engaged in criminal activity, and seven were noted to have a history of psychiatric disorder. Five of the offenders were killed during gun battles with police, and all others went to trial. The insanity defense was raised in 13 trials, but only 1 defendant was acquitted by reason of insanity. The death sentence was given five times; three prisoners had been executed when the articles were written. Twenty-two victims were strangers, twelve were friends or acquaintances, and nine were lovers. Two male victims were noted to have been homosexual, and at least seventeen female victims were prostitutes. Men were killed, but virtually never sexually molested; women were almost always sexually attacked before being killed.

Many of the articles contained detailed descriptions of violent acts. Colorfully explicit descriptions of wounds and crime scenes were universal. Stalking or surveillance of the victim, methods of investigation, investigative reconstruction of the events, and crime laboratory work were commonly described. Networks of informants played a pivotal role in almost all investigations, and extensive media publicity was emphasized. Arrests tended to be rapid and overpowering. Extensive coverage was afforded to trials, verdicts, and sentences. Many articles ended by reporting a substantial prison sentence and reminding the reader that the offenders, or others like them, were still at large or might soon be.

Case Reports

The following six case histories illustrate how detective magazines are used as a source of fantasy material. The facts are drawn from investigative files submitted to the FBI Academy Behavioral Science Unit (Cases 1, 5, and 6) or from case files developed in the course of forensic psychiatric evaluations (Cases 2, 3, and 4). Cases 1 and 2 depict multiple murderers who enjoyed detective magazines. The offender in Case 3 used detective magazines during masturbation, but reportedly never acted out his most extreme fantasy scenarios. The pedophile in Case 4 used detective magazines to facilitate his masturbation fantasies and may have begun to act out those fantasies. The offender in Case 5 used detective magazines in the commission of his offense. Case 6 describes the victim of an autoerotic fatality, who used detective magazines in the course of acting out his fantasies.

Case 1

A multiple murderer of the late 1950s had a collection of the covers of detective magazines. He told police investigators that he liked detective magazines "sometimes for the words, sometimes for the covers."

He approached two of his victims on the pretext that he wished them to model bondage scenes for detective magazines. In his statement to the investigating officers he said:

> I told her that I wanted to take pictures that would be suitable for illustrations for mystery stories or detective magazine stories of that type, and that this would require me to tie her hands and feet and put a gag in her mouth, and she [was] agreeable to this, and I did tie her hands and feet and put a gag in her mouth and I took a number of pictures, I don't remember exactly how many, of various poses and changing the pose from picture to picture.

He acknowledged that he never had any intention of submitting the photographs for publication, and added that he was impotent in the absence of bondage.

Case 2

A 35-year-old, married, white man was charged with approximately a dozen murders in several states.

He had never known his father, who had been executed for murdering a police officer and who also had killed a correctional officer during an escape. Shortly before being executed the father wrote: "When I killed this cop, it made me feel good inside. I can't get over how good it did make me feel, for the sensation was something that made me feel elated to the point of happiness . . ." He recalled his grandmother showing him a picture of his father and telling him that his father had been a heroic firefighter. Later, he learned that the photograph was from a detective magazine article about his father's murders and execution. Often told of his resemblance to his father, he came to believe that his father lived within him.

His mother was married four times and also had a series of short-term extramarital sexual partners. She frequently told her son that she had been raped by her father when she was nine. She ridiculed her son's bedwetting, which persisted to age 13, by calling him "pissy pants" in front of guests; he was also beaten for the bedwetting and for night terrors. For as long as he could recall he had had recurrent nightmares of being smothered by nylon similar to women's stockings and being strapped to a chair in a gas chamber as green gas filled the room. One of his stepfathers beat him relentlessly. For leaving a hammer outside, he was awakened by this stepfather burning his wrist with a cigar, which left a permanent scar. For playing a childish game while urinating, he was forced to drink urine. On the one occasion when his mother intervened, the stepfather pushed her head through a plaster wall. From then on she also actively abused her children from the earlier marriages.

Knocked unconscious on multiple occasions, he was once briefly comatose at age 16 and for over a week at approximately age 20. A computed tomography (CT) scan of the brain showed abnormally enlarged sulci and slightly enlarged ventricles. Results of the Halstead-Reitan Neuropsychological Battery and the Luria-Nebraska Neuropsychological Battery were interpreted as showing damage to the right frontal lobe.

As a juvenile, he had police contacts for vandalism, malicious acts, running away, and multiple burglaries (beginning at age seven in the company of an older brother). Apprehended for lewd contact with a 7-year-old girl at age 13, he was sent to reform school for a year. He was suspended from high school for misconduct and poor grades. At age 16, he was arrested for armed robbery, escaped, and later turned himself in to authorities.

At age 18, 2 weeks after the birth of his first child, he married the child's mother. Despite subsequent arrests for armed robbery, beating his wife, assault, burglary, auto theft, theft, parole violation, and other offenses, he was awarded custody of his daughter after divorcing his first wife. His second and third marriages ended in divorce after he beat his wives, and his fourth marriage ended in divorce for unknown reasons.

After many more arrests and a jail escape, he was eventually sentenced to prison on an armed robbery conviction. He initiated sexual contact with his seven-year-old daughter during a conjugal visit on the prison grounds. Prison records from his early 20s document a psychotic episode with paranoid delusions and suicidal ideation following the death of a brother. After he was paroled from prison he impregnated one woman and married another (his fifth wife). He separated from her after he was released from parole. His second through fifth wives appeared young enough to pass as teenagers.

In his early 30s, he lived as husband and wife with his 13-year-old daughter, whom he impregnated. The pregnancy was aborted. He continued to molest his daughter, who reported one of his rapes. He also sexually assaulted one of her girlfriends. He celebrated one of his birthdays by sodomizing his then 14-year-old daughter. Eventually she moved to her grandparents' home, and he began living and traveling with another woman, who became his sixth wife and his partner in a two-year series of rapes and murders.

His wife knew of his fantasies of torturing young girls and his desire for women he could control and abuse, and she assisted him in each of his known murders by selecting the victim, orchestrating the abduction, and concealing the evidence. He beat, tortured, and raped his victims, whom he forced to play the role of his daughter in fantasy scenarios that he directed. Available data suggest that he killed his victims to avoid detection and not because the killing gave him sexual pleasure.

His early victims were all teenage girls; his later victims included adults. After his initial murders, he again raped his daughter and her friend. They reported these offenses, and an arrest warrant was issued. The offender changed his identity, as he had on previous occasions, using falsified identification papers. A gun enthusiast, he bought and sold various firearms; shortly before his last arrest, he possessed two revolvers, an automatic pistol, a derringer, and a semiautomatic assault rifle. Those victim's bodies that have been located showed death by gunshot wounds or blows to the head. Some of the bodies were still bound.

Masturbation he regarded as shameful, dirty, and unmanly. The first sexually explicit pictures he could recall having seen were photographs of his mother with a man he did not recognize. Although familiar with sexually explicit men's magazines, he had never been to an adult book store or an X-rated movie "because I didn't want anybody to think I was in that category." He considered *The Exorcist* and *Psycho* influential in his life. In speaking of sexual deviations, he referred to "sadism-maschotism" [sic], but noted that this did not apply to him: "... sadism-masochism is where you like to be hurt while you hurt, and I don't think that's it. Maybe one half of it, cause I think I've been hurt enough." The imagery characteristic of bondage and domination pornography disgusted him: "That ain't me.... The ball in the mouth, the excess rope, I think what they've done is taken a fantasy and overdo it. The mask makes somebody look like out of Mars.... You're in a room and a girl walks out with a rubber suit or whip and she's subject to get shot." Asked about the covers of detective magazines, he responded by saying that they are what he really likes and that the interviewer seemed to read his mind, asking questions that allowed him to say what he was already thinking.

When he was 14, he learned that his fugitive father had been caught because his mother had told the police his whereabouts. After reporting this, he stated: "Sometimes I [think] about blowin' her head off.... Sometimes I wanta' put a shotgun in her mouth and blow the back of her head off ..." For years, his favorite sexual fantasy was of torturing his mother to death:

> I was gonna' string her up by her feet, strip her, hang her up by her feet, spin her, take a razor blade, make little cuts, just little ones, watch the blood run out, just drip off her head. Hang her up in the closet, put airplane glue on her, light her up. Tattoo "bitch" on her forehead ...

This fantasy gradually changed and came to include forced sexual activity and other forms of abuse and torture. After his first wife left him, she replaced his mother in the fantasy; eventually their daughter replaced her.

Case 3

A 35-year-old, single, white man was charged with unarmed robbery. He had had several psychiatric hospitalizations, each time receiving a diagnosis of chronic undifferentiated schizophrenia. He was suspected to have committed the current act to gain readmission.

He left school after the ninth grade and never worked. He admitted to bouts of heavy alcohol consumption, but denied using other drugs. He had been arrested previously for threatening the President, attempted strong-arm robbery, and attempted bank robbery. He admitted several indecent exposures and burglaries for which he had not been arrested. During the burglaries he had taken food and women's underclothing, searched bureau drawers, and torn up clothes. He also admitted to "peeping" and several episodes of crossdressing, donning panties, slips, dresses, and lipstick. On several occasions he had entered houses when the occupants were away and left notes threatening to kill them if they did not leave things for him to take. He denied urinating or defecating in these houses, although he had once thrown a litter box containing cat feces. He had also once tried to steal explosives.

At age ten he had engaged in sexual play with his sister and a niece; there had been at least one episode of intercourse. After he quit school at age 16, he lived briefly with a 14-year-old girl who became pregnant and miscarried. At some point thereafter he began having fantasies of forced vaginal intercourse, sucking and biting on breasts, and mutual oral sexual activity. He described subsequent enchantment with pornography depicting these activities and dated his first contact with detective magazines to approximately the same time.

By his mid-20s, his masturbatory fantasies were of lying on a woman, tying her with heavy, electrical wire, having intercourse with her, killing her by blows and strangulation, and then attacking her genitalia. He said that the detective magazines had not caused these fantasies, adding, "I had 'em before but the [detective] magazines bring them out." By his late 20s, he was having fantasies of mutilation, smearing and drinking blood, and continuing intercourse after his victim's death. He also had recurrent dreams of being a "bloodthirsty murderer."

He stated that he preferred masturbating while looking at the covers and contents of detective magazines. He regarded detective magazine photographs as the best match to his current sexual fantasies and as his most important source of sexual pleasure. He said he masturbated in his bathroom with detective magazine covers and pictures from explicitly erotic magazines so positioned that he could see himself and the pictures in a mirror. He particularly liked pictures in which women "look like whores," and he masturbated to orgasm while fantasizing about "killing whores."

He claimed never to have acted out his most extreme fantasies, but he believed that he might be "losing control over them." He admitted to having had intense "sexual thoughts" during the unarmed robbery, to "enjoying touching, feeling panties and bras," and to excitement at thoughts of women struggling.

A detailed review of his records uncovered no documentation of symptoms or signs of schizophrenia. He admitted to having feigned mental illness so that he could be stopped from acting out his fantasies.

Case 4

A 20-year-old, single, black man with no previous criminal record but several psychiatric evaluations was incarcerated for sexually molesting children. At least three complaints had been lodged previously against him without formal charges being filed.

He stood charged with two sexual assaults against prepubescent girls. In the first incident he asked a girl to go with him, claiming that a friend wanted to speak with her. He grabbed the girl, pulled her pants down, and fondled her genitals until someone appeared, when he fled. The second incident was similar, although reportedly more forceful, with the victim resisting more aggressively. He fled when the victim bit him. He denied any sexual contact with his victims, but did say that in one offense against a girl he "kept hitting until she was unconscious; I thought she was dead."

His father had been rarely present, and the family was on welfare. One of his brothers was said to be mentally retarded and institutionalized. He claimed to have had good relationships with family members and to have had friends. He completed ninth grade with below average grades; the school authorities had wanted him placed in special education classes, but his mother had refused. He was never married, had no military history, and worked intermittently in unskilled jobs. He acknowledged moderate use of alcohol and marijuana, but denied using other drugs.

206   JOURNAL OF FORENSIC SCIENCES

During the screening psychiatric interview he denied any symptoms suggestive of a psy-chotic illness. He claimed his present offenses occurred because he was "too scared to ask out women." Fearing that older women might reject him and tell him he was "too young, just a kid, and I can't handle that," he felt anger toward older women, "like I want to kill them." He admitted to daydreams about "beating them up" followed by intercourse. His masturbatory fantasies involved bondage in which the hands of the women were tied behind their backs, their mouths gagged, and their legs tied to bedposts. He denied masturbatory fantasies involv-ing other physical injury. He also denied crossdressing. He believed he would never act on his masturbatory fantasies: "I just couldn't see myself doing something like that; not if she don't do as I tell her. If I get mad I start tearing up stuff, but not kids; I like kids. If I had kids I wouldn't want someone doing that to them." He claimed his fantasies involved "mostly white girls" ages 12 to 13.

He said that he frequently used visual media to stimulate his masturbatory fantasies. His favorite images involved women wearing undergarments, such as brassieres and panties, or two-piece bathing suits, which he commonly found on detective magazine covers, but added that he found detective magazines less appealing than traditional pornography.

Case 5

A 34-year-old, white woman received a telephone call from a man claiming to represent a manufacturing firm that had developed a new line of brassieres and was conducting a market-ing survey in her area. She was invited to participate in the survey. She would be sent six free bras to wear for six months, when she would be asked to complete a questionnaire as to their comfort, durability, and washability. She agreed and provided her bust measurements to the caller.

Approximately seven months later, the same man called the second time and said that he would like to deliver the bras to her home. She asked that he call back in a few days as she wanted to discuss the matter with her husband. When he rang, she told him that she had de-cided not to participate in the survey. He responded, "I don't want to have intercourse with you, I just want to deliver the bras." She hung up immediately.

Five months later, upon receiving a package in the mail which contained four sketches de-picting her bound, in various stages of undress, she notified the police. Shortly thereafter, the man called again, asking for her opinion of the sketches.

A second package containing four sketches similar to the first ones arrived about four months later, again followed by a telephone call. During this conversation, the man requested that she meet him and said he would call again to arrange the meeting. He also described the wallpaper pattern in her bathroom. He used no profanity in the telephone conversations.

Approximately four months later he called for the sixth time, requesting a meeting. She hung up on him. Within days came another call during which she agreed to meet him at a shopping center near her home. She notified the police, who arranged surveillance. After wait-ing in vain for 45 min at the appointed location, she talked with the surveilling officers and drove home.

The following month, the man called and accurately described her movements at the ren-dezvous and her return home. He requested that she deliver two of her bras to a designated Salvation Army clothes bin. Again she notified the police and a surveillance of the drop site was arranged; however, the offender was able to pick up the bras undetected by entering the clothes bin from an opening in the rear. Shortly thereafter, she received a third package con-taining her bras, two pictorial pages, an advertisement page, and a cover from a detective mag-azine. The bras had semen stains and handwriting on them. The magazine cover and the pic-torial pages each showed a woman being threatened by a man holding a knife; her name was written above the women and the word "me" was written above the men. The advertisement was for Nazi paraphernalia. One month later he rang to ask what she thought about the package.

That same month, she received a letter containing polaroid photographs of a white male, nude except for a ski mask, masturbating in a hotel room. The letter said that he had rented the room, intended to kidnap her, and had bought rope with which to bind her and a camera with which to take pictures of her performing various sexual acts. He called her again shortly after she received the letter. The eleventh and final call came one month later.

From the photographs the police were able to identify the hotel, where they found that he had registered under his real name. He was later arrested, convicted, and sentenced to one year in jail. At the time of his arrest, the police seized a folder containing 30 detective magazine covers that depicted women in potentially lethal situations.

Case 6

A 30-year-old white man was discovered dead in his apartment. He was partially suspended in a doorway by a length of plastic clothesline which encircled his neck twice with a knot on the right. The clothesline went up to and through an airspace above the door and was affixed to a hinge beside the victim. His arms hung at his sides, and his feet touched the floor. A pair of wire cutters and more clothesline were found on a washing machine in the apartment. He wore eyeglasses, a brassiere, jockey shorts, and black calf-length socks.

Propped up on a stand directly in front of him was a detective magazine cover which depicted a man strangling a young woman who wore a black brassiere. Two lingerie advertisements taped to a nearby wall showed a woman from the waist up who wore only a brassiere and a woman wearing a brassiere and a panty girdle. A nearby phonograph was on, and the first song on the record was "Barbie Ann." An album cover lying beside the phonograph had a picture of a man with two young women wearing halter tops.

The decedent's wife, Barbara, had been separated from him for four months; she and their only child had moved to another state. He had appeared to be in normal spirits during a visit with his parents six days earlier. A friend with whom he had played pool on the evening before his death and who was the last person to see him alive described him as having been in good spirits at the time of their parting.

The death was ruled to be an accident occurring during autoerotic activity. The decedent's attire and visual props suggest a brassiere fetish, while the detective magazine cover in front of him depicting the sexual murder of a woman wearing a brassiere suggests that he entertained a sadistic fantasy that he had been enacting with his own body. The object of his fantasies may have been his wife. (This case has been reported in less detail elsewhere [20].)

Discussion

Detective magazines juxtapose conventionally erotic images (for example, pictures of scantily clad women or descriptions of sexual acts) with images of violence and suffering. Detective magazines are not the only source for this combination of images; many recent horror films, crime films, and rock video productions have similar characteristics. One study found that bondage and domination was the primary theme of 17% of the magazines sold in "adults only" bookstores [21]. Unlike these magazines, however, detective magazines, being inexpensive and available on many newsstands, have a large circulation. They are always openly displayed, unlike magazines showing nonviolent nudity, and there is no effort to discourage sales to minors.

The cases reported in this paper show that some readers who use detective magazines as sources of sexual fantasy material also act on their fantasies. MacCulloch et al [22] have described men who progress from sadistic masturbation fantasies to crimes that enact portions of

208 JOURNAL OF FORENSIC SCIENCES

the fantasy sequence, and thence to more serious offenses based on an elaborated fantasy sequence. A similar pattern can be recognized in Cases 3 and 4 above.

At least two previously published case reports mention the use of detective magazines as a source of sexual fantasy imagery. Graber et al [23] reported the history of a 36-year-old man who forced a woman to fellate him at knife-point in a women's restroom of a public park. This attack was followed several weeks later by "an abortive attack on a woman that ended when she was cut by his knife." The offender had no prior criminal record. He reported a lack of sexual experience, including masturbation, until marriage at age 23. The frequency of intercourse with his wife decreased after he experienced a business failure. About a year before his arrest he had begun masturbating while reading the sex crime articles in a detective magazine, which thereafter became his preferred sexual outlet. The offense for which he was arrested was inspired by a detective magazine article.

Wesselius and Bally [24] recorded the history of a 24-year-old man who practiced autoerotic asphyxia by self-hanging for ten years. He first masturbated at age ten while suspended from the bar of a swing set. He began using the pictures in *True Detective* magazine while masturbating around age 14. The authors report: "From this magazine he developed the idea of dressing in female clothing which he would take from the family laundry hamper. . . . " Within months, he became sexually aroused while watching a hanging scene in a cowboy film, and was particularly excited by the man's struggle and kicking feet. He then began masturbating while hanging himself. The authors noted that "[h]e continued to use *True Detective* magazines with only occasional use of other more common soft pornography publications." He would become most aroused by dressing in soiled women's undergarments and hanging himself. He also became aroused by wearing such clothing and binding his limbs and neck. He fantasized strangling a woman and was particularly aroused by imagining her helpless struggling and her kicking feet.

Goldstein and Kant [25] quoted a rapist as saying:

I can remember looking through *True Detective* and stuff like this and seeing articles about women that had been murdered or something. . . . I remember partially nude bodies. There was a lot of magazines on the stands I used to buy all the time, these horror stories, "trips of terror," weird stories, stuff like this. Soon after this, they banned 'em from the newsstands. I used to like to read them all the time.

While there is no doubt that detective magazines provide a rich source of sexually sadistic imagery, the role that these magazines play in the development of sexual sadism, if any, is unknown. To the extent that paraphilic responsiveness is acquired by repeatedly associating sexual arousal with particular images, the availability of sexually sadistic imagery may be important. Detective magazines are one source of such imagery.

The cases we have described do not prove that detective magazines "cause" sexual sadism or sadistic offenses. Only unethical experiments could prove or disprove such causation, and we do not encourage that they be contemplated. Tests of the arousal of normal men and of sexual sadists to the cover imagery we describe could, however, tend to support or refute our postulate and could be conducted in an ethical manner that minimizes the risk of harming the subjects.

We assume that conventionally erotic elements in detective magazines would arouse many males and that responsiveness to particular stimuli can be learned. We postulate that repeated pairing of arousal with the unconditioned stimuli in these magazines, such as depictions of bondage, domination, weapons, strangulation and other struggles, blood, and corpses increases the probability that the viewer will subsequently be aroused by exposure to these stimuli, whether or not they are presented in an erotic context.

We know that some boys and men repeatedly use detective magazines to achieve sexual arousal and that at least some of these individuals are sexual sadists. Of these latter, however, we do not know what proportion were sexual sadists before their exposure to detective magazines. We consider it plausible that some boys and young men turn to detective magazines for such conventional sexual imagery as scantily clad women or descriptions of sexual interaction, and through repeated exposure learn to be aroused by elements of the photographs and articles that otherwise would have had no sexual associations. We recognize, however, that horror movies and other films probably expose more boys and young men to the pairing of erotic and violent images.

Detective magazines might affect the established sexual sadist by reinforcing his paraphilia (particularly if he masturbates to orgasm while looking at or reading the magazines), by adding details to his fantasies and preferred imagery, and by providing consensual validation that lessens the extent to which he considers his preference abnormal or unacceptable.

Beyond their significance with respect to sexual sadism, detective magazines have other potentially criminogenic effects. None of these potential effects is unique to detective magazines. but each should be considered in assessing the social value of these magazines.

Detective magazines publicize particularly serious crimes. In an era in which many value fame more highly than esteem or freedom, the prospect of publicity serves as an inducement to crime. While detective magazines reach a smaller audience than network television, national news magazines, wire services, or the most widely read newspapers, they reach an audience with greater than average interest in crime, provide lengthier and more detailed accounts of particular offenders and offenses, and emphasize the degree of publicity received by the offender.

Detective magazines are an unsurpassed source of public information on techniques for committing crimes, on the errors of unsuccessful offenders, and on the methods available to law enforcement agencies for preventing crimes and apprehending offenders. We have examined and studied offenders who have sought out, filed, and used such information to commit crimes, but we also know law enforcement officers who use such information as a source of continuing education.

The advertisements in detective magazines provide access to information and paraphernalia that are sometimes used to commit crimes, including weapons, burglary tools, and car theft equipment. Police badges and other false identification obtained through these advertisements have been used by offenders to gain entry to dwellings or to stop motorists. Cases have been documented of persons murdered or otherwise victimized by persons whom they met through lonely hearts advertisements such as those appearing in detective magazines [26].

Conclusions

Detective magazines have a lengthy heritage and generate substantial sales. No doubt some readers examine detective magazines out of curiosity or casual interest. Sexual sadists, however, are particularly drawn to detective magazines, and some of these individuals translate their fantasies into action. Clinicians should learn to ask their patients about reading preferences and should also have sufficient knowledge of popular publications to be able to interpret the responses. Since few patients spontaneously mention sadistic sexual fantasies in the course of assessment or psychotherapy, inquiries about reading habits provide an important route through which to explore a patient's fantasy life.

Patients with a particular interest in detective magazines may have problems other than sexual sadism. In our experience, many individuals who are paranoid or preoccupied with violence read or collect detective magazines, mercenary magazines (such as *Soldier of Fortune, Commando*, and *Gung Ho*), and hunting and gun magazines. Peterson [27] noted that "the market of a medium [usually] coincides with that of its advertisements" and that advertisements generally reflect consumer needs and desires. Some of the advertisements in detective magazines cater to those with pronounced feelings of inadequacy by offering greater sexual control, appeal, or function; techniques of mind control; and certification of identity.

Our view that the harmful effects of detective magazines probably outweigh whatever contributions they may make to law enforcement, entertainment, and the economy is, of course,

210   JOURNAL OF FORENSIC SCIENCES

not entirely original. Writing at the end of the 19th century, Cesare Lombroso considered newspaper reports of crime the source of many imitative ("copycat") crimes, of which he gave multiple examples. He concluded:

> This morbid stimulation is increased a hundred-fold by the prodigious increase of really criminal newspapers, which spread abroad the virus of the most loathsome social plagues, simply for sordid gain, and excite the morbid appetite and still more morbid curiosity of the lower social classes. They may be likened to those maggots which, sprung from putrefaction, increase it by their presence [*28*].

We suppose that Lombroso put it too strongly, as was his custom. Nonetheless, we are concerned that detective magazines—today's equivalent of "really criminal newspapers"—may contribute to the development and persistence of sexual sadism; facilitate sadistic fantasies; and encourage crime by rewarding it with publicity, disseminating technical information, and easing access to criminal equipment.

We therefore urge policymakers to consider detective magazines in their deliberations concerning violence in the media and pornography. We recommend that the new national commission on pornography [*29*] include detective magazines and other sources of sexually sadistic imagery among the classes of materials that it studies. Whatever definition of pornography or obscenity emerges from the ongoing public policy debate should surely be formulated to encompass those materials that present the greatest risk of promoting the erotization of violence.

References

[*1*] Peterson, T., "British Crime Pamphleteers: Forgotten Journalists," *Journalism Quarterly*, Vol. 22, 1945, pp. 305-316.

[2] Mayhew, H., *London Labour and the London Poor. Volume I: London Street-Folk*, Charles Griffin and Company, London, ca. 1864, pp. 227-350.

[*3*] Mayhew, H., *London Labour and the London Poor. Volume III*, Charles Griffin and Company, London, ca. 1864, pp. 51-167.

[*4*] Jowett, G. S., Reath, P., and Schouten, M., "The Control of Mass Entertainment Media in Canada, the United States and Great Britain: Historical Surveys," in *Report of the Royal Commission on Violence in the Communications Industry. Volume 4: Violence in Print and Music*, J. C. Thatcher, Toronto, 1977, pp. 3-104.

[*5*] Monkkonen, E. H., *Police in Urban America. 1860-1920*, Cambridge University Press, Cambridge, 1981.

[*6*] Mott, F. L., *A History of American Magazines. Volume I: 1741-1850*, Belknap Press, Cambridge, MA, 1937, p. 481.

[*7*] Mott, F. L., *A History of American Magazines. Volume II: 1850-1865*, Harvard University Press, Cambridge, MA, 1938, pp. 185-187.

[*8*] Mott, F. L., *A History of American Magazines. Volume II: 1850-1865*, Harvard University Press, Cambridge, MA, 1938, pp. 325-337.

[*9*] Mott, F. L., *A History of American Magazines. Volume IV: 1885-1905*, Belknap Press, Cambridge, MA, 1957, pp. 199-200.

[*10*] Smith, G. and Smith, J. B., *The Police Gazette*, Simon and Schuster, New York, 1972.

[*11*] Morgan, W. L. and Leahy, A. M., "The Cultural Content of General Interest Magazines," *Journal of Educational Psychology*, Vol. 25, 1934, pp. 530-536.

[*12*] Kerr, W. A. and Remmers, H. H., "The Cultural Value of 100 Representative American Magazines," *School and Society*, Vol. 54, 1941, pp. 476-480.

[*13*] Hagood, P., *The Standard Periodical Directory*, 7th ed., Oxbridge Communications, Inc., New York, 1980.

[*14*] Otto, H. A., "Sex and Violence on the American Newsstand," *Journalism Quarterly*, Vol. 40, 1963, pp. 19-26.

[*15*] Lyle, J., "Contemporary Functions of the Mass Media," in *A Report to the National Commission on the Causes and Prevention of Violence. Volume XI: Mass Media and Violence*, D. L. Lange, R. K. Baker, and S. J. Ball, Eds., U.S. Government Printing Office, Washington, DC, 1969, pp. 187-216.

[*16*] Beattie, E., "Magazines and Violence," in *Report of the Royal Commission on Violence in the Communications Industry. Volume 4: Violence in Print and Music*, J. C. Thatcher, Toronto, 1977, pp. 161-221.

[17] Lazarsfeld, P. F. and Wyant, R., "Magazines in 90 Cities—Who Reads What?," *Public Opinion Quarterly*, Vol. 1, 1937, pp. 29-41.

[18] Friedman, H. L. and Johnson, R. L., "Mass Media Use and Aggression: A Pilot Study," in *Television and Social Behavior, Volume III: Television and Adolescent Aggressiveness*, G. A. Comstock and E. A. Rubinstein, Eds., U.S. Government Printing Office, Washington, DC, 1972, pp. 336-360.

[19] Lyle, J. and Hoffman, H. R., "Children's Use of Television and Other Media," in *Television and Social Behavior, Volume IV: Television in Day-to-Day Life: Patterns of Use*, E. A. Rubinstein, G. A. Comstock, and J. P. Murray, Eds., U.S. Government Printing Office, Washington, DC, 1972, pp. 129-256.

[20] Dietz, P. E., Burgess, A. W., and Hazelwood, R. R., "Autoerotic Asphyxia, the Paraphilias, and Mental Disorder," in *Autoerotic Fatalities*, R. R. Hazelwood, P. E. Dietz and A. W. Burgess, Lexington Books, Lexington, MA, 1983, pp. 77-100.

[21] Dietz, P. E. and Evans, B., "Pornographic Imagery and Prevalence of Paraphilia," *American Journal of Psychiatry*, Vol. 139, 1982, pp. 1493-1495.

[22] MacCulloch, M. J., Snowden, P. R., Wood, P. J. W., and Mills, H. E., "Sadistic Fantasy, Sadistic Behaviour, and Offending," *British Journal of Psychiatry*, Vol. 143, 1983, pp. 20-29.

[23] Graber, B., Hartmann, K., Coffman, J. A., Huey, C. J., and Golden, C. J., "Brain Damage Among Mentally Disordered Sex Offenders," *Journal of Forensic Sciences*, Vol. 27, No. 1, Jan. 1982, pp. 125-134.

[24] Wesselius, C. L. and Bally, R., "A Male with Autoerotic Asphyxia Syndrome," *American Journal of Forensic Medicine and Pathology*, Vol. 4, 1983, pp. 341-345.

[25] Goldstein, M. J. and Kant, H. S., *Pornography and Sexual Deviance*, University of California Press, Berkeley, CA, 1973, p. 71.

[26] Brown, W., *Introduction to Murder: The unpublished facts behind the notorious Lonely Hearts killers Martha Beck and Raymond Fernandez*, Greenberg, New York, 1952.

[27] Peterson, T., "Why the Mass Media are That Way," in *Mass Media and Communication*, 2nd ed., C. S. Steinberg, Ed., Hastings House, New York, 1972, pp. 56-71.

[28] Lombroso, C. (Horton, H. P., trans.), *Crime: Its Causes and Remedies*, Little, Brown, and Co., Boston, 1912, p. 211.

[29] "Child Pornography Law Signed; U.S. Study Commission Created," *New York Times*, 22 May 1984, p. A20.

Address requests for reprints or additional information to
Park Elliott Dietz, M.D., M.P.H., Ph.D.
School of Law
University of Virginia
Charlottesville, VA 22901

[7]

Adolescents' Motivations for Viewing Graphic Horror

DEIRDRE D. JOHNSTON
Hope College

This study identifies four motivations adolescents report for viewing graphic horror films: gore watching, thrill watching, independent watching, and problem watching. On the basis of a uses and gratifications model of media effects, it is argued that viewing motivations are predictors of responses to graphic horror. This study also seeks to extend Zillmann's excitation-transfer model of media effects to predict under what conditions viewing-generated arousal is transferred to positive or negative affect. The dispositional characteristics of fearfulness, empathy, and sensation seeking are found to be related to different viewing motivations, providing a viewing-related personality profile for the four different types of adolescent viewers. The four viewing motivations are found to be related to viewers' cognitive and affective responses to horror films, as well as viewers' tendency to identify with either the killers or victims in these films. Directions for future research addressing the role of viewing motivations in the relationship between violent media, cognitive and affective responses, and subsequent behavioral aggression are discussed.

The purpose of this study is to identify adolescents' motivations for viewing graphic horror and to identify the cognitive and affective reactions that correspond to different viewing motivations. The graphic-horror film genre, for example, *Halloween* (Hill & Carpenter, 1981), *Nightmare on Elm Street* (Shaye & Craven, 1985), and *Friday the 13th* (Cunningham, 1980), is characterized by prolonged terror and the modeling of sadistic torture and human mutilation. The violence is often directed toward sexually attractive young females (Cowan & O'Brien, 1990), and the triumphant killer often survives for yet another sequel. Although adolescent viewers are the primary target for graphic horror, adolescents have to make some effort to view these films through video rental, pay-per-view movie channels, or sneaking into movie theaters, because these movies are not ubiquitously available through standard television, and they carry restricted ratings. This "preexposure involve-

Deirdre D. Johnston (Ph.D., University of Iowa, 1988) is an assistant professor in the Department of Communication at Hope College, Holland, Michigan. An earlier version of this article was presented at the 1990 meeting of the Speech Communication Association (Mass Communication Division), Chicago. My appreciation is extended to James R. Dumerauf, MD, for contributions on an earlier version of this study, and to Howard Giles and the anonymous reviewers for their insightful comments.

Human Communication Research, Vol. 21 No. 4, June 1995 522-552
© 1995 International Communication Association

ment" (cf. Levy & Windahl, 1985) suggests that moderately powerful needs and motivations accompany adolescents' viewing behavior.

Research suggests that the viewing of graphic horror may have detrimental effects. Long-term exposure to female victimization is related to sexual violence and decreased empathy to victims of rape (Linz, 1985; Linz, Donnerstein, & Penrod, 1988), and viewers' beliefs about violence may be related to subsequent behavioral aggression (Rule & Ferguson, 1986). Yet we cannot assume equivalent processes and responses by all adolescent viewers of graphic horror. Viewers are active participants in the media experience, and media content is multifunctional, such that different viewers use a given genre to pursue varying psychological and social needs (Olson, 1989). This perspective on the effects of graphic horror suggests that different viewing motivations may activate different cognitive and affective processes and, consequently, different responses and effects.

The analysis of adolescents' viewing motivations in this study builds on two media effects theories: uses and gratifications, and excitation transfer. The uses and gratifications perspective posits a relationship between gratifications sought and gratifications obtained from media experiences (Palmgreen, Wenner, & Rayburn, 1980). Gratifications are believed to influence responses to media exposure by shaping individuals' interpretations of media content.

Current research taking the uses and gratifications perspective does not, however, adequately explain why adolescents view graphic horror. Much of this research seeks generalized media use motives across media categories and content genres (e.g., Bantz, 1982; Lull, 1980; Rubin, 1977, 1979, 1981, 1983). Comparisons of media motives across channels and content genres typically reflect how a particular media-usage group rates a typology of 6 to 11 media motives (e.g., information, passing time, companionship, escape, arousal, and relaxation; Armstrong & Rubin, 1989; Lin, 1993; Palmgreen et al., 1980; Rubin, Perse, & Powell, 1985). Although the use of a media motive typology is useful for systematizing research on varied topics under the auspices of uses and gratifications research (Rubin, 1993), it is limited by its tendency to sanitize the diversity of motives sought by different social groups and by its tendency to gloss over more specific motives encompassed by these generalized categories. The rich and varied reasons for seeking a particular type of media experience may be lost when media users are asked to respond to preestablished checklists of viewing motivations. This research focus, for example, may tell us why most people watch television, but "escapism" and "arousal" may provide only limited insight into why some adolescents are attracted to a particular type of media content, such as graphic horror.

In addition to the limitations of the media motive typology, several researchers have noted the need for the study of psychological variables

524   HUMAN COMMUNICATION RESEARCH / June 1995

in media effects research (Conway & Rubin, 1991). Wober (1986) contended that in much of the uses and gratifications research, viewing motivations are not differentiated from the cognitive traits that are posited to produce them. Moreover, much of the early uses and gratifications research focused on social variables—for example, social-contact opportunities, work experience, leisure behavior, and so forth (Blumler, 1979)—to the neglect of cognitive variables that also give rise to viewing motivations.

In recent research, Conway and Rubin (1991) have addressed this issue by identifying cognitive and affective dimensions that differentiate among media motivations. Specifically, Conway and Rubin (1991) found that the disinhibition dimension of sensation seeking, anxiety, creativity, parasocial interaction, and assertiveness are related to viewing motivations derived from previous research (e.g., Frank & Greenberg, 1980; Rubin, 1981).

In sum, researchers of uses and gratifications have sought to address the atheoretical charges levied against them (Blumler, 1979) by developing generalized categories of social conditions, media uses, and media responses. As a result, much of this research stops short of "speak[ing] to the viewing conditions" (Blumler, 1979) of the media user. In contrast, recent research on psychological predictors of viewing motivations (Conway & Rubin, 1991) begins to reveal the rich and varied experience of media viewers and allows for the possibility that the media may affect different types of viewers in different ways.

According to excitation transfer research on media effects, exposure to media may generate excitational states that intensify postexposure emotional responses (Zillmann, 1980). The physiological arousal generated by media exposure may be transferred (or labeled) by viewers in an effort to ascribe meaning to their experience. Research on graphic horror suggests that viewing-induced arousal may be transferred to feelings of distress or delight (Sparks, 1991; Zillmann, Weaver, Mundorf, & Aust, 1986). Yet, other than research addressing the role of gender roles in the prediction of delight or distress responses to graphic horror (Mundorf, Weaver, & Zillmann, 1989), research has not expanded the excitation-transfer model to identify those variables that predict the hedonic transfer of arousal. This study seeks to expand the excitation-transfer model by assessing the role of personality and viewing motivations in determining whether heightened arousal is transferred to euphoric or dysphoric feelings.

The uses and gratifications model in conjunction with excitation-transfer theory enhances our understanding of media effects. Uses and gratifications models have long noted the importance of a viewer's cognitive framework (i.e., gratifications sought) in predicting responses (i.e., gratifications obtained) to media experiences. It is proposed that the personality and motivations of the viewer are likely to influence the perceptual focus and processing of media information, which will, in turn, affect the activation of cognitive associations (Berkowitz, 1984) and the labeling of affect-laden arousal. For example, adolescents viewing graphic horror for the euphoric excitement of experiencing empathic distress and resolution are likely to activate much different cognitive associations and affective responses than adolescents viewing graphic horror to vicariously experience anger, aggression, and destruction.

This study seeks to integrate research in the uses and gratifications tradition by (a) identifying personality characteristics associated with various viewing motivations (Conway & Rubin, 1991), (b) identifying the viewing motivations unique to a specific social group and genre of media (Armstrong & Rubin, 1989), and (c) assessing the relationship between viewing motivations and reported cognitive and affective responses to media content (Perse, 1990). Moreover, this study will focus on the identification of viewers' reported motivations—as opposed to viewers' responses to generalized media motivations that are derived from previous research and are nonspecific to social group or media genre.

MOTIVATIONS FOR VIEWING GRAPHIC HORROR

Media-viewing motivations are reasons for seeking a particular media vehicle or content genre (Rubin, 1986); they reflect gratifications generated by the attributes, content, and social contexts of the media content and viewing experience (Katz, Gurevitch, & Haas, 1973). Adolescents' decision to view media stimuli that depict terror-ridden victims, startling special effects, powerful and terrifying killers, and grotesque mutilation is an intriguing phenomenon, yet existing research on adolescents' viewing motivations is limited.

Several studies have assessed reactions to graphic horror (e.g., distress and delight: Zillmann et al., 1986; enjoyment: Zillmann, 1980; fear: Sparks, 1986; and arousal: Tannenbaum, 1980, Zillmann, 1983, 1984), assuming that these reactions are consistent with motivations for viewing. Other studies have addressed conditions thought to lead to the viewing of graphic horror (e.g., sensation seeking: Zillmann & Bryant, 1985; arousal activation: Sparks & Spirek, 1988), assuming that psychological conditions that give rise to viewing motivations are the same as the motivations themselves. Yet the most significant limitation of this research is that the implied motivations are all researcher generated. These studies have not gone directly to the adolescent viewer and asked the viewer to generate reasons and motivations for watching this genre of violent media. Moreover, the motivations of college student viewers—the typical sample for horror movie research (Sparks, 1989, 1991; Sparks & Spirek, 1988; Tamborini, Stiff, & Zillmann, 1987; Zillmann et al., 1986)—are not likely to be consistent with the motivations of adolescents (the targeted audience for this genre). Thus this study will address the following research question:

RQ1: What are adolescents' motivations for viewing graphic horror?

PERSONALITY CHARACTERISTICS
AND VIEWING GRAPHIC HORROR

Research on personality variables influencing the selection of, and reaction to, graphic violence is limited. Viewing of graphic horror has been associated with "liking to witness destruction" (Tamborini & Stiff, 1987); the Machiavellian trait of deceit; and the disinhibition, experience-seeking, and boredom susceptibility dimensions of sensation seeking (Tamborini et al., 1987). Reactions to graphic horror (i.e., enjoyment, boredom, and fright) have been associated with the cognitive states of hostility, mutilation anxiety, perceived victimization vulnerability (Mundorf et al., 1989), and permissive sexual attitudes (Oliver, 1993). Although each of these studies enhances our understanding of people's attraction to graphic horror, there is little that ties these studies together to provide a comprehensive profile of the graphic-horror viewer.

Personality, according to Wober (1986), can "vary the form and intensity" (p. 209) of media messages, and different cognitive sets can determine people's involvement with, or detachment from, a media experience (Cantor, 1991). Therefore, sensation seeking, empathy, and fearfulness—three personality characteristics that would be likely to vary the viewers' involvement and the form and intensity of the graphic-horror media experience—were selected for analysis in this study. To explore the relationship between viewers' preexposure cognitive framework (i.e., personality and viewing motivations) and viewers' reported affect (i.e., transfer of excitation) following exposure to graphic horror, it makes sense to select personality characteristics associated with viewing-induced arousal. Even though all three personality characteristics are conceptually correlated with viewing-induced arousal, the interpretation of this arousal (i.e., excitation transfer) is likely to vary.

Sensation Seeking

Sensation seeking is associated with horror movie attendance (Zuckerman & Little, 1986), although the strength of the relationship between sensation seeking and liking of graphic horror varies from strong (Edwards, 1984) to weak (Tamborini & Stiff, 1987) to nonsignificant (Mundorf et al., 1989; Tamborini et al., 1987). These equivocal results may be an artifact of undergraduate, as opposed to adolescent, samples. Zuckerman (1988) reported that sensation seeking, which has biochemical bases, peaks in the teens and declines with age.

Tamborini (1991) argued that the relationship between sensation seeking and exposure to graphic horror may be "moderated by some other set of variables" (p. 314). Research has generally assumed that sensation-seeking graphic-horror viewers are motivated by arousal and respond to graphic horror with enjoyment. Sensation seekers, according to Zuckerman (1988), "prefer stimuli that are novel, complex, and ambiguous, and that elicit strong emotional reactions" (p. 180). Zillmann and Bryant (1985) contended that understimulated people are likely to seek arousing media content regardless of the negative or positive valence of the stimuli, and Zaleski (1984) reported that high-sensation seekers are more likely than low-sensation seekers to seek negative arousal generated by torture, executions, and corpses. To say that sensation seekers seek stimuli for negative as well as positive stimulation is rather circular. It is possible that viewing motivations may mediate the relationship between sensation seeking and graphic-horror exposure; sensation-seeking adolescents may have varying motivations for seeking the negative affect and arousal generated by graphic horror.

Empathy

The capacity for empathy leads to concordant affective responses to the acute emotional experiences of others. The dimensions of empathy most clearly related to responses to media depictions are (a) emotional contagion, that is, eliciting the same emotions observed in others (Davis, 1983, cited in Davis, Hull, Young, & Warren, 1987; Mehrabian & Epstein, 1972); (b) empathic concern, that is, warm, compassionate emotional responses to the experiences of others (Davis et al., 1987; Stiff, Dillard, Somera, Kim, & Sleight, 1988); and (c) fictional involvement, that is, vicariously experiencing the emotions of media characters (Tamborini & Mettler, 1990).[1]

Viewers with high and low dispositional emotional empathy must have different motivations for seeking exposure to graphic horror. High levels of empathy would enhance the needs of arousal-oriented persons who seek intense emotional, albeit negative, responses to frightening films (Sparks & Spirek, 1988). Yet, according to the research of Tamborini, Stiff, and Heidel (1990), nonempathic individuals are most attracted to graphic horror, and persons with high levels of empathy appear to experience negative affective reactions (e.g., hostility, depression, and anxiety) to violent film stimuli (Davis et al., 1987; Tamborini & Mettler, 1990). Tamborini et al. (1990) posited that nonempathic individuals like this genre of entertainment because their predisposition neutralizes their reactions to highly noxious stimuli. Nonempathic individuals must, therefore, have motivations other than arousal for seeking exposure to graphic horror, and empathic individuals must have powerful viewing motivations that override their negative reactions to graphic horror.

Fearfulness

Dispositional fearfulness reflects individual differences in the intensity of emotional responses to perceptions of threat or danger. Fear is most often discussed as a reaction to violent media, as opposed to a preexisting disposition influencing the interpretation of media stimuli (Cantor, 1991; Cantor & Reilly, 1982; Sparks, 1986, 1991).

One of the few studies that considers the dispositional characteristic of fearfulness was conducted by Neuendorf and Sparks (1988). They state that fear of particular objects and stimuli develops from sources other than exposure to horror films, and that fear of numerous objects and stimuli is related to frightening reactions to horror films. The most intense fright was reported by persons who found that a stimulus they perceived as frightening actually appeared in the horror film viewed in the study.

It follows that persons with varying levels of dispositional fearfulness will have different viewing motivations. The greater the number of stimuli a person is frightened by, the greater the likelihood that the person will experience elevated excitation, arousal, fear, or all when viewing horror films. Thus persons experiencing high levels of previewing fearfulness are most likely to satisfy arousal-related motivations by viewing graphic violence, and persons characterized by low dispositional fearfulness must, once again, have alternative motivations for seeking exposure to graphic horror. Persons reporting less intense fear responses to graphic horror films also report greater liking of these films (Mundorf et al., 1989); if these persons were seeking arousal experiences, more intense fear reactions should be related to increased liking of the films.

Although arousal motivations for viewing graphic horror have been widely touted (Frost & Stauffer, 1987; Sparks & Spirek, 1988; Zillmann & Bryant, 1985, 1986), arousal may not be the only motivation for adolescent viewing of graphic horror. Moreover, even when arousal is sought, it may not be a positive experience. Research suggests that personality variables, such as sensation seeking, empathy, and fearfulness, are intuitively related to viewing-induced arousal but are not all positively correlated with liking of graphic horror. Thus the following research question is raised:

RQ2: Are variances in the level of sensation seeking, empathy, and fearfulness related to different motivations for viewing graphic horror?

RESPONSES TO VIEWING SLASHER FILMS

Research suggests that there are individual differences in cognitive and affective responses to violent media. Sparks and Spirek (1988), for example, proposed that different responses are tied to individual differences in people's activation-arousal systems. Persons biased toward the activation system seek to retain constancy in internal representations and to neutralize affective experiences; on the other hand, persons biased toward the arousal system seek novel information and intensification of affect. However, this framework stops short of explaining the varied nuances of affective responses identified by Zillmann (1984). A review of excitation-transfer research indicates that residual arousal (such as that following the viewing of graphic horror) may be transferred to any number of affective responses, ranging from enjoyment and humor to anger, aggression, dysphoric empathy, and even sexual stimulation (Cantor, Bryant, & Zillmann, 1974; Cantor, Zillmann, & Bryant, 1975; Zillmann & Bryant, 1974). Researchers have not yet adequately explained these widespread differences in affective responses. One explanation is that emotional responses to media are consistent with pre-viewing affective states. Zillmann and Bryant (1993) concluded that people select media fare as a function of their affective states; O'Neal and Taylor (1989) reported that angry men who want to retaliate will select violent media to perpetuate their angry state, and angry men who will not have a chance to retaliate select calming media to relieve their anger. Thus viewing motivations may be a function of previewing affect or desired affective state, and individuals are likely to differ in their affect-driven viewing motivations.

There are also individual differences in beliefs about graphic horror. Males and females have different beliefs and preferences regarding graphic horror; some males, for example, seek exposure to graphic horror because they enjoy viewing female victimization (Tamborini et al., 1987). Tamborini et al. (1987) reported that males prefer movies with the most graphic victimization of females and that males are more likely than females to transfer viewing-generated distress to delight. These viewing-related beliefs are concerning in light of Rule and Ferguson's (1986) research linking beliefs that the "victim deserves her fate" to aggressive behavior. Moreover, Oliver (1993) reported that traditional attitudes toward females' sexuality are positively related to viewing graphic horror "to see the victims get what they deserve." Given this evidence for variance in preferences and beliefs regarding horror films, researchers need to provide a theoretical framework that explains gender differences in beliefs about graphic violence. Specifically, are different viewing motivations associated with different beliefs regarding graphic horror?

Another type of cognitive response to viewing graphic horror is identification with film characters. Viewers who identify with the female victim are more likely to experience distress during viewing (Zillmann & Cantor, 1977) and are not relieved of this distress by a happy resolution for their favorite character (Tannenbaum & Gaer, 1965). Empathic concern for the victim can lead to intense negative reactions, such as hostility, anxiety, and depression (Davis et al., 1987). In contrast, viewers who identify with the powerful, often victorious, male killer may experience aggressive responses (Geen & Thomas, 1986; Jo & Berkowitz, 1993). It is plausible that those identifying with the killer will have concordant responses (Zillmann & Cantor, 1977), such as power over women, control over fear, blunted affect toward the victim, and possibly even joy and delight for the killer's successes. Although little research has addressed viewers' identification with characters, character identification may add a great deal to our understanding of the viewing experience and responses of the adolescent graphic-horror viewer. It seems plausible that viewers identifying with the victim may have quite different viewing motivations than those identifying with the killer.

Uses and gratifications theory suggests that variance in viewing motivations may lead to individual differences in interpretation of media content. Excitation-transfer theory suggests that viewing-induced arousal may intensify postviewing affective responses. If adolescents view graphic horror for different reasons, these motivations may be associated with (a) viewers' positive or negative labeling of media-generated arousal, (b) viewers' beliefs and preferences regarding graphic-horror content, and (c) viewers' identification with film characters. To explore the role of viewing motivations on affective and cognitive responses to horror films, the following research questions are raised:

RQ3: Do different motivations for viewing graphic horror correspond with variance in the valence of adolescents' perceived viewing-related affect?

RQ4: Do different motivations for viewing graphic horror correspond with varying patterns of adolescents' beliefs regarding what makes a "good slasher movie"?

RQ5: Do different motivations for viewing graphic horror correspond with variance in adolescents' identification with the films' victims or killers?

RQ6: Do viewing motivations account for variance in viewing-related affect, content-related beliefs, and character identification after controlling for biological sex?

METHOD

Participants

The sample consisted of 12 freshmen and sophomore high school students who participated in a focus group discussion and 220 freshman and sophomore students from a medium-sized midwestern high school who participated in a survey study. Fifty-two percent of the survey sample were male and 48% were female. The age of the survey respondents ranged from 13 to 16.

According to the focus group study, adolescents use the term *slasher films* to refer to that group of contemporary horror films that feature graphic, grotesque horror and violence, startling special effects, and are typified by the stalking and killing of usually more than one victim. Ninety-five percent of the adolescents in the survey study reported viewing slasher films. To check the validity of this incidence of viewing measure, survey respondents were asked to list their favorite "slasher" movies to ensure that the survey respondents and researchers were referring to the same film genre. Ninety-two percent of the films the survey participants listed (e.g., *Halloween, Nightmare on Elm Street*, etc.) fit the definition given above; the remaining 8% were references to *Faces of Death* (Scott & LeClaire, 1978), which presents a "real" video of people succumbing to a variety of violent deaths.

Focus Group Procedure

Twelve high school freshmen and sophomores from a medium-sized midwestern high school volunteered to participate in a focus group to elicit their opinions regarding horror films. The 2-hour focus group discussion was videotaped. Participants first described the characteristics of the horror movies they watched and reported that they called these films "slasher movies." The participants identified the defining characteristics of slasher movies and the ensuing discussion focused on this specific genre, as opposed to horror movies in general. The facilitator asked questions and follow-up questions related to the following questions: "Why do you watch movies like *Halloween* and *Nightmare on Elm Street*?" "What characteristics make a good slasher movie?" "What are you doing and what feelings are you experiencing at the time you decide to watch a slasher movie?" and "What feelings best describe your mood after watching a slasher movie?" The participants' comments regarding the viewing of slasher films were transcribed, content analyzed, and used to generate scale items for the survey instrument.

Survey Research Procedure

The survey instrument was administered to students in their classrooms, with two research assistants and the classroom teacher present. It took the students no longer than 25 minutes to complete the instrument. The first part of the survey consisted of dispositional-fearfulness, empathy, and sensation-seeking scales. The personality scales were administered before the respondents were informed of the purpose of the study. The second part of the survey assessed respondents' viewing behavior, motivations for viewing, beliefs and content preferences, pre- and postviewing affect, and identification with "slasher" film characters.

Fearfulness Scale

Respondents rated the 36 anxiety-provoking items from Wolpe and Lang's (1964) dispositional-fearfulness assessment instrument on the degree to which they were disturbed by each item on 5-point scales anchored by (1) *not at all* and (5) *very much*. Wolpe and Lang's original 72 items were reduced to 36 by eliminating those fears that were unrelated to graphic-horror content, such as "social and interpersonal fears" (e.g., public speaking), "miscellaneous fears" (e.g., dull weather), and some "classic phobias" (e.g., vertigo and crossing streets). The remaining fear items (reflecting fear of blood, fear of death, fear of medical procedures, fear of the sick or deformed, fear of physical abuse, fear of places and sounds, fear of transportation, and fear of lights and shadows) were combined in the tradition of Wolpe and Lang (1964) into a generalized fearfulness score reflecting the number of different stimuli that a person finds frightening (Cronbach's alpha = .90). Fearfulness scores ranged from 41 to 137 (M = 73.85, SD = 18.59).

Empathy Scale

Participants rated the 22 items on Mehrabian and Epstein's (1972) trait empathy assessment instrument on 5-point scales ranging from (1) *strongly disagree* to (5) *strongly agree*. Although empathy has several dimensions (e.g., fictional involvement, perspective taking, emotional contagion, etc.), Mehrabian and Epstein's Emotional Empathy Scale is believed to be a general measure of chronic emotionality and emotional responsiveness. Davis et al.'s (1987) measure of Empathic Concern is strongly correlated with Mehrabian and Epstein's (1972) Emotional Empathy Scale. According to Davis et al. (1987), emotional empathy is more clearly related to affective responses to film stimuli than are other empathy dimensions.

Mehrabian and Epstein's scale items reflecting a general measure of chronic emotionality were highly correlated. Therefore, a principle components factor analysis with oblimin rotation was employed. The factor analysis of empathy items failed to converge in 25 iterations. The empathy items were therefore used to compute one empathy index (Cronbach's alpha = .79). Empathy scores ranged from 24 to 66, with a mean of 44.30, and a standard deviation of 7.89.

Sensation-Seeking Scales (SSS)

Respondents completed the SSS Form II described by Zuckerman (1971, 1988). Respondents rated sensation-seeking items on 5-point scales ranging from (1) *very unappealing* to (5) *very appealing*, with high scores reflecting high levels of sensation seeking. Because of evidence of orthogonal dimensions of sensation seeking (Zuckerman, 1988), a principal components analysis with varimax rotation was employed. Consistent with previous research, the factor analysis revealed four dimensions of sensation seeking: Proclivity for Substance Abuse (eigenvalue = 3.39, variance after rotation = .63), Adventure Seeking (eigenvalue = 2.56, variance after rotation = .65), Physical Risk (eigenvalue = 1.61, variance after rotation = .48), and Boredom Susceptibility (eigenvalue = 1.46; variance after rotation = .43). Using the .60/.40 criterion for factor loadings, four items comprised the Proclivity for Substance Abuse scale: smoking, drinking alcohol, smoking pot, and using cocaine (Cronbach's alpha = .81, range 4 to 19, $M = 6.77$, $SD = 3.77$), and three items comprised the Adventure Seeking scale: driving fast, gambling, and sensations of fast movement (Cronbach's alpha = .78, range 3 to 15, $M = 9.6$, $SD = 3.04$). Items related to physically risky and novel activities (e.g., parachuting, roller coasting, skate boarding), and boredom susceptibility (e.g., reading books, watching television, doing problem-solving tasks, and analytic thinking tasks) did not produce reliable scales.

Motivations for Viewing

The items employed on the viewing-motivations instrument were derived from the focus group transcript responses to the question: "Why do you watch movies like *Halloween* and *Nightmare on Elm Street*?" Motivations that were reiterated or elaborated by at least one other focus group member were used to create the viewing-motivations instrument. Only two of the motivations mentioned received no elaboration by other members of the focus group. The survey respondents rated the resulting 18 viewing motivations on 5-point scales ranging from (1) *strongly disagree* to (5) *strongly agree*.

Beliefs Associated With Graphic Horror

Scale items reflecting adolescents' beliefs regarding graphic-horror content were derived from the adolescent focus group transcripts. Responses to the prompts "Describe your favorite slasher movies," "What characteristics make a good slasher movie?" and "What characteristics make a particular movie your favorite?" were used to construct 22 scale items representing beliefs about slasher movies (e.g., the movies are scary, believable, real, funny; and the special effects, music, etc. are exceptional).

Beliefs regarding graphic-horror content were analyzed by asking the survey respondents to rate the 22 film characteristics according to what constituted a good slasher movie. If adolescents view these movies for different reasons, beliefs about graphic-horror content should be orthogonal. For this reason, a principal components analysis with varimax rotation was employed. The analysis revealed four dimensions of slasher movie beliefs, accounting for 62.2% of the variance: Preference for Graphic Violence (eigenvalue = 3.85, variance after rotation = .47), Preference for Excitement (eigenvalue = 2.49, variance after rotation = .47), Preference for True Stories (eigenvalue = 1.36, variance after rotation = .64), and Preference for Humor (eigenvalue = 1.05, variance after rotation = .64). The .60/.40 rule was used as the criterion for item selection for scale construction. The five items comprising the first factor, Preference for Graphic Violence, and their respective factor loadings are as follows: preference for torture (.75), random killings (.73), sexually stimulating content (.68), gory scenes (.64), and revenge killings (.62). These items were combined in the Preference for Violence scale (Cronbach's alpha = .75, range 5 to 25, M = 16.03, SD = 4.58). The factor loadings for the three items comprising the second factor, Preference for Excitement, are preference for suspense (.77), intense drama (.76), and lots of surprises (.74). These items were combined in the Preference for Excitement scale (Cronbach's alpha = .75, range 3 to 15, M = 13.13, SD = 2.34). The third and fourth factors, reflecting preferences for true stories and humor, failed to produce reliable scales.[2] Survey respondents also rated the extent to which they believed slasher movies were enjoyable, exciting, and funny; and these three items produced a reliable scale reflecting positive beliefs about slasher movies (Cronbach's alpha = .72, range 3 to 15, M = 9.84, SD = 2.63).

Viewing-Related Affect Associated With Graphic Horror

The scale items reflecting respondents' perceived viewing-related affect were derived from the focus group discussion prompted by

a. "Think about the last few times you've seen slasher movies. Think about who you were with, where you were, and what you were doing. What are you doing, and what feelings are you experiencing at the time you decide to watch a slasher movie?"
b. "Do you experience particular moods that make you want to watch these movies?"
c. "What feelings best describe your mood after watching a slasher movie?"
d. "Do you have teenage friends who experience different feelings before watching slasher movies? Do your friends experience different emotions after watching slasher movies? Please describe their feelings."

Respondents rated the degree to which nine different emotions generated by the focus group discussion characterized their perceived pre- and postviewing affect. Adolescents' *generalized perceptions* of their affective states are clearly important to the reinforcement of viewing behavior, to their interpretation of violence in different contexts, and to their beliefs and responses to graphic-horror exposure. Memories of cumulative affective responses may tell us more about adolescents' graphic-horror interpretive schemata than the measurement of affect following exposure to a single incidence of graphic horror.

Because of correlations among pre- and postviewing affect, a principal components analysis with oblimin rotation was employed. The factor analysis revealed four dimensions of affect, accounting for 66.6% of the variance: Positive Affect (eigenvalue = 5.22, variance after rotation = .51), Negative Postviewing Affect (eigenvalue = 3.63, variance after rotation = .62), Negative Previewing Affect (eigenvalue = 1.38, variance after rotation = .59), and Anxiety (eigenvalue = 1.10; variance after rotation = .56). Scales were created using the .60/.40 criterion for item selection. The seven items used to create the Positive Affect scale (Cronbach's alpha = .85, range 7 to 35, M = 22.21, SD = 6.00) and the factor loadings for each item are postviewing wildness (.77), postviewing excitement (.76), good postviewing feelings (.76), postviewing powerfulness (.69), previewing excitement (.71), previewing wildness (.70), and previewing powerfulness (.61). The Negative Postviewing Affect scale (Cronbach's alpha = .86, range 4 to 20, M = 9.334, SD = 3.87) included four items, and the factor loadings for each item are as follows: postviewing frustration (.81), loneliness (.80), anger (.77), and sadness (.77). The Negative Previewing Affect scale (Cronbach's alpha = .86, range 3 to 15, M = 6.55, SD = 2.73) included three items, and the factor loadings are as follows: previewing anger (.78), sadness (.76), and frustration (.76). The fourth factor, reflecting pre- and postviewing anxiety, did not produce a reliable scale.

Character Identification and Graphic Horror

Character identification issues emerged in the focus group discussion. Some of the teens reported liking the killers in these movies, acting out scenes of the movie with themselves as the killer, and dressing up like the killer. Others reported experiencing fear of victimization after viewing these films. An analysis of the focus group transcript revealed 13 character identification behaviors.

The survey respondents rated the 13 character identification items on 5-point scales ranging from (1) *very unlikely* to (5) *very likely*. Because of individual differences in viewing responses, the character identification items were believed to be orthogonal. Therefore, a principal components analysis with varimax rotation was employed. Four factors, accounting for 57.5% of the variance, emerged: Identification With the Killer (eigenvalue = 2.81, variance after rotation = .45), Identification With the Victim (eigenvalue = 2.00, variance after rotation = .61), Identification With the Survivor (eigenvalue = 1.46, variance after rotation = .46), and Behavioral

Identification With the Killer (eigenvalue = 1.20, variance after rotation = .83). Scales were created using the .60/.40 criterion for item selection. The six items comprising the Identification With the Killer scale (Cronbach's alpha = .76, range 5 to 25, M = 11.52, SD = 4.16) and the factor loadings for each item are as follows: "The victim usually gets what he or she deserves" (.76), "I think about slasher movies a lot" (.73), "the killer usually has a good reason for killing" (.67), "slasher movies are sexually stimulating" (.63), "I think slasher movies are funny" (.60), and "slasher movies are educational" (.60). The three items comprising the Identification With the Victim scale (Cronbach's alpha = .79, range 3 to 15, M = 9.13, SD = 2.94) and the factor loadings for each item are as follows: "I sometimes get scared to go out alone after watching slasher movies" (.86), "I don't like to be in dark places after watching slasher movies" (.85), and "I can see myself as the victim who gets killed" (.61). The third and fourth factors, reflecting identification with the survivor and propensity for dressing up as the killer, failed to produce reliable scales.

RESULTS

Adolescents' Motivations for Viewing Slasher Films

Respondents' reasons for watching slasher movies were factor analyzed using a principal components analysis with varimax rotation. The use of the varimax rotation is consistent with the premise of this study that posits that viewing motivations are represented by orthogonal dimensions. This analysis yielded six viewing factors, accounting for 64.1% of the variance. The .60/.40 rule was used as the criterion for item selection in scale construction. The primary factor (eigenvalue = 5.11, variance after rotation = .64) is labeled Gore Watching. The Gore Watching scale includes three items, and the factor loadings for each item are as follows: "I watch because I'm interested in the ways people die" (.88), "I like to see blood and guts" (.77), and "I like to see the victims get what they deserve" (.74). Scores on the Gore Watching scale ranged from 3 to 15 (Cronbach's alpha = .80, M = 6.37, SD = 3.14). The second factor (eigenvalue = 2.14, variance after rotation = .58) is labeled Thrill Watching. This scale includes four items: "I watch because I like to be scared" (.77), "I watch to have fun" (.77), "It's something I like to do" (.75), and "I watch to freak myself out" (.74). Scores on the Thrill Watching scale range from 4 to 20 (Cronbach's alpha = .75, M = 14.7, SD = 3.50). The third factor (eigenvalue = 1.33, variance after rotation = .57) is labeled Independent Watching. This scale includes three items: "I watch because it makes me feel brave" (.86), "Watching makes me feel mature" (.78), and "I watch to be different" (.61).

TABLE 1
Correlations Among Motivations for Viewing

Viewing Motivation	Gore	Thrill	Independence	Problem
Gore watching		.30**	.44**	.45**
Thrill watching			.23*	.21*
Independence watching				.53**

*p < .01; **p < .001.

Scores on the Independent Watching scale ranged from 3 to 15 (Cronbach's alpha = .79, M = 6.68, SD = 2.74). The fourth factor (eigenvalue = 1.03, variance after rotation = .60) is labeled Problem Watching. This scale includes three items: "I watch because I'm lonely" (.85), "I watch when I'm angry" (.79), and "I watch to avoid problems at home" (.68). Scores on the Problem Watching scale ranged from 3 to 15 (Cronbach's alpha = .82, M = 5.84, SD = 2.61). The fifth and sixth factors related to peer motivations (e.g., "Everybody else watches" and "I watch to fit in with my friends") and entertainment motivations (e.g., "I watch because there's nothing else to do" and "I watch because the films are stupid and I can laugh") did not produce reliable scales.

Each respondent has a score on each of the four motivations for viewing. A respondent's viewing profile may, therefore, include more than one motivation for viewing. Correlations among motivations are presented in Table 1.

Dispositional Characteristics and Motivations for Viewing

Because dispositional characteristics may covary, stepwise regression analyses were employed to determine the best predictors of each viewing motivation. Stepwise regression analyses were used to assess the relative effects of dispositional characteristics—empathy, fearfulness, and the two dimensions of sensation seeking (i.e., proclivity for substance abuse and adventure seeking)—in the prediction of each of the four motivations for viewing graphic horror (i.e., gore watching, thrill watching, independent watching, and problem watching).

Each viewing motivation was the dependent variable in an equation, and the four personality characteristics were evaluated for entry in each equation according to stepwise criteria. Results are presented in Table 2. To summarize, gore watching is characterized by low levels of empathy, low levels of fearfulness, and high levels of adventure seeking. Thrill watching is associated with high levels of adventure seeking and high dispositional empathy. Viewers motivated by independence are characterized by low levels of dispositional empathy, and viewers motivated by

TABLE 2
**Summary of Hierarchical Regression Analysis for
Personality Variables Predicting Viewing Motivations**

Viewing Motivation	F	df	R^2	β
Gore watching				
Step 1: empathy	27.56**	1,131	.17	−.42**
Step 2: adventure seeking	19.52**	2,130	.23	.25**
Step 3: fearfulness	15.74**	3,129	.27	−.21*
Thrill watching				
Step 1: adventure	7.04*	1,131	.05	.23*
Step 2: empathy	7.39**	2,130	.10	.24**
Independent watching				
Step 1: empathy	6.18*	1,131	.05	−.21*
Problem watching				
Step 1: substance use	8.94*	1,131	.06	.25*
Step 2: empathy	7.58**	2,131	.10	−.20**

*$p < .01$; **$p < .001$.

problems are characterized by high levels of proclivity for substance abuse and low levels of dispositional empathy.

Viewing Motivations and Viewing-Related Affect

Because the viewing motivations are not mutually exclusive, stepwise regression analyses were employed to assess the relative effects of the four viewing motivations (predictor variables) on viewing-related affect (dependent variables). The results of these analyses are presented in Table 3 and summarized below.

Two viewing motivations were significantly related to positive affect. Thrill watching was the first variable to reach the stepwise entry criteria, followed by independent watching. Cumulatively, the two variables accounted for 39% of the variance in positive affect. Thrill watchers and independent watchers were more likely to report feeling wild, powerful, excited, and good before and after viewing graphic horror than were gore watchers and problem watchers.

Two viewing motivations were significantly related to negative previewing affect (e.g., sadness, frustration, and anger). Problem watching and thrill watching reached significance first and second, respectively, in the stepwise regression equation. Viewers with low levels of thrill watching and high levels of problem watching were most likely to report negative previewing affect. Gore watching and independent watching did not contribute significantly to the prediction of negative previewing affect

TABLE 3
Summary of Hierarchical Regression Analyses for Viewing Motivations Predicting Viewing-Related Affect

Viewing-Related Affect	F	df	R^2	β
Positive affect				
Step 1: thrill watching	73.23*	1,144	.34	.58*
Step 2: independent	45.82*	2,144	.39	.54*
Negative previewing affect				
Step 1: problem watching	22.35*	1,144	.13	.37*
Step 2: thrill watching	17.69*	2,144	.20	−.26*
Negative postviewing affect				
Step 1: Problem watching	42.14*	1,144	.23	.48*
Step 2: Gore watching	23.83*	2,144	.25	−.16*

*$p < .001$.

after thrill watching and problem watching were entered in the equation. Cumulatively, thrill watching and problem watching accounted for 20% of the variance in negative previewing affect.

High motivations for problem watching and low motivations for gore watching were significantly related to negative postviewing affect (e.g., frustration, anger, loneliness, and sadness). In a stepwise regression analysis with viewing motivations as the predictor variables, problem watching was the first variable to meet the stepwise entry criteria, followed by gore watching. Cumulatively, problem watching and gore watching accounted for 25% of the variance in negative postviewing affect.

Viewing Motivations and Beliefs About Graphic Horror

Because of covariance among viewing motivations, three stepwise regression analyses were conducted to assess the relative effects of the four viewing motivations on (a) positive beliefs about slasher movies, (b) preference for graphic violence, and (c) preference for excitement in slasher movie content. Each of the belief scales was the dependent variable in an equation, and each of the four viewing motivations were considered for entry according to stepwise regression criteria. Results of these analyses are presented in Table 4 and summarized below.

Two viewing motivations were significantly related to positive beliefs about slasher movies. Gore watching was the first variable eligible for entry in the stepwise procedure, followed by thrill watching. Independent watching and problem watching did not meet the stepwise criteria for entry in the regression equation once gore watching and thrill watching had been entered. Cumulatively, gore watching and thrill watching ac-

TABLE 4

Summary of Hierarchical Regression Analyses for
Viewing Motivations Predicting Beliefs About Graphic Horror

Beliefs About Graphic Horror	F	df	R^2	β
Postive beliefs				
Step 1: gore watching	35.00*	1,144	.20	.44*
Step 2: thrill watching	21.77*	2,143	.23	.20*
Preference for graphic violence				
Step 1: gore watching	75.84*	1,144	.34	.58*
Preference for excitement				
Step 1: thrill watching	25.08*	1,144	.15	.38*

*$p < .001$.

count for 23% of the variance in positive beliefs about graphic-horror movie content. This suggests that gore watchers and thrill watchers believe that slasher movies are exciting, funny, and enjoyable, whereas independent watchers and problem watchers do not consistently hold these beliefs.

Gore watching was the only motivation that significantly contributed to the prediction of preference for graphic violence in a stepwise regression analysis. Gore-watching motivations accounted for 34% of the variance in beliefs reflecting a preference for graphic violence (e.g., beliefs that the best movies show torture, random killings, sex, gore, and revenge).

Thrill-watching motivations were significantly related to preference for excitement beliefs (e.g., beliefs that the best movies are suspenseful, intense, and filled with shocking surprises). Thrill watching accounted for 15% of the variance in preference for excitement beliefs. Gore watching, problem watching, and independent watching did not significantly contribute to the prediction of the preference for excitement beliefs after thrill watching was entered in the equation.

Viewing Motivations and Character Identification

Because of covariance among viewing motivations, two stepwise regression analyses were used to assess the relative effects of the four viewing motivations (predictor variables) on identification with the killer and identification with the victim (outcome variables). Results are presented in Table 5 and summarized below.

In a stepwise regression equation with identification with the killer as the dependent variable, and the four viewing motivations as predictor variables, gore watching was the only viewing motivation that met the

TABLE 5
Summary of Hierarchical Regression Analyses for
Viewing Motivations Predicting Character Identification

Identification With Film Characters	F	df	R^2	β
Identification with killer				
Step 1: gore watching	147.11**	1,169	.47	.68**
Identification with victim				
Step 1: gore watching	10.11*	1,166	.06	−.24*
Step 2: independent	9.76**	2,165	.11	−.24*
Step 3: problem watching	7.06*	3,164	.13	.20*

*$p < .01$; **$p < .001$.

stepwise regression criteria for entry in the equation. Gore watching accounted for 49% of the variance in identification with killer.

Low motivations for gore watching, high motivations for independent watching, and high motivations for problem watching were related to identification with the victim. Gore watching was the first variable to meet entry criteria in a stepwise regression analysis, followed by independence viewing motivations and problem-related viewing motivations. Cumulatively, the three viewing motivations only accounted for 13% of the variance in identification with victim.

Viewing Motivations and Biological Sex

Gore watching is the only motivation significantly related to biological sex ($r = .32, p < .001$); males are more likely to view graphic horror for gore motivations than are females.

Therefore, the covariance of gore watching and biological sex in the prediction of viewing-related affect, beliefs about graphic horror, and character identification was investigated to assess whether gore watching predicted cognitive and affective responses to graphic horror over and above the effects of biological sex (Table 6).

Although gore watching was a significant predictor of negative postviewing affect, a forced-entry regression equation with biological sex as the predictor variable and postviewing negative affect as the dependent variable was not significant.

To assess the covariance of biological sex and gore-watching motivations in the prediction of preference for graphic-violence beliefs, a regression analysis in which sex and gore watching were predictor variables was conducted. Using a forced-entry procedure, sex was entered first in the equation, followed by gore watching. Although sex was significantly

TABLE 6

Summary of Regression Analyses for Gore Watching and
Biological Sex Predicting Affect, Beliefs, and Character Identification

Responses to Graphic Horror	F	df	R^2	β
Affect (negative postviewing affect)				
Enter: sex	0.28	1,172	.002	.04
Beliefs (preference for graphic violence)				
Enter 1: sex	11.15*	1,180	.06	−.24*
Enter 2: gore watching	38.25*	2,179	.30	.52*
Identification with killer				
Enter 1: sex	16.46*	1,169	.09	−.30*
Enter 2: gore watching	74.72*	2,168	.47	.66*
Identification with victim				
Enter 1: sex	16.61*	1,170	.09	.30*
Enter 2: gore watching	9.39*	2,169	.10	−.11

*$p < .001$.

related to preference for graphic violence, such that males were more likely than females to profess a preference for violence, adding gore watching to the equation resulted in a significant increase in R^2 from .06 to .30.

To assess covariance of gore watching and biological sex in the prediction of identification with the killer, a regression analysis was conducted with sex and gore watching as predictor variables. Sex was entered first, using a forced-entry regression procedure. The results indicate that sex is significantly related to identification with killer such that males were more likely than females to identify with the killer in a slasher film. However, gore watching contributed to the prediction of identification with killer after biological sex was already in the equation, resulting in a .38 increase in R^2. Although biological sex is significantly related to identification with the killer, the cumulative variance accounted for by sex and gore watching is slightly less than the variance accounted for by gore watching alone.

To assess the covariance of biological sex and gore watching in the prediction of identification with the victim, a regression analysis using a forced-entry procedure was conducted with sex entered first, and gore watching entered second. Sex is clearly the best predictor of identification with victim; sex accounts for 30% of the variance in identification with victim, and gore watching did not meet the criteria for entry into the regression equation after sex was already entered. Results indicate that females were more likely to identify with the victim than were males.

It appears that the effects of gore watching on viewing-related affect, beliefs about graphic violence, and identification with the killer cannot be attributed to biological sex. However, the effects of low levels of gore watching on identification with the victim appear to be an artifact of the covariance between gore watching and sex.

DISCUSSION

The generation of viewing motivations by the focus group and the subsequent validation of these motivations by 220 adolescents suggests that viewers of slasher films have varying motivations for viewing graphic horror. These findings are consistent with the expectations of the uses and gratifications theory of media effects that predicts that viewers' cognitive framework (gratifications sought) is related to viewers' responses (gratifications obtained) from viewing experiences. However, rather than suggesting that gratifications sought mirror gratifications obtained, this study suggests that individual differences in viewing motivations explain variance in responses to graphic media and that the responses to a media experience may include serendipitous reactions that are predicted by, but are necessarily the same as, the reasons for viewing. Thus this study focuses more on viewers' lasting interpretation of their graphic-horror media experiences than on their satisfaction (i.e., gratifications) with these media experiences. Specifically, viewing motivations may mediate the relationship between violent media content and cognitive and affective responses to graphic horror; viewing motivations are related to different beliefs regarding the positive attributes of slasher movies, different content preferences, different patterns of pre- and postviewing affect, and different character identification. Moreover, the results support the notion that viewers with different motivations are characterized by different personality profiles.

This study also expands our understanding of excitation-transfer processes in response to viewing-induced arousal associated with graphic horror. Previous research suggests that gender is predictive of the transfer of viewing-induced arousal to feelings of delight or distress (Mundorf et al., 1989). This study suggests that the valence of perceived viewing-related affect is significantly related to adolescents' viewing motivations. Results indicate that thrill watchers and independent watchers were more likely to report positive affect in response to viewing graphic horror, and that low levels of gore watching and high levels of problem watching were related to perceived negative postviewing affect. That is, viewers who seek graphic horror for excitement and opportunities to demonstrate mastery over fear report positive affect both before and after viewing.

Further research is needed to assess whether the viewing of graphic horror intensifies these positive feelings, as predicted by excitation-transfer theory, or whether the previewing affect is consistent in both valence and intensity to the postviewing affect for thrill- and independent-watching viewers. In contrast, viewers who do not like gore and viewers who watch as a result of anger, loneliness, and personal problems report negative affect after viewing. Problem watchers also report negative affect prior to viewing, but the negative postviewing affect reported by viewers who do not watch for gore motivations appears to be attributed (by the viewers) to the viewing experience. Thus the valence of reported postviewing arousal appears to be consistent with previewing affect, except for those viewers who cannot relate to gore-watching motivations and who consequently react with negative affect to the experience of viewing graphic horror.

The viewing motivations identified in this exploratory study may reflect different aggression-viewing schemata (Schank & Abelson, 1977). According to this theory, scripts and schemata serve to organize our experiential knowledge, to determine the perception and salience of incoming information, to govern the integration of information with existing knowledge, and to dictate the inferences and interpretations we formulate. Rule and Ferguson (1986) proposed that aggression schemes can be used

> 1) to identify the cognitive processes that are used when viewers attempt to understand portrayals of media violence, 2) to assess how people with different cognitive structures respond to the form and content of aggressive episodes, and 3) to determine the interplay between the cognitive capabilities of the viewer and the violent content of the show. (p. 35)

Indeed, the four viewing motivations revealed in this study (gore watching, thrill watching, independent watching, and problem watching) suggest four very different cognitive and affective media experiences in response to graphically violent stimuli.

Gore-watching motivations may reflect a curiosity about physical violence ("I'm interested in the ways people die"), a vengeful interest in killing ("I like to see victims get what they deserve"), and an attraction to the grotesque ("I like to see blood and guts"). These motivations are consistent with gore watchers' strong and exclusive preference for graphic violent content in slasher films. Oliver (1993) provided additional validation of the Gore Watching scale.

The gore-watcher personality is characterized by low empathy, low fearfulness, and high adventure seeking. This combination of personality traits may lead gore watchers to seek isolated arousal generated by graphic portrayals of blood, death, and tissue damage and to blunt emotional responses to the psychological terror, physical suffering, and death of the film characters.

Gore watching is also related to high viewing frequency. This is consistent with Tamborini et al.'s (1990) finding that low-empathy people are most attracted to graphic horror and with Mundorf et al's (1989) finding that low fearfulness is associated with liking of graphic horror.

The relationships between gore watching and viewing-related affect may reflect emotional blunting consistent with the personality of low fearfulness and low empathy. Gore watching was not significantly related to the combined measure of pre- and postviewing positive affect. Nor was gore watching related to previewing negative affect. Gore watching was, however, negatively related to negative postviewing affect (e.g., feelings of sadness, nervousness, anger, frustration, and loneliness). Thus gore watching is not characterized by positive affect, it is not precipitated by negative affect, but the process of viewing results in low levels of negative affect. This suggests that viewing graphic violence for gore-watching motivations does not have dramatic effects on affective states.

Additional research is needed to assess the relationship between gore watching and aggression; it appears that of the four viewing motivations, gore watchers are most at risk for subsequent violence. Gore watching was strongly related to identification with the killer and males were less likely to identify with the victim. Research reviewed by Rule and Ferguson (1986) suggests that identification with the killer and insensitivity toward the victim are related to increased likelihood of subsequent aggression. In addition, Oliver (1993) found gore-watching motivations to be related to double standard beliefs about male and female sexuality; gore watchers were more likely to respond positively to scale items such as, "It is all right for males, but not for females, to have sex before marriage." This double standard was specifically correlated with the gore-watching scale item "I like to see victims get what they deserve." Moreover, beliefs in this double standard were related to greater reported enjoyment of female-victim videos. This finding is particularly revealing given the research of Cowan and O'Brien (1990), who conclude that women portrayed in asexual roles in slasher films survive and women portrayed in sexual roles are killed.

Thrill-watching motivations reflect the fun of being startled and scared. Thrill watching was strongly related to a preference for suspense and excitement in slasher movie content (cf. Oliver, 1993, for additional validation of the Thrill Watching scale). Whereas the gore watcher focuses on graphic depictions of blood and guts, the thrill watcher focuses more on the suspense. The personality of the thrill watcher is characterized by high levels of empathy and high levels of adventure seeking. Thrill watchers are also characterized by consistent positive affect both before and after the viewing experience. Whereas some research reports high levels of short-term postviewing distress for high-empathy viewers (Davis et al., 1987; Tamborini & Mettler, 1990), the findings of this study suggest that the long-term recollection of the pre- and postviewing states is positive. Moreover, the tendency for thrill watchers to report both pre- and postviewing positive affect suggests that slasher movies may serve to intensify existing excitement and arousal for these viewers. Interestingly, thrill watching was not significantly related to either killer or victim identification. Given the items on the Victim Identification scale (e.g., "I sometimes get scared to go out alone after watching slasher movies"), it is possible that thrill watchers empathize with the victim but do not perceive themselves at risk for victimization. Future research is needed to determine if thrill watchers distance themselves from victimization fears by dismissing the reality of slasher movie content.

It appears that independent watchers view slasher movies to play a role; this role is assumed to test the viewer's maturity and bravery. Independent watchers are characterized by low levels of dispositional empathy; however, empathy only accounts for 5% of the variance in independent watching, suggesting that there are yet unidentified personality traits that might further define this viewer profile.

Independent watchers show no preference for either violence or suspense, and they report experiencing consistently positive affect (e.g., wild, excited, powerful) both before and after viewing slasher movies. The independent-watcher viewing motivation provides some support for Zillmann et al.'s (1986) contention that some people use graphic-horror movies to play out socialized roles that call for the demonstration of mastery over fear. Although Zillmann et al. posit that male gender identification is motivated by mastery and female gender by dependence, no relationship was found between biological sex and independent viewing motivations in this study. Only gore watching was significantly related to sex, such that males were more likely to view for gore-watching reasons than were females. The findings that independent watchers identify with the victim, yet report positive affect related to the viewing experience, are consistent with Zillmann et al.'s conclusion that fear of victimization should inhibit enjoyment of horror, but that people seeking to demonstrate mastery may project themselves as being less fearful than they actually are (Mundorf et al., 1989). Mastery over fear was experimentally manipulated in the Zillmann study, and the responses of the independent watchers in this study provide some limited support for the existence of mastery motivations. Additional research is necessary to empirically validate the mastery hypothesis by assessing the independent watchers' actual viewing behavior.

Problem watchers report being angry and lonely. It is not surprising that the personality of the problem watcher is characterized by sensation seeking in the form of substance abuse and low dispositional empathy. Problem watchers' identification with the victim may be a reflection of their own perceived helplessness. Problem watchers were the only viewers who reported consistently negative affect both before and after viewing graphic horror. It is possible that the problem viewers' negative affect is a pervasive state that is not altered by viewing slasher films. Although, according to Zillmann (1982), if a viewing experience reinstates negative affect, there is unlikely to be a reduction in arousal and consequent aggression. Thus additional research is needed to determine if the negative affect reported by problem watchers is intensified, reduced, or unmodified by the viewing experience.

Significant relationships among viewing motivations were found. Thrill-watching motivations covaried with all the other viewing motivations, but the shared variance was minimal. Gore watching, independent watching, and problem watching covaried to a greater degree, and this is likely due to the low dispositional empathy common to all three of these viewing motivations.

In general, this study suggests that viewing motivations mediate the media experience. Much of the research on adolescents' use of graphic horror needs to be reexamined in light of these varying viewing motivations and gratifications. For example, the equivocal findings regarding the effect of media on the intensification of arousal (Zillmann, 1982), the transfer of arousal (Zillmann, 1984), and the habituation of arousal (Linz, Donnerstein, & Penrod, 1984; Thomas, 1982) may be explained by individual differences in viewing motivations. In addition, this study suggests that the equivocal findings regarding the relationship between sensation seeking and viewing of graphic horror may be explained by viewing motivations; only two of the four motivations for viewing in this study were related to the adventure-seeking dimension of sensation seeking. Moreover, the interaction of empathy, plot resolution, and postviewing enjoyment or distress (Zillmann, 1980) may be affected by viewing motivations; we would expect gore watchers' enjoyment to be independent of plot resolution, thrill watchers' and independent watchers' enjoyment to be dependent on plot resolution, and problem watchers' enjoyment to be more dependent on plot resolution if they are watching for escapism motivations. Finally, this study suggests the value of exploring the personality characteristics of graphic-horror viewers. Whereas previous research found only small effects for personality as a predictor of graphic-horror viewing, this study suggests that combinations of dispositional traits are useful for differentiating viewing motivation profiles.

The focus on cognitive and affective responses to media experiences in this study builds on the uses and gratifications research tradition but changes the focus from satisfaction with media experiences to interpretation of media experiences. Whereas beliefs about content preferences seemed to be intuitively reflective of viewing motivations, perceived affect and identification with the victim was not always perceived positively (i.e., as a gratification) by the viewer. In fact, it appears that negative reactions may be overridden by the powerful motivations that drive the decision to repeatedly view graphic horror. Thus meaning attributed to viewing, not gratifications per se, may most accurately reflect the varied responses to media viewing.

Additional research is necessary to assess the relationship between viewing motivations and affective and cognitive responses to media. Researchers need to assess, for example, the tenets of priming cognitive associational theory (Berkowitz & Rogers, 1986); that is, does the affective labeling of the viewing-induced arousal activate cognitive associations, and do viewing motivations interact with perceived affect in the prediction of cognitive responses and interpretations of graphic horror?

In conclusion, unlike previous research on the viewing of graphic horror, this study directly assesses the motivations of the adolescent viewer. The findings suggest that adolescents do not all watch graphic horror for the same reasons and that, consequently, graphic horror does not have consistent and ubiquitous effects on all adolescents. Although there is a subset of adolescents who view graphic horror for gore-watching motivations and who hold disturbing beliefs and responses to the viewing of graphic horror, other adolescent viewers appear to seek graphic horror for the thrill, enjoyment, and stimulation of the viewing experience, and their responses (positive affect and preferences for suspense) are not, at least explicitly, as concerning. It is also comforting that independent watchers—who seek mastery over their fears, are characterized by low empathy, and report positive affective responses—tend to identify with the victim rather than the killer in these movies. It is less clear how problem watchers cope with intensified postviewing negative affect and how their low dispositional empathy is related to some identification with the victim.

Viewing graphic horror does, clearly, have effects on adolescent viewers, although the type and intensity of these effects vary according to adolescents' motivations for viewing. Although researchers have long sought behavioral effects of media viewing, the existence of individual differences in viewing motivations opens a rich avenue for additional research on psychological effects, such as affective and cognitive responses associated with exposure to graphic horror. Rather than identifying one-time behaviors, the focus on psychological effects may lead researchers to identify gestalt patterns of thinking and reacting—that may be created, intensified, or maintained by media influences—that underly behavioral choices. Thus future research efforts need to expand the analysis of cognitive and affective responses, analyze responses over time (i.e., at the time of viewing, immediately after viewing, and some time after viewing), and empirically validate viewing motivations and responses.

NOTES

1. Perspective taking, often considered a key dimension of empathy, does not differentiate the emotional responses of viewers in the absence of instructional perspective-taking directions (Davis, Hull, Young, & Warren, 1987). Moreover, perspective taking is a precursor of emotional contagion, empathic concern, and fictional involvement in Tamborini and Mettler's (1990) model of empathic reactions to negative film stimuli. Thus perspective taking is a cognitive dimension of empathy that does not seem to be directly related to responses to negative film stimuli (Davis et al., 1987).

2. Full details about the items that did not meet the .60/.40 criterion for the factor analyses and about the factors that did not produce reliable scales are available from the author on request.

REFERENCES

Armstrong, C. B., & Rubin, A. M. (1989). Talk radio as interpersonal communication. *Journal of Communication, 39*, 84-93.

Bantz, C. R. (1982). Exploring uses and gratifications: A comparison of reported uses of television and reported uses of favorite program type. *Communication Research, 9*, 352-379.

Berkowitz, L. (1984). Some effects of thoughts on anti- and prosocial influences of media events: A cognitive neoassociationist analysis. *Psychological Bulletin, 95*, 410-427.

Berkowitz, L., & Rogers, K. H. (1986). A priming effect analysis of media influences. In J. Bryant & D. Zillmann (Eds.), *Perspective on media effects* (pp. 57-81). Hillsdale, NJ: Lawrence Erlbaum.

Blumler, J. G. (1979). The role of theory in uses and gratifications studies. *Communication Research, 6*, 9-36.

Cantor, J. (1991). Fright responses to mass media productions. In J. Bryant & D. Zillmann (Eds.), *Responding to the screen* (pp. 169-197). Hillsdale, NJ: Lawrence Erlbaum.

Cantor, J., Bryant, J., & Zillmann, D. (1974). Enhancement of humor appreciation by transferred excitation. *Journal of Personality and Social Psychology, 30*, 812-821.

Cantor, J., & Reilly, S. (1982). Adolescents' fright reactions to television and films. *Journal of Communication, 32*, 87-99.

Cantor, J., Zillmann, D., & Bryant, J. (1975). Enhancement of experienced sexual arousal in response to erotic stimuli through misattributions of unrelated residual excitation. *Journal of Personality and Social Psychology, 32*, 69-75.

Conway, J. C., & Rubin, A. M. (1991). Psychological predictors of television viewing motivation. *Communication Research, 18*, 443-463.

Cowan, G., & O'Brien, M. (1990). Gender and survival vs. death in slasher films: A content analysis. *Sex Roles, 23*, 187-196.

Cunningham, S. (Producer & Director). (1980). *Friday the 13th* [Film]. Los Angeles: Paramount.

Davis, M. H., Hull, J. G., Young, R. D., & Warren, G. G. (1987). Emotional reactions to dramatic film stimuli: The influence of cognitive and emotional empathy. *Journal of Personality and Social Psychology, 52*, 126-133.

Edwards, E. (1984). *The relationship between sensation-seeking and horror movie interest and attendance.* Unpublished doctoral dissertation, University of Tennessee, Knoxville.

Frank, R. E., & Greenberg, M. G. (1980). *The public's use of television: Who watches and why.* Beverly Hills, CA: Sage.

Frost, R., & Stauffer, J. (1987). The effects of social class, gender, and personality on physiological responses to filmed violence. *Journal of Communication, 37*(2), 29-45.

Geen, R. G., & Thomas, S. L. (1986). The immediate effects of media violence on behavior. *Journal of Social Issues, 42,* 7-27.

Hill, D. (Producer), & Carpenter, J. (Director). (1981). *Halloween* [Film]. Los Angeles: Media.

Jo, E., & Berkowitz, L. (1993). A priming effect analysis of media influence: An update. In J. Bryant & D. Zillmann (Eds.), *Media effects: Advances in theory and research* (pp. 43-60). Hillsdale, NJ: Lawrence Erlbaum.

Katz, E., Gurevitch, M., & Haas, H. (1973). On the use of the mass media for important things. *American Sociological Review, 38,* 164-181.

Levy, M. R., & Windahl, S. (1985). The concept of audience activity. In K. Rosengren, L. Wenner, & P. Palmgreen (Eds.), *Media gratifications research: Current perspectives* (pp. 109-122). Beverly Hills, CA: Sage.

Lin, C. A. (1993). Modeling the gratification-seeking process of television viewing. *Human Communication Research, 20,* 224-244.

Linz, D. (1985). Sexual violence in media: Effects on male viewers and implications for society. (Doctoral dissertation, University of Wisconsin—Madison, 1985). *Dissertation Abstracts International, 46,* 1382B.

Linz, D., Donnerstein, E., & Penrod, S. (1984). The effects of multiple exposures to filmed violence against women. *Journal of Communication, 34,* 130-147.

Linz, D., Donnerstein, E., & Penrod, S. (1988). Effects of long-term exposure to violent and sexually degrading depictions of women. *Journal of Personality and Social Psychology, 55,* 758-768.

Lull, J. (1980). The social uses of television. *Human Communication Research, 6,* 197-209.

Mehrabian, A., & Epstein, N. (1972). A measure of emotional empathy. *Journal of Personality, 40,* 525-543.

Mundorf, N., Weaver, J., & Zillmann, D. (1989). Effects of gender roles and self perceptions on affective reactions to horror films. *Sex Roles, 20,* 655-673.

Neuendorf, K. A., & Sparks, G. G. (1988). Predicting emotional responses to horror films from cue-specific affect. *Communication Quarterly, 36,* 16-27.

Oliver, M. B. (1993). Adolescents' enjoyment of graphic horror: Effects of viewers' attitudes and portrayals of victim. *Communication Research, 20,* 30-50.

Olson, S. R. (1989). Mass media: A bricolage of paradigms. In S. S. King (Ed.), *Human communication as a field of study* (pp. 57-83). Albany: State University of New York Press.

O'Neal, E. C., & Taylor, S. L. (1989). Status of the provoker, opportunity to retaliate, and interest in video violence. *Aggressive Behavior, 15,* 171-180.

Palmgreen, P., Wenner, L. A., & Rayburn, J. D. (1980). Relations between gratifications sought and obtained. *Communication Research, 7,* 161-192.

Perse, E. (1990). Involvement with local television news: Cognitive and emotional dimensions. *Human Communication Research, 16,* 556-581.

Rubin, A. M. (1977). Television usage, attitudes and viewing behaviors of children and adolescents. *Journal of Broadcasting, 21,* 355-369.

Rubin, A. M. (1979). Television use by children and adolescents. *Communication Research, 5,* 109-120.

Rubin, A. M. (1981). An examination of television viewing motivations. *Communication Research, 8,* 141-165.

Rubin, A. M. (1983). Television uses and gratifications: The interactions of viewing patterns and motivations. *Journal of Broadcasting, 27,* 37-51.

Rubin, A. M. (1986). Uses, gratifications, and media effects research. In J. Bryant & D. Zillmann (Eds.), *Perspectives on media effects* (pp. 281-301). Hillsdale, NJ: Lawrence Erlbaum.

Rubin, A. M. (1993). Media uses and effects: A uses-and-gratifications perspective. In J. Bryant & D. Zillmann (Eds.), *Media effects: Advances in theory and research* (pp. 417-436). Hillsdale, NJ: Lawrence Erlbaum.

Rubin, A. M., Perse, E. M., & Powell, R. A. (1985). Loneliness, parasocial interaction, and local television news viewing. *Human Communication Research, 12*, 155-180.

Rule, B. G., & Ferguson, T. J. (1986). The effects of media violence on attitudes, emotions, and cognitions. *Journal of Social Issues, 42*, 29-50.

Schank, R., & Abelson, R. (1977). *Scripts, plans, goals and understanding*. Hillsdale, NJ: Lawrence Erlbaum.

Scott, R. P. (Producer), & LeClaire, C. (Director). (1978). *Faces of Death* [Film]. Gordon Video.

Shaye, R. (Producer), & Craven, W. (Director). (1985). *Nightmare on Elm Street* [Film]. Los Angeles: Media.

Sparks, G. (1986). Developing a scale to assess cognitive responses to frightening films. *Journal of Broadcasting and Electronic Media, 30*, 65-73.

Sparks, G. (1989). Understanding emotional reactions to a suspenseful movie: The interaction between forewarning and preferred coping style. *Communication Monographs, 56*, 325-340.

Sparks, G. (1991). The relationship between distress and delight in males' and females' reactions to frightening films. *Human Communication Research, 17*, 625-637.

Sparks, G., & Spirek, M. M. (1988). Individual differences in coping with stressful mass media: An activation-arousal view. *Human Communication Research, 15*, 195-216.

Stiff, J. B., Dillard, J. P., Somera, L., Kim, H., & Sleight, C. (1988). Empathy, communication, and prosocial behavior. *Communication Monographs, 55*, 198-213.

Tamborini, R. (1991). Responding to horror: Determinants of exposure and appeal. In J. Bryant & D. Zillmann (Eds.), *Responding to the screen* (pp. 305-328). Hillsdale, NJ: Lawrence Erlbaum.

Tamborini, R., & Mettler, J. A. (1990, November). *Emotional reactions to film: A model of empathic processes*. Paper presented at the meeting of the Speech Communication Association, Chicago, IL.

Tamborini, R., & Stiff, J. (1987). Predictors of horror film attendance and appeal: An analysis of the audience for frightening films. *Communication Research, 14*, 415-436.

Tamborini, R., Stiff, J., & Heidel, C. (1990). Predictors of horror film attendance and appeal: An analysis of the audience of frightening films. *Communication Research, 14*, 415-436.

Tamborini, R., Stiff, J., & Zillmann, D. (1987). Preference for graphic horror featuring male versus female victimization. *Human Communication Research, 13*, 529-552.

Tannenbaum, P. H. (1980). Entertainment as vicarious emotional experience. In P. H. Tannenbaum (Ed.), *The entertainment functions of television* (pp. 107-131). Hillsdale, NJ: Lawrence Erlbaum.

Tannenbaum, P. H., & Gaer, E. P. (1965). Mood change as a function of stress of protagonist and degree of identification in a film-viewing situation. *Journal of Personality and Social Psychology, 2*, 612-616.

Thomas, M. H. (1982). Physiological arousal, exposure to a lengthy aggressive film and aggressive behavior. *Journal of Research in Personality, 16*, 7-81.

Wober, J. M. (1986). The lens of television and the prism of personality. In J. Bryant & D. Zillmann (Eds.), *Perspective on media effects* (pp. 205-231). Hillsdale, NJ: Lawrence Erlbaum.

Wolpe, J., & Lang, P. J. (1964). A fear survey schedule for use in behavior therapy. *Behavior Research Therapy, 2*, 27-30.

Zaleski, Z. (1984). Sensation seeking and preference for emotional and visual stimuli. *Personality and Individual Differences, 5*, 609-611.

Zillmann, D. (1980). Anatomy of suspense. In P. H. Tannenbaum (Ed.), *The entertainment functions of television* (pp. 133-163). Hillsdale, NJ: Lawrence Erlbaum.

Zillmann, D. (1982). Television viewing and arousal. In D. Pearl, L. Bouthilet, & J. Lazar (Eds.), *Television and behavior: Ten years of scientific progress and implications for the eighties* (DHHS Publication No. ADM 82-1196, Vol. 2, pp. 53-67). Washington, DC: U.S. Government Printing Office.

552   HUMAN COMMUNICATION RESEARCH / June 1995

Zillmann, D. (1983). Arousal and aggression. In R. G. Geen & E. Donnerstein (Eds.), *Aggression: Theoretical and empirical reviews* (pp. 75-102). New York: Academic Press.

Zillmann, D. (1984). Transfer of excitation in emotional behavior. In J. T. Cacioppo & R. E. Petty (Eds.), *Socio psychophysiology* (pp. 215-240). New York: Guilford.

Zillmann, D., & Bryant, J. (1974). Effect of residual excitation on the emotional response to provocation and delayed aggressive behavior. *Journal of Personality and Social Psychology, 30,* 782-791.

Zillmann, D., & Bryant, J. (1985). Affect, mood, and emotion as determinants of selective exposure. In D. Zillmann & J. Bryant (Eds.), *Selective exposure to communication* (pp. 157-190). Hillsdale, NJ: Lawrence Erlbaum.

Zillmann, D., & Bryant, J. (1986). Exploring the entertainment experience. In J. Bryant & D. Zillmann (Eds.), *Perspectives on media effects* (pp. 303-324). Hillsdale, NJ: Lawrence Erlbaum.

Zillmann, D., & Bryant, J. (1993). Entertainment as media effect. In J. Bryant & D. Zillmann (Eds.), *Media effects: Advances in theory and research* (pp. 437-461). Hillsdale, NJ: Lawrence Erlbaum.

Zillmann, D., & Cantor, J. (1977). Affective responses to the emotions of a protagonist. *Journal of Experimental Social Psychology, 13,* 155-165.

Zillmann, D., Weaver, J. B., Mundorf, N., & Aust, C. F. (1986). Effects of an opposite-gender companion's affect to horror on distress, delight, and attraction. *Journal of Personality and Social Psychology, 51,* 586-594.

Zuckerman, M. (1971). Dimensions of sensation seeking. *Journal of Consulting and Clinical Psychology, 36,* 45-52.

Zuckerman, M. (1988). Behavior and biology: Research on sensation seeking and reactions to the media. In L. Donohew, H. E. Sypher, & E. T. Higgins (Eds.), *Communication, social cognition, and affect* (pp. 173-194). Hillsdale, NJ: Lawrence Erlbaum.

Zuckerman, M., & Little, P. (1986). Personality and curiosity about morbid and sexual events. *Personality and Individual Differences, 7,* 49-56.

[8]
Ideological Homicide

R.S. Ratner

I Introduction

Serial murder, or recreational killing according to its more figurative description, now occurs with enough frequency to suggest something more than a bizarre, passing anomaly. We are forced to contemplate why our society inculcates violence to such an extent that people will kill without apparent motive or remorse. The statistical rarity of the phenomenon[1] and the solitary commission of the act have made serial murder chiefly the metier of psychiatry and criminal psychology,[2] but its congruences with widely shared cultural values are becoming harder to ignore. Reports of serial killing are certainly increasing, though whether the 1984 FBI announcement of an epidemic in such offences was exaggerated is difficult to determine since, as Egger states, the actual extent and prevalence of serial murder "is as yet unknown" (1990:29). The probability that serial murder researchers exceed the actual number of offenders attests to both the natural intrigue of the phenomenon and to the exponential drive for knowledge, especially where fears of individual security are concerned. Of course, attraction to the subject may be voyeuristically impelled (study of the ultimate perversion as it were); nevertheless, it deserves scrutiny, not as criminological exotica but in order to better understand patterns of violence that threaten to engulf us all.

Up to now, the study of serial killers has been conducted primarily through the medium of the psychodynamic approach,[3] usually exploring some combination of organic and environmental factors (Norris, 1988). The psychiatric categories of psychopath (Hare and Forth, 1922; Egger, 1990, ch.4) and antisocial personality type (Levin and Fox, 1985, ch.14) have strongly influenced psychological profiling, prediction scaling and court testimony. Typical profiles of serial killers have been constructed (e.g., Leyton, 1983) but, as yet, they have only rudimentary value for purposes of detection since thousands of individuals share the same general profile. Moreover, while serial killers are markedly different from non-offenders in some behavioural areas, they act much like normals most of the time. The preponderant similarities suggest the need for an approach that examines serial murder as expressive of, rather than alien to, mainstream culture; as perhaps, prototypical rather than atypical. At the same time, any such perspective would have to explain why it is that although millions are exposed to a roughly similar cultural programme, only a very small number become serial killers. Such attempts to address the issue at the level of cultural context (Holmes and DeBurger, 1988, ch.2) and social construction (Hickey, 1991, ch.4) have commenced, but it is my contention that these forays will prove insufficient until the understanding of serial murder is connected to the analysis of ideology. In the remainder of this essay I will attempt to underscore that relation and present the basis for a sociological interpretation of serial murder that can also incorporate psychodynamic research findings.

II Serial Murder as Ideological Homicide

What engages the sociologist about the subject of serial murder is not its alleged atypicality but the glimpse it affords of problems endemic in society. Could this highly singular phenomenon nevertheless signify something important about the abstract workings of ideological hegemony, i.e., the attempts, in and by ideology, of a dominant group to secure the consent and adhesion of subordinate groups to a world view favourable to its own interests? At first glance one is unlikely to query whether serial murder has anything at all to do with reinforcing or undermining capitalistic hegemony. To begin, however, what may seem an unusual line of enquiry, there is nothing contentious about viewing homicide as ideological if we presume that all acts are, at bottom, ideological.[4] As Marx observed, in whatever we do within society, we are all the trager or carriers of the social relations of production. Moreover, ideology is pervasive because people cannot act without rules of conduct, without orientations. Ideology, according to Althusser, is "indispensable in every society in order to shape men, to transform them and enable them to respond to the exigencies of existence" (1969:235). Thus, ideology is integral to the constitution of social life; it is the "social cement" through which human beings live as conscious objects within the daily totality of social relations (Giddens, 1979:179).

Setting aside this broader definition, we can recognize instances of what may be called "ideological homicide" when people kill on behalf of a belief or conviction, such as in cases of treason or insurrection.[5] In such cases the meaning of the concept is transparent. But there are more complex instances in which the ideological strain towards homicide is less apparent but nevertheless real. In Durkheim's formulation we have the conceptual basis for this more obscure form of ideological homicide. In describing anomic suicide, Durkheim writes that it "results from man's activity lacking regulation, and his consequent sufferings" (1955:258). Do we not find resonances of this concept (converted to the notion of anomic homicide) in the sociological problem of malintegrated cultural goals and institutionalized means so insightfully schematized by Robert Merton over a half-century ago[6] and aptly applied to the phenomenon of serial murder in Elliot Leyton's *Hunting Humans* (1986)?

I am arguing, therefore, for the necessity of situating serial murder ideologically in both the wider generic sense intended by Althusser and the inverted sense intended by Marx — as congruent (or incongruent) with the dominant hegemonic ideology reproduced within a web of institutions, social relations and ideas that obscure class predominance. Both usages mirror the paramount reality of capitalist society — that its hegemony must be constructed within an ideological grid that stabilizes relations of inequality and incorporates subordinated classes. Tolerable life-patterns must be constructed across the class hierarchy, which domesticate potential dissidence and which relieve failure and frustration in the dominant economic sphere. Yet whatever cautions are invoked, there remain blueprint failures — the deviant modes of adaptation sketched by Merton, yielding individuals sometimes unassimilable within the dominant hegemonic order and threatening its stability.

Returning to the immediate focus, our interest is in determining whether serial murder represents an instance of "ideological leakage," a shredding of the net, that "fabric of hegemony" (as Gramsci termed it) coming unspun and throwing into doubt the assumption of a regulated social order. The research literature, as previously noted, draws little attention to analysis of the phenomenon at this ideological level, although some concern is incipient in the characterizations of families as "crucibles of malformed identity" (Leyton, 1983:106), sources of "traumatization" (Hickey, 1991:65-73) and, more generally, "cradles of violence." While not articulating the links between ideological superstructure and family sub-systems, these studies clearly indicate that families of serial killers typically fail as carriers of cultural solutions. Although premature from the standpoint of confirmatory research, it may be useful, even at this early stage, to hypothesize the main trajectory along which ideological and family relations intersect in the lives of serial killers. Minimally, this offers a starting framework with which to organize ongoing research and suggest grounds for reconceptualization.

1. Ideological themes (especially those regarding wealth and power) linking the wider social order and the sub-cultural orders are inadequately fostered, regulated and sustained.

2. Social inequality tension-points (embedded in gender, race and class) are aggravated by the absence/erosion of ideological controls.[7]

3. Interpersonal relations are de-stabilized. The most vulnerable receptors of this disjointed state are children in ideologically dysfunctioning families who suffer flagrant abuse and neglect.

4. Such abuse/neglect is partially eroticized by the child as the only available means of rationalizing maltreatment and maintaining some form of necessary emotional contact.[8]

5. Since the abuse/neglect trauma cannot be understood or appropriately compartmentalized by the child, it must be repressed or anaesthetized. The deadening of emotion achieves pain reduction. Sociopathy — or excessive compartmentalization — is the long-term consequence.

6. Later expression of the repressed content is inevitable. Scripted eroticized violence becomes the means for cataclysmic fulfillment of long-cultivated fantasies. Overwhelming power asymmetries are symbolically neutralized and avenged; serial murder is the result.[9]

Implicit in the above is the argument that serial murder results from an ideological double illusion. The primary illusion is one to which all subordinated classes are ordinarily subject. The social inequalities generated by the capitalist mode of production reflect irresolvable contradictions that are concealed by ideological practices. In Marxian terms, this entails the cultural production of false consciousness among those classes for whom compliance with bourgeois hegemony is problematic. Under normal circumstances, the available stock of ideological distortions is adequate to ensure the reproduction of class hegemony. When regulatory controls break down, however, through increased hardships, sudden affluence, media provocation, etc., cultural codes harmonizing class goals and individual aspirations are no longer efficiently transmitted through weakened family units. Solutions to dire predicaments are sought through a second order of illusion, one based on individual fantasy rather than hegemonic manipulation, but which caricatures the latter and exploits the cultural inventory of valued goals/objects in terrifying asocial form. When, therefore, institutionalized ideological controls become inoperative, should we be surprised that a more idiosyncratic brand of illusion, bereft of scruples, is the result?

III Serial Murder and Bourgeois Hegemony

I have suggested that serial murder may be understood as one form of ideological displacement — however rare and macabre — stemming from asymmetrical power relations that can no longer be legitimately processed within certain family settings. Some victims of these regulatory breakdowns take flight in compensatory killings, which, as purely psychic solutions, conceal and misrepresent the real social contradictions that instigated the dilemma, which they were unable to address. Captive humans, reconceived within a narcissistic symbology of ritual possession, defilement and disposal, afford brief vengeance against the rejecting family/society.

As audience to these atrocities, we are appalled by the perverted manner of domination but entranced by the perverse will to dominate. Does serial murder, therefore, re-certify the dominant hegemony by its lurid apotheosis of power, or do its gruesome excesses bare a deeply flawed hegemony that must finally be renounced?

The paradoxical meaning of the phenomenon was astutely portrayed by Stuart Ewen in his analysis of the Charles Manson murders.

> Manson's occult unification of sensuality and death ... making love on one hand and lending 'sensuality' to the crime in the ritualization of murder, confronts people for whom sensuality has been commodified into violence, within the grievous rationality of their own lives. What stands between the legitimate partaker in sex-violence and Manson may be little more than an economic-political-rational structure which damns the one and celebrates the other .... Manson is acting out all of the myths that societies which are formulated on unfreedom create about freedom, about 'human nature', without the safeguards of controlling authority ... outside of the operational terminology of technological capitalist society. (1972: 35-36)

The bourgeois vision of utopia, expressed through the Manson murders, is attractive because it represents "a world of 'freedom' without restraints," but in Manson's barbarism we are reminded that freedom is dangerous, that such a utopia is intolerable and a threat to social order, and that "it is better to live in a world of law and order (even if these laws and that order inculcate sex-violence in restricted and socialized form) than in a world where 'freedom reigns'" (Ewen, 1972: 39). Thus, the impulse towards sensual fulfillment, fused with aggression, is a utopia we dare not practice, and the justice meted out to its satanic exponents is "...society's ritualized reminder that society is more dependable than utopia, albeit the vision of utopia conjured up to tantalize people through the authoritarian maze" (Ewen, 1972: 42).

We strike a delicate balance, therefore, between suppression and enticement of serial murder, sundering the constraints of bourgeois hegemony precisely in order to re-secure its dominance. But this homoeostatic function of serial murder can be overdrawn. As with other regulatory controls, its effects can be unpredictable and treacherous for the maintenance of bourgeois hegemony. Indeed, it must be asked whether there is not a limit to ideological stabilization capacities within societies marked by growing relations of inequality, and whether families can be expected to buffer the contradictions of capitalist society once ideological resources are spent or ground into irrelevance.[10]

What, then, is the role of the media in exploiting the drama of serial murder in the interest of bourgeois hegemony? Given that crime is a media staple, and that murder remains a primal topic, tabloid journalism knows almost no bounds on the subject of serial murder, particularly as sales increase and profits roll in. But what are the implications of public curiosity and the absence of regulation over journalists who see themselves in the business of titillation and who are also seeking individual celebrity status? Does the coverage of serial murder place us all on the same spectrum with serial killers, showing that what they covet are only widely shared cultural goals (lust, power, greed)? To what extent do the media depictions of women as available sex objects encourage serial killers to believe that women exist solely in order to gratify their bizarre fantasies?[11] The virtual glorification of serial killers in the film media[12] has also done little more than replay the confusion between normal and pathological currents in mass culture, leaving viewers with a disturbing yen for the unbounded freedoms of the bourgeois utopia. Nor can the imprinting of the faces of serial killers on trading cards sold to children be dismissed as mere commercialism, since the association of serial murder with youthful recreation may be preparatory to involvement.

But public indulgence can also shift to bafflement, fright and indignation, calling for a profound interrogation. What does it mean to wind up like that in this society? How is this person formed by us? By this community? He's a human being! Why him and not me/us? Such questions lead away from troubling ambivalence to dispassionate analysis of the causes of split families, the scale of domestic violence and the effects of abuse and neglect. Indeed, this debate is beginning to take place, opening out alternatives to sensationalist and politically conservative media agendas.[13]

So there is great potential for the media to provide unequivocal evidence of the problems in society, to expose the rage, alienation and loneliness that drive individuals to the depths of serial murder, to spread awareness about the warning signs, and to help break the domestic abuse cycle, if only by informing chronic victims about where and how they can take refuge. Whether the media take up these challenges must not depend on "What sells?" — although that is currently the chief modus operandi.

IV Conclusion

That the mass media do reinforce class dominance is everywhere evident, so there are certainly grounds for pessimism. But if we have not lost the capacity to recognize and react to problems, if we are not merely the carriers of self-reproducing structures, and if we do not, ourselves, expect to join the celebration of violence, then little that occurs in our society can escape scrutiny, least of all serial murder.

Studying serial killers is important because it informs us about what makes human beings people, and how society can expose people to degradation. First and foremost, this project requires that we study the family unit, which, as presently constituted, is ill-suited to our social structure, often incubating pathologies of which serial murder is the most notorious example. But larger social institutions cannot be left unexamined. We must pursue a critique of the forces that shape everyday life and of the ideological relations that link public and private realms.[14] Egger's proposed research agenda for serial murder (1990:211-213) makes no mention of the need to study serial murder in ideological context. Perhaps the topic of bourgeois hegemony seems too grandiose for criminological investigation. I believe that serial murder can be understood only by adopting this focus.

Endnotes

1   While only two to three per cent of all North American homicide victims share the same killer, the number of unsolved homicides is rising (approximately 5000 per year in the U.S.), suggesting more stranger-to-stranger killings. Estimates of the number of serial killers now at large in the U.S. range from 30 to 250. In Canada, estimates range from 5 to 30. It is interesting to note that the police search for the Green River Killer in Seattle, Washington identified over 10,000 suspects, 1000 of whom merited detailed investigation. These figures, and other information reported in this article, are based on a review of the research literature, journalistic accounts and interviews conducted with police in Vancouver and Seattle, RCMP, journalists and lawyers involved in serial killer cases and research.

2   Leyton (1983:98) noted that the little attention the subject had received from the academic community was "overwhelmingly non-sociological."

3   The forensic psychiatric approach is epitomized by Helen Morrison who writes, "the evidence shows that the killer's impairment is fixed by the end of the first year of life. As an infant, the future serial murderer cannot develop the ability to differentiate himself into a separate, distinct personality" (1991:9).

4   The reader will note that I am not using the very restrictive definition of "ideology" employed by Leyton in his keynote address at the Windsor conference ("a closed system of thought impervious to argument").

5   So labelled by Stephen Schafer (1971) as the "convictional criminal" — those who have a conviction of the justice of their cause and assume that only the commission of a criminal, even homicidal act, can promote it.

6   I am of course referring to Merton's classic article, "Social Structure and Anomie" (1938).

7   Interestingly, Jenkins (1988) notes that "waves" of multiple murders in the U.S. occurred in the 1910s-1930s, and more recently beginning in the 1970s. These are two periods in U.S. history subject to massive economic de-stabilization (rising affluence and decline), which, to follow Durkheim, can be seen as "anomic" periods involving a loss of ideological controls.

8   Widom (1989), in reviewing studies of the "violence breeds violence" hypothesis, concluded that the pathway from child to parental abuse is neither straight nor certain. Obviously, detailed exploration of serial killers' family backgrounds will answer the question for this particular group of offenders. Most case studies, thus far, point to a link.

9   Surprisingly, Morrison (1991:8) writes, "A serial killer may complain that he was abused as a child, either physically or sexually. Little or no evidence has demonstrated, however, that these complaints are consistent or that the alleged abuses have any real foundation. These claims could result from the disintegrating psychological state that is so characteristic of a serial killer." This assertion is radically inconsistent with the growing number of case studies developed by competent researchers about the lives of serial killers.

10   In a macabre twist, motivational commitment to the "system" was worn thin for the families of Clifford Olson's victims when the provincial government in British Columbia agreed to a $100,000 payoff (a trust fund to Olson's wife and child) in order to obtain Olson's help in locating the bodies of the children he had raped, tortured and slain (Mulgrew, 1990).

11 Paralleling this effect is the psychological resignation exhibited by women and other victimized groups who knowingly place themselves at risk, suggesting, in some instances, that they are awaiting pick-up.

12 The film, *Silence of the Lambs*, lionized psychopathic killers in the person of Hannibal Lecter, who was portrayed as super-human, awarded the film's punchline and allowed to escape to a tropical island. This, we may surmise, presumably with some hint of envy, is "justice" in the bourgeois utopia.

13 Commenting on the British journalistic scene, Soothill and Walby (1991:156) note, "While for feminists male sexual violence is quite common, and a wide social solution is necessary to give women real security, the conservative response suggests that it is the product of a few sex fiends, and that the solution is to lock them away for a long time. The evidence does not support the view that sex crime is a rare phenomenon caused by a handful of sex monsters, nor is the preferred solution of most rape victims that of long prison sentences. But such evidence is not welcome in the press."

14 As one of my respondents put it, "Our society is far too materialistic. People believe that money is everything. Everyone is too selfish. The family unit suffers — the children suffer — and the product of that family unit is anyone's guess."

References

Althusser, Louis. 1969. *For Marx*. London: Allen Lane.

Durkheim, Emile. 1951. *Suicide: A Study in Sociology*. London: The Free Press.

Egger, Steven A. 1990. *Serial Murder: An Elusive Phenomenon*. New York: Praeger.

Ewan, Stuart. 1972. "Charlie Manson and the Family: Authoritarianism and the Bourgeois Conception of 'Utopia': Some Thoughts on Charlie Manson and the Fantasy of the Id." *Working Papers in Cultural Studies* 3: 33-45.

Giddens, Anthony. 1979. *Central Problems in Social Theory*. Berkley, California: University of California Press.

Hare, Robert D. and E. Adelle Forth. 1992. "Psychopathy and Crime across the Lifespan." In R. Peters, R. McMahon and V. Quinney (eds.), *Aggression and Violence Across the Lifespan*. Newbury Park, California: Sage.

Hickey, Eric. 1991. *Serial Murderers and Their Victims*. Pacific Grove, California: Brooks/Cole Publishing Co.

Holmes, Ronald and James DeBurger. 1988. *Serial Murder*. Newbury Park, California: Sage.

Jenkins, Philip. 1988. "Serial Murder in England: 1940-1985." *Journal of Criminal Justice* 16: 1-15.

Levin, Jack and James Alan Fox. 1985. *Mass Murder: America's Growing Menace*. New York: Plenum Press.

Leyton, Elliott. 1983. "A Social Profile of Sexual Mass Murderers." In Tom Fleming and Livy Visano (eds.), *Deviance Designations: Crime, Law, and Deviance in Canada*, pp. 98-107. Toronto: Butterworths.

Leyton, E. 1986. *Hunting Humans*. Toronto: McClelland and Stewart.

Merton, Robert K. 1938. "Social Structure and Anomie." *American Sociological Review* 3: 672-682.

Morrison, Helen. 1991. *Serial Killers and Murderers*. Publications International Ltd.: Lincolnwood, Illinois.

Mulgrew, Ian. 1990. *Final Payoff*. Seal Books: Toronto.

Norris, Joel. 1988. *Serial Killers*. New York: Anchor Books, Doubleday.

Schafer, Stephen. 1971. "The Concept of the Political Criminal." *The Journal of Criminal Law, Criminology, and Police Science* 62(3): 380-387.

Soothill, Keith and Sylvia Walby. 1991. *Sex Crime in the News*. London: Routledge.

Widom, Cathy Spatz. 1989. "Does Violence Beget Violence? A Critical Examination of the Literature." *Psychological Bulletin* 106(1): 3-28.

Part III
Criminological Analysis

[9]

Criminal Justice Review
Volume 17, Number 1, Spring 1992

A MURDER "WAVE"?
TRENDS IN AMERICAN SERIAL HOMICIDE
1940-1990

Philip Jenkins

This study employs a historical and quantitative analysis to test the widespread suggestion that serial murder activity in the United States has increased dramatically since the late 1960s. The crime of serial murder appears to have occurred infrequently between 1940 and 1964, but a rapid acceleration is observable from about 1965. The rate of increase far exceeds the general upsurge in violent crime that occurred about that time. Also, the growth in activity cannot be explained simply in terms of changes in recording or reporting practices. In explaining the transition, particular emphasis is placed on factors such as demographic structure and aspects of the "youth culture" of the 1960s. It is also tentatively suggested that changes in the mental health system may have played an important role.

It is widely agreed that the frequency of serial murder in the contemporary United States is very high in comparison with similar societies, and probably in relation to most historical periods as well (Egger, 1990; Jenkins, 1988; Levin & Fox, 1985; Lindsey, 1984; Newton, 1990). It is common to write of an American "wave" of serial murder that began in the late 1960s. Murder sprees and serial homicide careers were by no means new in the 1960s, but events of this sort seemed to begin occurring with greater frequency and severity, establishing a macabre trend that continues unabated. Holmes and DeBurger (1988) have suggested a surge in "multicide" dating from about 1960. Norris (1988) comments, "Since 1960 not only have the number of individual serial killers increased but so have the number of victims per killer, and the level of savagery of the individual crimes themselves" (p. 19). Leyton (1986) suggests that reported acts of multiple homicide in the United States were 10 or 12 times more frequent after the 1960s than before. On a related topic, Fox has remarked that 1966 marked "the onset of the age of mass murder" (quoted in "Experts Say," 1988, p. A3).

However widespread it may be, perceptions of an "epidemic" leave a number of unanswered questions about the reality of the phenomenon and its causation. First, recent conditions are not without parallel in American history; in an earlier study, it was suggested that serial homicide little below the present scale and frequency did in fact occur in the United States in the early twentieth century, between about 1900 and 1940 (Jenkins, 1989). On the other hand, repeat homicide appears to have become much rarer between about 1940 and 1965. This is a matter of some importance for our understanding of recent developments. If the frequency of serial murder activity fell in midcentury and then increased sharply during the 1960s, this suggests that this type of crime is connected to wider social conditions that require explanation. We might explore factors that affect the prevalence of extremely violent behavior, the nature of criminal justice responses, or the availability of a victim population. Alternatively, we might hypothesize that apparent changes in multiple homicide merely reflect fashions in recording or reporting rather than substantive changes in behavior; the increase of reported cases from the late 1960s onwards would thus reflect new perceptions by the police or the mass media, and the "wave" might be a myth or an artificial construct.

Whichever approach proves more accurate, the historical study of serial murder offers significant theoretical lessons. It is particularly useful for examining the constructionist approach in sociology, which stresses that social problems are rarely as novel as they sometimes appear (Best, 1989, 1990). In this view, behaviors such as the use of violence against children or the elderly are endemic in society, but they ultimately come to be perceived and defined as new problems with names such as "child abuse" and "elder abuse." The task of the sociologist is to determine the social, political, and bureaucratic forces that lead to this new recognition and definition and to identify the claims-makers who shape the debate. A constructionist approach would favor the view that serial murder activity remained high throughout the century but that the phenomenon was only recognized (or rediscovered) in the mid-1960s. If indeed these years marked a real and significant increase of the behavior itself, this would provide an important exception to the constructionist model.

If there was a real and sudden growth in multiple homicide after 1960, then explaining it offers a challenge for sociologists and criminologists, and it is disappointing that so few of the current accounts have attempted a systematic explanation. One notable exception is that of Leyton (1986), who presents an ambitious chapter entitled "Towards an Historical Sociology of Multiple Murder." Leyton accepts the idea of a surge, which is attributed to the changing life opportunities of certain social groups and classes. The growing closure of avenues of opportunity in the 1960s led some to frustration and to consequent outbursts of violent protest, of which multiple murder was one dramatic manifestation. The theory may or may not have substance, but at least it attempts to place the observed phenomenon in a context of known social theory. It also marks a vital shift away from the largely individualistic and psychodynamic explanations that have long dominated the analysis of multiple homicide. An authentic increase in serial murder in the 1960s would have significance for policy makers no less than academics. Understanding the social context of offenders such as Ted Bundy or John Wayne Gacy might provide an opportunity for intervention, with the goal of removing or reducing the factors that promote this sort of crime.

These questions can only be answered by tracing the frequency of serial murder in the United States over a lengthy period before and after the apparent upsurge in offenses in the mid-1960s. Obviously there are major methodological difficulties in such an endeavor, and a comprehensive history would be impossible. However, it will be argued that the resources do exist for an admittedly tentative account that favors the objectivist approach to this problem. It will be argued that serial homicide was indeed rare in midcentury and has become much more frequent in recent years. This change will be explained chiefly in terms of the weakening of social control mechanisms from the mid-1960s onwards.

METHODOLOGY

The most important stage of this research involved compiling a list of all serial murder cases recorded in the United States between 1940 and 1990. Each case involved an offender associated with the killing of at least four victims over a period greater than 72 hours. Excluded were cases in which the offender acted primarily out of political motives or in quest of financial profit. Organized and professional criminal activity was thus excluded, although this limitation would not be accepted by all researchers. Of course, the list cannot include cases that did not come to the attention of law enforcement or in which neither the police nor the media recognized a linkage in a series of homicides. Also, the exact number of cases in a particular series is a highly controversial subject.

The issue of "association" poses a large and probably insurmountable problem. It is rare for any serial killer to be formally charged and convicted in all the cases in which he or she is a strong suspect, and we thus have to rely on much less certain evidentiary criteria to assess the real number of victims. In one well-known case, Ted Bundy was executed in 1989 for a murder committed in Florida, and the same state had tried and sentenced him for only two other homicides, but it has been suggested that Bundy was guilty of anywhere from 25 to 100 other murders across the United States. In the present study, an individual was included if law enforcement and mainstream media sources consistently reported that the offender was believed to be implicated in four or more deaths. Clearly this evidence is far from satisfactory, especially where it is based on confessions. Confessions might be a major source in some cases, but there are many factors that could lead a suspect to portray his or her criminal activity as either more or less serious than it truly was. It is also likely that media and police estimates are sometimes exaggerated or simply wrong, but such a reputational approach is perhaps the only means of proceeding in such a contentious area.

Cases were compiled from three major sources. The first involved three well-indexed and authoritative newspapers, the *New York Times*, *Los*

4   *Philip Jenkins*

Angeles Times, and *Chicago Tribune*. This material was supplemented from a variety of secondary sources on serial murder (Brian, 1986; Gaute & Odell, 1979; Wilson & Pitman, 1984; Wilson & Seaman, 1983), which have been fully listed in two earlier articles (Jenkins, 1988, 1989). Finally, a number of references were acquired from Michael Newton's recent "encyclopaedia" of serial murder, *Hunting Humans* (1990; compare Newton, 1988), an important source that requires discussion. Unfortunately, the book lacks a scholarly apparatus, and sources are cited only very generally, but the author's use of those sources is cautious and scholarly.

Hunting Humans is by far the most comprehensive available listing of serial murder cases, incorporating the vast majority of references that were found in the search of media and secondary sources. In fact, one of the major criticisms that can be levied against the book is that it is overcomprehensive, including many cases with only two or three reported victims. Although there are omissions—including some spectacular cases such as that of Stephen Nash—Newton has provided an excellent basis for the analysis of trends in American serial murder. (Less confidence can be placed in the book's reliability for other nations.) Combined with the evidence of newspapers and secondary sources, Newton's work permits the compilation of a thorough list of the reported serial murder cases of the last half-century.

CHANGES IN REPORTING PRACTICE

It thus becomes crucial to ask whether the rate of reporting was fairly constant over time. If a study of media sources in the 1940s or 1950s produces far fewer cases than can be found in the 1980s, can it be safely assumed that this reflects a change in the frequency of the offense, or might it simply reflect changes in the practices and interests of the mass media? There is some evidence that metropolitan papers such as the *New York Times* and *Los Angeles Times* did expand their coverage of regional news from the 1950s onwards. This arose not from changes in the marketing or journalistic practices of those particular papers but from wider changes in the newspaper industry as a whole.[1]

From the 1950s, local newspapers were increasingly likely to form part of large chains or corporate groupings, and those chains themselves grew from statewide or regional concerns to national status. About 29 percent of American newspapers were owned by chains in 1960, compared to 63 percent in 1988 (Gaziano, 1989). In the same period, the proportion of chains that were national in scope rose from 11 percent to 33 percent. One

---

[1] I am grateful to Dr. Daniel W. Pfaff of the School of Communications at Pennsylvania State University for discussions about the changing nature of regional press coverage in recent decades.

consequence of this was that stories that were of any sensational value were less likely to be confined to a purely local market and more likely to be disseminated throughout the chain. Stories would thus reach a national audience and would be picked up (or at least referred to) by other major journals such as the *New York Times*. As the trend towards chain ownership was most marked in the late 1960s, it is possible that the increased reporting of serial murder might, in part, reflect a growing "nationalization" of news.

On the other hand, this would not in itself be a sufficient explanation for any perceived changes. Throughout the century, major serial murder cases have usually been viewed as stories of great journalistic interest, and between about 1900 and 1940 the *New York Times* reported extensively and enthusiastically on serial murder cases as far afield as Colorado, Iowa, Alaska, and South Dakota. There is no reason to believe that media practices or public taste changed suddenly during the 1940s. Even so, the danger of overlooking cases prior to the 1960s is reduced by using Newton's *Hunting Humans*, which draws on regional and local newspaper files from no fewer than 25 states: papers such as the *Eagle-Beacon* of Wichita, Kansas; the *Daily News* of Anchorage, Alaska; and the *Clarion-Ledger* of Jackson, Mississippi. Even a search as wide as this apparently failed to find a large number of midcentury cases that escaped the attention of the major metropolitan press.

Also, newspapers, magazines, and books in midcentury all devoted abundant attention to spectacular crimes such as multiple homicide when they did occur, and this suggests that public interest remained high throughout the period. Magazines on the lines of *True Crime* and *True Detective* were popular. Moreover, cases that might seem comparatively minor or commonplace today would have received enormous attention in terms of column inches in the newspapers or in numbers of published books. Some of the most celebrated and widely discussed cases of these years involved three or four victims, as with Harvey Glatman, William Heirens, and Charles Howard Schmid, whereas modern studies tend to focus on extreme serial cases that claim 10 or 20 casualties. The suggestion is that, if more cases had occurred in earlier years, they would have been reported at length. If a case like that of Ted Bundy had occurred in, say, the early 1950s, it is hard to believe that its sensationalistic potential would have been overlooked.

It might also be suggested that cases were as likely to be reported in midcentury but that police agencies interpreted crimes differently before announcing their conclusions to the media. One possible hypothesis would be that a police agency arresting a suspect in the late 1940s might be slow to investigate his involvement in a series of crimes over many years in a number of states, whereas the agency's modern counterparts would be more familiar with patterns of serial homicide and would thus tend to speculate with greater freedom. Modern agencies also have superior record-keeping techniques and more experience of interagency cooperation, enhancing the likelihood that a suspect could be linked to a large number of earlier offenses.

This view is superficially attractive, but the contrast with earlier eras is too sharply drawn. Between 1900 and 1940, American police agencies often demonstrated their familiarity with the concept of serial murder and pursued investigations accordingly, so that such offenders were frequently detected and apprehended. Investigators traced the earlier movements of suspects and attempted to link them with crimes in other jurisdictions as a matter of course. There is no evidence that police agencies at midcentury were any less aware of these issues and problems, especially in the aftermath of widely publicized affairs such as the Cleveland torso murders of the 1930s (Nickel, 1989). In 1941, police from several states interrogated the newly arrested multiple murderer Jarvis Catoe in an attempt to link him with crimes in their jurisdictions (Newton, 1990). Moreover, the attention that focused on the "sex maniac" in the 1950s ensured that police and media were continually aware of the possibility that a sexually motivated attack might well be one of a lengthy series.

The reported cases analyzed below can only represent a portion of the real total, but apparent changes over time do not simply reflect differences in police or media reactions to homicide. A significant growth in the number of reported incidents is likely to reflect a real change in the frequency of the behavior itself.

THE FREQUENCY OF SERIAL HOMICIDE 1940-1990

On first impressions, it seems that serial murder in the 1940s and 1950s followed patterns that are quite familiar from more recent years. The actions of a multiple homicide such as Melvin D. Rees, for example, closely resemble those of sex-killers of the 1980s, especially those who operated on or near college campuses. Rees raped and killed a Maryland woman in 1957 and massacred a family of four in Virginia in 1959. He was also believed to have carried out four other "sex-slayings" near the University of Maryland. Equally "modern" in character was the case of Jake Bird, a drifter who killed two women in Washington state in 1947. When arrested, Bird confessed to more than 40 homicides in the previous decade, with confirmed offenses recorded in Illinois, Kentucky, Nebraska, South Dakota, Ohio, Florida, and Wisconsin. The reconstruction of his travels and crimes bears obvious resemblances to the investigations of more recent itinerant killers such as Henry Lee Lucas and Gerald Stano, and Stephen Nash of California resembles homosexual killers of later years.

And yet these resemblances can be misleading. There were serial killers of this sort, but they were far fewer than in more recent years. Between

1940 and 1969, there were a maximum of 49 serial murder cases recorded in the United States, and the real number might be smaller. Between 1970 and 1990, there was an absolute minimum of 187. An acceleration of activity is therefore indicated, and the change can be dated with some precision. The figures can be broken down into three periods: the age of very low serial murder rates between 1940 and 1964; a transitional period between 1965 and 1969; and the "murder wave" since 1970.

For the era between 1940 and 1964, Newton cites about 50 American cases of serial murder. This total is substantially reduced when cases with fewer than four victims are excluded. Several of the remainder should also be dismissed because of the clear profit motive underlying the offenses, which brings the crimes into the realm of organized fraud or professional criminal activity; examples include the cases of Alfred Cline, Louise Peete, Martha Beck, and Raymond Fernandez, as well as the medical rackets of Roland E. Clark.

According to these criteria, there remain about 30 cases for the whole 25-year period (see Table 1). Of that total, 7 are believed to be "extreme" cases involving eight or more victims. (These offenders were Jake Bird, Albert DeSalvo, Jarvis Catoe, Nannie Doss, Stephen Nash, Melvin Rees, and Charlie Starkweather.) This is assuredly not a comprehensive list of cases, even of those cases that came to the notice of the media or the authorities, but the sources consulted would have recorded any case that attained even limited or short-lived notoriety. The list of extreme cases is more likely to be valid, as these phenomena were especially likely to draw regional or national attention.

This is not a large number of incidents for a 25-year period, and a list of even this length can be achieved only by bending the criteria somewhat. It is by no means certain that Ed Gein killed as many as four people, although some sources have estimated far higher figures, and Gary Krist's inclusion here is particularly tenuous. Several of the cases also involved at least partial motives of profit and property crime and thus might be excluded. In terms of motivation, these 30 cases can be classified according to the following typologies:

1. **Lust murders**, that is, murders clearly associated with rape, sexual abuse, or perversion: 11 cases (Catoe, DeSalvo, Edwards, Floyd, Gein, Hill, the Illinois child murders, the "Moonlight Murderer," Morse, Nash, Rees).

2. **Irrational or "berserk" murders**, where one or more individuals embark on a killing spree without apparent motive. Property crime might be tangentially involved, but the violence used is wholly disproportionate to the encounter: 9 cases (Bird, Cook, Delage, Krist, McManus, Searl, the "Sidney Sniper," Starkweather, York and Latham).

3. Murders predominantly associated with **property crimes** such as robbery and burglary: 5 cases (Brown and Kelly, Hall, Hickson, Taborsky, Whitney).

8   *Philip Jenkins*

4. **Poison murders,** committed at least partly for financial motive: 4 cases (Archerd, Doss, Lyles, Martin).

5. **Other cases**: 1. (From this group, the Dudley and Gwyn case defies classification. This involved a couple killing six of their children over a prolonged period by a combination of abuse, violence, and conscious neglect.)

Table 1

Serial Murder Cases 1940-1964

Name	Dates active
Clarence Hill	1938-1941
Jarvis Catoe	1939-1941
Nannie Doss	1920s-1954
Jake Bird	1942-1947
Charles Floyd	1942-1949
James Waybern Hall	1945
Monroe Hickson	1946
the "Moonlight Murderer"	1946
Kenneth Dudley and Irene Gwyn	1946-1961
Rhonda B. Martin	1940s-1950s
William Dale Archerd	1947-1966
William Cook	1950-1951
Joseph Taborsky and Arthur Culombe	1951-1956
Frederick E. McManus	1953
Mack Ray Edwards	1953-1970
Anjette Donovan Lyles	1950s
Ed Gein	1954-1957
the Illinois child murders	1955-1957
Melvin D. Rees	1956-1959
Stephen Nash	1950s
Charlie Starkweather and Caril Ann Fugate	1958
George York and James Latham	1959
Hugh Bion Morse	1959
Dennis Whitney	1960
Richard Delage	1960-1975
Charles N. Brown and Charles E. Kelly	1961
Gary S. Krist	1961-1964
Albert DeSalvo	1962-1964
the "Sidney Sniper"	early 1960s
Ralph Ray Searl	1964

These categories cannot be regarded as hard and fast, and other observers might find little to distinguish between the cases in groups 2 and 3. On the other hand, this confirms once again that serial murder as such was uncommon in these years, and "pure" serial murder—lust murder or "berserk" and irrational crime—was especially rare. The limited number of cases makes it extremely difficult to discuss multiple homicide rates, except to say that this type of offense represented a tiny fraction of all murders. The relative lack of cases in midcentury contrasts dramatically with the experience of more recent years. Between 1970 and 1990, there was a minimum of 187 cases, 94 of which were "extreme" in the sense of involving eight or more victims. This number could easily be expanded by including other cases with strong links to robbery or professional crime.

In summary, between 1940 and 1964 a serial murder case was recorded every 10 months or so on average, and an "extreme" case every 43 months. Between 1971 and 1990 a serial case could be expected to emerge in the media every 39 days, and an extreme case every 77 days. By this coarse measure, serial murder cases overall can be seen to have been 8 times as likely in the later period as in the earlier, and extreme cases were reported more than 16 times as frequently. The conclusion seems inescapable: Serial murder has become far more frequent in recent years, and offenders tend to kill larger numbers of victims.

SERIAL HOMICIDE IN THE LITERATURE

The relative scarcity of serial murder in midcentury is confirmed by an examination of the contemporary literature on homicide and violent crime. The dominant intellectual trend of this period within criminology was psychiatric and psychoanalytic, and there was considerable interest in the life histories of strange or bizarre offenders who might illustrate unusual aspects of the human mind (Cassity, 1941; Catton, 1940). In addition, public concern about sex offenders and "sex psychopaths" led to widespread legislative action. In 1955, Tappan suggested that in popular mythology "tens of thousands of homicidal sex fiends stalk the land" (quoted in Cohen, 1980, p. 669). Collections of case studies were published by highly reputable scholars who devoted great attention to psychopathy (Abrahamsen, 1944; Bromberg, 1948; Karpman, 1954). There were numerous accounts of serial homicide and lust murder, and the important distinction between "mass" and "series" murder was beginning to enter the literature (Banay, 1956; Galvin & MacDonald, 1959; MacDonald, 1961).

Many offenders were described, but the overwhelming majority were drawn from countries other than the United States. The classic case studies were mainly of German murderers of the 1920s and 1930s, such as Fritz Haarman, Karl Denke, and Peter Kürten, each of whom claimed 10 or 20 victims in circumstances of extreme brutality and sexual perversion (MacDonald, 1961; Von Hentig, 1948; Wertham, 1949). A similar emphasis on European cases is also to be found in the sensationalistic literature, which recounted gruesome homicide cases in prurient terms (Masters & Lea, 1963). When the Cleveland torso murders became notorious, the affair was seized on by Nazi propagandists anxious to show that the Western nations also had crimes like those that had become so firmly linked to German cities like Hanover and Berlin (Nickel, 1989).

Modern accounts of multiple homicide would probably draw all their examples from American cases, but domestic examples did not then exist in anything like comparable numbers. In a sentence that today seems quite remarkable, Bromberg could write in 1948 that "the paucity of lust-murders in modern criminologic experience makes an analysis of the basic psychopathology difficult" (p. 146). There were "few actual cases" to compare with "Jack the Ripper or other legendary sex-fiends," and the author had to return to 1913 to find an American parallel (compare Karpman, 1954; Neustatter, 1957; and Wertham, 1966).

This is not to suggest that no American cases attracted interest, but the same small group of incidents was described repeatedly. Albert Fish occupied a central place in the literature for many years after his execution in 1936, due in large part to the detailed analysis of the case published by Fredric Wertham in 1949. Kittrie (1971) has suggested that it was this case in particular that helped to form the public perception of the sex offender as a multiple child killer (compare Schechter, 1990). In later years, Ed Gein, Charlie Starkweather, and Albert DeSalvo all earned a like celebrity, and a spate of books and articles began to stimulate renewed interest in multiple homicide (Allen, 1976; Chapman, 1982; DeFord, 1965; Frank, 1967; Galvin & MacDonald, 1959; Gollmar, 1981; MacDonald, 1961; Menninger, 1968; Reinhardt, 1960). The most comprehensive study of specifically American offenders was that of Reinhardt (1962), who described Starkweather, Melvin Rees, Dudley and Gwyn, Brown and Kelly, and Nannie Doss. In addition, writers on extreme violence often referred to the cases of William Heirens and Caryl Chessman, neither of whom falls within our definition (Chessman, 1960; Freeman, 1955; Kennedy, Hoffman, & Haines, 1947).

One remarkable point about such a list is that it omits some of the most spectacular killers, who bore the closest resemblance to the "classic" German cases. One searches in vain for extensive discussion of Jarvis Catoe, Jake Bird, or Clarence Hill, and this lacuna may suggest a political element in the selection of case studies. All three men were black, and in the context of these years it might well have been thought inappropriate or tasteless to focus on their acts. If unduly publicized, these events could have given ammunition to racists and segregationists anxious to justify their opinions about black violence and criminality. Whatever the reason, the consequence was to limit the range of cases available to contemporary criminologists.

The lack of concern about serial murder as a major American problem can be illustrated in a number of ways, but one of the most striking involves the numerous official reports and investigations published in the 1960s on the topics of violence and criminality. In the aftermath of political assassinations and racial disturbances, and against a background of rising crime rates, it became common to express concern about the prevalence of violence in the United States. There were several major investigations into different aspects of the perceived crisis, the most comprehensive undertaken by the National Commission on the Causes and Prevention of Violence from 1968 to 1969, which examined many aspects of violence, political and otherwise, but discussion of mass and serial homicide was conspicuous by its near absence. Some cases were mentioned in the context of different theories of the causation of crime, but the subject of multiple homicide occupied nothing like the role that it might be expected to play in a contemporary discussion. It is not even mentioned in the commission's influential final report (U.S. Government, 1969-1970; see especially volumes 11-13).

THE EVIDENCE OF POPULAR CULTURE

Also suggestive here is the relative absence of multiple homicide as a theme in American popular culture in midcentury. The celebrated serial cases of the 1920s were recalled in early 1940s films like *Stranger on the Third Floor* and even *Arsenic and Old Lace*, but later treatments rarely referred to contemporary cases (McCarty, 1986). *The Sniper* (1952) was one powerful exception that appeared in the next decade. It addressed the topic of serial murder with a sophisticated and sympathetic awareness of contemporary psychoanalytic and criminological theories, but the main real-life example chosen to illustrate the phenomenon, after so many years, was still Albert Fish. The compulsive nature of the "sniper's" violence also bears an explicit resemblance to the Heirens case, which formed the basis of *While the City Sleeps* (1956).

Only in the 1960s did real-life events once more attract attention, with films based on the careers of Ed Gein (*Psycho*, 1960), Albert DeSalvo (*The Strangler*, 1964, and *The Boston Strangler*, 1968), and Charlie Starkweather (*Badlands*, 1973); *Dirty Harry* (1971) freely synthesized the stories of Gary Krist and "Zodiac." Authentic incidents of mass murder similarly inspired *In Cold Blood* (1967) and *Targets* (1968). The resurgence of interest in multiple homicide was fueled by the steadily increasing reports of actual cases, and "Ripper" or "mad slasher" films have been a profitable, if controversial, genre during the last two decades. The recent vogue provides a dramatic contrast to the apparent absence of notable American cases in the 1940s and 1950s.

THE YEARS OF TRANSITION: 1965-1969

In the mid-1950s the United States enjoyed very low rates of serial homicide. Two decades later the country would be in the midst of an apparent "murder wave," and the transition between the two stages can be dated with fair precision to the mid-1960s. The increase of extreme and seemingly irrational homicide was frequently remarked during these years, and many writers focused on a short period during 1966. In July of that year Richard Speck killed 8 nurses in a Chicago hostel, in an act that may have been the culmination of an already lengthy career of murder, and in August Charles Whitman killed 16 people during a shooting spree in Texas. Less celebrated were the murder sprees perpetrated later that same year by Robert B. Smith in Arizona and by Kelbach and Lance in Utah.

12   *Philip Jenkins*

The media enjoy finding such symbolic events that can be claimed as the harbingers of wider social trends, but there seems to be little doubt that these events were indeed significant. Newton offers a total of 23 cases of serial murder that occurred between 1965 and 1969. Several of these cases that involved fewer than four victims should be removed from consideration, applying the same criteria that were applied to the earlier list, and several other incidents can be added from other sources. Finally, one can identify 19 serial murder cases that were reported during these five years, or an average of one every 96 days (see Table 2).

Table 2

Serial Murder Cases 1965-1969

Name	Dates active
Jerry Brudos	1968-1969
John Norman Collins	1967-1969
Antone Costa	1969
Janie Gibbs	1968
Walter Kelbach and Myron Lance	1966
Posteal Laskey	1965-1966
Charles Manson and followers	1969
John Meadows	1968-1971
Thomas Lee Penn and William Penn	1966
George Howard "Buster" Putt	1969
Mark Alan Smith	late 1960s
Richard Speck	1966
Leroy Snyder	1969
Richard Steeves	1960s-1980s
Richard Lee Tingler	1968-1969
Clarence Walker	1965
"Zodiac"	1968ff
the New Jersey hospital murders	1966
the New Jersey unsolved murders	1965-1966

Although this was below the rates of the 1970s, it was a sharp increase over conditions of the previous two decades, and, as the rate of serial murder intensified, so its nature changed. The new cases included fewer marginal or debatable incidents than had been reported in earlier years. There was an especially sharp rise in the number of "Ripper" crimes or "lust murders," of the sort that had been dismissed as so rare in the 1940s but that would become so commonplace after 1970. Between 1940 and 1964, only 11 cases could be classified as lust murders, but another 11 could be so categorized between 1965 and 1969 alone. These were the years of notorious offenders such as John Norman Collins (Keyes, 1977), Jerry Brudos (Rule, 1983a), Antone Costa (Damore, 1990), "Zodiac" (Graysmith, 1987), and others (Hilberry, 1987; Moser & Cohen, 1967). The picture was actually even worse than it appears, because several offenders now began careers of "lust murder" and serial homicide that would not be detected until the 1970s or later.

The frequency of serial homicide was accelerating at the end of the 1960s, but still more cases came to light in the following years (see Table

3). To take the single year of 1973, there were at least 10 arrests of serial killers as well as two incidents that remain unsolved, and the cases in this year included several extreme offenders such as Dean Corll, Herbert Mullin, Edmund Kemper, and Girard Schaefer.

Table 3

Growth of Serial Murder Cases 1970-1980*

Year	Serial killers arrested	Unsolved serial cases terminated	Total
1970	2	—	2
1971	5	—	5
1972	3	2	5
1973	10	2	12
1974	5	2	7
1975	7	5	12
1976	8	—	8
1977	4	4	8
1978	9	2	11
1979	6	2	8
1980	12	3	15
Totals	71	22	93

*This table must be regarded as especially tentative, as it combines two essentially different phenomena. However, this is the only way to suggest the changing scale of repeat homicide. The dates describe serial murder cases that were completed in a particular year, that is, (a) serial killers arrested in that year and (b) unsolved serial murder cases that apparently terminated in that year. The question of when an unsolved series of murders concludes is all but impossible to answer, and this part of the table frequently relies on estimates and opinions of law enforcement authorities.

A constructionist approach to the problem of serial murder might seek to emphasize the continuity in activity from the 1940s onwards and then attempt to understand the moral and political pressures that led commentators to describe an artificial "upsurge" from the late 1960s. By contrast, this case study supports the "objectivist" view that a genuine phenomenon was occurring and that no creative stereotyping was required to define the problem (compare Goode, 1989). Of course, a constructionist argument might still stress that the real scale of the problem was blown out of proportion or that the debate was shaped to benefit certain interests or ideologies; but new problem there certainly was. There simply were more serial killers, more of whom could be categorized as lust murderers. A new problem was identified because a new problem had come into being.

SOCIAL DIMENSIONS

We must therefore address the social factors that gave rise to this change. It is a commonplace that the mid-1960s marked a dramatic transition in many aspects of American life, and any attempt at explaining the growth of serial homicide must deal with an embarrassing surfeit of possible reasons. It would be rash to dismiss the status frustration postulated by Leyton, though additional factors can be suggested. It is often difficult to isolate any one type of causation, as the various elements so often intertwined. Fundamental was the changing demographic composition of the United States and the relative growth of the segment of the population consisting of people in their teens and twenties. This in itself contributed to a sharp rise in overall violence rates, and it may be asked whether the increase in serial homicide was merely a facet of the general growth in crime.

Almost certainly this was not the case. United States homicide rates did rise between the 1940s and the 1980s, but over the whole period they may only have doubled. From 1945 to 1966, the rate per 100,000 population fluctuated between about 4.5 and 6.0; it then began a rapid rise, from 6.0 in 1968 to 8.8 in 1974-1975, and by 1981 it exceeded 10.0. It then fell below 8.0 by the mid-1980s (Riedel & Zahn, 1985). There were particular regions and cities with far higher growth rates in homicide, but few could match the eightfold or tenfold increases that have been suggested for reported serial homicide (Block, 1987).

Simple demographics may have contributed a little to the upsurge in serial murder after 1965, but additional explanations are required. Some can be found in aspects of the distinctive youth counterculture evolved by the "baby boom" generation. Though avowedly pledged to peace and nonviolence, this culture may inadvertently have promoted overtly aggressive behavior, especially with sexual motivations. Only a small number of people might have been affected in this way, but the number of multiple homicide offenders is only in the hundreds nationwide. A vast increase in the availability and consumption of a wide range of drugs presumably had effects that are still difficult to quantify, which would have been especially severe in individuals already prone to violent or disinhibited behavior. From the mid-1960s there was also a rapid increase in the availability of sexually stimulating imagery, both through the media and in everyday life.

It is plausible that greater access to pornography or extremely violent visual material might have shaped the fantasies and consequent actions of some offenders, but neither drugs nor pornography would in itself be an adequate explanation of the changes observed. As has been argued elsewhere, the act of homicide may arise from any number of circumstances peculiar to the offender, but serial murder also presupposes social conditions that permit the creation of a victim population (Jenkins, in press). Such a population is accessible to the offender, and several victims can disappear or be found dead before the authorities become seriously concerned. The nature of responses by police and other justice agencies plays an important role in shaping such opportunities for victimization.

In this view, the vital changes in the 1960s might have been the greater independence of the younger generation and changes in their sexual behavior and attitudes. This greatly enhanced the opportunities for a potential offender to find himself or herself in intimate circumstances with a victim, and the increased physical mobility of these years made it less likely that a young person's disappearance would be immediately noticed. Similarly, the range of acceptable deviancy was greatly expanded in these years. Changes in mores increased a willingness to experiment with alternative belief systems and life styles and made many people less prepared to reject or suspect individuals who might appear strange or deviant. The sum total of these changes was to facilitate encounters between strangers that might have been far more difficult only a few years previously. At the same time, the political fragmentation of the late 1960s discouraged young people from invoking police assistance in what might have been seen as suspicious circumstances.

THE MENTAL HEALTH SYSTEM

Other possible factors do not directly involve the "baby boom" generation but would nevertheless have similarly encouraged a growth in both potential offenders and their victims. In the forefront were changes in the mental health system. The 1960s were marked by a reluctance to institutionalize deviants and the mentally ill for long periods, and it became difficult to commit a person on the strength of his or her outrageous or threatening acts. The average number of individuals incarcerated in state mental hospitals on any given day fell from 550,000 in 1955 to 200,000 in 1974, a decline of 65 percent (and in proportion to the overall population the fall was still greater). Despite the generally laudable intentions of the movement, the effects of decarceration have often been disastrous, and one tragic effect was to release onto the streets some genuinely dangerous offenders who would hitherto have been maintained in secure institutions (compare Isaac & Armat, 1990; and Johnson, 1990). This was also an incidental effect of the shortening of prison sentences and actual time served and the new emphasis on community care facilities.

Decarceration was part of a more general attack on therapeutic responses to crime and violence reflecting great skepticism about the possibility of predicting and preventing future acts. The assault was seen most clearly in the area of "sexual psychopath" laws, which faced increasingly successful courtroom challenges (Cohen, 1980; Katenbach, 1984; Scull, 1977). In discussing this movement, Kittrie (1971) even writes of the notion of "the illusive psychopath," almost suggesting that the condition itself was mythical. It is ironic that this new legal environment coincided with a probable increase in the number of seriously disturbed offenders in the aftermath of the rapid growth of drug abuse.

The notorious serial killers of the decade following 1965 included many individuals who had been committed or incarcerated periodically for acts of extreme violence but were released with what proved to be too little regard for public safety. To take a specific case, it is difficult to believe that a flamboyantly psychotic offender like Richard Trenton Chase would have escaped lengthy incarceration had he lived in the 1940s. However, the mental health system he encountered was that of 1970s California, where compulsory commitment was much more difficult, and he remained at liberty until the 1978 murder spree that earned him the title of the ''Vampire of Sacramento'' (Markman & Bosco, 1989).

In one of the most tragic examples of this sort, Carroll E. Cole, who was also from California, made repeated attempts to warn doctors and law enforcement authorities of his sadistic and violent impulses towards women, and he was committed to mental institutions sporadically in the 1960s and early 1970s. However, he remained at large, and he carried out the first of his 13 murders in 1970 (Newton, 1990). Chase and Cole may have represented extreme failures on the part of the courts and the medical profession, but very serious mistakes were also made in the cases of killers such as Jerry Brudos, ''Buster'' Putt, Herbert Mullin, Ed Kemper, Charlie Hatcher, John Wayne Gacy, and many others (Ganey, 1989; Lunde, 1976; Rule, 1983a, 1983b). All had been diagnosed at some stage as showing strong tendencies to future violence, yet all had been released from youth institutions or from psychiatric custody, often on several occasions. Attempts at predicting violent behavior have a long and controversial history, but it appears that in the 1960s even the most extreme warning signs failed to cause official intervention.

CONCLUSION

It would be tempting to draw facile political conclusions. If the upsurge in multiple murder from the mid-1960s was in a sense an outgrowth of the political and social liberalism that characterized that era, then one conceivable policy response would be to limit or reverse those trends, to emphasize traditional moral views on issues such as drug use and sexuality. Against this view it is important to stress the limited scale of the multiple homicide problem within the broad spectrum of violent crime and to avoid overemphasizing the purely negative changes associated with the 1960s. In addition, it remains uncertain how far any government could successfully shape moral attitudes and beliefs if the attempt ran against existing social currents. Similarly, it would be misleading to concentrate entirely on the bad effects of changes in the mental health system such as the decline of compulsory commitment laws. Most would agree that due process values were long overdue in the area of psychiatric confinement and treatment, even if the actual process of decarceration left a great deal to be desired.

Perhaps the most important lesson concerns the state of academic research in the area of multiple homicide. It appears that social, legal, and environmental factors play a major role in determining the prevalence of this crime, but the scholarly emphasis continues to focus on the individual offender. If the rate of serial murder is to be reduced, these underlying factors must be understood, and this can be achieved only if the killer is seen not merely as a disturbed individual but as an actor within a changing social context.

Serial killers appear to fall into several distinct psychiatric categories, with paranoid schizophrenics and sexual psychopaths both being frequently recorded, and some authorities would emphasize the role of biological factors no less than the role of psychological factors in causing acts of extreme violence (compare Norris, 1988). It may be that conditions that give rise to irrational violence occur to a similar degree in all human societies, or that social and developmental factors may make this behavior much more common in some societies than in others. In the 1950s, for example, psychiatrists would strongly have emphasized the role of factors such as child-rearing practices, which would be peculiar to a particular society at a given time. In this view, changes in family structure or in attitudes to children could account for variations in extremely violent behavior, as could changes in media depictions of violence or sexuality. It is quite possible that the frequency of aggressive behavior might indeed vary between societies, but that is a different matter from the specific phenomenon of serial homicide. An individualistic approach might account for how one person came to kill, but it cannot explain how he or she found the opportunities to evade detection until several murders had been committed, and it is this latter circumstance that makes an aggressive offender into a serial killer.

If the average number of victims claimed by serial killers rises or falls in a particular era or society, this is less a comment on the changing dynamics of the individual offenders themselves than a function of the social, moral, and bureaucratic context in which they all operate. It would be impossible to understand the murders of the medieval baron Gilles de Rais, "Bluebeard," without discussing the society in which he existed and the means by which he was able to entrap and murder so many innocent victims; it should be equally unthinkable to omit the social context of a modern case in Seattle or Houston. There is thus a crying need for scholarly studies, not merely of single offenders, but of all the cases of a particular region or decade, including discussion of how the killers exploited the opportunities in their particular situations or milieux.

In summary, an effective strategy against multiple homicide must draw on research from both social and individual perspectives. The social perspective will explore the broad victim environment while psychological analysis will aid investigators by profiling offenders and seeking more sophisticated means of predicting future violence. Both approaches must be used if serial homicide is to be reduced.

18   *Philip Jenkins*

REFERENCES

Abrahamsen, D. (1944). *Crime and the human mind*. New York, NY: Columbia University Press.

Allen, W. (1976). *Starkweather: The story of a mass murderer*. Boston, MA: Houghton Mifflin.

Banay, R. S. (1956). Psychology of a mass murderer. *Journal of Forensic Psychology*, *1*, 1.

Best, J. (Ed.). (1989). *Images of issues*. New York, NY: Aldine de Gruyter.

Best, J. (1990). *Threatened children: Rhetoric and concern about child victims*. Chicago, IL: University of Chicago Press.

Block, C. R. (1987). *Homicide in Chicago*. Chicago, IL: Center for Urban Policy, Loyola University of Chicago.

Brian, D. (1986). *Murderers die*. New York, NY: St. Martin's Press.

Bromberg, W. (1948). *Crime and the mind: An outline of psychiatric criminology*. Philadelphia, PA: J. B. Lippincott.

Capote, T. (1965). *In cold blood*. New York, NY: Random House.

Cassity, J. H. (1941). Personality study of 200 murderers. *Journal of Criminal Psychopathology*, *2*, 296-304.

Catton, J. (1940). *Behind the scenes of murder*. New York, NY: Norton.

Chapman, I. (1982). *Private Eddie Leonski: The Brownout Strangler*. Sydney, Australia: Hale and Iremonger.

Chessman, C. (1960). *Cell 2455, death row*. Englewood Cliffs, NJ: Prentice-Hall.

Cohen, F. (1980). *The law of deprivation of liberty*. St. Paul, MN: West Publishing.

Damore, L. (1990). *In his garden*. New York, NY: Dell.

DeFord, M. A. (1965). *Murderers sane and mad*. New York, NY: Abelard Schuman.

Egger, S. A. (Ed.). (1990). *Serial murder: An elusive phenomenon*. New York, NY: Praeger.

Experts say mass murders are rare but on the rise. (1988, January 3). *New York Times*, p. A3.

Frank, G. (1967). *The Boston Strangler*. London, England: Jonathan Cape.

Freeman, L. (1955). *Before I kill more*. New York, NY: Crown.

Galvin, J. A. V., & MacDonald, J. M. (1959). Psychiatric study of a mass murderer. *American Journal of Psychiatry*, *115*, 1057.

Ganey, T. (1989). *St. Joseph's children: A true story of terror and justice*. Lyle Stuart/Carol.

Gaute, J. H. H., & Odell, R. (1979). *The murderers' Who's Who*. London, England: Harrap.

Gaziano, C. (1989). Chain newspaper homogeneity and presidential endorsements. *Journalism Quarterly*, *66*(4), 836-845.

Gollmar, R. H. (1981). *Edward Gein: America's most bizarre murderer*. New York, NY: Pinnacle.

Goode, E. (1989). The American drug panic of the 1980s. *Violence-Aggression-Terrorism*, *3*(4), 327-348.

Graysmith, R. (1987). *Zodiac*. New York, NY: Berkeley.

Hilberry, C. (1987). *Luke Karamazov*. Detroit, MI: Wayne State University Press.

Holmes, R. M., & DeBurger J. (1988). *Serial murder*. Beverly Hills, CA: Sage.

Isaac, R. J., & Armat, V. C. (1990). *Madness in the streets: How psychiatry and the law abandoned the mentally ill*. New York, NY: The Free Press.

Jenkins, P. (1988). Myth and murder: The serial murder panic of 1983-1985. *Criminal Justice Research Bulletin*, *3*(11), 107.

Jenkins, P. (1989). Serial murder in the USA 1900-1940: A historical perspective. *Journal of Criminal Justice*, *17*, 377-392.

Jenkins, P. (in press). Chance or choice: The selection of serial murder victims. In A. Wilson (Ed.), *Dynamics of the victim-offender interaction*. Cincinnati, OH: Anderson.

Johnson, A. B. (1990). *Out of bedlam: The truth about deinstitutionalization*. New York, NY: Basic Books.

Karpman, B. (1954). *The sexual offender and his offenses*. New York, NY: Julian Press.

Katenbach, J. (1984). *First born*. New York, NY: Atheneum.

Kennedy, F., Hoffman, H. R., & Haines, W. H. (1947). A study of William Heirens. *American Journal of Psychiatry*, *104*, 113.

Keyes, E. (1977). *The Michigan murders*. London, England: New English Library.

Kittrie, N. N. (1971). *The right to be different*. Baltimore, MD: Johns Hopkins Press.

Levin, J., & Fox, J. A. (1985). *Mass murder: America's growing menace*. New York, NY: Plenum.

Leyton, E. (1986). *Compulsive killers*. New York, NY: New York University Press.

Lindsey, R. (1984, January 22). Officials cite a rise in killers who roam U.S. for victims. *New York Times*, p. A1.

Lunde, D. T. (1976). *Murder and madness*. New York, NY: W. W. Norton.

MacDonald, J. M. (1961). *The murderer and his victim*. Springfield, IL: Charles C Thomas.

Markman, R., & Bosco, D. (1989). *Alone with the devil*. New York, NY: Doubleday.

Masters, R. E. L., & Lea, E. (1963). *Perverse crimes in history*. New York, NY: Julian Press.

McCarty, J. (1986). *Psychos*. New York, NY: St. Martin's Press.

Menninger, K. (1968). *The crime of punishment*. New York, NY: Viking.

Moser, D., & Cohen, J. (1967). *The Pied Piper of Tucson*. New York, NY: New American Library.

Nettler, G. (1982). *Killing one another*. Cincinnati, OH: Anderson.

Neustatter, W. (1957). *The mind of the murderer*. New York, NY: Philosophical Library.

Newton, M. (1988). *Mass murder: An annotated bibliography*. New York, NY: Garland Reference Library of Social Science.

Newton, M. (1990). *Hunting humans*. Port Washington, WA: Loompanics.

Nickel, S. (1989). *Torso*. Winston-Salem, NC: John F. Blair.

Norris, J. (1988). *Serial killers*. New York, NY: Dolphin.

Reinhardt, J. M. (1960). *The murderous trail of Charlie Starkweather*. Springfield, IL: Charles C Thomas.

Reinhardt, J. M. (1962). *The psychology of strange killers*. Springfield, IL: Charles C Thomas.

Riedel, M., & Zahn, M. (1985). *The nature and patterns of American homicide*. Washington, DC: Justice Department, NIJ.

Rule, A. (1983a). *Lust killer*. New York, NY: Signet.

Rule, A. (1983b). *Want-ad killer*. New York, NY: New American Library.

Schechter, H. (1990). *Deranged*. New York, NY: Pocket.

Scull, A. (1977). *Decarceration*. Englewood Cliffs, NJ: Prentice-Hall.

U.S. Government. (1969-1970). *Report of the National Commission on the Causes and Prevention of Violence* (Vols. 1-13). Washington, DC: Government Printing Office.

Von Hentig, H. (1948). *The criminal and his victim*. New Haven, CT: Yale University Press.

Wertham, F. (1947). *Dark legend*. Garden City, NJ: Doubleday.

Wertham, F. (1949). *The show of violence*. Garden City, NJ: Doubleday.

Wertham, F. (1966). *A sign for Cain: An exploration of human violence*. New York, NY: Macmillan.

Wilson, C., & Pitman, P. (1984). *Encyclopaedia of murder*. London, England: Pan.

Wilson, C., & Seaman, D. (1983). *Encyclopaedia of modern murder*. New York, NY: Perigee.

[10]

Journal of Criminal Justice Vol. 16, pp. 1–15 (1988)
All rights reserved. Printed in U.S.A.

SERIAL MURDER IN ENGLAND 1940–1985

PHILIP JENKINS

Administration of Justice
Pennsylvania State University
University Park, Pennsylvania 16802

ABSTRACT

Recent American work on serial murder has begun to move away from exclusive reliance on case-studies to broader and more quantitative accounts of the total phenomenon as it involves both offenders and victims. This article discusses the phenomenon of serial murder over a long period by focusing on England, where homicide of this sort is sufficiently rare to have been studied in detail. A comprehensive list of offenders also was easily constructed. Offender characteristics are discussed, to show a sharp division between serial killers whose violence was apparent in early childhood and others who seemed relatively normal until well into adulthood. The article also considers the relative success of English police and courts in handling the special problems posed by serial homicide.

In 1983, a major report by the United States Department of Justice analyzed cases of extreme multiple homicide from the previous decade. The study was important in a number of ways, not least in contributing to something of a public panic about the threat posed by multiple murderers and the suggestion that these offenders might be responsible for thousands of deaths each year. The panic has now subsided, but the serious interest in multiple homicide appears to flourish. In the last decade a division has been made between "mass" and "serial" murder, with particular attention being focused on the latter type of offense.[1] There is a growing and impressive literature on multiple homicides and their victims (Fox and Levin, 1985; Egger, 1984, 1986; Hickey, 1986).

The most significant aspect of the recent work is that finally there have been attempts to quantify the activity of such offenders. The need for such research has been amply clarified by the recent media panic about this topic, in which quite reputable authorities placed the number of serial murder victims at anywhere between one and twenty percent of American homicides. The Justice Department study suggested that during the 1970s and early 1980s there might have been about thirty-five serial killers active at any given point. The figure can be challenged—either as excessive or too conservative—but the attempt to quantify this activity was an important innovation. Fox and Levin (1985) attempted to examine all cases of multiple homicide in the United States between 1974 and 1979, in a project whose detailed conclusions remain to be fully published.

Works such as these represent an important departure in the study of homicide, but

1

2   PHILIP JENKINS

they also indicate what remains to be done. There have been a number of general works on the murderers of a particular era or country, but these have not offered anything approaching scientific precision (Nash, 1973; Godwin, 1978; Wilson, 1972, 1984; Wilson and Seaman, 1983; Gaute and Odell, 1979, 1982; Lindsay, 1958). Such "Famous Murderers" books may be useful sources, but they cannot by themselves be a reliable guide to changes in the nature and frequency of social homicide.

What is most critically lacking in this research is what might be termed the "epidemiology" of multiple homicide and especially of serial murder, which are the focus of this article. It seems, for example, that this type of offense is far more common in some countries and eras than others. Partly, the evidence for this is impressionistic. Between 1920 and 1940, for example, Germany had a dozen cases in which a serial killer claimed over twenty victims, though such extreme examples were not common there either before or since. In the United States, there is more solid evidence for "waves" of multiple murder. Between 1950 and 1970 there were only two cases of an individual killing ten or more victims over a period of time; since 1970 there have been thirty-nine known examples. Such changes over time will not, clearly, be evident from short-term studies that focus on a particular era like the mid-1970s. In addition, comparative and historical study will make clear whether the current "wave" of serial murders in the U.S. is as unique or even extreme as was often stated in the public pronouncements about the subject in 1983 and 1984.

The case-study approach to serial murder must therefore be supplemented by more general research on the total phenomenon. Moves in this direction are currently taking place under the auspices of federal law enforcement authorities and specifically the newly formed National Center for the Analysis of Violent Crime. However, there is ample scope for criminological analysis of this topic, particularly for long-term studies (National Center for the Analysis of Violent Crime, 1986).

One problem in such studies is the sheer scope of the material. In the United States since 1960 alone, there have been over a hundred cases in which a serial killer committed five or more homicides, making analysis a very substantial task. The present article illustrates the questions that need to be asked about serial murder by focusing on a smaller jurisdiction, where there is, however, abundant material to aid the researcher. In England and Wales (hereafter described solely as England), there have been far fewer multiple homicides than in the United States, but these cases have been very extensively studied.[2] It is certain that the cases listed here are a comprehensive account, a statement that cannot be made so categorically for any period of American history. The relative scarcity of English serial killers also means that the phenomenon can be studied over a lengthy period. In this research, all cases between 1940 and 1985 have been included. Finally, no claim is made that the present article is a fully comparative study. However, each of the cases described here certainly exhibits close parallels to American cases (Godwin, 1978; Nettler, 1982).

Perhaps the most important lesson of a study like the present one is the very rudimentary state of our knowledge of serial murder, even when our access to the facts of particular cases is extensive. However, research on multiple homicide is necessary and important. As is shown here, this type of killer, though rare, can make a quite disproportionate impact on crime statistics, to say nothing of the more important area of the community's sense of security from violence (Nettler, 1982, 1984; Newman, 1979).

DEFINITION

Despite all the recent American work on multiple homicide, there is no universally accepted definition of serial murder. Fox and Levin defined "mass murder" as involving four or more victims, but did not differentiate between "mass" and "serial" killers. Egger (1984) also regarded four victims as the criterion for serial murder, though the Justice Department study chose six.

Also, "serial" killers kill over a period of time, but the exact time remains undefined. If someone kills repeatedly over some hours, this is a mass murder. If days elapse, then it might be seen as a "serial" offense. Furthermore, there is the problem of definition when an individual commits one murder and then another mass killing at a later date. Does that person become a serial or a mass killer? These points may appear pedantic, but they are important in developing a taxonomy of multiple murderers. It might be suggested that a mass murderer like Richard Speck was no different behaviorally or psychologically from a serial lust-murderer like Jack the Ripper. It merely happened that he found the opportunity to carry out so many of his fantasies at one place and time. Generally, though, there are substantial differences between mass killers like James Huberty (who killed over twenty people in a few hours) and a serial murderer like Ted Bundy (Michaud and Aynesworth, 1983).

Fortunately, the English cases under discussion do not offer serious problems on the question of timing; serial killers stand out clearly, and mass murder in the American sense is unknown. As for the number of victims, four has been taken as the minimum.

Other criteria of definition must be clarified. Excluded from the present study were killers acting from an explicitly political motive, such as the "Balcombe Street" IRA group responsible for at least nine deaths in 1974–75. Also omitted were professional, underworld, and "contract" killings, though here the lines of demarcation are rather thin. The study omitted Archibald Hall, a confidence trickster and thief who committed five murders in 1977–78 with the sole purpose of concealing his lucrative crimes (Lucas and Davies, 1979). In other cases, however, individuals have been included although monetary gain played at least some part in one or more of their murders. Again, this rather arbitrary criterion did not gravely affect the number of subjects discussed as "serial killers." Hall was the only case who might have been added to the list.

METHODOLOGY

Although murder remains a very rare crime in England, crime in general and murder in particular have long been a source of great public fascination, and unusual cases attract a great deal of attention (see for example McCormick, 1970; Farson, 1972; Forbes and Meehan, 1982; Heppenstall, 1973; Orwell, 1965; Rutherford, 1973; Sereny, 1972). Thus a number of secondary sources were consulted for the present article. Most important were reference books on murders and biographies of particular offenders (Gaute and Odell, 1979, 1982; Goodman and Will, 1973; Lindsay, 1958; Lisners, 1983; Wilson and Seaman, 1983; Wilson, 1972). Also examined was the large literature of police memoirs and accounts of and by forensic scientists (Andrews, 1973; Browne, 1956; Browne and Tullett, 1980; DuRose, 1971; Firmin, 1948; Greeno, 1961; Howe, 1965; Jackson, 1967; Millen, 1972; Simpson, 1978; Smyth, 1980; Tullett, 1979, 1986).

Many of these books are journalistic in character and very variable in quality. Some are sensationalistic *True Crime* genre pieces, but others are far better. For example, Masters's (1985) account of Dennis Nilsen is a work of real scholarship based on access to extensive diaries and writings of the subject. Other writers—like Norman Lucas and Tom Tullett—are experienced crime reporters with close associations to the police and excellent access to the investigations covered.

However, the most important point here is not so much the quality of the coverage as its comprehensiveness; and here, the books mentioned are reliable. It is unlikely in the extreme that a serial murder case would have escaped the attention of all these sources. Indeed, it is remarkable to see the attention lavished on relatively minor cases. In the early 1950s, John Straffen became a monster in public notoriety with a series of three child murders; whereas there are many books on domestic tragedies of only local note (Cornwell. 1984; Posner, 1973). The simple biographical facts about offenders and victims were easy to obtain and for the most part were confirmed by

4   PHILIP JENKINS

TABLE 1

SERIAL MURDERS IN ENGLAND 1940–1985

Name	When Active	Victims	Major Sources
Cummins, Frederick Gordon	1942	4	Tullett, 1979
Christie, John Reginald Halliday	1943–53	8	Kennedy, 1961
Haigh, John George	1944–49	6	Lustgarten, 1968
"Nudes Murderer"	1959–64	7	McConnell, 1974; DuRose, 1971
Brady, Ian	1963–5	5	Harrison, 1986; Williams, 1967
Morris, Raymond Leslie	1965–7	4	Hawkes, 1970
Young, Graham Frederick	1962–71	4	Wilson and Seaman, 1983
Mackay, Patrick David	1973–5	11	Clark and Penycate, 1976
Neilson, Donald	1974–5	4	Valentine, 1976
Dinsdale, Peter G. ("Bruce Lee")	1973–80	26	Wilson and Seaman, 1983
Sutcliffe, Peter	1975–80	13	Cross, 1981; Burn, 1984
Nilsen, Dennis	1978–83	15	Masters, 1985

several sources in addition to the primary account. Questions about the personality and motivation of a particular offender are obviously much more subjective and tentative, and sources are indicated more fully. Clearly, for such a small group, any statements that are made must be impressionistic and must not claim scientific validity.

Based on these sources, Table 1 presents a rough list of individuals who have been associated by a number of sources with four or more serial homicides in England since 1940.

Omissions from the list are apparent. It does not include individuals active either currently or in the past who have not yet become suspects in a series of homicides, and there may well be such. In 1973, for example, three teenage girls were murdered in the county of Glamorgan by an offender who remains unidentified. If he were to become associated with other killings, then this anonymous murderer ought to be included here.

Another problem is the 1947 case of Dr. Robert Clements, who committed suicide when he was suspected of poisoning his wealthy wife. Later investigation suggested strongly that his three earlier wives might also have died in the same manner. There may well be a "dark figure" in serial homicide, though cases like Clements's are much too tentative to form the basis of discussion (Gaute and Odell, 1979).

In this list, a number of "probable victims" has been assigned to each offender. One of the most intractable problems in discussing serial murder is the means by which it is possible to know the number of victims of a particular offender and thus to trace the person's career in detail. The issues here are obvious. At least until the abolition of capital punishment in 1967, it was vitally important for a suspect either to establish his or her innocence or to establish a plausible insanity defense. Some offenders would attempt to minimize their crimes, but others certainly exaggerated their murders. Haigh, for example, very probably killed six people. While in prison, he confessed to three further murders, although popular legend raised his "kill" into the hundreds. Overwhelmingly, writers on this case have dismissed the extra murders of the prison confessions and confidently claimed that he killed six victims. Of course, there is also the temptation for the police to boost the number of claimed victims in order to improve their apparent clearance rates. On the other hand, it is encouraging to study cases in which police attempted to associate disappearances with a particular offender like Brady or Mackay. Stringent criteria appear to have been applied in attempting to make such links, and the police appear to have been very conservative in claiming extra victims for an offender.

Studying multiple homicides raises rather delicate questions of terminology. In very few cases were all the murders commonly attributed to an offender charged against that individual and then proved in court; whereas, as has been shown, confessions are far from being an infallible source. The difficulty is illustrated by Ian Brady, who was *convicted* of three murders between 1963 and 1965. The case has been the subject of much research and writing, and it is commonly *accepted* that there were two other victims. It is widely *believed* that this may understate his criminal career. Early statements by the police at the time of his arrest suggested that he was connected with eight disappearances, and a recent book based on detailed interviews with Brady suggested that he might have been guilty of twelve or more killings. "Proved," "believed," and "accepted" facts are very different, and there are wide disparities in the number of victims attributed to most of these offenders. Patrick Mackay was charged with three murders, and he was the leading suspect in eight more.

In one sense, the British legal environment serves to limit the gross exaggeration of cases like those under discussion. British libel law is exceedingly strict, as demonstrated by a 1970s case in which a convicted killer named Roger Gleaves successfully sued journalists writing about his case. They had apparently "blackened his character" by charges of embezzlement. Even when an individual has been found guilty of several murders, it is still libellous to speculate too freely about his involvement in others, unless the evidence is quite overwhelming.

In summary, the list of serial killers provided here is likely to be accurate in the sense that each individual has been properly classified, and there are not likely to be serious omissions. The specific figures given for numbers of victims (and therefore, length of activity) can only be described as likely estimates, subject to considerable revision.

THE SCALE OF SERIAL MURDER

It goes without saying that the number of cases under consideration is small and that it is very difficult to make worthwhile statistical analysis. As a very rough statement, it can be suggested that in a country of forty-eight million people, there is usually at least one and occasionally two of these very unusual offenders pursuing a career of serial murder at any given time.

Such a general statement belies many short-term fluctuations. There were no serial killers active in England in the 1930s and only one known murder between 1954 and 1962, a 1959 killing by the "Nudes Murderer" (in addition, Scottish serial killer Peter Manuel killed at least one of his victims over the English border in 1957). By contrast, there have been periods when several serial killers were active at once. The murders of Jack the Ripper in 1888 were followed by a series of major cases—George Chapman, Frederick Deeming, Neill Cream, Amelia Dyer, and others. In the period discussed in this article, the mid-1970s were an equally noteworthy time, when four or five serial killers were active at once. The reason for such concentrations is unknown, but obviously the imitation of celebrated cases may play some part.

In Table 1, it was suggested that the twelve known "serial" cases accounted for 107 murders over a period of forty-six years. These represent a small proportion of British homicides—an average of 2.3 murders each year. In order to provide a context for this, it is necessary to understand the extremely low murder rate in England. Serial activity over the whole period accounts for 1.7 percent of English murders, the proportion rising to 3.2 percent for the period 1973–1983—one case in thirty-one.

Serial murder is thus a fringe phenomenon that assumes disproportionate importance because of the rarity of homicide in England. Moreover, even the apparently low homicide statistics of that country exaggerate the reality. In the worst year of the present century (1979), 629 homicide offenses were initially recorded by the police, or 1.11 per hundred thousand population. The comparable U.S. figure at the same point was over 20,000, or a homicide rate almost nine times that of England (Gibson and Klein, 1961; McClintock, 1963, 1968; Walker, 1968; *Criminal Statistics*, 1985).

But the 1979 figure is misleadingly high. About this time, the forensic scientist Dr. Keith Simpson (1978) wrote that the number of "real" murders each year in England was only 120. The figure requires explanation. First, since 1967, homicides in England have been recorded in two categories—"offenses initially regarded as homicide" and "offenses no longer recorded as homicide." Each year, about twelve percent of the first category fail to merit inclusion on the final list. The 1979 figure of 629 homicides thus became only 546 "real" homicides after further investigation. Of the second category, only some forty percent are ever charged as murder, as opposed to second degree manslaughter or infanticide (a separate offense in English law). By this criterion, there were about 200 "real" murders in England in 1979, a number much closer to Dr. Simpson's estimate (*Criminal Statistics*, 1985).

The Home Office compilers of the annual *Criminal Statistics* are commendably frank about the limitations of their figures and particularly about the possibility of deducing long-term trends in criminality. Between 1957 and 1966, for example, the available homicide statistics seem very low, but this is misleading. At this point, offenses found not to be homicide were excluded from the count for that year. After 1967, the major statistic

published (and publicized) was the "raw" number of suspected homicides, without later deductions. In consequence, there appears to have been a jump in the homicide rate about 1967, which conservative critics attributed to the loss of the deterrent effect of capital punishment. In reality, the serious increase did not occur until several years later, and the 1967 change can be seen as the result of statistical rethinking.

With these difficulties in mind, it is apparent that long-term trends in English homicide are by no means easy to trace. However, general estimates can be made with some confidence. Between 1940 and 1985, there were roughly 17,000 offenses initially regarded as homicide, of which 15,400 were finally classified as such. Of these, roughly 6,200 were technically murders, or 135 a year.

This provides the explanation for the remarkably high proportion of serial murder victims between 1973 and 1983. In a country with (then) perhaps 200 actual murders each year, at least five killers were active, committing a total of seven murders annually. In all the time from Jack the Ripper's day until 1970, no English murderer definitely had killed more than eight victims (John Christie in the 1940s and 1950s was credited with eight). Suddenly, after 1973 the scale of serial murder changed substantially. Peter Sutcliffe, the "Yorkshire Ripper," killed thirteen women in the red-light districts of Northern England. Dennis Nilsen became England's first serial killer to prey on the homosexual subculture, committing at least fifteen known murders. Patrick Mackay probably killed eleven victims in a variety of circumstances, ranging from people he mugged to casual strangers he met on the street or in a train. Finally, and the most unusual departure, England had its first serial killer who used arson to dispose of his victims. Peter Dinsdale ("Bruce Lee") was charged with twenty-six deaths by fire during the 1970s.

English serial murders thus attained a significance hard to appreciate unless the very low murder rate is taken into account. To take an earlier example, the shock caused by

Jack the Ripper's five or so murders may have been natural enough, but in addition to the intrinsically horrible character of these crimes, they represented over three percent of English murders for the year 1888. Moreover, for the present century, the proportion of English murders followed by the offender's suicide has remained steady at around twenty percent. Repeat homicides by a predatory stranger therefore appear even more bizarre and threatening than they might in another context.

In both England and the U.S.A., serial killers account for only a small proportion of murders—perhaps one or two percent in an average year. In both countries too, there has been a marked increase in this type of offense since the early 1970s (Jenkins, forthcoming).[3] There have been more offenders active, and they have claimed a larger number of victims before being apprehended or otherwise stopped. It is beyond the scope of this article to explain the reasons for this growth, except to suggest very tentatively that the real change lies in the opportunities available to killers and the increased chances of a crime remaining undetected.

Successful killers are those who prey on an environment with many transients, where a stranger is likely to pass unnoticed—such as a red-light district, a meeting place for casual homosexual contact, or a "skid row." There may or may not be more individuals prepared to kill, but in both England and America, the environments in which they can do so over long periods have proliferated in recent decades. Offenders achieve "success" by exploiting to the full the opportunities made available to them by changes in the broader culture (Goldstein, 1986; Nettler, 1982; Wolfgang and Weiner, 1982).

THE OFFENDERS

From such a small sample of offenders, generalization is of course difficult—or at least, it is unlikely to produce results of wider validity. Also, taxonomies of serial killers and similarly extreme offenders are currently very rudimentary. However, there are a number of points of interest both about the offenders and, more particularly, about the responses of the English criminal justice system towards them.

There are several possible ways of classifying such killers. It would be useful to adopt precise personality descriptions, but this presents problems. Terms like "psychopath" (the term most commonly used) change with time, and English and American approaches and diagnostic categories are different. English psychiatrists, for example, are far less likely to sympathize with Freudian or psychoanalytic terminology (See for example Abrahamsen, 1945, 1960, 1973; Blackburn, 1968, 1971; Brittain, 1970; Gibbens, 1958; Goldstein, 1986; Satten et al., 1960).

Less controversial is the classification of serial murderers according to their choice of victim, as most have tended to prey chiefly on one particular type. Of the twelve murderers in Table 1, the majority chose young women, and especially prostitutes. Cummins, Sutcliffe, Christie, and the "Nudes Murderer" all fell into this category, and the first two also imitated the original "Ripper" in mutilating their victims. Active female prostitutes accounted for the largest class of serial murder victims, twenty-four out of 107. The next major category is that of child murderers, represented by Ian Brady and Raymond Morris. Eleven of the total number of victims were under sixteen years old. Third, there are the killers who acted at least partly for gain but whose acts of violence were wholly disproportionate to the possible profit or need for concealment. Patrick Mackay, for example, killed victims encountered in petty street robberies, as well as passers-by. This class also includes Donald Neilson.

There are also three individuals who do not fit easily into a more general category, though the homosexual serial killer Dennis Nilsen has many counterparts in Germany in the 1920s and in the contemporary U.S.A. Finally, there are the obsessive psychopaths—Graham Young, the compulsive poisoner, and Peter Dinsdale, the pyromaniac.

The offenders can also be analyzed in terms of their "career profiles," patterns that

8   PHILIP JENKINS

can be sketched with some confidence and that suggest some consistency. First, most started their career of murder at a relatively late age. Of the twelve cases, the median age at which the first homicide was committed was thirty-three. Two began in their early teens and Christie not until his mid-forties; but otherwise, seven of the individuals began killing between the ages of twenty-four and forty. By the time of final apprehension, they were thus a rather elderly criminal population, with a median age of over thirty-six. This, of course, does not mean that their first contacts with the criminal justice system occurred at so late an age. Apart from Nilsen, all had extensive police records by the age of thirty.

The question of early criminality is obviously significant for the long and acrimonious debate over whether extreme violence can be predicted from early symptoms. Some of the English cases do offer considerable support for advocates of such predictability (see especially Newman, 1979; Dinitz and Conrad, 1980; Monahan, 1981; and the articles in Wolfgang and Weiner, 1982; Marsh and Katz, 1985). Patrick Mackay in particular is one of the best examples of what has been described as the "Macdonald triad" theory of the early signs of a multiple murderer (Macdonald, 1963; Hellman and Blackman, 1966). This suggests the importance of a complex of symptoms in a child—bed-wetting, arson, and the torture of animals. In Mackay's case, he had a lengthy and very disturbing record by the age of fifteen, including arson in a church, multiple attacks on family members and neighbors, at least one apparent murder attempt, and extensive and savage cruelty to animals. When Mackay was fifteen—some six years before he committed his first murder—a psychiatric report suggested that he was a "cold, psychopathic killer" (Clark and Penycate, 1976). Equally precocious were Graham Young and Peter Dinsdale, both of whom had apparently killed their first victim by the age of fifteen. By that age, each was firmly embarked on his respective obsession, whether poison or fire. In his early teens, Ian Brady had a wide reputation in his community for torturing both

children and animals, whereas recent interviews have led one author to suggest that he committed his first murder before he was ten years old. Like Mackay, he had a lengthy juvenile record for theft and violence (Compare Lewis et al., 1979, 1986).

These four individuals had a great deal in common, not the least of which was their very significant record of juvenile crime. There were many incidental resemblances. All had abundant fantasy lives of a particular nature. Dinsdale actually changed his name to that of the martial arts star, Bruce Lee. The others—Young, Brady, and Mackay—all worshipped Hitler and read anything they could find about the Nazi regime. In addition, Brady and Mackay spent much of their lives role-playing characters of this sort—world dictators, SS-men, and so on.

These cases suggest a number of common features in the personality of at least a few offenders. However, the picture is far from clear-cut. Most of the other offenders simply did not fall into the Brady/Mackay category. They did not have extensive juvenile records, they were not regarded as "problem" juveniles, and they often exhibited no early signs of violent tendencies. Regarding criminal records, most of the other eight killers had some prior arrests for petty theft, embezzlement, or forgery before committing their first homicide. Christie, Haigh, and Cummins all were well-known as persistent petty offenders. But, most of these encounters with the police occurred in early adulthood, when the subjects were in their early or mid-twenties. Moreover, with the exception of the four killers with strong juvenile records, none of the remainder had a recorded history of violence before their early twenties. Christie's only violent conviction before his first murder was an unlawful wounding charge at the age of thirty-one. The "Nudes Murderer"—if in fact he was correctly identified—showed the first manifestations of tendencies towards violence and assault at about the same age (DuRose, 1971; McConnell, 1974). In terms of "career," Peter Sutcliffe was typical. He had no criminal record before his mid-twenties, when he assaulted a prostitute and was caught carrying weapons. However, he did not commit his first murder until he was twenty-nine. He then killed a total of thirteen women until his arrest at the age of thirty-four.

In summary, the English cases offer no consistent answer to the question of predictability. In four cases, a combination of police record and psychiatric analysis might have predicted that these individuals were likely to kill at an early age and to kill repeatedly. In most of the other cases, the worst that might have been predicted was a career of chronic dishonesty and perhaps minor psychopathic tendencies. The division is striking. In fact, it may be reasonable to speak of a distinction between two categories—the "predictable" and the "respectable."

In the first case—the Brady type—the aggressive impulses were so overwhelming from an early age that it is highly unlikely that the offender could have progressed far into adulthood without arrest for at least one very serious offense. Also in the class of the very predictable was the Scot, Peter Manuel, who murdered at least ten people between 1956 and 1958. Although he did not kill his first victim until he was thirty, his extensive record for burglary, robbery, and rape dated back to age eleven. It may well be that only lengthy prison terms had prevented him from beginning to kill before such a relatively late age. In the 1968 case of Mary Bell, an eleven-year-old girl who murdered two small boys, prompt detection and incarceration almost certainly prevented a much worse series of killings (Sereny, 1972).

But there is a second category of offender, whose drift to violence might have been very belated. Of this group, most had achieved some respectability by their mid-thirties and lived down their early offenses. When they committed their first murders, no less than half the killers were married, had apparently stable family relationships, and had usually lived for several years in the same house. This was true of Christie, Cummins, Morris, Neilson, Sutcliffe, and the "Nudes Murderer." In terms of most guidelines for bail or parole, all these would have appeared to be excellent risks, up to the point when they actually fell under suspicion of murder. In addition, a number of the murderers had career records that suggested discipline and respectability. Six of the twelve had served in the armed forces, and three (Christie, Nilsen, and the "Nudes Murderer") had in addition served in the police. Nilsen and the "Nudes Murderer" had worked as security guards, an occupation they shared with a number of U.S. serial killers.

At the time of arrest, eight of the twelve murderers had stable jobs, and most of those were white-collar positions in middle-sized factories or businesses. Christie, Brady, and Nilsen were clerical officers; Morris was a factory foreman. Others were blue-collar workers—Sutcliffe was a truck driver and Young a shopfloor worker. Only four could be categorized as "drifters"; included in this group were Haigh and Mackay, both of whom were unable to hold down any job other than professional criminal, thief, or con-man.

One important aspect of the study of serial murder is estimating the rate at which such offenders commit their crimes, since this is important for assessing the scale of the problem in a particular society. The problem is illustrated by the U.S. Justice Department study of 1983 (see Jenkins, forthcoming), which claimed that at least thirty-five serial killers were active at any given time. As has been noted, this figure is a perfectly plausible estimate. However, in the ensuing debate, it was suggested that serial murder victims might total 4,000 or so annually in the U.S.A. This would mean that each killer would have to account for over a hundred victims annually, a grossly improbable figure. In reality, five or six is a much more likely annual total of victims for recent American serial murderers. This would suggest an annual total of serial victims closer to 400 than to 4,000.

In England, a serial killer is likely to continue his "career" for an average of just under four years. Naturally enough, someone who kills only a small number of victims each year is likely to continue unapprehended longer than another killer who begins a "murder rampage," because this in itself is likely to provoke intense law-enforcement atten-

tion. Overall, however, the murderer is unlikely to kill more than an average of four
people in any given year.

TABLE 2

HIGHEST RATE OF SERIAL MURDER ACTIVITY

Number of Cases	Largest Number of Victims in Calendar Year
1 (Dinsdale)	11
2 (Mackay, Nilsen)	7
3 (Cummins, "Nudes Murderer," Sutcliffe)	4
3 (Christie, Haigh, Neilson)	3
3 (Young, Brady, Morris)	2
12 (Total)	

In most accounts of serial killers, the actual dates on which murders occurred are
among the most solid evidence regarding the
"career" of a particular offender. Despite
this, it is extremely difficult to generalize
about any periodicity in an offender's urge
or wish to commit murder. In the great majority of cases, intervals between murders in
a series range from a few days to a year or
even longer. John Christie, for example,
committed his first known murder in 1943.
The second was over a year later. Five years
elapsed before the third and fourth victimizations, in 1949. The chief variable in his decision to kill appears to have been the presence of his wife. When she left to visit a
relative, he would kill. In 1952, he killed his
wife, and then killed three more women in a
two-month period (Kennedy, 1961).

For the purposes of investigating multiple
homicide, it would be convenient to believe
that killers acted on an urgent compulsion
that required them to defy any threat of capture. This is the picture that has emerged perhaps from historic American cases like the
1940s "Moonlight Murderer," who killed
once a month. The idea gains some support
from remarks like those of Ian Brady, "I've
killed three or four and I'll do another one,
but I'm not due for another one for three

months . . ." However, the urge to kill appears more related to opportunity than to
compulsion. The "Nudes Murderer" killed
his first victim in 1959 and waited over four
years before committing another crime. He
then killed six times in two years. The only
rule of periodicity that does appear to have
some validity is that in the career of each
murderer, the rate of killing has accelerated
over time. This is most marked in the cases of
Christie and the "Nudes Murderer." A common pattern has been for a year or more to
elapse after the first killing, which is followed
by three or four further murders in a year.
But, as in so many other issues regarding the
psychology of the multiple killer, the evidence simply does not exist to permit more
than such generalizations.

THE JUSTICE SYSTEM

In every case but one, the cases discussed
here ended with an arrest. From the police
point of view, the 1942 case of Frederick
Cummins represented a very creditable outcome—effective investigation and prompt arrest. Cummins murdered four women in a
week, causing a major panic in London. This
was all the more severe because the crimes
took place in the already traumatic setting of
the Blackout. A fifth attack was interrupted,
and he left behind belongings that led to his
identification. A series of killings thus led to
an intensive police investigation that ultimately caused the apprehension of the offender. This has been very much the pattern
of later "manhunts," which have often received melodramatic media attention—the
"Nudes Murderer," the "Black Panther"
(Neilson), the "Yorkshire Ripper" (Sutcliffe). All ultimately succeeded in catching
the perpetrator.

Furthermore, it is impossible to evaluate
police successes in this area because, by definition, a successful investigation catches an
offender *before* he or she becomes a repeat
killer. The case of Mary Bell has already
been noted, and it is representative of dozens of other incidents where an arrest prevented the near certainty of future crimes.

At first sight, the police response to serial murder has been very successful. At the time this article was written, there were in England no unsolved serial killings—at least, not cases in which an offender was known to have killed four or more victims but remained at large. Only in one case—the "Nudes Murderer"—did a killer escape apprehension, and it is very commonly accepted that this happened only because of the offender's suicide.

It should be noted, however, that the record of investigation of serial murder is by no means one of untrammelled achievement. In some cases, a series of murders continued for several years without interruption, although the existence of a serial murderer was known. Probably the most studied and the most notorious of these examples was the "Yorkshire Ripper" investigation of 1975–81. By mid-1977, excellent detective work had focused the investigation on Peter Sutcliffe's firm, but the trail was lost, and the police put mistaken credence in a series of letters and tapes purporting to come from the killer. Sutcliffe thus was enabled to kill eight more times, much to his amazement (he attributed his continued success to the Divine mission he claimed).

Also, it is common for serial murder cases to be identified as such only in retrospect, often when the killer has already been caught. No law enforcement agency was aware that the Christie or Nilsen murders had even occurred until bodies were found in their respective houses and the suspects made confessions. The murders committed by Young and Dinsdale were classified as accidental deaths until the flagrant behavior of those individuals attracted suspicion and then retrospective reexamination of the earlier cases.

Whatever the reasons, though, it can be stated that English serial murder cases do have common outcomes. Arrest is likely within about four years. Once he is in custody, the serial killer also has a predictable fate. He may well attempt a defense of insanity or diminished responsibility, but it is extremely unlikely that this will be successful. He will receive at least one life sentence (the mandatory minimum for murder). This is remarkable when the ease with which insanity defenses are accepted in England is considered. For most of this century, American scholars writing on murder repeatedly have remarked on the tendency of English courts to describe murderers as insane. In the 1950s, Wolfgang calculated that almost forty percent of people brought to trial at assizes were declared insane (Wolfgang, 1958:314–16; Compare Lunde, 1976:41–42).

Insanity defenses became rather rare in England when capital punishment declined in the 1960s. However, the new defense of diminished responsibility (introduced in 1957) reduced murder charges to manslaughter and was widely successful where attempted. In the 1960s, psychopaths were reluctantly included in this category (Walker, 1968:279). In that decade, over forty percent of those indicted for murder were found either insane or of diminished responsibility. Serial killers were thus far less fortunate than the "normally"abnormal (Chiswick et al., 1984; Gibbens et al., 1977).

All the cases discussed received strikingly consistent treatment from the courts, especially in the matter of medical and psychiatric evidence. Of the twelve cases, one was never brought to trial. Of the remainder, an insanity defense was attempted in eight cases. However, medical factors played a role in the outcome of only one case, that of Peter Dinsdale ("Bruce Lee"), who was detained without limit in a special hospital.

The lack of success of insanity defenses in other cases was remarkable. Before 1960, there were three serial cases, all of which resulted in the execution of the offender. In the Haigh case of 1949, psychiatric evidence of paranoia and psychosis was presented strongly, but was challenged by the prosecution on the grounds that any statement or words from the accused were invalid evidence, because he had so strong an interest in saving his life. This effectively excluded the vast majority of psychiatric or psychoanalytic evidence, but this scepticism was the view upheld by the jury, and Haigh was hanged.

More recently, the question of insanity has lost some of its importance because the accused no longer faces the death penalty. However, there are very anomalous cases. In 1981, Peter Sutcliffe was tried as the "Yorkshire Ripper," in a setting that seemed to favor an insanity defense. Both prosecution and defense psychiatrists wholeheartedly agreed on a diagnosis of extreme paranoid schizophrenia, but they were overruled by the judge, who insisted on Sutcliffe's fitness to stand trial. In the event, he was found guilty as charged and received a life sentence. Equally curious was the 1971 case of Graham Young, who had spent his teens in the Broadmoor hospital for the criminally insane. On release, he committed new murders, which led this time to a "regular" guilty verdict and a life sentence.

There has been great reluctance to accept defenses of insanity or diminished responsibility, even when (as in the cases of Brady or Mackay) it is freely admitted that the offenders were deeply psychopathic. Moreover, this reluctance has its curious aspects. Since the 1880s, the British insanity verdict has been "guilty but insane," and it leads not to normal psychiatric treatment but to incarceration in a prison-hospital like Broadmoor. Accepting an insanity defense is therefore less likely to be seen as in any sense letting the offender evade justice.

American courts have sometimes made controversial decisions about the sanity of offenders who would widely be seen as mentally ill—John Wayne Gacy, Edmund Kemper, and (most remarkably, perhaps) Herbert Mullin. This is a trait they share with their English counterparts, though the skepticism about insanity defenses is even more remarkable in England. Undoubtedly, one factor in both countries is the influence of hostile public opinion in very notorious cases, but the consistent reluctance to attribute insanity to extremely violent offenders is noteworthy. At the very least, it indicates the enduring hostility of the legal profession to that ill-defined but important type of personality, the aggressive psychopath (see Gaylin, 1983; Marsh and Katz, 1985; Wrightsman, 1987).

CONCLUSION

Serial killers in England and America have exhibited broadly similar patterns and personality types. Major differences that are immediately apparent have included the relative availability of firearms, a type of weapon favored by some American killers, which makes possible mass killings like those of Huberty. The U.S.A. is also a much bigger and more mobile society, and bodies can be more easily concealed in the U.S. for lengthy periods. This helps to explain why U.S. serial murderers might have been so much more "successful" than their English counterparts.

However, the English study does present one issue that is not familiar in the literature, and that is the dichotomy between the highly predictable killers and their more restrained counterparts. In eight of the English cases, it would have taken real insight to predict when the subject was twenty that serious violence lay in his future. In the other four cases, such a diagnosis could have been made with some confidence not long after the subject reached puberty. This distinction—between the Brady type and the far more controlled Christie—needs explanation.

No attempt has been made here to offer explanations in either biological or environmental terms, but both views would have their adherents. With the Brady type, the phrase "born to kill" seems apposite (Newman, 1979); for the others, minor psychopathic tendencies seem to have culminated in an explosive mid-life crisis in which alcoholism may perhaps have played a part. This suggestion emerges from four of the cases, but it remains merely suggestive. If violent tendencies are found to come on at particular ages (like the mid-twenties), it would be interesting to know how this chronology compares with the usual onset of common psychiatric illnesses, such as schizophrenia.

Several suggestions can therefore be made for future research on extremely violent offenders of this nature. But a vital first step must be to apply very traditional social science concepts of longitudinal and crosssectional research in order to define groups of offenders in a particular society or at a special time. Only thus can case-study techniques produce new taxonomies and new explanations that can be based on them. The serial murderer is too important a type to be left to the desultory attentions of the crime journalist and the police memoir.

NOTES

[1] Mass and serial killers both murder a large number of people, the precise number being undefined. Mass murderers kill at one place and time, serial killers act over a period of time.

[2] Of the four countries that make up Great Britain, England and Wales share a common legal system and are treated as a single entity for purposes of recording criminal statistics. Scotland has a very different legal system based on Roman law, with offenses being differently defined. Northern Ireland has a separate criminal justice system that has been profoundly affected by the terrorist crisis that has existed since 1969. In 1972, for example, the murder rate in Northern Ireland was over thirty-five times that of England and Wales.

[3] Since 1985 several new serial murder investigations have been in progress. Two men, Michele Lupo and Kenneth Erskine were each charged with four or more murders.

REFERENCES

Abrahamsen, D. (1973). *The murdering mind.* New York: Harper & Row.

———(1945). *Crime and the human mind.* New York: Columbia University Press.

———(1960). *The psychology of crime.* New York: Columbia University Press.

Adorno, T.W., et al. (1950). *The authoritarian personality.* New York: Columbia University Press.

Altick, R. D. (1973). *Victorian studies in scarlet.* London: Dent.

Andrews, A. (1973). *Intensive inquiries.* London: Harrap.

Baldwin, J., and Bottoms, A.E. (1976). *The urban criminal: A study in Sheffield.* London: Tavistock.

Bingham, J. (1973). *The hunting down of Peter Manuel.* London: Harrap.

Blackburn, R. (1968). Personality in relation to extreme aggression in psychiatric offenders. *Brit J Psychiat* 114:821.

———(1971). Personality types among abnormal homicides. *Brit J Crim* 11:237–45.

Borrell, C., and Cashinella, B. (1975). *Crime in Britain today.* London: Routledge Kegan Paul.

Boyle, J. (1977). *A sense of freedom.* London: Pan.

Brittain, R. P. (1970). The sadistic murderer. *Med Sci Law* 10(4).

Browne, D. G. (1956). *The rise of Scotland Yard.* London: Harrap.

———and Tullett, T. (1980). *Bernard Spilsbury.* London: Harrap.

Burn, G. (1984). *Somebody's husband, somebody's son.* London: Heinemann.

Calvert, E. R. (1927). *Capital punishment.* London: G.P. Putnam's.

Chiswick, D.; McIsaac, M.; and McClintock, F.H. (1984). *Prosecution of the mentally disturbed—Dilemmas of identification and discretion.* Aberdeen: Aberdeen University Press.

Clark, T., and Penycate, J. (1976). *Psychopath—The case of Patrick Mackay.* London: Routledge Kegan Paul.

Cohen, S. (1971). *Images of deviance.* London: Penguin.

Cornwell, J. (1984). *Earth to earth.* New York: Ecco.

Criminal Statistics England and Wales. (1985). London: Her Majesty's Stationery Office.

Cross, R. (1981). *The Yorkshire Ripper.* New York: Dell.

Dilnot, G. (1929). *Scotland Yard.* London: Geoffrey Bless.

Dinitz, S., and Conrad, J. P. (1980). The dangerous two per cent. In *Critical issues in juvenile delinquency,* ed. D. Shichor and D. H. Kelly. Lexington, MA: D.C. Heath.

Douthwaite, L.C. (1928). *Mass murder.* London: John Long.

DuRose, J. (1971). *Murder was my business.* London: W.H. Allen.

Egger, S. A. (1984). A working definition of serial murder. *J Police Sci Adm* 12:348–57.

———(1986). Utility of case study approach to serial murder research. Paper presented to American Society of Criminology, Atlanta, Georgia, in November, 1986.

Farson, D. (1972). *Jack the Ripper.* London: Michael Joseph.

Firmin, S. (1948). *Scotland Yard.* London: Hutchinson.

Forbes, G., and Meehan, P. (1982). *Such bad company.* Edinburgh: Paul Harris.

Fox, J. A., and Levin, J. (1985). *Mass murder: America's growing menace.* New York: Plenum.

Gaute, J.H.H., and Odell, R. (1982). *Murder: Whatdunit?* London: Harrap.

———(1979). *The murderers' who's who.* London: Harrap.

Gaylin, W. (1983). *The killing of Bonnie Garland.* New York: Penguin.

Gibbens, T.C. (1958). Sane and insane homicide. *J Crim Law* 49:121–34.

————Soothill, K.L., and Pope, P.J. (1977). *Medical remands in the criminal courts.* Oxford: Oxford University Press.

Gibson, E., and Klein, S. (1961). *Murder.* Home Office Research Report. London: Her Majesty's Stationery Office.

Godwin, J. (1978). *Murder USA.* New York: Ballantine.

Goldstein, J. H. (1986). *Aggression and crimes of violence.* 2nd ed. Oxford: Oxford University Press.

Goodman, J., and Will, I. (1984). *Underworld.* London: Harrap.

————ed. (1973). *The trial of Ian Brady and Myra Hindley.* Newton Abbott: David and Charles.

Greeno, E. (1961). *War on the underworld.* London: Harrap.

Hansford-Johnson, P. (1967). *On iniquity.* London: Macmillan.

Hare, R.D., and Schalling, D. (1978). *Psychopathic behavior.* New York: Wiley.

Harrison, F. (1986). *Brady and Hindley.* London: Ashgrove.

Hawkes, H. (1970). *Murder on the A34.* London: John Long.

Hellman, D.S., and Blackman, N. (1966). Eneuresis, firesetting and cruelty to animals. *Am J Psych* 122:1431–85.

Heppenstall, R. (1973). *The sex war and others.* London: Peter Owen.

Hickey, E. W. (1986). The etiology of victimization in serial murder. Paper presented to American Society of Criminology, Atlanta, Georgia: November.

Holdaway, S. (1979). *The British police.* Beverly Hills: Sage.

————(1983). *Inside the British police.* Oxford: Blackwell.

Howe, Sir R. (1965). *The story of Scotland Yard.* London: Arthur Barker.

Howgrave-Graham, H.M. (1947). *Light and shade at Scotland Yard.* London: Murray.

Jackson, R. (1967). *Occupied with crime.* New York: Doubleday.

Jenkins, P. (1988). Myth and murder: The serial killer panic of 1983–85. *Criminal Justice Research Bulletin* (forthcoming).

Kennedy, L. (1961). *Ten Rillington Place.* New York: Simon and Schuster.

Lewis, D. O.; Pincus, J. H.; Feldman, M.; Jackson, L.; and Bard, B. (1986). Psychiatric, neurological and psychoeducational characteristics of 15 death row inmates in the US. *Am J Psych* 143:838–45.

Lewis, D. O.; Shanok, S.; Pincus, J.H.; et al. (1979). Violent juvenile delinquents. *Journal of the American Academy of Child Psychology* 18:307–19.

Lindsay, P. (1958). *The mainspring of murder.* London: John Long.

Lisners, J. (1983). *House of horrors.* London: Corgi.

Lucas, N., and Davies, P. (1979). *The monster butler.* London: Arthur Barker.

Lucas, N. (1968). *The Flying Squad.* London: W.H. Allen.

————(1969). *Britain's gangland.* London: W.H. Allen.

Lunde, D.T. (1976). *Murder and madness.* New York: W.W. Norton.

Lustgarten, E. (1968). *The business of murder.* London: Harrap.

McClintock, F.H. (1963). *Crimes of violence.* London: Macmillan.

————et al. (1968). *Crime in England and Wales.* London: Heinemann.

McConnell, B. (1974). *Found naked and dead.* London: New English Library.

McCormick, D. (1970). *The identity of Jack the Ripper.* London: John Long.

Macdonald, J. M. (1963). The threat to kill. *Am J Psych* 120:125–30.

McNee, Sir D. (1983). *McNee's law.* London: Collins.

McVicar, J. (1979). *McVicar by himself.* London: Arrow.

Mark, Sir R. (1978). *In the office of Constable.* London: Fontana.

Marsh, F. H., and Katz, J., eds. (1985). *Biology, crime and ethics.* Cincinnati: Anderson.

Masters, B. (1985). *Killing for company: The case of Dennis Nilsen.* New York: Stein and Day.

Michaud, S.G., and Aynesworth, H. (1983). *The only living witness.* New York: Simon and Schuster.

Millen, E. (1972). *Specialist in crime.* London: Harrap.

Monahan, J. (1981). *Predicting violent behavior.* Beverly Hills: Sage.

Morris, T., and Cooper, L. B. (1964). *A calendar of murder.* London: Michael Joseph.

Moylan, Sir J. (1929). *Scotland Yard and the Metropolitan Police.* London.

Nash, J. R. (1973). *Bloodletters and bad men.* New York: M. Evans.

National Center for the Analysis of Violent Crime (1986). "The National Center for the Analysis of

Violent Crime." Behavioral Science Services, FBI Academy, Quantico, VA ("revised 4/7/86").

Nettler, G. (1982). *Killing one another.* Cincinnati: Anderson.

———(1984). *Explaining crime.* 3rd ed. New York: McGraw Hill.

Newman, G. (1979). *Understanding violence.* Philadelphia: Lippincott.

Orwell, G. (1965). *Decline of the English murder and other essays.* London: Penguin.

Palmer, S. (1960). *The psychology of murder.* New York: Thomas Y. Crowell Co.

Partridge, R. (1953). *Broadmoor.* London: Chatto and Windus.

Patrick, J. (1973). *A Glasgow gang observed.* London: Eyre Methuen.

Posner, M. (1973). *Midland murders.* Wolverhampton: Star Publications.

Prothero, M. (1931). *History of the CID at Scotland Yard.* London: Herbert Jenkin.

Revitch, E., and Schlesinger, L.B. (1981). *The psychopathology of homicide.* Springfield, IL: Charles Thomas.

Radzinowicz, Sir L., and Hood, R. (1986). *A history of the English criminal law and its administration Vol. 5.* London: Stevens.

Rutherford, W. (1973). *The untimely silence.* London: Hamish Hamilton.

Satten, J.; Menninger, K.; Rosen, I.; and Mayman, M. (1960). Murder without apparent motive. *Am J Psych* 117:486–95.

Sayeed, Z.A.; Lewis, S.A.; and Brittain, R.P. (1969). An EEG and psychiatric study of 32 insane murderers. *Brit J Psychiat* 115:306–11.

Scott, H. (1954). *Scotland Yard.* London: Andre Deutsch.

Sereny, G. (1972). *The case of Mary Bell.* London: Eyre Methuen.

Simpson, K. (1978). *Forty years of murder.* London: Harrap.

Slipper, J. (1981). *Slipper of the Yard.* London: Sidgwick and Jackson.

Smyth, F. (1980). *Cause of death.* London: Orbis.

Templewood, V. (1951). *The shadow of the gallows.* London: Gollancz.

Toch, H. (1969). *Violent men.* Chicago: Aldine (revised ed. 1980).

Tullett, T. (1986). *Clues to murder: Forensic murder investigations of Professor J.M. Cameron.* London: Bodley Head.

———(1979). *Strictly murder.* London: Bodley Head.

Valentine, S. (1976). *The Black Panther story.* London: NEL.

Walker, N. (1968). *Crime and punishment in Britain.* 2nd ed. Edinburgh: Edinburgh University Press.

———and McCabe, S. (1968–72). *Crime and insanity in England.* 2 vols. Edinburgh: Edinburgh University Press.

Webb, D. (1955). *Deadline for crime.* London: Muller.

Wertham, F. (1947). *Dark legend: A study in murder.* London: Gollancz.

———(1949). *The show of violence.* London: Gollancz.

Williams, E. (1967). *Beyond belief.* London: Hamish Hamilton.

Wilson, C. (1972). *Order of assassins.* London: Rupert Hart-Davis.

———(1984). *A criminal history of mankind.* London: Granada.

———and Pitman, P. (1962). *Encyclopaedia of murder.* New York: Putnam.

———and Seaman, D. (1983). *Encyclopaedia of modern murder.* New York: Perigee.

Wilson, J. G. (1959). *The trial of Peter Manuel.* London: Secker and Warburg.

Wolfgang, M., and Ferracuti, F. (1967). *The subculture of violence.* London: Tavistock.

Wolfgang, M. (1958). *Patterns of criminal homicide.* Philadelphia: University of Pennsylvania Press.

———and Weiner, N.A. (1982). *Criminal violence.* Beverly Hills, CA: Sage.

Wrightsman, L. (1987). *Psychology and the legal system.* Belmont, CA: Wadsworth.

Erratum

The following diagrams should appear on page 213.

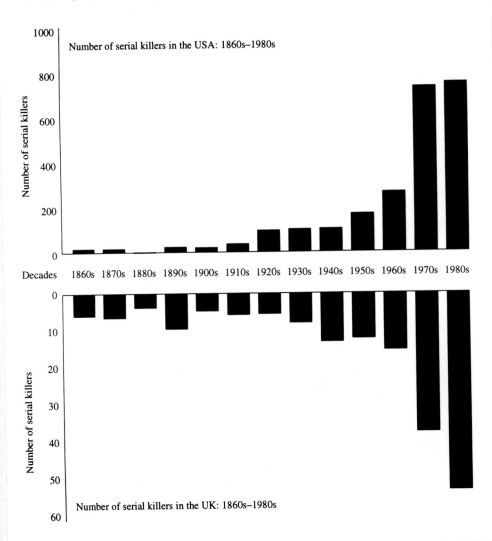

[11]

Canter, D., Missen, C., & Hodge, S. (1996) A case for special Agents *Policing Today* 2 (1) (April)

ARE SERIAL KILLERS SPECIAL?

David Canter, Christopher Missen and Samantha Hodge
Investigative Psychology Unit
Department of Psychology
The University of Liverpool

Synopsis:

Two or three times a year there is some outcry about the discovery of someone who has killed a number of people over a period of time; Fred and Rose West, Colin Ireland, John Duffy. This sets up media orchestrated outrage about the rapid increase in these types of offenders and what it implies. But what are the facts? Are serial killers really on the increase? Is this a crime of cross-national epidemic proportions as some FBI reports have claimed? Do we really need special international computer systems and their associated teams of 'experts' to fight the menace?

Drawn from a larger study of over 3000 serial killers that have been identified throughout the world over the past 150 years, a detailed analysis of the frequencies and varieties of serial killers has been carried out. These figures reveal that there has been an increase over the last 25 years, but that this increase directly reflects the growth in the number of homicides overall in that period. The figures for Britain mirror those for the USA and other countries in this regard. In other words, these crimes are a by-product of an increasingly violent society not some special 'plague'.

Examination of the background characteristics of US serial killers also show that their dysfunctional family backgrounds and extensive, wide ranging criminal histories are very similar to those of other violent offenders. They are not some, special 'breed' drawn from a limited section of the criminal population as some have claimed.

Study of the distances both US and UK serial killers travel to commit their crimes also show, as for other criminals, that serial killers do not usually make a habit of travelling long distances. Most commit their crimes locally to where they are living, although some do travel larger distances. The size of the area over which they travel does have implications for the ways in which linked investigations are set up.

The implications of these studies is that the way to investigate these crimes is to ensure that the resources available for 'conventional' murder investigations are in place, not to waste money on special systems just to investigate serial muder.

In 1936 H.Russell-Wakefield contributed a chapter to a book on "The fifty worst crimes of the last Hundred Years" . The chapter was about Henri Landru, a Frenchman who was guillotined in 1922 for the murder of at least 11 women. In the chapter H.Russell-Wakefield refers to "..serial murderers such as Landru who made homicide their career.." and in so doing established a term that gained currency over the subsequent 50 years until it was taken up by the thriller writer Thomas Harris (1987) to describe his homicidal characters and thereby passed into public awareness as a central concern of American crime fiction. Along the way, the US Law enforcement agency that often only has jurisdiction in homicide cases if they can be shown to be part of a series, the FBI, started to take a special interest in the characteristics of men who had committed a number of sexually related homicides (Ressler et al 1988).

Through their many lectures worldwide the FBI Behavioural Science Unit (Ressler and Shachtman 1994) encouraged the notion that serial killers were a special breed of offenders that required special systems to investigate their crimes. A centralised record of violent crimes (VICAP) was established in the USA with the intention of dealing with this 'growing menace'((Ressler et al 1988). A new clutch of 'experts' was also hatched to 'profile' this specific set of criminals. Furthermore, despite the lack of any systematic assessments of the efficacy of VICAP, or its Canadian descendant VICLAS, and the luke warm support for 'profiling' as anything more than a useful second opinion, (Pinizzotto 1984, Copson 1995) international examination of the possibility of introducing centralised record keeping systems and 'profiling teams' into many other countries and even of cross-national networking of the systems is currently being actively considered. It is therefore essential to consider the nature of serial killing and to question what the most appropriate investigative strategies are for dealing with it.

The Data Set

Defining a 'serial killer' simply as anyone who has committed more than two murders over a period of time, perhaps more technically 'episodic homicides', Christopher Missen has collected and collated information on serial killers world-wide, from every source he could identify. He has examined newspaper reports, accounts in books and magazines and where ever possible directly contacted the law enforcement agencies involved in investigating these crimes. By cross checking information from various sources it has been possible to build dossiers on 3,532 serial killers from over 30 countries, who were identified from 1860 up to the present day. Of course, much of the information in the sources available has to be treated with caution, accounts of child rearing practices in the killers' infancy, or the personalities of his parents may owe more to journalistic imagination than to actuality. But other information such as the locations in which bodies were found, the date of birth of the offenders, their convictions prior to the murders, and many of the details of how the murders were carried out, which tend to be a matter of public record, are found by corroboration to be reasonably accurate. This *corpus* of information is the basis for the present study. Of course, it can only be regarded as indicative. The very early cases are likely to be distorted through historical lapses, the most recent figures will be under representative because of offenders currently active who have not been apprehended. All of the information only relates to detected cases. But despite these caveats the corpus does provide some reasonable indication of the variety and prevalence of this significant phenomenon.

Are Serial Killers on the Increase?

By examining the frequencies of serial killers for each decade since 1860 a clear picture of their changing numbers can be established. By far the largest number of such murderers have been found in the USA, 2,617 , and so it is appropriate to consider the frequencies for that country as the bench mark against which to examine the situation for the UK. The figures make it clear that serial killers increased in number steadily until the 1970's when the rate of increase climbed considerably. This accords with Hickey's (1991) findings based on a sub-sample of 203 serial killers. His smaller sample gave him a less precise and more erratic distribution but nonetheless he draws attention to the fact that the great majority of US serial killers have come into being in the last 25 years. His graph shows a slight, optimistic decline in recent years, but from our figures that appears to be an artefact of his small sample.

Assuming that about 70% of all the US serial killers we have identified (i.e. 1,832) have been active in the last 25 years, that means that in any year about 73 (1,832/25) are active. This is within the range of 35 to 100 that Hickey (1991) argues from his much smaller sample, but far lower than the thousands sometimes claimed.

Figures for USA Serial Killers About Here

There can be little doubt then that the phenomena that has grabbed public attention and become the staple diet of Hollywood thrillers has indeed increased considerably over the last quarter of a century in the USA. However, there has been no similar comparison for other countries. Figures derived from the Missen Corpus do show that there are direct parallels. It has been possible to identify 164 serial killers in the UK since 1860. So although this is much smaller than for the USA the trend in these numbers is directly analogous to those for the USA with a large increase over the last quarter of a century. It is worth noting also that the 144 serial killers for France follow a similar pattern over the same period. The 165 such offenders for Germany also show the recent upsurge, but the figures for the earlier part of this century do not show the same steady increase, presumably because of the chaos of two world wars.

Using parallel calculations to those for the USA indicates about 5 such individuals a year may be active in each of Britain, France and Germany at the present time. This is an important number, but it does need to be set against the current annual homicide rate for England and Wales of around six hundred a year.

Figures for UK Serial Killers About Here

Relationship to General Homicide Figures

When looked at in isolation the inflation in serial killings over the last two decades can lead to the vision of the emergence of an entirely new form of killing and killer that requires new forms of investigation to combat it. Yet comparison with the general pattern of homicides is most instructive. The frequencies of homicides for the USA derived from US Justice Department statistics and for Britain derived from Home Office statistics have increased considerably since the second World War with a particular increase since the late 1960's. Indeed the figures follow each other with there typically being about 25 US homicides for every British one. Many matters need to be taken into consideration in explaining these variations in the frequency of murder, not least the changes in the demographic make up of both countries, but in considering the prevalence of serial murder they provide an important backdrop against which to assess the uniqueness of this phenomenon.

Up until the turn of the century, in broad terms in the USA, for every 250 homicides that took place in a year there was one serial killer active in the decade in which that year fell. From the turn of the century until the second world war the ration is nearer to 350:1. In Britain there was little difference around the turn of the century but up until the second world war the figure is closer to 55 homicides for one serial killer in the decade. After the second world war the rate increases, for the USA to around 30:1 and for the UK to 15:1.

These figures do deserve much closer attention and more detailed analysis, but three points can be drawn from them as they stand at present:

> 1. The recent increase in serial killer rates is a direct reflection of the recent increase in the general homicide rate.
>
> 2. The proportion of serial killers to homicides has increased since the second world war.
>
> 3. Most curiously of all, the proportion of homicides in the UK that can be related to serial killings is distinctly higher than in the USA.

This last finding is especially surprising but was noticed by Leyton many years ago (Leyton 1989). He wrote "...nations such as Britain or Germany, which have very low homicide rates, appear to have high multiple-murder rates." p.21. He is sensibly suspicious of inferring or explaining any trends when the incident rates are so low and the figures less than totally reliable.

However it is worth cautiously considering these comparisons because at first sight they appear to challenge the view that the USA is a more violent society. In such a context, if it is assumed that Serial Killing is an indicator of 'motiveless' violence against strangers then it would have been expected that a higher proportion of killings would have been committed by these extremely 'alienated' individuals. However the figures do make sense, and accord with the existing understanding of the differences between US and UK murder (as discussed recently by Leyton, 1995), if serial killing is seen as little different from conventional murder. Within this perspective a distinction needs to be drawn between violence and those particular aggressive acts that result in murder. If aggression breaks out within a violent society where weapons and the demonstration of coercive control is more acceptable then there is an increased probability that aggression will lead to a killing, but those forms of aggression that are at the heart of premeditated murder may be similar in most societies. If such is the case, then serial killing will be a standard, albeit small, component of this form of aggression. This leads to the proposal that there are a higher proportion of serial killers per homicide in the UK than the USA because there are fewer outbursts of emotional violence that turn into murder in the UK than in the USA.

These are proposals that require further elaboration and study. In particular it suggests the need for much closer attention to the proportion of different varieties of events that give rise to homicide in the different countries. Unfortunately such specific statistics are extremely difficult to come by. However, more detailed information is available on serial killers and their victims which can be used to test the view that serial killings have many characteristics commonly associated with other forms of homicide. Because the numbers are so much greater in the USA than in the UK more detailed analysis is possible in most cases for the USA.

Characteristics of the Victims

In order to consider the characteristics of serial killers a sub-sample of 217 US serial killers was identified on which reasonably full information was available. This allowed examination of the relationship with their victims that existed prior to the murder. The common assumption is that homicide in general grows out of a pre-existing relationship between victim and perpetrator but that serial killers are essentially killing strangers in a more random or *as hoc* way. The analysis shows that 68% of the victims were known to the offenders prior to the offence. In 45% of the cases the victim knew the offender as an acquaintance. Indeed it is common for at least one of the victims of a serial killer to be an associate (35%), neighbour (22%) or even family member (7%).

These bald figures hide a whole range of scenarios from offenders secretly targeting victims, giving unknown victims lifts as hitch-hikers, accosting prostitutes, taking casual acquaintances home and then killing them, through to killing their own tenants and family members. The central point though, is that this range of contacts is typical of all murder. So there are no obvious focus for the targets of serial killers that clearly distinguish them from other forms of homicide, other than a tendency towards more obviously vulnerable victims and people who also tend to have less obvious direct contact with the offender. They can therefore be looked upon as typical of those murders in which an obvious culprit may not be immediately apparent and which therefore pose some special difficulties of investigation.

Characteristics of the Offenders

If there are no very obvious distinguishing characteristics of the victims of these murderers then are there some obvious, special aspects of the offenders that mark them out from other killers?

5

Age

Wilson and Harston (1985) show that the peak age for violent crime in the USA in 1980 was in the late teens to mid-20's. Although other researchers using rather more narrowly defined categories of violence that include murder propose the average as being between 23 and 27 . There are many sociological and anthropological explanations of these results, but when compared with the 205 serial killers for whom we have details of their age at the onset of their series it can be seen that the distribution does overlap considerably with that well attested 'dangerous age'. The mean value of 28 years is only a little older than would be anticipated purely on the general figures for violent crime, but it does accord with the dominant age of British murderers as reported by the home office and is actually very close to the mean of 32 years old for 239 murderers in a sample of British cases that initially proved problematic to the investigators (Salfati 1995).

Criminal History

Furthermore, serial killers are clearly drawn from the general criminal population. Three-quarters of our 217 US serial killers had previous convictions, 24% of these having convictions for burglary and theft, 22% for violence and 17% for drug related offences with 16% having history of sexual offence convictions. Many of them had started their life of crime early, with 45% having a juvenile criminal history. Thus although the emphasis of their crimes is more towards violence and sexually related crimes than would be true for the criminal population as a whole they are certainly not law-abiding citizens prior to their killings. They thus share much with the criminal fraternity that finds its way into other forms of serious crime.

Family Circumstances

The domestic setting out of which they grow also is typical of most criminals. In a quarter of the cases it was known that the offender's immediate family had a history of criminality. Their families were typically dysfunctional in a variety of recognisable ways, an absent father (65%), frequent moves (45%), institutionalised (41%) a mother known for her promiscuity (38%), and much violence in the family (50%). These experiences left a sizeable minority of these men physically handicapped (18%), scarred (14%) or with a stutter or similar disorder (13%). Indeed, as has been noted for many sub-groups who are involved in violent crime a high proportion (45%) had suffered some serious head injury or other physical trauma at some point in their life prior to killing. This seems to reflect their life-styles rather than being a distinct cause of their crimes. They relate to the high proportion (63%) who had been physically or sexually abused during their childhood, many by family members (48%).

Educational History

The disruptive early years is also shown in the educational background of these offenders. The great majority of them (867%) dropped out of school many without any qualifications at all

(74%), some were illiterate (10%) . However, the general pattern does not indicate completely incompetent, 'drifters'. A notable proportion of them (47%) had held some sort of skilled manual occupation and a handful (4%) had professional level occupations. In fact court assessment of the IQ's of these individuals do indicate that a remarkable proportion (56%) scored in the high range (above an IQ of 120). This does not support the popular belief that these offenders are often near geniuses , indeed many of them are of the low intellectual ability associated with most criminals.

It is therefore reasonable to think of these murderers as often drawn from the more capable levels of the criminal population. They are less likely to be the totally incompetent offender who gets caught through obvious 'errors' , but they are certainly not some sort of 'super-criminal' as favoured by Hollywood. Many of them (73%) drink heavily, or take drugs (46%) around the time they commit their crimes and thus cannot be regarded as studious intellects set on some determined mission.

Distances Offenders Travel

Competent criminals may be the simplest way of describing people who manage to kill a number of times without getting caught. But a picture does not emerge of some very special sub-group that will only be detected by means not normally available to police investigations. Of particular importance in these considerations is the locations in which the crimes are committed and the relationship this has to the location at which the offender is based around the time he is carrying out his offences.

The idea that criminals are active at locations that bear a distinct relationship to where they live has been proposed for common crimes such as burglary for a considerable time (Brantigham and Brantigham, 1981). However the possibility that this is also true for more serious, serial crimes of an apparently impulsive nature such as rape has only recently been established for a UK sample (Canter and Larkin 1993). Deriving from that work has been the hypothesis that offenders have a natural *range* over which they operate. This is likely to be a function of their resources and capabilities(Canter and Gregory 1994). The simplest test of this hypothesis, proposed by Canter and Gregory, was that offenders would tend to live within an area defined by a circle the diameter of which was defined by the two offences furthest from each other. In their study of 45 serial rapists living in the area of London they found that 86% did indeed live within the area defined by the circle.

Taking the sample of US serial killers, for whom there was reliable geographical information on 121, it was found that the same 'circle hypothesis' accounted for 87% of the offenders. There is thus strong evidence that serial killers, like other criminals, tend to operate in an area that can be defined in relation to where they live. The difference between such offenders is therefore also likely to be the scale of area over which they operate. This further hypothesis that there is some range that is typical for any particular offender implies that there is a strong relationship between both the maximum distance the offender is likely to travel and the minimum distance. This can be directly tested and does indeed show strong correlations for the 121 US serial killers and for the 29 UK Serial killers on whom information was available.

7

Relationship of Maximum and Minimum Distances for US Offenders here.

Relationship of Maximum and Minimum Distances for UK Offenders here.

These results add further support to the view that these are not highly devious, specially gifted offenders who roam far and wide, but that like other offenders they seek out targets a comfortable distance from their base within the limits of their own resources and capabilities. The average distances involved also show how the scale of these ranges is a reflection of the life style mobility of the country.

Distance Travelled in Miles
By Serial Killers

	Average Minimum	Average Maximum
USA	22	68
UK	4	7

Thus although the figures for the USA are apparently quite large they still constitute local distances by the conventions of travel of that country. The UK distances are probably larger than for opportunistic burglaries but are also clearly at a local scale. Of course there are some individuals who do travel great distances, but these (as Hickey has also noted) are very much the minority. Often these people actually are moving their 'base' , living in a series of places. So if they were investigated in relation to local knowledge they could still come to police attention.

These findings are important both for individual investigations and for policy decisions about the systems that should be put in place in preparation for any major investigation. They suggest that intensive local effort should be the prime basis of any investigation with less recourse to national or cross-national systems.

Implications for Investigations

Serial killers aggravate the difficulties found in all police investigations in two especial ways; linking cases and identifying the offender. These problems come precisely from the fact that these murders are especially difficult to detect. If they were easier to detect then the offender would not have continued to murder time and time again.

Similarities in the victims and the styles of killing will draw police attention to the possibility that the crimes have been committed by the same person. Inability to make these links with confidence may therefore arise from two distinct matters. The first is the possibility that a crime has not been recognised as such. In this regard the reporting of missing people may be significant but it is especially challenging to investigations to decide whether or not that does imply that the missing person has been killed. Our data that indicates there is frequently association of some sort between the offender and his victims does at least show the importance of careful consideration of all reports of missing people in the vicinity of known killers.

The second difficulty in linking offences arises if there is no forensic evidence to provide clear indication that the same perpetrator is involved. In countries with relatively low murder rates the number of possible killings that may be the work of one individual, even over a ten year period is relatively low. A high proportion of identified homicide will relate to known offenders. This may be either domestic violence or violence between young men who do already know each other. The problem is therefore to link the remaining offences in some way. In Britain, as our results have shown, the distances over which serial killers travel to find different victims are relatively small, and certainly typically within the realm of very few police forces. Therefore it is likely, and indeed has been the case, that in the great majority of homicides that may be linked to one individual that they operate within a framework in which local police forces can draw together the strands in order to look closely at the cases in order to decide their linking. Of course, the problems of linking offences when there is no forensic evidence to provide clear connection is a challenging one and does require detailed behavioural analysis, but this problem only has very special demands when the offender's crimes are widely distributed over a large area and thus there is a risk that they cannot be brought into the pool for consideration as being linked.

Even in the United States the numbers of offenders who travel any distance are not large. There the problem is much more that there are many small law enforcement jurisdictions. As a consequence they have difficulty in linking any types of serial offences without some state wide or even national agency.

If the crimes are geographically very widely spread linking is only likely to be achieved with confidence when there is very clear forensic connection through fibres, body fluids or the like, or very distinct, signature behaviours. As a consequence those unsolved crimes that have a wide geographic distribution require very careful scrutiny by an individual or team that knows the sort of behavioural issues to consider. The scale of operation required for this is not very considerable against the backcloth of the number of such offences that occur within countries with relatively low murder rates. Furthermore, the sorts of distinguishing behavioural characteristics that may be relevant are likely to be rather special to each particular offender. It is therefore more likely that they will be identified by close scrutiny of the cases involved rather than by trying to develop some very generalised rather content free computerised system. It is therefore not surprising that American systems such as VICAP have been singularly ineffective in facilitating the linking of cases across large areas of the United States.

Indeed the investigation into the murders of Maxwell, Harper and Hogg, three young girls, was attempted by the use and creation of a major national computer system that recorded all murders and abductions of children over a thirty year period. Yet Robert Black who was eventually convicted of these murders, was not within this computer system. A more behaviourally oriented approach that had considered the possibilities that this type of offender was likely to have some previous history for offences against children and was likely to have a job that took him across the country and therefore provided the opportunity for crimes that were so widely distributed, may have been a more fruitful direction, requiring more direct intelligence than relying upon computer number crunching.

The nature of the challenge to police investigations of identifying the perpetrator of serial killings depends upon the assumption as to whether serial killers are very different from other murderers. If they were then it may be appropriate to have special investigative teams to examine their cases. However, our study has shown that their characteristics are very similar to those who commit other forms of homicide. The conclusion to be drawn from this is that they are therefore likely to come to police attention through normal good police investigative practices. They will be identified in house to house enquiries, through information offered by associates, or through examination of police records for local villains.

In the study reported serial killers have been considered in terms of their general statistical patterns. We have not reported on the examination of the patterns of their behaviour nor any speculation on their 'motivations'. It is quite possible that such considerations would reveal these offenders both to be distinguishable from criminals at large and also to have large variations between each other. This, however, is mainly of relevance to the explanation of these crimes and is only of relevance to investigations when the details can be shown to require different approaches to conducting an enquiry than is true for any other murder enquiry. At present the results indicate that serial killers do indeed pose particular demands on police investigators but this is mainly because like many other murderers they have found ways of killing that make detection difficult.

The figures presented have been largely drawn from US serial killers, however, making allowances for the increased violence and mobility of the USA there do appear to be many parallels with the British situation. Indeed, there is some intriguing evidence that serial killing may be some what more typical of UK murder in general than US murder in general.

There is a clear sense in which serial killers emerge because one-off murders are not solved. The results of this study also demonstrate there is a great deal in common between serial murderers and those people who may have gone on to commit a second or third murder if they had not been caught for the first. They are of a similar age, kill a similar range of victims and come from similarly dysfunctional family and criminal backgrounds. As a consequence the best strategy for tackling serial killings is to ensure that the investigation of all murders are as thorough and effective as possible. As in all types of crime a small sub-group of offenders do travel some considerable distance and therefore are particularly challenging to an investigation. But the results of the current study indicate that the majority have a preferred range of operation that tends to be within a few miles of where they live. Rather than set up special systems that are likely only to be relevant once such individuals have been identified and therefore most of the time will be of little value, it is better to use established findings to identify whether or not an offender falls into this sub-group and then put resources specifically into that investigation.

Acknowledgements:

We are grateful to Thandi Milner for her help in preparing this paper and to Malcolm Huntley for his help in computer programming.

10

References

Brantigham, P.J. and P.L. (eds) (1981), *Environmental Criminology. Beverly Hills: Sage.*

Canter, D. (ed.) (1985), *Facet Theory: Approaches to Social Research. New York: Springer-Verlag.*

Harris, T. (1987), *Red Dragon. New York: Bantam.*

Hickey, E.W. (1991), *Serial Murderers and their Victims. California: Brooks/Cole.*

Leyton, E. (1989), *Hunting Humans: The Rise of the Modern Multiple Murderer. London: Penguin*

Leyton, E. (1995), *Men of Blood: Murder in Modern England. London: Constable*

Ressler, R.K., Burgess, A.W. and Douglas, J.E. (1988), *Sexual Homicide: Patterns and Motives. Massachusetts: Lexington Books.*

Ressler, R.K., and Shachtman, T. (1994), *Whoever Fights Monsters. London: Simon and Schuster.*

Wilson, J.Q. and Herrnstein, R.J. (1985), *Crime and Human Nature. New York: Simon and Schuster.*

Canter, D and Gregory, A. (1994), `Identifying the residential location of rapists', *Journal of the Forensic Science Society,Vol 34, No.3, pp. 169-175.*

Canter, D and Larkin, P. (1993), `The Environmental Range of Serial Rapists', *Journal of Environmental Psychology, Vol.13, no.1, pp. 63-9.*

Copson, G, (1995), 'Coals to Newcastle? Police Use of Offender Profiling', *Police Research Group Special Interest Series: Paper No. 7 London: Home Office Police Department.*

11

Hickey, E. (1990a), The etiology of victimization in
serial murder, in Serial Murder: An Elusive
Phenomenon. New York: Praeger, 53-71. Copyright
by Steven A. Egger.

Pinizzotto, A.J., (1984) "Forensic Psychology: Criminal
Personality Profiling" Journal of Police Science and
     Administration vol 12 (1) 32-40

Salafati, G. (1995) Facet of Homicide (Internal Report,
University of Liverpool)

[12]

THE BRITISH JOURNAL

OF

CRIMINOLOGY

| Vol. 34 | Winter 1994 | No. 1 |

MULTIPLE MURDER

A Review

DAVID M. GRESSWELL* and CLIVE R. HOLLIN†

A review of the literature on multiple murder reveals little systematic research on this phenomenon despite widespread media interest and figures indicating that over 3 per cent of homicide victims in England and Wales die in incidents of multiple homicide. Difficulties in both defining multiple murder and estimating its prevalance are noted, although these can be seen as essential steps towards the formulation of a comprehensive psychological model of this type of crime. A review of the literature indicates that fantasy rehearsal of murderous and sadistic acts is commonly reported in this group, and stresses the importance of examining environmental factors that could elicit and control violent behaviour. It is concluded that further research is required in three areas: (1) detection and recognition of a multiple crime perpetrator from crime scene evidence; (2) identification and recognition of risk factors within imprisoned and clinical populations; (3) identification of the treatment needs and the appropriate disposal of these offenders.

Introduction

There are many different forms of multiple homicide, ranging from the large scale apparently politically motivated killings of Joseph Stalin or Idi Amin, through the seemingly motiveless killings of Peter Sutcliffe and Michael Ryan. In this paper, we will focus on the phenomenon of non-politically motivated homicide in England and Wales, particularly the type of perpetrator that clinicians and criminologists are likely to encounter through the criminal justice or secure hospital systems.

A comprehensive literature search conducted in preparation for this paper revealed

* Rampton Hospital and North Lincolnshire Health Authority.

† University of Birmingham and the Youth Treatment Service.

Any opinions expressed in this paper are those of the authors and not of North Lincolnshire Health Authority, Rampton Hospital, or the Youth Treatment Service.

This research was supported by a grant from the Rampton Hospital Research Fund. Requests for reprints should be sent to D. M. Gresswell, Francis Willis Unit, Lincoln County Hospital, Greetwell Road, Lincoln.

DAVID M. CRESSWELL AND CLIVE R. HOLLIN

that over 900 articles have been published on homicide since 1967 but of these only 26 focus on multiple murder. This low figure contrasts with the interest shown by the media in a form of offending that some authors believe constitutes a persistent and growing phenomenon with widespread repercussions for society (Levin and Fox 1985; Leyton 1987; Lowenstein 1989; Norris 1990). Until the 1980s there had been few systematic studies of multiple killers (Busch and Cavanaugh 1986) and what literature there was consisted mainly of post-hoc case studies (Arieti and Schreiber 1981; Bartholomew *et al.* 1975; Cheney 1976; McCully 1978, 1980) or summaries of clinical experience (Brittain 1967). Even the more ambitious contemporary studies, such as those of Holmes and De Burger (1985, 1988), Levin and Fox (1985), Leyton (1987), and Jenkins (1988) have relied on newspaper accounts, criminal records, and trial transcripts for information. Indeed, the only large published study, involving original data from interviews with the perpetrators of multiple murder as well as archival information, was carried out by the FBI Behavioral Science Unit (Ressler *et al.* 1988). However, Ressler *et al.* were investigating only sexually motivated murder, hence their sample may be atypical. Indeed Levin and Fox (1985) have estimated that 72 per cent of multiple murders have no sexual component. The applicability of the Ressler *et al.* findings to a non-American population is also questionable. For example, there are the widely differing homicide rates of 8 per 100,000 in the USA (Uniform Crime Reports, 1955–1984, cited in Holmes and De Burger 1985) against a rate of 1.3 per 100,000 in England and Wales (Home Office 1988).

In this review we have divided the material into the key areas of attempts to describe, categorize and estimate the prevalence of multiple homicide, predisposing factors and predictability, factors that maintain the homicidal behaviour, and triggering events. Finally we offer suggestions for future research.

Describing Behaviour: Definitions and Typologies

Many early studies of murder attempted to formulate classifications of offenders based on personality types, the relationship between the perpetrator and victim, the general circumstances of the offence, or legal categories (Abrahamson 1973; Boudouris 1974; Guttmacher 1973; Lester 1973; McGurk and McGurk 1979; Megargee 1966; Tanay 1976; Wille 1974; Wolfgang 1958). These early studies often saw multiple murder as a sub-type of homicide and attempted little further analysis. When attempted, sub-classification of multiple murder was generally in terms of dichotomies such as 'schizophrenic' versus 'sadistic' (Guttmacher 1973), or 'mass' versus 'serial' (Lunde 1976).

A widely accepted contemporary view (Holmes and De Burger 1988; Ressler *et al.* 1988) is that there are three major forms of multiple murder: *mass murder, spree murder,* and *serial murder.*

Mass murder

Mass murder is defined primarily by the length of time over which the murders take place. 'Classic' mass murder involves the taking of several lives in the same general area in a short period of time by a lone assassin. James Oliver Huberty who in 1984 shot and killed 21 people in a Texas restaurant provides an example of this type of murderer.

MULTIPLE MURDER

Dietz (1986), Rappaport (1988), and Rowlands (1990) divide mass-murderers into three further groups: *pseudo-commandos* who are younger men obsessed with fire-arms; *set and run killers* who plan the lethal episode sufficiently to facilitate their own escape; and *psychotic killers* who may commit either mass or serial murder. Holmes and Holmes (1992) offer three further categories: *disciples* who are members of cults such as Charles Manson's 'family'; *family annihilators* who are usually depressed men who kill their families before committing suicide; and *disgruntled employees* who retaliate against being dismissed or ill-treated by their employers.

Spree murder

With spree murder, several victims are murdered over a period of hours or days in different locations by an impulsive killer who appears to make little effort to evade detection. The victims often have some familial or symbolic significance for the offender and are killed in a 'frenzy'. At completion of the sequence this type of killer is unlikely to kill again; many commit suicide or are killed in shootouts with the police. A British example of this type of murderer is Michael Ryan who shot and killed his first female victim, drove to a petrol station and fired at an attendant, and then drove to a nearby town where he killed 15 more people before killing himself.

Not all commentators agree that spree murder is a separate form of multiple murder. Busch and Cavanaugh (1986), for example, argue that spree killings can be thought of as a sub-set of either mass or serial murder. However, unlike serial murder there is no emotional 'cooling off period' between offences, and unlike mass murder the killings may occur in several sequences. Yet further, it can be argued that family annihilation should be regarded as a separate and probably most common form of multiple murder (Dietz 1986; Malmquist 1980; Rappaport 1988; Rowlands 1990). Almost all mass and spree murderers are male with a racial composition 'that closely approximates that of the population itself' (Levin and Fox 1985: 51).

Serial murder

The central feature of serial murder is repetition, often over a long time period. Egger (1984) offers six characteristics in his 'working definition' of serial murder: (1) there are at least two murders; (2) there is no relationship between perpetrator and victim; (3) the murders are committed at different times and have no direct connection to previous or subsequent murders; (4) the murders often occur at a different location; (5) the murders were not committed for material gain, but are usually either compulsive acts, or are aimed at gratification of needs which have been developed through fantasy; (6) subsequent victims have characteristics in common with earlier or later victims. Peter Sutcliffe, who killed 13 women in Yorkshire, is a well-known example of this type of killer.

As with the previous groups, most serial murderers are loners, with rare exceptions such as Ian Brady and Myra Hindley, the 'Moors Murderers', or Angelo Buono and Kenneth Bianchi, the 'Hillside Stranglers' (Holmes and De Burger 1985). Serial murderers are generally white males (Levin and Fox 1985)[1] and there is no apparent victim precipitation (Ressler *et al.* 1986a).

---

[1] Because the majority of multiple murderers are male we will use the male pronoun throughout for convenience.

3

DAVID M. CRESSWELL AND CLIVE R. HOLLIN

As with mass and spree murder, the classification of serial killers may be further refined: Ressler *et al.* (1988) argue that the killer can be categorized as either 'organized' or 'disorganized' based on information from the scene of the crime. Holmes and De Burger (1985, 1988) suggest that the serial killer should be described in terms of his geographical mobility (stable or unstable) and then assigned to one of four types depending on the motives that are thought to predominate. These motives are:

Visionary   Such killers have hallucinations or delusional beliefs that lead them to kill particular types of victims. These individuals are unusual amongst serial killers in that they could be classified as psychotic (Holmes and De Burger 1985).

Missionary   This type of killer, apparently of his own accord, has decided to rid society of a particular group of people. He could not be classified as mentally ill and may function well in his local community.

Hedonistic   This group is a mixed one and includes three additional sub-types. The first sub-type includes the so-called 'lust murderers' for whom the act of killing is associated with sexual enjoyment. Members of the second 'thrill oriented' sub-type do not kill primarily for sexual reasons but for the sheer excitement of a novel experience. With both these sub-types the method of killing may be sadistic, involving mutilation and dismemberment with evidence of sexual activity both before and after death. Detection may be very difficult and this type of murderer may be active for several years. The third sub-type is the 'comfort-oriented' killer for whom the murder is likely to be 'act' rather than 'process' focused. The murderer's intention is to have the victim dead, the means being selected on purely pragmatic grounds, rather than the killer dwelling on the process of killing and so gaining satisfaction. The motivation for this type of killer is instrumental, with psychological or physical security and comfort being gained from insurance payouts or accumulation of victim's property.

Power and control   This type of killer is motivated by the wish to have complete life and death control over a victim. The primary aim is not sexual gratification, although as with the other sub-types sexual activity may take place.

Problems of Definition

These various definitions and typologies have been derived primarily by focusing on the perpetrator and on the events and circumstances of the murders. However, when situational and random factors are considered the classifications begin to look less useful. A principal danger lies in accepting the assumption that the perpetrator's actions followed his intentions and then imposing motivational patterns where none exist.

Cases where the killer's attacks have not gone according to plan can be found in the literature: for example, some perpetrators have underestimated the difficulty of subduing and killing a victim. Klausner (1981) in his study of the serial killer David Berkowitz ('Son of Sam'), describes how Berkowitz's first attack was quickly terminated when he ran off after the victim screamed and bled—something Berkowitz had not anticipated. Berkowitz was only 'successful' after he bought and began using a gun;

4

MULTIPLE MURDER

an option not widely available in all countries. However, even when firearms are available an intended mass killer may 'fail' because his victims survive. A recent example is Robert Sartin from the north-east of England who was arrested after shooting 18 people. Seventeen people survived despite Sartin's apparent intention to kill. Thus random unpredictable environmental factors may be as important as the competence, motivation, and intelligence of the perpetrator in determining the number of fatalities, when and if he gets caught, and the classification category to which he is eventually assigned.

Although the motivation for the murderous behaviour must be taken into account, the categories offered by Holmes and De Burger (1985, 1988) do have a number of shortcomings. First, they are not mutually exclusive: the motivation of the visionary and missionary types for example appear very similar and separated only by the purported psychosis of one group. Secondly, the list of categories is not exhaustive. 'Contract' or hired killers have been excluded on the grounds that in their case the motivation is extrinsic. However, killing for the money claimed from insurance companies, as may be the case with some hedonistic-comfort oriented killers, or to prevent a sexual assault victim identifying an assailant, may also be considered extrinsically motivated acts.

Finally the typologies generally fail to pick up interactions between the killer, the victims, and the environment, and do not appear to be flexible enough to accommodate a killer who may have different motives for different victims or changing motives over time. In his biography of Dennis Nilsen, a British serial killer, Masters (1985) describes how in the middle of his killing sequence Nilsen killed a man not for his usual idiosyncratic reasons but simply because the victim was annoying and in his way. Similarly Ressler *et al.* (1986*b*) describe a case where a killer's motivation changed over time. One of the killers in their sample reported that after being released from prison high levels of emotional arousal were associated with the dismemberment and concealing of a body whereas previously the arousal had been associated with the act of killing. Similarly a need to generate and maintain public interest may affect or exceed the original motivation. Several members of Ressler *et al.*'s (1988) sample of sexually motivated killers followed the reporting of their offences in the media or even attempted to participate in police investigations. This behaviour seemed to serve the function of maintaining high levels of excitement for the offender after the murder.

Overall there is a clear need for a typology based on analyses flexible enough to account for both psychological and environmental variables, and which also recognize that there is a process to multiple murder.

Estimating the Size of the Problem

Holmes and De Burger (1985) suggest that the true prevalence of multiple homicide is difficult to gauge: murders may go undetected and victims may not be attributed to the same killer. Rowlands (1990), in considering the work of Lunde (1976), has suggested that there were 30 multiple murderers 'at work' in the United States between 1970 and 1984. However, this may be an underestimate as further evidence supports the view that there has been a 'surge' in multiple homicides in the United States since the 1960s. Leyton (1987) surveyed both the literature and press reports to produce figures indicating an increase in multiple homicides this century in the United States. From

5

DAVID M. CRESSWELL AND CLIVE R. HOLLIN

the 1920s to the 1950s multiple murder was rare but thereafter it started to increase in frequency. During the 1960s Leyton estimates there was one new multiple-killer every 20 months but this jumped to one every seven months in the 1970s. From 1980 to 1984 there was a new multiple murderer being reported every 1.8 months. Leyton believes these figures to be an underestimate, but they could also reflect a growing media interest in a bizarre and exotic type of offending. Lowenstein (1989) suggested that the crime figures from 1982 to 1989 indicated a 270 per cent increase in serial murder, compared to a 12 per cent increase in 'general' murder over the same period.

Estimating the current prevalence of multiple murder is, however, fraught with difficulty. Holmes and De Burger (1988) estimated that between 3,500 and 5,000 people are killed by serial killers each year in America. They based their estimate on a figure of 5,000 murder victims for whom the assailant is unknown, that one-quarter to two-thirds of these are victims of serial killers, that there are a number of undetected victims, and that the typical numbers of victims per killer are 10–12. From this formula Holmes and De Burger calculated that there could be as many as 350 serial killers at large in the United States. Fox (1990), questioning the assumptions on which the estimates are based, has described these estimates as 'preposterous', and suggested the figures are probably ten times too great. Ressler *et al.* (1988) estimate that the number of multiple murderers in America probably ranges between the low 30s to over 100 individuals. Such figures are difficult to generalize from outside the United States. If the more conservative figures are applied to England and Wales and equated with the smaller population, then one might expect there to be between six and 20 killers active. However, if the general murder rate for England and Wales (six times less than in the United States) is taken into account, but assuming that detection rates are similar in both countries, an estimate of up to four active killers may be more realistic. Clearly such formulae make assumptions about consistency in detection rates and police efficiency. Indeed to some extent the number of active multiple murderers is a function of the average time to detection. There could, therefore, be fewer 'busy' murderers active at a time when a large proportion of murders are attributable to serial killers.

When considering the prevalence of incidents of multiple murder in England and Wales, the Home Office[2] figures given in Table 1 are informative. They show that there were 52 'incidents' of multiple murder, defined as three or more victims attributed to a killer or group of killers, recorded between 1982 and 1991. These offences involved 58 perpetrators and 196 victims, some of whom were killed before 1982.

When considering the recorded prevalence of serial murder Jenkins (1988) estimated that, between 1940 and 1985, serial killers (defined as four or more victims) accounted for 1.7 per cent of murders (which are defined differently from homicides) in England and Wales, rising to 3.2 per cent for the ten year period between 1973 and 1983. When Jenkins's figures are broken down decade on decade and combined with Home Office figures, as in Table 2, it can be seen that there is little empirical support for the idea of a dramatic increase in serial killers since the war. Although the decade 1970–9 produced a large number of killers and victims, 39 of the victims were killed by just two men: Peter Dinsdale (26 victims) and Peter Sutcliffe (13 victims).

In addition to the 52 incidents with known perpetrators, the Home Office lists a

---

[2] The authors would like to thank S1 Division of the Home Office for their help.

MULTIPLE MURDER

TABLE 1   *Description of Incidents of Multiple Homicide Recorded in England and Wales 1982–91*

	No. of victims in incident						All incidents
	3	4	5	6	7	16	
No. of incidents	37	6	5	1	2	1	52
No. of victims	111	24	25	6	14	16	196
No. of perpetrators	40	6	7	1	3	1	58[a]
No. of incidents followed by suicide of suspect	19	0	1	0	0	1	21
No. of incidents with multiple perpetrators	3	0	1	0	1	0	5
No. of female perpetrators	4	2	0	0	0	0	6

[a] Some incidents had multiple perpetrators.

TABLE 2   *Number of Serial Killers with 4 or More Victims Identified in England from 1940*

Period	No. of killers	No. of victims
1940–9	3	18
1950–9	1	7
1960–9	3	13
1970–9	5	60
1980–9	2	11

Killers are included in the year that they killed their first victim. Figures to 1981 from Jenkins (1988), figures from 1981 include data supplied by the Home Office for this study.

further eight incidents which are classed as multiple murders but where no perpetrator has as yet been apprehended. These eight incidents claimed a further 42 victims bringing the total up to 238. The figures indicate that approximately 3 per cent of homicide victims were killed in episodes of multiple killing during the ten-year period from 1982–91.

The majority of perpetrators recorded by S1 Division of the Home Office (89.6 per cent) and victims (58.6 per cent) are male. This compares with studies of murder in general which indicate that 82 per cent of murderers are male (Wolfgang 1958) and the majority (60 per cent) of victims are female (Gibson and Kline 1961). A high proportion of perpetrators (36.2 per cent) kill themselves: in all but two cases, after killing only members of their family. Indeed, 100 of the victims (51 per cent) were members of the killer's family, while a further 31 (15.8 per cent) were either acquaintances or friends.

It is likely, however, that these figures underestimate the true prevalence of multiple murder. The Home Office includes only detected crimes or cases where victims' bodies are clearly identifiable and attributable to a specific perpetrator. Perpetrators, on the other hand, often claim more victims: in one of the cases included above the

7

perpetrator claimed to have 12 victims, but as only six could be identified he was therefore convicted of six counts of murder along with two of attempted murder.

Analysis of Predisposing Factors

The literature considering the background of multiple homicide perpetrators has not generally been informed by the typologies described above. Furthermore the major studies have tended to concentrate on sexually motivated and sadistic killers, with comparatively little detailed research available on 'mass' or 'spree' killers. An exception is the work of Levin and Fox (1985), who reviewed the literature relating specifically to mass murderers. They noted the high prevalence of childhood trauma, such as sexual abuse, brutal beatings, and abandonment, in the histories of such killers. Burgess *et al.* (1986) and Liebert (1985), who consider the cases of sexually motivated multiple killers, suggest that an early history characterized by a failure of empathic bonding and attachment between the child and carer, with the child becoming aloof and cold, is the basis of multiple homicide. McDonald (1963) found early childhood behaviours such as enuresis, firesetting, and torturing animals to be common in the histories of more sadistic multiple killers. McDonald saw these behaviours as indicative of a lack of affective bonds between the child and others, and as precursors to similar acts ultimately directed towards people. Burgess *et al.* (1986), however, saw such behaviour as an expression of the child's developing revengeful sadistic fantasies.

These causal propositions rest on two assumptions: first, that the caretakers do not help the child cope with traumatic experience; secondly, that the child incorporates elements of his traumatic experience in violent sadistic day-dreams and fantasies. Burgess *et al.* (1986) argue that the child feels helpless but develops a private world where highly arousing fantasies give him a sense of power and control. He becomes increasingly dependent on fantasy to meet his emotional needs, experiences little effective intervention or control from parents and significant others, and misses opportunities to acquire pro-social values and skills. Thus he acquires an increasingly distorted view of himself and human relationships. According to Burgess *et al.*, the future sadistic or sexually motivated multiple killer adopts an increasingly anti-social position, alongside a belief that he is entitled to express himself in any way he chooses.

It seems unlikely that these background factors are adequate explanations in themselves of multiple murder. Such formative childhood experiences are unfortunately common, while multiple murder is very rare. Indeed in Jenkins's (1988) study, six out of 12 English serial killers had 'respectable' and superficially normal childhoods. Several of these background factors are at best predictive of anti-social behaviour in general (West 1982), rather than multiple murder specifically (Levin and Fox 1985). Indeed many of the factors outlined above are found in other psychological models of aggression. Bandura (1977), for example, stresses the role of three factors in aggression: *acquisition*, i.e., learning to be violent from observing others and from direct experience; *instigation*, i.e., expectations of the outcomes of aggression or of failing to be aggressive; and *maintenance*, the reinforcement that maintains the aggressive behaviour which for Bandura can be either overt or private self-reinforcement. Novaco (1978), in his cognitive model of anger and stress, emphasizes the role of cognitive processes, particularly appraisal of the nature of 'provocative' stimuli. The role of cognition with respect to multiple homicide is considered below.

8

MULTIPLE MURDER

Analysis of maintaining factors

Cognitive inhibitory processes Cognitive processes have been considered to have a major role in the aetiology of multiple murder: primarily in overcoming or preventing learning inhibitions to aggression. Burgess *et al.* (1986) argue that because of early childhood experiences, such as those described above, individuals who ultimately commit sadistic murder feel alienated and socially isolated. As a part of this experience, the individual 'filters out' any social feedback that could potentially inhibit his aggression. Burgess *et al.* (1986) make the case that sexually motivated murderers may never have acquired the ability to respond empathically to others. These authors also argue that cognitive processes such as depersonalization of victims, failure to internalize inhibitions against violence, and a belief that violence against others is legitimate, precede homicidal behaviour. Anti-social behaviours evident in childhood consequently escalate through minor criminal acts to assault, rape, and murder.

On the other hand, Ressler *et al.* (1981) offer an account of a rapist who appeared to have inhibitions against murder which he had to overcome—primarily by trying to ignore personal information and by focusing on the consequences of being caught—before killing some of his victims. It therefore seems unwise to assume at this stage that all multiple killers have failed to acquire inhibitory belief systems, rather than that they have had to learn means of overcoming them. Indeed cognitive processes such as those described by Burgess *et al.* can be seen in violent populations generally (Goldstein 1986) and in most cases do not escalate to multiple murder. Bandura *et al.* (1975) and Lerner (1980), for example, have observed that following aggression there is a tendency on the part of the aggressor to devalue the victim. The devaluation may be so 'successful' that the aggressor believes that further attacks are warranted. A cycle of attack and devaluation may, therefore, arise where the aggressor attributes faults to the victim for his or her own acts of aggression. Given this observation it must be questioned whether the characteristics of multiple murderers outlined above, based as they are on post-hoc studies, may be as much the products of, as the antecedents to, multiple murder. It is also worth considering whether such processes as depersonalizing of victims and overcoming inhibitions to murder could also occur during fantasy rehearsals of offences, as well as during overt aggression.

Cognitive facilitating processes A number of researchers have addressed the role of fantasy as both a precursor to serial offending, and as a means by which sadistic offenders cope with life's pressures (Brittain 1967; MacCulloch *et al.* 1983; Ressler *et al.* 1988). Brittain (1967) suggested that many sadists have a rich fantasy life that involves imagining their own and others' sadistic acts. MacCulloch *et al.* (1983) examined 16 patients detained in a maximum security mental hospital with a diagnosis of psychopathic disorder. They found that the sadistic behaviour of 13 of the patients was explicable only in terms of 'internal circumstances'. This group had a history of habitual use of sadistic sexual fantasies, often used as part of masturbation, and several had acted out elements or sequences of these fantasies prior to commiting their sadistic offences. Prentky *et al.* (1989) also found that fantasy preceded serial sexual murder. These authors compared 25 serial sexual murderers with 17 single sexual murderers. In their sample 86 per cent of the multiple killers disclosed a history of violent fantasy, compared to 23 per cent of the single murderers. There appears to be little research to

9

DAVID M. CRESSWELL AND CLIVE R. HOLLIN

date, however, on how pervasive sadistic fantasy is within the general population nor on the precise relationship between fantasy offending and real offending.

Operant processes Engagement in fantasy, trial runs, and murder appear to be rewarded in the short term by intense positive feelings of power and control, with associated changes of arousal, together with a simultaneous shift or distraction from aversive experience. Such behaviours are thus positively reinforced in that they lead to rewarding outcomes; and negatively reinforced in that they allow escape from the aversive realities of everyday life.

Gresswell (1991) suggested that there may be parallels between the experiences of addicted gamblers and multiple murderers. In particular, a psychological model of addictions may be useful in explaining the processes by which fantasy and try-outs are maintained. Brown (1987) suggests that: 'Many gamblers are trying to repeat a never forgotten "peak experience", perhaps of a big win after a long series of losses or quite often of the special feelings which accompanied their first big win' (p. 117): a description that is very similar to the experiences of some sadistic offenders and multiple murderers who engage in 'trial runs' in an attempt to make real experience match fantasy.

Prentky *et al.* (1989) have suggested that since a perfect match between fantasy and reality is never quite possible, the reality is never as satisfying as the fantasies promise. Further attempts with new victims are, therefore, enacted in an attempt to achieve a closer match between experience and fantasy. By their very nature such attempts are likely to be only partly successful, producing short-term effects and giving rise to intermittent schedules of reinforcement. Such reinforcement schedules inevitably make the behaviours resistant to extinction and susceptible to reinstatement.

In summary, the profile of a multiple murderer so far is of a male probably less than 35 years old, who has failed to achieve proper socialization. He is likely to have a well-rehearsed set of violent, sadistic fantasies which are used both to escape the aversive realities of everyday life, often at the expense of the development of other pro-social coping mechanisms, and to enhance sexual pleasure. He may have a history of rehearsing sequences of his fantasies. In addition, the potential multiple murderer has a thriving and self-maintaining set of beliefs that legitimize and normalize the use of violence and sadism. The same processes that support these beliefs may also be eroding any acquired constraints against killing. Individuals with these characteristics may well have a substantially increased potential for committing murder. Marshall and Barbaree (1984) emphasize, however, that the acquisition and erosion of inhibitions is not 'all or nothing' (p. 70), but is best viewed as a continuum. If we accept this view then the strength of acquired inhibitions is likely to determine the strength of the situational events that trigger the aggression. We consider the role of situational factors below.

Analysis of Situational Factors and Triggers

In Ressler *et al.*'s (1988) analysis of 36 convicted sexual murderers, financial, legal, employment, marital problems, and conflict (particularly with women and parents) were all found to be antecedents to murder. Thirty-four per cent of this sample said that they had not directly planned the murder in question but were in 'emotional states' that made them 'open for opportunities'. These emotional states included feeling frustrated, hostile and angry, agitated or excited; although depression, anxiety, and confusion were less commonly reported. Sixteen per cent of the murderers viewed their offences as purely spontaneous and unplanned.

Situational factors may play a role in triggering serial murders, as well as other forms of multiple murder. In the Prentky *et al.* (1989) study, evidence of fantasy rehearsal and forethought in the planning and execution of the murder was found to be highly correlated with the degree of organization of the crime. Prentky *et al.* (1989) also found that organized murderers were three times more common among serial sexual murderers than among single sexual murders. However, in comparing the planning of the actual offence—single sexual murder against the first murder in a sequence—there was no significant difference in the planning. It seemed that many of the single murderers had planned an offence (e.g., rape) but that the killing itself was unplanned. However, although the multiple killers had well thought-out plans, their first murder was often a reaction to adverse environmental events such as those noted above.

The question then arises of how an event can elicit anti-social behaviour. Mawson (1987) has suggested that a 'stressful event combined with the simultaneous absence or destruction of social bonds' (p. 20) can lead individuals who have previously been well controlled and law abiding to commit criminal acts. Briefly, Mawson's theory of transient criminality holds that an individual has a 'cognitive map' of familiar objects, people, places, values, beliefs, and sources of reinforcement. People are resistant to changes in their 'map' and seek familiar stimuli to maintain their equilibrium. Under extreme stress and emotional arousal, and in the absence of familiar social supports, the individual experiences a disintegration of his or her cognitive map. A person in this 'disintegrated state' becomes more suggestible and is likely to engage in 'stimulation seeking behaviour' usually directed at familiar objects. Because social rules, laws, and norms have been lost with the disintegration of the cognitive map, a variety of anti-social or criminal acts becomes possible. It seems reasonable to assume that under such adverse circumstances individuals who have well-rehearsed murder fantasies will be more likely to act them out than to engage in other, less prepared for, criminal acts. Levin's (1987) model of 'indiscriminate killing' (mass-murder) is similar to Mawson's model of transient criminality. Levin's model includes four factors: first, there is a basis of formative experience, the perpetrator has 'led a life of frustration'; secondly, he has access to and the ability to use firearms; thirdly, there is a precipitating event such as unemployment or divorce; and finally the perpetrator experiences a breakdown of 'social controls', for example a move to a new town or the loss of an important relationship.

We would suggest that although a killer trained in the use of firearms may be more effective than one using contact weapons this is not an essential feature. A more useful way of conceptualizing this component may be to consider that training in firearms in these cases is indicative of a style of coping with stress and problems of poor self-image/social competence that includes dependence on aggressive fantasies and role-play. The salience of these fantasies and experience of those processes outlined in earlier sections may be the best predictor of the 'choice' of a homicidally aggressive behaviour.

Research Issues

We have drawn together the literature as a preliminary step to developing appropriate cognitive–behavioural models of multiple murder. There are four main areas where

11

DAVID M. CRESSWELL AND CLIVE R. HOLLIN

further research could be usefully applied. First, this group of offenders are very difficult to detect and create a good deal of public anxiety. Further research may increase recognition of homicides that may have been perpetrated by a multiple murderer, and help to increase the utility of offender profiling. Profiling is the process by which psychological profiles of offenders are devised based on crime scene analysis, a process which Canter (1989) has described as 'far more of an art than a science' (p. 12). Secondly, correct identification and understanding of this group of offenders would facilitate correct disposal of the perpetrator after trial. Some perpetrators may for example be better dealt with through the health system rather than through the penal system, which may facilitate the development of homicidal fantasy by increasing frustration and further isolating the individual from normal social feedback.

Thirdly, the processes involved in the progression to multiple murder may have much in common with other, less extreme repetitive anti-social acts. Greater understanding of extreme behaviours such as multiple murder may facilitate our understanding of other solitary recidivistic offenders.

Lastly, it is known that some of these offenders have been in contact with therapeutic or professional supervisory agencies prior to or during the course of perpetrating their offences. Research that helps clinicians in the detection, targeting, and appropriate management of this group would have major benefits not only in terms of preventing the crime itself, but also in reducing the harmful effects of public anxiety which these crimes create.

The next step, we suggest, is to undertake functional analyses of a large number of multiple murder perpetrators to facilitate the development of appropriate, testable cognitive–behavioural models: our current research addresses this point (Gresswell and Hollin 1992, 1993) and is based on direct interviews with convicted perpetrators and study of official files on cases of multiple murder between 1982 and 1991.

REFERENCES

ABRAHAMSON, D. (1973), *The Murdering Mind*. New York: Harper and Row.

ARIETI, S., and SCHREIBER, F. R. (1981), 'Multiple Murders of a Schizophrenic Patient: A Psychodynamic Interpretation', *Journal of the American Academy of Psychoanalysis*, 9: 501–24.

BANDURA, A. (1977), *Social Learning Theory*. Englewood Cliffs, NJ: Prentice-Hall.

BANDURA, A., UNDERWOOD, B., and FROMSON, M. E. (1975), 'Disinhibition of Aggression through Diffusion of Responsibility and Dehumanization of the Victims', *Journal of Research in Personality*, 9: 253–69.

BARTHOLOMEW, A. A., MILTE, K. L., and GALBALLY, F. (1975), 'Sexual Murder: Psychopathology and Psychiatric Jurisprudential Considerations', *Australia and New Zealand Journal of Criminology*, 8: 143–52.

BOUDOURIS, J. (1974), 'A Classification of Homicides', *Criminology: An International Journal*, 11(4): 525–40.

BRITTAIN, R. P. (1967), 'The Sadistic Murderer', *Medicine, Science and the Law*, 10: 198–207.

BROWN, R. I. F. (1987), 'Classical and Operant Paradigms in the Management of Gambling Addictions', *Behavioural Psychotherapy*, 15: 111–22.

BURGESS, A. W., HARTMAN, C. R., RESSLER, R. K., DOUGLAS, J. E., and McCORMACK, A. (1986), 'Sexual Homicide: A Motivational Model', *Journal of Interpersonal Violence*, 1: 251–72.

BUSCH, K. A., and CAVANAUGH, J. L. Jr (1986), 'The Study of Multiple Murder: Preliminary

MULTIPLE MURDER

Examination of the Interface Between Epistemology and Methodology', *Journal of Interpersonal Violence*, 1: 5–23.

CANTER, D. (1989), 'Offender Profiles', *The Psychologist*, 2: 12–16.

CHENEY, M. (1976), '*The Co-ed Killer: A Study of the Murders, Mutilations, and Matricide of Edmund Kemper III*'. New York: Walker and Co.

DIETZ, P. E. (1986), 'Mass, Serial and Sensational Homicides', *Bulletin of the New York Academy of Medicine*, 62: 447–90.

EGGER, S. A. (1984), 'A Working Definition of Serial Murder and the Reduction of Linkage Blindness', *Journal of Police Science and Administration*, 12: 348–57.

FOX, J. A. (1990), 'Murder They Wrote', *Contemporary Psychology*, 35: 890–1.

GIBSON, E., and KLINE, S. (1961), *Murder*. London: HMSO.

GOLDSTEIN, J. H. (1986), *Aggression and Crimes of Violence* (2nd edn). New York: Oxford University Press.

GRESSWELL, D. M. (1991), 'Psychological Models of Addiction and the Origins and Maintenance of Multiple Murder', in M. McMurran and C. McDougall, eds, *Proceedings of the First DCLP Annual Conference* (Vol. 2). Leicester: The British Psychological Society.

GRESSWELL, D. M., and HOLLIN, C. R. (1992), 'Towards a New Methodology for Making Sense of Case Material: An Illustrative Case Involving Attempted Multiple Murder', *Criminal Behaviour and Mental Health*, 2: 329–41.

—— (1993), *English Female Multiple Homicide Perpetrators: 1982–91*. Paper presented at the European Conference of Clinical Psychology and Offenders, Royal Holloway and Bedford New College, University of London, Surrey.

GUTTMACHER, M. (1973), *The Mind of the Murderer*. New York: Arno Press.

HOLMES, R. M., and DE BURGER, J. (1985), 'Profiles in Terror: The Serial Murderer', *Federal Probation*, 49: 29–34.

—— (1988), *Serial Murder*. Newbury Park, CA: Sage.

HOLMES, R. M., and HOLMES, S. T. (1992), 'Understanding Mass Murder: A Starting Point', *Federal Probation*, 56: 53–61.

HOME OFFICE (1988), *Criminal Statistics for England and Wales*, Cmnd 498. London: HMSO.

JENKINS, P. (1988), 'Serial Murder in England 1940–1985', *Journal of Criminal Justice*, 16: 1–15.

KLAUSNER, L. D. (1981), *Son of Sam*. New York: McGraw-Hill.

LERNER, M. J. (1980), *The Belief in a Just World*. New York: Plenum Press.

LESTER, D. (1973), 'Murder: A Review', *Corrective and Social Psychiatry and Journal of Behaviour Therapy*, 19: 40–50.

LEVIN, J. (1987), 'Why His Last Shot Blew the Truth Away', *The Sunday Times*, 23 Aug., p. 23.

LEVIN, J., and FOX, J. A. (1985), *Mass Murder: America's Growing Menace*. New York: Plenum Press.

LEYTON, E. (1987), *Hunting Humans: The Rise of the Modern Multiple Murderer*. Harmondsworth, Middlesex: Penguin Books.

LIEBERT, J. A. (1985), 'Contributions of Psychiatric Consultation in the Investigation of Serial Murder', *International Journal of Offender Therapy and Comparative Criminology*, 29: 187–200.

LOWENSTEIN, L. F. (1989), 'Homicide: A Review of Recent Research (1975–1985)', *The Criminologist*, 13: 74–89.

LUNDE, D. T. (1976), *Murder and Madness*. San Francisco, CA: San Francisco Book Co.

MACCULLOCH, M. J., SNOWDEN, P. R., WOOD, P. J. W., and MILLS, H. E. (1983), 'Sadistic Fantasy, Sadistic Behaviour and Offending', *British Journal of Psychiatry*, 143: 20–9.

13

DAVID M. CRESSWELL AND CLIVE R. HOLLIN

McCULLY, R. S. (1978), 'The Laugh of Satan: A Study of a Familial Murderer', *Journal of Personality Assessment*, 42: 81–91.

—— (1980), 'Satan's Eclipse: A Familial Murderer Six Years Later', *British Journal of Projective Psychology and Personality Study*, 25: 13–17.

McDONALD, J. M. (1963), 'The Threat to Kill', *American Journal of Psychiatry*, 120: 125–30.

McGURK, B. J., and McGURK, R. E. (1979), 'Personality Types among Prisoners and Prison Officers: An Investigation of Megargee's Theory of Control', *British Journal of Criminology*, 19: 31–49.

MALMQUIST, C. P. (1980), 'Psychiatric Aspects of Familicide', *Bulletin of the American Academy of Psychology*, 8: 298–304.

MARSHALL, W. L., and BARBAREE, H. E. (1984), 'A Behavioural View of Rape', *International Journal of Law and Psychiatry*, 7: 51–77.

MASTERS, B. (1985), *Killing for Company: The Case of Dennis Nilsen*. London: Jonathan Cape.

MAWSON, A. R. (1987), *Transient Criminality: A Model of Stress-Induced Crime*. New York: Praeger.

MEGARGEE, E. I. (1966), 'Undercontrolled and Overcontrolled Personality Types in Extreme Anti-Social Aggression, *Psychological Monographs*, 80: 611.

NORRIS, J. (1990), *Serial Killers*. London: Arrow.

NOVACO, R. W. (1978), 'Anger and Coping with Stress', in J. P. Foreyt and D. P. Rathjan, eds, *Cognitive Behaviour Therapy*. Lexington, MA: Lexington Books.

PRENTKY, R. A., BURGESS, A. W., ROKOUS, F., LEE, A., HARTMAN, C., RESSLER, R., and DOUGLAS, J. (1989), 'The Presumptive Role of Fantasy in Serial Sexual Homicide', *American Journal of Psychiatry*, 146: 887–91.

RAPPAPORT, R. C. (1988), 'The Serial and Mass Murderer: Patterns, Differentiation, Pathology', *American Journal of Forensic Psychiatry*, 9: 38–48.

RESSLER, R. K., BURGESS, A. W., and DOUGLAS, J. E. (1981), 'Rape and Rape-murder: One Offender and Twelve Victims', *American Journal of Psychiatry*, 140: 36–40.

—— (1988), *Sexual Homicide: Patterns and Motives*. Lexington, MA: Lexington Books.

RESSLER, R. K., BURGESS, A. W., DOUGLAS, J. E., HARTMAN, C. R., and D'AGOSTINO, R. B. (1986a), 'Sexual Killers and their Victims: Identifying Patterns through Crime Scene Analysis', *Journal of Interpersonal Violence*, 1: 288–308.

RESSLER, R. K., BURGESS, A. W., HARTMAN, C. R., DOUGLAS, J. E., and McCORMACK, A. (1986b), 'Murderers who Rape and Mutilate', *Journal of Interpersonal Violence*, 1: 273–87.

ROWLANDS, M. (1990), 'Multiple Murder: A Review of the International Literature', *Journal of the College of Prison Medicine*, 1: 3–7.

TANAY, E. (1976), *The Murderers*. Indianapolis: Bobbs-Merrill.

WEST, D. J. (1982), *Delinquency: Its Roots, Careers and Prospects*. London: Heinemann.

WILLE, W. (1974), *Citizens who Commit Murder*. St Louis, MO: Warren Greene.

WOLFGANG, M. E. (1958), *Patterns in Criminal Homicide*. Philadelphia, PA: University of Pennsylvania Press.

14

[13]

Assessment of PTSD Symptoms in a Community Exposed to Serial Murder

▼

Michael J. Herkov
University of Florida

▼

Monica Biernat
University of Kansas

This study examined the presence of PTSD symptoms across time in a community exposed to serial murder. One hundred eighty four subjects (48% response rate) responded to the initial survey while 64 and 30 subjects, respectively, participated in the 9- and 18-month follow-up studies. Results indicated widespread endorsement of PTSD symptoms following the murders. The most severe reactions were found among residents demographically similar to the victims. PTSD symptoms, while not transient, appeared to decrease over time with few subjects still reporting symptoms at 18 months. These data suggest that violent acts such as serial murder can have far reaching psychological consequences for the community and result in vicarious victimization. © 1997 John Wiley & Sons, Inc. J Clin Psychol **53** 809-815, 1997

Post-traumatic stress disorder (PTSD) represents a psychiatric syndrome in which an individual experiences a severe anxiety reaction to an overwhelming psychosocial stressor "outside the range of usual human experience" (American Psychiatric Association, 1987). Hallmarks of PTSD include reexperiencing of the traumatic event, avoidance of stimuli associated with the event, psychological numbing, and persistent symptoms of increased physiological arousal.

Traditionally, the study of PTSD reactions has focused on individuals directly exposed to situations of extreme violence and carnage such as military combat (Oei, Lim, & Hennessy, 1990) or rape (Burgess & Holmstrom, 1974; Calhoun & Atkeson, 1991). However, other traumatic events can lead to PTSD reactions. DSM-III-R includes in its description of qualifying traumatic events "destruction of one's home or community; or seeing another person who has recently been, or is being seriously injured or killed as the result of an accident or physical violence." Investigations of populations who have been exposed to natural disaster (Horowitz,

Stinson, & Field, 1991) or accidents (Bromet, 1989) confirm that these stressors can also lead to PTSD reactions.

Recently, researchers have begun to examine whether people can experience psychological trauma through knowledge of, or indirect exposure to, violence. That is, can a person be traumatized through media or other information concerning violent acts such as murder, terrorism, or rioting in their community? Young (1989) describes this phenomenon as "vicarious victimization" and describes seven factors that can lead to increased likelihood of its occurrence including a realistic threat of death to all members of the community, extraordinary carnage, strong community affiliation, witnessing of event by community members, symbolic significance of victims to the community (children, etc.), need for numerous rescue workers, and significant media attention.

Terr (1985) observed this phenomenon among family and friends of the children who had been taken hostage in the Chowchilla kidnapping case. Terr noted that while none of the family members or friends had been directly exposed the incident, many appeared to have "caught" post-traumatic symptoms. These symptoms included frightening dreams and avoidance behaviors.

The purpose of the present study was to examine whether community residents in Gainesville experienced any post-traumatic symptoms following the serial murder of five college students. While once thought to be a rare event, recent Federal Bureau of Investigation statistics estimate that as many as 5,000 Americans a year may be murdered by serial killers (Holmes & DeBurger, 1985). The random and gruesome nature of the deaths, choice of students as victims, increased presence of rescue workers (i.e., police) and accompanying media coverage associated with the Gainesville murders meet virtually all of the conditions hypothesized by Young (1989) as setting the stage for community vicarious victimization. The presence of these symptoms in the community would provide additional empirical support for the concept of vicarious victimization.

METHOD

Subjects

Subjects consisted of 500 community residents arbitrarily selected from the local residential phone directory. Questionnaires were mailed to all subjects, however, 120 were returned for incorrect or inadequate addresses. Of the remaining 380 subjects, 184 returned completed questionnaires, representing a return rate of 48%. Table 1 provides demographic information on the sample as well as the general community. Community statistics were based on information obtained from the 1990 U.S. Census.

Comparison of the sample to the Gainesville population indicates that women were slightly overrepresented in the sample and minorities were underrepresented. While the current sample appears to be significantly older than the general community, the median age of the two groups is actually more similar than the statistics suggest. This is because census statistics include all possible ages, even those under age 18. Because this research used phone listings as a subject source, young residents would not have been included in the survey, thus increasing the age of the sample.

Measures

All subjects were administered a questionnaire designed to measure their psychological response to the serial murders, including a series of questions designed to assess PTSD symptoms. These questions were written to closely resemble the DSM-III-R criteria and all questions were designed

Table 1. *Demographic Characteristics of Sample
and Gainesville Community*

Variable	Sample	Community
Gender		
Female	59%	51%
Ethnicity		
White	95%	73%
Black	2%	21%
Hispanic	2%	4%
Median Age	38 years	27 years
Married	35%	37%
Education		
High School Graduate	21%	16%
College Degree	40%	29%
Graduate Degree	30%	15%
Median Income	$25.500	$21.077
Mean Income	$32.200	$29.844

to assess changes in the person's functioning *since* the serial murders. Where possible, DSM-III-R criteria were written exactly as they appear in the manual. For example, in assessing the increased arousal symptom of sleep difficulties subjects were asked "Since the murders: Have you had difficulty falling asleep?" Other criteria required modification to adjust for the subjects' lack of knowledge regarding psychiatric terms. For example, "increased physiological reactivity" was assessed by asking subjects "Since the murders: Have you had increased nervous attacks (e.g., sweating, heart racing, etc.)?" Subjects responded to each question using either a "yes/no" or Likert scale format, depending on the question content. The questionnaire assessed all three symptom clusters of PTSD including reexperiencing of the traumatic event, avoidance of stimuli associated with the trauma and psychological numbing, and symptoms of increased arousal.

Procedures

Data collection of the initial sample began 5 weeks following the murders. Additional follow-up data were collected on these same subjects at 9 and 18 months following the murders. Sample size decreased over time due to subject attrition. The 9- and 18-month samples consisted of 64 and 30 subjects, respectively. Much of the subject attrition appeared to be due to subjects' change of residence. In the 9 month sample, 40 (24%) of the questionnaires were returned because of incorrect address. While the number of incorrect addresses may seem quite high, the community is a "university town" where students move frequently and often do not leave forwarding addresses. This hypothesis is partially supported in Table 1 in which students comprised almost a quarter of the initial sample by only 9% and 3% of the 9- and 18-month follow-up samples.

Because of the substantial subject attrition, separate analyses were conducted on the 30 subjects who participated in all three data collections. Examination of these subjects' responses provides another analysis of longitudinal reactions to the murders by following specific subjects across time.

RESULTS AND DISCUSSION

Table 2 presents the frequency of PTSD symptoms reported by community residents across the three data collections. Symptoms are broken down into the categories in which they appear in

812   *Journal of Clinical Psychology, December 1997*

Table 2. *Frequency of PTSD Symptoms at Initial Data Collection and 9 and 18-Month Follow-ups*

Symptom	Initial	9 months	18 months
Reexperience of the traumatic event			
Distressing thoughts	34%	22%	7%
Distressing dreams	4%	0%	0%
Feelings of danger	10%	13%	0%
Avoidance and emotional numbing			
Avoidance of activities	28%	22%	17%
Loss of interest in activities	7%	3%	0%
Feeling distant from others	9%	6%	3%
Restricted affect	3%	3%	0%
Sense of foreshortened future	35%	19%	17%
Symptoms of increased arousal			
Difficulty falling asleep	19%	19%	0%
Increased irritability	4%	5%	0%
Concentration difficulties	11%	8%	0%
Increased startle response	35%	34%	10%
Physiological reactivity	18%	25%	3%

DSM-III-R. As illustrated by Table 2, substantial numbers of subjects reported PTSD symptoms immediately following the murders. Symptoms most commonly reported were sense of foreshortened future (35%), increased startle response (35%), and distressing thoughts (34%), each representing a different symptom cluster.

Nine months following the murders over one-third of subjects were still reporting increased startle response and nearly one-fifth reported distressing thoughts, avoidance of activities, difficulty falling asleep, and increased physiologic reactivity. By 18 months, however, virtually all symptoms had significantly decreased. In fact, only two symptoms (sense of foreshortened future and avoidance of activities) were reported by 10% or more of subjects. The most dramatic decreases were observed in the increased arousal and reexperiencing of the trauma categories. Thus, while symptoms appeared to resolve over time, there were by no means transient. This pattern of reduction of symptoms is similar to that observed in individuals who have been direct victims of violence (Calhoun & Atkeson, 1991). Thus, it would appear most subjects were able to experience "psychological healing," although the process took over 1 year.

These results are consistent with the meta-analysis study of post-disaster psychopathology conducted by Rubonis and Bickman (1991). In the meta-analysis of 32 studies, Rubonis and Bickman reported an overall psychopathology effect size of .174, with anxiety symptoms demonstrating the largest effect size (.309). Similar to our results, these authors found that the psychopathology diminished over time.

Because of the severe attrition in subject participation across time, the possibility exists that the follow-up results reflect methodological artifact rather than actual decrease of symptoms. That is, individuals most affected by the murders dropped out of the study. To control for this possibility, and analysis of the reported symptoms of the 30 subjects who responded to all three questionnaires was conducted.

As illustrated in Table 3, the pattern of observed symptoms of this subsample is remarkably similar to the results presented in Table 2 both in terms of initial symptoms and resolution of symptoms over time. These data suggest that the observed decreases in subject reported symptoms represents a real attenuation of the community's psychological response and is not solely due to attrition of the more distressed subjects.

Table 3. *Endorsement of PTSD Symptoms by Subjects Responding to the All Three Data Collections*

Symptom	Initial	9 months	18 months
Reexperience of the traumatic event			
Distressing thoughts	27%	12%	4%
Distressing dreams	0%	0%	0%
Feelings of danger	4%	0%	0%
Avoidance and emotional numbing			
Avoidance of activities	31%	19%	16%
Loss of interest in activities	4%	0%	0%
Feeling distant from others	4%	4%	4%
Restricted affect	4%	4%	0%
Sense of foreshortened future	19%	15%	20%
Symptoms of increased arousal			
Difficulty falling asleep	8%	12%	0%
Increased irritability	4%	4%	0%
Concentration difficulties	4%	4%	0%
Increased startle response	19%	19%	7%
Physiological reactivity	12%	19%	4%

Young (1989) hypothesized that vicarious trauma reactions are most likely to occur among individuals who closely identify with the actual victims. To test this hypothesis, psychological distress was analyzed by student status (all victims were college students) and gender (four of five victims were female). It was expected that students and women would experience the most severe psychological reactions. Comparison of students and non-students across all PTSD symptoms revealed significant differences on only two symptoms: avoidance of activities (x^2 (1) = 6.90, $p < .009$) and sense of foreshortened future (x^2 (1) = 13.17, $p < .004$). The finding that avoidance of activities was more often noted in students is not surprising in that this segment of the community is most likely to engage in high risk activities (walking alone at night, going out to bars at night) that would tend to be avoided following a series of murders.

Gender, on the other hand, appeared to be closely related to psychological distress. As illustrated in Table 4, significantly more women reported PTSD symptoms following the murders than men. Specifically, women reported significantly more distressing thoughts, avoidance of activities, sense of foreshortened future, sleep difficulties, startle response, and physiological reactivity than men. Interestingly, the only symptom reported more frequently by men was increased irritability. While these findings may reflect the identification of Gainesville women with the student victims, another explanation may be that groups such as women that have been historical victims of violence may be more susceptible to traumatization through vicarious means.

While the above analyses provide information about the general presence of PTSD symptoms, they do not assess the magnitude of distress, i.e., the number of PTSD symptoms experienced by the individual subject. To evaluate the level of psychological distress reported by subjects, individual records were evaluated for presence of a PTSD "diagnosis" using DSM-III-R criteria. The term "diagnosis" is used only as a convenience to describe those subjects who reported PTSD symptoms from all DSM-III-R diagnostic clusters. The authors are clearly not asserting that these subjects experienced a clinical PTSD and recognize that such a diagnosis would require a clinical interview which was not part of this research. DSM-III-R decision rules were followed for all categories except C (avoidance/numbing). Because the questionnaire only sampled five of the seven category C criteria, the threshold for presence of this category was reduced from three to two criteria.

814   **Journal of Clinical Psychology, December 1997**

Table 4. *Frequency of PTSD Symptoms by Gender at Initial Data Collection*

Symptom	Males	Females	p
Reexperience of the traumatic event			
Distressing thoughts	23%	42%	.008
Distressing dreams	1%	7%	.09
Feelings of danger	5%	13%	.09
Avoidance and emotional numbing			
Avoidance of activities	7%	42%	.000
Loss of interest in activities	3%	9%	.14
Feeling distant from others	5%	11%	.333
Restricted affect	3%	4%	.67
Sense of foreshortened future	4%	55%	.000
Symptoms of increased arousal			
Difficulty falling asleep	11%	25%	.014
Increased irritability	7%	3%	.325
Concentration difficulties	5%	14%	.116
Increased startle response	12%	51%	.000
Physiological reactivity	1%	29%	.000

In the initial sample, 25 subjects (14%) endorsed sufficient criteria for a diagnosis of PTSD. While the lack of data on these subjects before the murders makes it difficult to judge the significance of this finding, epidemiological studies of PTSD in other communities indicate prevalence rates of between 1% and 3% (Davidson, Hughes, Blazer, & George, 1991; Helzer, Robins, & McEvoy, 1987). Thus, the magnitude of reported symptoms in the present sample is well above that expected in the community and suggests that the increase in PTSD prevalence reflects psychological sequela associated with the serial murders. However, it is important to note that the community studies of PTSD cited above utilized the Diagnostic Interview Schedule (Robins, Helzer, Croughland, Williams, & Spitzer, 1981), a structured interview with more stringent criteria than that used in the present study. Had such measures been used in the present study the prevalence of PTSD may have been lower. Still, the finding that 14% of the present sample reported multiple symptoms from all PTSD symptoms clusters indicates that these individuals experienced significant psychological distress following the murders.

These PTSD subjects were further analyzed to determine how they differed from those individuals who did not meet diagnostic threshold or reported less magnitude of symptoms. Results indicate that the PTSD subjects were significantly younger ($F(157, 24) = 2.35$, $p < .016$) and more likely to be female ($x^2(1) = 15.44$, $p < .000$) compared to the general sample. In fact, only one PTSD subject was a male.

These subjects also appeared to cope with their fears differently than the rest of the sample. For example, individuals who met diagnostic criteria for PTSD were much more likely to choose the coping behavior of purchasing a firearm than the general sample ($x^2(1) = 9.97$, $p < .001$). This trend was not observed in the purchasing of other self-defense devices such as mace ($x^2(1) = 2.07$, $p > .10$). This is especially interesting in that virtually all of these subjects were women, a group not traditionally associated with firearm use. While this illustrates the intensity of fear experienced by these subjects, it is somewhat unsettling that the group with the most serious psychological reaction chose to protect themselves with the most deadly force.

Comparisons between groups on other variables such as whether the murderer would kill again, was in police custody, or would eventually be caught were not related to diagnosis of PTSD. However, other variables such as home distance from the murder sites and status as a student, while not significant, showed some relationship to this diagnosis. For example, 43% of the PTSD subjects lived within one mile of the murder sites while only 27% of the community respondents lived within that area. Similarly, a larger proportion of these subjects were students (41%) compared to the general sample (28%). Longitudinal study of these PTSD subjects indicated a substantial reduction in diagnoses. For example, in the 9-month follow-up sample only four (6%) of the respondents still had symptoms sufficient to meet this diagnostic threshold. No subjects in the 18-month follow-up received a PTSD diagnosis. Thus, these subjects, similar to the overall sample, appeared to return to psychological equilibrium with time.

This study provides a model for understanding how communities respond to violence such as serial murder. While methodological concerns such as response rate, subject attrition, and absence of a control sample limit the generalizability of the findings, results do indicate that large numbers of Gainesville residents experienced significant psychological trauma following the student murders. Further, this distress was not transient with many subjects requiring over a year to recover. These data clearly illustrate how a community can be traumatized by violence perpetrated on a few members. The nature of the killings, media response, and cohesion of a university town clearly met the criteria identified by Young (1989) factors associated with vicarious victimization, thus making Gainesville particularly vulnerable to experiencing community vicarious victimization. In conclusion, this study suggests that the sense of community that binds people together also renders them vulnerable to the harm befalling only a few. It is, apparently, empirically true that communities are bound to each other emotionally and not simply geographically.

REFERENCES

AMERICAN PSYCHIATRIC ASSOCIATION. (1987). *Diagnostic and statistical manual of mental disorders.* (3rd ed., revised). Washington, DC: Author.

BROMET, E.J. (1989). The nature and effects of technological failures. In R. Gist & B. Lubin (Eds.), *Psychosocial aspects of disaster* (pp. 61–85). New York: Wiley.

BURGESS, A., & HOMSTROM, L.L. (1974). Rape trauma syndrome. *American Journal of Psychiatry, 131,* 981–985.

CALHOUN, K.S., & ATKESON, B.M. (1991). *Treatment of rape victims: Facilitating psychological adjustment.* New York: Pergamon.

DAVIDSON, J.R., HUGHES, D., BLAZER, D.G., & GEORGE, L.K. (1991). Post-traumatic stress disorder in the community: An epidemiological study. *Psychological Medicine, 21,* 713–721.

HELZER, J.E., ROBINS, L.N., & McEVOY, M.A. (1987). Post-traumatic stress disorder in the general population: Findings of the Epidemiologic Catchment Area survey. *New England Journal of Medicine, 317,* 1630–1634.

HOMES, R.M., & DEBURGER, J.E. (1985). Profiles in terror: The serial murderer. *Federal Probation, 49,* 29–34.

HOROWITZ, M.J., STINSON, C., & FIELD, N. (1991). Natural disasters and stress response syndromes. *Psychiatric Annals, 21,* 556–562.

OEI, T.P., LIM, B., & HENNESSY, B. (1990). Psychological dysfunction in battle: Combat stress reactions and posttraumatic stress disorder. *Clinical Psychology Review, 10* (3), 355–388.

ROBINS, L.N., HELZER, J.E., CROUGHLAND, J.L., WILLIAMS, J.B.W., & SPITZER, R.L. (1981). *NIMH Diagnostic Interview Schedule Version III.* Public Health Service (PHS), publication ADM-T-42-3 (5-8-81). Rockville, MD: NIMH.

RUBONIS, A.V., & BICKMAN, L. (1991). Psychological impairment in the wake of disaster: The disaster-psychopathology relationship. *Psychological Bulletin, 109,* 384–399.

TERR, L.C. (1985). Psychic trauma in children and adolescents. In *Psychiatric clinics of North America* (Vol. 8, No. 4, pp. 815–835). Philadelphia, PA: W.B. Saunders Company.

YOUNG, M.A. (1989). Crime, violence, and terrorism. In R. Gist & B. Lubin (Eds.), *Psychosocial aspects of disaster* (pp. 61–85). New York: Wiley.

Part IV
Psychiatric Diagnosis and the Law

[14]

SUPPLEMENT

AMERICAN PSYCHIATRY AND THE CRIMINAL : A HISTORICAL REVIEW [1]

SEYMOUR HALLECK, M.D.[2]

Behavior which communicates personal suffering is a traditional concern of psychiatry. When the patient experiences unbearable pain in the form of anxiety or despair he seeks relief. He comes to the physician with a spirit of cooperation hopefully expectant that his suffering will be alleviated. The role of the psychiatrist in this situation is relatively clear. A tradition of 2500 years provides a model which defines the limits and potentialities of medical involvement.

Another aspect of human behavior of interest to psychiatrists involves conduct that is harmful to the society or to the person himself. In this situation the role of psychiatry is less clear. The patient may be aware of little personal suffering. While alteration of the noxious aspects of this person's behavior may be applauded by the community it may at the same time be unwelcome to the individual. The application of the medical model in this situation leads to agonizing complications. Yet, since the beginning of the 19th Century the search for biological explanations of deviant behavior has been unremitting. This is particularly true of that deviant behavior which is labelled as criminal.

Throughout history the criminal has intrigued the medical profession. This is because he bears many startling resemblances to those whom we call mentally ill. When incarcerated (and sometimes before) the offender often proved to be a miserable, unhappy person who could be observed to suffer in the same way as the mental patient. Psychoanalytic psychiatry taught us that those psychological mechanisms which produced neurotic suffering were also operant in individuals who demonstrated criminal behavior. These observations fostered psychiatry's hopes of contributing to the understanding and attenuation of criminal behavior. Although these hopes have at times been realized, progress in this area has not come easily. The medically oriented approach to criminality never has achieved major influence in any society. Moralistic and socially directed concepts have invariably predominated. Where psychiatrists have made contributions they have amalgamated their own thinking with those of other disciplines or idealogies. Many of the techniques and theories that have resulted bear little resemblance to traditional medical models.

With this introduction the author proposes to examine one important part of the story of psychiatry and the criminal. From the beginning of the 19th Century American psychiatrists have made significant contributions to the science of criminology. A few of the names that appear in this history are those of our most respected members. Most of the contributors have, however, been relatively unheralded. There can be little question as to what motivated these men. Material rewards were meager and recognition or honors even more rare. Many who ventured into this work abandoned lucrative practices in pleasant surroundings in exchange for underpaid, unrespected positions in the most depressing of environments. Two motivations emerge as the most plausible explanations of this unusual dedication. First, a scientific quest to better understand and alter a perplexing variety of human behavior. Second, a humanistic desire to both alleviate the suffering of the criminal and to improve his plight. This latter motivation combined

[1] Many individuals have devoted considerable time and effort to assist the author in the preparation of this material. The author is especially indebted to Drs. Rinck, Smith and Settle of the Federal Prison System, Dr. Kuehnert in Calif., Dr. Abrahamsen in N.Y., Dr. Russell in Mass., and Mr. Uehling in Wisc.

[2] Associate Professor, Univ. of Wisconsin Medical School.

i

the medical mandate to relieve pain together with the reformer's zeal to change those conditions which perpetuate it.

Certain aspects of the relation of psychiatry to the criminal will not be emphasized in this paper. The successful offender who manages to evade apprehension has never been studied by psychiatrists. Our knowledge of the psychological problems of a large group, perhaps the majority, of offenders is meager. Psychiatric criminology has concerned itself only with the unsuccessful criminal. The historical relationships of psychiatry and the law while certainly relevant to any study of criminology raise too many diverse issues to be adequately studied in a short project. Legal problems will be considered only

when it is essential to maintain an overview of the total picture of psychiatry's relation to the criminal. Similarly the problems of the youthful offender will not be examined in detail.

The chart of 100 milestones in the history of American psychiatry and the criminal covers the period from 1800 to 1960. The events are listed to honor those moments which the author has judged to be the most significant. Many important events and individual contributions may have been neglected. Hopefully these omissions are the result of personal selection rather than insufficient research. The reader may find the chart useful in following the major trends discussed in the descriptive and theoretical parts of the paper.

ONE HUNDRED SIGNIFICANT EVENTS IN THE HISTORY OF AMERICAN PSYCHIATRY AND THE CRIMINAL

1812—Benjamin Rush publishes first American psychiatric text which emphasizes medical causes of deviant behavior.

1817—New York State begins to utilize a system of parole, the first indeterminate sentencing in this country.

1824—Charles Caldwell becomes principal advocate of phrenological theories of criminal behavior.

1938—Isaac Ray publishes **A Treatise on the Medical Jurisprudence of Insanity.**

1841—Practice of probation begins in Boston, Massachusetts.

1844—**American Journal of Insanity** begins publication under editorship of Amariah Brigham (many early articles devoted to criminally insane).

1855—New York State opens first institution for the criminally insane adjacent to Auburn State Prison (moved to Matteawan in 1892).

1881—Trial of Charles J. Guiteau the assassin of President Garfield involves many prominent psychiatrists.

1883—Michigan authorizes the building of Ionia State Hospital for the Criminally Insane.

1895—Massachusetts opens "Asylum for Insane Criminals" (name changed to Bridgewater State Hospital in 1904).

1895—Hamilton D. Wey a prison physician at Elmira Reformatory, New York, becomes principal American advocate of anthropological theories of crime (the "criminal brain").

1899—First juvenile court established in Chicago.

1903—William Alanson White appointed superintendent of St. Elizabeths Hospital.

1908—Guy Fernald begins work as psychiatrist at Massachusetts State Reformatory.

1909—Bernard Glueck begins work at St. Elizabeths.

1909—Indiana sterilization law of 1907 is expanded to provide for sterilization of criminals.

1909—William Healy appointed to examine offenders in Chicago Juvenile Court Clinics (the first psychiatrist to work in a court clinic).

1911—Massachusetts passes law providing for segregation of defective delinquents.

1912—Clinic established at Chicago House of Corrections for the study of nervous and mental diseases.

1912—Major Edgar King begins psychiatric work with prisoners at Ft. Leavenworth.

1913—A. Warren Stearns begins psychiatric work with prisoners at Massachusetts State Prison.

1913—V. V. Anderson helps establish and provide psychiatric service to adult court clinic in Boston.

1913—John D. Rockefeller establishes laboratory of social hygiene to allow for psychiatric examination of all persons committed to Bedford Reformatory (under direction of Dr. Edith Spalding).

1913—New York Probation and Protective Association institutes studies of female delinquents (later carried out by Augusta Scott and Anne T. Bingham).

1914—William J. Hickson begins work at first adult clinic in Chicago.

1915—Paul E. Bowers psychiatrist at Indiana State Prison presents comprehensive clinical studies of the relationship of mental illness to crime.

1916—Committee on the Mental Hygiene of the Prisoner organized under chairmanship of Dr. Thomas W. Salmon.

1916—Bernard Glueck begins psychiatric studies of prisoners at Sing Sing.

1917—W. A. White as chairman of Committee for Sterilization of Criminals of the Institute of Criminology concludes that scientific evidence is insufficient to warrant this practice.

1917—Psychiatric clinic established to assist police department in New York City.

1917—William Healy and August Bronner leave Chicago to continue their work at Judge Baker Foundation in Boston.

1917—Herman Adler replaces Healy at Juvenile Court Clinic in Chicago and is also appointed state criminologist.

1917-18—Bernard Glueck begins to report on his studies at Sing Sing and to make vigorous recommendations for changes in the New York Prison System.

1919—Benjamin Karpman begins work with criminally insane in Howard Hall section of St. Elizabeths.

1920—Permanent "psychopathic clinic" established at Sing Sing Prison.

1921—Department for Care of Defective Delinquents opened at State Hospital at Bridgewater, Massachusetts.

1921—Briggs law passed in Massachusetts largely through efforts of Dr. Vernon Briggs.

1921—Dr. John R. Oliver and Dr. Ronald Jacoby become directors of court clinics in Baltimore and Detroit.

1922—National Committee for Mental Hygiene creates a division for the Prevention of Delinquency (traveling court clinic team approach).

1924—American Orthopsychiatric Association founded "to meet the needs for a central organization of those dealing with the psychiatric aspects of delinquency."

1924—Psychiatric services at Wisconsin Correctional Institutions started by Dr. William Lorenz and Dr. Frank Richmond.

1924—Briggs Law extended to include examination of convicted felons already imprisoned.

1924—Benjamin Karpman holds first symposium on the problem of psychopathy.

1924—APA sets up Committee on Legal Aspects of Psychiatry.

1926—Committee on Legal Aspects of Psychiatry presents report to the APA recommending ideal conditions for psychiatric treatment of crime.

1926—Karl A. Menninger presents Committee on Legal Aspects of Psychiatry's recommendations to the American Bar Association.

1926—Herman Adler begins teaching psychiatric aspects of criminology in university setting (Univ. of California, Berkeley).

1927—Amos T. Baker appointed director of Sing Sing psychopathic clinic.

1927—Colorado passes law allowing for examination by public facilities for any criminal who wishes to plead insanity.

1928—American Prison Association recommends use of a standard psychiatric classification for offenders.

1928—Winfred Overholser conducts first survey of psychiatric services available to correctional institutions and courts.

1929—American Bar Association concurs with APA and AMA in recommending that all felons be examined psychiatrically before sentencing and before release.

1929—Congress appoints committee to study conditions in Federal Prisons.

1929—Prison riots in New York and Ohio give impetus to prison reform—particularly in Federal system.

1930—Dr. V. C. Branham becomes Deputy Commissioner of Corrections of New York State.

1930—Manfred Guttmacher becomes director of Baltimore court clinic.

1930—Congress passes law re-organizing Federal Prisons and authorizing Public Health Service to provide medical services to prisons.

1931—New York City Court of General Sessions begins to examine all offenders (under direction of Karl Bowman and later Walter Bromberg).

1931—Behavior Clinic begins to examine offenders at the Criminal Court of Cook County.

1932—First psychiatrist in California system appointed at San Quentin.

1933—Medical Center for Federal Prisoners opens at Springfield, Missouri.

1934—James L. McCartney reports on survey of psychiatric services available to prisons.

1934—APA forms Section on Forensic Psychiatry under Chairmanship of William Alanson White.

1935—Lowell S. Selling appointed director of Recorder Court in Detroit.

1935—Dr. Peter Bell becomes chief of Wisconsin Psychiatric Field Services.

1937—Dr. Winfred Overholser appointed superintendent of St. Elizabeths hospital following the death of William Alanson White.

1937—National Committee for Mental Hygiene holds symposium on "The Challenge of Sex Offenders" (participants E. A. Strecker, A. H. MacCormick and W. Overholser).

1937—Michigan passes "pioneer" sex psychopathic law—later found unconstitutional.

1937—James Bennett becomes director of Federal Bureau of Prisons.

1938—Illinois passes first constitutional sex psychopathic law.

1939—Sing Sing psychopathic clinic abolished.

1940—**Journal of Criminal Psychopathology** begins publications under editorship of Dr. V. C. Branham.

1940—Medical Correctional Association organized under the guidance of Dr. Ralph Banay.

1941—Pennsylvania begins first specialized training program in prison psychiatry under direction of Dr. Philip Roche.

1941—William Haines becomes director of the Behavior Clinic of the Criminal Court of Cook County.

1944—Reception-Guidance Center for psychiatric examination of offenders opened at San Quentin.

1945—Group therapy begins to be utilized in U.S. Army.

1948—Group therapy begins to be utilized in New Jersey prison system.

1949—Redevelopment of active court clinics begins in Massachusetts.

1949—Public Law 285 authorizes psychiatrists in Federal Prisons to diagnose and detain for treatment persons who are too mentally ill to stand trial.

1949—California refines legal procedures so as to develop a workable sex crime's law.

1949—Forensic Committee of Group for Advancement of Psychiatry presents report criticizing current practices and offering suggestions for change.

1950—California Medical Faculty opened at Terminal Island under the direction of Dr. King.

1950—Dr. Douglas M. Kelley becomes first psychiatrist appointed as a full-time faculty member in a department of criminology (Univ. of California, Berkeley).

1950—New Jersey Sex Offender Act approved and begins realistic operation.

1950—New York State reports on systematic study of sex offenders (Abrahamsen) and passes workable legislation.

1950—California begins intensive research on the problems of sex crimes under directorship of Dr. Karl Bowman.

1950—Association for the Psychiatric Treatment of Offenders is founded.

1951—Maryland passes "defective delinquency" law.

1952—First Isaac Ray Award presented to Dr. Overholser.

1952—Wisconsin begins operation of first sex crimes program with adequate provisions for treatment.

1954—**Journal of Social Therapy** (Medical Correctional Association) begins publication).

1954—Durham decision in District of Columbia encourages further psychiatric interest in the offender.

1955—Pantuxet Institution for Treatment of Defective Delinquents opens in Maryland.

1955—Vacaville Medical Facility opened in California.

1957—Warren S. Willie surveys psychiatric facilities in correctional institutions.

1957—**Journal of Offender Therapy** begins publication (then called APTO Journal).

1958—Massachusetts passes legislation for care of dangerous sex offenders.

1955—**Journal of Criminal Psychodynamics** begins publication under editorship of Benjamin Karpman.

1958—Public Law 752 passed providing for commitment of convicted federal offenders for psychiatric study before imposition of sentence.

The story of American psychiatry and the criminal begins in the 19th Century. For convenience the discussion will be broken down into sections of historical time periods.

1800 TO 1900

The 19th Century was one of emphasis on the enlightened treatment of the mentally ill. While the treatment of the criminal did not improve accordingly, he was not neglected by psychiatrists. Benjamin Rush, often considered the first American psychiatrist, devoted considerable space to consideration of deviant behavior in his writings(1). These were to influence the subsequent contributions of an impressive number of physicians who interested themselves in psychiatry.

From the beginning the uniqueness of American psychiatry's approach was a concern with the criminal rather than with the crime. It was the medical profession that made the initial and significant efforts to study the criminal as an individual.

While all 19th Century physicians focused primarily on organic determinants of behavior, their interest took two basic directions. There were those who believed that almost every crime could be understood as the result of the influence of a single biological determinant. This monistic approach took many forms. For a time phrenological theories championed by Charles Caldwell took precedence(2). Later the hereditary approach predominated and was loaned impetus by the publication of Richard Dugdale's *The Jukes* (3). Inherited "perversion of the moral senses" and congenital feeble-mindedness were concepts that fitted in well with the moralistic attitudes of that day. Hereditary theories of crime were supported by such prominent figures as O. W. Holmes, R. E. McVey and A. Drahms. In later years they helped to create a rationale for eugenic approaches to the criminal. Towards the turn of the century the influence of Lombroso was deeply felt in this country. His concept of a criminal type of brain based on both anatomical and physiological findings found a number of supporters among American prison psychiatrists such as H. Wey in New York and H. McCorn in Wisconsin.

Other psychiatrists, such as Isaac Ray, directed their attention to separating the insane criminal from the ordinary offender. This was more than a theoretical concern. For at that time, even more than today, the difference in the treatment of the criminal and the mentally ill was profound. In his writings Ray(4) considered the problems of mental illness and motivation as they related to the prevailing law. Even today his publications stand out as erudite and practical commentaries. Ray and other 19th Century psychiatrists who concerned themselves with the issue of criminal insanity sought to help and treat those who could be adjudicated as mentally ill. But their efforts contributed little to the welfare of the great majority of offenders. The offender was either mentally ill or a criminal. As a criminal he was often rejected as a worthy subject for medical treatment. This "either-or" attitude pervades the pages of the *American Journal of Insanity* throughout its publication during the 19th Century. In the very first edition(5) Amariah Brigham criticized the *Journal of Prison Discipline* for degrading the insane by publishing statistical reports of both mental hospitals and prisons in the same issue.

The trial of Charles Guiteau in 1884 heightened interest in the issue of criminal responsibility. Psychiatrists were divided in opinion as to Guiteau's insanity. Their testimony, often eloquent(6), presents a clear picture of the predominant psychiatric thinking of the time. Most of those psychiatrists who testified were deeply influenced by the "either-or" attitude of their time. The doctrine of "moral insanity" was thoroughly discussed and re-discussed before Guiteau was finally found guilty. In reading the conflicting testimonies of various psychiatric witnesses one cannot help but be struck by the great disagreements within a discipline which was then just beginning to collect a scientific body of knowledge. In 1884 as today psychiatric involvement in legalistic rather than scientific decisions often resulted in confusion and ineptness.

For some 19th Century psychiatrists a broader view of the criminal was possible which took neither a wholly monistic nor an "either-or" attitude. By 1894 H.E. Allison(7), the superintendent of Matteawan State Hospital in New York, advocated the psychiatric examination of all men who were convicted of crimes. He himself was not fully committed to any single theory of causation. But he did recognize that many criminals not legally designated as insane were nevertheless disturbed individuals who could benefit from psychiatric attention.

There were still other important innovations in the 19th Century. The prison system itself developed the practices of probation and parole which in later years were to offer increased opportunity for the employment of psychiatric skills. And a great humanitarian step was taken when hospitals for the criminally insane were constructed in Massachusetts, New York, Michigan and Illinois. In summarizing the work of psychiatrists during the 19th Century it is easy to dismiss much of their theorizing as unsound, unscientific and naive. But Fink(8), the most prominent student of the psychiatric criminology of the 19th Century warns us that "there is need to evaluate the contribution of these physicians in the light of the knowledge and experience of their day. If they were in error at times it was the error which they shared with their generation."

Nineteenth Century psychiatry did give us an individual approach to the problem of crime. It attempted to discover scientific explanations for the behavior of criminals rather than relegating them completely to moral condemnation or to pessimistic theories of social inevitability. As a byproduct of this scientific concern many humanitarian changes were made. In the 19th Century American medicine was the most potent and promising force for an enlightened criminology.

1900 TO 1910

In the first decade of the 20th Century psychiatry's concern with separating the criminal from the insane continued. Publications related to medico-legal matters continued to outnumber those more clearly directed to the problem of criminality. Still, signs of a mounting interest in the problem of psychiatric criminology began to appear. In this decade both William Alanson White and Bernard Glueck began their work at St. Elizabeths and were deeply influenced by their experiences with the criminally insane they encountered in the Howard Hall section of that institution. Walter Fernald in Massachusetts and Frank Christian in New York became interested in the problems of feeble-mindedness as related to criminal behavior. Guy Fernald undertook studies of reformatory inmates at the Massachusetts State Reformatory. In this decade there appeared for the first time a major development independent of the Eastern Seaboard states of New York and Massachusetts or the District of Columbia. In 1909 William Healy began to examine juvenile offenders at the court clinic in Chicago. His experiences led to the development of techniques and theories that were to have a revolutionary impact upon the entire field.

Anthropological and hereditary theories of crime began to receive harsh scrutiny and questioning. By the end of this decade there had been an abandonment of belief in the existence of a "criminal brain." Fink notes that, "By 1910 the study of the criminal had shifted from the anatomy and physiology of the brain to the function of the human being as a whole." This change undoubtedly reflected major trends in all areas of psychiatry, particularly a growing interest in environmental and social determinants.

But the doctrine of hereditary criminality could not be laid to rest quietly. This concept continued to appeal to those who could envision the utilization of medical techniques for the control of a social problem. With the perfection of the operation of vasectomy in 1899 sterilization became a relatively simple procedure. During the first decade of this century the medical profession and others concerned with the problem of crime began to advocate denial of procreative rights to those who had transgressed against the law. In Indiana, for example, 465 criminals were sterilized between 1899 and 1907. In other states more punitive measures, such as castration, were recommended and carried out. In 1909 the state of Indiana legalized the sterilization of criminals and by 1914 thirteen states had passed similar laws. This practice was not effectively discouraged until 1915 when Edith Spalding and William Healy presented damaging evidence against the hereditary theory(9). Finally in 1917 William Alanson White, as head of a study committee on sterilization of criminals, concluded that there was insufficient evidence to justify continuation of this practice(10).

However benevolent were the motivations of those who advocated such procedures their efforts led to a dark period in the history of American psychiatry and the criminal. The coercive use of medical procedures to control socially deviant behavior is a risky business, whether such procedures are based on proven fact or on conjecture. It is not in the finest tradition of medicine and particularly when exercized without necessary legal restraints constitutes a threat to democratic institutions. Although coercive medical procedures appear intermittently throughout the history of psychiatry and the criminal, the sterilization furor of the early years of the 20th Century constitutes the most gruesome warning of their potentiality for abuse.

The first decade of the century was noteworthy in at least one other respect. Since the time of Isaac Ray the relationship of mental defect to crime had intrigued psychiatrists. In 1908 Walter Fernald and Charles Burr provided a classification of feeble-mindedness in their paper "The Imbecile and Criminal Instinct"(11). They maintained that every feeble-minded individual, especially the high grade defective, was a potential criminal. With this concept they anticipated some of the theories of feeble-mindedness and crime that were to flourish and to produce violent controversy for the next two decades.

1910 TO 1920

In this decade one of the most important trends was influenced by new developments in the field of psychology. Until

1965]　　　　　　　　SEYMOUR HALLECK　　　　　　　　vii

1910 when Henry H. Goddard introduced the use of the Binet-Simon Intelligence Test to this country, the diagnosis of feeble-mindedness was made by psychiatrists through interview techniques, observation, and clinical judgment. When Goddard began formalized testing of criminals he discovered that 25% of his population performed at a feeble-minded level (12). By 1914 he was convinced that this figure could be raised to 50%. In the meantime prison psychiatrists, particularly the Fernalds, had come to believe that most crime was rooted in intellectual deficiency. Psychiatric reports of the incidence of feeble-mindedness in criminal populations were varied but fell within the range of 28% to 89%.

As Lombroso's doctrine of physical types of criminals declined, the psychiatrists swung to the doctrine of the inborn mental type, the defective. The criminal who was also believed to be feeble-minded was given many labels, the most prominent of which were moral imbecile and defective delinquent. The first name soon disappeared from medical usage. Defective delinquency, a term suggested by Walter Fernald, remained viable for many years and continues to be applied to certain classes of intellectually limited or troublesome offenders. It was not until psychological tests were standardized with army recruits in World War I and not until other inadequacies and errors in test administration were discovered that the doctrine of the feeble-minded criminal began to decline. Even into the 1930's mental defect was considered by many as the primary cause of crime. During the decade 1910 to 1920, however, this doctrine was at its peak. Few at that time would have disagreed with Walter Fernald when he stated, "Feeble mindedness is the mother of crime, degeneracy and pauperism."

In spite of these ultimately unprofitable controversies the years 1910-1920 also represent a period in which psychiatry made revolutionary contributions to the study of the criminal. In 1919 V.V. Anderson, who worked both in the Boston Court and New York Prison System summarized(13) the findings of 9 physicians who had made extensive studies of prisoners in different institutions. New "psychopathic laboratories" appeared in prisons staffed by such individuals as Frank Christian, John Harding, Guy Fernald, Edith Spalding, Louise Bryant, Bernard Glueck, Frank Heacox, Paul Bowers and A. Warren Stearns. Importantly these men and women identified themselves not only as prison physicians but also as psychiatrists. Using the best available techniques of their time they discovered that large groups of the criminal population (from 35% to 63%) fit into diagnostic categories ordinarily reserved for the mentally ill. These pioneer prison psychiatrists employed a variety of organic and environmental theories in their work. They did not cling to any single global theory of criminality. The social usefulness of their work had expanded far beyond the limited benefits of separating the insane criminal from the general class of offenders.

The group of psychiatrists employed in court clinics was smaller but probably even more influential than the prison psychiatrists. Beginning in juvenile court clinics, William Healy and later Augusta Bronner intensively studied large numbers of delinquents. They submitted reports to judicial agencies which were instrumental in influencing the social treatment of the child. As a result, probation, foster home placement and other specialized dispositions were utilized more frequently. To a limited extent psychotherapeutic techniques were employed in treating the individual delinquent. These children's court clinics were the forerunners of the child guidance clinics of today. They also laid the groundwork for the formation of adult clinics during the same decade.

The psychiatric heroes of this era were Bernard Glueck and William Healy. In 1918 Glueck reported(14) on the examination of 608 inmates at Sing Sing Prison in New York. He noted that 58% of his population demonstrated some form of nervous or mental disease. Glueck's examinations were not based on a linear model of causation but rather took cognizance of all psychiatric data available at that time. He recognized the influence of the environment on mental disorders and at the same time did not neglect the importance of biological factors. His recommendations for the reorganization of the New York State Prison System were far-reaching but practical. He advocated psychiatric examination for all convicted offenders and pleaded for the segregation of different classes of criminals in specialized institutions. He also suggested a practical classification of criminal types based on current psychiatric thinking.

Healy's major contribution was the application of the case study method to the individual delinquent. This technique provided information that precluded classification of the offender as a type and discouraged naive speculation as to linear causality. His approach was what we would today call dynamic, combining medical observations with the study of man in society. This amalgam of social and medical approaches represented a revolutionary change in psychiatry's view of the criminal. Together with Spalding he helped lay to rest hereditary theories of criminality(15). Throughout his career he collaborated with other individuals such as Bronner(16) and Alexander(17) to produce a remarkable number of useful publications. His influence was deeply felt throughout the second, third, and fourth decades of this century.

Still other important developments in the history of psychiatry and the criminal occurred during the years 1910-1920. Many more states created specialized facilities for the criminally insane and provided levels of staffing on a par with those of mental hospitals. It was also during this and the following decade that psychiatric criminology gained its highest level of respectability. Psychiatrists who chose to work in prisons or court clinics received a comparatively high level of respect and honor. Many of them were the acknowledged leaders of the profession.

The dislocations caused by World War I did not materially impede progress. Some individuals such as Herman Adler and H. Warren Stearns merely switched the focus of their interest to the military offender. In 1920 Thomas Salmon, then medical director of the National Committee for Mental Hygiene, summarized the major psychiatric contributions to criminology(18) up to World War I and prophesized even greater developments in the postwar era. Subsequent history was to prove the accuracy of his predictions.

1920 TO 1930

The third decade of this century was one of continued expansion of psychiatric services to prisons and courts. In 1928 Overholser(19) reported that 93 correctional institutions were utilizing the service of full- or part-time psychiatrists. Almost 10% of the courts of the country had obtained similar services. This growth was mainly clustered around the states of California, Illinois, Massachusetts, Michigan, New York, Ohio and Pennsylvania. Some of the stimulus to expansion of court clinics was generated by the efforts of the National Committee for Mental Hygiene which set up a traveling psychiatric team to assist municipalities in developing their own court program. The mobile team idea also appeared in Wisconsin where a centralized agency was formed to provide psychiatric field service to all state institutions. In spite of the social usefulness of such activities, treatment based on psychotherapeutic principles was still a rarity. The court clinics' psychiatrists were mainly interested in disposition or in helping judges and correctional workers to better understand offenders. Prison psychiatrists focused on diagnosis and classification or in cooperating with and influencing the rehabilitative techniques of the correctional administrators.

St. Elizabeths Hospital continued to influence psychiatric criminology mainly because of the work of William Alanson White(20) and Benjamin Karpman(21, 22). By this time the concept of the psychopathic personality had emerged as an important link to the understanding of criminal behavior. Karpman's fascination with the psychopath began in this decade and was later to produce an extraordinary number of comprehensive studies of this special class of offenders.

The Leopold and Loeb trial in 1924 furnished a spectacular battle of psychiatric experts but as in the Guiteau trial of the preceding century psychiatric testimony did not appreciably influence the final verdict. The significance of this trial for psychiatry is that it offered the first public forum for the exposition of psychoanalytically oriented viewpoints as applied to the criminal.

Had the Leopold-Loeb trial taken place in Massachusetts instead of Illinois, psychiatric knowledge might have been utilized in a more scientific manner. Largely through the efforts of Dr. Vernon Briggs the state of Massachusetts in 1921 passed legislation requiring psychiatric examination of those offenders charged with a capital offense or for those charged with a felony where there had been a previous conviction of a felony. The Briggs law was heralded as an enlightened approach to the criminal. It provided increased opportunities for practical utilization of existing knowledge. An attractive feature of this law was that it provided the courts with impartial psychiatric reports and helped to eliminate the embarrassing "battle of the experts." The Briggs law not only offered a partial solution to many of the dilemmas of forensic psychiatry but it was also useful in providing machinery for the psychiatric examination of thousands of offenders. It has been thoroughly studied(23-25) and has influenced the development of similar laws in other states (Colorado, Kentucky, Michigan).

The formation of the Section on Legal Aspects of Psychiatry of the American Psychiatric Association in 1926 was soon followed by efforts to codify standards of psychiatric services to the criminal. Karl Menninger, William Alanson White and Herman Adler worked devotedly to explain the psychiatric position to both the American Medical Association and the American Bar Association. In 1927 the Section on Criminal Law of the American Bar Association heard Karl Menninger recommend the following psychiatric services as an indispensible adjunct to enlightened criminology: 1. a psychiatrist available to every court, 2. psychiatric report made available before sentencing any felon, 3. a psychiatric service in every correctional institution, 4. a psychiatric report on every felon before release, 5. a psychiatric report before any parole or transfer between institutions. In 1929 the ABA approved these recommendations. Such unanimity of opinion between the legal and psychiatric professions was truly remarkable. It must be considered a tribute to the degree of respect offered to the psychiatric criminologists of that day. This level of interprofessional cooperation was not destined to be maintained in later years. And the programs that had been agreed upon were never to be realized. In 1959 Karl Menninger(26) lamented the fact that no state in the union could provide services that 30 years earlier had been recommended by the APA, the ABA and the AMA.

1930 TO 1940

The year 1929 was one of disorganization throughout the country. The prison system was not exempted. Serious riots occurred in New York State and in Ohio. In the same year a Congressional Committee was established to study conditions in federal prisons. This committee uncovered dangerous overcrowding and unsatisfactory conditions throughout the country. In 1930 the Federal Bureau of Prisons was reorganized with a new commitment to a program of "treatment and custody based on the individual needs of offenders." The United States Public Health Service was enlisted to provide medical and psychiatric services to the Bureau of Prisons and in 1933 the Center for Defective Delinquents, a predominantly psychiatric institution, was opened at Springfield, Missouri. This institution, later renamed the Medical Center for Federal Prisoners, was designated as the facility for care of those inmates who had been classified as psychotic, homosexual, or psychopathic.

Throughout the 1930's the Federal Prison system grew in esteem and attracted the services of many excellent psychiatrists. The attitude of the time was well summarized by Sanford Bates, first director of the reorganized Bureau of Prisons, when he said, "The psychiatrist is in the prison business to stay. All we ask of him is that he work with us and not apart from us, that he realize the tremendous difficulties of our work, that he not content himself with telling us what is (or was) wrong with our offenders, but that he takes his coat off and goes into the operating room with us to help correct and cure them"(27). This hospitable attitude was maintained when James Bennett became director in 1937 and throughout his tenure psychiatry continued to be an integral part of the Federal correctional process.

In the meantime, similar expansion occurred in the state of Wisconsin. Under the direction of Dr. Frank Richmond and later of Dr. Peter Bell a team of mental health specialists was formed to serve the needs of the state. This was a true "field service" which provided psychiatric consultation to all correctional institutions, to probation agents, to judges, to the parole board and to the hospital for the criminally insane. There were probably a number of unrecognized men like Dr. Peter Bell who worked quietly with exceptional modesty to create meaningful statewide programs. The dedication of this man was profound. He worked 12 to 16 hours a day, 6 days a week, without vacations. Through the years 1934-1936 he personally examined 5,000 offenders at the Wisconsin State Prison alone. No inmate entered the institution or left it on parole without having consulted with Dr. Bell.

One senses this kind of commitment in other areas of psychiatric criminology throughout the early years of this decade. Bromberg and Thompson at the New York Court of General Sessions reported(28) on the examination of 7100 offenders in a four-year period. Dr. Lowell Selling was similarly active at the Recorder Court in Detroit and Dr. Manfred Guttmacher began his work in Baltimore directing a court clinic that was to be the most influential model for the next two decades.

The liveliness of psychiatric criminology in this era is marvelously illustrated in the transactions of meetings of local psychiatric societies published in the *Archives of Neurology and Psychiatry*(29-31). The depth of interest and sophistication present at that time was truly remarkable. The comments of such lively figures as Phillip Roche, Abraham Myerson, Winfred Overholzer, Menas Gregory and others could not be more meaningful and poignant if they were made today. This was an era in which it was possible for a physician, Dr.

Victor C. Branham, to be director of the State Correctional System of New York.

The major theoretical trend of the years 1930-1940 was the acceptance of psychoanalytic theories of criminal behavior. With the introduction of Franz Alexander's concept of the neurotic character(32) many varieties of criminal behavior could be related to mental mechanisms that were familiar to most psychiatrists. The psychodynamics of individual criminal acts began to be studied(33). Without resorting to oversimplified doctrines it was possible to relate the problems of crime to the mainstream of psychiatric interest. Further elaboration of the psychodynamics of that most difficult group of criminals known as psychopaths was presented by Karpman(34), Partridge(35) and Wittels(36). The psychoanalytic movement was also influential in finally laying to rest theories of criminality based on mental deficiency, heredity or "criminal psychosis." Since the 1930's the criminal has been studied through combined biological and social approaches; not as man as an isolated physical being but as man who lives in relationships to others and who is often driven to act by forces outside of his awareness.

In 1934 Dr. James McCartney(37) surveyed psychiatric services to correctional institutions and optimistically discussed the activities of the 83 full- or part-time psychiatrists then working in American prisons. At this time neither he nor others had any reason to believe that the field of psychiatric criminology would soon experience a sharp cessation of growth. But somehow or other this is exactly what happened. In the later years of the 1930's psychiatrists began to lose interest in working with the offender. Except for isolated programs the feeling of enthusiasm that characterized the previous two decades and the early 1930's began to wane. In 1939 the Sing Sing psychopathic clinic was closed. In the same year most of the Wisconsin Psychiatric Field Service was wiped out. It is questionable if the field of psychiatric criminology ever reversed this decline or was again able to reach the peak it had obtained in 1934. In 1939 two psychiatrists, J. C. Wilson and M. J. Pescor, published a comprehensive book on *Problems in Prison Psychiatry*(38).

It is significant that no similar text has since been written.

1940 TO 1950

American psychiatry's interest in the criminal began to decline in 1939. This retrogression continued during World War II and throughout the early postwar years. Prison services actually decreased and new court clinics failed to appear. The absence of activity during World War II is understandable. But the pre-war recession and the failure of this field to revitalize in the postwar years is more difficult to comprehend. No such interruption of progress followed World War I. A partial understanding of this puzzling trend may be found through examination of the problems of psychiatric criminology up until the 1940's and through consideration of the changing nature of psychiatric practice during the postwar years.

The heavy emphasis on diagnosis and disposition of offenders during the 1920's and 1930's undoubtedly was helpful to the individual criminal. But for the most part such services were even more valuable to the correctional administrator. As long as psychiatry cooperated in making the task of the court and of the prison more simplified, it was welcome. Unfortunately, this was a role of psychiatry that was almost entirely sociological, employing medical models to assist society in efficient management of its deviants. Psychotherapy for the offender was practically non-existent. Even in the 1930's some psychiatrists wondered if they were accomplishing little more than improving the "housekeeping" of correctional agencies. Disillusionment lurked around the corner.

With the rise of psychoanalytic doctrine the major interest of psychiatrists shifted to psychotherapy. After World War II psychiatrists began to value most highly those gratifications that came with treating motivated individuals. Although psychoanalysis provided a theoretical model of criminal behavior it did not provide a practical rationale for treatment of the criminal. The problem of how to apply the values of psychoanalytically oriented therapy to a person who is to be made to conform to the law is not simple. The correctional psychiatrist learned quickly that what was good for the prison community was not always good for the individual. To a large extent the decline of psychiatric interest in criminology may have reflected this inability of both physicians and correctional administrators to reconcile the values of individual psychotherapy with those of social rehabilitation. In later years a disillusioned Bernard Glueck was quoted by Zilboorg (39) as having made the melancholy observation that "prison psychiatry seems to make the prisoner a better prisoner and not a better citizen." As late as 1949 Brancale had expressed doubt as to the plausability of ever doing adequate psychotherapy under existing prison conditions.

In the postwar years there was a general movement away from all types of institutional or agency work. Private practice with a focus on individual psychotherapy became the most prestigious psychiatric role. The great number of physicians who sought psychiatric training in the postwar years were not inclined to wrestle with the problems of the community but were rather attracted to methodologies that promised relief of individual suffering. With the many new horizons opening for the psychiatric profession there was little time or interest left over for the criminal.

The major developments of the decade 1940-1950 centered around specialized programs for selected classes of offenders. Beginning in the late 1930's several states passed or considered legislation designed to utilize psychiatric skills for the control of certain kinds of sexual behavior. These laws directed the psychiatrist to assist in the commitment of selected sex offenders to institutions where they were to remain without fixed sentences. This principle of indeterminate sentencing was of course not new. It was inherent in the use of parole from the early part of the 19th Century. The Massachusetts' program for defective delinquents instituted in 1911 had provided for an even broader kind of indeterminate sentencing.

The possibility of releasing prisoners after treatment and recovery rather than after having spent a fixed number of years behind bars has always appealed to psychiatrists. If a simplified medical model is applied to criminal behavior the following logic seems to be relevant. "Releasing prisoners at a fixed time is as unscientific as insisting that all patients with pneumonia be released from the hospital after a specified number of days. Obviously some prisoners will be ready for release quickly; others only after long stays or, perhaps, never." Indeterminacy has special appeal when applied to behavior that can be labelled as dangerous. If it appears that an individual is likely to repeat behavior which the community has defined as dangerous, the possibility of that individual losing his civil rights through an indeterminate sentence is far less disturbing.

Unfortunately, the first laws involving large-scale indeterminate sentencing in this country were passed without sufficient regard either to legal safeguards or to defining the issue of dangerousness. They were directed towards the control of the ill-defined sexual psychopath and too often they were founded on fear and hysterical public opinion. Under these early laws a sex offender could be committed even before conviction of a crime if so recommended by a psychiatrist. In the absence of reliable scientific criteria for defining sexual psychopathy such practices carried an inherent danger of depriving citizens of their civil liberties. Furthermore, provisions for treatment of the committed sex offender were not offered.

For a variety of fortunate reasons these laws were rarely utilized in practice. It is to the credit of our profession that much of the vigorous questioning of these statutes was done by psychiatrists. (Although sociologists such as Tappan did not shun a critical role.) Ellis and Brancale(40) studied a large group of sex offenders in New Jersey and concluded that the largest proportion were not dangerous and did not tend to be recidivistic. They and others(41) stressed the difficulties of defining a diagnostic class of sexual psychopaths. The report of the Group for the Advancement of Psychiatry in 1947(42) was critical of sex psychopath legislation up to that time and suggested realistic guidelines for future programs. Subsequent laws passed in New York, New Jersey,

California, Wisconsin and Massachusetts took cognizance of the need for preserving legal rights and in the case of the latter three states made provisions for treatment.

Other events in the years 1940-1950 centered around organizations, publications and programs. Under the guidance of Ralph Banay the Medical Correctional Association was formed in 1940 "to band together all those especially concerned with or interested in the medical aspects of crime." In 1941 Phillip Roche initiated a formal training program in psychiatric criminology. The *Journal of Criminal Psychopathology* began publication in 1940. Significant books appeared by Karpman(43), Bromberg(44) and Cleckley(45). An encyclopedia of criminology with a distinctly psychiatric orientation was edited by V. C. Branham and S. B. Kutash(46).

The most encouraging trends of this decade occurred in California. Following a thorough study of the prisons by a legislative investigating committee in 1943, a special session of the legislature passed a bill which revised the entire prison system and set up a modern professionally organized program under the direction of Richard A. McGee. Legislation was passed insuring that certain activities would be required by law. One provision established a diagnostic center at San Quentin for the psychiatric team examination of all males committed to prison. The first so-called "reception-guidance center" opened at San Quentin in the fall of 1944.

1950 TO 1960

In the most recent decade of this century there was some upsurge of activity centered for the most part in the programs of selected state and federal organizations. Although group and individual therapy were used sporadically during the 1940's, the first large-scale effort to treat offenders through psychotherapeutic techniques was initiated by the Association for Psychiatric Treatment of Offenders (APTO). This remarkable organization, under the guidance of Mellita Schmideberg, enlisted personal practitioners who at considerable personal sacrifice committed themselves to psychotherapeutic treatment of offenders. Founded in 1950, it was incorporated by the State of New York in 1952 and in later years chapters were formed in Massachusetts, Florida and California. Its members have demonstrated an almost missionary zeal in experimenting with specialized therapeutic techniques. They have repeatedly deplored pessimistic attitudes with regard to psychiatric treatment of the offender. The degree to which psychiatry had moved away from the older biological models of deviant behavior is illustrated by the following formal statement of the APTO orientation. "It is because psychotherapy is a social as well as a medical science that it has an important role to play in handling the offender. Modern psychotherapy is in actuality an educative or re-educative process which aims to enable to treat an individual to live in harmony with his culture and to channelize his energies into activities which are socially acceptable and, if possible, useful. Therefore, psychotherapy must inevitably take its place among the other disciplines which society uses to protect itself from the dangers of uncontrolled behavior." This philosophy called for an integration of biological and social theories in a manner that closely reflects the attitudes of most modern-day psychiatrists.

A similar growth of outpatient facilities for the offender developed in Massachusetts centered around a program of court clinics. Beginning with a single clinic in Norfolk County in 1949, the Massachusetts program, under the direction of Donald Hayes Russell, had by 1963 expanded to an organization of 15 clinics conducting over 15,000 interviews annually. The emphasis went beyond diagnosis or disposition and focused on psychotherapy. No other state has come close to providing such extensive outpatient facilities for the offender.

In 1957 Warren Wille(47) surveyed psychiatric services to prisons and reported on the activities of 82 full- and part-time psychiatrists and 51 consultants. For the most part these men identified themselves with one of a relatively small number of active programs. By 1955 New York and Massachusetts had recovered services that had been seriously weakened in the postwar era. And interesting innovations in prison psychiatry began to appear in Maryland, Wisconsin, California and the Federal Bureau of Prisons.

In 1955 the State of Maryland opened the Pautuxet Institution for the treatment of defective delinquents. This institution conducted a revolutionary and truly indeterminate program. It called for specialized treatment of the defective delinquent who was defined as "an individual who by the demonstration of persistent aggravated anti-social or criminal behavior evidences a propensity towards criminal activity and is found to have either some intellectual deficiency or emotional imbalance or both as to clearly demonstrate an actual danger to society." This is a broader definition of the term defective delinquent than was employed at the turn of the century and would obviously include many who might be called "psychopathic." The program aimed to treat the most difficult behavior disorders and to utilize psychiatric intervention for indeterminate control when treatment was not successful. Its usefulness and its potential threat to civil liberties has been seriously scrutinized. The Maryland "defective delinquency" program, nevertheless represents the most comprehensive effort yet made to treat the dangerous offender through psychiatric techniques.

Wisconsin began a similar program of indeterminate sentencing for certain classes of sex offenders in 1952. The emphasis here was on diagnosing the so-called deviated offender and providing him with psychiatric treatment. Parole as in Maryland was dependent on the decision of a Special Review Board. The author(48) has previously discussed the immense technical and moral problems of maintaining such a program. The issue of defining who is a "deviated" offender is not a simple one and grows more rather than less difficult with increased sophistication. Nevertheless, by 1962 the Wisconsin program had treated over 500 serious sex offenders with strikingly low rates of recidivism. It represented the first sex crimes program to provide realistic facilities for psychiatric treatment of the convicted offender.

In evaluating legislation such as the Wisconsin Sex Crimes Law or the Maryland Defective Delinquent Law it is useful to pause for a moment and review certain inherent problems. Any system of indeterminate sentencing can be abused if the offender is denied full legal rights through due process. It can also be abused, however, if treatment is supposed to be provided but is actually not available. To commit an offender indefinitely without providing resources for his rehabilitation makes for a mockery of the democratic tradition of justice. Such a man could languish in prison for years without help and without hope for release. Programs of indeterminate sentencing can be justified only if they maintain adequate staff levels and realistic facilities for treatment. In the absence of such resources they represent a use of psychiatry for punishment rather than for treatment.

During the decade 1950-1960 California made important steps to provide psychiatric treatment for incarcerated offenders. The Vacaville Medical Facility began full-scale operation in 1955. This institution included a diagnostic reception center but its primary function was to provide treatment for emotionally disturbed offenders. As was true in Maryland and Wisconsin group therapy became the main modality of treatment, Today as many as 800 Vacaville inmates are receiving some form of psychotherapy. Importantly, other California institutions stimulated by the work of Vacaville began similar expansions in group and individual therapy.

The Federal Bureau of Prisons through the 1940's and 1950's was able to maintain a high standard of psychiatric care under the medical directorship of Harold Janney. The hub of activity was the Springfield Medical Center for Federal Prisoners where psychiatrists such as Charles Smith, Edward Rinck and Russell Settle worked to build a truly treatment oriented institution. In the post-war years the Public Health Service was in the advantageous position of being able to recruit psychiatrists who fulfilled military obligations by taking positions with the Federal Bureau of Prisons. By 1956 a career training program was initiated which insured a steady recruitment of at least a few well-trained psychiatrists. During the late 1930's and the early 1940's the Springfield Institution had

attempted specialized treatment programs for homosexuals and so-called "constitutional psychopathic inferiors." Diagnostic work became much more important in 1949 with the passage of Public Law 285 and again in 1958 when Public Law 752 was passed. The first law provided for the examination of offenders to determine their competency to stand trial. The second law offered the sentencing judge a means of obtaining psychiatric examination at a federal institution prior to imposition of final sentence. These laws significantly altered the patient population at Springfield and in themselves helped to shape a more psychiatrically competent diagnostic and treatment program.

Publications related to psychiatric criminology were numerous in the decade 1950-1960 but for the most part they were slanted towards legal issues. A great deal of discussion of the problem of criminal responsibility was encouraged by the Isaac Ray awards and by the hopefulness for legal reform which followed the Durham decision. Books more directly related to psychiatric criminology were published by Guttmacher(49), Abrahamsen(50), Banay (51), McDonald(52) and Karpman(53). The publications of Abrahamsen represent unusually comprehensive and thoughtful expositions of modern psychiatric theories of crime.

EVALUATION OF PSYCHIATRIC CONTRIBUTIONS TO CRIMINOLOGY

The author in chronicling the above information has striven to emphasize the sincerity, dedication and effectiveness of those psychiatrists who made the most important efforts to understand and treat criminal behavior. Only the most intellectually arrogant would attempt to deprecate their contributions in the light of modern developments in psychiatry, psychology, or sociology. For those who study the behavioral sciences have learned repeatedly that the prevailing theories and sciences of one era may to subsequent generations appear only as dogma and pseudoscience. An evaluation of the contributions of American psychiatry to the criminal is nevertheless in order. The effectiveness of our efforts will be discussed under two headings, 1. the development of psychiatric services to offenders and, 2. the impact of psychiatry on the American system of criminal justice. The reader is forewarned that the discussion to follow is heavily weighted with the author's personal opinions and biases.

The major contribution of American psychiatry to the criminal has been the development of theories of behavior that emphasize the individual. Psychiatric theories of criminality have deeply influenced every aspect of therapeutic work with the offender. They have become a permanent part of the criminological science of the disciplines of social work and psychology. American psychiatrists have presented criminology with a theoretical framework that can be debated and criticized but that is nevertheless here to stay as one enlightened approach to the criminal.

In caring for physical needs, in supplying emotional support and in recommending humane disposition, psychiatry up until recent years performed a necessary service for the offender. In the last 15 years, however, there has been increased evidence that psychotherapy offers the individual criminal an opportunity to change his behavior in a manner that is often beneficial to himself and to society. Where psychotherapy has been attempted with the criminal it has yielded encouraging results and has been regularly welcomed. Programs for group and individual therapies with probationers in court clinics and with convicted offenders in prisons have been established in several areas throughout the country. About the only discouraging things that can be said about these activities is that there have not been enough of them. Nowhere in the United States has there ever been a program of psychotherapeutic services for the criminal that begins to approach modern standards of treatment of the mentally ill. Programs for the treatment of the offender are invariably understaffed, overworked, and forced to resort to "expedient methods." Those who would argue that psychotherapy does not help offenders should first understand that it has never been utilized in an optimum manner.

Psychiatrists as educators have also done much both to provide service to the offender and to influence the entire field of correctional administration. There is first of all the acknowledged usefulness of psychiatric consultation to other mental health professions. Perhaps even more important is the impact of a psychodynamic orientation on other correctional workers. Probation officers, prison chaplains, teachers, wardens and prison guards have been able to increase their effectiveness through better understanding of individual behavior. Counselling procedures administered by relatively untrained personnel represent only one method of reaching large groups of offenders. The educative potentialities of psychiatry for training and supervising nonprofessionals in techniques of individual and group counselling have not yet begun to be fully exploited. The unlimited possibilities of these techniques represent both an opportunity and a challenge to the profession of psychiatry.

Aside from the effects of education American psychiatry has been unable to materially influence the American system of criminal justice. We have not clarified the issue of legal insanity. We have failed to create adequate programs for the criminally insane. We have been unsuccessful in interesting realistic numbers of psychiatrists to work with the criminal. And finally, our efforts to promote humane prison reform have produced negligible results.

In spite of an enormous preoccupation with the problems of legal insanity there has been little change in the treatment of offenders suspected of mental illness since the time of Isaac Ray. The psychiatrists' role in the legal process remains unclear. As early as 1925 Sheldon Glueck(54) and later Winfred Overholser(55) advocated that the courts rule only on the issue of whether or not the offender had committed a crime and that a tribunal of psychiatrists, sociologists, and other experts be allowed to assist the judge in proper disposition. This enlightened suggestion has never been put into practice. Over the years men of such diversified orientation as Karl Menninger, Philip Roche, William Haines and Thomas Szasz have at one time or another deplored the sanity trial and have sought means for its abolishment. Yet the endless debates over criminal responsibility continue. Whether testifying under the McNaughton or the Durham rulings psychiatrists are still forced to engage in a frustrating exercise of deciding man's responsibility; an issue that has to do with morality and value judgement rather than with scientific fact.

Many psychiatrists agree that it would be better to find a way of treating all offenders as responsible and then utilizing psychiatric skills for disposition and treatment. But there has been no concerted effort to implement this policy. It must of course be granted that the existence of the death penalty has made such stands difficult to maintain in capital cases. But capital cases are rare, and it is difficult to understand how the preoccupation of psychiatrists with the issue of criminal responsibility has helped many offenders. Indeed, by diverting many of our most proficient colleagues from the problem of psychiatric treatment of offenders such interests may actually have served to impede progress.

Some psychiatrists would argue that separating the insane criminal from the ordinary offender remains a useful function since it provides the opportunity to offer treatment rather than punishment for at least some individuals. This is a valid argument only if facilities for the treatment of the criminally insane actually are adequate. Unfortunately, since the 1920's the level of care in these institutions has fallen sharply behind that which is offered in other mental hospitals. Of course there are exceptions such as St. Elizabeths, the Medical Center for Federal Prisoners and Atascadero State Hospital in California. But in many, perhaps most states, treatment for the criminally insane is no better (and sometimes worse) than treatment for the convicted criminal. In 1857 Edward Jarvis(56) wrote the following eloquent words, "But the insane criminal has nowhere any home. No age or nation has provided a place for him. He is everywhere unwelcome and objectionable. The prisons thrust him out, the hospitals are unwilling to receive him, the law will not let him stay in his home and the public will not permit him to go abroad. And yet humanity and justice, the sense

of common danger and a tender regard for a deeply degraded brother man all argue that something should be done for him." With certain exceptions psychiatry has not yet succeeded in finding a "suitable home" for the criminally insane.

In the 1920's and 1930's the psychiatrist who worked with the criminal held a relatively esteemed position. From the late 1930's to the present his prestige has steadily declined. This trend is reflected in the unwillingness of the younger generations of American psychiatrists to engage in the problems of the offender. The accompanying chart indicates an amazing lack of growth of psychiatric personnel in correctional settings.

The figures are not entirely comparable since in 1928 and 1961 different kinds of measurements were being made. There are also today many psychiatrists who spend briefer periods of time consulting to correctional institutions and their influence is difficult to evaluate. Even if we grant full allowance for these factors it still appears that between the years 1934 and 1960 the availability of psychiatric services did not keep up with the growth of the prison population. It is likely that the average incarcerated criminal today receives less psychiatric treatment than he did in 1934. This is a shameful fact. It is particularly shameful if we consider the impressive numerical growth of the psychiatric profession during this same span of years. With each passing year the proportion of psychiatrists who work actively in the field of criminology decreases. Figures are not available with regard to court work but there is no reason to suspect that the situation there would be any different.

In an earlier part of this paper the author considered some of the reasons for the decline of psychiatric criminology during the late 1930's and early 1940's. The changing nature of psychiatric practice and the difficulty of resolving some of the social dilemmas involved in correctional work are probably the most important factors. But certain problems of status and recognition have served to block a meaningful revitalization of this once esteemed field.

The psychiatrist who elects to work with the criminal today is afforded little of the

Surveys of Psychiatrists in Correctional Settings

	1928 OVERHOLSER SURVEY	1934 McCARTNEY SURVEY	1957 WILLIE SURVEY	1961 APA SURVEY
	29 institutions had at least one psychiatrist.	48 full-time psychiatrists in prisons.	43 full-time.	65 reported spending over 30 hours a week in correctional institutions.
	64 institutions had at least one part-time psychiatrist.	35 part-time psychiatrists in prisons.	39 part-time.	45 reported spending between 15 and 29 hours a week in correctional institutions. (many psychiatrists reported that they spent a few hours a week consulting to correctional settings)
Prison Population	1934 — 118,000			
	1960 — 213,000			

respect granted to his colleague in private practice or mental hospital work. The public knows practically nothing of his work. Rarely does the prison or court administrator accept him as a trustworthy, cooperating member of the correctional team. The more academically oriented sociologists scoff at his naiveté and lack of sophistication in perceiving social problems. Social workers and psychologists are respectful but have difficulty in understanding why they are paid only half of his salary for doing similar work. At best, psychiatric colleagues treat him as though he were a misguided but harmless zealot. At worst, they sometimes tell him that(57) only psychiatrists with strong authoritarian needs are attracted to correctional work. All these factors have discouraged our younger psychiatrists from identifying themselves as psychiatric criminologists. How many psychiatrists today could list the names of 10 or even 5 prominent colleagues in this field? With but few exceptions the Healys, the Gluecks, the Fernalds, the Stearns and the Spaldings have disappeared.

In the field of forensic psychiatry the situation is somewhat different. In 1961, 975 psychiatrists listed this sub-specialty as a major interest. There are many forensic psychiatrists who sincerely believe that psychiatry will eventually be of most benefit to the criminal through that education of the public and judges which takes place in the public forum of the courtroom. This position is advanced most eloquently by Benjamin Karpman in a reply to a letter from Dr. Russell Settle published in the *Journal of Criminal Psychodynamics* (58). Dr. Settle's letter was critical of the legalistic and academic flavor of Dr. Karpman's journal. He maintained that psychiatry could do the most for a criminal by going to work and treating him where he was, namely in the prison. This kind of debate still rages today. Most psychiatrists would probably agree with Dr. Karpman. But the logic of Dr. Settle's position deserves careful consideration.

Throughout its history psychiatric criminology in America has been a "passionate" specialty. Running through perhaps a majority of reports in the professional journals is an exhortative trend, a plea for prison reform and for changes that would reflect current psychiatric theory and facts. But has American psychiatry been an important influence in changing the structure of criminal justice ? The answer must be a qualified no. It is of course difficult to measure those benefits accrued as a result of stimulation of interest in the criminal as an individual. And it must be conceded that isolated programs have at times reflected current psychiatric thinking, and that some institutions have made changes because of the influence of individual psychiatrists. A good example of such reform is the work of Dr. Norman Graff(59) in the 10 South section for acutely disturbed prisoners at Springfield. Unfortunately such changes have been dependent upon the energy and persuasiveness of individual personalities. They are more likely to have been the result of the dynamic personality of an isolated psychiatrist than of the dynamic impact of psychiatric knowledge. For the most part, American prisons have changed little and psychiatry can take little credit for those small improvements that have been made. Zilboorg(60) has pointed out that the history of penal reform suggests that it is mostly likely to come about through the actions of enlightened and benevolent laymen and that the professions of both law and psychiatry have been ineffective in promoting change.

Psychiatric criminologists have rarely been able to divorce a humanistic zeal for correctional reform from the medical mandate to treat and study. It is of course extremely difficult to separate these roles. Few men can experience a correctional or legal setting and restrain themselves from crying out against the inhumanities which man fixes upon his fellow man. But perhaps there is some merit in at least making an effort to separate those psychiatric activities which are scientific from those which are humanistic. This does not mean that either need be neglected. It is simply a matter of putting things where they belong. The pages of scientific journals are not the appropriate places for polemics or exhortation. It would be better if they were reserved for reports of theoretical and research activities. At the same time there is no reason why psychiatrists as especially

well-informed private citizens, should not be free to agitate for humanitarian changes. Active participation by 100 psychiatrists in The League for the Abolishment of Capital Punishment might in the long run lead to more beneficial changes than publication of 100 "scientific" articles which lament and criticize the backwardness of the law and penology.

A MORAL PROBLEM FOR PSYCHIATRY

Psychiatry has always had its critics. But their arguments have been most incisive when they have examined our interest in deviant behavior(61, 62). When psychiatrists go beyond the less complicated models of medical healing and begin to participate in the problems of social change they are most vulnerable to censure. Wertham(63) has discussed the danger of psychiatry being utilized to provide medical rationalizations for problems that have important moral and political determinants. He fears that the psychiatrist might become an apologist for the existing social order and even a force for the resistance of progress. Wertham has given this role the unflattering title of "praetorian psychiatry" and sees such psychiatric services as being comparable to the function of the praetorian guards of ancient Rome. A similar concern was voiced by Margaret Curti(64) as early as 1926. In trying to explain the persistence of feeble-mindedness as an explanation of delinquency she made the following indignant observations. "How is it possible this deep rooted belief regardless of evidence, in the inherent inferiority of the criminal ? The belief is in my opinion simply a rationalization of the status quo in relation to delinquency. Why are some people constantly guilty of antisocial conduct ? Why do they burn, rob and murder ? Surely it cannot be because anything is radically wrong with the organization of society ; it must be that these delinquents are made of inferior stuff."

More recently, Thomas Szasz(65) in his book *Law, Liberty and Psychiatry* has implied some of these same concerns. He is deeply troubled by the current tendency to label many forms of deviant behavior as mental illness. Once behavior is so labelled, he argues, great infringements of civil liberties can take place under the guise of medical care. Szasz would be wary of any criminal commitments that take place before conviction, or of any type of indeterminate sentencing that could deprive the offender of "due process."

Unfortunately the history of American psychiatry and the criminal suggests that the haunting voices of the critics can not be dismissed too lightly. Psychiatry, like any discipline that involves itself in the problem of social change, must face the troubling possibility that its theories will be used for apology, for rationalization, or even for abuse. There is no way to assess to what extent psychiatry has provided society with some rationalization for avoiding encounter with those social problems that contribute to criminal behavior. Certainly so long as men could believe that criminals were hereditary degenerates or feeble-minded it was easier to avoid the moral problems of slums, poverty and inequalities of justice. The sterilization practices of the early part of this century suggest that psychiatry can also be used in a punitive manner.

Modern psychiatric theory is more cognizant of social and moral determinants of behavior. There is therefore reason to be hopeful that abuses of psychiatry are less likely to occur in the future. There exists, nevertheless, a persistent and nagging moral dilemma for those psychiatrists who chose to treat deviant behavior. Is there some danger that psychiatric treatment itself can serve to discourage types of rebelliousness that might be socially useful? Could psychiatrists, in an effort to treat, find themselves becoming agents for coercive social control? History seems to say that the likelihood of this happening is remote. Isolated events and trends warn, however, that it is not an impossibility.

SUMMARY

The history of American psychiatry and the criminal is the history of individuals who through unselfish motives have committed themselves to helping a portion of society that is ordinarily abused and neglected. In some instances they have been dramatically effective; in others they have failed. The growth of psychiatric crimi-

nology has been an uneven one. In the 19th Century physicians led the way in initiating social reform and in urging society to examine the criminal as an individual. For the first 40 years of the 20th Century psychiatrists made progress in explaining criminality in psychological terms and involved themselves deeply in the social treatment of the offender. Following the postwar surge towards private practice models of psychiatry, interest in the offender diminished. It did not begin to show signs of revival until this past decade. The newer psychiatric criminology shows some promise. Reflecting the social conditions of our era it seems to be concerned with organized programs rather than with the efforts of individual psychiatrists. Such programs have made encouraging progress in demonstrating how techniques of dynamic psychotherapy can be applied to correctional problems.

This history can be viewed in a somewhat different perspective. The manner in which medical practice has been modified so as to be applicable to problems of deviant behavior in itself makes for an interesting study. The naive biological models of the 19th Century are no longer useful. Similarly, utilization of medical skills to control social problems has proven to be dangerous and unrewarding. For a time psychiatrists were pessimistic of ever being able to treat the offender in settings dominated by the punitive attitudes of correctional administrators. But more recently, those who despaired of treating the criminal through techniques designed for "free individuals" have begun to take a second look. With careful attention to the biological needs of the individual as balanced against the needs of the community it has been possible to devise sociopsychological techniques of treatment that do help. It is true that these techniques are dependent upon theoretical models that still present many puzzling contradictions. Those individuals who have chosen to work with the criminal have repeatedly experienced the agonizing intellectual and emotional exercise of trying to reconcile the needs of the individual with those of society. More than other psychiatrists, they have come to appreciate the staggering complexities involved in this problem. Arrogance, unreflectiveness, and dogma tend to disappear in the face of this bewildering dilemma.

The younger generation of psychiatrists has been trained with the image of private practice and emphasis on psychotherapy of selected patients as the ideal professional career. The pendulum, however, has recently begun to swing. We now seem to be moving in a new direction. Psychiatrists are being called upon to assist the community in the resolution of its social problems. It is doubtful if we could resist such demands, even if we wanted to. But community involvement will require new models of medical care and will necessitate the development of extremely complicated roles for the psychiatric profession. If psychiatry is to concern itself with the social problems of our time, its practitioners would do well to learn from those who have had the most experience with such problems. The body of knowledge accumulated by those American psychiatrists who have worked with the criminal provides a bountiful source for study. If we can learn from their enthusiasm, from their dedication, from their thoughtfulness and from their mistakes we may yet come to fully honor those psychiatrists who have given so unselfishly to their less fortunate brother men.

BIBLIOGRAPHY

1. Rush, Benjamin : Medical Inquiries and Observations upon the Diseases of the Mind. Philadelphia : 1812.
2. Caldwell, Charles : New Views on Penitentiary Discipline. Phrenological J. (Edinburgh), VII : 1831.
3. Dugdale, Richard : The Jukes. New York : Putnam, 1877.
4. Ray, Isaac : A Treatise on the Medical Jurisprudence of Insanity. Boston : 1838.
5. Brigham, Amariah : Editorial in Am. J. Insan., 1 : 1844.
6. Review of the trial of Charles J. Guiteau, *Ibid.*, 38 : 353, 1882.
7. Allison, H. E. : *Ibid.*, 51 : 54, 1894.
8. Fink, Arthur E. : Cause of Crime. New York : A. S. Baines, 1938.
9. Spaulding, Edith R., and Healy, William : Bull. Am. Acad. Med., 15 : 27, 1914.
10. White, William A. : Report of Chairman of Committee on Sterilization of Crimi-

nals. J. Am. Instit. Crim. Law Criminol., 1917.
11. Fernald, Walter E. : Am. J. Insan., 65 : 731, 1909.
12. Goddard, Henry H : Proc. Am. Prison Ass., 355, 1912.
13. Anderson, Victor V. : Ment. Hyg., 3 : 147, 1919.
14. Glueck, Bernard : *Ibid.*, 2 : 85, 1918.
15. Spaulding, Edith R., and Healy, William : Bull. Am. Acad. Med., 15 : 4, 1914.
16. Healy, William, and Bronner, Augusta : Delinquents and Criminals. New York : Macmillan, 1925.
17. Alexander, Franz, and Healy, William : Roots of Crime. New York : Knopf, 1935.
18. Salmon, Thomas : Ment. Hyg., 4 : 29, 1920.
19. Overholser, Winfred : *Ibid.*, 12 : 801, 1928.
20. White, William A. : Am. J. Psychiat., 7 : 493, 1928.
21. Karpman, Benjamin : Psychiat. Quart., 13 : 1, 1929.
22. ———— : *Ibid.* : 370, July 1929.
23. Overholser, Winfred : Ment. Hyg., 12 : 807, 1928.
24. Glueck, Sheldon : *Ibid.*, 11 : 287, 1927.
25. Thom, Douglas H. : Am. J. Psychiat., 80 : 219, 1923.
26. Menninger, Karl A. : Verdict Guilty. Now What?; Harper's Magazine, August, 1959.
27. Bates, Sanford : Ment Hyg., 14 : 628, 1930.
28. Bromberg, Walter, and Thompson, Charles B. : J. Crim. Law Criminol., 28: 70, 1937.
29. Proceedings of the Philadelphia Psychiatric Society, Arch. Neurol. Psychiat., 38 : 13, 1936.
30. Proceedings of the New York Psychiatric Academy, *Ibid.*, 34 : 13, 1934.
31. Proceedings of the Michigan Psychiatric Society, *Ibid.*, 44 : 14, 1940.
32. Alexander, Franz : The Neurotic Character : (1930) In The Scope of Psychoanalysis. New York : Basic Books, 1961.
33. Bromberg, Walter, and Keiser, Sylvia : Am. J. Psychiat., 94: 1441, 1938.
34. Karpman, Benjamin : J. Crim. Psychopath., 3 : 137, 1941.
35. Partridge, G. E. : Am. J. Psychiat., 87 : 53, 1930.
36. Wittels, F. : Psychoanal. Rev., 24 : 276, 1937.
37. McCartney, James L. : Am. J. Psychiat., 90 : 1183, 1934.
38. Wilson, J. G., and Pescor, M. J. : Prob-

lems in Prison Psychiatry. Caldwell, Idaho: Paxton Printers, 1939.

39. Zilboorg, Gregory: *In* V. C. Branham and S. B. Kutash: Encyclopedia of Criminology. New York: Philosophical Library, 1949.

40. Ellis, Albert, and Brancale, Ralph: The Psychology of Sex Offenders. Springfield, Illinois: C. C Thomas, 1956.

41. Bowman, K., and Rose, M.: Am. J. Psychiat., **109**: 177, 1952.

42. Report No. 9: Psychiatrically Deviated Sex Offenders. New York: Group for the Advancement of Psychiatry, 1949. Revised February 1950.

43. Karpman, Benjamin: Case Studies in the Psychopathology of Crime. Washington, D. C.: Medical Sciences Press, 1948.

44. Bromberg, Walter: Crime and the Mind. Philadelphia: J. B. Lippincott, 1948.

45. Cleckley, Hervey: The Mask of Sanity. St. Louis: C. V. Mosley, 1941.

46. Branham, V. C., and Kutash, S. B.: Encyclopedia of Criminology. New York: Philosophical Library, 1949.

47. Wille, Warren: Am. J. Psychiat., **114**: 481, 1957.

48. Pacht, A. R., Halleck, S. L., and Ehrmann, John C.: *Ibid.*, **118**: 802, 1962.

49. Guttmacher, Manfred: Sex Offenses. New York: Norton, 1951.

50. Abrahamsen, David: The Psychology of Crime. New York: Columbia University Press, 1960.

51. Zilboorg, Gregory: The Psychology of the Criminal Act and Punishment. New York: Harcourt Brace, 1954.

52. MacDonald, John: Psychiatry and the Criminal. Springfield, Illinois: C. C Thomas, 1958.

53. Karpman, Benjamin: The Sexual Offender and His Offenses. New York: Julian Press, 1954.

54. Glueck, Sheldon: Mental Disorder and the Criminal Law. Boston: Little, Brown, 1925.

55. Overholser, Winfred: Ment. Hyg., **11**: 306, 1927.

56. Jarvis, Edward: Am. J. Insan., **13**: 195, 1857.

57. Powelson, Harvey, and Bendix, Reinhard: Psychiatry, **14**: 73, 1951.

58. Letters to the Editor Section, Arch. Crim. Psychodyn., **1**: 525, 1958.

59. Graff, Norman: Bull. Menninger Clinic, **20**: 85, 1956.

60. Zilboorg, Gregory: Am. J. Psychiat., **100**: 757, 1943.

61. Hakeem, Michael: Law and Contemporary Problems—Crime and Correction, School of Law, Duke University, **23**: Autumn, 1958.

62. Szasz, Thomas: Psychiatry, **20**: 313, 1957.

63. Wertham, Fredric: Am. J. Psychother., **17**: 404, 1963.

64. Curti, Margaret: J. Crim. Law Criminol., **17**: 246, 1926.

65. Szasz, Thomas: Law, Liberty and Psychiatry. New York: Macmillan, 1963.

[15]

THE INSANITY PLEA: A FUTILE DEFENSE FOR SERIAL KILLERS

I. INTRODUCTION

Despite its publicity, the insanity plea is rarely used. When defendants do invoke the insanity plea, the defense is rarely successful. With the recent trial of Jeffrey Dahmer,[1] the debate has arisen again[2] as to whether or not the insanity plea should be abolished.

Dahmer's case captured headlines around the world. With this exposure, however, came fear. There was fear of Dahmer himself, fear of a person being capable of committing the acts that he did, and fear that a finding of insanity would be Dahmer's escape hatch to freedom. Fear of Dahmer's re-entry into society was largely unfounded. This Article addresses six factors that virtually insure that a serial killer will not be found not guilty by reason of insanity. First, however, the Article will review the history of the insanity plea and examine its application.

II. HISTORY OF THE INSANITY PLEA

The insanity plea traces its origins to mid-thirteenth century England.[3] During the reign of Henry III (1216-1272), the life of an insane criminal could be saved only by a pardon from the king upon a showing that the criminal was of unsound mind and that irrational occurrences were not unusual for that person.[4] In the late thirteenth century, during the reign of Edward I (1272-1307), "complete madness" became an established criminal defense, and

---

1. Jeffrey Dahmer pleaded not guilty by reason of insanity to the murders of fifteen men and boys in Milwaukee, Wisconsin. Edward Walsh, *Jury Finds Dahmer Was Sane*, WASH. POST, Feb. 16, 1992, at A1. The jury held that he was sane at the time he committed the murders and he was sentenced to fifteen consecutive life sentences. Annie Schwartz, *Milwaukee Serial Killer Dahmer Sentenced to 15 Life Terms*, REUTERS, Feb. 17, 1992. Wisconsin does not have the death penalty. Edward Walsh, *Jury Finds Dahmer Was Sane*, WASH. POST, Feb. 16, 1992, at A1.

2. In 1981, John Hinckley attempted to assassinate President Ronald Reagan. He was found to be not guilty by reason of insanity; his acquittal was the cause of much debate. Irving Kaufman, *The Insanity Plea on Trial*, N.Y. TIMES, Aug. 8, 1982 (Magazine), at 16.

3. RITA JAMES SIMON, THE JURY AND THE DEFENSE OF INSANITY 16 (1967).

4. *Id.*

it was no longer necessary to receive a royal pardon.[5]

Despite its acceptance as a criminal defense as early as the thirteenth century in England, the first recorded acquittal of a defendant by a jury on the ground of insanity was not until 1505.[6] In 1581, William Lambard, a noted legal authority, espoused "knowledge of good and evil" as the test for criminal responsibility.[7] In his handbook, *Eirenarcha*, Lambard stated, "[i]f a madman or natural fool, or a lunatic in the time of his lunacy . . . do kill a man, there is no felonious act . . . for [he] cannot be said to have any understanding will."[8]

In 1723, Justice Tracy set the standard which would be applied in English courts throughout the eighteenth century.[9] In his instruction to the jury in the trial of Edward Arnold,[10] Tracy articulated what came to be known as the "Wild Beast Test": "In order to avail himself of the defense of insanity a man must be totally deprived of his understanding and memory so as not to know what he is doing, no more than an infant, a brute, or a wild beast."[11]

Justice Tracy's wild beast test was briefly rejected in *Hadfield's Case* in 1800.[12] In that case, the court rejected two concepts which it had previously accepted. It rejected the argument that the defendant "must be totally deprived of all mental faculty before . . . acquitt[al]; and it severed the tie between insanity and the ability to distinguish . . . right from wrong."[13] However, this rejection was short-lived. Within twelve years of the *Hadfield's Case* decision, the English courts had returned to the wild beast test as formulated by Justice Tracy.[14]

---

5. *Id.*

6. Rita James Simon & David E. Aaronson, The Insanity Defense—A Critical Assessment of the Law and Policy in the Post Hinckley Era 10 (1988).

7. Simon, *supra* note 3, at 17.

8. J. Richard Ciccone, *Murder, Insanity, and Medical Expert Witnesses*, 49 Am. Med. Ass'n Archives Neurology 608 (1992) (quoting C. B. Coventry, *Medical Jurisprudence of Insanity*, J. Insanity 1.134-144 (1844)).

9. Report of the Board of Trustees, *Insanity Defense in Criminal Trials and Limitation of Psychiatric Testimony*, JAMA, June 8, 1984, at 2967; *see also* The Trial of Edward Arnold, 16 State Trials 1695 (1723).

10. The Trial of Edward Arnold, 16 State Trials 1695 (1723).

11. Simon, *supra* note 3, at 17.

12. *Id.* at 18-19 (citing *Hadfield's Case*, 27 State Trials 1281 (1800)).

13. *Id.* at 19.

14. *Id.*

A new standard for determining insanity, the irresistible impulse test, was developed in England in 1840.[15] It states: "If some controlling disease was, in truth, the acting power within [the defendant] which he could not resist, then he will not be responsible."[16] Under this test, insanity was recognized as a defense when a "mental disease prevent[ed] the defendant from controlling his or her conduct."[17] The test also required a causal relationship between the mental disorder and the crime.[18]

In 1843, a landmark decision, *Daniel M'Naghten's Case*, established the fundamental standard for criminal insanity to be used in both England and the United States for nearly a century.[19] *M'Naghten* set out the rule:

> [I]t must be clearly proved that, at the time of the committing of the act, the party accused was labouring under such a defect of reason, from a disease of the mind, as not to know the nature and quality of the act he was doing; or, if he did know it, that he did not know he was doing what was wrong.[20]

The history of the insanity plea in the United States begins with the *M'Naghten* decision. Within a decade, the test for insanity which *M'Naghten* espoused was adopted in federal and most state courts in the United States.[21] Rita James Simon, Dean of the School of Justice at American University, and David Aaronson, professor of criminal law at American University, state that this quick acceptance of the *M'Naghten* rules in the United States indicates that American courts lacked an adequate test for insanity at that time.[22]

Soon after the *M'Naghten* rules became established as the insanity defense in the United States, the irresistible impulse test surfaced as well. In *Parsons v. State*,[23] the judge initially in-

---

15. SIMON & AARONSON, *supra* note 6, at 15 (quoting Regina v. Oxford, 175 Eng. Rep. 941, 950 (1840)).

16. *Id.*

17. *Id.*

18. Donald H.J. Hermann, *The Insanity Defense*, 44 OHIO ST. L.J. 987, 1001 (1983) (reviewing WILLIAM J. WINSLADE & JUDITH WILSON ROSS, THE INSANITY PLEA (1983)).

19. Report of the Board of Trustees, *supra* note 9, at 2971.

20. *Daniel M'Naghten's Case*, 8 Eng. Rep. 718, 722 (H.L. 1843).

21. SIMON, *supra* note 3, at 25.

22. SIMON & AARONSON, *supra* note 6, at 14.

23. 81 Ala. 577, 2 So. 854 (1887).

structed the jury on the *M'Naghten* test.[24] However, he added to these instructions that, even if the *M'Naghten* test was not met, the defendant could still not be held responsible if the following two conditions existed:

> (1) If, by reason of the duress of such mental disease, he had so far lost the *power to choose* between the right and wrong, and to avoid doing the act in question, as that his free agency was at the time destroyed;
> (2) And if, at the same time, the alleged crime was so connected with such mental disease, in the relation of cause and effect, as to have been the product of it *solely*.[25]

The irresistible impulse test is used in the United States primarily as a supplement to the *M'Naghten* rules. A criticism of the *M'Naghten* test is that, although it excuses those who suffer from mental illness because they cannot tell the difference between right and wrong, it does not excuse those who know their conduct is wrong but cannot control their actions.[26] Consequently, some states have expanded the *M'Naghten* rules to include the irresistible impulse standard in an effort to remedy this deficiency.[27]

In 1954, yet another test to determine insanity was established in the United States. In *Durham v. United States*,[28] the district court applied the *M'Naghten* rules.[29] On appeal, the District of Columbia Court of Appeals discarded the *M'Naghten* rules and established what is now known as the *Durham* test.[30] Under the *Durham* test "an accused is not criminally responsible if his unlawful act was the product of mental disease or mental defect;"[31] thus, this standard is a broader test than the *M'Naghten* rules.

In 1964, the American Law Institute (ALI), through the Model Penal Code, established a test that is seen as a compromise between the *M'Naghten* rules and the overly broad *Durham* approach.[32] The ALI standard is as follows:

---

24. Simon & Aaronson, *supra* note 6, at 15.
25. *Parsons*, 81 Ala. at 597, 2 So. at 866-67.
26. Report of the Board of Trustees, *supra* note 9, at 2971.
27. *Id.*
28. 214 F.2d 862 (D.C. Cir. 1954).
29. Simon, *supra* note 3, at 30.
30. *Id.* at 31.
31. *Durham*, 214 F.2d at 874-75.
32. Report of the Board of Trustees, *supra* note 9, at 2971.

> A person is not responsible for criminal conduct if at the time of such conduct as a result of mental disease or defect he lacks substantial capacity either to appreciate the criminality [wrongfulness] of his conduct or to conform his conduct to the requirements of law. [T]he terms "mental disease or defect" do not include an abnormality manifested only by repeated criminal or otherwise anti social conduct.[33]

Judge Irving Kaufman, of the Second Circuit Court of Appeals, describes the ALI test as "focus[ing] not only on the defendant's understanding of his conduct, . . . but also on the defendant's ability to control his actions."[34] He states that this test would absolve from criminal punishment an individual who knows what he is doing, yet is driven to crime by delusions, fears, or compulsions.[35]

The ALI test was the law in the federal courts until October, 1984.[36] But, as a result of the acquittal of John Hinckley by reason of insanity for the assassination attempt of President Ronald Reagan, the Insanity Defense Reform Act of 1984 was passed.[37] This Act was the first federal codification of the insanity defense.[38] Subsection (a) of this Act states:

> [A]t the time of the commission of the acts constituting the offense, the defendant, as a result of a severe mental disease or defect, was unable to appreciate the nature and quality or the wrongfulness of his acts. Mental disease or defect does not otherwise constitute a defense.[39]

The newer test does not recognize a defendant's inability to conform his conduct to the law as a valid insanity defense.[40]

The mens rea approach, adopted by the American Medical Association,[41] abolishes the insanity defense. States which have adopted this approach "permit consideration of mental disease or defect [only] as a factor in the mitigation of punishment at the

---

33. MODEL PENAL CODE § 4.01 (Proposed Official Draft, 1962).
34. Kaufman, *supra* note 2, at 19.
35. *Id.*
36. SIMON & AARONSON, *supra* note 6, at 44-45.
37. *Id.* at 45.
38. *Id.* at 22, 45.
39. 18 U.S.C. § 17(a) (1988).
40. SIMON & AARONSON, *supra* note 6, at 22.
41. Wallace D. Riley, *Reform Not Abolition*, JAMA, June 8, 1984, at 2947.

sentencing stage of the trial."[42] The mens rea approach "allow[s] acquittal only when a defendant, as a result of mental disease or defect, lack[s] the state of mind required as an element of the offense charged."[43]

As of 1992, nineteen states, and the District of Columbia, used the ALI approach in its proposed form. Eight states used some derivation of the ALI approach. Sixteen states used some form of the *M'Naghten* rules while five states used *M'Naghten* supplemented by the irresistible impulse test. One state used the *Durham* test.[44] Two states had abolished the insanity plea altogether[45] and, as stated earlier, federal courts now follow the standard set out in the Insanity Defense Reform Act of 1984.

III. FREQUENCY OF USE

According to the Washington Post, "[i]n a study of eight states, . . . researchers found that a defense of insanity was offered in slightly less than one percent of [all felony cases]."[46] When a defendant does plead not guilty by reason of insanity, chances are very slim that he or she will be successful. According to this study, the insanity defense was successful in only twenty-five percent of the cases in which it was offered.[47] A study by Jeffrey Rodgers, Dr. Joseph Bloom, and Dr. Spero Manson indicated that roughly eighty percent of successful insanity defense cases are a result of the prosecutor stipulating to the insanity verdict.[48] Another study conducted by Policy Research Associates concluded that only seven percent of not-guilty-by-reason-of-insanity acquittals are by a jury.[49] These statistics are disheartening for a defendant who seeks to invoke the insanity defense in a jury trial.

---

42. Report of the Board of Trustees, *supra* note 9, at 2981.

43. Riley, *supra* note 41, at 2947.

44. Michelle Migdal Gee, Annotation, *Modern Status of Test of Criminal Responsibility—State Cases.* 9 A.L.R. 4th 526 (1981 & Supp. 1992).

45. SIMON & AARONSON, *supra* note 6, at 151.

46. David Brown, *Insanity Defense: Setting a Benchmark of Human Intellect and Will*, WASH. POST, Jan. 27, 1992, at A3.

47. *Id.*

48. Jeffrey L. Rogers, Joseph D. Bloom & Spero M. Manson, *Insanity Defenses: Contested or Conceded?*, 141 AM. J. PSYCHIATRY 885, 886 (1984).

49. Andrew Blum, *Debunking Myths of the Insanity Plea*, NAT'L L.J., Apr. 20, 1992, at 9.

IV. The Application of the Not-Guilty-By-Reason-of-Insanity Plea to Serial Killers

The statistics demonstrate that the insanity defense is rarely successful. However, a plea of insanity does seem to be more successful for some defendants than for others. The Jeffrey Dahmer case suggests that a not-guilty-by-reason-of-insanity verdict is virtually impossible for serial killers to obtain.

There are six factors which make the not-guilty-by-reason-of-insanity plea more difficult to establish for serial killers than for other defendants. First, a serial killer is not likely to suffer from a psychological abnormality.[50] Second, a defendant's bizarre or gruesome behavior when committing the crime is not sufficient to show that he or she is insane.[51] Third, a serial killer is methodical and in control of his actions,[52] making it hard to view him as either crazy or out of control. Fourth, the jury feels a great deal of pressure to convict in these cases.[53] Fifth, there is the fear that, if sent to a mental hospital as a result of an acquittal, the defendant will be released back into society within a short period of time.[54] Lastly, it is difficult to accept that a serial killer is not responsible for his or her crimes.[55]

Before exploring the six factors set out above, some background on *State v. Dahmer*[56] is instructive. Because of the gruesome facts, however, details will be provided only to the extent necessary to demonstrate the six factors previously mentioned.

Jeffrey Dahmer entered a guilty plea in connection with the

---

50. *Why Mass Murderers Kill*, McLeans, Apr. 21, 1986, at 6 (an interview with Elliot Leyton, professor of anthropology and criminology at Memorial University in St. John's, Newfoundland, and author of six books, including Hunting Humans: The Rise of the Modern Multiple Murderer).

51. William Grady, *Shocking, Bizarre Cases Often Renew Insanity Defense Debate*, Chi. Trib., Feb. 16, 1992, at A18.

52. Eric Houston, *New York Serial Killer Pushes Insanity Plea*, USA Today, Dec. 11, 1990, at 3A (quoting James Fox, author of a book on mass murderers).

53. Rogers Worthington, *Dahmer Trial to Draw World Audience*, Chi. Trib., Jan. 26, 1992, at C1 (quoting Elissa Benedek, specialist in criminal insanity and a professor of psychiatry at the University of Michigan Medical School).

54. Hermann, *supra* note 18, at 988.

55. Stephen M. Glynn, *If Dahmer's Not Crazy, Who Is?*, Nat'l L.J., Mar. 9, 1992, at 13.

56. Special Verdict in State v. Dahmer, case # F-912542, was rendered in Milwaukee, Wisconsin Circuit Court before Judge Laurence Gram, Jr., on February 15, 1992.

murders of fifteen men and boys in Milwaukee, Wisconsin. As a result of Wisconsin's bifurcated system, a separate jury trial was held in order to determine whether or not Dahmer was insane at the time he committed the murders. On February 15, 1992, a jury found Dahmer to be sane.[57] He was sentenced the next week to fifteen consecutive life sentences. The fact that Dahmer committed multiple murders is not the most frightening aspect of the case; rather, it is the gruesome method which he used to kill his victims. Stephen Glynn, a Milwaukee attorney, described it succinctly, while maintaining some sense of dignity: "[h]e drill[ed] holes in his living victims' heads, pour[ed] in chemicals to 'zombify' them, ha[d] sex with the corpses' viscera, and ke[pt] some body parts in his refrigerator, occasionally eating them."[58] Those parts that he did not eat, Dahmer either pulverized with a sledge hammer or put into a vat of acid so as to prevent them from being recognized as human.[59] An even more tragic aspect of the case is that one of Dahmer's victims, a fourteen year old boy, escaped, nude and bleeding, and found a group of police officers in the street. Dahmer caught up with the boy while he was talking to the police and convinced the police that they were homosexual lovers who had just had a fight. The police returned the boy to Dahmer, and the fourteen year old became his next victim.[60]

As stated above, Jeffrey Dahmer was found to be sane. In reviewing the facts of his case in the context of the six factors discussed below, it seems that serial killers have little, if any, hope of acquittal when they rely on the insanity plea as their defense.

A.   Serial Killers Do Not Suffer from Mental Defects or Diseases

Serial killers, generally, are not insane.[61] They are "not deranged or drooling idiots," but are very much in control of what they are doing.[62] They do not display any biological abnormality, and very few of them display any clinical symptoms of a psycho-

---

57. Wisconsin uses the American Law Institute's standard in determining whether a defendant is insane. Simon & Aaronson, *supra* note 6, at 263.

58. Glynn, *supra* note 55.

59. Joe Treen, *Probing the Mind of a Killer*, Time, Feb. 3, 1992, at 75.

60. Edward Walsh, *Jury Finds Dahmer Was Sane*, Wash. Post, Feb. 16, 1992, at A1.

61. *Why Mass Murderers Kill*, *supra* note 50, at 6.

62. *Id.*

logical abnormality.[63] In contrast to mass murderers who kill many people at one time, serial killers have not tripped over into paranoid schizophrenia and, therefore, do not qualify for the insanity defense.[64] Instead of being insane, serial killers tend to suffer from personality disorders. But "personality disorders do not necessarily excuse criminal behavior."[65] Accordingly, extending the insanity defense to persons with personality disorders is considered to be a major error.[66] Because serial killers tend to suffer from personality disorders rather than insanity, they rarely satisfy the "mental disease" component of the *M'Naghten*, irresistible impulse, and ALI tests.

Serial killers are often victims of cruel or neglectful parenting, and many have suffered physical, emotional, or mental abuse.[67] They come from troubled backgrounds, and tend to feel that they are low in the social order.[68] These circumstances sometimes lead to the development of personality disorders. For example, Jeffrey Dahmer grew up in a home in which there was no warmth.[69] A parole officer's report quotes his father, Lionel Dahmer, as saying that his son was sexually abused by a neighbor when he was eight years old.[70] Several "psychiatrists said that Dahmer's psychopathology was most likely linked to childhood trauma."[71] He was diagnosed as suffering from alcoholism, a personality disorder (an anti-social personality with obsessive-compulsive and sadistic components), and a sexual disorder.[72] Despite these diagnoses, the jury was not willing to conclude that his condition constituted a mental illness as defined by the court.[73]

---

63. *Id.*

64. Michael Conlon, *Mass Murderers, Serial Killers Alike, Experts Say*, REUTERS, Oct. 17, 1991.

65. Brown, *supra* note 46.

66. Loren H. Roth, *Tighten But Do Not Discard*, JAMA, June 8, 1984, at 2949.

67. Treen, *supra* note 59.

68. *Why Mass Murderers Kill*, *supra* note 50.

69. Jean Latz Griffen, *Dahmer's Lawyer Says His Pursuit of Insanity Ruling Was for Science*, CHI. TRIB., July 16, 1992, at C2 (quoting Gerald Boyle, Jeffrey Dahmer's attorney).

70. Dahmer himself denies this. Treen, *supra* note 59, at 75.

71. Griffen, *supra*, note 69.

72. Joan Ullman, *"I Carried it Too Far, That's for Sure": Report from Jeffrey Dahmer Trial*, PSYCHOLOGY TODAY, May 1992, at 28.

73. Griffen, *supra* note 69.

B.   Taken Alone, Bizarre Conduct Is Insufficient to Prove Insanity

Many people look at serial killers' acts and conclude, "To have done that, they must have been crazy!" In the lay person's view, there is no explanation for these acts other than sheer madness. However, bizarre and shocking acts, in and of themselves, do not create a legal presumption that the defendant is, or even could be, insane.[74] "The fact that a defendant's conduct can be characterized as 'bizarre' or 'shocking' does not compel a finding of legal insanity."[75] This is especially true when there is expert testimony that the defendant was sane at the time he committed the crimes.[76] Charles Krauthammer, author and columnist, states that it would be "absurd to permit the heinousness of the crime to become self-acquitting."[77] To allow this, he claims, would establish a perverse standard that the more terrible the crime, the crazier (and less culpable), the offender is.[78]

Dahmer's attorney did try, however, to prove Dahmer's insanity by attempting to show that only a crazy man would have drilled holes into the skulls of human beings. He argued that Dahmer's cannibalism and murders were themselves proof of his innocence.[79] Dr. Frederick Berlin, the psychiatrist who testified as Dahmer's expert witness, said of Dahmer's acts "If this isn't mental illness, . . . I don't know what is."[80] However, the jury's decision suggests that a serial killer's acts per se are not sufficient proof of mental illness.[81]

C.   Consistent Behavior and a Sense of Control Do Not Support a Finding of Insanity

Serial killers are methodical. They are organized, and they cover their tracks.[82] They try to "conceal [their] action[s] and kill

---

74. Treen, *supra* note 59, at 75.

75. Grady, *supra* note 51.

76. *Id.*

77. *So Guilty, They are Innocent*, NAT'L REV., Mar. 2, 1992, at 17.

78. *Id.*

79. *Id.*

80. *World News Tonight With Peter Jennings* (ABC television broadcast, Feb. 10, 1992).

81. *So Guilty, They are Innocent, supra* note 77, at 17.

82. Houston, *supra* note 52.

over a long period of time."[83] Because of this consistency and perceived element of control, serial killers frequently fail to meet the volitional and cognitive prongs in the *M'Naghten*, irresistible impulse, and ALI tests. Consequently, they are rarely found to be insane. In contrast, defendants who carry out a single crime are more likely to use the insanity defense successfully.[84] Those who carry out a single crime "stand a better chance of convincing a jury that they are mentally imbalanced."[85] This seems to stem from "the common sense notion that truly 'irresistible urges' are short lived, . . . [suggesting that the insanity defense] cannot apply to crimes that require elaborate preparation."[86] Jurors in serial killer trials rationalize that someone who commits a crime time after time, in a planned, organized, and rational manner cannot be insane.[87]

This sense of planning and organization resulted in a finding of sanity in *Dahmer*. Dahmer killed again and again over an extended period of time, committing his first murder at the age of sixteen.[88] His conduct seemed to involve a certain amount of planning and rationality.[89] In fact, Karl W. Stahle, one of the jurors in the Dahmer trial, stated that he did not think that Dahmer was insane because of evidence that the killings were planned in advance.[90] Dahmer's trial revealed that he "chose his victims carefully, . . . always targeting men who did not have a car because he knew that automobiles could be used to trace missing persons,"[91] and that he dismembered the bodies "to get rid of the evidence."[92] The fact that he "had enough sense to hide his deeds . . . [could be seen as] evidence enough of sanity [to satisfy] the law."[93]

Dahmer always seemed to be in control. This control contributed to a finding that he was sane while committing these acts. Stephen Glynn, one of the authors of Wisconsin's insanity law,

---

83. Conlon, *supra* note 64.

84. Michael Conlon, *Jurors May Not Believe Milwaukee Serial Killer Was Insane*, REUTERS, Jan. 16, 1992.

85. *Id.*

86. Brown, *supra* note 46.

87. Conlon, *supra* note 64.

88. Griffen, *supra* note 69.

89. Grady, *supra* note 51; *see also*, Conlon, *supra* note 64.

90. Walsh, *supra* note 60.

91. *Id.*

92. *Id.*

93. *So Guilty, They are Innocent*, *supra* note 77, at 17.

said that "Dahmer's ability to control himself convinced the police that [he] was not a dangerous man."[94] In a graphic example, "a psychiatrist said Dahmer had proved his sanity by 'remembering to reach for a condom' before copulating with [the corpses]."[95] He "testified that Dahmer's capacity to delay gratification and his capacity for impulse control showed he could conform his conduct to social norms" and thus was proof of his sanity.[96]

D.   The Community Places Pressure on the Jury to Convict

The community exerts pressure on the jury in two ways. First, the jury does not want to hand down a verdict that will result in community outrage.[97] Therefore, the jury feels a duty to reach a verdict that will satisfy the community at large.[98] Jury verdicts in insanity trials involving the death penalty reflect the idea that punishing someone who is insane instead of treating him gives society some satisfaction; society feels that it has gotten something from the system by "getting rid of" this person.[99]

Secondly, community pressure to convict is felt in that the jury itself is made up of members of the community. Therefore, the jury carries with it any biases or understandings that the community as a whole may have.[100] In fact, the jurors' individual attitudes toward crime and insanity probably developed from popular

---

94. *World News Tonight With Peter Jennings, supra* note 80.

95. Ullman, *supra* note 72, at 28.

96. *Id.*

97. Worthington, *supra* note 53.

98. Don J. DeBenedictis, *Sane Serial Killer: Experts Say Insanity Plea Alive and Well, Thanks Partly to Dahmer Trial*, A.B.A. J., Apr. 1992, at 22.

99. *Sonya Live* (CNN television broadcast, April 29, 1992) (interviewing Robert Ressler, author and FBI agent).

100. Voir Dire does not always result in an impartial jury. Often, jurors either "consciously or unconsciously lie" (Broeder, *Voir Dire Examinations: An Empirical Study*, 38 S. Cal. L. Rev. 503, 528 (1965)) about their views because they do not want to openly admit their feelings, beliefs or prejudices. They would rather give socially desirable responses and fill a basic need to be correct and please. Therefore, they try to give the "right" answer in order to get approval from the judge. (John L. Carroll, *Speaking the Truth: Voir Dire in the Capital Case*, 3 Am. J. Trial Advoc. 199, 200-201 (1979); Margaret Covington, *Jury Selection: Innovative Approaches to Both Civil and Criminal Litigation*, 16 St. Mary's L.J. 575, 581 (1985); Newton Minnow & Fred H. Cate, *Symposium Issue on the Selection and Function of the Modern Jury: Article: Who is an Impartial Juror in an Age of Mass Media*, 40 Am. U. L. Rev. 631, 651 (1991)).

culture.[101] Unfortunately for defendants, popular culture is not very supportive of the insanity plea. The community's view of the insanity plea is that too many criminals escape punishment by pleading insanity,[102] and if acquitted, those defendants will return to society quickly.[103] When jurors take these beliefs into a trial, it is not surprising that they are not likely to return a not-guilty-by-reason-of-insanity verdict.

Fear of community outrage seems to have influenced the jury's decision in the Dahmer trial. Dahmer's attorney, Gerald Boyle, stated that the jury "probably decided that [they were] not going to let the world at large think that [sexual deviations] in Wisconsin are mental diseases."[104] Theresa Smith, whose brother was one of Dahmer's victims, said that the verdict "brought back the faith I lost in the justice system."[105] As stated in the *ABA Journal,* "[t]here [was] little protest, . . . [because the] jury did what the community wanted [it to do]."[106]

E. The Community Fears that if a Defendant is Found to be Insane, He Will Be Released Too Quickly

Society fears that a defendant found not guilty by reason of insanity will be released from a mental hospital prematurely. This fear may be carried into the trial by individual jurors, resulting in a higher likelihood that the jury will convict.

The public perceives "that those who successfully plead the insanity defense are freed from any institutional restraint or, . . . are released too quickly by mental health authorities."[107] As a result, serial killers are rarely found not guilty by reason of insanity because society, and therefore the jury, does not want to bear the risk that violent offenders, including serial killers, will be released prematurely and again be a threat to the community.[108]

---

101. Ibtihaj Arafat & Kathleen McCahery, *The Insanity Defense and the Juror,* 22 DRAKE L. REV. 538, 539 (1973).

102. Hermann, *supra* note 18, at 987.

103. *Id.* at 988.

104. Jerry C. Smith, *Dahmer Sanity Verdict Brings Mixed Reaction,* Proprietary to UPI, Feb. 16, 1992.

105. Dirk Johnson, *Milwaukee Jury Says Dahmer Was Sane,* N.Y. TIMES, Feb. 16, 1992, at 24.

106. DeBenedictis, *supra* note 98.

107. Hermann, *supra* note 18, at 988.

108. Ruth Marcus, *Justices Weigh Louisiana's Criminal Sanity Law; Can*

Ralph Slovenko, of the Wayne State Law School, may have said it best: "No serial killer is [found to be insane.] They don't want this type of person walking the street."[109] Accordingly, based on the facts of the Dahmer case, it is easy to understand that the fear of his release would influence the jury's decision. Members of the community, along with the jurors themselves, would fear for their safety if he was not detained.[110]

F. Responsibility for the Crime Committed

Individuals who have mental disabilities should not be held legally responsible for their crimes. Their disabilities "deprive[ ] them of even the minimal capacity for rational and voluntary choices on which the law's expectation of responsibility is predicated."[111] The insanity defense was developed so that those who cannot be held legally responsible for their actions will not be punished.

As stated above, the insanity plea is designed to protect the severely mentally disordered.[112] The defense is rarely successful, however, because although a defendant does suffer from mental disabilities, he or she, nevertheless, committed the criminal acts. When society hears about someone who commits these crimes, it wants to hold the offender responsible;[113] an actor deserves to be punished when he or she has failed to comply with the law.[114] Therefore, even if a defendant does suffer from a mental defect that could excuse him from legal responsibility, society's need to hold someone accountable often compels a conviction.

The belief that we should hold people responsible for their actions is especially strong with regard to serial killers. To find that a serial killer is not guilty by reason of insanity is to hold that he or she is not responsible for the deaths of his or her victims. Even if a serial killer's conduct may warrant the label "crazy," it is difficult

---

Confinement Continue When Patient is No Longer Mentally Ill, But May Be Dangerous?, WASH. POST, Feb. 24, 1992, at A3.

109. DeBenedictis, *supra* note 98.

110. *Dahmer Case is No Reason to Trash Insanity Defense*, USA TODAY, Feb. 6, 1992, at 8A.

111. SIMON & AARONSON, *supra* note 6, at 4.

112. Grant Morris, Acquittal by Reason of Insanity *in* MENTALLY DISORDERED OFFENDERS 65, 67 (John Monahan & Henry J. Steadman eds.).

113. *See* text *supra* part IV. D.

114. Hermann, *supra* note 18, at 85.

to find that he or she is not responsible for his or her criminal conduct.[115] A basic tenet of criminal law is that individuals should be held accountable for their actions if they are acting deliberately.[116] Since serial killers are methodical, demonstrate control, and tend not to have psychological abnormalities, they are thought to be acting under their own free will and, consequently, are held accountable for their actions.

With regard to the Dahmer case, "almost no one . . . considered Mr. Dahmer to be anything but responsible for the horrendous acts he described in 60 hours of police confessions."[117] Even if Dahmer was "crazy," or perhaps insane, a jury was not willing to say that he should not be held accountable for the brutal murders and dismemberment of fifteen young men.[118] The crimes were too brutal for a jury to decide otherwise.

V. CONCLUSION

In light of these six factors, the insanity defense is not a viable option for serial killers. Serial killers cannot meet the requirements of the insanity tests in the United States. They do not meet the mental disease requirement because they tend to suffer from personality disorders instead of mental illnesses. They also fail the cognitive and volitional prongs of the various insanity defenses because of the control they demonstrate and the methodical nature of their actions.

Moreover, serial killers are not acquitted since they often have jury trials. Juries are not likely to acquit serial killers due to community pressure and their own prejudices and beliefs. These beliefs include the fear that the serial killer may be released too soon if sent to a mental hospital upon acquittal.

Despite all the fear of acquittal surrounding the trial of Jeffrey Dahmer, some of the fear was unfounded. It was justified to fear Dahmer himself and to fear that a fellow human being is capable of such acts. Nevertheless, the paranoia that Dahmer may have

---

115. Glynn, *supra* note 55, at 13.

116. SIMON & AARONSON, *supra* note 6, at 4.

117. Glynn, *supra* note 55, at 13.

118. *Id.*

208   Law & Psychology Review   [Vol. 17:193

been acquitted under the insanity plea was clearly unjustified because the insanity plea is an ineffective defense for serial killers.

Anne C. Gresham

[16]

Contributions of
Psychiatric Consultation
in the Investigation
of Serial Murder

John A. Liebert

Abstract: *This article focusses on enhancing communication between investigative officers assigned to serial murder cases and their psychiatric consultants. In view of the interdisciplinary interest in this topic, it must be pointed out that my purpose in presenting this article is not for the validation of psychiatric diagnosis of psychodynamic formulations. For those who are primarily interested in the validity of psychiatric formulations as applied to violent crime and predictions of dangerousness, standard texts are recommended where metapsychological issues are thoroughly discussed, and the very important issues of the validity of psychiatry. The reader, if not already acquainted with the literature of "Antipsychiatry", of Laing (1967), and the literature of Szasz (1961) can read these authors concerning the issues of validity in the field of psychiatric consultation to the criminal justice system. A well-known dilemma in clinical psychiatry is the retrograde reconstruction of clinical material, both fantasy and behavior, to presumed etiological antecedents. A definitive, unitary psychological model for serial murder does not exist today. Hence, this is an attempt to assist in communications between law enforcement personnel with the duty of investigating serial murder and their psychiatric consultants. The article is divided into three sections: 1) Overview, 2) Psychological Formulation of Serial Murder, 3) Profiling.*

OVERVIEW

The problems of definition and identification in serial murder are issues best left to discussion by law enforcement and criminology experts. It is of note, however, that serial murders are identified at a point where a threshold of awareness is broken at the interface of the community and its police force. For example, a serial murder was identified retrospectively and prospectively when two separate reports of missing girls were entered with one police department, thereby initiating the "Ted Case" in Seattle. These two cases of missing persons were inactivated for lack of other suspects after Bundy's conviction for murder in Florida. It is typical in these cases for investigative doubt and confusion to persist for months concerning the actuality of a single murderer's responsibility for

187

multiple victims over time and multiple police jurisdictions. The current Green River serial murder case in Washington State may span years and multiple states as did the "Ted" case which allegedly included Washington, Oregon, Wyoming, Colorado, Utah and Florida. When an apprehension is made, unsolved murders going back decades may be brought to investigative light once the neighborhood of the suspect has been discovered.

The problem of definition in serial murder is subject to interpretation of the crime scene for theories regarding motivation for murder. The assumption formulated when conceptualizing apparently random events under the term *serial murder* is that one or more persons are murdering over a span of time and definable space and that there is a common denominator of motivation in the otherwise random appearing killings. The serial murder, therefore, must be conceptualized in terms of whether it appears to be motivated by lust (Bundy); terrorism (Atlanta); cultism (Zebra) or delutional thinking (Ecology, Santa Cruz). Psychiatric expertise may help in cases of terrorism, cults, and organized crime—such as child exploitation cases of lust murder where a pathological equivalent of coitus in the violent act of murder is compulsively repeated over time, appear especially appropriate for psychiatric consultation. For that reason, gangland slayings will not be discussed which may occur consecutively but have "rational" motivation.

Besides problems of definition and the identification of serial murder, the additional problem of excitement generated within a community upon identification far exceeds its morbidity and mortality risks. Excessive public excitement can create a self-feeding cycle between public sensibilities and newspaper coverage ultimately interfering with the process of investigation. Police administration must insulate the investigative staff from the demands for quick solutions and bizarre theories. Serial murders are notoriously difficult to investigate and require patient plodding work not popularized on television. Attention must be given to the possibility of a ritualized murder by a cult, terrorism, or the organized crime of "white slavery". The difficulty of defining a set of circumstances as serial murder, both spatially and temporally, indicates that organized murder of cultism or terrorism are apparently not operating. It is unlikely that bizarre symbolization of a ritualized cultist murder would go unnoticed long enough for an investigative staff to be in doubt as to whether a chain of serial murders exist. Likewise, a politically motivated group attempting to bring attention to itself or elicit change in the system via apparently random murders is extremely unlikely. *Serial murder is a product of extremely primitive emotions.* Investigators, however, must be alert for signs of symbolism at the crime scene which may link apparently random cases. The phases of the moon at which time the killings occur, for example, could have peculiar meaning to the killer without being a part of a cultist murder conspiracy. Without creating insensitivity to an apparent symbolic presentation at the crime scene, *murder theme* priorities must be set as early as possible. Evidence of symbolism within the spatial or temporal organization of the crime scene could provide clues regarding the identity of the killer. Excessive preoccupation with this can lead to wasteful distractions and disruptions in the investigation. Apparently motiveless serial killings of young males or females where intimate physical contact obviously preceded death, demands the investigation of Lust Murder. Retvitch (1965) explains in "Sex Murder and the Potential Sex Murderer",

> "Attacks and murders may be described by the police and courts as attempts at robbery and theft or assault and battery. The underlying sexual dynamics may be completely disregarded. In a case previously reported a man arrested for assault with intent to rob had attacked a woman with a black jack; he rationalized that he needed money and that a woman was the easier victim. Under intravenous sodium amytal, he revealed long-standing fantasies of tying female legs and that this was the purpose of the attack. A noose, a rifle and a book, *Psychopathia Sexualis,* found in his car were not considered clues. Only in isolated incidents were these cases examined as sex offenders."

To enhance the investigative focus on lust murder a psychiatrist or clinical psychologist may be consulted in order to make sense of an otherwise senseless killing spree.

Psychological Formulations of Serial Murder

If lust murder is the working hypothesis regarding apparently random violence, the clinician is expected to explain motivation and thereby help identify a suspect. Investigators need to be familiar with the language and concepts utilized by psychiatrists in their formulations of sex and aggression.

Rada (1978) in his publication, "Clinical Aspects of the Rapist" states,

> "Williams suggests that sexual crimes directed against females occur on a continuum from minor assaults at one end to lust murder at the other. The findings of other investigators, however, suggest that the rape-murderer and the lust murderer are quite different in terms of motives and personality dynamics. The rapist who murders rarely reports any sexual satisfaction from the murder and does not perform sexual acts on the dead victim. Rape murder occurs subsequent to sexual assault and does not appear to have sexual connotations itself. The lust murderer, on the other hand, frequently needs the murder to arouse his sexual interest and desires. Often he does not perform intercourse with the victim, dead or alive. He may, however, experience intense sexual pleasure and orgasm at the time of the murder—some compulsively dismember or disembowel the victim and masturbate to orgasm. J. Rhinehart points

190   International Journal of Offender Therapy and Comparative Criminology

out that the potential sex killer may have committed previous offenses and may even have been caught, but his known criminal offenses usually do not arouse suspicion of a potential sex killer. The true sex killer is generally a very inept lover and can be a well-mannered, gentle, reserved, religious and timid man. Unlike the rapist, the great majority of lust murderers appear to be either overt or latent psychotics with poor control and explosive breaks with reality.

I believe that the lust murderer and the rapist are basically different types of offenders and not simply a variance on a continuum. Rapists are capable of murder but usually for different reasons. In some rapists, however, there appears to be a progressive increase in aggresive fantasies toward women which over time may eventually lead to murder.''

In a study of eight murders and thirty-four unprovoked assaults on women by males, Retvitch (1965) found introversive tendencies, feelings of isolation, detachment and lowering of reality boundaries to be among the most common findings in this series. Retvitch wrote:

"In our material, 19 cases were considered schizoid or dynamically schizophrenic and nine cases overtly clinically schizophrenic. Five cases were diagnosed as mentally defective, and only ten cases could be classified in a category of personality pattern or personality trait disturbance. The psychiatric diagnoses are not precise, frequently overlap and should be viewed on a continuum rather than as a tightly fixed category.

Today, most likely many of these cases would be considered Borderline or Narcissistic Personality Disorders, or, the "Latent Pyschotics" of Rada's (1978) text.

Traditional resistance within the criminal justice system to the psychiatric concept of lust murder is evidenced in the discussion of diagnostic consideration. Retvitch (1965) has written:

"In reviewing the literature one gains an impression that the great majority of recorded sadistic acts were perpetrated by either overt or latent psychotics with poor control or explosive breaks with reality. Vacher the Ripper was manifestly a case of paranoid schizophrenia with a history of hospitalization in an insane asylum for 'persecution mania'. Yet the experts of his time declared him 'sane' and a 'common criminal'. In the case of Verzeni, Krafft-Ebing quoted the experts as saying: 'There was nothing in his past that would indicate a mental disorder' but in describing his personality, the experts added: 'His character was peculiar; he was silent and inclined to be solitary'. In the case of John F. Roche, the newspapers reported the following 'Three psychiatrists found the 27-year plumber's helper sane and capable of standing trial'. Psychiatrists found Roche free of mental disorder and declared that in him the more primitive sadistic forces of murder, rape, etc. were mobilized into a habit pattern'. A week later one read: 'the sullen defendant told his lawyer that he would not cooperate with them, and throughout the day Roche wrote and sat expressionless in his seat in front of two prison

Contributions of Psychiatric Consultation 191

> guards while prospective jurors were questioned, and shook his head
> negatively each time one of his attorneys tried to consult with him. Time
> after time he snarled answers to questions but most of the day he just sat
> grimly. 'Roche is not interested in a trial at all', said Mr. Murray.
> 'Talking to him is like sticking pins into an iceburg'. It is interesting that
> another expert diagnosed Roche as a case of schizophrenia which aroused
> the anger of the court."

In order to communicate with a psychiatric consultant about the latent psychotic individual, a familiarity with the concepts of Borderline and Narcissistic personality underpinnings and Clinical Disorders and their manifestations is necessary. Research on psychological separation and individuation is crucial for understanding how destructive aggression can be intertwined with bonding abnormalities between child and mother. Preoedipal aggression in psychiatric language distinguishes aggression unique to the parent/child relationship preceding the onset of identification and the triangular, competitive relationships between child and parents known as the oedipal period beginning at age three. Preoedipal developmental issues emphasize the diadic relationship between mother and child. It is this diadic development preceding the competitive, triangular strivings of the Oedipal Period that is of primary concern in the psychogenesis of Latent Psychotic Borderline or Narcissistic Personality Disorder. McDevitt (1983) described deviant sadomasochistic interactions between the male child and his mother during this preoedipal period including obviously painful pinching. Lansky (1983) further develops the relationship between impulsive behavior and attachment in his paper, "The Explanation of Impulsive Action". According to Lansky, impulsive behavior can be considered restorative, because the impulse can restore emotional equilibrium in adults suffering from disorders of attachment in the preoedipal first three years of life. He describes a profound sense of "absence" in adult attachment disorders followed by restoration of more normal feelings following impulsive behavior. Podolsky (1965) in "The Lust Murderer", has stated:

> "the typical lust murder characterized by 1) periodic outbursts due to
> recurring compulsions by paroxysmal sexual desires, 2) nearly always
> cutting or stabbing, particularly the breasts or genitals, frequently with
> sucking or licking of the wounds, biting of the skin and sometimes a
> desire to drink the blood and eat the flesh of the victim, 3) sometimes
> erection and ejaculation followed by violation of the victim—often there
> is no attempt at intercourse, 4) behavior usually returns to normal until
> the next outburst".

The columnist, Lerner (1957) wrote, "In many cases of sexual brutality and murder the sex act is never committed. Violence serves as a substitute for it".

Retvitch (1965) has elaborated on the restorative function of violent sexual impulses.

> "Either murder or assault on a female is an expression of a compulsive need and provides satisfaction with or without accompanying sexual manifestations such as erection and ejaculation. The assaults are usually repetitive and are frequently committed in a similar ritualistic manner...the accumulation of tensions released through the attack may be of long duration or it may be a displacement of suddenly induced, hostile emotions from mother or mother-surrogate to the victim. Krafft-Ebing in reporting the case of the 20-year-old-male who stabbed girls in the genitals stated, 'For a while he succeeded in mastering his morbid cravings, but this produced feelings of anxiety, and perspiration would break out on his entire body.'"

The restorative value of impulsive behavior for reintegration of personality may explain Podolsky's (1965) findings that "behavior usually returns to normal until the next outburst after the lust murder". The intertwining of sadomasochistic aggression and attachment anomalies evidenced in the early childhood observations of McDevitt (1983) may lead to a clearer psychodynamic formulation of sadomasochistic aggression in the Latent Psychotic or Borderline and Narcissistic Personality Disorders. It is the aggressive and destructive elements of the early mother and child relationship that are "introjected", or, absorbed excessively into the personality structure of the Borderline or Narcissistic Personality Disorders and remain *"unmetabolized"* as dissociated elements, or elements that can be split off and "projected" outward on the external world. Hence the Narcissistic or Borderline Personality Disorder has incorporated too much of the bad from the maternal relationship and can split this "introjected" badness from his own personality and perceive it as originating from outside. In this psychodynamic formulation, the individual no longer possesses the "badness"—it is the other person, the female victim who "has it". He may either project his introjected, dissociated badness on to his victim and justify his own violence or displace his violence toward his bad mother on to the victim and destroy the mother's badness. The lack of sound personality boundaries in these individuals creates confusion regarding the location of the "badness" between people. In absorbing elements of the badness and aggression of mother and recycling of this badness through projection or displacement, female targets become psychotic disorganization with a lack of realistic perception and true identification of the potential victim. The latent psychotic in the process of lust murder is unlikely to have adequate personality integration and reality testing to know the nature of the victim as an actual human being or target of his own aggression. Kernberg (1982), discussing sexual aggression and introjection in his article, "An Ego Psychology and Object Relations approach to the Narcissistic Personality", has stated,

Contributions of Psychiatric Consultation   193

"One prognostically crucial dimension along which one can explore narcissistic personality structures is the extent to which aggression has been integrated into the psychic apparatus. Aggression may be integrated into the pathological, grandiose self, or it may remain restricted to the underlying, dissociated, and/or repressed primitive object relations against which the pathological grandiose self represents the main defensive structure. One may, in fact, describe the developmental sequence of this integration of aggression into the psychic apparatus including, 1) primitive dissociation or splitting of aggressively invested object relations from libidinally invested object relations, 2) later condensation of such primitive aggressive object relations with sexual drive derivatives in the context of polymorphous, perverse sexual striving and 3) predominant channeling of aggression into a pathlogical, narcissistic character structure with direct investment of aggression by the pathologic grandiose self...When primitive aggression is directly infiltrated in the pathological, grandiose self, a particularly ominous development occurs perhaps best described as characterological sadism. In this last group we find narcissistic patients whose grandiosity and pathological self idealization are reinforced by the sense of triumph over fear and pain achieved by inflicting fear and pain on others. We also find cases where self esteem is enhanced by the direct sadistic pleasure of aggression linked with sexual drive derivatives. Some of these narcissistic personalities may pursue joyful types of cruelty...A final factor that has crucial prognostic significance is the extent to which the antisocial trends are built into the patient's narcissistic character pathology...

Antisocial tendencies go hand and hand with a lack of integration and normal superego functions, and also with a lack of development of a modulated capacity for depressive reaction. The qualtiy of object relations is also an inverse relation to antisocial trends. Naturally when antisocial trends are present in the patients who also present a sadistic infiltration of the pathological grandiose self or direct expressions of severely sadistic sexual behavior, the prognosis is significantly worsened."

It seems likely that the contemporary concepts of Narcissistic or Borderline Personality Disorders with antisocial, sadistic impulse disorders are referred to in the literature as latent psychotics and lust murder. It is the clinical elucidation of rage, violence, aggression, and sadomasochistic sexual perversion, or polymorphous perverse sexuality, which Kernberg developed from his clinical research. Psychoanalysis cannot prove causative linkage between the clinical manifestations of sexual perversion, violence and sadomasochism presented by their adult patients and events from the mother-child diad of the first three years of life; yet well organized clinical case material can be dramatically convincing. It is this function, clinical effectiveness of psychoanalytic reconstruction from adult symptom to childhood event that is the traditional psychodynamic foundation for conceptualizing lust murder and latent psychosis.

It is the fusion of destructive impulses from disorganized sexual impulses evolving out of the preoedipal matrix of these individuals, together with the incapacity for empathic bonding typical of the sociopath, that provides a motivational model for comprehension of the serial lust murderer. With this model the investigative staff may be able to better comprehend the unobtrusive, superficially adjusted individual in society who appears to behave and relate normally but is incapable of true social integration, true intimacy or consistent psychological integration. It is this individual who may appear to be a "good family man" and a "good citizen" but one driven by a crescendoing evolution of antisocial, aggressive sexual impulsivity into a repetitious pattern of lust murder. It is this person who can be transiently psychotic and, via impulsive behavior such as murder and yet reintegrate to a superficial appearance of social and psychological adjustment. It is this individual who charges fragmentary sexual behavior, such as collecting female shoes, with destructive aggression.

Guttmacher's (1963) series of sexually aggressive offenders shows the relevance of polymorphous perverse sexual behavior, or the predilection of a substitute for intercourse, in the histories of these men, i.e., fetishism. Guttmacher (1963) has written:

> "Only one case had a previous conviction for exhibitionism. Of great importance for prediction of potential violence with sexual motivation seem to be the following combination of factors: 1) unprovoked assaults on women, particularly choking or stabbing, 2) offenses of breaking and entering committed solo and in bizarre circumstances, 3) fetishism of female underclothing...confusion of sexual identity as elicited on projective tests....and blurring of reality boundaries.

It is certainly not proven in the cases of lust murderers that history of polymorphous perverse or, synonymously, paraphilic behavior is a common antecedent to the murdering; however, lust murderers are frequently uncooperative in volunteering psychological information. The *Comprehensive Textbook of Psychiatry,* (1980), defines paraphilia as follows:

> "Paraphilias are characterized by specialized sexual fantasies, masturbatory practices, sexual props and requirements of the sexual partner. The special fantasy, with its unconscious and conscious components, is the pathognomonic element, arousal and orgasm being variously dependent upon the active elaboration of the illusion. The influence of the fantasy, of its elaborations on behavior, extend beyond the sexual sphere to pervade the person's life. Paraphilia, also referred to as perversion and sexual deviation, at one end of the spectrum shades into the psychosis and gender identity disorders...Overall, paraphilia shares more common grounds with Borderline Personality Disorders...in fetishism the sexual focus is on objects such as shoes, gloves, corsets or hose that are intimately associated with the human body and are relatively indestructible. The particular fetish is linked to somebody closely involved with the

Contributions of Psychiatric Consultation 195

patient during his childhood and has some quality closely associated with that loved, needed and traumatizing person. It serves the magical, hence fetish, bridge to relatedness, as a binder against aggression and as a representation of the female phallus.

Sexual activity may be directed toward the fetish itself, such as masturbation, with or into a shoe, or the fetish may be incorporated in sexual congress with, for example, the demand that high heel shoes be worn.

Fetishization has been viewed as the central process in all sexual arousal, perverse and normal. Stoller, however, broadened fetishization to a more general process of dehumanization and believed that the fetish stands for the human, rather than solely for the missing maternal phallus. McDougal also suggested that fetishism is one concrete means of compensating for the gap in reality sense left by the disavowed sexual reality, that is, disavowal of the anatomical distinction between the sexes.''

The individual who is borderline in character structure—and so sociopathic and incapable of social bonding as to be capable of multiple murder—likely manifests fetishist behavior early in his criminal career. For that reason, Guttmacher's (1963) cases may have shown a high incidence of "fetishism of female underclothing, expressions of hatred, contempt and fear of women, primitive fantasy life, confusion of sexual identity and a high incidence of offenses of breaking and entering, committed solo and in bizarre circumstances''. The mutilated victim of lust murder can be conceptualized therefore as a failure of the fetish. For example, Podolsky (1965) says,

"In a crime pronounced as sexual murder, the type of injuries is of considerable importance; the most frequent are mutilation of the genital organs or the cutting out thereof; next comes disembowelment, the plunging of a stick or umbrella into the vagina or anus, the tearing out of the hair, the severing of the breast and throttling...

In genuine cases of sexual murder, the killing replaced the sexual act. There is, therefore, no sexual intercourse at all. Sexual pleasure is induced by cutting, stabbing and slashing the victim's body, ripping open her abdomen, plunging the hand into the intestines, cutting out and taking away her genitals, throttling her, sucking her blood. These horrors, which surpass in frightfulness everything that has been committed by human beings even under the effects of war psychosis, constitutes, so to speak, pathological equivalents of coitus.''

Weinsel and Calef (1972) have formulated an hypothesis which further assists in bridging the phenomena of the paraphilias with lust murder,

"Mention should also be made of the role of the necrophelia theme in that group of sexual perversions (paraphilias) which, loosely, are considered together under the label of 'bondage' fantasies and practices. Here too the helplessness of the sexual object is the crucial dynamic element: most frequently the object is tied-up or bound in some other fashion; but

→ the numerous variations include the object's being a slave, being drugged or anaesthetized, asleep, hypnotized or paralysed. Sexual gratification for these individuals is often possible only when the object is in this helpless condition, for practical purposes—dead! We recognize that no one single determinant is responsible for such fantasies and behavior, and both the products or regression from an oedipal conflict and more primitive pregenital (preoedipal) fixations play some role in the formation of these tendencies. Further, it is our experience that at least in some of these cases the wish to re-enter and to explore the interior of the mother's body may be an important dynamic ingredient; and it is our further impression that the more immediate causal element is related to the traumatic impact of viewing the paternal phallus together with a defensive identification with it. It should be added that in all of these fantasies the mechanism of turning passive into active is a crucial factor.''

Here we begin to see the bizarre destructive acts of the lust murderer as primitive aggression fused with the polymorphous, perverse sexuality described by Kernberg (1982) as well as the possible final outcome of crescendoing development of paraphilia to ultimate breakdown of the binding power of the fetish, hence personality disintegration and resultant psychosis. Therefore, masturbation into a shoe which has been burglarized from a woman's bedroom may be only a quantitative leap from disembowelment in terms of disavowal of sexual reality. The lust murderer who mutilates and disembowels his victim, in other words, is dehumanizing his victim, and denying the threat of sexual differences to a far greater extreme than the foot fetishist. Mutilation and disembowelment
→ of the victim in lust murder and the foot fetish, however, share similar paraphilic roots in the service of the magical functions in the Borderline Personality Disorder, or latent psychotic, who is defending from psychological disintegration. Stoller (1980) in his discussion of Transsexualism describes brutally violent hypermasculinity in primitive tribal warriors whose attachment with their mothers was so powerful that denial of female identification, through hypermasculine aggression and dehumanization of the female, was necessary for defense against symbiotic anxiety, and, consequently, dissolution of psychological boundaries and ultimate psychosis.

Profiling

In order for a psychiatrist to be of assistance in the investigation of serial murder there must be a clear and frank discussion of the nature of the process being investigated. If investigative personnel believe that a serial murderer is basically a bad person who behaves offensively because he has chosen a particularly nefarious habit, the psychiatrist can be of little assistance. Psychiatrists are only of value in serial murder investigations if there is receptiveness within the investigative staff to a mutual learning process concerning lust murder. The repulsive nature of this crime, particularly if associated with necrophilia or mutilation, may result in resistances within the staff that can lead to wasteful diversions. Evidence can be missed or destroyed to avoid disgust or threatening emotional feelings. Acceptance that the Borderline or Narcissistic Personality Disorder with severe sociopathic and sadistic trends can commit murder as a substitute for normal erotic pleasure or even nonviolent perversion is the foundation for exploration of motivation in serial murders. With a mutually respectful desire to learn about the bizarre world of the lust murderer the investigator and psychiatric consultant can enhance their sense of "type" for a suspect. The investigator is less likely to make a mistake in judging the grandiosity of pathological narcissism and the manipulativeness of sociopathy with "normalcy". The lust murderer can present a facade of relationships and effective, perhaps, even superior performance. Not infrequently, he will be in the bright-superior intelligence range and, therefore, potentially a skilled imposter. Ted Bundy served as a government sexual-assault expert and a crisis clinic counselor. This does not mean that the lust murderer, despite his appearance of superior function and normal relationships, is otherwise a normal person who has consciously selected a criminal career in life. The lust murderer has primitive personality abnormalities making him incapable of normal intimacy. I know of no lust murderer who was in intensive psychotherapy and therefore provided evidence of his capacity to bond in a human relationship. Lust murderers may be able to maintain effective facades as imposters, immitating normal people, but they are not normal enough to tolerate the intensive bonding demands to meaningful psychotherapy. The not uncommon expectation that a serial murderer is the intimate acquaintance of practicing psychiatrists is, of course, totally contradictory to the psychodynamic formulation of lust murder. Lust murder represents the extreme sadomasochistic and sociopathic end of the Borderline-Narcissistic Personality Disorder spectrum—consequently the least treatable part of the spectrum. Their inability to attach, hence their intolerance of intimacy, may be manifested in their propensity to drive great distances frequently crossing state lines. The clinical manifestation of disturbed bonding in sociopathic personality disorders along with manifestations of confused and fragmented, or polymorphous perverse sexuality may be observed in the suspects' prior histories. Sensitivity to polymorphous perverse sexuality in these individuals, hence to fetishistic and paraphilic sexual behavior, will lead to concentration on these aspects of a suspect's biography. This perspective on lust murder is, of course, questionable practical value, because the vast majority of personality disorders who manifest sadomasochistic behavior and polymorphous perverse behavior are extremely unlikely to commit serial murder, but ruling them in or out while ignoring this dimension is reckless.

As previously mentioned, there may be resistance within the criminal justice system to uncovering sexual motivation for crime. To assume that previous convictions and F.B.I. rap sheets are in any way a comprehensive and valid representation of a person's predilections for violent offenses is inexcusable within this type of investigation. Any suspect with a history of burglary or assault must be thoroughly investigated for a history which has either been distorted by the court or inadequately investigated. These individuals have extremely damaged self images. Therefore, any manifestation of normalcy is in fact that of an imposter. They are devious in their apprehension of victims. It is not coincidental that Ted Bundy worked in a sexual assault program or Wayne Williams as a talent scout. Their heightened ability to be effective imposters and dedicate this skill to a successful predatory existence is an important factor of their narcissistic and sociopathic personality structure. Devices as disguises, impersonations, and other manipulations of the environment are not uncommon, in contrast to the authenticity of their own identity which they cannot experience. Sensitivity to the manifestations of sadomasochism and polymorphous perverse sexual behavior is likewise of importance to the coroner's office. To examine the victim of a serial murder case without looking carefully for evidence of symbolic mutilation, vampirism or oral aggression and cannibalism in the form of bite marks suggests a non-professional orientation. The bite marks in the Chi Omega case which resulted in the conviction of Ted Bundy, were nearly destroyed.

Summary and Suggestions:

Lust murder cases appear to be increasing. It is unrealistic to expect urban and suburban police departments to invest major resources of tracking these individuals with the hope of reducing the vulnerability to society. It is doubtful that a full-time metropolitan intelligence department can be dedicated to the tracking of serial murders. It is important that one investigator, within a region, be highly trained and educated regarding this type of crime. If a network of experience and information is available regionally and/or nationally, police departments can turn to these agencies for assistance in the event their communities are victimized by a serial lust murderer. The value of this type of accessibility depends on liason between specialized investigative resource for lust murder and the administrations of the various departments. All too often investigations are disrupted and confused by interdepartmental breakdowns in communication.

The value of specialized resources depends upon the soundness of information and assistance provided. Behavioral science profiling can be superficial, phenomenological and, perhaps, even worse, distracting. There is no evidence that we know enough about lust murderers to make very

Contributions of Psychiatric Consultation 199

many phenomenological generalizations. True, some cross state lines, but Wayne Williams did not, even though he drove a great deal. Many lust murderers are extremely bright and extraordinarily clever; yet some are nearly retarded. Lust murders have been know to infiltrate the investigation. Their major interest revolves around their potential apprehension. Superficial behavioral scientific profiling that rigidly reduces serial murder to a few observable parameters can lead an investigation astray. It is better to search for what distinguishes any given serial murder in its uniqueness, then build a profile of a potential suspect against the psychopathology of the Narcissistic or Borderline Personality disorders particularly the severe forms. Their biographies will likely show overt but, perhaps, subtle antisocial, polymorphous perverse and sadistic trends not registered often on police records. The mutual study of suspects' biographies by investigators with a psychiatric consultant can reduce wasteful diversions and rigidity within the investigtion.

REFERENCES

Comprehensive Textbook of Psychiatry (1980) Baltimore, Md. Williams and Wilkins Co.

Guttmacher, M. (1963) "Dangerous Offenders," *Crime and Delinquency. Vol. 9:* 381-390.

Kernberg, O. (1982) "An Ego Psychology and Object Relations Approach to the Narcissistic Personality." In The American Psychiatric Association, *Psychiatry, 1982, Annual Review.* Washington, D.C.: American Psychiatric Association Press (510-523).

Laing, R. (1967) *"The Politics of Experience."* London: Penguin.

Lansky, M. (1983) "The Explanation of Impulse Action." Paper presented at the Seventh World Congress of Psychiatry, Vienna, Austria.

Lerner, M. (1957) New York Post, Apr. 22.

McDevitt, J. (1983) "Emergence of Hostile Aggression and Its Modification during the Separation Individuation Process." Paper presented to the Seattle Psychoanalytic Society.

Podolsky, E. (1965) "The Lust Murderer," *Medico-Legal Journal.* Vol. 33: 174-178.

Rada, R. (1978) *"Clinical Aspects of the Rapist,"* New York: Grune & Stratton.

Retvich, E. (1965) "Sex Murder and the Potential Sex Murderer," *Diseases of the Nervous System.* Vol. 26: 640-648.

Stoller, R. (1980) "Cross Cultural Observations about General Identity." Paper presented to the Seattle Psychoanalytic Society.

Szasz, T. (1961) *"The Myth of Mental Illness."* New York: Harper & Row.

Weinshel, E. and Calet, V. (1972) "On Certain Neurotic Equivalents of Necrophilia," *International Journal of Psycho-Analysis.* Vol. 53: 67-75.

John A. Liebert, M.D.
Assistant Professor:
University of Washington Medical School

Consulting Psychiatrist:
Green River Murder Task Force
Atlanta Children's Murder Task Force
"Ted" (Bundy) Task Force, Washington

Private Practice:
27 100th Ave. N.E.
Bellevue, Washington 98004
U.S.A.

[17]

The Sexually Sadistic Criminal and His Offenses

Park Elliott Dietz, MD, MPH, PhD; Robert R. Hazelwood, MS; and Janet Warren, DSW

This is an uncontrolled, descriptive study of 30 sexually sadistic criminals. All were men, and all intentionally tortured their victims in order to arouse themselves. Their crimes often involved careful planning, the selection of strangers as victims, approaching the victim under a pretext, participation of a partner, beating victims, restraining victims and holding them captive, sexual bondage, anal rape, forced fellatio, vaginal rape, foreign object penetration, telling victims to speak particular words in a degrading manner, murder or serial killings (most often by strangulation), concealing victims' corpses, recording offenses, and keeping personal items belonging to victims.

Sexual sadism was named by Richard von Krafft-Ebing[1] after the Marquis de Sade. whose writings describe a pairing of sexual acts with domination, degradation. and violence. The century that has passed since Krafft-Ebing's description has produced case histories extending along a spectrum from accounts of sexually sadistic dreams or fantasies related by neurotics in the course of psychoanalysis to the continuing stream of popular biographies of sexual sadists who have been convicted of sensational crimes. The innocuousness of those who only fantasize contrasts dramatically with the viciousness of those sexually sadistic offenders whose translation of fantasy into criminal actions causes them to be seen in the practice of forensic psychiatry and criminal investigation. To understand the entire spectrum of sexual sadism, it is necessary to study not only the neurotically conflicted, but also the sadist unencumbered by ethical, societal, and legal inhibitions.

Among the most useful publications to forensic psychiatrists are the clinically informed case histories of those who have committed serious crimes, such as those reported by Krafft-Ebing,[1] Stekel,[2] Macdonald,[3,4] or Groth.[5] Such cases occur so infrequently in any one jurisdiction, however, that it has proved difficult for researchers to gather information about a series of cases that can permit more generalized observations than can be made on the basis of the small number of cases typically accumulated in a

Dr. Dietz has a consulting practice in forensic psychiatry based in Newport Beach. CA. and is a consultant to the F.B.I.'s National Center for the Analysis of Violent Crime and to the Forensic Sciences Unit of the New York State Police. Special Agent Hazelwood is an Instructor at the National Center for the Analysis of Violent Crime. F.B.I. Academy, Quantico. VA. and a member of the Adjunct Faculty of the University of Virginia. Dr. Warren is an assistant professor in the General Medical Faculty. Division of Medical Center Social Work and Department of Behavioral Medicine and Psychiatry. University of Virginia. Address all correspondence to Dr. Dietz. Threat Assessment Group. Inc., 410 W. Coast Highway. Newport Beach. CA 92663.

single individual's practice. For this article we used the unique resources of the National Center for the Analysis of Violent Crime to study a series of sexual sadists who have engaged in remarkably predatory behavior.

Although the men in this series were serious criminals, it is important to recognize that sexual sadists, like other paraphiles, do not necessarily engage in any actions in fulfillment of the paraphilia.[6] Indeed, it is possible that a majority of sexual sadists never engage in a sexually sadistic act, much less a crime. Among those who act on their fantasies, there are those who limit their actions to lawful behaviors with consenting partners or to behaviors with paid partners. In some cases, however, the sexual sadist does not content himself with lawful or quasi-lawful adaptations, but rather indulges himself at the expense of unwilling partners.[7] It is this latter group of sexually sadistic offenders that poses the greatest problem for society.

Sexual sadism has often been confounded with other mental disorders, particularly where a psychotic offender has cruelly harmed someone or where a patient has described bizarre fantasies. In our experience the extremities of behavior among sexually sadistic offenders prove perplexing to even seasoned clinicians, who find themselves tempted to ascribe psychosis to those who engage in extraordinarily cruel acts despite the absence of delusions, hallucinations, or markedly illogical thinking. Compounding the diagnostician's difficulty, the offenders generally conceal the truth—sometimes even in the face of compel-

ling evidence of guilt—and even when they reveal it, it is so bizarre as to invite disbelief.

This report focuses on 30 sexually sadistic criminals who probably have character pathology in addition to the Axis I condition of sexual sadism, but this does not mean that sexual sadism is invariably associated with such pathology. Presumably, sexual sadism can occur in the absence of any other diagnosable mental disorder or in combination with any other diagnosis. Even here, however, diagnostic errors are common. The behavior of a sexual sadist with antisocial personality disorder may be markedly different from one with schizoid personality disorder, for the latter may be so shy as to have limited the number of victims attacked and so odd when examined as to invite a psychotic diagnosis. Likewise, the clinician may find it difficult to differentiate the individual who engages in sexual behavior of a seemingly sadistic nature only when psychotic from the individual with an established pattern of sexual sadism who subsequently becomes psychotic. Only the latter is a sexual sadist, as all manner of sexual thoughts and behaviors can occur during psychosis without a diagnosis of a paraphilia being warranted.

A variety of cruel sexual and criminal acts has evoked attributions of sexual sadism, even by so astute an observer as Stekel.[2] Rada[8] has surveyed the varied, often contradictory, definitions of sadism that have been offered by psychiatrists of various camps. To be clear, we must state our position, which is that only those crimes reflective of an endur-

The Sexually Sadistic Criminal

ing pattern of sexual arousal in response to sadistic imagery ought to be regarded as sexually sadistic offenses.

Although such varied actions as mutilation followed by murder, murder followed by mutilation, and cannibalism have been said to provide sexual excitement to sadistic murderers,[3] these actions are not necessarily indicative of either sexual excitement or sexual sadism. Sexually sadistic offenses must be differentiated from seemingly similar crimes, such as genital mutilation motivated by other than sadistic sexual arousal patterns[9] (e.g., the severely disturbed prostitute who emasculates her client while he sleeps or the schizophrenic murderer who dissects his victim from pelvis to neck); cruelty motivated by revenge or other nonsexual motives (e.g., the gang which tortures and castrates a man in retaliation for his liaison with a gang member's "girl"); pathological group behavior (e.g., atrocities against civilians in a combat zone); torture during interrogation; ritualized human sacrifice (e.g., within the Aztec culture); or institutionally sanctioned cruelty (e.g., concentration camp atrocities). Likewise, acts such as those that occur in sexually sadistic role-playing (e.g., by prostitutes or others who enact a sadistic role for the benefit of their clients, partners, or pornographers) and sexually sadistic acts among psychotics or sexual experimenters must be carefully distinguished from acts indicating sexual sadism.

Although not universally true, some sexual sadists have considerable insight into their sexual deviation and devote significant energy to self-scrutiny. One of the clearest definitions of sexual sadism comes from the writings of a man who kidnapped, kept captive, raped, sodomized, and in some instances murdered victims in several states over an extended period of time. Audio tapes of his sexual torture of his fourth wife and of one of his stranger victims, photographs he took of foreign object penetration of another captive victim 20 years earlier, and his own written plans for building an "S & M play area," cells, and an incinerator, confirm an enduring pattern of sexual arousal to the suffering of his sexual partners. He wrote:

> *Sadism:* The wish to inflict pain on others is *not* the essence of sadism. One essential impulse: *to have complete mastery over another person,* to make him/her a helpless object of our will, to become the absolute ruler over her, to become her God, to do with her as one pleases. To humiliate her, to enslave her, *are means to this end,* and the most important radical aim is to make her *suffer* since *there is no greater power over another person than that of inflicting pain on her* to force her to undergo suffering without her being able to defend herself. The pleasure in the complete domination over another person is the very essence of the Sadistic drive. [Emphasis in original.]

Although it is possible that he may have copied this material from a published source, a diligent search has failed to disclose a similar passage in any of the writings on sexual sadism. The passage is consistent with both the other writings of this man and his enduring pattern of behavior. More importantly, it is consistent with the behavior of all of the sexually sadistic offenders we have studied.

Methods

Case files were drawn from a pool of cases referred to or studied by the National Center for the Analysis of Violent Crime (NCAVC). When President Ronald Reagan announced the establishment of the NCAVC in 1984, he identified its primary mission as that of identifying and tracking repeat killers.[10] The NCAVC today encompasses four programs: the Profiling and Consultation Program (now the Criminal Investigative Analysis Program), the Violent Criminal Apprehension Program, the Research and Development Program, and the Training Program.[11] The NCAVC is a tertiary referral center for unsolved crimes and particular types of extreme offenses, providing services to law enforcement agencies and prosecutors analogous to the services provided by the Centers for Disease Control to state and local health departments[12] such as epidemiologic surveillance, intelligence, specialized consultation, training, and research.

The sampling universe for the present study consisted of all cases identified as possible sexually sadistic criminals that were submitted to the NCAVC for analysis or were sent to specialists within the NCAVC for teaching and research purposes between 1984 and 1989. Each case within this universe was screened by the authors for the presence of an enduring pattern of sexual arousal in response to images of suffering or humiliation. For a case to be admitted to the study, all three authors had to agree that a factual basis was available for finding that the subject had been sex-

ually aroused in response to images of suffering or humiliation on two or more occasions spanning an interval of at least six months. Most often the evidence of sexual arousal consisted of documented sexual acts or self-reported sexual arousal occurring simultaneously with a victim's expressed suffering. Most of the cases that others had believed to be possible sexual sadists but that were eliminated through this screening process were those in which an offender committed a single rape or murder with torture or mutilation, but without evidence of an enduring pattern of arousal to such activities, or cases in which cruel behaviors occurred at times other than those at which the victim was conscious and the offender aroused. Thus, for example, we excluded cases in which a rapist injured or killed his victim if there was no evidence of sexual arousal accompanying the injury or killing and cases in which sexual activity or mutilation occurred only after a victim was unconscious or dead. The sample thus consists of consecutively referred sexually sadistic offenders, but two of the offenders admitted to the study had committed their crimes many years before the case files were referred for teaching and research purposes.

For each case, information was available from at least two of the following sources: police investigative reports, crime scene photographs, victim statements, reports of interviews with family members, confessions, psychiatric reports, grand jury or trial transcripts, presentencing reports, and prison records. In addition to these, materials pro-

The Sexually Sadistic Criminal

duced by the offenders such as manuscripts, diaries, photographs, sketches, audio tapes, videotapes, and threatening letters were available in the majority of cases. Five of the 30 subjects have been interviewed at great length by at least one of the authors, with informed consent. In six of the 30 cases, published book-length biographies were used to supplement available investigative information. The many published biographies of serial killers include some notoriously unreliable and inaccurate volumes (including some with fabricated data), but the ones used here are among the most reliable of such books according to investigators familiar with the cases. For two of the cases the book proved the more complete source of data, but in the other four the investigative information was superior to the book-length account.

Each of the 30 men on whom this report is based meets stringent criteria for sexual sadism, having engaged in repeated fantasies and actions evidencing sexual arousal to the suffering and humiliation of other persons for periods in excess of six months. Each of the 30 also engaged in extensive patterns of antisocial behavior in adulthood. The available evidence does not often include juvenile police records (which were generally sealed) or extensive information on the adolescence of the men. It is thus not possible to be certain how many of the men would meet DSM-III-R[13] criteria for antisocial personality disorder. None of the individuals studied was psychotic at the time of onset of a pattern of sexually sadistic behavior, but one became psychotic later in life.

All of the data reported in this article must be regarded as minimum estimates of the true frequency of the variables studied among this population because of variations in the quantity of information available about particular cases. The data about which we are least confident are those on reported physical and sexual abuse during childhood, because no systematic effort was made to collect such data or to verify spontaneous claims of abuse.

Results

Offender Characteristics Table 1 presents the characteristics of offenders in the sample. Note that each of these characteristics is also found among persons who are neither sexual sadists nor offenders. Without comparable data on males in the general population or other comparison groups, these data must be interpreted cautiously. Each of the offenders was male, and all but one was white. Forty-seven percent of the men came from homes characterized by parental infidelity or divorce; approximately equal proportions reportedly had been physically abused (23%) or sexually abused (20%) in childhood. While committing offenses, 43 percent were married. The nine who were incestuously involved with their children comprised 30 percent of the total sample, but 60 percent of the 15 subjects who had children.

Forty-three percent were known to have had homosexual experiences, excluding childhood sex play and two cases

Dietz *et al.*

Table 1
Characteristics of Sexually Sadistic Criminals

Characteristics	n	%
Male	30	100.0
White	29	96.7
Parental infidelity or divorce	14	46.7
Physically abused in childhood	7	23.3
Sexually abused in childhood	6	20.0
Married at time of offense	13	43.3
Incestuous involvement with own child	9	30.0
Known homosexual experience*	13	43.3
Known cross-dressing	6	20.0
Known history of peeping, obscene telephone calls, or indecent exposure	6	20.0
Shared sexual partners with other men	6	20.0
Education beyond high school	13	43.3
Military experience	10	33.3
Established reputation as solid citizen	9	30.0
Drug abuse (other than alcohol)	15	50.0
Suicide attempt	4	13.3
Excessive driving	12	40.0
Police "buff" (excessive interest in police activities and paraphernalia)	9	30.0

* Excluding childhood sex play.

in which suspected homosexual activity could not be confirmed. Nonsadistic paraphilic activities included cross-dressing (20%) and minor sex offenses (peeping, obscene telephone calls, or indecent exposure; 20%). Six men shared their consenting sexual partners with other men (including three who shared their wives).

Forty-three percent had been educated beyond the high school level. Of the 10 known to have military experience, eight served in the ground forces. At least five had been honorably discharged, and one received a medical discharge for unknown reasons. The occupations of these subjects were baker (two), cook, chef, candy maker, bartender, restaurant owner, musician, bouncer/truck driver, laborer, rancher, logger, television repairman, barber/nude

photo studio proprietor, amusement park train conductor, mechanic, construction worker, construction contractor, house painter, upholsterer, salesman, sales manager, real estate developer/race car driver, photographer, cardiovascular technician, security guard, sheriff's deputy, law student, military officer, and banker. Note that the majority of these occupations involve contact with the public. Thirty percent of the offenders had established reputations as solid citizens through involvement in civic activities, volunteer work, charitable contributions, political activity, and sound business dealings.

Half of the offenders were known to abuse drugs other than alcohol. Thirteen percent had a history of at least one suicide attempt. These four men had a total of six parasuicidal episodes, includ-

The Sexually Sadistic Criminal

ing hanging (two). carbon monoxide poisoning. industrial chemical ingestion, wrist cutting. and drug overdose.

Excessive driving. defined as driving with no clear goal or driving long distances only to spontaneously change course in another direction, characterized 40 percent of the men. Thirty percent of the men were police "buffs" who habitually showed excessive interest in police activities and paraphernalia. This interest ranged from collecting literature dealing with police technology to having complete police uniforms, counterfeit identification and badges, and vehicles modified to resemble police cars (black wall tires, two-way radio, Bearcat scanner, whip antenna, flashing red lights, and siren).

Seventeen (57%) of the men had no known arrest history prior to their arrest for the sadistic offenses described below. Thirteen (43%) had prior arrests for a variety of nonsexual and nonsadistic sexual offenses.

Eighty-three percent of the men maintained collections of items related to sexual or violent themes or both. The most commonly occurring collection was pornography (53%), followed in frequency by guns (37%), bondage paraphernalia (27%), and detective magazines (23%).[14] Smaller proportions of men collected knives (10%), *Soldier of Fortune* magazine (7%), sexual devices (7%), and women's undergarments (3%). As with the offender characteristics given in Table 1, the collections specified here are not necessarily associated with either sexual sadism or criminality.

Offense Characteristics Characteristics of the offenses are given in Table 2. Eleven (37%) of the men committed at least some of their offenses with a partner who assisted in all phases of the crime. These 11 offenders were assisted by 11 male partners and seven female partners. Two of the male partners were the offender's fathers. Five of the female partners were wives of the offenders, and one was a victim who had been held captive for weeks before she began assisting in the abduction and torture of other victims. Five of the offenders shared sexual access to their victims with 11 other men.

Ninety-three percent of the offenders were judged to have carefully planned their offenses, as evidenced by such behaviors as studying law enforcement procedures; studying and collecting weapons; constructing a torture rack or a specially equipped torture room; altering' a vehicle for use in abduction and torture (soundproofing a van, disabling windows and door handles, or installing police vehicle accessories); preparing a "torture kit" containing binding materials, torture implements, weapons, cameras, recording devices, and burial equipment (e.g., a shovel and lime); taking provisions for travel to remote locations (e.g., water and food for the desert; extra fuel to fly to a remote island); conducting systematic surveillance and stalking of victims; impersonating a police officer in the commission of the offense (23%) or other elaborate ruses; wearing gloves to avoid leaving fingerprints; and taking the victim to a location selected in advance (77%).

Dietz et al.

Table 2
Characteristics of Offenses

Characteristics	n	%
A partner assisted in offense	11	36.7
Careful planning of offense	28	93.3
Impersonation of police in commission of offense	7	23.3
Victim taken to preselected location	23	76.7
Victim kept in captivity for 24 hours or more	18	60.0
Victim bound, blindfolded, or gagged	26	86.7
Sexual bondage of victim*	23	76.7
Anal rape of victim	22	73.3
Forced victim to perform fellatio	21	70.0
Vaginal rape of victim	17	56.7
Foreign object penetration of victim	12	40.0
Variety of sexual acts with the victim†	20	66.7
Sexual dysfunction during offense	13	43.3
Unemotional, detached affect during offense	26	86.6
Told victim what to say during assault	7	23.3
Intentional torture	30	100.0
Murdered victim	22	73.3
Committed serial murders (three or more victims)	17	56.6
Concealed victim's corpse	20	66.6
Victim beaten (blunt force trauma)	18	60.0
Recorded the offense‡	16	53.3
Kept personal item belonging to victim	12	40.0

* Sexual bondage is distinguished from bondage for the sole purpose of restraining the victim's movements by the use of a variety of positions, excessive binding, symmetrical bindings, and neatness.

† A variety of sexual acts is defined as having subjected the victim to at least three of the following: vaginal rape, forced fellatio, anal rape, foreign object penetration.

‡ Includes recordings through writings, drawings, photographs, audio tapes, or videotapes.

The most commonly used means of gaining access to the victim was determined for each of the 30 offenders. The largest number (27 or 90.0%) used a "con" approach,[15] openly approaching the victim under a pretext such as requesting or offering assistance, asking directions, or making an arrest. For example, one man hired models to pose in photo sessions, ostensibly to be used for the covers of detective magazines, but would take the victims to the desert, photograph, and strangle them. Two men tended to use "surprise" approaches, in which they suddenly grabbed the victims to gain control. One used a "blitz" approach, suddenly striking the victims over the head with a blunt object.

Sixty percent of the offenders kept one or more of their victims captive for periods ranging from 24 hours to six weeks before killing or releasing them. Three offenders persuaded or coerced former captives to return for additional abuse. Victims were kept captive by being bound or locked in a confined area, by the continuous physical presence of the offender, or by a combination of these. Eighty-seven percent of the offenders bound, blindfolded, or gagged one or more victims. Seventy-seven percent of the offenders engaged in sexual bondage of one or more victims. Sexual bondage

The Sexually Sadistic Criminal

refers to restriction of movements or use of the senses to enhance the sexual arousal of the offender. It is distinguished from binding for the sole purpose of restraining the victim's movement by the use in sexual bondage of elaborate and excessive binding material. unnecessarily neat and symmetrical binding. and binding the victim in a variety of positions. often while being photographed.

As shown in Table 2. the sexual acts forced on victims by the largest numbers of offenders (in decreasing order) were anal rape. forced fellatio. vaginal rape, and foreign object penetration. Sixty-seven percent of the offenders forced one or more victims to engage in at least three of these activities. Forty-three percent of the offenders experienced sexual dysfunction during their offenses. including retarded ejaculation (11). premature ejaculation (one). and conditional ejaculation (one). In addition to the sexual acts listed in Table 2. small numbers of offenders engaged in other sexual acts with their victims. including inserting a finger into the vagina or anus (three): performing cunnilingus on the victim (two): forcing the victim to masturbate self or offender (two): forcing two victims to engage in sexual activity with one another (two): forcing the victim to drink urine or eat feces (two): urinating on the victim (one): penetrating the rectum with a fist (1); and postmortem intercourse (one).

The demeanor of the offenders during the commission of offenses could be ascertained from victims' statements, recordings made by the offender. or interviews in a sufficient number of cases to know that at least 87 percent had an unemotional. detached affect. Twenty-three percent instructed their victims to utter particular words during the offense, sometimes from written scripts. Such forced utterances included descriptions of the sexual acts occurring. self-deprecating phrases, and role playing of third parties.

One hundred percent of the offenders intentionally tortured their victims, mostly with extreme and obvious methods as listed in Table 3. To illustrate the extremity of torture used by these 30 men, we cite only the two least offensive examples: The first was a man who bound and suspended his daughter with ropes in painful positions and with painfully tight bindings from ages two to eight while he photographed her. The second was a man who forced his captive rape victim to watch as he raped and killed a second woman. Individual of-

Table 3
Methods of Physical Torture Used by Sexually Sadistic Criminals

Method of Torture	n	%
Instruments	8	26.7
Painful insertion of foreign objects	7	23.3
Beating	6	20.0
Biting	5	16.7
Whipping	5	16.7
Painful bondage	5	16.7
Electrical shock	4	13.3
Twisting breasts until victim unconscious	4	13.3
Asphyxiation until victim unconscious	4	13.3
Burning	3	10.0
Other*	7	23.3

* Other methods of torture included amputation (two). threatening with snakes (two). cutting (one). pulling out hair (one). insertion of glass rod in male urethra (one). injection (one), and submersion (one).

fenders often used multiple means of torture. Psychological torment through humiliation, degradation, and threats was often combined with physical methods of torture to heighten the victim's fear. The importance to the offender of the victim's terror is underscored by the caution taken by several offenders to insure that their victims retained consciousness while being tortured and the resuscitation of near-dead victims by two offenders in order that they might cause additional suffering before their victims died.

Twenty-two (73%) of the 30 men were known to have murdered; together they had 187 known murder victims. Five men were responsible for 122 of the known murders, and the other 17 known murderers killed 65 known victims. The total number of murders committed by the 22 known killers is suspected to be more than 300. Seventeen of the men (57% of offenders and 73% of murderers) were known to have been serial killers,[16,17] having murdered three or more victims in separate incidents. (Three other murderers were suspected of serial killings that could not be proved.) All but two of the murderers' concealed at least one of their victims' corpses. This was not consistent behavior, however, as some victims were left where they would be seen by intimates or easily found, and others were disposed of carelessly.

The 187 known murder victims died from a variety of causes. Cause of death could be established for 130 cases (see Table 4). The most striking difference between the causes of death in these

Table 4
Cause of Death of 130 Murder Victims

Cause of Death	n	%
Ligature strangulation	42*	32.3
Manual strangulation	34†	26.1
Gunshot wounds	32‡	24.6
Cutting and stabbing wounds	13	10.0
Blunt force trauma	4	3.1
Hanging	2	1.5
Suffocation	1	0.8
Torture	1	0.8
Exposure	1	0.8

* One man was responsible for 32 of these murders.
† One man was responsible for 25 of these murders.
‡ One man was responsible for 17 of these murders.

murders and the distribution of causes of death among murder victims generally is the relatively high proportion of asphyxial causes of death (61%), and the relatively low proportion of gunshot wounds (25%). Serial killers were inconsistent in the means by which they killed their multiple victims, with the exception of one man who manually strangled all 25 of his murder victims and one man who shot all 17 of his murder victims. Although beatings caused death in only three percent of the murders, 60 percent of the offenders beat their victims. Cause of death could not be determined for victims whose bodies were destroyed by fire (17), decomposed (28), or skeletonized (7); and of the three men responsible for these murders, two denied involvement in the crime and one committed suicide after arrest and before questioning. (For five victims, cause of death data were missing.)

Fifty-three percent of the offenders recorded at least one offense in writings, drawings, photographs, audio tapes, or videotapes. The amount of detail in such recordings varied from making an en-

The Sexually Sadistic Criminal

crypted notation on a calendar to a videotape of torture or a book-length autobiography detailing every nuance of the crimes. Several offenders maintained extensive records of their offenses, including collections of photographs of the victims (13%), collections of audio tapes of the crimes (7%), and collections of videotapes of the crimes (7%). Forty percent of the offenders kept one or more personal items belonging to the victim (undergarments, shoes, jewelry, wallets, driver's license, or other identification), which were often found hidden among the mementos of the offender.

Victim Characteristics Ninety-seven percent of the offenders victimized only whites. The sole black offender victimized only whites, and one white offender victimized both whites and blacks. Eighty-three percent of the offenders focused their crimes primarily on strangers. Seventy-three percent victimized only females, 17 percent only males, and 10 percent both females and males. Fifty-seven percent victimized only adults, and 17 percent victimized only children. It is noteworthy that 43 percent of the offenders victimized one or more children.

In only five (17%) of the 30 cases was there some evident resemblance between the victims chosen and someone of psychological significance in the offender's life. For example, one man who killed at least two women had been married to a woman with long black hair. His victims had dark hair, and he referred to his actions with them as "practice" for what he would do when he gained control over his former wife. He

prepared written scripts for his victims that echoed the words he had forced his former wife to utter during tape-recorded sessions in which he brutalized her.

Discussion

Although the sexually sadistic offenders studied were responsible for large numbers of serious crimes, we must caution that there are far larger numbers of sexual sadists who commit less extreme crimes and thus would not have been referred to the National Center for the Analysis of Violent Crime. While these data may not be generalizable to the entire class of sexually sadistic criminals, they provide insight into a class of offenders who are the most proficient and destructive of all sexual criminals. These cases are not extreme in the severity of their sexual sadism but in the severity of their criminality. If these are "terminal" sexual sadists whose crimes are particularly extreme, we believe they differ from less destructive sexual sadists not in the "severity" of the paraphilia, but in the character pathology that permits them such uninhibited expression of their sexual desires.

The clinician evaluating someone who may suffer from sexual sadism must be able to elicit an adequate history without undue shock or disbelief. It is not within the customary clinical repertoire to inquire as to the particular forms of torture that the interviewee finds most appealing or the subject of the most arousing fantasies, yet questions about such taboo areas of inquiry are necessary if the interviewer hopes to elicit the relevant diagnostic information. Such inquiries are relevant not only to forensic assessments of persons who have committed sexually sadistic offenses, but also in taking a sexual history from anyone who has given evidence of paraphilic patterns of arousal. Even the best of interviews, however, will fail to elicit the complete truth in most cases. Where there is reason to suspect sexual sadism, the clinician would also be wise to seek information from sources other than the interviewee, such as the sources on which this article is based.

A few of the observations reported here require some explanation. The meaning of excessive driving was aptly captured by one man who described the "sense of freedom" "to go where I want, when I want, with no one telling me what to do." Fascination with police activities and paraphernalia reflects the offenders' fantasies of and strivings for power. Sexual partners are shared with others as a means of humiliation. Victims are held captive for ready access, to reshape their behavior through "training," and to prolong their suffering. Victims are told what to say during assaults in order to recreate previously fantasized scenarios with idealized partners. Victims' corpses are concealed—in contrast to the body being left at the death scene as occurs in most homicides—to reduce the likelihood of rapid discovery and therefore of apprehension. Personal items belonging to victims are kept as trophies of the offenders' "conquests" or as stimuli to facilitate arousing recollections. Strangers are selected as victims

to reduce the odds of their being linked to the offender.

One particularly intriguing observation is that larger proportions of these offenders committed forcible penetration of the anus and mouth than of the vagina. Although this might be thought an artifact of the number of male victims, it remains true even among those whose victims were all females. Among the possible explanations for this observation are that the high proportion of offenders with a history of homosexual activity in adulthood predisposes to anal and oral sexual contact and that anal and oral penetration are intended to be more degrading to victims than vaginal penetration.

One of the most important findings from this study is that 53 percent of sexually sadistic offenders produced and retained records of their crimes. Although some have shared these records with crime partners, they are otherwise their most secret possessions, intended to be seen by no one else. These records—whether writings, drawings, photographs, or electronic recordings—are sources of unusual depth for understanding the offender, his fantasies, and his behavior.

Through the offenders' personal records, it is possible to uncover his secret world, otherwise hidden during interviews with mental health or law enforcement professionals. Although offenders sometimes are forthcoming about their criminal acts, they are rarely forthcoming about the pattern of sexual arousal that motivates or accompanies the crimes.

The Sexually Sadistic Criminal

The unemotional, detached affect of the offenders during their crimes contrasts dramatically with the emotionally intense crimes of so many other violent offenders, and is consistent with their highly methodical offenses. As one listens to the recordings of their crimes, one is struck by the deliberate manner in which the offender maintains a calm, instructional tone in the face of his victim's obvious and intense distress. Although anger sometimes surfaces, there is never a hint of any loss of control or dominance over the situation. We consider the unemotional, cold tone of the offenders during their crimes as evidence—if any more were needed—of their lack of empathy for their victims. This lack of empathy may reflect psychopathy, narcissism, an extraordinary capacity to dehumanize victims, or a combination of these.

Although systematic data were not collected on the features of narcissistic personality disorder in these men, we noted that all were interpersonally exploitive and many were grandiose, lacked empathy, responded to criticism with rage, and demanded a show of admiration from those victims they kept captive. These narcissistic features are related to the subjects' self-consciousness of their status as "super criminals." For example, one subject recently wrote one of the authors a demeaning letter criticizing the author's previous writings, bragging that someone is writing a book about him, and suggesting that with sufficient incentive he might be willing to share a few of his insights with the researcher. We have no basis for believing that sexual sadism is generally associated with narcissism; rather, it is the psychopathy of these subjects that is probably associated with narcissism. These observations are reminiscent of Leaff's opinion that "psychopathic personalities represent one form, a severe form, of a narcissistic personality structure."[18]

The men described herein engaged in crimes that are regarded as grotesque, bizarre, and horrible, yet not one was perceived as particularly odd by those who knew them well before their offenses. More importantly, none of the men received any psychiatric or psychological attention for their sexual sadism before the commission of their crimes, though many had been examined in connection with military discharge, incarcerations for earlier offenses, or for other purposes.

Their contacts with clinicians were strikingly ineffective, as illustrated by a few examples. One, at age 12, was taken to a physician by his mother because she had discovered that he was hanging himself (he was engaging in autoerotic asphyxiation[19]). The physician told her the boy would outgrow it, but he remained sexually attached to ropes as he strangled a series of three women. Another consulted a psychiatrist when he found that sexually sadistic rapes were no longer gratifying and grew concerned at his thoughts of adding murder to his repertoire. As he described his fantasies of murder, his elderly psychiatrist fell asleep; the offender walked out of the session, never to return. Another who had been arrested for enticing young boys to his home to photograph them as they defecated and held knives to one another using ketchup or red ink to simulate wounds was committed to a state hospital; he eloped, murdering one young boy and wounding another. In yet another case a psychologist asked the offender to write out his most bizarre fantasies as part of psychotherapy. The offender wrote detailed descriptions of his actual crimes, but the therapist did not recognize that these were recollections, not fantasies. Other cases met with equal failure.

Even more disturbing than the treatment failures are the failures of ordinary personal security measures to prevent their crimes and the failures of ordinary police methods to capture the offenders after the first offense. As one offender responded when asked how a woman could prevent being raped:

> [T]here's a lot of steps you can take to help eliminate the average criminal [who is] just spontaneous and reckless and careless.... If somebody wants somebody bad enough ... it's nearly impossible [to prevent].... They could have the best security in the world. They could have guards and dogs and everything else. But if you have the time and the patience, the opportunity is going to arise when you can hit somebody.

Conclusions

We have described the characteristics of 30 sexually sadistic criminals, their offenses, and their victims, including some of the details of the offenses that constitute patterned behaviors to be expected in this offender group. It is important to recognize that the noncriminal characteristics described in this population each occur among persons who are neither sexually sadistic nor

criminal. We do not suggest, for example, that the characteristics given in Table 1 are predictive of sexual sadism. On the contrary, we would maintain that the necessary condition for a diagnosis of sexual sadism is the presence of sexually arousing fantasies about the kinds of behavior in which this sample of offenders actually engaged. When such fantasies are identified, for example when a patient volunteers bondage fantasies or when an investigator learns of a subject's drawings of torture, the possibility of sexual sadism should be considered and explored by further inquiry into the other behaviors described here.

The factors associated with sexual sadism have not previously been described in sufficient detail to permit universal recognition of this pattern of behavior by clinicians or by law enforcement officials. Among clinicians, it has not become sufficiently common to take a history of paraphilic patterns of sexual arousal, to ask patients' consent to obtain police records, or to offer behavior therapy or antiandrogens to known paraphiles. Among police investigators, it has not become sufficiently common to recognize the distinction between sexually sadistic offenses and other brutal crimes or to anticipate the importance of written records, drawings, audio tapes, videotapes, and souvenirs of offenses when applying for and executing search warrants in such cases.

Because this was an exploratory, uncontrolled study of a highly selected group of offenders, it would be inappropriate to draw conclusions about sexual sadists in general from the data reported

The Sexually Sadistic Criminal

here. We would, however, recommend that researchers studying more representative populations of sexual sadists and with access to comparable data on normal and criminal control subjects address the following questions:

1. Are parental infidelity or divorce or a history of physical or sexual abuse during childhood predisposing factors for sexual sadism even among nonoffenders?

2. Are nonsadistic paraphilic activities, adult homosexual experiences, sharing of sexual partners with others, excessive driving, interest in police activities and paraphernalia, and collecting pornography, bondage paraphernalia, weapons, or detective magazines associated with sexual sadism even among nonoffenders?

3. Are sexual dysfunction, minor sexual offenses, and incestuous involvement with their own children complications of sexual sadism even among those sexual sadists who do not commit violent offenses involving torture?

Each of these features was observed among the 30 men on whom this report is based, but it is not possible to determine from the data reported here which features are associated with sexual sadism and which are associated with criminality or character pathology. Drug abuse, for example, is known to be associated with criminality[20,21] and may have no independent association with sexual sadism. Nonsadistic paraphilias, on the other hand, are known to be associated with sexual sadism[22] and may have no independent association with criminality.

Our data do allow us to draw conclusions about the features of crimes by the most dangerous sexually sadistic offenders, which is the group fairly represented by the 30 men studied. The hallmark of their offenses is intentional torture of the victim to sexually arouse the offender. We conclude that such offenders tend to commit crimes that often but not invariably involve the following features: selection of strangers as victims; advance selection of a location to which the victim is taken; participation of a partner; careful planning (including impersonating a police officer); use of a pretext in approaching victims; beating victims; keeping a victim captive; binding, blindfolding, or gagging a victim; sexual bondage of a victim; anal rape, forced fellatio, vaginal rape, foreign object penetration; performing multiple sexual acts with victims; telling victims to speak particular words in a degrading manner; intentional torture; murder or serial killings (most often by strangulation); concealing victims' corpses; recording offenses; and keeping personal items belonging to victims.

Acknowledgments

In this research, Dr. Dietz was supported by the Sesquicentennial Associateship Program of the Center for Advanced Studies, University of Virginia. The authors are grateful to Herbert C. Thomas, M.A., of the University of Virginia School of Law for invaluable research assistance, to the contributors of case files from law enforcement agencies throughout the United states, and to those mental health professionals and attorneys who facilitated access to subjects for interviews.

References

1. von Krafft-Ebing R: Psychopathia Sexualis: A Medico-Forensic Study. Translated by Klaf FS. New York, Stein and Day, 1965
2. Stekel W: Sadism and Masochism: The Psychology of Hatred and Cruelty. Translated

by Brink L. New York, Horace Liveright, 1929

3. Macdonald JM: The Murderer and His Victim. Springfield, IL, Charles C Thomas, 1961

4. Macdonald JM: Rape: Offenders and Their Victims. Springfield, IL, Charles C Thomas, 1971

5. Groth AN: Men Who Rape: The Psychology of the Offender. New York, Plenum, 1979

6. Dietz PE: Sex offenses: behavioral aspects, in Encyclopedia of crime and Justice. Edited by Kadish SH. New York, Free Press, 1983, pp 1485–93

7. MacCulloch MJ, Snowden PR, Wood PJW, Mills HE: Sadistic fantasy, sadistic behaviour and offending. Br J Psychiatry 1983; 143:20–9

8. Rada RT: Sexual psychopathology: historical survey and basic concepts, in Clinical Aspects of the Rapist. Edited by Rada RT. New York, Grune and Stratton, 1978, pp 1–19

9. Hazelwood RR, Douglas JE: The lust murderer. FBI Law Enforcement Bull 49(4):18–22, Apr 1980

10. Roessner BT: President extols "war on crime." The Hartford Courant, June 21, 1984, pp A1, A14

11. Depue RL: An American response to an era of violence. FBI Law Enforcement Bull 55(12):2–5, 1986

12. Depue RL: Following the medical model. 1988 Annual Report. Quantico, VA, National Center for the Analysis of Violent Crime, FBI Academy, 1989

13. American Psychiatric Association: Diagnostic and Statistical Manual of Mental Disorders (ed 3), revised. Washington, DC, American Psychiatric Association, 1987

14. Dietz PE, Harry B, Hazelwood RR: Detective magazines: pornography for the sexual sadist? J Forensic Sci 31:197–211, 1986

15. Hazelwood RR: The behavior-oriented interview of rape victims: the key to profiling. FBI Law Enforcement Bull 52(9):8–15, Sep 1983

16. Dietz PE: Mass, serial, and sensational homicides. Bull NY Acad Med 62:477–91, 1986

17. Dietz PE: Patterns in human violence, in Psychiatric Update: American Psychiatric Association Annual Review. Edited by Hales RE, Frances AJ. Washington, DC, American Psychiatric Press, 6:465–90, 1987

18. Leaff LA: The antisocial personality: psychodynamic implications, in The Psychopath: A Comprehensive Study of Antisocial Disorders and Behaviors. Edited by Reid WH. New York, Brunner/Mazel, 1978, pp 79–117

19. Hazelwood RR, Dietz PE, Burgess AW: Autoerotic Fatalities. Lexington, MA, Lexington Books, 1983

20. Bureau of Justice Statistics: Prisoners and Drugs. Washington, DC, US Department of Justice, 1983

21. Guze SB, Goodwin DW, Crane JB: Criminality and psychiatric disorders. Arch Gen Psychiatry 20:583–91, 1969

22. Abel GG, Becker JV, Cunningham-Rathner J, et al: Multiple paraphilic diagnoses among sex offenders. Unpublished manuscript, Behavioral Medicine Institute, Atlanta, Georgia

Part V
Psychological Perspectives

[18]

A STUDY OF WILLIAM HEIRENS

FOSTER KENNEDY,[1] M.D., HARRY R. HOFFMAN,[2] M.D., AND
WILLIAM H. HAINES,[3] M.D.

During the year 1945 and early in 1946 the citizens of Chicago were horrified by newspaper reports of three atrocious murders and the beating of a nurse. All the murders followed a pattern, in that they occurred in small apartments and no evidence of burglary or other apparent motivation was found. In one apartment, in which an ex-Wave was brutally killed, appeared in lip stick on the wall, "For heaven's sake catch me before I kill more; I cannot control myself." In another, a child of six years was kidnapped and her body dismembered and thrown into various sewers and drains. A ransom note was written and delivered to her parents. In addition, hundreds of burglaries were reported in a residential area in the north side of Chicago.

On June 26, 1946, a young man was intercepted after an attempt at burglary. In endeavoring to make his getaway he was hit on the head with a flower pot and finally subdued by a policeman off duty, who was returning from a nearby bathing beach. A routine arrest followed, until an alert police official noticed the similarity of a curve flourish in his signature and the ransom note. By this time several days had elapsed and no formal charge had been booked against the youth. He was, it developed, a 17-year-old University of Chicago student. He was being held in the hospital of the House of Correction in Chicago, suffering from scalp wounds. Here he refused to answer questions, and mimicked his questioners. Saturday afternoon, June 29, 1946, he was seen by Drs. Francis J. Gerty and William H. Haines for an opinion of his mental status. It was thought that he was malingering. Another interview was arranged and he was examined the same night by Drs. Roy R. Grinker and William H.

Haines, at which time a conclusion was reached that he was malingering. During the following week he made a full confession to his attorneys regarding the atrocities and brutal murders.

In examining his record it was found that he had been arrested for burglary at the ages of 13 and 15. Finger prints were not taken because he was held by the Juvenile Court authorities. He was also arrested for carrying a gun, while returning from rifle practice at the university. This arrest occurred after the perpetration of the atrocities. The case was dismissed and he was told to register his gun.

While in jail awaiting trial, three notes he had written were intercepted. In one of these he denied all the crimes, and in the others—to his parents—he admitted the burglaries.

A psychiatric examination was ordered by the court before trial, at the request of his attorneys and the state's attorney. This commission consisted of Dr. Harry R. Hoffman, state alienist and director of the Neuropsychiatric Institute; Dr. William H. Haines, director of the Behavior Clinic of the Criminal Court of Cook County, and a third member to be from outside the State of Illinois. Dr. Foster Kennedy, director of the neurological service at Bellevue Hospital in New York City and ex-president of the American Neurological Association, was selected. Dr. Francis J. Gerty, head of the department of Psychiatry at the University of Illinois, and Dr. Francis J. Braceland, ex-chief of Psychiatry in the Navy and now at Mayo Clinic in Rochester, Minn., were also contacted, but were unable to serve because of other commitments.

The Supreme Court in Illinois had handed down opinions regarding the mental status of defendants at the time of going to trial, to wit: "BEFORE TRIAL.—He is not considered a lunatic or insane if he is capable of understanding the nature and object of the proceedings against him and if he rightly comprehends his own condition in reference

---

[1] Director Neurological Service, Bellevue Hospital, New York, N. Y.

[2] Director Neuropsychiatric Institute, Chicago, Ill.

[3] Director Behavior Clinic of the Criminal Court of Cook County, Chicago, Ill.

to such proceedings and has sufficient mind to conduct his defense in a rational or reasonable manner, although upon some other subjects his mind may be deranged or unsound." [4] The examiners were agreed in their opinion that the defendant was able to stand trial and submitted a joint report of 32 pages.[5] In this report to the court many of Heirens' answers were given verbatim. These have been condensed in this article to conserve space.

Report to the Court Dated September 3, 1946

William Heirens was examined pursuant to an order of the Honorable Harold G. Ward, Chief Justice of the Criminal Court of Cook County. This order was entered after a conference between the state's attorney and the counsel for the defense. We were asked to make a comprehensive report. To this end we were instructed to obtain all necessary expert advice, and we were provided by both prosecution and defense with all documents pertinent to the case in their possession.

This patient, in our opinion, is not suffering from any psychosis, nor is he mentally retarded: he has average intelligence. He has a deep sexual perversion and is emotionally insensitive and unstable. He has sufficient intelligence to understand the nature and object of the proceedings against him. He rightly comprehends his own position in regard to these proceedings and has sufficient mind to conduct his defense in a rational and reasonable manner. He has repeatedly stated to us that he has always been aware of the nature and purpose of his acts, which acts are the basis of the present proceedings against him.

Our study has included a careful survey by the social service department of the patient's early life and environment. We have interviewed the patient's parents and his roommate at the university. We have read the patient's statements to the state's attorney regarding his acts charged in the indictments

---

[4] Insanity and the Criminal, William H. Haines, M.D., and Harry R. Hoffman, M.D., Medical Clinics of North America, January 1945.

[5] To be published in full in the Journal of Criminal Law and Criminology.

against him. We have spent with him in close investigation, singly or together, with the presence of a stenographer and without, about 5 or 6 hours a day since the 12th of August. These investigations were conducted privately in the quiet of the chapel of the Cook County Jail.

In addition, he was subjected to a series of carefully selected and conducted psychological tests calculated to reveal trends, both conscious and underlying consciousness. The quality of intellect was carefully tested and he was found to have an intelligence quotient of 110, an average figure. The Rorschach test was used and failed to reveal any psychosis.

At the Illinois Neuropsychiatric Institute several electroencephalographic tracings were taken and found completely normal. X-ray studies of skull and spinal column were normal. The basal metabolic rate was normal. A complete blood study, insulin tolerance and urine test proved normal. The spinal fluid was normal, as were also the Wassermann and Kahn tests of the blood.

We have examined his notebooks made during the past three years. We have studied the post-mortem reports of the murders.

Social History

The patient is a 17½-year-old white boy, born in Evanston, Ill., of native-born parents of Luxemburg descent. The family history, as given, is negative as to insanity, epilepsy, alcoholism or mental defectiveness. The father grew up in a floral business with his father, and opened a store and conservatory of his own soon after marriage, flower arrangements being his specialty. The family occupied a flat in connection with the store. With the depression, the business failed and although several attempts were made to reestablish themselves in different locations, none was successful. After a period of irregular employment, the father secured work on the police force of Carnegie Steel Company, about 8 years ago, and has now worked up to the position of special investigator. In addition, he works several evenings on the Lincolnwood Village police force. The mother has worked much of the time since marriage, both to supplement the income and because she enjoyed it, working in their own and other florist shops, in a bakery as a fancy pastry maker, and more recently designing and executing custom made clothes. The mother handles the family finances. The patient expressed some concern over his mother's work, feeling it was done to pay his school tuition, but she preferred to do so and employ someone to do the housecleaning, etc.

The patient is the elder of two brothers. Family religion is Roman Catholic. Early in the pregnancy with the patient, the mother feared she would miscarry. Labor was long (62 hours) and delivery difficult with high forceps employed. The patient weighed 8 pounds and 5 ounces and was 24 inches long at birth. Breast feedings were inadequate and extremely painful to the mother and were supplemented by bottle feedings almost from the beginning. Weaning from the breast was completed by age of one month. He presented a feeding problem from the beginning—he "vomited in a gush" after every feeding and was sickly and severely underweight for the first 3 months. Thereafter under different care and diet he began to gain weight. Teething presented no problem. The ages of walking and talking are unknown; the mother reports "the usual age." The mother reported that toilet training was completed early; after 8 months there was no nocturnal wetting and by one year, daytime bladder and bowel control had been established. No relapses were reported.

At 7 months while unattended he fell from his buggy to a cement basement area 12 feet below, injuring his head. He was not unconscious when his mother found him. At age 8 or 9 he fell from a trapeze and sustained a compound fracture of the bones of the right arm, necessitating an open reduction. When about 12, he fell down some cement stairs at school, cutting his head over the eye. Patient fainted then. At the age of 8, he had a tonsillectomy with severe hemorrhage and some complications. He also had chicken pox and measles as a child. In the summer of 1942 and again in the spring of 1946, he complained of severe headaches. Otherwise the health history is negative.

He was a solitary child and youth, sensitive but difficult to know. Apparently no one ever had a close or confidential relationship with him. Certainly his parents did not. As a child he was with his brother a good deal

and had to fight his battles for him. He never had any real friends and preferred to be alone. In the 7th and 8th grades excessive day dreaming was reported. He had some mechanical interests and considerable skill, according to the parents, repairing electric motors, repairing or making radios from old parts. He was interested in collecting and recently had a considerable coin collection. Very early he was eager to earn his own money—worked delivering orders for a food store the summer he was 12, delivered for a liquor store the summer he was 14, and worked in the steel mills with his father the summers of 1944 and 1945. He was very frugal with his money, spent little on himself, just saved it. His only "splurge" was in gifts for the family, buying expensive presents out of proportion to his earnings. Very early he learned not to whimper or cry when hurt and could endure considerable physical pain.

He attended public school kindergarten for a few months at age 5 and entered parochial school at 6. He attended three parochial elementary schools, as the family moved, and graduated from 8th grade (receiving his diploma *in absentia* since he was then in the Juvenile Detention Home) at age of 13.

In June, 1942, at the age of 13, he was first apprehended by the police trying to break into a basement storeroom. Subsequently he admitted 9 burglaries within the preceding 6 months. Following the juvenile court hearing, he was committed to Gibault School for Boys and remained there from July 5, 1942 to June 4, 1943. Except for an attempt to run home 3 weeks after commitment, he presented no discipline problem and exteriorly was a conformist according to report received. He was obedient and cooperative, with good attitude toward authority. He completed his first year of high school here with scholastic averages all in the 80's. He was quiet and serious, "definitely an introvert," and would often be found away from campus completely alone. He had few friends and preferred to be by himself. He was not interested in athletics; team games especially did not appeal to him. He expressed a good attitude toward religious obligations, frequently took Holy Communion, went to confession less regularly at school than

Serial Murder

lately. He did not want to know anyone intimately.

Two months after his return from Gibault, he was again arrested, charged with burglary. In Juvenile Court the case was heard before a visiting judge who acceded to the family's wishes. The patient was placed on probation to go to St. Bede's Academy at Peru, Illinois, where he remained from September, 1943 to May 27, 1945, but was at home for summer vacation in 1944 and 1945. He completed 2d and 3d years of high school there. This school report showed grades of "A" and "B" in all subjects for his sophomore year, from "A" to "F" (English) in junior year. His adjustment was good, no discipline problem, he had no confidential relationship with anyone and preferred to be alone. Probation was terminated January 19, 1945.

In September, 1945 he entered the University of Chicago, taking placement tests, remaining there until his apprehension during the summer quarter of 1946. His scholastic record there was average and below. He had many absences from academic and physical education classes. According to the mother, he was active in the Calvert Club (a Catholic organization, social and religious). He seemed to have at least a superficial relationship with a few students and finally began to have a few "dates" with girls, though with no close friends.

According to the parents, the patient never displayed any of the usual sexual curiosity as a child nor displayed any jealousy of his brother three years younger. No sex instructions were given by the parents. At the age of about 13, there was an incident of sex play which patient witnessed in the boys' toilet at school and reported to his mother, at which time he was warned about venereal disease. This was a few months before the first known burglary. The parents were unaware of his delinquencies until after he was apprehended, but since his earlier court appearance have been constantly fearful of a repetition, though trying to trust him.

Physical Examination.

The patient was carefully examined physically. He is a well built young man weighing 159 pounds. There were no deformities excepting a scar on right forearm, the result of a compound fracture when aged about 10. No evidence was found of any structural abnormality in the central, autonomic or peripheral nervous systems. The hands were moist and over-cold and without tremor. There was a remarkable reduction to the perception of pin pricks, however strong, as "pain." This was present all over the body with the exception of the glans penis. Sharp pin pricks inside the nose on the mucous membrane and the soles of the feet were denied as being painful and no motion of withdrawal was made there or elsewhere. This was also true as regards the mucous membrane of the lip, and the scrotum and body of the penis. A sharp needle could be pressed more than four millimeters under the nails without inducing pain or defense withdrawal movements. As the sensory examination proceeded, this "analgesic cloak" deepened in quality under suggestion, so that below a sharp circle round both arms level with the upper edge of the anterior wall of the armpits he became unable to feel pin prick as other than "not blunt." The corneal reflexes at first were greatly reduced, and at the close of this examination had disappeared so that it became possible to tap the eyeballs with a closed safety pin without his winking or giving any motor sign of sensation. Deep pain produced by pressure on calf muscles and Achilles tendons and the testes was also reduced. As regards his ability to perceive light touch, he missed two out of three stimulations in scattered distribution over the body. The perception of vibration and the other forms of sensation were normal. The visual fields were found to narrow progressively as the test continued, so that they became finally almost pin-point. This phenomenon is known as "a spiral" or "helicoid" visual field, and is a positive objective indication of profound hysteria.

This striking reduction of power to appreciate painful stimulation as such, together with its remarkable deepening as the result of suggestion, is to us a clear proof of the patient's hysterical personality.

The blood pressure, heart, lungs and abdomen were normal. He is powerfully built with fine muscular development; he excelled in wrestling.

Psychiatric Examination

The psychiatric interviews, to which allusion has already been made, consisted in

1947] F. KENNEDY, H. R. HOFFMAN AND W. A. HAINES 117

quiet, persistent questioning, while noting the answer and its emotional accompaniment. He was informed of his constitutional rights and in reply promised his full cooperation. His statements to the state's attorney are on record and indeed have been published. The patient was, of course, taken over every point of these. We shall try here not to repeat that information but to give enough of our great mass of material to display new evidence and new viewpoints on the dynamic forces at work in this patient.

We propose now to give as briefly as possible an account of the significant actions and emotional reactions of this patient insofar as they could be discovered. When quotation marks are used, the quotations will be patient's own words.

When aged 9, the patient began to be interested in "the feeling and color" and then "the stealing" of women's underclothing. He began to take these at first from clothes lines, then from basements, and later from strange houses, the doors of which he found open or ajar. Dresses or other articles of women's apparel made no appeal to him nor was he interested in the undergarments of his immediate family. Having secured a pair of women's panties or drawers, he would take it to a basement or home, put it on, experience excitement and sexual completion. Most garments he then threw away, some he replaced, and some he hoarded in his grandmother's attic.

We believed it important, if possible, by objective evidence to prove the truth of his statement of fetishism. An investigation brought to light, in the spot he had described, "a cardboard box" containing some 40 pairs of women's old, used panties or drawers, mostly made of rayon and brightly colored.

When 12 or 13 years of age, he secured the desired garments by going into houses through windows. This furnished more excitement. After three such expeditions, he took objects ("guns or money") other than underclothes; a change which was again an added stimulation. "It seemed sort of foolish to break in and not take anything." When he had thus changed his objective, the interest in underclothes largely evaporated and was replaced by the excitement experienced on "making an entrance" through the window. Often he would struggle against his desire to leave his room at night, but

when he did leave it was for the purpose of committing burglaries. He had sexual excitement or an erection at the sight of an open window at the place to be burglarized. Going through the window he had an emission. Later it took several entrances to produce the emission. If startled in the act of burglarizing he immediately killed, stating, "It was the noise that set me off, I believe. I must have been in a high tension and the least bit of noise would disturb me in that manner." In describing the disposal of the 6-year-old Degnan girl's body, he said, "It is just like a floor with holes in it. I've tried to look through the holes to see what is down below. There is not enough holes to find out" —referring to his memory. His phrase "sexual excitement" was expanded: "I nearly always have to urinate or have a bowel movement—it always preceded the urge; when I first noticed it, I was in the basement and I had a bowel movement." Often when sexual completion occurred in the entered room it was accompanied or preceded by defecation or urination, or both. He would leave the consequences in the room or would find them later in his own clothes. After an emission, he would always leave the entered house without taking anything with him. After assaulting Miss Peterson, the nurse, he had an orgasm and without striking her again he left and returned to his room at the university. He later returned to the Peterson apartment, administered first aid, and tried by telephone to get help for her.

After an emission was the only time he felt he had done wrong. We believe, from other statements, by this remark he meant that only immediately after orgasm did he suffer from the pang of conscience. This compelling "urge" had clearly a dynamic sexual origin, and the emptying of bowel and bladder was due to an overflow spinal reflex; so we asked him had he never relieved this tension by manual manipulation. On one occasion he indignantly denied even the attempt despite all his experience with underclothes, occurring as often as four times a week. Later he said he tried this method twice without success. In the same manner, he at first denied ever having attempted any sex play with girls. Two days later with one of his rare shows of emotion he said, looking much ashamed, that twice, later correcting himself to eight times, he had touched girls "on the breasts" and then pressed "on the leg." Always, having done this, he would immediately burst into tears and "be upset and unable to sleep." It should be noticed that no uncomfortable emotions followed either burglaries or murders. He forcibly denied ever having made any more intimate advances, except that he "kissed them" sometimes. "They wanted to kiss; I didn't."

It was clear that normal sex stimulation and experience were unpleasant, indeed "repulsive," to him, and these efforts afterward created in him a negative emotional state. He found them improper in the conduct of others; he never spoke of them except in condemnation, as for example of the young men in the university who had brought a girl into their rooms at night.

He was interested in books on sex and crime. "I read around the subject of masochism, fetishism, sadism, flagellation, also Kraft-Ebbing and dreams, some parts of Freud." At one time he said he could not read Freud because it was "dirty"—about sex. Asked which was most obnoxious, sex, burglaries or murder, he replied "sex and murder." When asked to choose between sex and murder, he nodded his head, then replied "murder." In observing the patient, he was noted not to nod his head in speaking. We believe that William Heirens nodded his head to indicate that subjectively he felt sex was worse than murder, but in verbalizing stated murder.

He felt masturbation was worse than carrying a loaded revolver or the act of burglary. However, he replied that he felt murder was worse than masturbation.

He felt he was just as "responsible as any for his burglaries." As for the murders, "Whether it is my imagination or not, I seem to be blaming everything on George. It seems so real."

The patient struggled often against the "urge" to go out and seek excitement: "I would just put my hand on the table, then the headache would get too strong and I thought if I could just get out it would help. I had to get into any old thing. When I got these urges I would take out plans and draw how to get into certain places. I would burn up the plans; sometimes they helped. I was playing a game with myself. I would draw up plans and then burn them or tear them up. I must have drawn about 500 plans on how to enter a house or rob a train or things of that sort."

In his room, as has been already said, the urge to go out was often ushered in by a desire to go to stool. Although he knew the urge to go out could be abolished by satisfying this desire, he often neglected to do so and, accepting the "urge," went out anyway. At no time did he, despite his struggling sometimes strongly and sometimes not at all, ever seek help from anyone. He told no one. The early peccadilloes in fetishism were confessed to the priest, but the burglaries and the murders never. He sought no help from the church, his family, medicine, nor even from a charlatan. "I'd no confidence that they would not have me arrested and also that they would help me." . . . . "On one occasion I took off my clothes and thought if I did that I would not be able to get out. I would get ready for bed. I resisted for about two hours. I tore sheets out of place and went into a sweat. My roommate came back from the Calvert Club, and he asked me what was wrong, and I told him I had been drinking. I had to give him some excuse. I told him to go outside until I could get things fixed up. I put on my clothes and went out. I told him I was going out for a walk. I went out and burglarized that night. . . . . I had locked my clothes in the closet and put the key in the washroom. I got in bed and then the urge came on. I just stayed in bed and tried to talk him (George) out of it, but it did not work. . . . . I did this about three times. It was about Christmas time once that I had locked the door and that time there were people out in the corridor. I did not want them to see me go out and I went out of the window into the gutter and went down the fire escape. At that time when I could come in there would be snow on my feet."

He denied masturbation or any sexual relationships.

A reference has been made earlier to a mysterious individual named "George," whom the patient invokes from time to time as having responsibility for the patient's crimes. Some excerpts follow from our conversation on this subject: "He was just a realization of mine. I just stuck him in for no good reason. Before he seemed real to me. At Gibault things were so vague when I went out on burglary, it seemed to me that George was doing it. He seemed to be real. I cannot introduce him to anybody but he is there." . . . . "Usually when I had to get out I would ask him where he was going. We would talk back and forth that way. He would say, down to the lake, and I would say, what are you going to do there? He said he would get some things. I would ask him why he was going and he said, because he wants to. It would be just that way. I would argue with him to stay and then I would get a headache. I would argue in every way possible with him but he always wanted to get out.". . . . "I don't want you to laugh. It seems so darn real to me. Previous to this, I had given the whole matter a name. I just had a faint memory of these things, as to temperature or color of things. When I would go out it would make no difference to me if I had a summer suit on with freezing weather. I could not feel any temperature. I gave it the name of George." . . . . "When I went out I had some vague ideas of what I would do. I took him as a benefactor for money or anything else I would take. If I did not throw the things away and have them in the morning. I would look them over and take out what I wanted and I attributed this to George. It was just a little game I was playing. . . . . I would write letters to myself. I would talk to him. When I wanted to get out he would ask me where I was going, why I was going out, and what time I would be back and things of that nature. I begged him to stay. I had a headache almost all the time I was doing that. I was just stimulated to get out. One of the letters I had written was to George M. S. I figured if I could send him to Mexico. . . . ." . . . . "I gave him a name after I came out of Gibault. He came into the picture before I started to burglarize in 1942. In the beginning I always tried to resist and after that I tried to talk to him, and later on developed writing to him. . . . . When I tried to resist him, I would get a headache. It seemed like my head was a balloon filled with water. When I would lay down it would fill the balloon and I would get

a pain. . . . . He wrote about burglary. He would say that the best way to burglarize was to go in windows. He would give names of people like Mike, Joe and Harry. . . . . Sometimes in the letters I would ask him for things I needed at school. I would ask him if I could borrow money from him. . . . . When this urge would come out, I would tell him there would be a letter in the drawer for him. Sometimes he would answer after I wrote and then when I would read it, it would all seem new to me. I don't remember writing the answer and would not know I had written what was written. . . . . I made a pact with George if I ever got caught through him that I would kill myself and kill him too. I thought that would scare him away but it never did. . . . . He has to be part of me. . . . ."

Asked, "In the last note you wrote, 'Catch me before I kill again; I cannot help myself,' what could you not help yourself from doing?" he answered, "From the murders. That was 'George' and I could not help what I was doing, and he was myself."

These conversations regarding "George," in our opinion, reveal a power for hysterical fantasy to be expected in a hysterical individual passing through long sustained emotional conflict. By hysteria we mean a condition produced by suggestion to an individual suffering from deep division in his emotional life. It is to be noted that in 1942 he went twice, just before George's invention, to see the movie, "Dr. Jekyll and Mr. Hyde," which "made a great impression" upon him. When asked, in his psychological examination, the name of his favorite movie, he said at once this title which was partially written down when he asked to change to, of all possible others, "Robin Hood." Only rarely did the patient for short periods lack insight into the true nature of the device he had constructed whereby he could account to himself for his actions, and at the same time enable him to continue doing them while he led otherwise an exemplary life and could continue his religious observances.

Suicide Talk

He made, after his arrest, several feeble, theatrical, puerile gestures toward suicide.

The original letters to his mother and father were given to us. These have been released to the daily press so we will not discuss them. He repeatedly stated he would commit suicide in order to do away with George. . . . . In the jail he collected cigarette stubs, aspirins, pennies and small pieces of soap which he repeatedly stated were his plans for suicide.

Leadership

There is in this young man an immense egocentricity. Despite his continuing failures to rule himself he has no anxiety, fears or lack of confidence in his abilities and powers. His reading revolves around the power principle: Nietzsche, Schopenhauer, and even Spinoza, of which he grasped nothing. Pictures of Hitler, Goering and Goebbels are in his scrap books and his favorite studies were a sketchy intellectual interest in "mass psychology." He writes in his notebook at school: "Just who am I? I begin to wonder after all I could be human as the rest are but to myself, I would laugh at such a thought. Oh these seem so much more superior. In plain words I think I'm a worm. It's from being a worm though, I like it: insignificant and obsolete. That's just what I need. Maybe if I'm all wrong in writing this. Probable I'll change my attitude soon. It's odd but I begin to like my habits now. Probably just a passing phase. I'll most likely hate myself when I do things disagreeable to myself. . . . . I wonder why I can't run the world. It seems only great men have that choice. It's funny but I don't understand why I haven't the same equal chance. I guess they probable know just where to start & I don't. Wouldn't it be great to have that much power. Men sacrifice their lives for it. There must be an easier and faster way to gain control. . . . . Why am I thinking these things. It's all nonsense. Probable never ever entered another mind. You've got a good imagination, Bill, but I doubt whether you'll get far with it. So far it's gotten you into trouble. Real trouble. Well, I guess that's life for you.

"Why the fish did I ever go out for football. I detest the game and yet I go in for the sport. That's some sign of you loosing your head. In about three years you'll probable end up in a coo-coo house. . . . .

"Whoever got the idea that I could do great things and so sent me to school. It's sure a mystery. Maybe if I come down to earth I'll learn sum'min. . . . .

"You god damned nincompoop. Why the hell do you live is all I can wonder. Your one of the most unworthy persons I've understood to be able to live. Your sure not following your golden rules for control. In fact you've been standing still for the last two weeks."

Great News 7:20 Sept. 26 '45

"I'm now shaking with excitement. My hopes and prayers have been answered in one of my biggest chances in life. If I can only use my chance to the best advantage. The University of Chicago has accepted me into its enrollment. This is my first chance at showing how good I am to society and I intend to show even better signs. Tonight I feel as if the world were mine. All I have to do now is pray, giving thanks and vowing to do my best as humanly possible."

"Plot VII

"Considering my present college status, considering my inability to control society, considering that I am loosing my moral code slightly; I hereby intend to change my whole way of living. Since I have devoted more time to psychology it should be easy. My plan described in this plot should be carried out fully. I shall attack human nature to my fullest extent."

The patient, as has been seen, had no emotional disturbance whatsoever after the completion of each of three murders. After the Brown murder "The dog barked and the lady started hollering. She had on a night gown. She jumped up and hollered. Then I took the knife and stabbed her—through the throat—just to keep her quiet. Going in I had an erection. When I realized what was going on I was in the living room. The knife was at the end of the bed. I took the knife out real quickly and washed it off." Asked if he read about the act he replied, "Yes, just like anything else in the paper. It did not bother me, no remorse—I read just the beginning; then I got tired."

After the Ross murder: "She screamed— I just stabbed her once. I went to a show downtown. The next day I went back to work." Asked if it bothered him he replied, "No." Asked, "Do you feel you have done wrong now?" referring to the three murders, he replied, "I do, yes—I'm in here—but I don't feel anything about the whole matter. I never did."

Laboratory Reports

The laboratory reports of the various tests taken at the Illinois Neuropsychiatric Institute are as follows: The basal metabolism rate was − 10%, at which time the pulse was 80 and the blood pressure 125/80. The urine examination revealed a PH of 6 with no sugar or albumin, cells or casts. The blood pressure revealed a hemoglobin of 16.6 gm.; the color index was .89; the red cells were 5,690,000; the white cells were 5,650. The differential count revealed 27% lymphocytes, 7% monocytes, 66% neutrocytes. The blood serology was negative in the Kahn and Wassermann tests. The insulin tolerance test is reported within normal limits. The report of the electroencephalogram is as follows: "Low voltage electroencephalogram with some 9-11 per second activity. No focal abnormality. No seizure discharges. Big build-up with over-ventilation. Normal EEG for age. No evidence of damage or epileptiform activity in the accessible cortex." The spinal serology was normal. An x-ray of the skull reveals a skull of normal configuration and density. The vascular markings are normal. The pineal body is not calcified. The sella turcica is normal in size and configuration. There is no evidence of fracture or other pathology. The frontal sinuses are heavily calcified, though reasonably well pneumatized. The impression is a normal skull. X-rays of the lateral, anterior and posterior positions of the spine revealed no evidence of trauma or disease in the cervical, thoracic or lumbar spine. The flat plate of the abdomen revealed no foreign bodies.

Psychologist's Report

William Heirens was submitted to a series of carefully selected and conducted psychological tests, calculated to reveal trends, both conscious and underlying consciousness.

The quality of intellect was carefully tested and he was found to have an intelligence quotient of 110—an average figure. He was cooperative, readily understood instructions, attempted all items offered, and answered questions freely.

On none of the psychological tests was there any indication of a psychosis or of malingering.

On personality questionnaires he was found to be outgoing and dominant with a lack of self-consciousness or feelings of inferiority. It must be remembered, however, that these questionnaires represent the subject's own evaluation of himself and may not necessarily conform with his actual behavior.

An evaluation of all the psychological techniques used, indicated a definite emotional insensitivity and instability severe enough to be considered abnormal, as well as a blunting of moral concepts.

The majority of tests tend to suggest hysteria.

We regret the lengthiness of this report; it represents, however, only a fraction of our total material. We believe that it conveys the reasons for the opinion expressed at the beginning of our statement; that William Heirens is not suffering from any psychosis nor mental retardation; that he has a deep sexual perversion and is as emotionally insensitive within, as he is incapable of feeling pain without. He is unstable, and hysterically unpredictable, and most of his actions can be swayed from time to time by the suggestions coming from his environment.

Legal Disposition

On September 4, 1946 William Heirens was arraigned in the Criminal Court of Cook County on Indictments 46-1465 to 46-1493 inclusive, and 46-1593, 46-1594 and 46-1654. He pleaded guilty to thirty of the charges and on September 5, 1946 received sentences on 24 burglaries of 1-year to life, to run concurrently; on 3 murders, natural life, to run consecutively; 1 robbery, 1-20 years to run consecutively; 1 burglary, 1-year to life to run consecutively; 1 assault to commit murder, 1-14 years to run consecutively. He was delivered to the Department of Public Safety of the State of Illinois at Stateville, Illinois on September 6, 1946.

[19]

The International Journal of Clinical and Experimental Hypnosis
1984, Vol. XXXII, No. 2, 67-101

THE BIANCHI (L.A. HILLSIDE STRANGLER) CASE: SOCIOPATH OR MULTIPLE PERSONALITY?[1]

JOHN G. WATKINS[2]

University of Montana, Missoula

Abstract: The case of Kenneth Bianchi (the Los Angeles "Hillside Strangler") has been controversial ever since he was first arrested in January, 1979. This contributor saw Bianchi as a consultant on March 21st and 22nd, 1979. Under hypnosis, he manifested what appeared to be a multiple personality. An underlying personality, "Steve," whose existence was apparently unknown to Bianchi, claimed responsibility for the 2 murders in Bellingham and those in Los Angeles. As a consequence, the court appointed 5 other consultants to examine the defendant. On April 20, 1979, I activated the Steve personality without a hypnotic induction. It described many murders in Los Angeles, indicating which ones he (Steve) had done and which ones Bianchi's cousin (Angelo Buono) did. The major personality (Ken) appeared to be amnesic to all this. 2 additional "personalities" were elicited by Martin Orne, another consultant. However, Orne would not accept the diagnosis of multiple personality. He diagnosed Bianchi as an "Antisocial Personality" (Sociopath) and claimed that he was a clever malingerer. He also asserted that Bianchi had never been hypnotized. The evidence, Rorschach tests, intelligence tests, handwriting samples, art creations, plus recorded sessions by Watkins, Orne and others, are analyzed. This writer concludes that the diagnosis of multiple personality is strongly supported.

> If only there were evil people somewhere insidiously committing evil deeds, and it were necessary only to separate them from the rest of us and destroy them. But the line dividing good and evil cuts through the heart of every human being. And who is willing to destroy a piece of his own heart [p. 168]?
>
> From *The Gulag Archipelago* (Solzhenitsyn, 1973)

In late March, 1979, I was asked to go to Bellingham, Washington to examine a man charged with murdering two college girls some 2 months earlier. The circumstantial evidence against Bianchi was conclusive, and there was no doubt that he had perpetrated the crimes. However, he not only insisted that he was innocent, but refused to allow his attorney to plead an insanity defense. He claimed that on the night of the killings he was at his office (where he served as a security guard). The next thing he knew was finding himself near Fairhaven Park on the other side of town 2 hours later. He also reported having had frequent blanking-out episodes in his life. His attorney, Mr. Dean Brett, asked me to see if I could

Manuscript submitted June 25, 1982; final revision received September 18, 1983.

[1]An earlier version of this paper was presented in E. E. Levitt (Chm.), A case of multiple personality? An invited symposium presented at the 32nd annual meeting of the Society for Clinical and Experimental Hypnosis, Chicago, October 1980.

[2]Reprint requests should be addressed to John G. Watkins, Ph.D., Department of Psychology, University of Montana, Missoula, MT 59801.

recover his memories for the night of the killings through hypnosis—and perhaps during other such amnesic episodes.[3]

I found Kenneth Bianchi to be a pleasant, mild young man who seemed to be earnestly seeking to understand what had happened and why he was in jail charged with two murders. In describing his childhood, he stated that he had always thought well of his mother ("I would have fought anyone who said anything against her."), but that he had recently been shown medical records which had brought many doubts to his mind. Reports of his many visits to physicians, school counselors, social workers and examining psychologists portrayed his mother as having been dominating, overconcerned, trotting him from one clinic to another for his "nervous" problems (petit mal, allergies, tic, incontinence, face twitching, many phobias), and refusing to accept psychiatric opinions of an emotional basis to his symptoms. She was also reported to have been both seductive (showing him nude pictures) and cruel (punishing him by holding his hand over a stove burner and beating him with a belt).

I spent an hour building a relationship and getting acquainted with his life. He lived with a common-law wife with whom he had a small child. She reported that he was a good husband and father.

My first concern was that he might be a very clever sociopath, and that I was being "conned." Both in the practice of psychotherapy for some 33 years (Army, Veterans Administration, and private) and as Consulting Psychologist for the Montana State Prison for 12 years, I had examined and treated many sociopaths — the tough, aggressive, violent types and the smooth, manipulative, conniving types. Kenneth Bianchi did not seem to fit any of these. He interacted quite normally, admitted weaknesses ("I lie at times."), but unlike most offenders I had examined showed little interest in what might happen to him at the hands of the law. He reported some nightmare dreams and seemed worried about his "self," especially his amnesic episodes. He said that he had been afraid to seek psychiatric help. Not once did he show any concern for his legal fate, only what was happening to him internally.

The *DSM-III* (American Psychiatric Association, 1980) lists the criteria for diagnosis of a sociopath (currently termed "Antisocial Personality Disorder") as follows:

> a history of continuous and chronic antisocial behavior in which the rights of others are violated, persistence into adult life of a pattern of antisocial behavior that began before the age of 15, and failure to sustain good job performance over a period of several years. . . .
>
> Lying, stealing, fighting, truancy, and resisting authority are typical childhood signs. In adolescence, unusually early or aggressive sexual behavior, excessive

[3]A transcript of the videotaped clinical examination which took place in March and April of 1979 has been deposited with the National Auxiliary Publications Service (NAPS). For 137 pages, order Document No. 04180 from NAPS c/o Microfiche Publications, P. O. Box 3513, Grand Central Station, New York, NY 10163. Remit in advance in U.S. funds only, $48.85 for photocopies or $4.00 for microfiche, and make checks payable to Microfiche Publications — NAPS. Outside the United States and Canada, add postage of $18.20 for photocopies, $1.50 for microfiche postage.

drinking, and use of illicit drugs are frequent. In adulthood, these kinds of behavior continue, with the addition of inability to sustain consistent work performance or to function as a responsible parent and failure to accept social norms with respect to lawful behavior [pp. 317-318].

Except for the present crimes with which he was charged, almost none of these characterized his childhood, his adolescence, his jobs, or behavior as a husband and father. His grades were poor, and he did miss a great deal of school, but more from illnesses than from truancy. He admitted to occasional lying, but his high school days were normal, his job performance acceptable to his employers, and there was not one record of prior arrest or childhood crime, minor or major.

For such a diagnosis the *DSM-III* requires that, not only must there be evidence that it began before the age of 15, but that the pattern of continuous antisocial behavior must be maintained "with no intervening period of at least five years without antisocial behavior between age 15 and the present time . . . [p. 321]." In fact, as a child Kenneth was overly socialized and conforming.[4] But if Bianchi was not a sociopath, then what

[4] The *DSM-III* specifically states that, "By definition the disorder begins before the age of 15 [p. 318]," and that the first symptoms in males "are usually obvious in early childhood [p. 318]." One must search with a magnifying glass to meet even the minimal "history" of three or more of the following [p. 320]" before the age of 15 required for such a diagnosis:

Truancy. No evidence. Ken's mother kept him out of school frequently for health reasons.

Expulsion or suspension from school for misbehavior. Negative.

Delinquency (arrested or referred to juvenile court because of behavior). Negative.

Running away from home overnight at least twice while living in parental home. Negative.

Persistent lying. Some evidence here. He did lie at times. However, reports from school did not stress "lying." Medical examiners also did not note this behavior, nor did the social work examiners. Most of the accusations of lying were made by his mother who was, herself, obsessed with the concept stating that, "I have never lied." She would beat him for "lying." Over and over in Ken's evaluations the mother was described as: "deeply disturbed," "probably much more the real problem than Kenneth," "preoccupied with the sex life of Kenneth," "not capable of cooperating with anyone in really treating the basic problem — herself," and having "apparent paranoid trends." Lying would be a normal defense for a child trying to cope with "smothering," cruel punishment, and pressures to get him to make accusations against the doctors.

Repeated drunkenness or substance abuse. Negative.

Thefts. Very little evidence before age 15. Many thefts after 19 when apparently the dissociation of Steve and Billy became overt.

Vandalism. An isolated instance or two of being with a group of boys who planned some violence.

School grades markedly below expectations in relation to estimated or known IQ. Ken's tested IQ prior to age 15 was 106 to 110, slightly above average. His grades were poor to mediocre, but one wonders what can be expected of a child hauled from one clinic to another, burdened by recorded physical and psychosomatic disabilities and kept out of school for extended periods by a "seriously disturbed" mother.

Chronic violations of rules at home and/or at school. Few reports of school "violations." Most of such claims were by the mother.

Initiation of fights. Negative. Quite the opposite. He avoided fights. His mother often kept him out of school as she reports "to avoid the taunts and jibes of his classmates" for wetting his pants.

All in all, the picture is that of an abused, neurotic child, shy, afflicted with enuresis, tics, fainting spells and a number of physical and psychosomatic symptoms, but not the aggressive, hostile, sociopathic behaviors which only appeared later in life — after the taking over

(Footnote 4 cont. on p. 70)

was he? Here at the age of 27 he is charged with brutal crimes quite out of line with all we knew about his earlier life, as a child, an adolescent and a young adult. Yet, his guilt was not in doubt—except by him.

Hypnosis is the best approach for breaking through amnesias, so I reassured his expressed fears about hypnosis and secured his cooperation to proceed. He voiced many self-doubts such as, "I've never faced up to the fact that I might have a problem. . . . There's been a lot of times when I, I can't justify my actions. There are things that I can't account for. . . . Who am I? . . . Why do I do the things I do; why do I lie . . .?" Concerning hypnosis he remarked, "I thought about . . . suppose I do open this door, suppose I do find out things that I—I never knew about, like things that really scare me, things that—that are just beyond my comprehension . . .?"

When I started to administer suggestibility tests, he showed his fear of being hypnotized by changing the subject and digressing in order to postpone the actual hypnotizing. This resistance is not at all typical of one who wishes to fake hypnosis, an issue raised later by Dr. Orne.

At this time much anxiety appeared. I ceased efforts at hypnosis, and we discussed his life with Kelli (his common-law wife) and his son. His childhood experience in the early grades included a repetitive, nightmare dream in which he would be in a dark room. "There was something there. . . . It was something in there that put such a fear in me . . . I can remember waking up screaming." Kenneth had been adopted when about 3 weeks of age. His real mother was a girl of the streets. He reported having no interest in finding her.

After much stalling, he agreed to try hypnosis again. An arm-drop induction, plus relaxation, fantasies of resting on a green slope, slowly descending stairs (40 of them) plus a hand levitation brought little response. Kenneth was very fearful of what he might discover inside himself. My thoughts were that I would probably not succeed in hypnotizing him, and I was prepared to give up. Had I done so, it is quite possible

---

(Footnote 4 cont.)

of the Steve personality. Even as a 9-year old, his answers on a Rohde Sentence Completions (Rohde, 1953) test were typical of an over-controlling, conforming youngster who denied all hostility.

The statement that, as an adult, he lacked all "empathy" with others is very questionable. Kelli, his common-law wife, although aware of his "scams" still described him as:

> One thing about Ken that I really liked was he did a lot of nice, nice things just because he wanted to do them because it made him feel good. [Examples given.] He was pretty considerate towards me. Always considerate to [our son]. He couldn't do enough for that baby. I moved in with Ken because it was handy and I cared for him and he cared for me.

Regarding her acquiring VD in a rape-affair,

> He was hurt, but he was really understanding about it. I was shocked—more understanding than I expected him to be. He's always cared more deeply for me than I have for him. He still does. That's never changed our relationship, etc.

All this occurred at the time that the brutal Steve was demonstrating his hatred of women by raping and murdering indiscriminately. True sociopaths do not show such alternation of behavior. But when the sociopathic aspects are dissociated then it becomes possible to lead a double life with "caring," gentleness and tenderness toward wife and child on the one hand, and psychopathic violence on the other.

that he would simply have been convicted on circumstantial evidence of the Bellingham murders. His connection to the Los Angeles killings might not have been revealed. The Los Angeles police already had reason to suspect him, and the conditions of the Bellingham murders were similar to those in Los Angeles. However, at that time there was no objective evidence which could have convicted him of the "Hillside Strangler" slayings.

Gradually little movements began to appear in one of his fingers during the hand levitation. With much repetition, I secured a complete levitation of the hand to the face. Hypnotic involvement began. Another long deepening procedure, rotating wheels (Watkins, 1984a, in press), and we had at last achieved a substantial degree of hypnotic depth.

I then gave a suggestion which has often been successful in breaking through an amnesia, activating a covert ego state or inducing a multiple personality to become overt. It is similar to the suggestions used by E. R. Hilgard in first eliciting the "hidden observer" phenomenon (E. R. Hilgard & J. R. Hilgard, 1975). It was as follows (excerpted from tape recording):

> I've talked a bit to Ken, but I think that perhaps there might be another part of Ken that I haven't talked to, another part that maybe feels somewhat differently from the part that I've talked to. And I would like to communicate with that other part.

No suggestion was made as to *the content* of such a "part." My experience has been that if there is no "other part," no underlying or covert entity, such a suggestion is simply ignored, even in good hypnotizable subjects.

At this point Bianchi began weaving back and forth and mumbling, much of which I could not understand. I then said, "Part, are you the same thing as Ken, or are you different in any way?" It replied, "I'm not him." The communications then proceeded as follows:

> W: You're not him. Who are you? Do you have a name?
> B: I'm not Ken.
> W: You're not Ken. Okay. Who are you? Tell me about yourself. . . . Do you have a name I can call you by?
> B: Steve. . . .
> W: You're not Ken. Tell me about yourself, Steve. What do you do?
> B: I hate him.
> W: You hate him. You mean Ken?
> B: I hate Ken. . . . He tries to be nice.

Steve then talked about "his" (meaning Ken's) mother, whom he hated. He stated that, "I make him [Ken] lie." This was followed by "I fixed him but good. . . . I fixed him good when he went to California." He then described Ken walking in on his cousin, Angelo Buono, when Angelo was "killing this girl" and later stated that, "I wouldn't let him remember that." He vividly described how he (Steve) had strangled and killed "all these girls," reiterating that "I fixed him [Ken] up good. He doesn't even have any idea."

It was shockingly obvious to me now that I was talking with "the Hillside Strangler." After getting Steve to describe the details for the killings, both in Bellingham and Los Angeles, I told him he could go where he needed to go and asked to talk to Ken (still under hypnosis). Ken returned. I asked him if he knew about Steve. He replied, "Who's Steve?" I then told him he would come to know about Steve and what he had done when he, Ken, felt ready to do so. This was a mistake as we will see later. When I counted up to 5, Ken came out of hypnosis showing the usual reactions of a subject emerging from a deep state. He was quite surprised that so much time had elapsed.

In cases of amnesia there is usually a "part" of the ego that is aware of what has happened, whether we call this an "ego state" (J. G. Watkins & H. H. Watkins, 1981) or a cognitive structural system ("hidden observer", E. R. Hilgard, 1977). Dissociation is a defensive process in normal individuals which reduces anxiety by keeping apart cognitively dissonant elements. Only in its most extreme form is it manifested as a true multiple personality.

"Ego states" can be activated by hypnosis and when studied are found to operate within the self like "covert" multiple personalities, creating conflict and influencing the primary executive state. However, their appearance under hypnosis is not to be considered justification for diagnosing a multiple personality.[5] While underlying personalities *can be* hypnotically activated, the diagnosis of multiple personality should be given *only* if these states emerge spontaneously, overtly and without any hypnotic induction. Furthermore, while ego states can be found in many normal and neurotic individuals, such as clients seeking help for conflicts related to stopping smoking or weight reduction (J. G. Watkins & H. H. Watkins, 1982), hypnotic suggestion cannot create true, overt, spontaneously activated multiple personalities unless the splits are already pres-

---

[5]It has been intimated that Bianchi was cued into an attempt to fake a multiple personality by suggestions given him by me; the social worker, Mr. Johnson; and Bianchi's attorney, Mr. Dean Brett, prior to the first appearance of Steve. The record needs to be set straight. First my wife, Helen H. Watkins, and not me was contacted by Mr. Johnson, who, as a former social work professor at the University of Montana, had worked with Helen as a colleague on various cases. This occurred while I was away from Missoula on a week's business trip. She was asked only about the possibility of using hypnosis to lift amnesias. She preferred not to take the case and suggested me. I returned to Montana on March 19th, contacted Mr. Johnson on March 20th, and traveled immediately the morning of March 21st to Bellingham, at which time I held my first interview with Bianchi. There was absolutely no time for my vita, publications, etc. to have been given to Mr. Brett prior to my arrival. He was aware only of my general background, although having read a paper of Helen's and mine on ego states.

Mr. Brett stated that Bianchi was told only that I was "an expert" in hypnosis. In no way was there any mention of multiple personality or ego states to Bianchi prior to Steve's first appearance. To check this, I have recently called Brett, who when asked about any such discussion, suggestion or intimation replied, "Definitely not." I did discuss with Brett the possibility of dissociation upon first arriving, but there was no contact between Brett and Bianchi prior to my eliciting the Steve personality. Although I did call for "another part," I was completely surprised at the appearance of the Steve personality, having anticipated only some possible lifting of amnesia by another segment (covert ego state) of Ken's personality. Brett was almost indignant when asked about the possibility of his having suggested multiple personality as a defense and replied, "I certainly know enough not to spoil the possibility for our experts to secure a correct diagnosis."

ent and severe. In the highly suggestible subject, a therapist's suggestions can cause many artifacts or pseudo-multiple personalities to appear temporarily, especially when the patient is rewarded by much interest and enthusiasm on the part of the therapist for bringing in a new one each day. These should not be confused with true, overt multiple personalities, which are generally few in number. I am always suspicious when large numbers of separate personalities are reported. Usually only a few are significant dissociated entities; many of the others are transitory states, perhaps created to please the therapist.

The first multiple personality I treated was in 1946 (J. G. Watkins, 1949). Since then, I have evaluated and treated a number of them intensively (50 to several hundred sessions each), both in and out of hospitals. Most of these were finally recognized and treated only after having been in a series of psychiatric hospitals and clinics misdiagnosed as "Schizophrenia," "Psychotic Depressive Reaction," "Psychomotor Epilepsy" — especially when irregularities in the EEG were found. The most common misdiagnosis is that of "Sociopath" (Antisocial Personality Disorder).

Multiple personality has been defined by the American Psychiatric Association (in *DSM-III*) as a condition characterized by "the existence within the individual of two or more distinct personalities, each of which is dominant at a particular time [p. 257]." The most well-known cases of multiple personality are those described by Janet (1907), Prince (1906), Schreiber (1973), and Thigpen and Cleckley (1957). Published descriptions of over 100 cases are available (Ellenberger, 1970). During the period when a secondary personality is overt or "executive," the original or primary personality is not conscious, and upon its return is usually amnesic as to what transpired at that time (J. G. Watkins, 1984b, in press; J. G. Watkins & Johnson, 1982). They walk in and out of the offices of psychiatrists and psychologists mislabeled, mistreated, and rightfully angry. This is partly because we have all been taught by the textbooks that multiple personalities are "extremely rare." We are not supposed to see them — and so we do not. Many practitioners do not really believe they exist. Such a negative set operates to blind examiners to the reports of frequent short periods of amnesia, slips of the tongue, and the little "object-type" behaviors by which dissociation is manifested (such as a feeling of being pulled into a bar when one did not really want to go there). Furthermore, many an examiner has listened to reports of auditory hallucinations without inquiring (possibly through hypnosis) into just *who is doing the speaking*. While the "believer" may be overly sensitized to these phenomena, the "skeptic" may be insensible to such signs and fall back on the much safer diagnosis of "Sociopath" or "Antisocial Personality Disorder." This latter is a good "waste-paper" diagnosis when we do not really understand what is going on dynamically within a patient or causing his surprising behavior.

It is also unlikely that a secondary personality will spontaneously appear during a brief office visit — especially if it is a malevolent state. The clinician sees an apparently normal or neurotic individual reported to be engaging in antisocial behaviors. Accordingly, his own statements about spells of amnesias are often dismissed as simple lying. The trick, of course, is to distinguish between the true amnesia case and the conscious liar or simulator.

The following day (March 22, 1979) Bianchi was again hypnotized. After about 20 minutes of induction and deepening, Steve was activated. The next 2 hours were spent exploring the relationship between Steve and Ken, the rigidity of the boundary which separated them, the reality of Ken's amnesia, plus Steve's views of life, himself, others in his world, and the killings. His reactions about his ability to come out, his relative ego strength compared to Ken's, his ability to keep Ken dissociated and ignorant of what happened when Steve was executive were most typical of a number of other multiple personality cases I have seen over the years. Steve insisted that "me and Angelo" did the killings, not Ken. When Steve wanted to kill, he "made him [Ken] go away." He described how he and Angelo took turns killing the girls in Los Angeles. He bragged about being "smart enough to pull it off." When asked about the newspaper accounts of the killings, he replied, "Hey, you know, what can I say? When you're popular, you're popular. . . ."

I asked if there was another personality, and Steve mentioned a "Bill." In his report, Dr. Orne stated that "Billy," a third personality, was "produced" only after he, Orne, had suggested that a "real" multiple personality had at least three different entities (not true—some of them are only bi-modal). Orne argued that this showed that Bianchi was faking, apparently not having noticed that a "Bill" was mentioned 2 months earlier in my March 22nd session. At that time, I did not activate and explore this personality.

Steve described traumatic incidents in Ken's childhood during which he, Steve, took over. I pressed strongly to determine to what extent Ken could have been aware of Steve: "Surely, there must've been some time along the way when he became aware of you or something, wasn't there?" His reply, "Shit—no, because I would stay out until I felt like it. I'd stay out until after everything was done and then I let him come back again, and sit there and think about it. Stupid ass-hole, ha, ha, ha." When asked what Ken would think about when coming back, Steve said, "How would you feel, if you had to figure out where the fucking hour went to? . . . Oh man, he lost more time than a broken clock!" The two personalities behaved differently in almost every respect: manner, attitude, language, posture, gestures, speech, behaviors, values. When asked if he, Steve, "gave him [Ken] any hints about . . . being around," he replied, "Fuck no, it would ruin me. . . . he's not aware . . . that I am what I am. . . . He just figures it's, it's a thought out of nowheres . . . he's just totally puzzled." Steve then claimed that he could put thoughts into Ken's head anytime he wanted to. His remarks about Ken's legal predicament were, "I hope they fucking roast him," and then "he would be out of my hair." Here we see the concrete thinking (trance logic) so typical of secondary personalities (and hypnotic "reals") who cannot generalize that harm to the primary personality may be destructive to them also. Such "logical inconsistencies" are manifested by multiple personalities and by deeply hypnotized subjects.

The judge and prosecuting attorney viewed the tapes of my sessions with Bianchi and decided that the case now transcended the circumstantial evidence of the killing of two girls in Bellingham. Accordingly, the court appointed six experts to examine the defendant in much greater detail. The two recommended by the prosecution were Martin T. Orne, M.D., Ph.D., and Saul J. Faerstein, M.D. of Los Angeles. The defense selected Donald T. Lunde, M.D., Professor of Psychiatry in the Stanford Law School (an expert witness along with Dr. Orne in the Patty Hearst case), and myself. The court then called on Charles M. Moffett, M.D., a Bellingham psychiatrist, and Ralph B. Allison, M.D., who is well-known for his work in the field of multiple personality. An additional psychiatrist, Ronald Markman, M.D., had also been employed independently by the defense. These specialists spent over 65 hours of time evaluating Bianchi — all audio- and videotaped. The exact scripts were available and quotes in this paper are taken from them.

I was asked to return 1 month later (April 20, 1979) to continue my evaluation of the case. Dr. Allison had seen Ken for several days and was convinced that he was a genuine multiple personality. He had "introduced" Ken to Steve under hypnosis (another error, in my opinion, since this eroded the dissociative boundary between Ken and Steve and made more difficult the diagnostic task of Drs. Orne and Faerstein who did not see Bianchi until 2 months later). Ken knew, now, of the existence of Steve.

I felt that two points were important in determining whether Bianchi was a true multiple personality: (*a*) I must try to activate Steve without hypnosis. A genuine multiple personality (which is not merely a covert ego state) can emerge by itself. No hypnotic induction preceded the activation of Steve at the time of the crimes. (*b*) Psychological tests, especially the Rorschach (Rorschach, 1942), which is most difficult to fake, should be administered separately to Steve and Ken.

During my session with Bianchi on April 20th (during which no hypnotic induction was used), Ken described his first awareness of the existence of Steve and his "readiness for the fight." Later he mentioned having intermittent headaches. It is very typical in multiple personalities that, when a secondary state attempts to emerge in spite of the resistance of the primary state, the individual often experiences this struggle as a headache (sometimes described as a "migraine" headache). This fact is not generally known — at least among the lay public.

Accordingly, when Ken reported feeling bad during our interview, I focused on this point and asked him repeatedly *why* he felt bad. With an angry snarl, Steve emerged voicing his dislike of me and loudly complaining of his difficulty in getting out now that Ken knew about his existence.

> All these fucking years I had it made. I could come and go as I pleased. He never knew about me. But, now he does. I have some feeling it's partly your fault. You started this whole fucking thing. . . . I try to come out. Instead I stay where I'm

at. and he complains about fucking headaches. . . . I'd like to give him a big fucking headache.[5]

In most cases the boundaries are usually permeable in one direction. The secondary state knows about the primary, but not vice versa. Since Steve reported being aware of Ken's thoughts, I decided to administer the Rorschach to Steve first. I also won the cooperation of Steve by showing him a magazine page which had on it pictures of the girls killed in Los Angeles by "the Hillside Strangler." Steve was delighted and pointed out to me just which ones he had killed and which ones Angelo Buono (Ken's cousin) had killed. After that, he refused further cooperation and was given the Rorschach. Ken was re-activated. He emerged feeling that he had been "asleep" for only a few minutes. The two Rorschachs were totally different from one another.

Even though I have taught, administered and interpreted Rorschach over the years, I felt it extremely important that a blind analysis be done by even more experienced Rorschachers who were not informed at all about the case. In this respect, I followed the recommendations of Orne's (1959) significant paper which showed that otherwise judges could not be truly objective. One of the two highly experienced Rorschach experts to whom I sent the Ken and Steve protocols was Dr. Richard Ball, who had been Chief Psychologist at a number of V.A. hospitals and former Dean of Students at the Albert Einstein Medical School. The other was Dr. Erika Fromm, Professor of Psychology at the University of Chicago, Clinical Editor of the *International Journal of Clinical and Experimental Hypnosis,* and a former president of the Society of Clinical and Experimental Hypnosis. She is widely known for her publications both in Rorschach and in hypnosis. They were told only to evaluate "these two Rorschach protocols," which were identified merely by the letters K (for Ken) and S (for Steve). Although both were quite familiar with my work in multiple personalities, neither of them recognized the Rorschachs as coming from the same individual.

I quote from the letter sent by Dr. Fromm:

> At first I wondered why you had sent me the record of Mr. K, a normal looking person, no more neurotic than you and I and most of our friends—together with this absolutely outrageous record of Mr. S who clearly is a rapist, a killer, and a most dangerous man. That is, I understood that Mr. S could be a court case, would *have* to be a court case; but I could not see why Mr. K should be in court. He seemed so utterly normal.

Her report on Ken concluded with the following statements:

> Mr. K is a relatively normal individual with a very mild neurosis. He is quite introverted and somewhat egocentric; but all of this is within the normal range. He has good reality orientation, his thinking is logical and orderly, he seems to have good relations with other human beings notwithstanding the mild egocentricity. . . .

[*]During the April 20th session, Steve was activated with a hypnotic induction (as clearly shown on the videotape). Ken was asked simply to close his eyes and tell me why he had been feeling bad. Steve spontaneously emerged.

Her report on Mr. S (Steve) was as follows:

> This is one of the sickest Rorschachs I have seen in working with this test for more than 40 years. It is clearly that of a patient in whose mind sexuality and violent aggression against women are fused. I would expect him to be a rapist and a killer, a most dangerous and violent person. He can be carried away by his own fantasies, to the point where he loses all judgment and reality orientation. He becomes overwhelmed by his sexual and aggressive drives, his Ego becomes passive and he will headlong run, rape and murder. . . .
>
> Mr. S is not a psychopath; he could be a schizophrenic . . . . What is clear, however, beyond any doubt, is that he is compulsively driven, driven, driven into attacking women violently.

She also indicated that knowing of my interest in multiple personalities the thought that these might be one had crossed her mind, but had been dismissed.

These Rorschachs were also analyzed by a well-known psychologist secured by Dr. Orne. His Rorschacher gave the diagnosis of "Sociopath." One specific criticism might be made of her evaluation. She reported a "Delta Index" of 0% for both Ken and Steve. The Delta Index on the Rorschach is a measure of the extent to which primitive, concrete (psychotic) ideation has invaded reality testing. I originally devised, researched and published the measure (J. G. Watkins & Stauffacher, 1952). Ken did score 0%, but Steve's Delta should have been scored 25% — clearly within the psychotic range.[7]

Orne also asked Dr. Harrison G. Gough, Professor at Stanford University and the originator of the California Personality Inventory (CPI; Gough, 1964) to evaluate those tests — which had been given separately to Ken, Steve and Billy by Dr. Allison. Dr. Gough's report gave little support for either the sociopath or the multiple personality diagnosis. He discussed both pros and cons for each with such statements as:

> If there are different personalities in this case, it seems clear that Steve is the one to be found guilty. . . . The profile for Billy is what one would expect from a naive, immature, rebellious, and dissatisfied fifteen-year old. . . . It cannot be

---

[7]Dr. Edwin Wagner, who apparently has published the only paper on Rorschach tests with multiple personality cases, wrote (in a personal communication to me August 2, 1983) that Ken's record "did not conform with the other cases" he had studied. However, he also stated, "I don't think Bianchi is a sociopath either." His study (Wagner & Heise, 1974) was based on three female cases. In only two of them were Rorschachs separately administered to the secondary personalities. The paper does not indicate whether they were activated under hypnosis (e.g., were only covert "ego states" as is found so often in the literature on presumed multiple personalities), nor whether the secondary personalities (who are usually aware of all that happens to the primary one) were tested *prior* to the primary one — as was done in Bianchi's case. The major criteria which they stated as differentiating multiple personalities seem to apply equally well to Bianchi, namely: large number of M responses, F and F plus relatively normal (true for Ken), color responses labile (true for Steve), decrease of M with successive personalities (Ken 6, Steve 3), tendencies toward simplification and reintegration with successive emergence of new personalities (Ken's protocol 17 responses; Steve's 11 responses). And Bianchi's characteristics of reported headaches, confusion and amnesia on return of primary personality, plus an opposite and at times violent secondary personality are also similar to Wagner and Heise's (1974) description of their cases.

> claimed that they are in fact, merely different roles or variants. . . . Are Ken,
> Billy, and Steve the different selves of a multiple personality? It is possible that
> they are, in particular the selves constituted by Ken and Steve.

And finally, "It must first be admitted that we are venturing into territory uncharted by sound, empirical research."

Unfortunately, Orne's psychologists not only did not have the opportunity to make blind evaluation, but they were also considerably briefed on the expectations of the prosecution. They were both informed that this was the case of Kenneth Bianchi, "the Hillside Strangler." Orne's transmittal letter to one of them (July 16, 1979), now a public court record, included the following:

> One of the key questions is whether the three personalities represent distinct
> individuals living on [sic] one body as some theories of multiple personality would
> propose. Alternative explanations must, of course, also be considered, the most
> likely being that these are not personalities in a true sense but represent roles
> which the individual plays, perhaps not only for others but also for himself.

Orne then gave the example of "The Secret Life of Walter Mitty," a film played by Danny Kaye in which "a variety of fantasies were acted out; while superficially very different, they certainly were not true personalities, though they may have appeared like it to a casual observer," and "It would now be important to learn whether the other two personalities (Steve, Billy) have any real substance or are relatively superficial expressions of the role." This letter concluded with: "I would appreciate your keeping track of the time devoted to this matter and your billing me appropriately. These costs would ultimately be borne by the prosecutor's office since it was he who retained my services." It should be noted that professionals can be influenced by suggestion as well as subjects or patients — as discovered by Orne (1979) in his simulation studies.

To minimize such suggestive influence neither of my psychologists were told anything about the case or informed as to which side was employing my services. Dr. Ball diagnosed Ken as follows:

> There does not appear to be any clear evidence of 1) low intelligence; 2) psycho-
> pathic personality, 3) organic brain impairment, 4) psychotic process either affec-
> tive or schizoid. I lean toward a diagnosis of hysterical neurosis, dissociative type.

His diagnosis of Steve: "Sadism."

When informed later that both Rorschachs came from a single individual and asked to write an integrated report on K and S, Dr. Ball concluded that: "There is no evidence, in either state, that he might be malingering; indeed both records have a clearly authentic consistency far beyond any capacity of his to dissemble."

The MMPI (Dahlstrom & Welsh, 1960) was given to Ken, but not to Steve. Its profile showed high peaks on Hysteria (80), Psychopathic Deviate (82) and Schizophrenia (82). There are no norms available on the MMPI (or CPI) for multiple personality. However, a computer analysis of the MMPI concluded as follows: "The preferred diagnosis . . . psycho-

FIG. 1. Handwriting of Bianchi's various personalities.

neurosis, hysteria, dissociating reaction, consisting of sudden episodes of unaccustomed behavior, related to hysterical acting out, possibly even with true amnesia."

Further Evidence Favoring a Diagnosis of Multiple Personality

Samples of handwriting were obtained by Dr. Allison from Ken, Steve, Billy and another personality uncovered by Dr. Orne, "Friend." Each was asked to write his name, address and name of parents. Steve and Billy wrote, "no parents." The samples differed widely. "Friend" wrote: "Dear Dr. Lunde, please help Ken. Just ask for me if you want. It's no problem. Thank you.", signed "Friend." It was almost illegible and in a florid, totally different type of script as compared to the neat orderly writing of Ken and the exaggerated cruder writing of Steve (see Figure 1). Each sample was consistent within itself as to style, but differed widely from the others.

The wife of a psychologist who attended a professional meeting at which I had discussed the case contacted me. She was a certified graphologist, had not been present at the meeting, but requested that she be permitted to analyze the handwriting samples. She, unlike my Rorschachers, did not have the benefit of making her evaluations blind. Her analysis was made many months after closing of the case, so Dr. Orne and the other consultants (as well as myself) did not have the advantage of considering it during our evaluations. However, in her report Ken was described as

a mild, humble, reserved, good natured individual of average intelligence, eager to please, avoiding conflict, a conformist. . . . Steve, a completely different

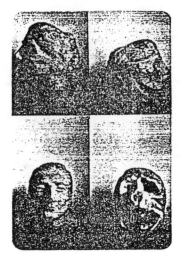

FIG. 2. Sculpture carved by Kenneth A. Bianchi as a high school student.

FIG. 3. Dissociated figure drawn by Bianchi while in jail.

BIANCHI CASE: SOCIOPATH OR MULTIPLE PERSONALITY?   81

Fig. 4. Figures drawn by Bianchi while in jail.

individual interested in his own gratification. He is cold in feelings, furiously angry.

It noted "many telling likenesses," but summarized that "a handwriting expert would find it difficult to build a case that would convince a jury that these handwritings were in fact done by one and the same person."

Ken smoked only filter-tip cigarettes. Steve could not stand filters and tore them off before smoking — to the confusion of Ken when he re-emerged.

During high school, Ken, who was somewhat of an artist, sculptured a Janus (two-faced) head (see Figure 2). One side is that of a normal person; the other that of a monster. Many sketches made by Ken in jail consisted of fragmented human figures (see Figures 3 & 4). Projective test specialists would consider these productions as indirect evidence of a dissociative reaction.

The Los Angeles Police Department and the police in Bellingham found that in Los Angeles Bianchi had at one time posed as a "psychologist," having secured a copy of a psychologist's diploma by the name of "Steve Walker." They considered this as evidence of conscious misrepresentation. However, both Steve and Billy reported doing this without the knowledge of Ken. The brief "practice" had a total of one client.

Incidents of cooperation with Angelo Buono in prostitution were also uncovered. However, in none of these do we know just which personality was responsible. Steve reported that he often used the name of "Ken" to get "that turkey" into trouble, and even to fool Angelo. None of the findings of the police would be evidence for or against a hypothesis that Ken was a multiple personality since we have no way of knowing which entity was involved at any given time.[5] Ken reported many instances during these years of amnesic episodes when he "lost" periods ranging from 1 hour or 2 to an entire day. Police investigations were not able to corroborate these. However, patients suffering from amnesic episodes often conceal them from others to avoid embarrassment.[9]

During the next 2 months, following my sessions with Bianchi, the other examiners, Drs. Lunde, Moffett, Allison, Orne and Faerstein made evaluations. These involved over 65 hours of interviews, audio- and videotape-recorded. Copies of all tapes and scripts were furnished each of us to help in making our diagnoses. Thus, each examiner had ample opportunity to study the interviews of the others before submitting his report.

Conclusions of Prosecution, Defense and Court Examiners

Dr. Faerstein	(Prosecution)	Sociopath. Not insane.
Dr. Orne	(Prosecution)	Anti-Social Personality. Not insane.
Dr. Lunde	(Defense)	Dissociative Reaction, extremely severe, bordering on psychosis. Insane.
Dr. Watkins	(Defense)	Dissociative Reaction: Multiple Personality. Insane.
Dr. Moffett	(Court)	Insane.
Dr. Allison	(Court)	Multiple Personality. Insane.
Dr. Markman	(Defense)	Severe multiple personality and the possibility of (brain) disorder.

Dr. Lunde wrote in his report:

> My own examination indicates that Bianchi is not psychologically sophisticated enough nor is he intelligent enough to have constructed such an elaborate history which might afford him a mental defense if he were subsequently charged with a crime. Furthermore, one would have to assume that Bianchi began plotting his strategy for these crimes and his defense at about age nine, since this is when the first documented symptoms of his mental disturbance occurred. Bianchi does not simply suffer from "convenient lapses of memory". He appears to have genuine amnesia for various events which have been documented over the years and which have no bearing on present criminal charges or any other conceivable criminal charges.

Dr. Allison administered the CPI separately to Ken, Steve and Billy and had them computer analyzed. After completing all his examinations of Bianchi, he concluded in his report to the judge that Steve was *not* "created by Dr. Watkins at the first hypnotic session." Rather, "this hyp-

[5]The description of Bianchi's "scams," his lying, his stealing, his running of prostitutes, his posing as a psychologist, etc. carefully documented for his stay in Los Angeles are, indeed, typical of a sociopath. However, Billy and Steve reported that they frequently carried these out under the name of Ken. There is no argument about the reality of these behaviors, only "Who was on first" when they were done. The complete alternation of behavior and manner from tender, caring husband and father, friendly colleague, etc. to brutal rapist and killer makes more sense as a multiple personality, in which one half was "normal" and the other half "sociopathic"—such as demonstrated in the Rorschachs.

[9]It has been stated that nobody observed these personality changes until I had "activated" Steve. However, Bonnie W., Kelli's roommate, states that on January 11 (just before the Bellingham killings)

> When Ken got here, if I didn't see his face and, you know, it just wasn't him. It um, there was just something totally different about him then, you know, when I talked to him before. —It was just really weird. Um, I [was] frightened when he came through and I didn't want him around me. —I've always liked him and he and I, well, we've talked; we have always had a good relationship. —To me, that wasn't Ken; I didn't understand it.

notic session allowed Steve to come out." He reported at that time that "Steve is an alter-personality which was made by Ken at the age of nine, while hiding under his bed, terrified with another rampage by his mother." According to the tests he found Steve "psychotic." And in a personal communication (August 16, 1979) he stated:

> During my last visit to Bellingham, I was perfectly willing to prove Ken a liar and deceiver. But I could not do it when the evidence was presented to me. He is the 50th multiple I have seen—so I think that I have enough clinical experience to judge when somebody is putting something over on me.

Questions have been raised why Dr. Lunde diagnosed Bianchi as "Dissociative Reaction" and Dr. Allison and I reported the diagnosis of "Multiple Personality." Yet each of us called him legally "insane." Dissociative reactions are classified in the *DSM-III* as neurotic, not psychotic disorders. Multiple personality, however, is more severe than most neuroses. Many workers in this area believe it is closer to psychosis. "Insanity" is a legal term and not necessarily equivalent to "psychosis" although there is much overlap. Definitions of insanity differ between states. However, the essential elements are usually: (*a*) that the defendant cannot appreciate the criminality of his actions, and (*b*) that he does not have the ability to control them and conform his actions to the requirements of the law. Ken could not "appreciate" the actions of Steve, and he did not have the ability to control them. Accordingly, I considered him "insane."

Because of erosion of the separating boundary, Drs. Orne and Faerstein did not have the opportunity of examining Bianchi when he demonstrated the dissociative reaction more clearly 2 months earlier. Although he "remembered" some of the crimes this seemed to be more like an intellectual insight. Bianchi reported the crimes to Orne and Faerstein as if his "self" was not involved ("Then, *the girls* were strangled." Not, "Then *I* strangled the girls."). The dissociative defense was still working to keep Ken from a full awareness of the enormity of Steve's behavior, but it was now less effective.

By October, 1979, Ken had become "convinced" that "he" had actually committed the crimes and was persuaded by his attorney to plead guilty to the 2 Bellingham murders and 5 of the 10 Los Angeles killings. He also agreed to testify against his cousin, Angelo Buono, in return for a dropping of the death penalty. He was sentenced to life imprisonment and then transferred to the Los Angeles jail to await the trial of Buono.

Dissociation is generally a defense to separate cognitively dissonant elements in a personality (J. G. Watkins & Johnson, 1982. The personality structures of Ken (a friendly, mild conformist) and Steve (a violent, hating rapist) were about as cognitively dissonant as two parts of an individual could be. Accordingly, I had predicted that if ever Ken *really* became aware of Steve's crimes (a true, experiential insight in which he had to take personal responsibility for them) it would likely precipitate a psychotic reaction. It was not surprising, therefore, that shortly after being moved to the Los Angeles jail Bianchi went into a deep, catatonic withdrawal — from which he apparently emerged by a re-establishing of denial and dissociation.

The prosecution in Los Angeles had subscribed to the minority diagnosis of "Sociopath." They viewed Bianchi as consciously faking both hypnosis and multiple personality, and they treated him accordingly. Ted Schwarz, a science writer, had been researching the case in preparation of a book (Schwarz, 1981). In late 1980, he sent me a copy of a long letter he had received from Bianchi and asked for an analysis of it. It was plain that massive dissociation had once more become Ken's defense. There was a complete denial of that which had been found in Bellingham and an almost paranoidal preoccupation with efforts to "prove" his innocence of all the crimes. In his view, he (Ken) could not possibly have done those things. If not a split again into a multiple personality, at least a new amnesia for all those events had been erected. Since now he had already been convicted and sentenced (he would spend his life in prison; he would not be executed), the imputation that he was faking it all to escape punishment was not very tenable. As before, he was striving to secure peace of mind and resolve his inner problem more than his external one. Dissociation or psychosis were his only defenses.

I wrote Mr. Schwarz an evaluation of the letter and made the following prediction which he published (Spring 1981) in the appendix of his book (Schwarz, 1981, pp. 247-248):

> Ken will be of no value to the prosecution of Buono, because he (Ken) now knows nothing of the crimes. Steve could be a witness if he were activated but may be scared and resist emerging again. Had the prosecution accepted the dissociation diagnosis and treated Ken appropriately, they could have had a credible witness against Angelo. Incidentally, if Ken (in his present state) testifies against Angelo Buono and states that he knows of Buono's killing, he will be lying. He may do this to please the prosecution or to secure some promised benefit. But Ken now (the one who wrote that letter) is no more aware of Buono's crimes than he is of Steve's. He can be easily tangled up by opposing attorneys since he will not know the correct details.

The only error in this prediction was the word "lying." It should have been "confabulating." As E. R. Hilgard and Loftus (1979), Loftus (1979), and Orne (1959) have pointed out, when pressure is placed on a witness to remember what he does not know, confabulated material will emerge.

This is precisely what took place. It was a fiasco for the prosecution. In July, 2 months after publication of Schwarz's (1981) book, Bianchi was placed on the witness stand. He accused Buono of various crimes and then (in a beautiful example of concrete thinking, hence "trance logic") claimed complete innocence for himself. The prosecution, with their star witness no longer "credible," moved to dismiss the murder charges against Buono. In an unprecedented move, the judge refused to permit this and ordered the case transferred to the California State Attorney General for prosecution.

The new prosecution team seemed to have learned nothing from the experience of the original one. They still based their case on the assumption that Bianchi was not a multiple personality, but a sociopath consciously simulating dissociation. One wonders what they had to gain by trying to present as a credible witness an individual diagnosed as a "sociopath" — the most prominent characteristic of which (according to the *DSM-III*) is lying. The situation was even more complicated by the fact that the California Supreme Court (primarily because of the testimony of Drs. Orne and Bernard L. Diamond) had ruled (March, 1982) that any witness who has been hypnotized was no longer legally credible.

The Question of Possible Faking or Simulation by Bianchi of Either Multiple Personality or Hypnosis

At all times uppermost in the minds of those of us who examined Bianchi was the possibility that he was faking a dissociation reaction to escape punishment. A summary of the evidence against this being a likelihood is overwhelming. First, for many months he adamantly refused to let his attorney plead insanity. Second, he was always much more concerned with what was going on within himself than his possible conviction and punishment. (During my interviews, he almost never mentioned what might be his fate if convicted.) Third, the striking changes of behavior, motivation, ethical concepts, perception of events, posture, gestures, manner, values, attitudes and thought processes which characterized the Steve personality as contrasted with the Ken personality were consistent throughout all interviews. Only after substantial erosion of the dissociating boundary (prior to the examinations of Orne and Faerstein) did fragments of memory concerning the crimes come through to Ken. Fourth, if he really wanted to fake a multiple personality (in spite of his refusal to permit an insanity defense) he would have had to be a fool to try to simulate such a complex condition. It would have been much easier to pretend to delusions and hallucinations. And simultaneously, he would have to be a well-informed genius to carry off successfully a simulation of this intricate and widely misunderstood psychiatric disorder. The viewpoint maintained by the prosecution was that he was a very brilliant sociopath who managed to fake both a multiple personality and hypnosis, and so to fool a majority of the examining consultants. Let us consider the evidence related to such a hypothesis.

Since my own diagnosis and final report to the court had been derived almost as much from frequent observation and intensive study of Orne's tapes as my own, I was astonished when I first read his report. I had seen Orne brilliantly hypnotize Bianchi many times, re-induce, deepen, and activate both Steve and Billy on numerous occasions. I had noted the same tremendous difference in the behavior of Ken and Steve, and the many cues which Bianchi displayed confirming his dissociation. I, too, had given special attention to the possibility of Bianchi's faking hypnosis, and, though "nominated" by the defense, had at all times considered myself as working for the court. In fact, I had written the judge that "Dr. Orne . . . is perhaps the world's authority on the danger of possible simulation" and called attention to his extensive publications in this area (Orne, 1969, 1971). I also noted to the judge that Dr. Orne had elicited and observed the same phenomena as I had. My final report was submit-

JOHN G. WATKINS

ted to the judge before I saw Orne's, and it never occurred to me that his evaluation would differ so significantly from mine.

In his report, Dr. Orne emphasized what to me was a pseudo-issue, namely, whether Bianchi had or had not been hypnotized by Orne, Allison and myself, the only consultants who used induction techniques. He apparently reasoned that if Bianchi could be shown to have faked hypnosis this would mean that he had also faked multiple personality. The question of multiple personality need not hinge on whether he had been hypnotized since a secondary personality in a true multiple emerges without hypnosis (although hypnosis is often used in treatment to facilitate activating it). The matter only became an issue almost 3 years later after the California Supreme Court ruling. However, I must concede if one favors a neo-dissociation theory of hypnosis (E. R. Hilgard, 1977) that multiple personalities are generally hypnotizable. An inability on the part of Bianchi to be hypnotized would lessen confidence in the diagnosis of Dissociative Reaction. Accordingly, the issue must be seriously addressed.

In his interview of May 28, 1979, Orne said to Bianchi,

> Ken is a very bright person. . . . I've got good evidence for that. I've got an IQ test that shows it. . . . You have the IQ necessary to have gone through college and gone through graduate school. . . . And that's a fact. . . . That's not a dispute. This is fact.

The fact is that Bianchi's IQ (frequently tested) was 116, 112 verbal (WAIS tested in jail; Wechsler, 1955), 110 (SIT at age 14; Slosson, 1963), 107 (high school placement at age 14) and 106 (Henmon-Nelson at age 14; Henmon & Nelson, 1957). He had a long record of poor grades and borderline academic performance. There is absolutely nothing to support the hypothesis that he was "very bright" and able to go "through graduate school."

Much has been made of the fact that a number of books on "psychology" were discovered in his house after his arrest, most of these of the *I'm OK — You're OK* (Harris, 1969) type. Ken reported trying to read the chapter on testing in the *Handbook of Clinical Psychology* (Wolman, 1965), but could not understand it. Also found was a small pamphlet on hypnosis which was handed to him when, as a security officer, he knocked on the door of a local lay hypnosis establishment. His attorney reported that, contrary to statements made, Ken had never taken a course in hypnosis nor read a publication by Orne (1959) which he, Dean Brett, had reported to Orne reading for himself. Kelli, his common-law wife, stated that Ken seldom did any reading at home. The books he had read suggested more the kind of reading of a disturbed adolescent who was concerned about his inner self. It is highly unlikely that they could have taught him either hypnosis or how to simulate a complex psychiatric disorder like multiple personality. I am in agreement with the conclusions of Dr. Frank Putnam, noted researcher in multiple personality with the National Institute of Mental Health, that this condition cannot be succesfully faked over any extended period of time (see Hale, 1983)

Was Bianchi Ever Really Hypnotized?

In his report to the judge, Dr. Orne stated that, "I do not believe that Mr. Bianchi was ever hypnotized. I am certain that he was not in hypnosis during the sessions when I worked with him. . . . it is my opinion that Mr. Bianchi does not have a multiple personality."

Orne argues that the essential ingredient in a state of hypnosis is the phenomenon of "trance logic." This has been described as the ability of a truly hypnotized subject to freely mix his perceptions derived from reality with those that stem from his imagination. It is a tolerance of logical inconsistencies. Orne (1959) states that trance logic is "intimately related to primary process thinking or autistic thinking [p. 295]." I agree. Another term might be "concrete" thinking (Kasanin, 1944), which characterizes regressive, psychotic ideation, the reasoning of children and some sufferers from organic brain damage. Whether or not it is the essential element in hypnosis, it is certainly highly correlated with it. This concept stems from an "altered state of consciousness" theory of hypnosis.

Orne (1971) has reported that even expert hypnotists (including himself) can often be fooled by simulators. However, he did not state just how many "expert hypnotists" were fooled, over how many trials, and for what length of time. No claims seem to have been made that the simulator can continue to fool the hypnotist if sufficient time and experiments are undertaken. The "fooling" was during "single sessions" with a restricted number of operations. It should be recalled that Bianchi had over 65 recorded hours of evaluation from seven different consultants, three of whom employed hypnotic techniques for over a total of 15 hours, and that each had the benefit of repetitive, objective observation of the taped sessions of the others.

Orne administered a number of "objective" tests of hypnosis to Bianchi and claimed that such tests were a more valid and scientific measure of the reality of hypnosis than the intensive, lengthy clinical evaluations done by me, Dr. Allison, and himself.

While such a conclusion may be controversial, I am in complete agreement that truly objective, scientific and rigorously controlled tests can carry great weight in arriving at a clinical diagnosis. In fact, the video-taped recordings of Orne administering these tests to Bianchi significantly influenced my own final diagnosis and deserve most careful study. The samples of behavior involved in these "objective" tests required less than 15 minutes (13 minutes 34 seconds for the significant ones). That is slightly over 1% of the total time during which Bianchi was "hypnotized." For such samples to outweigh the long, intensive study of several experienced clinicians, the "tests" must truly meet certain criteria: (a) there should be a general agreement among scientists as to their validity; (b) they must have been administered very objectively with rigorous controls; (c) the differentiating criteria must be clearly applicable to the individual being examined; and (d) the responses of that individual must significantly be consistent with one of the two hypothesized alternatives — being truly hypnotized (a "real") or only a simulator. A careful examination of the taped recordings of these tests showed that they were substantially wanting in many of these criteria. The four tests administered were the chevreul pendulum, the double-hallucination, the circle-touch, and the source-amnesia.

The *chevreul pendulum test*. This involves focusing attention of a subject onto a weight on a cord and suggesting that "it" will move, "back and forth," "around clockwise," etc. Tiny muscle reactions cause the movements of the weight. These are experienced by the individual as "object," hence, as not self-initiated. Orne's instructions to Bianchi to "will it [the weight] to stop," rather than "it" will now stop, are close to asking him to *make* it stop, almost a voluntary action. Nevertheless, Bianchi responded as a typical, hypnotically susceptible person would. Of course, this test can be consciously faked, so it cannot differentiate between a "real" and a simulator.

Both the concept of "trance-logic" and the *double-hallucination test* have elicited a considerable amount of research (Barber, 1972; Blum & Graef, 1971; E. R. Hilgard, 1972; Johnson, Maher, & Barber, 1972; McDonald & Smith, 1975; Peters, 1973; Sheehan, 1977). There is inadequate time here to review all their findings. However, there does seem to be general agreement on some of the criteria in this test which differentiate "reals" from simulators.

A hallucination is suggested to the presumably hypnotized subject that he will see a person, whom he knows, sitting in front of him. His eyes are opened, and his reactions to the hallucination noted. His attention is then directed to the real person, who has been stationed behind him, with the question, "Then who is this?" He is confronted with a conflict between a hallucinated image of the person (internal stimuli) and a real perception of the same person (external stimuli). His reactions to this logical inconsistency have been found to differentiate significantly between simulators and "reals."

1. Reals commonly acknowledge seeing both images. Simulators rarely do. In fact, since they have already committed themselves to having perceived the hallucinated image, in their efforts to behave like a hypnotized individual and fool the experimenter, they often deny seeing the real person. Orne (1959) reported that, "of approximately 30 'faking' Ss, only two acted as if they saw two images of the same individual [p. 296]." Bianchi passed this test as a "real" by seeing two Dean Bretts (his attorney).

However, Orne argues that the perception simultaneously of the two is not a valid indicator if "undue concern" or surprise is evinced by the subject. (Bianchi said, "If Dean Brett is here and Dean Brett is here, how can he be in two places?") According to Orne, to demonstrate "trance logic" the subject must accept the inconsistency with little concern. This finding is not reported by any of the other investigators, nor does Orne present experimental evidence to support this claim. Moreover, in the giving of demonstrations and the making of teaching tapes (J. G. Watkins, 1975) we have found it quite common that when a hypnotized subject (of known hypnotizability) is presented with a hallucination (someone they know is made invisible) and simultaneously with a real perception (a book is handed to the invisible individual) there is often surprise, great concern and attempts to resolve the inconsistency. The qualification that visualization of the two images in this test must be accompanied by a lack of concern is definitely not a valid criterion.

2. About half of the "reals" report seeing the hallucinated image as transparent ("I can see the chair through him."). Simulators never respond this way, and doing so is considered in all the studies as a specific indication of a "real." Bianchi did not spontaneously use the word "transparent" when describing Dean Brett's hallucinated image. However, later, when Orne quizzed him about it, he said, "The images weren't clear. It was like looking at a strobe light. You know, how a strobe light just gives you little bits and pieces." Orne did not inquire further to determine if this could be the *equivalent* of a "transparent" response. Sheehan (1977) reported a significant ($p < .001$) group difference in favor of hypnotized subjects who reported images of their original hallucination indicating "a lack of solidity, or a transparent quality [p. 198]." By this criterion (lack of solidity), Bianchi again indicated he was a "real."

Evans and Orne (1971) found that when reals and simulators were given a task like foot-tapping to "hallucinated" music, the simulators stopped the action when the experimenter left the room; the "reals" continued doing it. Orne left the room while Bianchi was conversing with the hallucinated Dean Brett. Bianchi continued the conversation while Orne was gone, even leaving spaces between each of his remarks to "Brett" appropriate to conversational responses. (Orne: "I'll leave you to talk to him for a few moments. I'll be back." Bianchi to hallucinated Brett: "Did your wife have the baby yet? — No, not yet?" — "So, what's new?" — "What are we gonna do now?", etc.)

3. Blum and Graef (1971) and Orne (1979) found that, when confronted with the inconsistency of the two images, the "reals" would look back and forth between the two images. The simulators did not. When Bianchi was asked which one of the Brett images was real, he looked back and forth, finally identifying the real one and stating that the other was "not there anymore" — a verbal response found both in "reals" and in some of the few simulators who admitted to seeing both images. By the "looking back and forth" criterion, Bianchi again is indicated as a "real."

In the administration of the test to Bianchi, confusing suggestions were given.

> (O: Now shortly I'm going to ask you to open your voice. your eyes . . . and when I do, you're going to see . . . that Mr. Brett will have come in and he will be sitting in the *chair right beside you*. . . . As you open your eyes. there's a *chair in front of you* . . . where Mr. Brett will be sitting.")

The subject is already being cued for double images by the confusing suggestions. Nevertheless, Bianchi's responses on the double hallucination test support the conclusion that he is a "real."

The *circle-touch test*. Orne (1980) reported that if one draws a circle on a subject's arm, "hypnotizes" him, and gives suggestions that there will be no feeling inside the circle, the "reals" respond differently from simulators when touched inside the circle. The subject is given a "catch 22" type instruction: "When I touch you outside the circle where you can feel it, you say 'Yes'; when I touch you inside the circle where you cannot feel it, you say 'No.'" Reals should manifest trance logic by responding "No" when touched inside. Simulators, recognizing the incongruity, should make no response when touched inside.

While this makes sense logically, until recently no controlled experimental studies have tested this hypothesis. Eiblmayr (1980) carried out a study designed to test Orne's hypothesis. Since it is not yet in print, some description of it is in order.

Three groups of 10 Ss each (insusceptible, moderately susceptible, and highly susceptible) were selected on the basis of scores on the Stanford Hypnotic Susceptibility Scale, Form C, and the Stanford Profile Scale of Hypnotic Susceptibility, Form I (Weitzenhoffer & E. R. Hilgard, 1963a, 1963b). Insusceptibles were given instructions to simulate hypnosis using the language recommended by Orne (1979). The two susceptible groups were hypnotized. A 1.5 inch circle was drawn with a felt pen on the palm of each S in all three groups. Those in the simulating group were told to feign anesthesia within the circle while Ss in the susceptible groups were given the suggestion of anesthesia within the circumscribed area. A second E, blind to the hypotheses, and able to see only each S's hand, administered the experimental tasks while the hypnotist was absent from the room. Thirty trials, using a Von Frey hair calibrated to a constant pressure of 4.56 g of pressure, were randomly administered under three conditions (10 trials each): inside the circle, outside the circle, no touch. The Ss were instructed that each trial would begin with a buzzer sound and to report "Yes" when touched outside the circle and "No" when touched inside. Four seconds were allowed for each trial.

There were no significant differences between groups when touched outside the circle or not at all. When touched inside the circle, the test did significantly distinguish moderately susceptibles from simulators, but not highly susceptibles from either of the other two groups. However, this differentiation was *the opposite* from that predicted by Orne. It was the "Yes" and the "no response" responses, *not* the "No" responses, which discriminated the "reals" from the simulators. A postinquiry revealed that the "reals" had resolved the inconsistency by reporting "Yes" when touched inside, but displacing its source to a point on the rim of the circle; hence, to just outside. Displacement, rather than "trance logic," was the mechanism used. Hypnotic subjects typically rationalize their responses to suggestions when these are inconsistent with reality.

Orne administered the circle-touch test twice to Bianchi. The first time his back obscured the video camera, so we do not know which response was given to which touch. However, the audibly recorded responses were: "Yes . . . No . . . Yes . . . Yes . . . Yes . . . Yes . . . Yes . . . Yes": one "No" and seven "Yesses."

According to Orne's criterion, the single "No" response should have indicated a "real." It is assumed that the second touch was inside the circle, since subjects practically never give a "No" when touched outside. However, it is unlikely that Orne touched inside the circle only once out of the eight trials. It is more likely that about half the touches were inside (as they were during his second administration of the test later). If *any of these* were "Yes," then according to the Eiblmayr (1980) study they would specifically indicate Bianchi as a "real."

During the second administration of the test much later, the camera had an unobscured view of the subject. All touches outside the circle (5) evoked responses of "Yes." All touches inside the circle (4) evoked no response. Eiblmayr (1980) found that the "no response" response also significantly differentiated simulators from *moderately susceptible* reals; however, *not from the highly susceptibles* (which one would expect a multiple personality to be). Postinquiry revealed that the highly susceptibles, unlike the simulators, gave the "no response" reactions because they really did not feel the touches at all. In other words, the area was truly anesthetized. Only the postinquiry could make this distinction, and no postinquiry was made by Orne in Bianchi's case.

Many other sources of bias and lack of control appear in the videotaped-record of the tests administered to Bianchi:

1. The circle (only outlined and not actually drawn) was placed on the back of Bianchi's hand where there is a greater possibility that the moving stylus brushing against hairs before reaching the point of impact will stimulate them, thus confusing the site of the touch. If the circle had been drawn on the palm (as in the Eiblmayr, 1980, study), this possible contaminating factor would have been eliminated, as well as providing an area richer in sensory endings, and hence more physiologically discriminating.

2. By touching the areas informally with a pen point instead of a Von Frey hair (where the pressure is constant), there is also no way of knowing whether the inside and outside areas received equal impacts.

3. In pilot studies, Eiblmayr (1980) found that a minimum of 4 seconds should be allowed between touches. Otherwise a "no response" could simply represent a delayed reaction which the subject did not have time to give before being confronted with the next touch. A minimum permitted time of 4 seconds is especially necessary if one is testing a deeply hypnotized individual, given the known retarded and lethargic reactions often found in such subjects. Because of the camera's obscurement we cannot view the first rendition of the test, but during the second administration Orne allowed an average of only 2.3 seconds between touches.

A breakdown of these is even more significant. When the touch was outside the circle (answered in each case with a "Yes"), the average time elapsing between touches was 2.7 seconds. However, when the touch was inside the circle (eliciting each time a "no response"), an average of only 1.8 seconds was permitted between touches.

An outside touch (responding "Yes" to feeling it) is a simple, almost reflex reaction. However, an inside touch requires much more complex mental processing. The subject at a covert level must first be aware of the touch, then collate it with the suggestion to say "No" before responding. It should require a *longer* period of time. Yet Orne allowed Bianchi *much less* time to make a response when the touch was inside the circle. No wonder all four of the inside touches brought a "no response" reaction. During this second administration of the circle-touch test, the total "touching-and-responding time" equaled only 15 seconds—an infinitesimal and unreliable behavior sample on which to base crucial decisions.

The *source-amnesia test*. This procedure has been found (Evans, 1971; Evans & Thorn, 1966; Orne, 1971) to significantly differentiate simulators from "reals." Thus, Orne (1979) states that, "it is frequently found in deeply hypnotized individuals. On the other hand, simulating Ss do not show this phenomenon . . . [p. 550]." He described it as follows: "Ss were taught a number of obscure facts during hypnosis, such as that amethysts, when heated, turn yellow. They then were wakened with suggestions of amnesia . . . [pp.549-550]." They were next asked general questions which included the obscure facts. Many good hypnotic subjects, while unable to recall the events that transpired under hypnosis, nonetheless were able to answer these questions correctly. "When asked about where they learned this information, they were unable to correctly specify the *source* of their knowledge [p. 550]." For the test to be successful, it is necessary to assure that the subject really learned under the hypnosis that he correctly remembered its *content* afterwards, and that he either did not know the source or confabulated another source.

During his May 27th session with Bianchi, Orne administered a 4-minute 55-second induction. The source-amnesia instructions were then given as follows:

O: I want you to tell me what the capital of England is.
B: London.
O: That's right. And what is the capital of Arkansas?
B: I don't know.
O: It's Little Rock, Arkansas. Now, the amethyst is a blue or purple gem stone. What color does it turn when it's heated?
B: I don't know.
O: Yellow. That's right, and you can just relax and sink deeper, it doesn't matter, you're forgetting all about it. . . .

Further deepening suggestions followed.

At this point the circle-touch test was administered, followed by further deepening. Then, "You're going to be able to let yourself go enough so that a part who has not heretofore talked to people will be able to come forward. . . [suggestions similar to mine in first activating Steve]." A frightened, weeping "Billy" personality emerged. This was followed by a discussion with Billy about Ken, Steve and the killings. Next, Orne made an attempt to activate "another part, that I suspect may be there." "Part" lifted its hand as a signal of its presence, but it did not want to talk. Billy was then re-activated followed by more discussion with him. Finally, Ken was brought back still under hypnosis. Forty-five minutes had elapsed since the source-amnesia items were implanted.

Orne now said,

> When you wake up you're going to forget what has happened until I ask you, "Now you can *remember everything* [emphasis mine]." And then you can remember things that happened. [Resistance from Ken.]
> O: Does that bother you? Would you like that? You wouldn't like it? You don't want to remember what you told me? You want it to be forgotten? You do want to remember? I'm confused.
> B: Wait.
> O: You want to wait? Okay. Then you won't have to remember it. You'll remember only as much as you feel comfortable with.

In being asked to "remember everything," Bianchi has been told to destroy his dissociative defense, relinquish his multiple personality, and bring to conscious awareness "everything" which transpired during the past hour. This includes the presence of Billy, the crimes which Steve did, plus many other events which for years he has been trying to avoid by dissociation. If successful, it could have precipitated an acute psychotic reaction. No wonder Bianchi was resistant and said, "Wait."

Dr. Orne, as a good clinician, must have recognized that, because he immediately reversed his field ("Then you won't have to remember it."). But now that Ken does not have to remember, he does not have to remember anything, such as that amethysts when heated turn yellow. Both Orne and Bianchi are "confused," and the source-amnesia test is irretrievably spoiled.

Bianchi was awakened, and questioning regarding the test was as follows:

> O: Do you remember anything of what has happened since you last closed your eyes? Okay. And the capital of Arkansas?
> B: Arkansas. Where is Arkansas?
> O: Middle west, somewhere. Towards the south. My geography's terrible.
> B: There's a song, wait a minute—Little Rock. It's a song I remember a long time ago.

Bianchi knows the answer, but ascribes it to *a different source*. He thus passes this test item as a "real," in spite of the confusing suggestions given to him.

In the "amethyst" item, Bianchi responded as follows: Orne: "The amethyst—it's a blue or purple gem stone—what color does it turn when it's heated?" Bianchi: "I'm sorry, I don't. . . . " No content memory which must first be present before the source memory can be tested. Possibly he did not learn it in the first place. Merely telling him this answer once under hypnosis does not assure that it was learned, and no check was made while he was under hypnosis to see if it had actually been learned.

Accordingly, this test item fails. No judgment can be made on it as to simulator versus "real."

Summary

The alternations of personality (behavior, perception, motivation, speech, mannerisms, handwriting, attitudes, amnesias, and Rorschach responses) and the consistencies within each of the respective personalities all point to a real dissociation and not to a simulation of this complex disorder.[10] This diagnosis is further supported by subsequent behavior (catatonic episode, inconsistent memory of crimes and confabulation when pressed), which was publicly predicted (Schwarz, 1981, pp. 247-248) on the basis of that diagnosis.

A diagnosis of "Antisocial Personality Disorder [Sociopath]" does not meet the specific criteria set down in *DSM-III*, namely, that this diagnosis is not made unless there is "a history of continuous and chronic antisocial behavior . . . [p. 317]," "with no intervening period of at least five years without antisocial behavior between age 15 and the present time . . . [p. 321]," an "inability to sustain consistent work performance . . . [p. 318]," none of which characterized Bianchi prior to his first arrest at age 26.

Numerous art productions by Bianchi, such as the monster face sculptured on back of Janus head when he was in high school, and fragmented human faces and figures drawn while in jail projectively suggest a dissociative disorder.

The prosecution position that Bianchi is a brilliant sociopath faking a multiple personality in order to escape punishment is contraindicated by the following: (a) his many months of refusing to allow his attorney to plead an insanity defense; (b) his total lack, during the early interviews, of concern about his legal position combined with intense curiosity about his inner mental state; (c) his moderate intellectual abilities (IQ repeatedly tested between 106 and 116); (d) his minimal reading (attested by his wife) and naïveté regarding psychological matters; and (e) his lack of any experience with hypnosis. Furthermore, since multiple personality is not classed as a psychosis, even a successful simulation of this disorder would not ensure an insanity defense. It would take a fool to attempt a simulation of this complex psychiatric disorder and a genius to carry it off—neither of which Bianchi is.

Whether he was hypnotized or not is irrelevant to the diagnosis since true multiple personalities emerge without hypnosis. However, since Dr.

[10]Psychodynamically the case might be formulated as follows: An abused child creates as a defense an imaginary playmate (Ken reported this). As a dissociated ego state, this entity becomes the repository for all the boy's anger, thus permitting him to behave in the overcontrolled and conforming ways which so characterized Bianchi's childhood. The price, however, was multiple psychosomatic symptoms for which he was hauled to one medical clinic after another.

Repressed throughout childhood and early adolescence, this child state, loaded with anger, becomes "executive" in early adulthood and emerges as a full-blown multiple to rape and kill symbolic mother figures.

Orne has based much of his conclusions on so-called "objective" tests of the reality of hypnosis, this issue was addressed.

The videotapes show repeated hypnotic responses to the inductions of Orne, Allison, and Watkins. The four tests administered by Orne: chevreul pendulum, circle-touch, double-hallucination and source-amnesia (in spite of poor wordings, confused suggestions and lack of controls) when interpreted in the light of research findings point to Bianchi as being a "real" and not a "simulator."

Finally, the adherence of the prosecution to a sociopathic diagnosis has had one unfortunate consequence. For the successful prosecution of his accomplice, Angelo Buono, they are greatly in need of data which can corroborate the circumstantial evidence secured by the police, the memories of which lie dissociated within that part of Bianchi known as "Steve." Since the prosecution will not admit the existence of Steve, no attempt in the last 3 years has been made to communicate with that personality. Steve could probably have been activated either hypnotically, or, as in my April session, nonhypnotically. Instead, they have been continually and futilely trying to pressure the Ken personality (who was not psychologically present at the killings) to give consistent testimony concerning the guilt and collaboration of his cousin. The result (as would have been predicted from studies in memory [Loftus, 1979]) has been inconsistency, confabulation and a complete discreditation of what could have been their star witness.

As long as the prosecution contends that the confusion and frequent change of testimony manifested by Ken represent simply conscious uncooperativeness, I do not believe that they will ever secure credible and verifiable testimony from him. And it may well be that "the other half" of the Hillside Strangler will go free.

After the Buono trial is over, and Bianchi has been transferred from his present isolated and protected cell in the Los Angeles jail to a prison where he will be in continuous contact with other brutal and hardened felons, it would be logical to expect a new dissociation. Steve can much better adjust to prison environment than Ken and may re-emerge. Perhaps Steve will then achieve the goal he voiced during our first interviews: "I want to destroy him. — I want to be free. — He won't last; he's not strong. — He'll die and I'll live."

Retrospect

Looking back, the question should be asked: "What might one have done differently?" I cannot accept the contention that my asking for another "part" of Ken could in itself initiate such a drastic reorganization of personality as to create a violent, cursing Steve, who described and bragged of his crimes in contrast to the mild, friendly, passive Ken, who was observed repeatedly and tested in the clinical interviews. After all, the "Hillside Strangler," a murderer and rapist, had to be precisely the kind of personality manifested by Steve. Yet Ken was reported by his employers and the woman who lived with him as being totally unlike the picture of Steve. In fact, they were unbelieving when he was apprehended. Hypnotic suggestion cannot make that drastic a change in personality functioning (which was manifest over many months in 1979), although many hypnotherapists might wish their modality had that power. In our experience with covert ego states, we have also found that these could not be activated (even in highly suggestible subjects) through requests for underlying "parts" which did not exist. However, if in March, 1979, I had suspected a multiple personality, it would have been better to have tried to activate Steve initially without a hypnotic induction—as was done during my April 20th interview. Failing this, the reported amnesias could have been explored under hypnosis. Perhaps regression to the time of the crimes would have brought out Steve without the necessity of asking for another "part."

In view of the recent Hitler diary episode (see Magnuson, 1983), it would seem advisable that, in cases of possible multiple personalities, analysis of the handwriting of the different states by one or more competent graphologists is indicated. This procedure should have been suggested at the time of our consultations. Study of writing styles might throw further light on the extent of dissociation present.

There is some evidence that different multiples have different EEG patterns. I did suggest that an EEG be given to Steve as well as to Ken, but it was not done. Current findings by Putnam (Hale, 1983) indicate that the different personalities manifest different brain scan pictures. These findings were not available in 1979. However, brain scans on both Ken and Steve might still be done if the authorities did not consider the diagnosis closed and refuse to permit attempts (hypnotic or nonhypnotic) to re-activate Steve.

At the time that Steve did emerge, we should have inquired in greater detail into the Los Angeles crimes. Such information would have been invaluable in the prosecution (or defense) of the case against Angelo Buono, then apparently at an impasse. But those matters were not considered by me or the other examiners in Bellingham back in 1979.

It has been suggested that an unconsidered alternative to a diagnosis of multiple personality was that Ken murdered the women in a dissociated and totally uncontrolled rage, and that the hypnosis merely consolidated these into the entity manifested by "Steve." While possible, I consider this as highly unlikely. Steve's description of the murders showed planning, coolness, integrated behavior and collaboration with Angelo Buono, not uncontrolled rage. The girls were picked up and went willingly to Buono's house where they were raped by Bianchi and Buono, who then took turns in killing them. Such integrated behavior cannot be so rapidly organized simply by a request to communicate with another part of Bianchi. Furthermore, Steve described many incidents when he was "out" which were unrelated to the violent crimes and for which Ken was amnesic.

More material should have been secured from the Steve entity related to early childhood incidents for which Ken may have had amnesia. Not enough exploration of Steve, his origins and emergences through the years were undertaken by any of us.[11] Faerstein, Moffett, and Lunde did not use hypnosis and did not contact Steve, but Allison, Orne and Watkins did. Such data might also have verified dissociation in earlier years.

Finally, better differential diagnosis and the legal questions of responsibility in these cases await our deeper understanding of the nature of dissociation. The multiple personality appears like an organism manifesting inconsistent behaviors which are under the control of two or more separate cognitive structural systems that are relatively independent of one another. An analogy might be that of a physical machine (the body) being controlled either by independent computers or by a single computer alternating from one program to another. A secondary personality in one of my patients put it as follows: "We were . . . uh . . . like Marylou's a robot, and we're kind of . . . we're . . . we're the dials inside, see? We just operate her like a TV tube."

In earlier papers (J. G. Watkins, 1976, 1978) my views have been discussed as to conditions which should govern the assessment of legal responsibility in cases of dissociation. To repeat them here would go beyond the bounds of this paper. However, further research and sound theoretical construction is badly needed to improve adjudication in ways which will both protect society and be fair to defendants. We must accept this challenge.

[11]Much has been made of "changes" in Steve's manner from his first appearance with me to his later ones with Dr. Orne. Although he did threaten me if I told Ken about his existence during my first (March) sessions, he did appear to be more belligerent later. This seemed to represent his increased anger at being revealed to Ken and the world, a normal consequence of the many questionings and evaluations. In my April 20th session, Ken noted that, "I've been discovering more and more about Steve." And as angry Steve voiced his reaction as follows:

> B: I keep trying to get out and I can't. . . .
> W: You've told me you've been getting out. . . .
> B: I got out any god-damn time I pleased. Now I can't. . . .
> W: Well, last time I talked with you you said he didn't even know about you.
> B: He didn't. . . . Between these fucking guys and all these other people that's been seeing him, he knows about me now. . . . I have some feeling it's partly your fault. You started this whole fucking thing. . . .
> W: Why does he get headaches?
> B: I try to come out. Instead I stay where I'm at and he complains about fucking headaches. . . .
> W: That's you trying to get out?
> B: That's fucking right.

It is to be regretted that Dr. Orne did not have the opportunity to see Bianchi until some 2 months later when the dissociative boundary had become less clear, Ken was strengthened, and able to "remember" many of the criminal actions previously carried out by Steve.

98   JOHN G. WATKINS

REFERENCES

AMERICAN PSYCHIATRIC ASSOCIATION. *Diagnostic and statistical manual of mental disorders (DSM-III)*. (3rd ed.) Washington, D.C.: APA, 1980.

BARBER, T. X. Suggested ("hypnotic") behavior: The trance paradigm versus an alternative paradigm. In E. Fromm & R. E. Shor (Eds.), *Hypnosis: Research developments and perspectives*. Chicago: Aldine-Atherton, 1972. Pp. 115–182.

BLUM, G. S., & GRAEF, J. R. The detection over time of subjects simulating hypnosis. *Int. J. clin. exp. Hypnosis*, 1971, *19*, 211–224.

DAHLSTROM, W. G., & WELSH, G. S. *An MMPI handbook: A guide to use in clinical practice and research*. Minneapolis: Univer. of Minnesota Press, 1960.

EIBLMAYR, K. H. An examination of the phenomenon of trance logic using objective measurement and limiting the hypnotist/subject relationship. Unpublished master's thesis, University of Montana, 1980.

ELLENBERGER, H. F. *The discovery of the unconscious: The history and evolution of dynamic psychiatry*. New York: Basic Books, 1970.

EVANS, F. J. Contextual forgetting: A study of source amnesia. Paper presented at the 42nd annual meeting of the Eastern Psychological Association, New York, April 1971.

EVANS, F. J., & ORNE, M. T. The disappearing hypnotist: The use of simulating subjects to evaluate how subjects perceive experimental procedures. *Int. J. clin. exp. Hypnosis*, 1971, *19*, 277–296.

EVANS, F. J., & THORN, W. A. F. Two types of posthypnotic amnesia: Recall amnesia and source amnesia. *Int. J. clin. exp. Hypnosis*, 1966, *14*, 162–179.

GOUGH, H. G. *Manual for the California Psychological Inventory*. Palo Alto, CA.: Consulting Psychologists Press, 1964.

HALE, E. Lives in pieces: Multiple personality and the mind. A Special Report by the Gannett News Service, Washington, D.C., 1983.

HARRIS, T. A. *I'm OK -- You're OK*. New York: Avon, 1969.

HENMON, V. A. C., & NELSON, M. J. *The Henmon-Nelson Tests of Mental Ability*. (Grades 6-9, Form A) Boston: Houghton Mifflin, 1957.

HILGARD, E. R. A critique of Johnson, Maher and Barber's "Artifact in the 'essence of hypnosis': An evaluation of trance logic," with a recomputation of their findings. *J. abnorm. Psychol.*, 1972, *79*, 221–233.

HILGARD, E. R. *Divided consciousness: Multiple controls in human thought and action*. New York: Wiley, 1977.

HILGARD, E. R., & HILGARD, J. R. *Hypnosis in the relief of pain*. Los Altos, CA: Kaufmann, 1975.

HILGARD, E. R., & LOFTUS, E. F. Effective interrogation of the eyewitness. *Int. J. clin. exp. Hypnosis*, 1979, *27*, 342–357.

JANET, P. *The major symptoms of hysteria*. New York: MacMillan, 1907.

JOHNSON, R. F. Q., MAHER, B. A., & BARBER, T. X. Artifact in the "essence of hypnosis": An evaluation of trance logic. *J. abnorm. Psychol.*, 1972, *79*, 212–220.

KASANIN, J. S. (Ed.) *Language and thought in schizophrenia*. Berkeley & Los Angeles: Univer. of California Press, 1944.

LOFTUS, E. F. *Eyewitness testimony*. Cambridge, MA: Harvard Univer. Press, 1979.

MAGNUSON, E. Hitler's forged diaries. *Time*, May 16, 1983, p. 36.

McDONALD. R. D., & SMITH, J. R. Trance logic in tranceable and simulating subjects. *Int. J. clin. exp. Hypnosis*, 1975, *23*, 80–89.

ORNE, M. T. The nature of hypnosis: Artifact and essence. *J. abnorm. soc. Psychol.*, 1959, *58*, 277–299.

ORNE, M. T. Demand characteristics and the concept of quasi-controls. In R. Rosenthal & R. L. Rosnow (Eds.), *Artifact in behavioral research*. New York: Academic Press, 1969. Pp. 143–179.

ORNE, M. T. The simulation of hypnosis: Why, how, and what it means. *Int. J. clin. exp. Hypnosis*, 1971, *19*, 183–210.

ORNE. M. T. On the simulating subject as a quasi-control group in hypnosis research: What, why, and how. In E. Fromm & R. E. Shor (Eds.). *Hypnosis: Developments in research and new perspectives*. (2nd rev. ed.) New York: Aldine. 1979. Pp. 519–565.

ORNE, M. T. Presented in E. E. Levitt (Chm.), A case of multiple personality. An invited symposium presented at the 32nd annual meeting of the Society for Clinical and Experimental Hypnosis, Chicago, October 1980.

PETERS, J. E. Trance logic: Artifact or essence of hypnosis? Unpublished doctoral dissertation, Pennsylvania State University, 1973.

PRINCE, M. *The dissociation of a personality*. New York: Longmans Green, 1906.

ROHDE, A. R. *Rohde Sentence Completions*. Beverly Hills. CA: Western Psychological Services, 1953.

RORSCHACH, H. *Psychodiagnostics: A diagnostic test based on perception*. (2nd ed.) (P. Lemkay & B. Kronenberg, trans.) New York: Grune & Stratton, 1942.

SCHREIBER, F. R. *Sybil*. New York: Warner Books, 1973.

SCHWARZ, T. *The Hillside Strangler: A murderer's mind*. Garden City, NY: Doubleday, 1981.

SHEEHAN, P. W. Incongruity in trance behavior: A defining property of hypnosis? In W. E. Edmonston, Jr. (Ed.), Conceptual and investigative approaches to hypnosis and hypnotic phenomena. *Ann. N.Y. Acad. Sci.*, 1977, 296. 194–207.

SLOSSON. R. L. *Slosson Intelligence Test (SIT)*. East Aurora. NY: Slosson Educational Publications, 1963.

SOLZHENITSYN, A. I. *The Gulag Archipelago 1918–1956: An experiment in literary investigation, I–II*. (Thomas P. Whitney, trans.) New York: Harper & Row, 1973.

THIGPEN. C. H., & CLECKLEY, H. M. *The three faces of Eve*. New York: McGraw-Hill. 1957.

WAGNER. E. E., & HEISE. M. R. A comparison of Rorschach records of three multiple personalities. *J. pers. Assess.*, 1974, 38, 308–331.

WATKINS. J. G. *Hypnotherapy of war neuroses*. New York: Ronald Press, 1949.

WATKINS. J. G. *Hypnotic phenomena: Part 1. Induction and suggestion. Part II. Deep trance*. Missoula, MT: Instructional Materials Services. Univer. of Montana. 1975. (Videotapes)

WATKINS J. G. Ego states and the problem of responsibility: A psychological analysis of the Patty Hearst case. *J. Psychiat. Law*, 1976. 4, 471–489.

WATKINS. J. G. Ego states and the problem of responsibility II. The case of Patricia W. *J. Psychiat. Law*, Winter, 1978, 519–535.

WATKINS. J. G. *Clinical hypnosis:* Vol. 1. *Hypnotherapeutic technique*. New York: Irvington Press. 1984, in press. (a)

WATKINS, J. G. Multiple personality. In R. Corsini (Ed.). *Encyclopedia of psychology*. New York: Wiley, 1984, in press. (b)

WATKINS, J. G., & JOHNSON, R. J. *We, the divided self*. New York: Irvington, 1982.

WATKINS. J. G., & STAUFFACHER, J. C. An index of pathological thinking in the Rorschach. *J. project. Tech.*, 1952, 16, 276–286.

WATKINS. J. G., & WATKINS, H. H. Ego-state therapy. In R. Corsini (Ed.), *Handbook of innovative therapies*. New York: Wiley, 1981. Pp. 252–270.

WATKINS. J. G., & WATKINS, H. H. Ego-state therapy. In L. E. Abt & I. R. Stuart (Eds.), *The newer therapies: A workbook*. New York: Van Nostrand Reinhold, 1982. Pp. 137–155.

WECHSLER. D. *The Wechsler Adult Intelligence Scale*. New York: Psychological Corp., 1955.

WEITZENHOFFER, A. M., & HILGARD, E. R. *Stanford Hypnotic Susceptibility Scale, Form C*. Palo Alto, CA: Consulting Psychologists Press, 1963. (a)

WEITZENHOFFER, A. M., & HILGARD, E. R. *Stanford Profile Scales of Hypnotic Susceptibility. Forms I & II*. Palo Alto, CA: Consulting Psychologists Press, 1963. (b)

WOLMAN. B. B. (Ed.) *Handbook of clinical psychology*. New York: McGraw-Hill, 1965.

100   JOHN G. WATKINS

Der Bianchifall (L. A.-Erwürger vom Bergabhang): Soziopath oder multiple
                              Persönlichkeit?

                              John G. Watkins

Abstrakt: Der Fall des Kenneth Bianchi (der Los Angeles-"Erwürger vom Bergabhang")
ist umstritten gewesen, sobald er im Januar 1979 verhaftet wurde. Dieser Mitarbeiter
sah Bianchi als fachärztlicher Berater am 21. und 22. März, 1979. Unter Hypnose mani-
festierte er, was eine multiple Persönlichkeit zu sein schien. Eine unterliegende Persönlichkeit, "Steve", deren Existenz Bianchi offenbar unbekannt zu sein schien, reklamierte
die Verantwortung für die 2 Morde in Bellingham und jene in Los Angeles. Infolgedessen
ernannte der Gerichtshof 5 andere Fachberater, den Angeklagten zu untersuchen. Ich
aktivierte die Steve-Persönlichkeit am 20. April, 1979, ohne eine Hypnoseinduktion. Sie
beschrieb die vielen Morde in Los Angeles, indem sie die bezeichnete, die er (Steve)
begangen hatte und jene, die Bianchis Cousin (Angelo Buono) begangen hatte. Die Haupt-
persönlichkeit (Ken) schien für all dies amnestisch zu sein. 2 Zuzügliche "Persönlichkeiten"
wurden von Martin Orne, einem anderen Berater, ans Licht gebracht. Jedoch akzeptierte
Orne nicht die Diagnose einer multiplen Persönlichkeit. Er diagnostizierte Bianchi als
eine "Anti-soziale Persönlichkeit" (Soziopath) und behauptete, daß er ein gerissener Si-
mulant sei. Weiterhin bestand er darauf, daß Bianchi niemals hypnotisiert worden war.
Das Beweismaterial, Rorschachtests, Intelligenztests, handschriftliche Muster, künstler-
ische Schöpfungen sowie auf Tonband aufgenommene Sitzungen von Watkins, Orne und
andern, werden analysiert. Dieser Schriftsteller kommt zu dem Beschluß, daß die Diagnose einer multiplen Persönlichkeit in starkem Maße Unterstützung findet.

Le cas Bianchi (L'Etrangleur de Hillside, L.A.): Sociopathe ou personnalité multiple?

                              John G. Watkins

Résumé: Le cas de Kenneth Bianchi (l'étrangleur de Hillside, L.A.) fut controversé dès
sa première arrestation en janvier 1979. L'auteur a vu Bianchi, en consultation, les 21 et
22 mars 1979. Sous hypnose, il manifesta ce qui semblait être une personnalité multiple.
La personnalité sous-jacente "Steve" semblait inconnue de Bianchi, mais revendiquait la
responsabilité des deux meurtres de Bellingham et ceux de Los Angeles. En conséquence,
la cour demanda à 5 autres consultants d'examiner le prévenu. Le 20 avril, je fis resurgir
la personnalité de Steve sans induction hypnotique. Elle décrivit plusieurs meurtres Los
Angeles indiquant lesquels elle (la personnalité Steve) avait commis et lesquels le furent
par le cousin de Bianchi (Angelo Buono). La personnalité principale (Ken) semblait amné-
sique de tout cela. Deux "personnalités" additionnelles furent mises en évidence par
Martin Orne, un autre consultant. Cependant, Orne n'acceptait pas le diagnostic de
personnalité muliple. Selon lui, Bianchi n'était qu'un sociopathe (personnalité anti-sociale)
doublé d'un simulateur intelligent et qu'il n'aurait jamais été hypnotisé. Les données
provenant du test Rorschach, de tests d'intelligence, d'échantillons d'écriture, de créations
artistiques et de sessions enregistrées par Watkins, Orne et d'autres sont analysées.
L'auteur conclut que ces analyses supportent le diagnostic de personnalité multiple.

El caso Bianchi (El estrangulador de Hillside, L.A.): ¿ Sociopatía o personalidad
                                múltiple?

                              John G. Watkins

Resumen: Desde su primer arresto en enero de 1979, el caso de Kenneth Bianchi (el
estrangulador de Hillside, Los Angeles) ha sido polémico. Requerido como consultante, el

BIANCHI CASE: SOCIOPATH OR MULTIPLE PERSONALITY?   101

autor de este artículo entrevistó a Bianchi el 21 y 22 de marzo de 1979. En estado de hipnosis presentó lo que pareció ser un caso de personalidad múltiple. Una personalidad subyacente, "Steve", cuya existencia era, aparentemente, desconocida para Bianchi, declaró ser la responsable de las 2 muertes de Bellingham y de las de Los Angeles. Como consecuencia de ello, la corte designó otros 5 consultores para examinar al detenido. El 5 de abril de 1979, sin inducción hipnótica activé la personalidad de Steve. Esta describió los numerosos crímenes de Los Angeles, indicando cuáles habían sido cometidos por Steve y cuáles habían sido llevados a cabo por un primo de Bianchi (Angelo Buono). La personalidad más importante (Ken) parecía amnésica a todo lo ocurrido. Dos personalidades adicionales fueron despertadas por Martin Orne, otro de los consultantes. Sin embargo, Orne no aceptó el diagnóstico de personalidad múltiple. Este consultante diagnosticó a Bianchi como una personalidad antisocial (sociópata), ademas declaró que era un simulador inteligente. Afirmó que Bianchi no había sido nunca hipnotizado. Se analizaron todos los materiales disponibles: Tests de Rorschach, tests de inteligencia, muestras de escritura, creaciones artísticas, además del registro de las sesiones hechas por Watkins, Orne y los otros especialistas consultados. El autor concluye que el diagnóstico de personalidad múltiple es altamente probable.

[20]

The International Journal of Clinical and Experimental Hypnosis
1984, Vol. XXXII, No. 2, 102-117

DIFFICULTIES DIAGNOSING THE MULTIPLE PERSONALITY SYNDROME IN A DEATH PENALTY CASE

RALPH B. ALLISON[1]

Morro Bay, California

Abstract: The problems involved in diagnosing the multiple personality syndrome in a rape-murder suspect are illustrated by the case of Kenneth Bianchi and the Hillside Stranglings. Hypnotic investigations of his amnesia revealed "Steve," who admitted guilt for the rape-murders. "Billy" later emerged, claiming responsibility for thefts and forgeries. Attempts to evaluate Kenneth Bianchi with methods used in therapy yielded an original opinion that he was a multiple personality and legally insane. Later events showed the diagnosis to be in error. A new diagnosis was made of atypical dissociative disorder due to the effects of the examining methods themselves. Warning is given that it may be impossible to determine the correct diagnosis of a dissociating defendant in a death penalty case.

The diagnosis of the multiple personality syndrome is difficult enough in the case of clinical patients, with their extensive use of denial, repression, and dissociation. The difficulty is greatly compounded when the individual under consideration is charged with first degree murder and is facing the death penalty. Because of the rarity of the occurrence of the multiple personality syndrome in the general population, guidelines for diagnosis are based on samples of limited size (Allison, 1978; Coons, 1980). When faced with the question, the forensic psychiatrist has to view these guidelines in the context of the legal situation, with its many differences from the clinical setting (Allison, 1981). All these difficulties existed in the case of 27-year-old Kenneth Bianchi and the Hillside Strangler case (Schwarz, 1981).

THE CRIMINAL CASES

In the fall and winter of 1977-78, the nude bodies of 10 women were found on various hillsides of Los Angeles County. All had been raped and then strangled. Extensive police investigation failed to identify the killer or killers.

On January 11, 1979, 22-year-old Karen Mandic and 27-year-old Dianne Wilder were raped and then strangled in a vacant house in Bellingham, Washington. Their clothed bodies were found in the Mandic car several hours after their friends notified police, since they had not reported to work on time. Immediate police investigation revealed physical evidence

Manuscript submitted August 11, 1982; final revision received November 29, 1982.

[1]Reprint requests should be addressed to Ralph B. Allison, M.D., 3240 Main Street, Morro Bay, CA 93442.

which led to the arrest, the following day, of Bianchi as the sole suspect. The Los Angeles Hillside Strangler Task Force was notified, and their detectives interviewed Bianchi, who had lived in the Los Angeles area when the 10 killings occurred in 1977-78. After their interrogation of him, the detectives did not consider him a likely suspect.

When first questioned by his defense attorney, Dean Brett, Bianchi claimed to have been driving his car some distance from the crime scene when the victims were killed. When confronted with facts which made his alibi impossible to believe, he then claimed he had fabricated the story to fill in the gap in his memory for the time span in question. Brett called in the first forensic psychiatrist, Donald T. Lunde, M.D., from the Stanford School of Law. Lunde reported that Bianchi gave a history of repeated spells of amnesia since childhood and recommended calling in someone experienced in the use of forensic hypnosis. John G. Watkins, Ph.D., Professor of Psychology at the University of Montana, was called in by Brett. During Watkins's hypnotic interview, what appeared to be an alter-personality, "Steve," appeared, claiming responsibility for the 2 local killings and involvement in 9 of the 10 Los Angeles deaths.

On March 30, 1979, the defense entered a plea of not guilty by reason of insanity, based on the possibility that Bianchi suffered from the multiple personality syndrome at the time of the offenses. Along with Charles W. Moffett, M.D., a Bellingham psychiatrist, the present author was appointed by the Court to examine the defendant, with specific instructions to determine whether or not he suffered from the multiple personality syndrome. Subsequently, the prosecution appointed Martin T. Orne, M.D., Ph.D., Professor of Psychiatry at the University of Pennsylvania and Saul J. Faerstein, M.D., of the University of Southern California Institute of Psychiatry and the Law, Los Angeles.

Evaluation Strategy

Since I had identified my first multiple personality syndrome patient in 1972 (Allison, 1974), I had seen 48 other individuals who appeared to have the multiple personality syndrome, 40 females and 8 males. My forensic experience included court appearances in seven cases (involving five males and two females). The crimes involved were bank robbery, forgery (see Ashby, 1979), embezzlement, theft, assault, drunken driving (see Hawksworth & Schwarz, 1977), and arson. The arsonist was later convicted of two murders, but the multiple personality syndrome diagnosis was not offered as a defense in those trials (Allison & Schwarz, 1980, pp. 159-182). Thus, the Bianchi case was to be the first one I was involved with where the charge was murder, the maximum penalty death, and the only possible defense legal insanity based on a diagnosis of the multiple personality syndrome.

After serious consideration of my options, I decided that the only way I could determine if the multiple personality syndrome diagnosis was correct was to match Bianchi's performance against that of multiple personality syndrome patients I had known best (i.e., those who had been in long-term therapy with me). This meant asking Bianchi to act like a patient, even though he would not actually be in the patient role with me. I knew of no other way to secure his cooperation in doing the mental maneuvers I needed him to perform so that I could compare him with my patient sample. The areas to be compared were family and psychiatric history, performance on several hypnotic procedures, and certain psychological tests.

I knew there was a risk in approaching Bianchi in the forensic setting as a pseudo-patient, when I was not under contract to be his therapist, but I saw no other way to accomplish the task for which I had been appointed. Prior to my first visit to Bellingham, I asked Brett to tell Bianchi to have ready some questions he wanted answered regarding a specific period of his childhood, in order to give me a logical reason to use hypnotic age regression, my main therapeutic modality for multiple personality syndrome. Also, the Minnesota Multiphasic Personality Inventory (MMPI; Dahlstrom & Welsh, 1960) had already been given to Bianchi on April 9, 1979. I asked John Johnson, a psychiatric social worker assisting Brett, to give Bianchi a California Psychological Inventory (CPI; Gough, 1964) before my arrival. Further CPIs were completed in June, 1979 by Bianchi and his two "alter-personalities."[2]

The clinical examination was carried out in two separate visits, one in April and one in June of 1979, each lasting 1.5 days.[3] After the April visit, Bianchi was seen again by Watkins for further hypnosis and Rorschach testing. Bianchi was also seen by Orne, Faerstein, and Moffett before my second visit.

THE APRIL, 1979 INTERVIEWS

Structure

The first several hours were devoted to obtaining a detailed history and listening to the reactions Bianchi expressed to the interview with Lunde. Lunde had noted the discrepancy between Bianchi's view of his mother as a saint and the documented history of her maternal psychopathology. While discussing his feelings about her, Bianchi willingly played the patient role, thus cooperating in my plan. He also admitted to a history of senseless lying to his wife, but claimed that he would do his best to give us the true facts as he knew them, with so much at stake. Per my prior

---

[2]These tests were computer scored by Behaviordyne, Inc. of Palo Alto, CA.

[3]A transcript of the videotaped clinical examination which took place in April and May of 1979 has been deposited with the National Auxiliary Publications Service (NAPS). For 255 pages, order Document No. 04181 from NAPS % Microfiche Publications, P. O. Box 3513, Grand Central Station, New York, NY 10163. Remit in advance in U.S. funds only, $78.25 for photocopies or $4.00 for microfiche, and make checks payable to Microfiche Publications — NAPS. Outside the United States and Canada, add postage of $28.00 for photocopies, $1.50 for microfiche postage.

instructions to Brett, he asked to know what important events had happened at age 8 when he had lived on Villa Street in Rochester, New York. I then explained the use of ideomotor signals to help answer his question.

The second session of the day began with ideomotor signals under hypnosis, which indicated that the ages of 9 and 13 were significantly related to the current problems. Regression to age 9 was accomplished, then progression to age 13. With progression to age 27, the criminal entity, "Steve," emerged. I then called on Ken to replace "Steve." Dehypnotizing Ken did not seem necessary. Next, I used ideomotor signals to determine if there were any other entities besides Ken and "Steve" and received a negative answer. Then I suggested that Bianchi might have a dream that night which would help him learn to cope with "Steve." (I did this because Watkins had already suggested that Ken would have increasing awareness of "Steve" but not what he was to do with that awareness.) I suggested that he use "the highest elements of helping power inside [his] mind," in an attempt to activate an Inner Self Helper, which has been of great help to the victims of the multiple personality syndrome (Peters & Schwarz, 1978). The following morning, he reported a dream of being with a twin brother, "Sticks," at one age, then with him again at an older age, when the twin was called "Steve Walker." Next, I asked Bianchi to conduct a dialogue with "Steve" as if he were talking to him on the telephone. This he did, speaking only as Ken but never as "Steve."

Results

1. *Regression to age 9*. Bianchi remained in a trance-like state, talking in the present tense. He did not behave as a conscious 9-year-old boy, in a state of revivification, as many multiple personality syndrome patients do. He reported his best friend to be Billy Thompson, the boy next door. Only when I asked if he ever hid inside his head did he mention talking there to "Steve Walker, my second best buddy." This reportedly occurred while he was hiding under his bed to escape his mother's wrath when she was very angry with his father for gambling too much.

2. *Regression to age 13*. This time Bianchi told of arguing by neighbors and between his parents, sneaking out to visit school buddies, and "Stevie" trying to talk him into running away from home. Only after I asked about the biggest problem that year did he mention his father's sudden death at work. No mention was made of any new personality being created thereby, as I had expected.

3. *Appearance of "Steve."* "Steve" was seen in full bloom, out of trance. He was very crude and nasty, using the word "fuck" in every sentence. He lunged at Johnson, who was operating the video camera behind my right shoulder. He talked about Ken in the third person, constantly putting him down. He freely admitted to strangling the two local victims "'cause I hate fuckin' cunts." He committed the crime, he said, to get Ken out of the way, so that he could control the body full-time. He further admitted to killing four of the Hillside Strangler victims and watching his

cousin, Angelo Buono, kill the other five victims. He denied there were any others like him inside Ken. When I called for Ken and put my hand in front of his forehead, "Steve" slumped into his chair and was replaced by a very tired Ken.

4. *"Telephone" conversation with "Steve."* Ken talked to "Steve" about childhood friends in Rochester, a psychological clinic evaluation done at age 9, and the two local killings. Ken appeared to know "Steve," accept his existence, and know that "Steve," who considered himself above the law, had committed the murders. Ken, in contrast, considered himself a law-abiding citizen who knew it was wrong to kill.

THE JUNE, 1979 INTERVIEWS

Goals

Since April, 1979, Bianchi had been hypnotized by Watkins and was seen by Orne. Information from Los Angeles indicated Bianchi had secured fake diplomas as a psychologist, using the name "Thomas Steven Walker," but giving a mailing address of "% Mrs. K. Bianchi." He had rented a psychologist's office in the evenings and had passed out professional cards at the title company where he worked. Numerous items found in Bianchi's apartment in Bellingham were found to have been stolen from a store where he had worked as a security guard. None of this could have been explained by the existence of "Steve," the killer.

The videotape of Orne's "hypnotic" session with Bianchi showed Orne telling "Steve" that he, Orne, could not believe "Steve" had been interested in working in a title company. Orne asked "Steve" if he were aware of another part within him that Ken did not know about. Following "Steve's" denial, "Steve" was replaced by a crying 9-year-old "Ken," who was followed by a 14-year-old "Billy," who admitted responsibility for the false diplomas, the psychologist role-playing, and the various thefts. When Orne asked if there was a higher level source of information present, Bianchi nodded in the affirmative, but he refused to talk to Orne in that mode.

Therefore, my goals in the second trip to Bellingham were to interview "Billy" and to talk to that higher source of knowledge. I had a long list of questions for both of them.

Structure

The first several hours were spent trying to get Bianchi's cooperation in these tasks, as he claimed he had amnesia for all the material he had produced during the various hypnotic sessions, and he was tired of seeing those sessions first reported in the newspaper. He appeared quite depressed and claimed to have tried to hang himself after his interview with Faerstein.

The second period was spent getting handwriting samples and questioning the Inner Self Helper, the higher source of knowledge. Many answers were quickly and clearly provided by "Ken's friend," as this entity called itself. I then asked Ken to enter into a dialogue with "Billy," which he could not do. I called out "Billy," secured his handwriting samples, and then asked him to initiate a dialogue with Ken. I could hear both voices this time. Ken then carried on a dialogue with "Steve." Finally, "Billy" came out to take the CPI.

During the third period, Bianchi made pictures of the faces of "Billy" and "Steve," using the Identi-Kit, under the supervision of Detective Fred Nolte. Then I called out "Steve" and persuaded him to take the CPI. The test booklet was left with Johnson so Ken could take that test again, also.

Results

To reach "Ken's friend," I had to appeal to that part of Ken's mind that had refused to talk to Orne. He initially talked in the first person and then switched to the third person in referring to Ken. After one question of his own, Ken asked me to give the questions. He told of "Steve's" beginning, of his killing, and pimping in Los Angeles. "Billy" was defined as "a source of secrets, of denial of facing up to the facts," having been created when Ken went daily to his father's casket prior to burial. "Billy" and Ken were co-conscious, while Ken was amnesic for all "Steve" did. "Billy" was the thief and pretended to be a psychologist as a new way to meet people. "Steve's" emotions were "anger, hate, and violence, while 'Billy's' were non-violent, such as deceit."

A week after Bianchi had been infected with gonorrhea by his wife, who claimed to have been raped while on vacation, "Steve" had killed the first of the Los Angeles victims, a prostitute. Bianchi's feeling of being betrayed was considered by Brett and Johnson to be a logical motive for this first murder. But "Ken's friend" denied the psychological connection, explaining that the physical weakness resulting from the infection had left Ken defenseless against "Steve's" coming out.

"Billy" appeared to be a shy, quiet, 14-year-old boy, who now wanted to cooperate with Ken in dealing with "Steve." He took the CPI quickly, calmly, and cooperatively.

When "Steve" and Ken spoke together this time, I could hear both voices while they talked of "Steve's" plan to send the coat and scarf of one of the local victims to cousin Buono. Bianchi reported that talking to "Steve" left him with a chill at the end of his spine, but he was comfortable talking with "Billy."

While making the Identi-Kit pictures, Bianchi repeatedly closed his eyes and appeared to visualize each face inside his head, carefully correcting the features to his satisfaction. Neither picture looked at all like Bianchi, and both matched the personality characteristics seen on interview.

When "Steve" returned to take the CPI, he was initially quite resistant, but he finally gave in, expending much energy in foot shuffling and pencil jabbing.

Psychological Test Results

The Behaviordyne computer reports a series of diagnoses in the order of preference. Both the MMPI and CPI scales can be run off using the CPI answer sheets.

1. *MMPI taken by Ken on April 9, 1979.* Preferred diagnosis: psychoneurosis, hysteria, dissociation reaction, consisting of sudden episodes of unaccustomed behavior, related to hysterical acting out, possibly with true amnesia.

2. *CPI taken by Ken in April, 1979.* Preferred diagnosis: personality with risk of a drinking problem. Second diagnosis: personality trait disorder, dissociating (hysterical) personality with sociopathic and passive aggressive features, emotional instability, and unpredictable (hysterical) acting out of unconscious impulses.

3. *CPI taken by Ken in June, 1979.* Preferred diagnosis: personality pattern disorder, paranoid personality, with passive hostile behavior.

4. *CPI taken by "Billy" in June, 1979.* Preferred diagnosis: personality trait disorder, dissociating [hysterical] personality.

5. *CPI taken by "Steve" in June, 1979.* Preferred diagnosis: psychosis, schizophrenia, paranoid type, with aggressive hostile behavior.

Forensic Conclusions

Following my April evaluation of Bianchi, I had reported to the Court that Bianchi suffered from the multiple personality syndrome, was legally insane at the time of the offenses, and because of the amnesia for the time period of the offenses, was unable to stand trial. After my June evaluation, I concluded that he was now able to stand trial, but my other opinions remained the same. I submitted 124 pages of reports detailing the data which supported the diagnosis of multiple personality syndrome. Space limitations prevent me from repeating any more of that material here. He was also believed to be insane by Lunde, Moffett, and Watkins. Both Faerstein and Orne considered him sane. With this split opinion, Bianchi agreed to a plea bargain in which he would plead guilty to 2 counts of first degree murder in Washington and to 5 counts of first degree murder in California in exchange for his testimony against Buono. On October 18, 1979, Bianchi was sentenced to 2 consecutive life terms in Washington. On October 22, 1979, he was sentenced to 6 concurrent life terms in California. Buono had been arrested on October 19, 1979 and is currently on trial for 10 counts of first degree murder. Bianchi has been the prime prosecution witness against him, but his stories keep changing, and no one can tell what version he is going to relate the next time he testifies.

The Aftermath

Letters from Jail

Seven letters were sent to me by Bianchi, from the Los Angeles County Jail, between October 14, 1979 and December 4, 1979. These letters were all from Ken, but in them he referred to "Steve" and "Billy" as himself in different states of mind. I had hoped, in responding to his first letter, that he would clear up some of the still unanswered questions about the

Washington crimes. In a letter dated November 10, 1979, he laid the blame on a man he named only as Greg, whom he knew had died in an accident after Bianchi's arrest. He claimed that he and Greg had invited the two victims to the house for a blind date. He claimed that, as "Billy," he had gone to the store, and, when he returned, Greg was in the process of hanging the two women. There was indeed a man named Greg who lived in the area at the time of the crime, but police investigation proved he could not have been at the crime scene with Bianchi the day of the killings.

The Compton Case

On September 6, 1980, an envelope was delivered to my home, post-marked "Seattle, Washington," but with a return address of "LAPD, Homicide." Inside I found a brassiere and an unlabeled cassette tape. On the tape was the voice of a young man claiming to have framed Bianchi for the murders in Washington, in return for money. Nothing on the tape told me who he was or where I could contact him. The package was turned over to the local police, who contacted the Bellingham Police Department. Two similar tapes were delivered in Bellingham, one to a clergyman and one to the Whatcom County Sheriff's Department. The latter tape had been hand delivered, and the messenger was able to provide a description of the woman who had given it to him at the Seattle airport. On September 29, 1980, the same woman lured a Bellingham woman into a motel room and tried to strangle her. The victim escaped and 24-year-old Veronica Lynn Compton was arrested for attempted murder. She was identified as a scriptwriter from Los Angeles County, a frequent visitor to Bianchi, and the owner of several other tapes on which were recorded threats against my daughters. In March, 1981, she was convicted of attempted murder in the first degree and sentenced to 5 years to life in prison.

Other New Information

With the list of boyhood friends supplied by Bianchi, detectives searched Rochester to find anyone who could remember his having complaints of lapses of memory or who had observed sudden personality changes in him. No one could be found to corroborate that history which he had given. When his wife was interviewed on television, she denied having noticed any personality changes she could now attribute to the existence of "Steve." None of the psychiatric staff at the Los Angeles County Jail reported meeting either "Steve" or "Billy."

Only in 1980 did the use of the Rorschach for specifically diagnosing multiple personality syndrome come to my attention (Wagner & Heise, 1974). When Wagner independently reviewed the Rorschach protocols of Ken and "Steve," he concluded,

> My considered opinion is that this is *not* a multiple personality. . . . Ken is what I would call . . . a paranoid with a psychopathic overlay. . . . Such cases

are quite dangerous and, as might be expected, tend to be diagnosed as psycho-pathic *or* paranoid . . . Ken is exclusively self centered and preoccupied with his own ideas. He is a compulsive ruminator with a marked incapacity to derive pleasure from interpersonal relationships. He is intimidated by women because of a love-hate relationship with his mother and, under conditions of lowered consciousness (e.g., fatigue, alcohol), is capable of a revenge type of rape-murder. Normally, because he can't share his thoughts with anyone, he seems quite dull to the casual observer. Qualitatively, it is interesting to note that he makes frequent references to his childhood. This often occurs with people who find themselves in threatening circumstances from which they feel they cannot escape. I believe that "Steve" represents Ken's escape hatch (a last desperate measure).

Steve's Rorschach does reveal hostility and sexual preoccupation but there is a perverse, deliberate aspect about it which smacks of psychopathic intent. The refusal to respond and desire not to "play" is psychopathic, not schizo-phrenic . . . . What is frightening about Ken is that his murders were probably committed without much affect and with a certain detachment.

Structurally, the basic inconsistency is that . . . the two Rorschachs are cogni-tively similar. From my experience, alter-personalities are always contained within (and break off from) the major or first personality. This is not the case with Bianchi. Ken and Steve appear to be mirror images — one "good" and the other "bad," like Dr. Jekyll and Mr. Hyde. This type of patterning is viable from a literary but not a psychological point of view.[4]

Later, in 1981, I started working full-time in a state prison after spend-ing 3 years working in a county jail part-time. In the prison, I began hearing the tales of convicted felons who claimed to have fabricated stories prior to trial so as to create insanity defenses. Having failed at that goal, they were now finding those histories of "mental illness" haunting them when they sought paroles from the Board of Prison Terms. I also met rapists who explained to me some of the mental aberrations they had undergone during their crime sprees, when they acted as law-abiding citizens by day and rapists at night, being, to a great degree, unaware of the two lives they were leading until they were apprehended and con-fronted with the evidence. These seemed to be honest reports of some type of a dissociative process which only occurred during a limited span of time.

THE BUONO TRIAL

In October, 1981, I was called to testify in Los Angeles in the prelimi-nary hearing for Angelo Buono. The main issue of debate was whether or not Bianchi had ever been "really hypnotized," since a positive judicial decision on that question would cast doubt on the reliability of his testi-mony. That issue was easily settled in my mind with the concept that there is no way to prove any person is in a state of hypnosis, since there is no universally accepted standard of behavior or objectively measurable physiological process which is accepted as being indicative of a hypnotic state of mind.

But the night before I was due in court, I reviewed all the transcripts of my sessions with Bianchi, as well as the events mentioned above. I

[4]Wagner, E., personal communication, February, 1980.

discovered that, in making the original diagnosis of multiple personality syndrome, I had inadvertently ignored certain items which, at the time, did not fit into a neat pattern. This was not an unusual situation for me in working clinically with multiple personality syndrome patients, as many times bits of data emerged which could not, at that time, be understood in the total context. Further digging into the repressed material usually clarified the problem and allowed me to fit that piece of data into the total picture. This was why I maintained contact with Bianchi by mail in the first place. The facts which I now looked at with more attention, however, fitted a dissociative disorder, but not what I knew to be the multiple personality syndrome.

In court, I testified that I had come to a new conclusion regarding Bianchi's psychiatric diagnosis. I now believe that, although he had to have been extremely disturbed to have committed the lust-murders at all, he did not have multiple personality syndrome at the time he committed the crimes. My new view was that all of the pathological elements we had seen as "Steve" and "Billy" had existed in Bianchi's mind for years, but had not "crystallized" into the forms we saw until he was first hypnotized by Watkins (for "Steve") and Orne (for "Billy"). (I knew that Watkins had testified that he believed Bianchi was in hypnosis when he first found "Steve" and that Orne had testified that Bianchi had never been really hypnotized by any of the examiners, including himself. While viewing the videotapes of Bianchi with Orne, I believed that Orne did have Bianchi in a hypnotic trance, which gave Bianchi a chance to show his psychopathology in a most dramatic fashion via "Steve" and "Billy.") I was quite willing to take responsibility for bringing out "Ken's friend." The Assistant Attorney General carrying out the cross-examination later told me that Bianchi said to her, "It was the best way I could think of at the time to explain to the doctors how my mind was working then." Once the trial was over, Bianchi no longer needed to explain his motives to the psychiatrists, so neither "Steve" nor "Billy" were necessary for him to bring forth. Ken apparently felt he had the capacity to deal with the problems in Los Angeles County completely on his own.

Before I list the factors in this particular case which caused me to change my original diagnosis, I must emphasize that there is no typical patient with multiple personality syndrome against which to match any future patient. To assume that the presence of the exact opposite of these listed characteristics would guarantee the diagnosis of multiple personality syndrome is faulty logic. Diagnosis from any list of necessary findings, as is implied by *DSM-III* (American Psychiatric Association, 1980) leads one into the pigeonhole myth (Dirckx, 1977, pp. 111-112). Human beings are much too complicated to view in that fashion, and more complex methods, such as factor analysis, may be more realistic. But the average clinician has to use the "list of criteria" method to start with, and these points are only guidelines to help those who may come across such individuals in their own local courtrooms.

1. *Personality characteristics of Ken.* Ken, as himself, seemed to be able to express a full range of emotional feelings. He was not unable to experience anger, resentment, fear, sexual pleasure, and other such feelings that multiple personality syndrome patients learn, from their families, are forbidden and thus require expression through their alter-personalities. That is one reason for creating an alter-personality, to express the forbidden thought and emotion.

2. *Regression to age 9.* Bianchi did not mention "Steve" as an imaginary playmate until I brought up the idea of hiding inside his own head. In retrospect, it would have been better not to have brought up that concept and to have left Bianchi to his own devices. Unfortunately, any question and tone of voice used gives some message as to the acceptable answer. Bianchi had a very strong need to please authority figures, of which we psychiatrists were the latest version. Multiple personality syndrome patients in therapy can and do ignore what I want to hear and do want to tell their story in age regression. They hint at subjects they are ashamed to mention and just need encouragement to continue, with assurance that they will not be punished for telling the truth.

3. *Origin of the villainous "Steve."* Bianchi reported no new or different physical or mental trauma the day he claimed he first heard "Steve" talking to him, while hiding under his bed. A dissociative process in multiple personality syndrome usually occurs when trauma of a life-threatening nature occurs, is too stressful for the child to handle in any physical fashion, and mental mechanisms must be used instead. Had his mother set his clothes on fire or chased him with a hatchet in her hand, the story would have been more convincing.

4. *The boy next door.* Bianchi's first choice as a best friend was a living boy, a fact which ruled out the need for an imaginary playmate. Multiple personality syndrome sufferers were very lonely children and usually felt there was no one — child or adult — to whom they could turn in times of crisis.

5. *School.* Both Ken and "Steve" disliked going to school. If "Steve" really existed in those days, he should have had a different attitude than that of Ken, not necessarily the opposite. Ken could have liked going to school and "Steve" could have just ignored the whole scene, since it held no interest for him. If there had been a hostile teacher who whipped the boys, "Steve" would have been the one who threw ink on her when her back was turned, and then allowed Ken to take the punishment.

6. *Buddies.* Bianchi reported many neighborhood friends in his later school years. With so many friends, he would not have needed to keep "Steve" around. In addition, "Steve's" obnoxious behavior would have driven away those children who tried to befriend Ken, keeping him in a lonely state of mind.

7. *Regression to age 13.* The error here was that Bianchi first mentioned fights of neighbors and between his parents, but nothing new. If that was

when "Billy" was created, at his father's death, he should have mentioned the death first. Only when I asked about the main difficulty that year did he bring up the subject of his father dying.

8. *Creation of "Billy."* "Ken's friend" reported that "Billy" was created during repeated visits to his father's casket at the funeral home. An alter-personality would have been more likely to have been created when news of his father's death was first brought by the messenger from work. It was reported by the family that Ken did go into hysterics when told the tragic news.

9. *The murder victims.* None of the victims had any emotional tie to Bianchi. They were not threats to him in any way. They were only the objects of the transference of his hatred for his mother, a common reason for lust-murder (Macdonald, 1971, pp. 132-139). Defendants with multiple personality syndrome, whom I have met since the Bianchi case, each killed a spouse or a parent-figure when their anger towards that individual overwhelmed their repressive abilities.

10. *Fatigue after hypnosis.* Fatigue after only switching personalities is not common with multiple personality syndrome patients, since each alter-personality has its own source of energy and it does not need to draw energy from the primary personality or each other. After age regression, fatigue is common, since much energy is expended in the lifting of repression in psychotherapy.

11. *Internal dialogue.* The first time he had internal dialogue, Bianchi followed my suggestion too literally and talked to "Steve" as if on a telephone. No multiple personality syndrome patient has ever done that in front of me, even when given the same instructions. Also, Ken claimed to have amnesia for all he said in the internal dialogue, while multiple personality syndrome patients usually have full recollection of both sides of the dialogue. The purpose of the exercise is to bring that repressed material to consciousness. This is one procedure I would now avoid in a forensic case, since there is a clear standard of the "proper" response and few defendants are ready to become aware of unconscious material during the trial phase of their incarceration. After conviction, they are much more likely to be willing to look at their faults and try to correct them.

12. *Ideomotor signals.* Bianchi's fingers answered "No" to the questions about the presence of entities other than "Steve" being present. This was a lie, if "Billy" had been present in the first interview. But it was a truthful answer, if "Billy" did not crystallize until Orne challenged "Steve" as being an inadequate explanation for the role-playing as a psychologist. It is quite logical to believe that Bianchi then had to produce "Billy" to satisfy Orne's objections.

Then there is the question of the basic reliability of ideomotor signals for telling the "unconscious truth." These signals may be very useful in therapy where the social consequences are minimal, but that procedure certainly does not have the sanction of research and judicial decision as a

lie detection process. Until the procedure has passed such tests of reliability and validity, it is not acceptable in a court of law and must be
reserved for therapeutic and research purposes only.

13. *Dehypnotizing*. Bianchi did not seem to need dehypnotizing after
the age regression and first appearance to me of "Steve." He was so alert
that I did not think any procedure was necessary. Was he really hypnotized
or not? In another case, when I forgot to dehypnotize a multiple personality syndrome patient who resisted and broke out of an age regression
session, she reported being very uncomfortable the next day until she
realized she was still in trance and dehypnotized herself.

14. *Blaming Greg for the murders*. Multiple personality syndrome
patients who have been arrested for crimes know, at some level, that they
are guilty of some wrongdoing, but they are not sure what it is they did.
They usually take their punishment, since they feel that they deserve it;
they do not blame another individual.

15. *The Compton case*. Again we see an attempt to lay blame elsewhere. At first, I was perplexed as to why Bianchi should have chosen to
send that package to me, instead of to anyone else involved in the case.
Gerald Chaleff, Buono's attorney, because of his knowledge of Bianchi's
current state of mind, identified this as a hostile act towards me. I tend
to agree, since Bianchi had expected that I would be involved in his
psychotherapy in the California prison system and may have seen me as
a rescuing father-figure. When he found himself locked in the Los Angeles
County Jail for an indefinite period of time, he may have felt betrayed by
me and used Comptom to strike back. Ex-patients with multiple personality syndrome have generally been appreciative of my recognition of the
reasons for their distress and have remained friendly towards me, even if
they did not agree with me at the time of first contact.

16. *Bianchi's lying*. Bianchi admitted to being a chronic liar, as Ken,
even regarding facts which were unimportant. Multiple personality syndrome patients, because of their many amnesic spells, learn to pay careful
attention to what happens when they are in charge. They pride themselves
on their excellent memory of those events of which they are aware. The
charges of lying come about because of their refusal to admit to misdeeds
which have been done by an angry alter-personality.

17. *No witnesses to personality changes*. None of his family members
or friends admitted witnessing personality changes, and jail staff witnessed
none, even when they had reason to look for them. Multiple personality
syndrome patients in hospitals or prisons do show different personalities
to different staff members, depending on their feelings about each staff
member. Thus, the patients tend to polarize the staff into camps of
believers and non-believers in multiplicity. None of this happened with
Bianchi in either jail. Now, I would say that if the institutional staff is not
split on the question of the diagnosis of multiple personality syndrome,
and very strongly so, the patient most likely has some other mental
disorder.

CONCLUSIONS

The first principle to remember is that the human mind can do anything. The only limits are those we put on it, with our own narrow view of what is possible. A man under the threat of death, who has never before been a defendant in any criminal action, is not bound by any rules of conduct involving honesty, decency, or fair play. The only rule is to save his own skin; if he has to use mental gymnastics, so be it. Consciously, he may believe he is telling only the truth; unconsciously, he must act in whatever manner he believes will prolong his life. That is why the unconscious mental mechanisms of defense exist in the first place.

The second principle is that it is extremely difficult — if not impossible — to be sure that a defendant who has not been in psychotherapy for the disorder really has the multiple personality syndrome, since we have no firm criteria against which to measure him. Clinical patients have such different situations and motives and show such variations in behavior, mood, and thinking patterns that there is no typical multiple personality syndrome patient. That is why there can be only general guidelines for determining who is and who is not disturbed in this particular fashion. A clear understanding of the psychodynamics underlying the disorder seems to be the best protection against error.

A third principle is that it may be impossible to determine the state of mind of a defendant claiming amnesia at the time of the crime, with his unverified statements being the only available historical evidence of mental status. Bianchi's story supported an insanity plea, but no other evidence could be uncovered to support the idea that he had a diagnosable dissociative disorder while in Rochester, Los Angeles, or Bellingham. He clearly had a long-standing personality disorder, but, without documented psychiatric observation or witnesses to provide evidence of any mental disease, defect, or disorder, I have no other data supporting any dissociative disorder diagnosis during those years of his criminal activity. My support of his insanity plea was based on the assumption that the dissociative disorder shown to the forensic examiners had existed prior to his arrest and was causally related to the commission of the crimes. Since that assumption no longer seems warranted, my forensic opinion now is that there is insufficient evidence to support an opinion that he was legally insane at the time of the crimes. His urges to rape and kill most likely arose from repressed unconscious conflicts, as is true in many crimes of violence, but that concept does not justify an excuse from legal sanctions in our courts today. Because the determination of his mental state during the crimes was hampered by his habitual tendency to lie, the truth may remain a mystery for many years. My prison experience indicates that such an individual defends against insight until faced with parole board hearings when his clear understanding of those unconscious motivations is required before release from prison can be considered.

My diagnoses of Kenneth Bianchi, as of the time of the forensic examinations, are as follows:

Axis I 300.15 Atypical Dissociative Disorder (see *DSM-III*, p. 260), occurring under stress of intensive and extensive psychiatric evaluations, while under threat of the death penalty, and limited in duration to the period of time between arrest for murder and sentencing.

Axis II 301.89 Mixed Personality Disorder (see *DSM-III*, pp. 329-330), with antisocial, paranoid, and histrionic features.

I do not believe Bianchi was deliberately and consciously faking the multiple personality syndrome clinical picture. He possessed the drives to lie, steal, rape, and kill in his unconscious mind since childhood. Certain triggering situations caused the resultant criminal behavior to occur. He may well have chosen to forget a large portion of his criminal behavior over the years to be able to live his version of a normal life at work and at home. But his amnesias were not due to the sudden control of his body by alter-personalities which had been created by psychosexual traumas occurring at the ages of 9 and 13. He found his targets for his negative transference feelings in those women he identified as the street-walking prostitutes of Los Angeles, even while he was employing other young women as prostitutes himself. Then, for some still unknown reason, he raped and killed two completely innocent women in Bellingham. I believe that he also unconsciously set himself up to be caught in Bellingham so that he could be stopped forever. Fortunately, the Bellingham Police Department, in their thoroughly professional manner, cooperated in his plan.

REFERENCES

ALLISON, R. B. A new treatment approach for multiple personalities. *Amer J clin. Hypnosis*, 1974, *17*, 15–32.

ALLISON, R. B. On discovering multiplicity. *Svensk Tidskrift för Hypnos*, 1978, 2, 4–8.

ALLISON, R. B. Multiple personality and criminal behavior. *Amer. J. forens. Psychiat.*, 1981, 2, 32–38.

ALLISON, R. B., & SCHWARZ, T. *Minds in many pieces*. New York: Rawson, Wade, 1980.

AMERICAN PSYCHIATRIC ASSOCIATION. *Diagnostic and statistical manual of mental disorders (DSM-III)*. (3rd ed.) Washington, D.C.: APA, 1980.

ASHBY, A. Esther Minor: Multiple personalities in court. *Forum*, 1979, *6*, 3–30.

COONS, P. M. Multiple personality: Diagnostic considerations. *J. clin. Psychiat.*, 1980, *41*, 330–336.

DAHLSTROM, W. G., & WELSH, G. S. *An MMPI handbook: A guide to use in clinical practice and research*. Minneapolis: Univer. of Minnesota Press, 1960.

DIRCKX, J. H. *Dx + Rx: A physician's guide to medical writing*. Boston: Hall, 1977.

GOUGH, H. G. *Manual for the California Psychological Inventory*. Palo Alto, CA: Consulting Psychologists Press, 1964.

HAWKSWORTH, H., & SCHWARZ, T. *The five of me*. New York: Regnery, 1977.

MACDONALD, J. M. *Rape: Offenders and their victims*. Springfield, IL: Charles C Thomas, 1971.

PETERS, C., & SCHWARZ, T. *Tell me who I am before I die*. New York: Rawson, 1978.

SCHWARZ, T. *The Hillside Strangler: A murderer's mind*. Garden City, NY: Doubleday, 1981.

WAGNER, E. E., & HEISE, M. A comparison of Rorschach records of three multiple personalities. *J. pers. Assess.*, 1974, *38*, 308–331.

Schwierigkeiten im Diagnostizieren des multiplen Persönlichkeitssyndroms bei einem mit der Todestrafe verbundenen Falles

Ralph B. Allison

Abstrakt: Die Probleme, die mit dem Diagnostizieren des multiplen Persönlichkeitssyndroms verbunden sind, werden durch den Fall des Kenneth Bianchi, unter Verdacht von Verwaltigungsmord und den Erwürgungen am Bergabhang illustriert. Hypnotische Investigationen seiner Amnesie offenbarten "Steve", der die Schuld an den Vergewaltigungsmorden zugab. "Billy" trat später auf und nahm die Verantwortung für Diebstähle und Fälschungen auf sich. Versuche, Kenneth Bianchi durch gebräuchliche Therapiemethoden zu bewerten, ergaben eine ursprüngliche Meinung, daß er eine multiple Persönlichkeit darstelle und gesetzlich irrsinnig sei. Spätere Ereignisse zeigten, daß diese Diagnose irrtümlich war. Eine neue Diagnose einer atypischen, dissoziativen Störung wurde auf Grund der Effekte gestellt, die sich aus einer Prüfung der Methoden selbst ergaben. Es wird ein Warnungszeichen gegeben, daß es unmöglich sein mag, die korrekte Diagnose eines dissoziierenden, zum Tode verurteilten Angeklagten zu bestimmen.

La difficulté de diagnostiquer le syndrome de personnalité multiple dans un cas de peine capitale

Ralph B. Allison

Résumé: Le cas de Kenneth Bianchi, l'étrangleur de Hillside, sert à illustrer les problèmes impliqués dans le diagnostic du syndrome de personnalité multiple pour le cas d'un accusé soupçonné de meurtres avec viols. L'investigation hypnotique de l'amnésie révéla la personnalité "Steve" qui admit la culpabilité pour les meurtres avec viols. La responsabilité des vols et des usages de faux fut admise par "Billy" une personnalité qui émergea plus tard. Les tentatives d'évaluation de Kenneth Bianchi, au moyen des méthodes utilisées en thérapie, aboutirent à l'opinion originale qu'il souffrait du syndrome de personnalité multiple et qu'il était donc légalement irresponsable de ses actes. Des événements ultérieurs démontrèrent que ce diagnostic était erroné. Un nouveau diagnostic de désordre dissociatif atypique, causé par les méthodes d'examens elles-mêmes, fut alors posé. L'avertissement est donné qu'il est peut-être impossible de poser un diagnostic correct de dissociation dans un cas de peine capitale.

Dificultades en el diagnóstico de la personalidad múltiple en un caso de peli... de muerte

Ralph B. Allison

Resumen: El caso de Kenneth Bianchi y las estrangulaciones de Hillside ilustran los problemas que presenta el diagnóstico del síndrome de personalidad múltiple en un sospechoso de violación y asesinato. La investigación hipnótica de la amnesia reveló a "Steve", el cual admitió ser culpable de las violaciones y homicidios. Luego apareció "Billy", el cual se declaró responsable de robos y falsificaciones. Los intentos de evaluar a Kenneth Bianchi con los métodos utilizados en terapia condujeron al diagnóstico de personalidad múltiple y a que era, por lo tanto, legalmente insano. Hechos posteriores demostraron que el diagnóstico estaba equivocado. Se hizo un nuevo diagnóstico de perturbación disociativa atípica, debido a los efectos de las evaluaciones psiquiátricas y a la amenaza de pena de muerte. Se previene que a veces es imposible determinar el diagnóstico correcto de un acusado disociado en el caso de pena de muerte.

[21]

The International Journal of Clinical and Experimental Hypnosis
1984, Vol. XXXII, No. 2, 118-169

ON THE DIFFERENTIAL DIAGNOSIS OF MULTIPLE PERSONALITY IN THE FORENSIC CONTEXT[1, 2]

MARTIN T. ORNE, DAVID F. DINGES, AND

EMILY CAROTA ORNE[3, 4]

The Institute of Pennsylvania Hospital and University of Pennsylvania, Philadelphia

Abstract: The problems of diagnosing multiple personality disorder in a forensic context are discussed, and illustrated by the case of *State v. Kenneth Bianchi* (1979), a defendant who was both charged with first degree murder and suspected of having the disorder. Because of the secondary gain (e.g., avoiding the death penalty) associated with the diagnosis of multiplicity in such a case, hypotheses had to be developed to permit an informed differential diagnosis between multiple personality and malingering. If a true multiple personality disorder existed, then (a) the structure and content of the various personalities should have been consistent over time, (b) the boundaries between different personalities should have been stable and not readily altered by social cues, (c) the response to hypnosis should have been similar to that of other deeply hypnotized subjects, and (d) those who had known him over a period of years should have been able to provide examples of sudden, inexplicable changes in behavior and identity, and evidence to corroborate his claimed intermittent amnesias. None of these proved to be the case. Rather, the content, boundaries, and number of personalities changed in response to cues about how to make the condition more believable, and his response to hypnosis appeared to reflect conscious role playing. Further, the life history indicated a persistent pattern of conning and deliberate deception. It is concluded that Mr. Bianchi was simulating a multiple personality and the diagnosis of Antisocial Personality Disorder with Sexual Sadism was made. Differential diagnoses and the clinical aspects that appeared to account for his behavior are discussed.

Multiple personality is a fascinating phenomenon where more than one "person" appears to inhabit the same physical body. Diagnostic criteria of multiple personality are described in *DSM-III* (American Psychiatric Association, 1980) as follows:

Manuscript submitted February 16, 1983; final revision received October 3, 1983.

[1]A preliminary version of this paper was presented by the first author in E. E. Levitt (Chm.), A case of multiple personality? An invited symposium presented at the 32nd Annual Meeting of the Society for Clinical and Experimental Hypnosis, Chicago, October 1980.

[2]The review and evaluation upon which the substantive theoretical outlook presented in this paper is based was supported in part by grant #MH 19156 from the National Institute of Mental Health, U.S. Public Health Service, and in part by a grant from the Institute for Experimental Psychiatry.

[3]We are especially grateful to Germain F. Lavoie, Campbell Perry, Ralph B. Allison, Matthew H. Erdelyi, Fred H. Frankel, Neville D. Frankel, Robert A. Karlin, Eugene E. Levitt, and David A. Soskis for their incisive comments on an earlier version of this paper and to Stephen R. Fairbrother, Mary Fleming Auxier, Barbara R. Barras, and Mae C. Weglarski for preparation and formatting of the manuscript.

[4]Reprint requests should be addressed to Martin T. Orne, M.D., Ph.D., Unit for Experimental Psychiatry, 111 North 49th Street, Philadelphia, PA 19139.

> The essential feature is the existence within the individual of two or more distinct
> personalities, each of which is dominant at a particular time. Each personality is
> a fully integrated and complex unit with unique memories, behavior patterns,
> and social relationships that determine the nature of the individual's acts when
> that personality is dominant [p. 257].

Typically, the predominant personality is not aware of the other personalities; consequently, reports of unaccounted for gaps in memory (amnesic
periods) are characteristic of such patients.

Though the syndrome has been recognized for over a century (see
reviews by Ellenberger, 1970; Sutcliffe & Jones, 1962; Taylor & Martin,
1944), during the past decade an increasing number of case studies have
appeared in the literature describing personal histories and symptoms
that frequently accompany the disorder (e.g., Allison & Schwarz, 1980;
Bliss, 1980; Braun, 1984; Coons, 1980; Greaves, 1980; Gruenewald, 1971;
Kluft, 1982). Once considered extremely rare, a review of the literature
shows that at least two to three times as many cases of multiple personality
have been reported in the last 10-15 years than in the entire 100-150 years
prior to 1970.[5]

There has been controversy, however, particularly since the well-known
cases reported by Prince (1906), over the role of the therapist in the
development of the syndrome (e.g., Ellenberger, 1970; Harriman, 1942;
McDougall, 1926; Sutcliffe & Jones, 1962); the discovery or exploration
of the alter personalities typically occurs in a hypnotic interaction between
patient and therapist. Though it is now widely believed that hypnosis as
such does not create alter personalities, it is also argued that implicit and
explicit suggestions in the hypnotic context can shape the expression of
ego fragments such that the therapist's interest in what may be considered
nascent "selves" serves to reify the fragments into personalities — which

[5]Taylor and Martin (1944) published an exhaustive review of reported cases of multiple
personality where the case description met criteria similar to the current criteria provided
in *DSM-III*. For the period from 1811 to 1944 they noted a total of 76 cases, and estimated
that there might be twice as many worldwide. Greaves (1980) could find only 14 cases of
multiple personality during the 25-year period from 1944 to 1969. Thus, the range of total
number of reported cases of the disorder for the 150 years prior to 1970 is 90-165. Greaves
(1980) reviewed the literature on reported cases from 1970 to 1980, finding a total of 50.
Bliss (1980) reported 14 cases not covered by Greaves, that same year, and has informally
indicated that he has seen roughly 40 additional cases. Kluft (1982) reported on 70 cases,
but stated that these were among 130 cases of multiple personality "interviewed in the last
10 years [p. 233]." Braun (1984) reports having made the diagnosis of multiple personality
59 times, and Allison (1978) mentions that a Honolulu psychiatrist has seen 50 cases of the
disorder, and a Phoenix psychiatrist 30 cases. Thus, since 1970 (and primarily from 1970 to
1980) over 370 cases of multiplicity have been claimed. If one includes informal assertions
(such as newspaper articles), a minimum of another 100 cases would have to be included.
    The total therefore goes from between 90 and 165 cases in the 150 years prior to 1970, to
between at least 370 and 450 cases after 1970. Braun (1980) states that "500 cases, conserv-
atively, have been seen in the past eight years [p. 210]." Nevertheless, it is not at all clear
whether the disorder has become more prevalent, whether criteria for diagnosing it have
changed, whether there has been a shift in tendency to uncover the disorder, whether a
very small proportion of therapists are contributing a disproportionately large percentage
of current cases, or whether some combination of these factors accounts for the dramatic
increase in claimed cases.

may evolve their own histories, temperaments, and motivations (see Gruenewald, 1977, 1978). This may help explain why some therapists see a high incidence of multiple personality among their patients, while other therapists who are familiar with the syndrome — even those who use hypnosis — view it as a relatively rare entity, as does *DSM-III*.

Though it remains controversial as to how much of the recent dramatic increase in the incidence of diagnosed multiple personality is due to iatrogenic factors, there is little doubt that once the syndrome is developed — iatrogenically or not — it can be subjectively real to the patient. What makes the syndrome so compelling to the observer is that the behavior of the individual changes dramatically in accordance with the professed temperament and motivations of the personality elicited.

Frequently, personalities will be opposites; if one is standoffish or prudish, another will be sexy and seductive, or if the main personality is ambivalent or passive, one of the alter personalities will be hostile and aggressive. So striking are the behavioral differences between personalities that the assertion is often made that one would need to have the dramatic skills of Sarah Bernhardt or Sir Laurence Olivier, along with a detailed knowledge of psychiatry, to effectively simulate such radically different persons. Moreover, it is often claimed that the differences among the various selves are reflected in behavior on psychological tests (e.g., projective tests, personality inventories, mood checklists), which are then used as evidence to buttress the view that these personalities are "real" and different. For these reasons, it has been argued that the successful malingering of a multiple personality disorder is unlikely, if not impossible.

PSYCHIATRIC DIAGNOSIS IN THE FORENSIC CONTEXT

In a forensic situation, with a defendant accused of murder, facing imprisonment or even the death penalty, it is essential to recognize that the individual would benefit greatly if he is able to convince the examining clinician that he suffers from a major disorder, which would relieve him of responsibility for the actions of which he is accused. Indeed, from the defendant's point of view such behavior is adaptive. In discussing this issue and the role of the psychiatrist in the forensic setting, Rappeport (1982) comments:

> In addition, the forensic psychiatrist must be aware that the patient is consulting the physician not in a therapeutic sense but for help in dealing with a third party. There is a great likelihood that the patient will not be as truthful as he or she would be in other circumstances. . . . the psychiatrist must shift attitude completely; not only may he or she not believe everything the patient says but he or she must suspect malingering as opposed to denial, suppression, or distorted perception. He or she must therefore obtain information from any source that will help. In criminal cases such sources as police reports, confessions, and interviews with witnesses, victims, and relatives are most useful. . . . In forensic work the psychiatrist may look rather foolish if the patient or the patient's attorney has distorted the facts and he or she has not been keen enough to suspect this and attempt to determine the truth [p. 333].

It is for these reasons that *DSM-III* (p. 331) emphasizes that purposive exaggeration of symptoms as well as outright malingering must be considered as an alternative diagnosis in any context that involves clear secondary gain.

The importance of making a specific differential diagnosis between any mental disorder and malingering in the forensic context is no less an issue with multiple personality disorder — in fact, this point is specifically emphasized in the discussion of multiple personality in *DSM-III* (p. 259). The defendant's symptom reports simply cannot be taken at face value without independent verification, nor can it be assumed that the defendant's primary interest is necessarily to obtain relief from private suffering caused by the disorder. Therefore, the diagnostic problem in a forensic situation is quite different from that normally encountered in therapy. Only after malingering has been successfully excluded can we begin to apply usual diagnostic criteria. In evaluating the possibility of multiple personality disorder in a clinical context, the problem of malingering is rarely relevant to treatment; indeed, it has been argued that a false positive diagnosis is the more conservative diagnostic error (e.g., Greaves, 1980). This position cannot be justified in the forensic context.

The focus of this paper is not whether multiple personality is a common or rare form of pathology, or whether an individual who suffers from the disorder really does demonstrate autonomous selves. Rather, the issue under consideration is whether it is possible for a motivated individual to successfully fake multiplicity (i.e., without experiencing feelings of being a totally different individual at different times as a consequence of amnesic barriers between at least the main personality and the alter personalities). Specifically, a number of clinical hypotheses were set forth in an effort to differentiate behavior characteristic of malingering as an adaptive response to the demands of the forensic situation, from that of a spontaneously evolved, long-standing multiple personality. Formulating such hypotheses required us to think through in advance the kinds of situations where the response is likely to be different for an individual who is malingering versus one who has a multiple personality.

The Case of Kenneth Bianchi

The case of *State v. Bianchi* (1979) serves to illustrate particularly well the problems of diagnosing multiple personality in a defendant charged with first-degree murder and facing the death penalty. What makes this case especially informative is the fact that a large amount of clinical and forensic information is available as a result of many hours of videotape recording of the interviews by six different clinicians, in addition to extensive life history material gathered by both the police and the defense, as well as information about Mr. Bianchi's behavior subsequent to his incarceration.

By court order all videotape and interview materials were made available to all experts. Dr. John G. Watkins (called by the defense), Dr. Ralph B. Allison (an *amicus curiae*), and Dr. Martin T. Orne (called by the prosecution) each had experience with multiple personality and used hypnosis in the evaluation of the defendant.[6,7] Since both Dr. Watkins and Dr. Allison examined Kenneth Bianchi prior to the first author's interviews with him, and they each described their approaches to the case earlier in this issue (Allison, 1984; J. G. Watkins, 1984a), we will seek to discuss only what the first author of the present paper tried to do, his reasons for doing it, the findings, and the outcome.[8]

Forensic Aspects

Ten murders occurred over a 4-month period in 1977-1978 and were given wide publicity as a result of the brutality and sadistic quality of the killings, involving young, attractive females who were raped and strangled. Because some victims were conspicuously displayed nude on hillsides in the Los Angeles area, the killer was called the Hillside Strangler. The female population of Los Angeles was terrorized for months, and despite intensive police effort, the perpetrator(s) was not apprehended at the time.

Eleven months later, however, on January 11, 1979, a similar murder of two young women took place in Bellingham, Washington. In this instance, circumstances led to the rapid apprehension and arrest on January 12 of a 27-year-old, 5-ft. 10.5-in., 193-lb., Caucasian male, Mr. Kenneth Bianchi, a supervisor for a private security company. Despite evidence against him, Mr. Bianchi insisted that he was innocent, and initially denied knowing either victim. When counsel was appointed to him, he maintained that he was totally ignorant of what had happened, and insisted that he had not committed the crimes. But the evidence made it clear that Bianchi was guilty of the Bellingham murders — physical evidence linked him to the crime scene and the young women were known to have been in his company near the time of the crime (though he had instructed them to keep their association with him a secret).

[6]Transcripts of the videotape interactions of the three experts (Drs. Allison, Orne, & Watkins) who used hypnosis were prepared by the defense, and are available from the National Auxiliary Publications Service (NAPS). For the 168-page transcript of the videotape interaction with the senior author, order Document No. 04179 from NAPS c/o Microfiche Publications, P. O. Box 3513, Grand Central Station, New York. NY 10163. Remit in advance in U.S. funds only, $52.15 for photocopies or $4.00 for microfiche, and make checks payable to Microfiche Publications — NAPS. Outside the United States and Canada, add postage of $19.30 for photocopies, and $1.50 for microfiche postage. For the transcript of the videotape interaction with Dr. Allison, order Document No. 04181 (see Allison, 1984, p. 103, footnote 3). For the transcript of the videotape interaction with Dr. Watkins, order Document No. 04180 (see J. G. Watkins, 1984a, p. 68, footnote 3).

[7]The three experts who did not employ hypnosis in their evaluation and whose views are thus not presented here, were as follows: Dr. Donald T. Lunde (called by the defense), Dr. Charles M. Moffett (an *amicus curiae*), and Dr. Saul J. Faerstein (called by the prosecution); in addition, Dr. Ronald Markman served as a consultant to the Los Angeles Public Defender's Office but his diagnosis has remained privileged (Personal communication, 1984).

[8]While we are familiar with the videotapes, reports to the Court, and testimony of the five colleagues involved in this case, at Dr. Watkins's request, his manuscript and this paper were not exchanged prior to acceptance.

Because Mr. Bianchi had a driver's license with a Los Angeles address, the Bellingham police contacted law enforcement authorities in Los Angeles the day after Mr. Bianchi's arrest. A number of pieces of circumstantial evidence suggested his possible involvement in the Hillside Strangler murders, and two detectives from Los Angeles arrived to examine the Bellingham crime scene evidence and victims on the following day. They returned to Los Angeles with a handprint which was identified immediately by the fingerprint expert assigned to the Hillside Strangler case as that of the individual for whom they were searching. This information was released to the Los Angeles newspapers, and published by them. Within 7 days of his arrest, the *Bellingham Herald* (1979) published a story that Mr. Bianchi was also a "prime suspect" in the Los Angeles murders. Mr. Bianchi made headlines daily, and when he was formally charged on January 29 for the Bellingham murders, it had already been publicized that he was the prime suspect in the Los Angeles Hillside Strangler case. Further, within 10 days of his arrest, his (as yet unnamed by Bianchi) alleged accomplice in the Los Angeles murders was under surveillance from the Los Angeles police. Throughout this time Mr. Bianchi had access to both newspaper and television reports, and his awareness of his alleged implication in the Hillside Stranglings was acknowledged by his lawyer (Trial trans., *People v. Buono*, 1983, p. 37,192-37,196; 37,934).[9]

Shortly after the two Bellingham murders, Mr. Bianchi provided a series of alibis for his whereabouts at the time of the murders; these included attending a Sheriff's Reserve meeting, working elsewhere, and driving around. None of the alibis could be confirmed, and other evidence and witnesses placed him in the vicinity of the location where the bodies were found. During the following 6 weeks, up to February 27, Kenneth Bianchi attempted to devise a number of additional alibis that could not be easily refuted (Trial trans., *People v. Buono*, 1983, p. 36,990-36,997). These included claiming that he was with another individual (who had since died) at the time of the murders, though the police proved that this could not have happened. He also attempted to use his mother and a woman friend to create alibis for him. These latter two alibis were the most elaborate.

In the first of these, Mr. Bianchi involved his mother by writing to her requesting that she type a letter (while wearing rubber gloves to avoid fingerprints) to the *Seattle Times*. This letter was to be an anonymous confession to the Bellingham murders. She was to fly to Seattle (from Rochester, New York) and mail the letter without leaving fingerprints on

[9]For corroboration of key elements of the chronology of the Forensic Aspects section, we have cited the defense attorney's testimony rather than that of the defendant. More than any other person, the defense attorney, Mr. Dean Brett, compiled material on Mr. Bianchi, saw him on a regular basis, and had records of his behaviors and reactions during incarceration. In this instance, Mr. Bianchi's plea bargain agreement to testify in Los Angeles against his alleged accomplice (Mr. Angelo Buono) waived his client/lawyer privilege and made it possible for his attorney to be subpoenaed to testify in *People v. Buono* (1983).

the envelope and without telling anyone. His mother notified his lawyer of this request, and did not carry it out (Trial trans., *People v. Buono,* 1983, p. 36,869). To construct the second alibi, shortly after his arrest in Bellingham, during a 4-week period Mr. Bianchi wrote extensive letters to, and had numerous conversations with, a woman friend — repeatedly suggesting how helpful it would be if someone had seen him or been with him on January 11 between 8:10 p.m. and 9:50 p.m., which was the time of the murders. Eventually, this young woman did claim that she was with Mr. Bianchi at that time, and he offered this as his alibi. However, his attorney recognized, and the woman later admitted, that this was not true (Trial trans., *People v. Buono,* 1983, p. 36,947-36,969).

Though the Bellingham police continued to uncover evidence against him, Mr. Bianchi continued to assert (throughout the 2 months following his arrest) that he was innocent, that he was driving around on the night of January 11, that the police were attempting to frame him, and that he was now, and had been in the past, psychologically healthy. This last point was contradicted by a psychiatric work-up at the DePaul Clinic in Rochester, New York, when Kenneth Bianchi was 11 years old, which his lawyer had obtained. This confusing picture prompted the defense counsel to ask Dr. Donald T. Lunde from Stanford University to confidentially examine Mr. Bianchi. The defense counsel reported that following this examination, Dr. Lunde informed him that Mr. Bianchi was a "pathological liar," that he had a "shell" of psychological defenses, and suggested that either narcosynthesis or hypnosis should be used to "break through the shell" [Trial trans., *People v. Buono,* 1983, p. 36,882-36,885]. The day after Dr. Lunde's evaluation of Mr. Bianchi, the defense attorney provided Bianchi with a copy of the DePaul Clinic report, and 2 days later, actually read the report aloud to Bianchi, in an effort "to suggest to him the viability or possible viability of a not guilty by reason of insanity defense [Trial trans., *People v. Buono,* 1983, p. 37,254]."

Within a day of having the DePaul Clinic report read to him, Mr. Bianchi requested to see another psychologist, and it was arranged for Mr. John Johnson, a psychiatric social worker, to spend time with him. (There were no transcripts, video- or audiotapes, or even clinical notes made available concerning the details of any of these interactions, which occurred before and between the examinations carried out by the six clinical experts.) At the suggestion of Mr. Johnson, Dr. Watkins was contacted (Trial trans., *People v. Buono,* 1983, p. 36,889). The defense counsel, Mr. Dean Brett, subsequently testified that he had read Dr. Watkins's work on ego state analysis, and that prior to Dr. Watkins seeing Mr. Bianchi, Mr. Brett discussed with Dr. Watkins the possibility that there might be another "part" of Mr. Bianchi (Trial trans., *People v. Buono,* 1983,p. 36,921-36,922).

After an initial interview with Kenneth Bianchi, Dr. Watkins induced hypnosis. Directly after induction, Dr. Watkins requested to speak to another "part"; this was followed by the appearance of "Steve," who took credit for the two Bellingham killings (and also implicated himself in the

Hillside Strangler killings) but insisted that he had done no wrong because killing women was the appropriate thing to do.

Under hypnosis, "Steve" explained the specifics of the murders he had committed and was able to provide a myriad of details to which only the guilty party would have been privy. However, after hypnosis Kenneth Bianchi continued to assert his innocence and lack of knowledge of the events that took place and disclaimed knowledge of "Steve." Dr. Watkins diagnosed Mr. Bianchi as a multiple personality, and 1 week later, the defense entered a plea of not guilty by reason of insanity.

Clinical Aspects

During all of the psychiatric interviews (excepting those times that a belligerent "Steve" spoke), Kenneth Bianchi was pleasant, cooperative, and ready to assist in the task of clarifying the possible reasons for his difficulties. While somewhat ingratiating, he displayed considerable charm, a good sense of humor, a good vocabulary, and rather than appearing street-wise, he presented a veneer of sophistication. He appeared to actively take part in the psychiatric interviews, was generally willing to consider various conjectures raised by the clinicians, and he had a certain ingenuous quality that invited explanation and engendered positive feelings. Mr. Bianchi was both physically and mentally attractive, and when not specifically stressed, he had an urbane manner that made it difficult to imagine that he could have been involved in the crimes with which he was charged. Though he would occasionally complain (about the news reports of his case or about the jail food), or express concern (about his infant son) or dysphoria (during the time he was in solitary confinement), superficially his appearance and interpersonal style during the clinical evaluations (as can be seen on the videotapes) was that of a sincere, young man who was apparently emotionally stable, and in control of himself.

It is not possible to review here the literally thousands of pages of material that were made available concerning Mr. Bianchi. Relevant facts may be summarized as follows. Kenneth Bianchi was raised by adoptive parents from 3 months of age. He had a history of being troubled as a child, with persistent partial urinary incontinence during the daytime, and had a horseshoe kidney with complications. Up until age 11 his adoptive mother took him to numerous urologists in an unsuccessful effort to find an organic basis for his urinary incontinence—which disappeared when his mother went to work. It is likely that he was severely disciplined and perhaps abused during his childhood by his mother toward whom he was intensely ambivalent. According to an investigative report, his mother stated that he was a habitual liar from an early age.

He had a full-scale IQ of 116 on the WAIS (Wechsler, 1955), when tested in Bellingham. However, his school grades were often considered to be below his estimated ability. He finished high school and took some courses at a junior college; overall his scholastic record ranged from indifferent to poor. The only area in which he showed promise was in the arts, which he did not pursue.

Mr. Bianchi had a good deal of other medical attention as a child. There are reports of a tendency to lose his balance and fall easily, which resulted in a broken nose on two occasions. He was reported to have hurt himself in other instances from falls. At 5.5 years of age a physician made the diagnosis of petit mal seizure based upon history and a tendency for his eyes to roll backwards. No record of childhood EEG studies was available, though adult studies (obtained after arrest) were negative. At age 11 Kenneth Bianchi was seen by a psychiatrist at the DePaul Clinic, referred by his school because of absenteeism, tics, enuresis, asthma, and many behavior problems. Psychotherapy was recommended but this suggestion was not acceptable to his mother. (This is the report that Mr. Brett, the defense attorney, made available and read to Kenneth Bianchi before Dr. Watkins's sessions with him.)

Though there were only partial school records available concerning attendance and behavior, there are reports by teachers in high school indicating that he was often absent when exams were to be given, and some teachers felt that he was unsuitable for the school. He was apparently not well liked by many of his teachers and not particularly popular with his peers. While there was no record of overt violent behavior, other than the killing of a cat and a dog (neither of which was independently confirmed), there was considerable rebellion at home during his early high school years, perhaps related to the death of his adoptive father when Kenneth Bianchi was 13.

In his adult life Mr. Bianchi was unable to sustain any consistent career aspirations except a wish to be a police officer, which was not supported by a willingness to persist at a junior college program in police science. He repeatedly applied to police departments without success, but was able to obtain employment as a security guard. He had at least 12 different jobs during the 9-year period following high school.

He grew up in Rochester, New York, and at age 19 married a high school girl friend, but the marriage lasted less than 8 months, ending in annulment. He had been quite active sexually (bordering on promiscuity) since age 16, and continued this pattern, forming no other permanent relationships. At age 26 he began to live with a young woman in a common-law relationship.

His history of lying persisted throughout this period, and by his own admission he stole a variety of merchandise, while working as a security guard to prevent shoplifting in a number of stores in Rochester. At the age of 24 he moved to Los Angeles, where he was involved in a number of illegal and antisocial activities including stealing, selling of drugs, the use of stolen credit cards, the pimping of juvenile prostitutes, attempted blackmail, and misrepresenting himself as a movie agent and as a California Highway Patrolman. He frequently defaulted on debts, resulting in repossessions of property. He was a compulsive liar, used aliases, and borrowed money from friends and acquaintances with no apparent intention of repayment.

It is particularly noteworthy that during the last year that he was in Los Angeles, he set himself up as a psychologist.[10] After discussing theories and treatments with a legitimate psychologist, Mr. Bianchi persuaded this doctor to allow him the use of his office and answering service. It appears that his common-law wife actually believed that he had become a psychologist, and she reports that on one occasion he took her to his office and administered "inkblot tests." In addition, he carried out an elaborate and shrewd scheme to obtain false diplomas by the placing of a classified ad in the *Los Angeles Times*, offering a position to a recently graduated psychologist — requiring that applicants send resumes and transcripts to Dr. R. Johnson, at Mr. Bianchi's then current address. Using the hundreds of applications he received, he obtained the information necessary to secure transcripts and blank diplomas to which he forged his name.

The closest that Mr. Bianchi came to establishing an ongoing relationship was with his common-law wife, though during this time he continued to have casual sexual encounters with other women. While he and his common-law wife maintained an unstable relationship for nearly 2 years with frequent prolonged separations (cohabiting only 8 of 25 months), he seemed to express affection toward their child who was born approximately 1 year after they met. During her pregnancy his common-law wife learned about his frequent absenteeism from work, and confronted him with her concern, whereupon Mr. Bianchi invented an elaborate story about his having cancer and requiring regular treatment. He maintained and embellished this story over a period of time, going so far as to have his common-law wife accompany him to the hospital and wait in the car while he went in for "treatment." Even though he was in fact healthy and his common-law wife was in the late months of pregnancy and worried about the stability of his job and their future, he responded to her worries by telling her that he had only a short time to live.

Curiously, it was during the time that Kenneth Bianchi used his purported cancer treatments as an excuse for time missed from work that the Hillside Strangler murders were being committed.

[10]When Kenneth Bianchi was taken into custody, police searched his apartment and found that 14 of the 27 books on the premises concerned psychology, including a book entitled *Handbook of Hypnotic Techniques*, by Garland H. Fross, D.D.S. (1966). Most of the psychology books found were contemporary textbooks dealing with therapy and assessment, rather than lay books. For example, these included: *Dictionary of Behavioral Science* (1973), *Handbook of General Psychology* (1973), *Dialogues for Therapists* (1976), *Diagnostic Psychological Testing* (1968), *Annual Review of Behavior Therapy: Theory and Practice* (1976), *Psychoanalysis and Behavior Therapy* (1977), *Modern Clinical Psychology* (1976), and *A Harry Stack Sullivan Case Seminar: Treatment of a Young Male Schizophrenic* (1976). Despite this somewhat impressive collection of clinical texts, Mr. Bianchi insisted that he never read the books, that they were obtained through a mail-order book club that automatically sent them each month, that he could not understand the jargon, that he had no knowledge or interest in psychology, and that he had never taken a psychology course in college.

Emergence of an Alter Personality

The failure of his various alibis to be substantiated, his vague story of driving around when the Bellingham murders were taking place, and his denial of a documented psychiatric history, led his defense attorney to suspect that there might be "another part" of Kenneth Bianchi, and he arranged for Dr. Watkins to hypnotize Mr. Bianchi on March 21, 1979.

Prior to the induction of hypnosis, Ken indicated that he did not really know very much about hypnosis, saying, "I've read a few things about it, but it was very minor, just in a small pamphlet once." In establishing rapport, Dr. Watkins then went on to explain what hypnosis was and was not, making it clear that it could help people "remember things about themselves better. . . . memories which are normally kind of pushed out of their minds . . . to recall things, and experience themselves a little bit more, look at sides of themselves." During this, Bianchi inquired as to "How far back can you go with hypnosis?" He was told that some "people go back to the first year of life . . .," but that "I [Dr. Watkins] don't know enough about you to know what you're capable of doing. . . . You see probably, Ken, what happens is that everything that happens to us is recorded somewhere in our brain. . . . But hypnosis is a way of getting back, and maybe gaining some access to those things." At this point Ken acknowledged a desire to "know what I'm all about." As the discussion of using hypnosis to help him remember continued, Dr. Watkins indicated that no matter what was eventually remembered in hypnosis, Ken could "forget the whole thing if you want to, that's up to you."

Following the establishment of rapport, a 28-minute hypnotic induction took place, and Mr. Bianchi went into what appeared to be deep hypnosis. At this point, the following exchange occurred between Dr. Watkins and Kenneth Bianchi:

> W: And now while you're relaxed Ken I want you to stay in your deeply relaxed state. But I would like to kind of talk to you. And I've talked a bit to Ken, but I think that perhaps there might be another part of Ken that I haven't talked to, another part that maybe feels somewhat differently from the part that I've talked to. And I would like to communicate with that other part. And I would like that other part to come to talk to me. And when it's here and then the left hand will lift up off the chair to indicate to me that that other part is here that I would like to talk to. Part, would you please come to communicate with me? And when you're here, lift that left hand off the chair to signal to me that you are here. Would you please come, Part, so I can talk to you? Another part, it is not just the same as the part of Ken I've been talking to. Would you lift the left hand to indicate to me that you are here when you are here and you're ready to communicate with me?
> Part, would you come and lift Ken's left hand to indicate to me that you are here? All right. Part, I would like for you and I to talk together, we don't even have to —we don't have to talk to Ken unless you and Ken want to. But, I would like for you to talk to me. Will you talk to me by saying, "I'm here"? Would you communicate with me, Part? Would you talk with me, Part, by saying, "I'm here"?
> B: Yes.
> W: Part, are you the same thing as Ken, or are you different in any way? Talk a little louder so I can hear you. Huh?

MULTIPLE PERSONALITY IN THE FORENSIC CONTEXT   129

> B: I'm not him.
> W: You're not him. Who are you? Do you have a name?
> B: I'm not Ken.
> W: You're not Ken. Okay. Who are you? Tell me about yourself.
> B: I don't know.
> W: Do you have a name I can call you by?
> B: Steve.
> W: Huh?
> B: You can call me Steve.
> W: I can call you Steve, okay. Steve, just stay where you are, make yourself comfortable in the chair and I'd like to talk to you. You're not Ken. Tell me about yourself, Steve. What do you do?

"Steve" was quick to say that, "I hate Ken. . . . I hate a lot of people. . . . I hate my mother." When asked who Ken was, he replied, "That's the other person. . . . Who tries to do good." "Steve" went on to claim that, "I make him lie. . . . I like starting arguments . . . making him lose his temper . . . I fixed him good." At this point, just a few minutes after this apparent alter personality emerged, Bianchi (as "Steve") began implicating himself in the Hillside Strangler murders along with his adoptive cousin Angelo Buono. Somewhat later in the same session he discussed killing the two Bellingham women.

Near the end of this hypnotic session, Dr. Watkins called the "Ken" personality back, and asked him, "Do you know anything about Steve?" to which Ken replied, "Who's Steve?" When asked if he wanted to find out things about himself, Ken said, "I don't know. Not a whole lot. Not all at once." Dr. Watkins then sought to help therapeutically by saying the following:

> W: Okay. Let me tell you something Ken; during the coming days and weeks, at your own speed, and in your own way, you will find out about Steve, who he is, what he has done, and what has happened. And you will find it out in such a way that you can become stronger and stronger and stronger with each passing day. Do you understand that?
> B: Yes.
> W: You will become stronger and stronger, and Steve will become weaker and weaker and weaker, and you will find out more and more, through thoughts, memories, dreams and so forth, who Steve is, what he has done to you and what it's all about, until you fully understand. Do you understand that?
> B: Yes.
> W: But, as you do this, you are going to get stronger and stronger and you will be stronger than Steve. You will have more energy — more of the energy of your whole body is going to flow into Ken, give him strength and courage and memory, until pretty soon, there is just Ken. Do you understand that?
> B: Okay.

While undoubtedly intended to help Mr. Bianchi, Dr. Watkins's treatment of the symptoms manifested by Kenneth Bianchi during this first hypnotic session also served to confuse the forensic picture by legitimizing the disappearance of amnesic barriers, as Ken came to "find out" about Steve.

Thus, this initial hypnotic session with Dr. Watkins was the first time in the Bianchi case that the "Steve" alter personality emerged, identified himself, and confessed to knowledge of, and involvement in, the murders.

It would, of course, not be the last time, as "Steve" appeared when summoned the next day by Dr. Watkins, and again over the subsequent 2 months, for Dr. Allison and the first author. However, the character of "Steve" and the way in which he interacted changed dramatically over time.

The "Steve" that emerged for Dr. Watkins this first time, and confessed to the murders, displayed pleasure in "fixing" Ken, and showed no remorse for the rape/stranglings. His behavior at this time, however, was not threatening, he spoke in a low voice, frequently laughed mockingly, did not curse, was relatively polite, made no demands, and was motorically passive; he sat in the chair, his head resting back and rolling from side to side as "Steve" talked. The next day when the second hypnosis session took place with Dr. Watkins, "Steve" began to change; he was more animated, laughed somewhat less, was more hostile, and used some profanity. However, by the time Dr. Watkins interviewed him a month later (a few days after Dr. Allison had interviewed Bianchi), "Steve" had changed dramatically; he was aggressive, threatening, insulting, no longer laughed, was very active and demanding, talked loudly, was extremely crude and obsessively profane, chain smoked, and appeared as a caricature of a macho man. This was the "Steve" that Dr. Allison saw, and who emerged in subsequent sessions when "Steve" was called forth in hypnosis. This evolution of the character of "Steve" from the first session to later sessions is incompatible with the pre-existence of a distinct, well-integrated alter personality.

"Steve" also insisted to Dr. Watkins during the second interview that in terms of his last name, "I don't know what I am. . . . I don't know. I just like first names." A month later, Dr. Allison asked Ken during hypnosis, while regressed to age 9, what "Steve's" last name was, to which Ken replied, "Walker." The next day, in the wake state, Bianchi reported that he had a dream where "Steve" was asked by Ken what his last name was, and he replied "Walker." In addition, Dr. Allison elicited, by way of finger signals in hypnosis, that "Steve" claimed to have first emerged at age 9. Unfortunately, Dr. Allison also gave suggestions directed toward fusing the personalities, thereby confounding the forensic picture even further.

The Court's Charge and the Diagnostic Problem

A week after Dr. Watkins's first two hypnotic sessions with Bianchi, and "Steve's" admission to the murders, Mr. Bianchi pleaded not guilty by reason of insanity on March 29, 1979, and the defense requested that the Court concern itself with Bianchi's sanity, and responsibility for the crimes. The Court therefore charged six clinical experts with determining the state of the defendant's mind at the time of the crime, and at the time of the examination in order to establish whether Mr. Bianchi could stand trial and assist in his own defense, and whether he was sane under the laws of the State of Washington (M'Naghten Rule).[11] If the psychiatric experts — particularly those familiar with multiple personality and hypnosis — were to concur on the diagnosis of multiplicity, the insanity defense might prevail, and Mr. Bianchi could thereby avoid the death penalty and perhaps even prolonged imprisonment; instead, he would spend time in a psychiatric treatment center and look forward to being released once the personalities had been fused.[12] Thus, the secondary gain for being diagnosed as a multiple personality was potentially a matter of life or death.

Mr. Bianchi was examined by the first author after Drs. Watkins, Moffett, and Allison had interviewed him. The videotapes of these interviews provided an opportunity to compare his behavior with different clinical evaluators, as it evolved over time. The pattern of interactions suggested the need to be particularly attentive to Mr. Bianchi's response to social cues. Perhaps even more important was the massive amount of life history material uncovered by the police and the defense, which in large part was not available to the earlier evaluators before their initial interviews, but which revealed a persistent pattern of carefully thought out deception

[11]Under Washington state law, the M'Naghten Rule for insanity is phrased as follows:
> To establish the defense of insanity, it must be shown that: (1) at the time of the commission of the offense, as a result of mental disease or defect, the mind of the actor was affected to such an extent that: (a) he was unable to perceive the nature and quality of the act with which he is charged; or (b) he was unable to tell right from wrong with reference to the particular act charged. (2) the defense of insanity must be established by a preponderance of the evidence.

[12]It has been argued by Dr. Watkins, that Bianchi "would also be stupid, if he were going to simulate insanity, to try to simulate multiple personality, because multiple personality per se is not insanity [Trial trans., *People v. Buono*, 1983, p. 2,549–2,550]." It is true that multiple personality disorder is not a form of psychosis. However, a consensus by the experts about the diagnosis of multiple personality disorder would likely have prevented the criminal proceedings, and Mr. Bianchi would have been dealt with less by the penal system and more within the framework of the mental health system. Further, the three experts who diagnosed Mr. Bianchi as dissociative reaction or multiple personality also reported to the Court that he was insane. It is particularly noteworthy that the use of multiple personality as an insanity defense had been successful in another case (*State v. Milligan*, 1978). The similarity between the Bianchi case and the Milligan case was pointed out in the context of an interview with Dr. Watkins by *Time* magazine (1979). In that article it was reported, "A judge found Milligan not guilty by reason of insanity, and he was committed to a mental hospital [p. 26]." In February, 1984, Milligan was granted release from the mental health center where he had been institutionalized (*Post*, 1984).

Not only was the multiple personality defense the basis of a plea of not guilty by reason of insanity in the Milligan case, but this fact received nationwide attention during the period immediately prior to the January, 1979 Bellingham murders. A full-page article on the multiple personalities of the defendant, Milligan, appeared in *Time* magazine (1978), prior to his trial, and another full-page article was published in *Newsweek* (1978), the week after the Court accepted Milligan's not guilty by reason of insanity plea. While there is no way of knowing whether Mr. Bianchi read these articles on the Milligan case, or had knowledge of them from other sources, prior to his not guilty by reason of insanity plea, it is interesting that Bianchi placed the emergence of the initial alter personality at age 9, which was the age that the *Newsweek* (1978) article had reported Milligan's "personality shattered [p. 106]."

that did not seem to fit the history of individuals with multiple personality. Because the sum total of the available data might well indicate purposive deception in the psychiatric interviews, it seemed especially important to provide a number of opportunities for Mr. Bianchi to demonstrate that he had genuine amnesic barriers, that he was hypnotized, and that the diagnosis of multiple personality was appropriate. Therefore, clinical criteria had to be developed that could be used to explore Bianchi's apparent symptoms and reports. This process, however, was seriously confounded by the fact that Kenneth Bianchi had access to many records in the case as part of his participation in his defense. He admitted to various experts that he had read the medical and psychiatric reports from his childhood; that he had read many of the police reports on evidence and interviews with various individuals such as his wife; and that the credentials of the examining clinicians preceded them. [13]

Moreover, as Ken, he often complained about what he read in the newspapers concerning his case, and indicated that he was "told" what various people had said about him to lawyers and investigators. The assessment of multiple personality versus the possibility of malingering was made more difficult by the fact that he had reported having seen the film "Three Faces of Eve"[14] some years earlier and the likelihood that he had seen the film "Sybil"[15] in his cell shortly before the sessions with Dr. Watkins, since these films illustrate the central role of amnesic barriers and the emergence of sudden shifts in behavior as typical of multiplicity.

Despite these problems, there was a large body of clinical data to evaluate, and an effort was made to determine the extent to which his behavior reflected a multiple personality disorder, rather than a response to demand characteristics within the situation (see Orne, 1962). One of these criteria concerned whether Kenneth Bianchi was hypnotized.

The Question of Hypnosis

Because the alter personality "Steve" was brought out during hypnosis, and because the ability to enter deep hypnosis has traditionally been

[13]During his early interviews with Dr. Watkins and again in his later interviews with Dr. Faerstein and the first author, Mr. Bianchi indicated that he had knowledge of the report on the psychiatric examination of him at the DePaul Clinic at age 11. Similarly, he indicated to Dr. Moffett and Dr. Faerstein that he had read the police reports, saying to Dr. Faerstein, "I've read police reports and everything else. Uh, you know, I've got all kinds of reports." Finally, he indicated to Dr. Watkins that, "Ah, yes, your credentials preceded you [March 21, 1979, p. 7]," and the attorney indicated to the first author that he (Mr. Brett) had enjoyed reading an article the first author wrote on hypnosis and simulation, though he subsequently testified that he had not shown it to, or discussed it with, Mr. Bianchi.

[14]This film shows the original personality, Eve White, troubled by severe headaches as a presenting complaint. It makes clear that these headaches are a symptom of an alternate personality attempting to emerge. Though headaches played an insignificant role in Mr. Bianchi's prior history, it is noteworthy that headaches assumed a prominent role following Dr. Watkins's uncovering of "Steve."

[15]The Bellingham jailer, Mr. Kovacks, reported that the television was on in Mr. Bianchi's cell while the film "Sybil" was being shown, a week before he saw Dr. Watkins.

reported to be associated with multiple personality (Bliss, 1980; Sutcliffe & Jones, 1962), determining whether Mr. Bianchi was deeply hypnotized would also help clarify the likelihood of his being a multiple personality. If it could be shown that Kenneth Bianchi was deeply hypnotized when the alter personality emerged, it would not prove that he was a multiple, but it would be consistent with that diagnosis. Conversely, evidence that hypnosis was being simulated would not prove that the symptoms of multiple personality were also simulated, but it would lend support to such a view.[16] Regardless of the relationship between hypnotizability and multiple personality, if simulation of deep hypnosis were observed, this would call into question the overall reliability of the individual.

In normal clinical practice the simulation of hypnosis is hardly ever encountered, since psychotherapists avoid problems of this kind by making certain that they do not lend themselves to satisfying secondary gains of the patient by means of their therapeutic interventions. Consequently, there is little motivation for the private patient seeking help to purposively deceive the therapist. In the usual clinical context, therefore, there is neither the need nor the opportunity to assess whether a patient is simulating hypnosis.

Nevertheless, contrary to popular assumptions, it is possible for untrained naive subjects to simulate deep hypnosis and fool even very experienced hypnotists,[17] by behaving in ways that they think a hypnotist wants (Orne, 1959, 1972). The variability of hypnotic behavior is sufficiently great that without having had the opportunity of comparing many hypnotized and simulating subjects (while blind to their actual status) with subsequent feedback concerning their actual status, it is simply not possible to reliably diagnose whether an individual is in fact hypnotized.

Over a period of years, however, in the context of resolving a number of basic research issues, criteria were developed for discriminating simulators from deeply hypnotized subjects (see Orne, 1977). Certain responses were rarely if ever seen in simulators, while other behaviors were rarely seen among deeply hypnotized individuals. Though there remains overlap between behaviors of hypnotized and simulating individuals, it has become possible to make reasonable probabilistic differentiation in

[16]It should be noted that this proposed use of hypnosis in evaluating a case of suspected multiple personality where secondary gain exists, is different from that suggested in *DSM-III*, where it is stated that malingering of multiple personality may be resolved by using hypnosis (or amytal interview). The implication in this latter case is that hypnosis can be used as a quasi lie detector; whatever the individual says in hypnosis is considered to be true. Such a claim has no basis in fact. Individuals can lie when deeply hypnotized as well as when simulating hypnosis (or for that matter, when under the influence of amytal). The strategy proposed here is not to attempt to use hypnosis as a lie detector, but rather, to assess the likelihood that an individual with a presumed diagnosis of multiple personality might be faking hypnosis.

[17]For example, in 1960, Dr. Milton H. Erickson participated in our studies of simulation and hypnosis. He sought to identify simulators using whatever procedures he saw fit. He was unable to discriminate between simulators and deeply hypnotized subjects, despite his vast experience with many thousands of subjects and undisputed mastery of the field.

the laboratory setting. Evaluating the presence of hypnosis in a single individual in any context, however, is, in the final analysis, a diagnosis.

As in most clinical differential diagnoses, it is unwise to base one's judgment on any single behavior—truly pathognomic symptoms or signs are rare in psychiatry. Rather, one studies specific situations and looks for patterns of behavior which permit inference about the underlying processes one seeks to diagnose. While some of these situations are structured to elicit behaviors of diagnostic significance, it would be inappropriate to conceive of such situations merely as "test items" which can be "passed" by giving "correct" responses. Instead, it is essential for a trained observer to evaluate the quality of the responses as they occur within the totality of the interaction and to make inferences about the cognitive processes that they reflect.

The Context in Which Hypnosis was Induced

The first author was introduced to Mr. Bianchi as an expert for the prosecution, a circumstance which might well imply an adversary relationship. Indeed, in two other cases of defendants charged with murder, the first author found that there was considerable resistance to the induction of hypnosis. Therefore, in this case, care was taken to avoid any confrontation and to both establish and maintain good rapport with Mr. Bianchi. This was apparently successful because when hypnosis was induced the response was that of a highly hypnotizable individual capable of entering hypnosis rapidly and apparently experiencing the most profound hypnotic phenomena. In addition, comments in Mr. Bianchi's diary, remarks made by Mr. Johnson, and testimony of Mr. Brett (Trial trans., *People v. Buono,* 1983, p. 36,913) all indicated that Mr. Bianchi felt that there was a positive relationship throughout the sessions with the first author. From the standpoint of Mr. Bianchi's behavior during the hypnotic sessions, there was no possibility that he was an individual of average hypnotizability; his behavior was such that he was either a hypnotic virtuoso or someone who was simulating deep hypnosis. His response to hypnosis in these sessions was consistent with what had been observed in the videotapes of the hypnotic sessions of Dr. Watkins and Dr. Allison. In a true sense, this diagnostic problem provided a real-life analog of the laboratory model which compares individuals who are either highly hypnotizable or simulating deep hypnosis.

In evaluating Kenneth Bianchi, the objective was to identify a group of behaviors that are typical of hypnosis, or to discern patterns of behavior characteristic of an attempt to simulate. The first step was to examine Mr. Bianchi's response to specific situations that have been useful to trained observers in distinguishing the deeply hypnotized individual's behavior from that of an individual simulating deep hypnosis.

Double hallucination. This procedure designed to elucidate the thought processes of a deeply hypnotized individual involves presenting the subject with a perceptual conundrum. After it has been suggested that the subject hallucinate a person — in this case, Mr. Brett — and he has talked to the hallucination for some time, he is asked where the person is and he obviously points to the hallucination. He is then instructed to turn toward an area (that had previously been outside his field of vision) where the actual person is sitting, and is asked, "Who is this?" If this is done in a manner that does not cue the subject as to what is desired, most simulators will indicate that they do not know who is sitting there, or that there is no one there, or that it is someone other than the person actually sitting there. In a laboratory situation, when no longer in the simulating role, the subject will upon inquiry explain that he was supposed to be hypnotized and hallucinate the person sitting in front of him, so he could not admit that he could see the other (real) person since the same person can be in only one place at a time.

In contrast, the deeply hypnotized individual does not appear to be bound by this logical stricture, but instead, shows what is called trance logic. That is, when faced with the perceptual conundrum, the hypnotized individual will correctly report the presence of the individual actually sitting there. though he may be puzzled by it when acknowledging that there are two of them (and may do a double-take), but he does not appear distressed or verbally excited; in short, this situation tends to elicit what is clinically referred to as *la belle indifference*.

The response of Kenneth Bianchi to the double hallucination of his attorney was superficially consistent with that of a hypnotized individual; he looked back and forth, admitted to two Dean Bretts being present, and inquired as to how there could be two of them. On the other hand, the manner in which the acknowledgment of both a real and a hallucinated Mr. Brett was conveyed was inconsistent with the style of a hypnotized individual. Mr. Bianchi spontaneously went to considerable effort to explain his response (without any request for elucidation). When asked, "Who is this?" (pointing to the real Mr. Brett), instead of what would be the usual slightly puzzled response, "Dean Brett," he replied in an agitated, insistent way with a question: "If Dean Brett is here and Dean Brett is here, how can he be in two places? Dean, Dean! How can Dean Brett be in two places? . . . How can Dean Brett be in two places?" After correctly responding to a request to indicate which one is the real Dean Brett, he was asked, "How do you know?" to which he replied, "Cause he's not there anymore. How can I see him in two places?"

We have never seen a deeply hypnotized subject volunteer his reaction to the double hallucination in this fashion. One does not generally observe a hypnotized person addressing the conundrum by answering with a question; particularly a question that highlights the simulator's logic problem ("How can I see him in two places?"). The repeated question almost seemed designed to assure the hypnotist that the experience was bona fide. In our view. this reaction is incompatible with that of a deeply hypnotized subject.

Single hallucination. One kind of behavior often seen in deeply hypnotized individuals is the mixing of percept and hallucination. Thus, the subject who is asked to see (hallucinate) someone in a chair across from him may spontaneously report seeing the individual *and* seeing an outline of the chair (the percept) through the hallucinated person. Note that this is not suggested nor is the subject asked whether he sees the chair through the hallucination, since such an inquiry would clearly indicate that a positive response may be expected. Among deeply hypnotized subjects, only about one-third will spontaneously describe some kind of transparency or other unusual feature of their hallucination, reflecting a mixing of the true percept with hallucination. However, this kind of response has not been observed occurring spontaneously in subjects simulating hypnosis.

When a suggested hallucination was induced, Mr. Bianchi did not evidence any mixing of percept and hallucination, despite being asked to, "describe Dean to me in some detail. . . . Describe him more. Describe every detail. . . . Is there anything unusual about him at all?" Since two-thirds of hypnotized subjects also fail to indicate transparency or mixing of percept and hallucination, a negative response has no diagnostic value (whereas a spontaneous transparency response from Mr. Bianchi would have been support for concluding that he was hypnotized). However, there are more subtle features of Mr. Bianchi's behavior — when he interacted with his hallucination and the examiner — that are worthy of comment.

In hypnosis it had been suggested that he would be able to see his attorney, Mr. Brett, in the chair in front of him, and then talk with him for a while. At this point Mr. Bianchi manifested a response that we have never observed with any hypnotized individual who is interacting with a hallucination: namely, Mr. Bianchi spontaneously leaned forward, shook hands with the hallucination, and sat back again. Characteristically, hypnotized subjects do not volunteer a physical interaction (e.g., handshake) with their hallucination, unless it is specifically suggested.

What followed was a conversation on the part of Mr. Bianchi with the hallucinated Mr. Brett; more information was volunteered and asked for than is typically seen with hypnotized individuals. Most striking, however, is what Mr. Bianchi said when it was suggested to him that he again see the hallucinated Mr. Brett:

> B: Oh, Dean. Boy, did you give me a start! So what's going on? What we gonna talk about, the three of us?

The first author then said, "Well, I want you to describe Dean to me in some detail. What does his. . . . Is he shaven?" to which Mr. Bianchi replied:

> B: Oh, no! His beard. God, you can see him. You must be able to see him?!

On the surface such responses may appear to merely reflect the compelling quality of the hallucination, by making it seem impossible that the hypnotist should not also be sharing in the hallucination; the "three of us" refers to Ken, the hallucinated Mr. Brett, and the hypnotist. However, we have never seen a hypnotized individual respond to the request to talk with the hallucination by implicitly demanding that the hypnotist participate in a three-way conversation. Similarly, we have never observed a deeply hypnotized subject who, in response to the suggestion that he describe his hallucination, instructs the hypnotist that "you must be able to see him."

Typically, the hypnotized subject describes the hallucinated person without involving the hypnotist in the hallucination (even though the hypnotist is behaving as if he also sees the hallucination), just as a non-hypnotized subject would describe an actual person or object, if asked to do so in a psychiatric interview. In other words, whether hallucinated in hypnosis or actually seen while not hypnotized, the subject describes what he sees when requested to do so. The deeply hypnotized subject interacting with a hallucination has no need to persuade the hypnotist of the reality of his experience. Only if the subject does not actually see the hallucinated event—but nevertheless desires to convince the interviewer that he does see the hallucination — would he be expected to refocus attention away from his response and emphasize what the hypnotist ought to see. With this behavior the subject reveals what is foremost in his own mind. Therefore, we interpret Mr. Bianchi's behavior in this situation as not that of a deeply hypnotized individual, but rather that of someone trying to convince the hypnotist that his hallucination is real.

Suggested anesthesia. This procedure was first described in print by a lay hypnotist, Mr. Harry Arons (1967); it consists of drawing an imaginary circle on the back of the hypnotized subject's hand. Anesthesia is induced by suggesting to the subject that the skin inside the circle will have no feeling whatsoever; once the subject's response indicates that he is experiencing localized anesthesia within the circle, he is instructed to close his eyes (if they are not already closed). The subject is then told that when he is touched in a place where he can feel it, he should say "Yes," and when he is touched in a place where he cannot feel it, he should say "No."

Hearing or reading these instructions, a paradox seems obvious. If for the deeply hypnotized subject there is no feeling inside the circle, why would anyone say "No" when touched there? This is precisely the conundrum facing a simulator. Thus, he/she responds to various touches outside the circle, saying "Yes" each time, but tends to remain logical by saying nothing when touched inside the circle. Deeply hypnotized subjects, on the other hand, typically are not bothered by the logical incongruity inherent in following the instructions, and therefore tend to respond "No" when touched in the anesthetized area. (If the anesthesia is not complete,

138   ORNE ET AL.

as is characteristic of only moderately hypnotizable subjects, touching inside the circle elicits an appropriate "Yes" response — interestingly, individuals feigning deep hypnosis do not say "Yes" when touched inside the circle.)[18]

The anesthesia procedure was carried out twice with Mr. Bianchi because the videotape camera was partially blocked on the initial trial. At that time, Mr. Bianchi responded by saying "Yes" . . . "No" . . . "Yes" . . . . "Yes." The suggestion for anesthesia was then reiterated "Okay. Now you can feel absolutely nothing inside of this circle." This was followed by a series of "Yes" responses interspersed with pauses. Some hours later this procedure was repeated and the camera filmed the stimuli being applied inside and outside of the imaginary circle. During this administration, Mr. Bianchi responded "Yes" when touched outside of the circle and failed to give a response when touched inside of the circle.

At the time the procedure was first conducted, the response Mr. Bianchi gave was taken by the first author to be indicative of simulation. However, on examining the audio portion of the videotape of the first administration, there is an initial "No" response, and the second absence of response when touched inside the circle (indicated by a delay between "Yes" responses) cannot be documented visually. For these reasons, as well as the possibility of inadvertent bias, we feel little weight should be placed on the results of this procedure as a means of distinguishing between simulation and deep hypnosis in this case.

Source amnesia. Another procedure that has some utility in identifying deeply hypnotized subjects concerns the loss of the origin or source of knowledge originally learned under hypnosis, even though the acquired information is recalled after the termination of hypnosis. The phenomenon is called source amnesia (Evans & Thorn, 1966; Thorn, 1960), and it has been found to occur in approximately one-third of all deeply hypnotized subjects, but not at all among subjects simulating hypnosis (Evans, 1979; Peters, 1973). Like the hallucination transparency, therefore, a positive response to the source amnesia procedure provides support for inferring that a subject was hypnotized, but a negative response does not indicate simulation.

---

[18]At the time of this evaluation, there were no published studies using this procedure. Subsequently, Eiblmayr (1981) reported a study, using a variation of the real/simulator model where "the simulating group were told to feign anesthesia within the circle" and using a modification of the circle procedure. In an attempt to employ psychophysical controls, the nature of the paradox inherent in the instructions to the subject seems to have been minimized. Further, it is unclear in the report whether the hypnotized subjects actually indicated that they experienced complete anesthesia, particularly since a group of only moderate hypnotizability was included. Despite these possible limitations, the data show that 7 out of 10 simulators, as opposed to only 2 out of 10 deeply hypnotized subjects, showed an absence of response when touched inside the circle. The data from moderately hypnotizable subjects (who tended to say "Yes" when touched inside the circle — indicating incomplete anesthesia) cannot be considered as relevant to the present case, since Mr. Bianchi was either highly hypnotizable or simulating deep hypnosis.

The procedure consists of asking the subject, during a hypnotic interaction, a number of simple questions to which he knows the answers,
such as "What is the capital of New York?" and then asking a question(s)
to which he is not likely to know the answer(s), such as, "The amethyst is
a blue or purple gemstone. What color does it turn when heated?" When
the subject indicates not knowing the answer to the difficult question, he
is given in hypnosis the correct answer (in this case, "yellow"). Later in
the hypnotic interaction the subject is given suggestions of amnesia, that
when he wakes up he will remember nothing of the events that occurred
in the session. After hypnosis is terminated, the individual is asked what
occurred in hypnosis, and at this time both simulators and most deeply
hypnotized subjects will indicate that they cannot remember what transpired. Following this, the difficult question(s) asked (and answered) in
hypnosis is again posed, embedded in easy questions.

Some subjects who have genuinely been hypnotized experience source
amnesia as evidenced by the fact that they will give the correct answers
to both the easy questions *and* the difficult question; they will not, however, remember where they acquired the answer to the difficult question,
and if pressed, will give a rationale such as, "I must have learned it in my
geology course at college." Thus, source amnesia is characterized by the
subject's forgetting the *source* of the information but not the content.
Simulating subjects never show source amnesia (Evans, 1979; Peters,
1973), since they would be careful not to admit to knowledge acquired in
hypnosis after having reported that they had amnesia for the events that
occurred during hypnosis.

A brief version of the source amnesia procedure was carried out with
Mr. Bianchi. Three easy questions were asked (e.g., capital of a state),
and only one very difficult question (the amethyst . . .); however, in
hypnosis Bianchi had to be told the answer to not only the difficult
question, but also to one of the relatively easy questions (i.e., the capital
of Arkansas).[19] Immediately after bringing him out of hypnosis (having
suggested amnesia prior to this), the four questions were administered.
Mr. Bianchi correctly answered the easy questions, but he did not know
the answer to the difficult target question that was the criterion for source
amnesia, a finding that does not discriminate between hypnosis and simulation.

Clinical Aspects of the Amnesia Behavior

A substantial number of Mr. Bianchi's hypnotic behaviors and responses
during the interviews with him seem best understood as exaggerated

---

[19]The difficult or target items for source amnesia were selected by Evans and Thorn (1966)
so as to be virtually certain that subjects would not have known the information before being
told the answers in hypnosis. If easier items were used as targets, one could not distinguish
between source amnesia and either momentary blocking in hypnosis or reminiscence effects
in the wake state. Though in hypnosis Mr. Bianchi did not know the answer to an easy
question (capital of Arkansas) but did recall the answer in the wake state, such a relatively
easy item cannot serve as a criterion for source amnesia.

demonstrations of his apparent desire to authenticate his hypnotic experience. We have already noted his spontaneously shaking hands with the hallucination, his insistence that the hypnotist must be able to see the hallucinated Mr. Brett, and his pointed questioning spelling out four times the conundrum of the double hallucination. An additional illustration of this kind of overacting, uncharacteristic of deeply hypnotized subjects, is worth noting, because it relates directly to the major symptom of multiple personality, *amnesia*.

During the first author's initial meeting with "Steve" (the confessed killer "personality"), which occurred on May 27, 1979, in a hypnotic interaction "Steve" aggressively insisted that he could not talk unless he had a cigarette, and consequently, some filter cigarettes were obtained for him. Consistent with his exaggerated macho style, he tore off the filter tips and smoked a half-dozen of the cigarettes during the interview, leaving a small pile of the torn off filters in front of him. When the interview with "Steve" was concluded, Ken was asked to return. Mr. Bianchi suddenly became his urbane self, looked at the hypnotist, looked at the desk in front of him, and then expressed utter surprise at the presence of the pile of filter tips, asking in an amazed voice what they were doing there and who could possibly have put them there.

We have rarely observed this kind of response in a person who has been repeatedly hypnotized. It was as if Kenneth Bianchi were using the opportunity to illustrate how strong his amnesia was for the behavior of "Steve Walker"; instead of saying that he could not remember what had just transpired, he was vividly demonstrating by his behavior that he had no awareness of what had occurred.

What is especially troubling about the cigarette tips incident is that Mr. Bianchi had previously demonstrated similar behavior separately with both Dr. Allison and Dr. Watkins. Already with Dr. Allison, almost 6 weeks earlier on April 18, 1979, he expressed surprise (as Ken) at finding his cigarettes missing and the tips in front of him. Two days later with Dr. Watkins, he expressed surprise (as Ken) over similar events. This dialogue is particularly revealing:

> B: What's my rosary doing here?
> W: Huh?
> B: What's my rosary doing on the table?
> W: Didn't you put it on the table?
> B: No. I remember I hid it in my pocket.
> W: Yeah. I thought you put it on the table. No?
> B: No.
> W: No. Okay. Well what do you think happened?
> B: Steve again?
> W: Yeah.

Mr. Bianchi had clearly had similar episodes of apparent surprise at finding that he did not remember moving objects around in hypnosis, as "Steve." Assuming bona fide amnesia (as he expressed), Ken should have known after this happened repeatedly that "Steve" was doing it, especially since he frequently inquired about it. Indeed, he indicates an awareness to Dr. Watkins that "Steve" had moved his rosary when he explains the phenomenon as "Steve again." Why then would he have shown such naive amazement when (for the third time or more) the Ken personality returned and found cigarette tips? This is especially striking since by this time he admitted to having learned a great deal about "Steve," who had emerged more than 2 months previously. The reenactment of this demonstration for each clinician who hypnotized him not only casts serious doubt on whether he was hypnotized, but calls into question the profound amnesia he displayed as part of his multiple personality.

The Question of Multiple Personality

Clinical psychiatry and psychology lack the benefit of the kind of feedback that the Clinico-Pathological Conference provides for general medicine — feedback about the cause of death and a determination of the clues that were available prior to death which could have led to the correct diagnosis. Such feedback hones the diagnostic skills of medical practitioners, and provides a criterion for assessing what can be learned from consensual validation and the clinical course over time. While the latter two criteria for determining diagnostic accuracy are basic to the clinical practice of psychiatry, in a forensic setting it is not generally possible to evaluate the defendant's clinical course over time. Nor is consensual validation particularly feasible in the context of the adversary system. Thus, a different approach is needed to help distinguish whether the defendant is suffering from a major psychiatric disorder or whether he is malingering.

Besides developing procedures to evaluate whether Kenneth Bianchi was deeply hypnotized, we endeavored to find criteria that would directly permit some discrimination of the alternatives of malingering versus experiencing the multiple personality symptoms. These discriminators centered on the number and the nature of the personalities that Mr. Bianchi displayed, as well as on the amount of external corroboration for the multiplicity symptoms that Bianchi appeared to have. In addition, other information purporting to confirm or disconfirm the suspected diagnosis of multiplicity was examined.

More so than with the procedures for simulation of hypnosis, the hypotheses directed at evaluating the authenticity of multiple personality involved comparing Mr. Bianchi's responses during the first author's interviews with him to his responses during the other psychiatric interviews as well as to data gathered by the forensic teams investigating the case. Not only was corroboration of multiplicity symptoms sought, but an effort was made to determine if the symptoms and personalities expressed by Kenneth Bianchi could be modified by a casual comment designed to unobtrusively alter the demand characteristics (see Orne, 1973). To the extent that the personality boundaries, which had previously been clearly documented by other experts, could be changed simply be redefining for Mr. Bianchi behavior characteristic of a multiple personality, malingering must be considered.

Thus, the stability of the presumably rigid boundaries between personalities and corroboration of multiple personality symptoms were the core criteria of these procedures. As with the hypnosis evaluation, no attempt was made to confront Kenneth Bianchi over the authenticity of his responses during the first author's interviews, nor was he challenged concerning any doubts that the interviewer may have had relating to any aspect of his behavior or symptoms. Quite the contrary, throughout the interview any positive attributes, such as his bright normal intelligence, were emphasized to facilitate rapport.[20]

The Number of Personalities

This case presented a unique situation where two clinicians, intimately familiar with multiple personality and hypnosis (Drs. Watkins and Allison), had worked with the defendant over a 2-month period and only one alter personality ("Steve") had emerged. Further, while Mr. Bianchi was hypnotized, Dr. Allison had explicitly tried to elicit additional personalities without success. Under these circumstances, it became reasonable to assume that Kenneth Bianchi had only two distinct, autonomous personalities, and an attempt by another clinician to bring forth yet a third personality under hypnosis would not be successful. It should not matter whether this clinician had previously communicated the expectation in the wake state that there ought to be a third personality.

On the other hand, if Mr. Bianchi was malingering, then a communication that made it clear that the clinician believed that "real" multiples always have at least three personalities should cause him to produce an additional alter personality, when given the opportunity to do so during a subsequent hypnotic interview. In other words, under these circumstances the production of the additional personality would be an instrumental act to convince the interviewer of the authenticity of his disorder.

Accordingly, Mr. Bianchi was asked during the initial interview with the first author to explain what he had learned about himself since talking with the clinicians. The relevant comment made prior to hypnosis was provided during the following apparently casual interaction:

> B: So one thing led to another and I was seeing all these experts and I went through a couple of sessions of hypnosis, and uh, I was told that there was a possibility that I had what's called a multiple personality. Which means that, that there are two separate distinct personalities within the same body, I guess.
> O: That's pretty rare for there to be two, actually, that's one of the things I'm curious about.
> B: Yeah, um, they mentioned only the two. I don't know, I, you know, I really don't know that much, much about the field. It's just as new to me as it is to, you know, a lot of other people. . . .

When subsequently hypnotized in this same session, Mr. Bianchi appeared as though he were in deep trance and eventually, on request,

[20]This emphasis of positive attributes of Mr. Bianchi to maintain rapport was similar to the approach taken by Dr. Watkins during interactions with "Steve"; for example, at one point Dr. Watkins said to Mr. Bianchi, "You're going so damned fast. I'm not that smart. Okay. I'm not as bright as you are so let's cool it and slow it down a bit [March 21, 1979, p. 43, Line 10, dialogue on videotape but omitted from transcript]."

"Steve" emerged. After "Steve" was sent away, the possible presence of another personality was explored and resulted in an apparently spontaneous regression to a 9-year-old boy who said his name was Ken, and who was crying and afraid of being hit — an ego fragment that appeared to relate to some earlier discussions with Drs. Watkins and Allison. The first author then asked to talk to that "part" that was neither Ken nor "Steve," in the same way the earlier interviewers sought additional personalities. At this time a new "personality" emerged, and responded that it needed more "time" before coming out. It said its name was "Billy," and he agreed to come out during the next session, which would be after dinner.

When Mr. Bianchi was hypnotized after dinner, "Billy" emerged with little difficulty. He was neither the aggressive, brutal, crude "Steve Walker" nor the urbane Kenneth Bianchi, but rather, an enthusiastic, pleasant hustler. His specialty was getting what he wanted or getting out of difficult situations by lying. He took responsibility for various cons (which previously were ascribed to "Steve") such as the psychologist scam. Whereas Kenneth Bianchi was ingratiating but somewhat aloof, "Billy" was not only cooperative, but extremely eager to offer superficial insights into both "Steve" and "Ken," in an almost collegial manner, yet throughout he maintained the demeanor of a hail-fellow-well-met.

It had been predicted that if Mr. Bianchi was feigning multiple personality, a third "personality" would emerge in response to the social cue given in the wake state, and thus the appearance of "Billy" further brings into question the validity of Mr. Bianchi's behavior. Not only would it have been unlikely for a true multiple personality to come forth as "Billy" after having failed to produce another personality for either Dr. Watkins or Dr. Allison, but also the manner in which "Billy" came forth fits this hypothesis. Thus, in our view, his unwillingness to talk before dinner can be understood if one considers that the idea of having an additional personality was brought up during the first interview that day, and he did not have the opportunity to think about what this personality should be like. The dinner break provided over 2 hours in which he could think about and put together the role of "Billy." It seems reasonable to assume that it was the casual comment which caused Mr. Bianchi to create an additional "personality."[21]

[21]It has been questioned whether "Billy" emerged for the first time as a result of the "casual comment" or rather was originally observed by Dr. Watkins. The latter does not appear to be the case. When first speaking with "Steve," Dr. Watkins inquired as to whether he had another name to which "Steve" replied, "Oh, Bill . . . Yeah, I've always liked Bill." Later, "Steve" responded to a question about who his childhood friends were, saying "Bill Peterson." These two are the only mention of the name "Bill" in Dr. Watkins's interviews. Similarly, during a hypnotic age regression to age 9, Ken mentioned to Dr. Allison that, "Billy Thompson" was his best friend as a child. Thus, at no time did any "Billy" personality emerge as an identifiable third personality prior to the communication that it was rare to have only two personalities — though additional personalities had been explicitly looked for previously by Dr. Allison. It is not surprising that if Mr. Bianchi was pushed to provide a third personality in response to the interviewer's expectations, that he would name it "Billy," as this was the name he used to describe a childhood friend, and he was keenly aware of all the attention and interest that the other experts had shown over his childhood — though "Billy" maintained that his name came from someone calling Bianchi that name by mistake.

As Dr. Allison's later interviews with Mr. Bianchi confirmed, "Billy" was as eligible as "Steve" to be accepted as an example of an alter personality. Our concern was not, however, to document whether phenomena closely resembling alter personalities could be produced by hypnotic suggestions (as had been already shown by Kampman, 1976); instead, the concern was with establishing whether an additional autonomous personality had existed prior to Mr. Bianchi's arrest. Since Dr. Allison had already probed for such a pre-existent personality, without success, and the major difference between his approach and that of the first author was only the addition of a hint in the wake state, it is extremely unlikely that "Billy" in fact represented a pre-existent alter personality.

Rather, the additional apparent alter personality, "Billy," was created by the simple expedient of implying that another such personality ought to exist. If such a hint had failed to produce an additional "personality," it would have lent support to there being firm barriers between the personalities — outside of Mr. Bianchi's conscious control — consistent with the diagnosis of dual personality. However, if a casual comment can parlay two personalities into three, then it seems likely that Kenneth Bianchi had far greater control over the management of his ego boundaries than he admitted to, or than would be expected in a patient with a multiple personality disorder.

Changes in Personality Boundaries

In describing the emergence of "Steve" earlier, it was noted that this "personality" changed considerably over a period of 2 months, becoming remarkably more aggressive and profane, which would be unusual for a fully developed alter personality that allegedly pre-existed for 19 years. Another way to evaluate the extent to which Mr. Bianchi was responding to demand characteristics in the situation (rather than portraying the reality of his condition), was to hint that Ken's personality would be more plausible if he acknowledged one or another flaw of his character. Thus, the first author indicated to Mr. Bianchi, outside of hypnosis, that he would be more credible if he (Ken) actually had some faults; as it was, he presented himself as a "plaster saint," particularly in claiming never to have taken advantage of any opportunity to steal or to have sexual encounters with the prostitutes working for "Steve."

During the interview with Dr. Faerstein, only 4 days later, Mr. Bianchi allowed that, as Ken, he had some involvement with these women, that he had stolen from the very stores which had hired him as a security guard, and he acknowledged recollections of the psychology scam. These reallocations of responsibility, which occurred with Dr. Faerstein and later with Dr. Allison, cannot be convincingly explained from the perspective of a multiple personality diagnosis. Had there been rigid barriers between the personalities, the basic "Ken" personality should have remained unchanged in Dr. Faerstein's interview. As it was, the boundaries of the three "personalities" were altered by straightforward social cues provided outside of hypnosis.

On the other hand, the quasi-therapeutic interventions that had occurred earlier with Drs. Watkins and Allison permit an alternative explanation to be offered; that is, the fusion process had been initiated, resulting in leakage across the previously impermeable amnesic barriers. Unfortunately, in the course of these quasi-therapeutic interactions, Mr. Bianchi was not only told that he was suffering from a multiple personality, but he was also instructed concerning the symptoms involved, that he would become more and more aware of things done by his personalities, and that this awareness would come to him over a period of time. Thus, Kenneth Bianchi was given *carte blanche* to "remember" whatever he wanted to, whenever he wanted to. Once the differential diagnosis between malingering and multiple personality has been resolved, providing such detailed information to a defendant about diagnosis, symptoms, and the expected clinical course may be appropriate as a therapeutic maneuver; but if in a forensic context, therapy is initiated prematurely, differential diagnosis becomes far more difficult.

In this case however, "Billy" was created during the session with the first author, long after these therapeutic interventions. While changes in the barriers between "Steve" and "Ken" could perhaps be explained on the basis of a therapeutic intervention, these interventions cannot be invoked to explain either the appearance of "Billy," or the reallocation of responsibility to "Ken" for different activities following "Billy's" emergence.

External Corroboration

The most fundamental criterion for diagnosing multiple personality in any situation involving secondary gain, is the *independent* corroboration of the pre-existence of distinct, autonomous personalities with specific "behavior patterns and social relationships [*DSM-III*, p. 257]." Additional symptoms typically considered characteristic of the disorder are discussed in *DSM-III* as well as by various writers (see Coons, 1980), and include amnesia, dramatic behavior changes, erratic interpersonal relationships, auditory hallucinations, hysterical physical symptoms, and childhood trauma. Since the disorder is considered to develop quite early in life, typically between the ages of 4 and 8, symptoms usually can be documented from adolescence on through adulthood. In classic cases, parents, spouses, relatives, friends, co-workers, and neighbors may be found who can verify at least some of these symptoms, especially profound shifts in behavior and amnesia for recent personal actions.

Certainly, Kenneth Bianchi ultimately displayed to those experts who used hypnosis what appeared to be three very different personalities.

Given the extreme differences between "Ken" and "Steve," corroboration of the pre-existence of these two personalities should have been relatively easy. Despite the expenditure of massive amounts of time, effort, and resources by both the police and defense to corroborate Mr. Bianchi's statements concerning his earlier symptoms, no corroboration of pre-existing alter personalities was found.

Though Mr. Bianchi's mother confirmed his difficult childhood and he likely suffered from her discipline and his father's death, none of the people who knew him, including his mother, ever reported that he displayed erratic behavior changes. Most disturbing of all is the fact that his wife, friends, and co-workers could recall no instances where he suddenly went from pleasant "Ken" to raging "Steve." Though he is reported to have been occasionally angry, this reaction was not accompanied by insisting that he be called by another name, by outrageous profanity, or by behavior that was totally uncharacteristic of him.

Similarly, while after the initial psychiatric interviews Mr. Bianchi reported that he had experienced blank episodes earlier in his life, no one was found who could verify such episodes. He never reported auditory hallucinations. He claimed to have headaches while incarcerated, but at other times, he denied having headaches prior to being incarcerated. (It had been explained to him very early in the clinical evaluations that headaches were due to another "part" of him trying to get out.)

The lack of corroborating evidence for the key symptoms of multiple personality is particularly disturbing in this case, given the extraordinary amount of effort expended at researching Mr. Bianchi's past. It is unlikely that the past of any other individual suspected of being a multiple personality has ever been so thoroughly investigated. The headaches as symptoms are at best equivocal, and only an extremely small proportion of children who suffer serious physical abuse or psychological trauma develop a multiple personality.

Another point that has received much attention concerns Mr. Bianchi's sculpture (during adolescence) of a head with two faces—one side with a normal appearance and the other with a monstrous look. It is difficult to assess the psychological significance of such an isolated projective creation, but it is noteworthy that Mr. Bianchi himself stated to Dr. Lunde in his interview that the two heads were an "accident" in that Bianchi had difficulty forming the back of the head and it therefore became a joint project wherein another student sculpted the "ape's" face (transcript of July 12, 1979, interview, Tape 1, Side 1, p. 8). In a letter dated July 12, 1979, to the experts, Mr. Brett, the defense attorney, also indicated that the sculpture was "done as a class project by Ken Bianchi and Tom Thornton in Jim Wickham's sculpture class in 1968 . . . [p. 2]."

Somewhat more substantial data in support of multiplicity derives from Kenneth Bianchi's psychological evaluation at age 11 at the DePaul Clinic.

This workup reflected the psychological impact of his mother's controlling and demanding behavior, in particular as it related to his inability to express masculine feelings and strivings, except in his wish to be a policeman. Following Mr. Bianchi's arrest, the defense counsel wrote to the psychologist who had evaluated Kenneth 16 years earlier; the psychologist replied, concluding retrospectively:

> It does not take great psychological acumen to see the possibility that the hostile, aggressive side of himself could have further retreated into the background only to be expressed in ways that would be so subtle, devious or indirect so as not to be recognized by his own conscious awareness. There are, of course, several ways of such expression but, to reiterate, multiple personality is among them.[22]

Thus, what little corroborative evidence can be located is at best consistent with the diagnosis of multiple personality, but fails to validate any of the crucial symptoms and can hardly be taken as evidence for it. Given the amount of data that was collected about Mr. Bianchi and the inevitable distortions in retrospective recollections, it is in fact surprising that more meaningful evidence in support of the diagnosis was not found.

On the other hand, a considerable amount of data inconsistent with a diagnosis of multiplicity has already been noted. Some additional points deserve mention. The nature of the crimes committed — ranging from the seemingly minor phony psychologist scheme to the Bellingham murders themselves — displayed a calculation and planning spaced out over days, weeks, or months. It is difficult to see how Kenneth Bianchi could have undergone the alleged personality shifts required to so often vacillate between the good and evil "personalities," in order to execute these schemes, and yet no one noticed the personality shifts, and he told no one of the amnesias that he later alleged.

One of the more interesting pieces of police work involved the search for "Steve Walker." After Mr. Bianchi displayed the "Steve" personality, the police set out to determine whether anyone had ever known Bianchi as "Steve Walker." In their search they discovered that there was indeed a real Steve Walker, and that Kenneth Bianchi knew a good deal about this individual. In order to obtain additional forged diplomas, Mr. Bianchi placed a classified advertisement for a psychologist on May 4, 1978. Thomas Steven Walker, M.A., was one of the many applicants who forwarded his college and graduate school transcripts in response to the ad — his scholastic records were particularly outstanding. Mr. Bianchi then wrote to the relevant institutions as "Steve Walker," requesting new diplomas, enclosing the appropriate fee, and asking that they "forward the *fully completed* diplomas *EXCEPT* for my name . . . I have at an additional expense retained a calligrapher that will print my name in a fancy script of my choice." He indicated that they should be sent to "Thomas Steven

[22]Letter dated June 8, 1979, from Robert M. Dowling, Ph.D., p. 2, to the defense attorney.

Walker, c/o Mrs. K. Bianchi." After obtaining the blank diplomas, he had a calligrapher affix "Kenneth A. Bianchi" to them.

This not only shows the planning that is involved in the kind of scams perpetrated by Mr. Bianchi, but clearly establishes that he knew of the real Steve Walker, and used his name. It is difficult to explain how "Steve Walker" could have been the alter ego that supposedly emerged during his childhood. If one assumes that by some bizarre coincidence an alter ego with the name of "Steve Walker" did exist independently of the psychologist Steve Walker, then one would expect that when Mr. Bianchi became aware of his alter personality that he would have shared the coincidence with the psychiatrists who evaluated him.

Finally, one needs to consider an analog to clinical follow-up, that is, what happened after Mr. Bianchi pleaded guilty (following the submission of the psychiatrists' reports) and the secondary gain for malingering a multiple personality was no longer as obvious. While Mr. Bianchi assiduously kept a diary of his emerging "insights" throughout the clinical evaluations — knowing that it was regularly distributed to the examining clinicians — he no longer maintained the diary after he pleaded guilty. He also developed a new story as to the killings in Bellingham, blaming them on another individual (named Greg) who is known to have lived in the area but who had been killed in an accident since the murders. The police definitively proved that Greg was not involved and that Bianchi knew of Greg's death. The most dramatic incident following Mr. Bianchi's guilty plea involved a young woman who had become interested in him, visited him frequently in prison, and then attempted a murder in the style of the Hillside Strangler. When apprehended, she admitted that this had been discussed with Mr. Bianchi and was an attempt to show that the killer was still at large. Shortly after learning of the woman's apprehension, Bianchi is reported to have become "catatonic." This time, however, there was no interest shown in his "mental illness," and the symptoms disappeared as quickly as they had come.

Clearly, even after Mr. Bianchi had pleaded guilty in order to avoid the death penalty, he continued his schemes to avoid responsibility for the crimes by a variety of means different from feigning multiple personality, but equally instrumental in terms of achieving the desired goal of raising doubts about his guilt.[23]

---

[23]Because Mr. Bianchi continues to provide different versions of what actually took place when the crimes were committed (as well as whether he was involved or even knew about them), it does not follow that he is necessarily a multiple personality. Individuals with antisocial personality disorders are chronic liars, and a prediction could easily have been made that he would continue to lie, distort, and misreport his involvement, even after pleading guilty. In his present situation it can be argued that there is nothing to lose by telling the truth, yet there is little to gain either. This erratic behavior may in part also be contributed to by a tendency toward paranoid ideation; in any case, however, he continues his pattern of blaming others for his difficulties.

Psychological Tests

Clinical investigations of suspected cases of multiple personality have more recently included psychological tests such as the Minnesota Multiphasic Personality Inventory (MMPI) of Dahlstrom and Welsh (1960), the California Personality Inventory (CPI) of Gough (1964), and the Rorschach (1942), in an effort to document clear differences among personalities (e.g., Brandsma & Ludwig, 1974; Larmore, Ludwig, & Cain, 1977; Miller, 1984; E. E. Wagner & Heise, 1974). This same approach was taken with Kenneth Bianchi; though the MMPI was administered only to Ken, the CPI was first administered to Ken and later to all three personalities (Ken, "Steve," and "Billy"), while a Rorschach record was obtained from Ken and "Steve."

At first glance, psychological testing may appear to be a simple and elegant way to authenticate the different, autonomous personalities of a suspected case of multiple personality. However, the evaluation and interpretation of these tests in such situations is considerably more complex. Psychological tests were designed to be given to an individual in order to permit inference about that unique individual's psychological and emotional makeup. Thus, when an expert evaluator is given a series of psychological test protocols to score blind, he would expect that each protocol was from a different individual. Unless the evaluator is involved in a special experiment, or told otherwise, it is reasonable for the expert to score and interpret each protocol as being from a separate person.

On the other hand, when the purpose of the psychological tests is to determine whether an individual who is a presumed multiple has separate, autonomous, and distinct personalities, the manner in which the protocols are presented to the evaluator creates a conundrum. The usual control for bias — to keep the evaluator blind — would tend to result in a description of two different personalities. Conversely, to inform the evaluator that two test records were produced by the same body would tend to result in the protocols being interpreted as coming from one personality. In the absence of extensive research there is no satisfactory resolution to this dilemma. The problems of applying psychological tests to the diagnosis of multiple personality are well illustrated in the case of Kenneth Bianchi, where tests were used to both support and refute claims of multiplicity.

The administration and initial scoring of the Rorschach records were conducted by Dr. Watkins, who then had two experts also each score the records blind (marked only as "K" and "S"), without any mention that they might be from a multiple personality. The blind evaluators interpreted the records as coming from two distinct individuals; this was submitted as proof of Mr. Bianchi's multiple personality.

Rather than infer multiplicity because the expert treated the protocols as coming from two different individuals, we chose to share with the evaluator that the problem was to determine whether the Rorschach records reflected different personalities that are essentially autonomous, or whether they did not. Recognizing the unavoidability of some form of bias, we treated this issue as a clinical problem, where an independent expert, experienced in blind analysis of Rorschach records, was asked to make a differential diagnosis based solely upon the psychological test protocols.

Accordingly, the Rorschach records (obtained by Dr. Watkins) were independently submitted to Dr. Margaret Singer (who is well known for the systematic analysis of blind Rorschach tests; see Singer & Wynne, 1965), with the clinical question of whether or not the records indicated separate personalities. In her evaluation of Record 1 ("Steve"), Dr. Singer[24] observed:

> With only a casual glance at how seemingly different the surface content and the quality of the way he treats the examiner, a reader might think this record comes from a second person. However, close inspection reveals that the thought, attention and associative properties that one sees at a formal level are almost identical. The underlying formal thought properties are so similar as to be striking. It is granted that the content is vastly different from that given in Test #2 (Ken), and the man treats the tester politely on that test, but here acts the role of the irritable, rude, uncooperative person who wants out of the situation and merely cuts off participating.

In summarizing her observations, Dr. Singer wrote:

> I regard these two records to be simply reflections of one man, who is a sociopathic personality. On Test 2 he was cooperative, on the #1 he said aloud a number of sexual contents. Over the years I have tested many sociopaths and this is one of their predictable ways of handling others. They are expert at "reading" what shocks other persons, namely saying shocking sexual or body function acts aloud. . . . There is no real cognitive slippage in these records even though some testers may get amazed at the sexual content; if they have tested enough similar persons in similar situations, they will no doubt see as one does here, the stark underlying similarities.[25]

[24] Letter dated June 20, 1979, from Margaret T. Singer, Ph.D., to the first author.

[25] In a letter (dated July 14, 1981) offering help to the District Attorney of Los Angeles (a letter introduced on October 26, 1981, in Trial trans., *People v. Buono*, 1983), Dr. Watkins indicated that his Delta Index (J. G. Watkins & Stauffacher, 1952) of the Rorschach for "Steve" should have been scored 25% — in the psychotic range — rather than 0% as scored by Dr. Singer. This index is based upon Dr. David Rapaport's classic studies (Rapaport, Gill, & Schafer, 1946) where he enumerated various types of deviant verbalizations in an effort to specify aspects of schizophrenic thinking as they could be detected in the Rorschach. He emphasized the need to evaluate a deviant Rorschach response in the context of the individual's overall interaction with the examiner. Thus, overt sexual responses are most commonly seen in psychotic records but they are then associated with a poor form response (F−), which is not the case here. If, as Dr. Singer points out, an individual uses street language, then the use of overt sexual content as well as the use of profane adjectives are likely to reflect a communicative style rather than cognitive slippage. Careful analysis shows that a number of responses that might superficially be interpreted as loss of distance are better understood as expressing an attempt to intimidate and shock the examiner. Fortunately, Dr. Watkins's codification of Dr. Rapaport's concept is generally quite useful, because one rarely encounters a nonpsychotic individual who goes out of his way to lard his speech with profane street language in the testing situation.

More recently, Dr. Allison (1984) took a similar approach to the Rorschach interpretation, requesting Dr. Edwin Wagner to review the records—Dr. Wagner has published the only paper (E. E. Wagner & Heise, 1974) on Rorschach tests with authenticated multiple personality cases. Dr. Wagner independently concluded that Bianchi's Rorschach records did not resemble those of the multiple personality cases he had seen, but rather were indicative of a sociopathic[26] or psychopathic person faking different profiles.[27]

The same kinds of interpretive issues that arose with the Rorschach records also existed for the CPI, which was administered to all three "personalities." Dr. Harrison Gough was asked to evaluate the three CPI protocols from Ken, "Steve," and "Billy" to determine whether or not these were distinct, autonomous personalities. Consistent with Drs. Singer and Wagner, he[28] concluded:

> the three personalities (Ken, Billy, and Steve) do not seem to be three distinct and different individuals, but rather roles or variations developed from a common core. . . . Are Ken, Billy, and Steve the different selves of a multiple personality? It is possible that they are, in particular the selves constituted by Ken and Steve. But against this must be mentioned the push toward fraudulence in the two profiles of Ken, and his tendency to persuade himself of the truth and legitimacy of whatever accrues to his own advantage. It would be tempting indeed for such a person, faced with his present difficulties, to fabricate two other selves and to try to shift all the blame and responsibility to one of them.

Finally, the MMPI was administered only to Ken by Mr. John Johnson. The protocol was evaluated blind by Dr. David E. Cummins who was

[26]Though there is a remarkable agreement in the Rorschach analyses of Dr. Singer and Dr. Wagner. Dr. Wagner notes that, "For the record, I don't think Bianchi is a sociopath either, at least not the garden variety type [Letter from Dr. E. E. Wagner to Dr. Watkins, August 2, 1983, with permission from Dr. E. E. Wagner]." Rather, as he states in a recent manuscript: "It is our contention that Bianchi is really a special kind of sociopath, a paranoid with a psychopathic overlay which, for lack of a better term, could be referred to as a 'psychopathic paranoid' [E. E. Wagner & C. F. Wagner, Diagnosing multiple personality with the Rorschach: The case of the Hillside Strangler, manuscript in preparation, p. 15]." Dr. Wagner's position has not changed since his February 22, 1980 letter to Dr. Allison wherein he stated:

> My considered opinion is that this is *not* a multiple personality. I am basically in agreement with Dr. Singer although I would hasten to add that this is not a typical psychopath. Ken is what I call (for lack of a better name) a paranoid with psychopathic overlay. . . . Such cases are quite dangerous and, as might be expected, tend to be diagnosed as psychopathic or paranoid [p. 1].

[27]Notwithstanding claims to the contrary, both Drs. Singer and Wagner concur that it is possible even for uninformed individuals to successfully fake Rorschach protocols evaluated by experts—especially if the experts have had little experience with the *blind* analysis of Rorschach records. In a recent study, for example, using as judges Fellows of the Society for Personality Assessment, protocols from Uninformed Fakers "received as many Psychotic diagnoses as did the actual Psychotic protocols [Albert, Fox, & Kahn, 1980, p. 118]"; further, protocols from Informed Fakers (informed about the disorder to be faked, but given no information about the Rorschach test), were actually diagnosed psychotic far more frequently than the protocols from actual psychotics.

[28]Harrison G. Gough, Ph.D. (Confidential report on Kenneth Bianchi, July 31, 1979; People's exhibit No. 227, Trial trans., *People v. Buono*, October 19, 1981).

selected by the defense, and who used a computer scoring of the protocol as one source for his evaluation. His[29] conclusions were:

> Based solely upon the MMPI, I am inclined to suggest a diagnosis of psychopathic personality disorder, with a tentative secondary diagnosis of latent schizophrenia. Before being in any way comfortable with that diagnosis, however, I would require that the possibility of subclinical idiopathic seizure disorder be ruled out.

While it is clear that the psychological test data do not support a diagnosis of multiple personality, there is a lack of normative data documenting how effectively individuals malingering multiple personality could produce psychological test data that would support a diagnosis of the disorder.[30] Specifically, research is needed to determine how well clinicians can distinguish between test data derived from authenticated multiple personality cases, versus data from individuals role-playing or faking multiplicity, versus records from different individuals submitted as though they were obtained from a suspected multiple personality. Until such data are available, psychological tests cannot be taken as definitive evidence to document a diagnosis of multiple personality.

Differential Diagnosis

Is Kenneth Bianchi a Multiple Personality?

It has been generally agreed that the diagnosis of multiple personality demands the pre-existence of autonomous, separate identities, with different values, pasts, and social relationships (e.g., *DSM-III*). Though different authors focus on different aspects of the definition as central to the diagnosis of multiplicity—some emphasizing the importance of amnesias and sudden unexplained behavior changes, and others focusing on child abuse, a history of headaches, hallucinations, hysterical reactions, and the emergence of other selves during crises—they generally concur that multiplicity must have existed prior to contact with the therapist. Gruenewald (1971), for example, points out, "that to be judged an authentic case, the patient should have led two or more lives independently prior to his coming to psychiatric attention [p. 41]." Though these diagnostic

---

[29]MMPI Interpretive Report dated April 14, 1979, from David E. Cummins, Ph.D., p. 2.

[30]Problems of interpretation, bias, and malingering also apply to personality inventories such as the MMPI and the CPI, but in these cases the issues tend to polarize around validity indicators. The MMPI has been used to document multiple personality, largely due to a misunderstanding of the lie scale in the MMPI. Dr. Grant Dahlstrom (personal communication, January 20, 1983) points out that it is often assumed that if one obtained different personality patterns without an elevated lie scale, these could be taken at face value. However, the validity indicators are intended to indicate not only whether an otherwise normal individual is malingering a psychiatric disorder, but also whether the respondent is denying the presence of symptoms. On the other hand, when normal individuals role play a certain sort of person in specific circumstances, the validity indicators do not necessarily detect the role playing. Further, little work has been done on individuals suffering from emotional or characterological problems, who are asked to avoid revealing those problems on one of a number of test administrations. Thus, a role-playing approach by a disturbed individual who is clearly motivated to portray two or more sides of himself could well go undetected on an otherwise reliable personality inventory. Consequently, when evaluating the possibility of multiple personality, reliance on validity indicators from such tests cannot be taken as definitive evidence of multiplicity.

criteria have evolved in clinical settings, they are obviously of even greater importance in a forensic evaluation.

In the case of Kenneth Bianchi, as discussed earlier, there is a total absence of any independent evidence that would corroborate the pre-existence of "Steve" or "Billy," despite extensive interviews with Mr. Bianchi's mother, wives, friends, co-workers, and former employers. The only time either "Steve" or "Billy" was seen was with the three clinicians who had used hypnosis.[31] Neither the other clincians, Mr. Bianchi's law-yer, his social worker, his priest, nor his jailers ever reported independently observing behavior characteristic of the alter personalities. Moreover, the evidence about the real Steve Walker from whom Mr. Bianchi at age 27 had arrogated to himself a Master's degree in Psychology, is difficult to reconcile with the information Bianchi provided during hypnosis that the alter personality, "Steve," had emerged at age 9. Further, the fact that "Steve's" essential characteristics changed considerably over several successive interviews would seem to belie the possibility that he was a pre-existing, fully formed alter personality. Similarly, the emergence of "Billy" following a hint by the first author that three personalities would make the diagnosis more credible, along with concomitant shifts in the boundaries of the personalities, appears inconsistent with the diagnostic criterion of multiple personalities each with pre-existent, well-defined boundaries outside of conscious control.

Thus, in our view, whatever Kenneth Bianchi's diagnosis might be, he does not meet the criteria required for an authenticated case of classic multiple personality.

Would a Less Stringent Criteria of Multiple Personality Be Useful in Describing Kenneth Bianchi?

Recently, it has been pointed out that "the symptomatology of multiple personalities lies on a continuum from mild and/or transient to severe and/or long lasting [Gruenewald, 1977, p. 385]," and that such a view is useful therapeutically. Dr. Watkins (1976) suggests that,

> personality and behavioral functioning are organized into ego states separated by boundaries, the permeability of which lie on a continuum from easy accessibility between the respective contents of two states to complete impermeability—such as appear to exist in the true multiple personality [p. 476].

He sought to apply this view to forensic issues by asking,

> At what point is an individual in ego-state A to be held responsible for actions committed by ego-state B? It may well be that "the person" who pleads not guilty to a crime when unimpeachable testimony proved that "his body" committed the

---

[31]The traditional view that evidence for a pre-existent alter personality with an independent past and its own social relationships must be available to document a genuine multiple personality has recently been operationalized by Dr. Watkins to mean that "The distinguishing characteristic of the true multiple personality is that they manifest the multiple personality without being hypnotized [Trial trans., *People v. Buono*, 1983, p. 2,496]." While we agree that this is a necessary condition, it is not a sufficient one. Thus, the fact that "Steve" came out without formal hypnosis during Dr. Watkins's final session with Mr. Bianchi (on April 20, 1979) cannot be taken as evidence that "Steve" had existed *prior* to Dr. Watkins's first session — particularly given the repeated elicitations of "Steve" by hypnosis in intervening clinical sessions.

crime is not simply lying. The ego state testifying to the judge does not realistically
and sincerely consider itself guilty of the act. It was not present when the crime
was committed [p. 476].

More recently, Dr. Watkins (1984b, in press) explained that

Such "ego states" are found in good hypnotic subjects and may be created by
many normal individuals for adaptation and defense. In these cases the dissociated
entities do not emerge spontaneously as in multiple personalities but require
hypnotic intervention for their activation [p. 4].

In the case of Kenneth Bianchi, however, Dr. Watkins made the diagnosis of multiple personality disorder because he felt that the alter personality "Steve" emerged outside of hypnosis, both while committing the
murders, and on the last interview day with Dr. Watkins, in response to
being told "Close your eyes, Ken" (April 20, 1979, Tape 73, Side A, p.
10). Though we do not concur with Dr. Watkins's diagnosis, it is worthwhile to consider the position that even if Kenneth Bianchi was not a
classic case of multiple personality, could he not have been relatively close
to this extreme on the continuum of dissociative states? That is, the "ego
state of Ken" might not have been present at the time of the murders,
though this would not have been obvious to outside observers since
"Steve" was disguised as Ken — and the undisguised "Steve" did not
emerge without hypnotic intervention.

In his discussion of Kenneth Bianchi, Dr. Watkins explains on the basis
of ego state theory that the reason why others had not seen "Steve" — a
somewhat unforgettable character — is because he typically acted disguised as Ken. "Steve" not only could ostensibly affect Ken's thinking,
but actually act as though he were Ken. In Dr. Watkins's words:

Steve said that even Mr. Buono thought that it was always Ken when he was
there. So Steve, in a sense had a rather perfect disguise [Trial trans., *People v.
Buono*, 1983, p. 2,611].

Thus, the reason that others might not have seen the sudden dramatic
shifts in behavior is that "Ego states act like 'part-persons' or 'covert'
multiple personalities [J. G. Watkins & H. H. Watkins, 1979, p. 218]." In
essence, then, one would apply less stringent criteria to the diagnosis of
multiple personality disorder — criteria that do not require evidence of
pre-existing, spontaneously emerging alter identities.

The application of these kinds of less stringent diagnostic criteria may
be useful in a therapeutic context, but they raise serious practical problems in a forensic context. In the previous section we specified the data
that caused us to reject the diagnosis of a classic multiple personality
disorder in the case of Kenneth Bianchi. Once less stringent clinical
criteria for the diagnosis are employed, however, the failure of others to
have observed dramatic behavior shifts, bizarre behavior that is uncharacteristic of the person, or the spontaneous emergence of an identifiable
alter personality, becomes irrelevant.

The one externally verifiable criterion that remains is lapses of memory which should logically occur when "ego state Ken" is unaware of the actions carried out by "ego state Steve," and subsequently becomes aware that he (Ken) cannot recall what transpired in the immediate past. Thus, from this perspective it would be understandable why an observer might not be aware of a shift between "ego state Ken" and "ego state Steve" (since there would be no observable change in behavior), but there should be obvious confusion when "ego state Ken" returns and is unable to account for passages of time, where he is, or how he got to be doing what he is doing. In other words, even with this loosening of criteria others ought to have observed the behavioral consequences of the amnesia, and Ken's ensuing puzzlement—but they did not.

In the absence of such corroboration, the only evidence available to help assess the diagnosis of multiple personality with less stringent criteria is what occurs during the psychiatric interviews, and of these, only the ones conducted by the three experts who used hypnosis permit an evaluation of the alter "personalities" when they are not disguised and are clearly identified as themselves. The role of hypnosis thus becomes crucial, since the alter "personalities" were initially uncovered and explored with this technique. Hence, one of the very few possibilities of addressing the question of malingering is to evaluate the validity of the hypnotic state itself.

Though there is research on the simulation of hypnosis, the criteria that discriminate individuals simulating from those who are hypnotized do so on a probabilistic basis, and one must therefore deal with the problem of distinguishing between malingering and hypnosis in a single individual as a diagnosis. The first author's extensive experience in working with deeply hypnotized and simulating subjects (blind as to their status, but with subsequent feedback as to the accuracy of diagnosis), as well as his clinical experience with forensic evaluations including several capital cases where the possibility of malingering hypnosis had to be assessed, was used as the basis for his diagnosis that Kenneth Bianchi was faking hypnosis. If Mr. Bianchi did not experience hypnosis, it throws into doubt whatever else he reported about his private, non-verifiable experience, and strongly suggests that he was also malingering the amnesia and other symptoms of multiple personality.

While in our view there is adequate evidence in the case of Kenneth Bianchi to dismiss the diagnosis of multiple personality disorder (even with less stringent criteria), it is worth noting that as the criteria become less stringent, the possibility of ever falsifying the diagnosis becomes increasingly tenuous.

Does Kenneth Bianchi's Assertion That He Could Not Recall the Events of the Crimes Represent a True Amnesia?

Even if we reject the diagnosis of multiple personality, it may still be reasonable to assume that Kenneth Bianchi's purported amnesia was at least partially valid due to some degree of dissociation during and after the crimes. Thus, reports of amnesia after homicides are frequent — ranging from 40% to 70% (cf. Bradford & Smith, 1979). Interestingly, this observation has been used not only to document the dissociation caused by the arousal concomitant with murder, but also to illustrate the profound unreliability of a defendant's verbal reports. These reflect the polarized positions that result from accepting the defendant's statements at face value as opposed to relying only on those assertions of the defendant that are verifiable. The problem, of course, stems from the fact that there is no way currently available to prove whether an individual is truly unable to recall, or whether he chooses to assert that he has no recollection while knowing full well the facts for which he denies knowledge.

From a legal point of view, the question whether an individual is actually able to remember is of crucial importance; not only does it determine whether the defendant can assist in his own defense, but also it may be closely related to the question of whether he knew right from wrong at the time of the crime — in other words, whether he was responsible for his actions or sane, in a legal sense. The issue is no less important from a clinical perspective, particularly in relation to the spectrum of dissociative disorders.

While the legal point of view seeks to distinguish between these two positions, the clinician is more likely to conceive of amnesia on a continuum of dissociation, ranging from a total inability to remember at one extreme, through various degrees of partial amnesia, to the very few individuals who show no dynamically determined memory loss on the other extreme. Many a murderer, particularly in the case of a heinous crime involving socially repugnant motives, would after having committed the crime fervently wish that it had not occurred, and experience the whole episode as ego alien to the point of working hard to keep his own participation in the matter out of consciousness. While the individual may not truly forget the crime, he may succeed in keeping it out of active awareness by continually working to suppress his recollection. Even the individual, who would have no difficulty in remembering the crime and asserts that he cannot recall because he has no way of justifying his behavior, may still find it easier to avoid thinking about what happened, so that it would not be in his immediate phenomenal awareness.

While these distinctions are interesting and at times clinically important, they are always difficult to make even if one is in a clinical context, where the patient is as eager to clarify the matter as the therapist. Often it is very difficult for us to tell just how unable we are to recall something, unless we actively attempt to do so, and then retrospectively judge the difficulty of recall that we originally experienced. In a forensic setting, where the defendant may have much to gain by maintaining his total inability to recollect, there is no way of reliably assessing the precise place on the continuum of ability-to-recollect where an individual might fall.

However, partial dissociation and partial amnesia are so ubiquitous that from a legal perspective they have little relevance. Thus, in a forensic context what is relevant is a true inability to recollect rather than a wish — no matter how fervent — that the events in question had never happened. This means that we must concern ourselves with the evidence that would indicate a rigid amnesic barrier, and recognize that anything other than such a profound amnesia has little relevance in answering the questions put to us by the Court.

While one cannot prove definitively whether an individual has amnesia, one can form a diagnostic judgment (especially when a history of amnesic episodes is claimed) by relying not only upon the clinical interview, but also upon extensive information concerning the individual's reported recollections to a number of people over time, upon examination of the manner in which he reports his amnesia, and upon a detailed study of amnesia-like events in his life history. In the case of Kenneth Bianchi, no corroborating evidence has been found of any amnesic episodes prior to his arrest. After his arrest, over a period of 2 months, Kenneth Bianchi did not claim amnesia for his whereabouts or actions the night of the Bellingham murders, but rather attempted to construct a series of false alibis that were outlined earlier.

Most of these alibis were potentially quite plausible — such as the assertion that he had been at the Sheriff's Reserve meeting — and were abandoned only after it was clear that they were specifically negated by incontrovertible evidence. Other alibis — such as the claim that he had been with Greg, an individual he knew had died — were apparently created in the hope that they would be more difficult to discredit. Finally, the alibi which he sought to induce his mother to create for him, showed careful and concerted planning, a characteristic that was even more evident in his writing numerous letters to induce a female acquaintance to provide him an alibi for the specific time of the crime. It does not appear to us that these kinds of activities are consistent with the behavior of an individual who in his interviews with the doctors displays an intense concern with learning about himself, and who seems so sincere in his preoccupation with his intrapsychic problems that he expresses more concern about these matters than about his reality predicament!

The issue of amnesia was first raised by the defense attorney because Mr. Bianchi had denied a psychiatric history, but the attorney had obtained the DePaul Clinic report of his psychiatric examination at age 11. The evidence that Dr. Lunde — who, in a confidential unrecorded interview, was the first to examine Mr. Bianchi — used as an indication of amnesia concerned Mr. Bianchi's denial of a psychiatric history, his denial of feelings of hostility toward his mother, and the vagueness of his description of his activities the night of the Bellingham murders (see Trial trans., *People v. Buono*, 1983, p. 2,274-2,280). Thus, as far as we were able to ascertain, Mr. Bianchi never spontaneously claimed a lack of memory for the time period when the murders were committed to the police, to his mother, or to his common-law wife, and only began to complain of this difficulty almost 2 months after his arrest after his lawyer had confronted him with the DePaul Clinic report and the fact that the evidence against him was overwhelming, in order to suggest to him the possible viability of an insanity defense.

Thus, while we feel that it is entirely likely that Kenneth Bianchi did try to put the crimes themselves out of mind, such as when Ken indicated to the first author that he did not wish to remember all that "Steve" knew about the crimes, examining all of the behavior relevant to lack of recall, we find it is not consistent with the diagnosis of psychogenic amnesia[32] — that is, a true inability to recall rather than an unwillingness to do so.

Was Kenneth Bianchi Insane?

It is a widely held view that anyone who commits a series of heinous, apparently senseless murders must *ipso facto* be considered insane. The more bizarre a murder, the more likely will it be viewed as the work of a "madman."

Nevertheless, the courts require that the diagnosis of insanity be based upon very specific criteria, such as the ability to tell right from wrong. Thus, an individual who is a paranoid schizophrenic and believes that God is telling him to eliminate "impure and dangerous creatures of the devil," would most likely be considered not guilty (of a murder) by reason of insanity because his illness prevented him from understanding that it was wrong to kill. The reason that such an individual is considered to be deranged is because his motive is incomprehensible to someone who does not share the patient's paranoid system. In the case of Mr. Bianchi, there is no evidence of a thought disorder or psychosis; but the crimes do not seem to be based upon any rational motive, which may lead to the inference that the perpetrator must have been insane.

What could be considered a rational motive for murder? There is a group of mass murderers, who are rarely if ever considered insane — at least by the criminal justice system — because their motive is financial

---

[32]In his July 23, 1979 report to the Court, Dr. Lunde argued that Mr. Bianchi could not have been malingering amnesia or a dissociative reaction, pointing out, "Furthermore, one would have to assume that Bianchi began plotting his strategy for these crimes and his defense, at about age nine, since this is when the first documented symptoms of his mental disturbance occurred [p. 7]." Such a view should require that the personal history demonstrate clear evidence of amnesia and dissociation — that is, these symptoms should have been noted by others years ahead of his apprehension for murder. Since no such corroboration was found, it is only Mr. Bianchi's unsupported statements (during the psychiatric evaluations after his arrest) about his childhood that form the basis of the clinical judgment concerning dissociative reactions and amnesias in childhood. There would have been little difficulty for Mr. Bianchi to pick up on the cues that were provided him and invent a personality split retrospectively, if he felt it was expedient to do so after other alibis had failed.

gain. These are the professional or contract killers who may or may not have thought disorders, can be severely disturbed, and even psychotic, but who nevertheless are presumed to commit their crimes for reasons that are considered rational, though deviant.

During the examination of Mr. Bianchi, it became clear that the motive for the murders was sexual gratification. This was documented by the physical evidence at the scene of the crimes, by the way that Bianchi, as "Steve," talked about the crimes, and was clarified further by Ken during his interviews with Dr. Faerstein and Dr. Allison. There is no doubt that Kenneth Bianchi is quite "sick" in the sense of having a perverted sexual need which allows him to obtain gratification from killing women, and one may reasonably assume that this is related to the profound ambivalence that characterizes his relationship with his mother. It is probably also not an accident that the Hillside Strangler murders began during his common-law wife's pregnancy and ceased with the birth of his son.

The Bellingham murders occurred during a period when his wife was nursing, and he had lost sexual interest, which he ascribed in a puzzled fashion to observing his wife nursing their child. That Kenneth Bianchi was at times capable of normal sexual relations was confirmed by his common-law wife.[33] However, when he learned that she was 2.5 months pregnant in August, 1977, Bianchi's frequency of sexual contact with her decreased dramatically from this time on through the birth of their son in February, 1978. It was during this period that the Hillside Strangler murders occurred, beginning in October, 1977, and ending on February 17, 1978, 6 days before the birth of his son. Following the birth, his wife moved to Bellingham, Washington, where Bianchi joined her 3 months later. While they resumed sexual relations at this time, the frequency decreased over 2 months, and virtually ceased again, except during a 10-day visit they took to Mr. Bianchi's mother in August, 1978, when Bianchi's interest in sex briefly returned to normal. By his wife's report, his interest in sexual relations with her ceased immediately upon their return from visiting his mother, and they never had intercourse thereafter (Interview on March 23, 1979, by attorney Dean Brett, p. 46). The Bellingham murders occurred in January, 1979.

The apparently satisfactory sexual relationship with his common-law wife, that had lasted for several months, became unsatisfactory for Kenneth Bianchi as soon as he became aware that she was pregnant, long before there was visible evidence of the pregnancy. The knowledge that she was a mother seemingly intensified the profound ambivalence that he

---

[33]While his common-law wife reported that sexual relations occurred at times with a satisfactory frequency, she did not indicate whether Kenneth Bianchi enjoyed the relationship. However, a comment by his first wife indicates early problems in this area: "And after we did have sex I always think he looked at me as a little soiled, you know. I don't think he got any pleasure out of it at all. It was more of a once and awhile duty . . . [p. 102; Inv. Report No. 960-78, Public Defender, County of Los Angeles]."

felt toward his own mother — perhaps one of the areas where his true feelings really were unconscious. It seems likely that he continued to be unaware of his actual feelings, even as he would glibly discuss hating his mother with the psychiatrists; a discussion that would have been far more difficult and would have involved genuine affect if it had been based upon a true awareness of his feelings. In any case, the Hillside murders, which almost certainly were an expression of rage against his mother, occurred at a time when he had ceased to be physically attracted to his wife while she was in a role of a mother-to-be.

With the birth of his son, he sought to resume the relationship with his common-law wife, and had some sexual interest when he moved back in with her in Bellingham. However, he found that her nursing of the child sharply diminished her sexual attractiveness. Particularly striking is the fact that when they visited his mother, the ambivalent feelings were again focused on his mother, and his sexual attraction to his common-law wife reappeared dramatically — only to disappear as suddenly as it appeared immediately upon their return to Bellingham. It is of interest that the common-law wife had positive feelings toward Kenneth Bianchi's mother, and described herself as being similar to her in many regards, most particularly in having a "take charge" manner (Interview on March 23, 1979, by attorney Dean Brett, pp. 48-52).

While these dynamic considerations may help explain aspects of the murders, they do not in our view indicate insanity. On the contrary, once we recognize the sexual motivation for the murders, it becomes clear that the acts represent criminal behavior to gratify a "sick" impulse. Unfortunately, the perverted nature of Mr. Bianchi's sexual needs resulted in murder. It may put the matter in perspective to consider that a sexual impulse that an individual seeks to gratify with an unwilling adult partner is rape — similarly here the motive is understood by judge and jury, and therefore the act is not considered insane, but is viewed as deviant and criminal. It is in this sense that we view the murders as motivated by a comprehensible, albeit severely disturbed, sexual impulse. Yet gratifying any sexual impulse by force or in a manner that brings injury to others is clearly a criminal act.

One final aspect of the crimes themselves deserves comment. While Mr. Bianchi, as "Steve," flatly denied that there was anything wrong with the killing of women and asserted that such behavior was appropriate, he, even as "Steve," clearly recognized that an individual carrying out such behavior would be punished if caught. Further, he acknowledged that he had gone to great length to avoid being caught. While "Steve" spoke of wanting "Ken" to be held responsible for the crimes — a seemingly bizarre and self-destructive view — his behavior before and after the Bellingham murders does not fit such a claim.

Indeed, Kenneth Bianchi, under his own name and demeanor, clearly planned the January 11, 1979, murders days in advance; on January 8, he told one of the guards at the security agency (where Bianchi was a supervisor) that he would assume the patrol of the area including the house where the murders occurred and that the guard was not to check on this area on either Thursday or Friday (January 11 or 12); on January 9 he called one of the victims to arrange for her to watch the house for 2 hours (ostensibly while the burglar alarm was being repaired) in return for $100, and instructed her that for security reasons she should discuss this with no one; he arranged that the daughter of the owner of the house where the murders were committed would not visit the evening of the killings, and phoned in advance to excuse himself from the Sheriff's Reserve meeting that night; on the eve of the murder he reported throwing his gun out of the window of his apartment to prevent his wife from seeing him take it that evening; he also prepared for the crimes by taking a yellow plastic bag (which he would later use to dispose of the evidence) and placing ace bandages, cord, a rubber glove, and condoms in it. All of these careful preparations before the crimes were matched by an equally systematic cleanup after the crimes. Mr. Bianchi left the crime scene neat and orderly, without any obvious evidence, as reported by the police on their initial visit. He had placed the bodies in one of the victim's cars; driven it to an isolated location; and disposed of the bandages, cords, and victims' belongings.

It was only because, contrary to Mr. Bianchi's explicit instructions, one of the victims had told her boyfriend about the lucrative and unusual arrangement that Kenneth Bianchi had recruited her for, that Bianchi became a suspect as soon as the girls were reported missing. It is by no means clear whether Mr. Bianchi would have been apprehended if the victims had followed his instructions to tell no one. All of this suggests that: (a) the crimes showed careful advance planning and premeditation; (b) Mr. Bianchi attempted to avoid being apprehended; and (c) the motive for these crimes was the acting out of a perverted sexual need. For these reasons and the fact that upon examination he showed no evidence of thought disorder or psychosis, we believe that Kenneth Bianchi was sane and knew what he was doing when he committed the Bellingham murders.

Diagnostic Summary

A careful review of the clinical data as well as the extensive biographical material that is available strongly urges a diagnosis of psychopathic or sociopathic personality, which in *DSM-III* is classified as Antisocial Personality Disorder, 301.70. Such a diagnosis requires at least 3 of 12 criteria being met prior to the age of 15. While there is some question whether Kenneth Bianchi's repeated absences from school were truancy, the history indicates that (a) he persistently lied from an early age; (b) his school grades were consistently below his estimated intellectual ability; and (c) he chronically violated rules at home and in school. For example, a priest at a grade school that Kenneth Bianchi attended described how Kenneth was part of a small group of boys who were caught with an unusually dangerous array of weapons that they were planning to use on their peers, including a bat studded with nails (Inv. Report No. 960-78, Public Defender, County of Los Angeles). In discussing the matter with Kenneth's mother, she insisted that Kenneth was a good boy,[34] and that the others must have made him do it, but a few days later called the priest to say that she had also found some evidence of his involvement with the weapons.

Further, the diagnosis of Antisocial Personality requires at least 4 of 9 manifestations of the disorder after age 18. Since the age of 18, Kenneth Bianchi displayed (a) an inability to sustain consistent work behavior reflected by at least 12 jobs in 9 years; (b) a failure to accept social norms with respect to lawful behavior, as evidenced by repeated thefts and pimping; (c) an inability to maintain an enduring attachment to a sexual partner — his first marriage was annulled, he had many transient sexual encounters, and though he knew his common-law wife for over 2 years, he lived with her for less than 8 months but continued to have casual sexual relations with others during this time; (d) a failure to honor financial obligations demonstrated by repeatedly borrowing money that he did not repay, and failing to support his common-law wife; and (e) a disregard for the truth as reflected by repeated lying and the "conning" of others for personal profit.

Another basic manifestation of the disorder, required for diagnosis, is a pattern of continuous antisocial behavior in which the rights of others are violated. This is illustrated even in Mr. Bianchi's relationship with people close to him. For example, a relative employed him out of gratitude to Kenneth's mother (who had been good to him as a child). During the time that the 19-year-old Bianchi worked for his relative, whom he had gotten along with very well, he was repeatedly irresponsible in work duties, and systematically stole increasing amounts of money from the business. Throughout this period, he maintained a pleasant facade, denying any wrongdoing. Perhaps most indicative of the callousness of his behavior is the cancer scam, where in order to quiet his pregnant wife's inquiries into his absenteeism from work while living in Los Angeles, he faked having cancer and receiving treatments. He went so far as to forge medical reports to convince his wife of the seriousness of his condition. He eventually told her that his cancer was in remission, but she remained concerned and when he was arrested in Bellingham, she told the police about his cancer. Thus, he maintained for well over a year the cruel fiction that he had cancer to the wife for whom he presumably cared.

[34]The absence of a police record is of interest in what otherwise is a clear example of an antisocial personality disorder. However, an examination of interviews with family and teachers reflects the mother's role in preventing the development of a police record. The weapon incident in grade school would normally have been brought to the attention of the police and recorded. Another example that was uncovered involved the police being called in when, in a fit of pique, Mr. Bianchi broke the apartment window of a girlfriend who had locked him out. His mother reported that she had managed to have the incident expunged from the police record, and complained that some evidence had survived in the files. It is also noteworthy that while living in the Los Angeles area, it is documented he engaged in a variety of felonious activities, yet he managed to avoid any police record prior to his arrest in Bellingham.

Finally, the diagnosis of Antisocial Personality Disorder requires that the behavior cannot be due to either severe mental retardation, schizophrenia, or manic episodes. None of these conditions were present when Mr. Bianchi was examined following his arrest.

Thus, despite his facade of being a husband, a good employee, and a responsible security officer, his wife repeatedly found it necessary to leave him, he stole from the very stores he was hired to protect from shoplifters, and he used his position with the security company to provide the setting and opportunity for the Bellingham murders. Throughout his adult life, Kenneth Bianchi maintained a pattern of antisocial behavior that has traditionally been described as psychopathy (see Cleckley, 1964). One of the characteristics of this condition, while not emphasized in *DSM-III*, seems nonetheless particularly germane for the understanding of this individual, that is, an inability to empathize with others.[35] The lack of empathy helps explain the callousness of such individuals because they are not constrained by feeling the discomfort and pain that they inflict upon those around them.

To document that Kenneth Bianchi is a psychopath does not, however, explain the murders he committed. In other words, if he had not committed the murders and was, for example, instead arrested for his participation in forcing underage minors into prostitution, he would still be appropriately classified as having an Antisocial Personality Disorder. In the sense of accounting for the murders, Antisocial Personality alone is not a sufficient diagnosis.

Earlier we discussed that Mr. Bianchi showed clear evidence of a Psychosexual Disorder, which would be classified by *DSM-III* as Sexual Sadism, 302.84. However, this disorder in and of itself rarely leads an individual to commit murder, even though he may find such a fantasy arousing. It is the combination of Antisocial Personality Disorder *with* Sexual Sadism that in our view creates the potential for Kenneth Bianchi to act out these impulses.[36] Thus, he not only has the perverted sexual impulse, but also the lack of empathy that removes many of the normal barriers that would prevent the acting out of such behavior. It is for reasons such as these that the earlier literature often spoke of the "true sexual psychopath" (McCary, 1967). This diagnosis would be expressed in *DSM-III* as an Antisocial Personality Disorder on Axis II (principal diagnosis), and as Sexual Sadism on Axis I.

Though the pattern of Kenneth Bianchi's psychopathic behavior goes back many years, the sexual psychopathy was manifested overtly for apparently only a relatively short period of his life. What were the factors

[35]Murray, H. A., personal communication, November 28, 1950.

[36]The literature has described individuals who are remarkably similar to Kenneth Bianchi, as lust murderers (Reinhardt, 1957), as compulsive murderers (Revitch, 1965), as sadistic murderers (Brittain, 1970), and as sexual sadistic murderers (Lunde, 1979). In a recent clinical study of 13 such rapists and murderers, MacCullouch, Snowden, Wood, and Mills (1983) emphasize that once apprehended this type of offender is often a model prisoner, but "given the opportunity he is likely to murder again and he knows it [p. 21]."

that could have translated the impulse into overt action? We may speculate that the relationship with an older male with whom he carried out a number of illegal activities, most particularly the running of juvenile prostitutes in Los Angeles, and who shared a similar sexual perversion, may have played a crucial role in causing Mr. Bianchi to actually commit a series of sexually motivated murders. Further, given the profound ambivalence toward his mother, it also seems likely that the stress from living with his common-law wife during her pregnancy in Los Angeles (as she was becoming a mother) and his negative response to her mothering of the baby in Bellingham, essentially eliminated sexual relations with his common-law wife. However, his heightened ambivalence towards women was not expressed as overt aggressive behavior toward either his common-law wife or his mother; rather, it contributed to the transformation of his perverted sexual impulses into acts of murder. Thus, we believe that while no single diagnosis is fully adequate to explain Kenneth Bianchi's behavior, the two combined aspects of the *DSM-III* diagnosis, along with situational factors, resulted in the multiple murders, though not in multiple personality.

IMPLICATIONS FOR DIAGNOSIS IN A FORENSIC SETTING

Though it is clear that Kenneth Bianchi has a severe personality disorder and is in many ways disturbed, it also is evident that he was almost successful in simulating multiple personality. The case of Kenneth Bianchi highlights in our view the distinction between forensic and clinical settings and underscores the limitations of clinical diagnostic procedures when applied in another context.

Rosenhan (1973) has demonstrated that it is a straightforward matter for motivated students to be diagnosed as psychotic by a psychiatric hospital staff and admitted to the hospital. Equally striking is his report concerning an outstanding university-based psychiatric service whose chief had argued that this could not occur in a service such as his. After Rosenhan (1973) obtained permission to introduce pseudo-patients to the service, and the staff diagnosed several newly admitted patients as malingerers for the first time in the history of the service, it turned out that in fact no pseudo-patients had been introduced during that period! These data emphasize the profound influence of the clinician's set upon diagnosis, both in terms of a false positive diagnosis of psychopathology, as well as a false positive diagnosis of malingering.

In a therapeutic setting, however, with no obvious secondary gain for appearing mentally disturbed, a patient who presents himself for admission to a psychiatric institution or even one who seeks outpatient treatment, must be assumed to be in need of help. Under these circumstances the therapist should not be concerned about whether the patient is malingering; in the clinical context, it is the therapist's responsibility to help the patient understand why he is doing what he is doing, and to cope with the stressors that have made it necessary for him to act in this fashion.

MULTIPLE PERSONALITY IN THE FORENSIC CONTEXT 165

While clinical skills are essential for making an appropriate diagnosis in any context, to the extent that these skills have been honed with a population of patients who seek help to alleviate their private anguish, they have only limited transfer to the problems encountered in a forensic setting. Here individuals may appropriately perceive that convincing the examining clinician that they are suffering from some particular form of mental disorder is the only route to freedom that is available to them. Under these circumstances the assumption that what the defendant says necessarily reflects his phenomenal experience, is no longer justified. Further, it is often difficult to determine in evaluating an individual in a forensic situation, whether there is a true therapeutic alliance in the sense of a troubled individual seeking help, as opposed to the defendant playing a role as an instrumental act. Recognizing the ease with which the clinician's set can bias him in either direction, there is a need to seek external corroboration, and it is desirable to include at least some procedures that elicit counterintuitive responses as part of the evaluative process.

REFERENCES

ALBERT. S., FOX. H. M., & KAHN, M. W. Faking psychosis on the Rorschach: Can expert judges detect malingering? *J. pers. Assess.*, 1980, *44*, 115–119.

ALLISON. R. B. On discovering multiplicity. *Svensk Tidskrift för Hypnos*, 1978, *2*, 4–8.

ALLISON, R. B. Difficulties diagnosing the multiple personality syndrome in a death penalty case. *Int. J. clin. exp. Hypnosis*, 1984, *32*, 102-117.

ALLISON, R., & SCHWARZ, T. *Minds in many pieces*. New York. Rawson. Wade, 1980.

AMERICAN PSYCHIATRIC ASSOCIATION. *Diagnostic and statistical manual of mental disorders (DSM-III)*. (3rd ed.) Washington, D.C.: APA, 1980.

ARONS. H. *Hypnosis in criminal investigation*. Springfield, IL: Charles C Thomas. 1967.

Bellingham Herald. Bianchi refused bail reduction. January 19, 1979, p. 1, 4.

BLISS, E. L. Multiple personalities: A report of 14 cases with implications for schizophrenia and hysteria. *Arch. gen. Psychiat.*, 1980, *37*, 1388–1397.

BRADFORD, J. McD. W., & SMITH, S. M. Amnesia and homicide: The Padola case and a study of thirty cases. *Bull. Amer. Acad. Psychiat. Law*, 1979, *7*, 219–231.

BRANDSMA, J. M., & LUDWIG, A. M. A case of multiple personality: Diagnosis and therapy. *Int. J. clin. exp. Hypnosis*, 1974, *22*, 216–233.

BRAUN, B. G. Hypnosis for multiple personalities. In H. J. Wain (Ed.), *Clinical hypnosis in medicine*. Chicago: Year Book Medical, 1980. Pp. 209–217.

BRAUN, B. G. Hypnosis creates multiple personality: Myth or reality? *Int. J. clin. exp. Hypnosis*. 1984, *32*, 191–197.

BRITTAIN, R. P. The sadistic murderer. *Med. Sci. Law*, 1970, *10*, 198–207.

CLECKLEY, H. *The mask of sanity*. St. Louis: Mosby, 1964.

COONS. P. M. Multiple personality: Diagnostic considerations. *J. clin. Psychiat.*, 1980, *41*, 330–336.

DAHLSTROM, W. G., & WELSH, G. S. *An MMPI handbook: A guide to use in clinical practice and research*. Minneapolis: Univer. of Minnesota Press, 1960.

EIBLMAYR, K. An examination of the phenomenon of trance logic using objective measurement and limiting the hypnotist-subject relationship. Paper presented at the 33rd Annual Meeting of the Society for Clinical and Experimental Hypnosis, Portland, October 1981.

ELLENBERGER, H. F. *The discovery of the unconscious: The history and evolution of dynamic psychiatry*. New York: Basic Books, 1970. (Chaps. 1–4)

EVANS, F. J. Contextual forgetting: Posthypnotic source amnesia. *J. abnorm. Psychol.*, 1979, *88*, 556–563.

EVANS, F. J., & THORN, W. A. F. Two types of posthypnotic amnesia: Recall amnesia and source amnesia. *Int. J. clin. exp. Hypnosis*, 1966, *14*, 162–179.

FRANKS, C. M., & WILSON, G. T. *Annual review of behavior therapy: Theory and practice*. New York: Brunner Mazel, 1976.

FROSS, G. H. *Handbook of hypnotic techniques*. Newark, N.J.: Power Publishers, 1966.

GOUGH, H. G. *Manual for the California Psychological Inventory*. Palo Alto, CA: Consulting Psychologists Press, 1964.

GREAVES, G. B. Multiple personality: 165 years after Mary Reynolds. *J. nerv. ment. Dis.*, 1980, *168*, 577–596.

GRUENEWALD, D. Hypnotic techniques without hypnosis in the treatment of dual personality. *J. nerv. ment. Dis.*, 1971, *153*, 41–46.

GRUENEWALD, D. Multiple personality and splitting phenomena: A reconceptualization. *J. nerv. ment. Dis.*, 1977, *164*, 385–393.

GRUENEWALD, D. Analogues of multiple personality in psychosis. *Int. J. clin. exp. Hypnosis*, 1978, *26*, 1–8.

HARRIMAN, P. L. The experimental production of some phenomena related to the multiple personality. *J. abnorm. soc. Psychol.*, 1942, *37*, 244–255.

KAMPMAN, R. Hypnotically induced multiple personality: An experimental study. *Int. J. clin. exp. Hypnosis*, 1976, *24*, 215–227.

KLUFT, R. P. Varieties of hypnotic interventions in the treatment of multiple personality. *Amer. J. clin. Hypnosis*, 1982, *24*, 230–240.

KORCHIN, S. J. *Modern clinical psychology*. New York: Basic Books, 1976.

KVARNES, R. G., & PARLOFF, G. H. *A Harry Stack Sullivan Seminar*. New York: W. Norton, 1976.

LARMORE, K., LUDWIG, A. M., & CAIN, R. L. Multiple personality — An objective case study. *Brit. J. Psychiat.*, 1977, *131*, 35–40.

LUNDE, D. T. *Murder and madness*. New York: Norton, 1979.

MacCULLOCH, M. J., SNOWDEN, P. R., WOOD, P. J. W., & MILLS, H. E. Sadistic fantasy, sadistic behaviour and offending. *Brit. J. Psychiat.*, 1983, *143*, 20–29.

McCARY, J. L. *Human sexuality*. Princeton: Van Nostrand, 1967.

McDOUGALL, W. *Outline of abnormal psychology*. New York: Scribner's Sons, 1926.

MILLER, R. D. The use of hypnosis in the treatment of multiple personality: Auto-hypnosis as a defense and a resistance. *Int. J. clin. exp. Hypnosis*, 1984, *32*, 236–247.

Newsweek. The ten faces of Billy. December 18, 1978, p. 106.

ORNE, M. T. The nature of hypnosis: Artifact and essence. *J. abnorm. soc. Psychol.*, 1959, *58*, 277–299.

ORNE, M. T. On the social psychology of the psychological experiment: With particular reference to demand characteristics and their implications. *Amer. Psychol.*, 1962, *17*, 776–783.

ORNE, M. T. On the simulating subject as a quasi-control group in hypnosis research: What, why, and how. In E. Fromm & R. E. Shor (Eds.), *Hypnosis: Research developments and perspectives*. Chicago: Aldine-Atherton, 1972. Pp. 399–443.

ORNE, M. T. Communication by the total experimental situation: Why it is important, how it is evaluated, and its significance for the ecological validity of findings. In P. Pliner, L. Krames, & T. Alloway (Eds.), *Communication and affect*. New York: Academic Press, 1973. Pp. 157–191.

ORNE, M. T. The construct of hypnosis: Implications of the definition for research and practice. *Ann. N.Y. Acad. Sci.*, 1977, *296*, 14–33.

People v. Buono, No. 81-A354231 (Cal. Super. Ct. November 18, 1983).

PETERS, J. E. Trance logic: Artifact or essence of hypnosis? Unpublished doctoral dissertation, Pennsylvania State University, 1973.

Post. Milligan granted release. February 6, 1984, p. 1.

PRINCE, M. *The dissociation of a personality*. London: Longmans Green, 1906.

RAPAPORT, D., GILL, M., & SCHAFER, R. *Diagnostic psychological testing: The theory, statistical evaluation, and diagnostic application of a battery of tests*. (Vol. II) Chicago: Year Book, 1946.

RAPAPORT, D., GILL, M. M., & SCHAFER, R. *Diagnostic psychological testing*. New York: International Universities Press, 1968.

RAPPEPORT, J. R. Differences between forensic and general psychiatry. *Amer. J. Psychiat.*, 1982, *139*, 331–334.

REINHARDT, J. M. *Sex perversions and sex crimes: a psychocultural examination of the causes, nature and criminal manifestations of sex perversions*. (Police Science Series). Springfield, IL: Charles C Thomas, 1957.

REVITCH, E. Sex murder and the potential sex murderer. *Dis. nerv. Syst.*, 1965, *26*, 640–648.

RIOCH, M. J., COULTER, W. R. & WEINBERGER, D. M. *Dialogues for therapists*. San Francisco, CA: Jossey Bass, 1976.

RORSCHACH, H. *Psychodiagnostics: A diagnostic test based on perception*. (2nd ed.) (P. Lemkay & B. Kronenberg, trans.) New York: Grune & Stratton, 1942.

ROSENHAN, D. L. On being sane in insane places. *Science*, 1973, *179*, 250–258.

SINGER, M. T., & WYNNE, L. C. Thought disorder and family relations of schizophrenics: III. Methodology using projective techniques. *Arch. gen. Psychiat.*, 1965, *12*, 187–200.

State v. Bianchi, No. 79-10116 (Wash. Super. Ct. October 19, 1979).

State v. Milligan, No. 77-CR-11-2908 (Franklin County, Ohio Dec. 4. 1978).

SUTCLIFFE, J. P., & JONES, J. Personal identity, multiple personality, and hypnosis. *Int. J. clin. exp. Hypnosis*. 1962, *10*, 231–269.

TAYLOR, W. S., & MARTIN, M.F. Multiple personality. *J. abnorm. soc. Psychol.*, 1944, *39*, 281–300.

THORN, W. A. F. A study of the correlates of dissociation as measured by post-hypnotic amnesia. Unpublished honors thesis, University of Sydney, Sydney, Australia, 1960.

Time. The man with ten personalities: Experts unravel the psyche of an Ohio rape suspect. October 23, 1978, p. 102.

Time. Murderous personality: Was the Hillside Strangler a Jekyll and Hyde? May 7, 1979, p. 26.

WACHTEL, P. L. *Psychoanalysis and behavior therapy*. New York: Basic Books, 1977.

WAGNER, E. E., & HEISE, M. R. A comparison of Rorschach records of three multiple personalities. *J. pers. Assess.*. 1974, *38*, 308–331.

WATKINS, J. G. Ego states and the problem of responsibility: A psychological analysis of the Patty Hearst case. *J. Psychiat. Law*, 1976, *4*, 471–489.

WATKINS, J. G. The Bianchi (L.A. Hillside Strangler) case: Sociopath or multiple personality? *Int. J. clin. exp. Hypnosis*, 1984, *32*, 67–101.(a)

WATKINS, J. G. Multiple personality. In R. J. Corsini (Ed.), *Encyclopedia of psychology*. New York: Wiley, 1984, in press.(b)

WATKINS, J. G., & STAUFFACHER, J. C. An index of pathological thinking in the Rorschach *J. project. Tech.*, 1952, *16*, 276–286.

WATKINS, J. G., & WATKINS, H. H. Theory and practice of ego state therapy: A short-term therapeutic approach. In H. Grayson (Ed.), *Short-term approaches to psychotherapy* (Vol. III. *New Directions in Psychotherapy* Series). New York: Human Sciences, 1979. Pp. 176–220.

WECHSLER, D. *Wechsler Adult Intelligence Scale*. New York: Psychological Corp., 1955.

WOLMAN, B. B. *Dictionary of behavioral science*.New York: Van Nostrand Reinhold, 1973.

WOLMAN, B. B. *Handbook of general psychology*. Englewood Cliffs, NJ: Prentice-Hall, 1973.

Über die Differentialdiagnose einer multiplen Persönlichkeit im forensischen
Zusammenhang

Martin T. Orne, David F. Dinges und Emily Carota Orne

Abstrakt: Probleme des Diagnostizierens einer multiplen Persönlichkeitsstörung im forensischen Zusammenhang werden hier diskutiert und durch den Fall *Staat wider Kenneth Bianchi* (1979) illustriert. Dies war ein Fall, wo der Angeklagte des Mordes beschuldigt wurde sowie unter dem Verdacht stand, diese Störung zu haben. Um einen sekundären Gewinn, der mit einer Diagnose der Vielfachheit in solch einem Fall verbunden ist, zu erzielen (z. B. der Todestrafe zu entrinnen), mußten Hypothesen entwickelt werden, die eine belehrende Differentialdiagnose zwischen multipler Persönlichkeit und dem Vortäuschen einere Krankheit erlauben. Würde eine wahre, multiple Persönlichkeitsstörung existieren, dann hätten (a) Struktur und Wesen der verschiedenen Persönlichkeiten über längere Zeit hin beständig sein müssen, (b) die Grenzen zwischen den unterschiedlichen Persönlichkeiten widerstandsfähig sein müssen und nicht leicht durch gesellschaftliche Anspielungen verändert werden können, (c) die Reaktion auf Hypnose hätte der von andern, tief hypnotisierten Subjekten vergleichbar sein müssen und (d) Personen, die ihn über eine Periode von Jahren hin gekannt hatten, hätten in der Lage sein müssen, Beispiele von plötzlichen, unerklärlichen Veränderungen in Benehmen und Identität zu liefern wie auch Beweismaterial, das seine behauptete, intermittierende Amnesie bestätigte. Keiner dieser Faktoren bestätigte sich als angebracht. Vielmehr änderten sich das Wesen, die Grenzen und Anzahl der Persönlichkeiten als Reaktion auf Anspielungen, wie diese Kondition glaubhafter gemacht werden könnte, und seine Reaktion auf Hypnose schien ein bewußtes Rollenspiel zu reflektieren. Weiterhin deutete seine Lebensgeschichte ein beharrliches Modell des Schwindelns und absichtlichen Betrügens an. Es wurde daher beschlossen, daß Herr Bianchi eine multiple Persönlichkeit simulierte, und die Diagnose einer Antisozialen Persönlichkeitsstörung mit Sexuellem Sadismus wurde gestellt. Unterschiedliche Diagnosen und die klinischen Aspekte, die für sein Benehmen verantwortlich zu sein schienen, werden diskutiert.

Le diagnostic différentiel de personnalité multiple dans le contexte légal

Martin T. Orne, David F. Dinges, et Emily Carota Orne

Résumé: Les problèmes de diagnostic du trouble de personnalité multiple dans un contexte légal sont discutés et illustrés par l'affaire l'Etat contre Kenneth Bianchi (1979), une cause impliquant un individu accusé de meutre au premier degré et soupçonné de souffrir de ce désordre. A cause des gains secondaires (e.g. l'évitement de la peine de mort) associés au diagnostic de personnalité multiple dans un tel cas, il importe de formuler des hypothèses qui permettent d'établir un diagnostic différentiel bien étayé de la personnalité multiple ou de simulation. L'existence d'un véritable problème de personnalité multiple implique: (a) que la structure et le contenu des diverses personnalités soient consistants à travers le temps, (b) que les frontières entre les diverses personnalités soient stables et non modifiées par des indices sociaux, (c) que la réponse à l'hypnose soit semblable à celle de d'autres sujets profondément hypnotisés et, (d) que les personnes l'ayant connu durant plusieurs années soient capables de présenter des exemples de changements soudains et inexplicables dans le comportement et l'identité, ainsi que de corroborer ses affirmations d'amnésies intermittentes: Rien n'a été prouvé en ce sens. Bien plus, le contenu, les frontières et le nombre de personnalités changeaient selon les indices pouvant lui permettre de rendre sa condition plus plausible, et, sa réponse à l'hypnose reflétait un jeu de rôle conscient. De plus, son histoire en est une de fraude et d'agression constantes. En conclusion, Monsieur Bianchi simulait une personnalité multiple et le diagnostic en est un de personnalité antisociale avec sadisme sexuel. La discussion porte sur les diagnostics différentiels et les aspects cliniques importants de son comportement.

MULTIPLE PERSONALITY IN THE FORENSIC CONTEXT   169

Diagnóstico diferencial de la personalidad múltiple dentro del contexto forense

Martin T. Orne, David F. Dinges y Emily Carota Orne

Resumen: Los problemas del diagnóstico de la personalidad múltiple dentro de un contexto
forense son discutidos e ilustrados a partir del caso caratulado Estado de Washington
contra Kenneth Bianchi (1979), el cual involucraba un acusado a quien se le incriminaba
un asesinato en primer grado; además, se presumía que el mismo padecía el mencionado
trastorno. Debido a la ganancia secundaria (evitar la pena de muerte) asociada al diagnóstico de personalidad múltiple, se desarrollaron ciertas hipótesis para permitir un diagnóstico diferencial entre personalidad múltiple y simulación de enfermedad. Si
verdaderamente existía personalidad múltiple deberíamos encontrar que: (a) la estructura
y el contenido de las varias personalidades debieran haber sido consistentes a través del
tiempo; (b) los límites entre las diferentes personalidades debieran haber sido estables y
no fácilmente alteradas por indicadores sociales; (c) la respuesta a la hipnosis debiera haber
sido similar a aquellas de otros sujetos muy sugestionables y (d) aquellos que lo conocieron
durante un cierto período de tiempo hubieran sido capaces de dar ejemplos de cambios
súbitos e inexplicables en su conducta e identidad, además de mostrar evidencias que
corroboraran sus reclamos acerca de amnesias intermitentes. Ninguno de estos elementos
pudo comprobarse. Más aún el contenido, límites y número de personalidades cambiaron
en respuesta a indicadores acerca de cómo hacer esta perturbación más creíble y su
respuesta a la hipnosis pareció reflejar un juego de roles conciente. Además, la historia
personal indicó un patrón persistente de conductas fraudulentas y decepciones deliberadas.
Se concluyó que el señor Bianchi simuló una personalidad múltiple y se hizo el diagnóstico
de Personalidad antisocial con componentes sádico-sexuales. Se discutieron el diagnóstico
diferencial y los aspectos clínicos que parecen dar cuenta de su conducta.

Criminal Behaviour and Mental Health, 2, 329–341, 1992 © Whurr Publishers Ltd   329

Towards a new methodology for making sense of case material: an illustrative case involving attempted multiple murder

DAVID M. GRESSWELL Psychology Department, Rampton Hospital, UK
CLIVE R. HOLLIN School of Psychology, University of Birmingham, and
    Glenthorne Youth Treatment Centre, UK

ABSTRACT Functional analysis provides a method of understanding behaviour in terms of its consequences for the individual concerned. The suggestion is made here that the application of this method to past behaviour will be useful to both practitioners and researchers. It offers benefits in terms of organising case material, understanding the aetiology of the behaviour, planning interventions and predicting dangerousness. It should be noted, however, that this is not an exercise in developing causal models of specific offences. In this paper multiple sequential functional analysis methodology is described and the problems of applying it retrospectively to criminal behaviours discussed. The methodology is illustrated with the case of a man who formulated a plan to kill 20 people and was convicted of two counts of attempted murder.

One of the challenges in trying to understand human behaviour is in making sense of complex case material. Practitioners attempting to understand criminal behaviour may face particular difficulties because the behaviour is not directly observable. They therefore must rely on indirect sources such as archival records, witness statements, reports from police, and the offender's self-report. A coherent formulation of the offence is, however, important for making decisions about the likelihood of further offences, for designing clinical programmes, and for writing effective court reports.

Many cases generate a wealth of often complex and contradictory information, giving rise to the need to organise what is known in a meaningful, consistent manner. Functional analysis is one means of making sense of information gathered during assessment (Hollin, 1990). As the name implies, a

The opinions expressed in this article are those of the authors and do not necessarily reflect those of the Special Hospitals Service Authority.

functional analysis is an attempt at understanding what function a behaviour has for the individual. A functional analysis is often presented in terms of an 'A:B:C' sequence: 'A' refers to the environmental events antecedent to 'B', the behaviour, which produce environmental consequences 'C'. Thus, 'A' and 'C' are events outside the person and 'B' is what the person does, including covert behaviours such as thoughts, feelings, physiological activity, and overt behaviours such as physical actions.

An A:B:C analysis is not a 'static' view of the world: as time passes one A:B:C sequence becomes part of an individual's learning history and hence an antecedent to another set of behaviours. Such analyses use an 'A:B:C' rather than an 'A → B → C' format to emphasise that the analysis does not assume causality or always explain behaviour. A functional analysis suggests that certain events occur in a particular order and so may have some functional relationship (Skinner, 1974; Bandura, 1977; Blackman, 1980, 1981; Owens & Ashcroft, 1982; Haynes & O'Brien, 1990).

Functional analyses are conventionally idiographic and are used to guide clinical practice with individual subjects in applied and clinical settings (Herbert, 1978, 1981; Owens & Ashcroft, 1982; Barlow & Hersen, 1984; Arco, 1987). However, functional analysis has also been used nomothetically and analyses have been constructed for a range of clinical presentations such as self-injury (Iwata, Dorsey, Silfer, Bauman & Richman, 1982), anorexia nervosa (Slade, 1982), and for criminal behaviours such as firesetting (Jackson, Glass & Hope, 1987) and delinquency (Jones & Heskin, 1988).

When analysing the development of complex behaviours there is a tendency to place the subject's experience before the analysis in one huge 'A' category with a subsection for specific triggers for the current behaviour. This results in a long list of variables that impedes the examination of functional relations. Items of analysis may also be intermixed, with cognitive events in particular frequently included in 'A' and 'C' as well as the 'B' categories. Another commonly used method of organising case material has been the construction of multicomponent flow diagrams, again using long lists of antecedents and consequences for a particular behaviour (Slade, 1982; Bromley, 1986; Burgess, Hartman, Ressler, Douglas & McCormack, 1986; Jackson et al., 1987). Such diagrams can result in a static picture lacking a sense of chronology and development, thereby under-stressing the important notion that functional relationships can vary over time. Such diagrams have the added risk that they can lead to unfounded inferences of causality (Jones, 1983). However, Hollin (1990) organised case material into a series of conventional 'A:B:C' sequences where the first sequence became the antecedent for the second sequence, both of these for the third sequence, and so on. This style of organisation of case material breaks down event sequences in to meaningful and manageable chunks which can be examined for internal logic and best fit as outlined by Bromley (1986). The purpose of multiple sequential functional analysis as developed here is to assist in the ordering of case material, but it avoids making statements of causality (although the ordering of the material may lead to hypotheses about causality). The method is elaborated here in a number of ways: first by suggesting the key learning for each A:B:C sequence; secondly, by increasing the flexibility and parsimony of the methodology by allowing the inclusion of new antecedent material at each stage; thirdly, by separating the 'behaviour' category into overt (directly observable action) and covert (thoughts, feelings, physiology) sections.

To illustrate the methodology we have chosen the case of D, a seemingly motiveless offender where an understanding of the offence is difficult to obtain from conventional psychiatric and psychological assessment. This is a case with a wealth of material to be sorted, assimilated, and understood. The material includes approximately 12 hours of interviews with D, 2 hours with his father and sister, 2½ hours with his psychotherapist and GP, and over 300 pages of witness statements, contemporary psychological, psychiatric, and social enquiry reports.

CASE STUDY

D is a man who had formulated a plan to kill 20 people; he had already attacked two by the time he was caught. Both victims survived and D pleaded guilty to two counts of attempted murder. He was classified as having a psychopathic disorder and ordered to be detained for treatment at a maximum security hospital under Sections 37/41 of the Mental Health Act 1983 without limit of time.

Early experiences

D claimed that both his parents were cold and found it difficult to relate to him warmly. He felt that other family members were different from him, more emotionally robust and able to 'laugh off' troubles. His reported coping strategy was the development of a fantasy life in which idealised caring parents would come to save him. Since D also felt he could not know his parents 'naturally', he got to know them by searching through their possessions and insisting that they report details of their conversations. The parents' reaction to this was to treat it as a family joke, so reinforcing D's perception of himself as different.

During early adolescence D had had an operation to lower an undescended testicle. He recalls his father making him show the scars and the humiliation of his mother's embarrassed laughter. He also developed cystic acne and despite repeated washing and facial remedies was unable to control the disfig-uring spots, and was also unable to control the teasing and rejection he conse-quently received from his peers. With an ever-increasing feeling of powerlessness and a sense that he could not make others like him D made the first of three suicide attempts at the age of 14 by putting his fingers in a lamp socket. D learned to cope with problems by isolating himself from others

TABLE 1: Stage 1 – early experience

A
    Emotionally absent parenting and 'insensitive' family behaviour.
    Operation for undescended testicle.
    Development of cystic acne.
    Rejected and tormented by peers at school.

B/covert
    An increasing sense of alienation and of being different from family and friends.
    Feelings of being unable to control body or other people.
    Increasing reliance on fantasies of real parents coming to collect him, miracle cures
    for acne, and revenge.
    Development of a protective belief system that he is better than other people.

B/overt
    Searches parents' possessions.
    Repeated face washing.
    Isolates self.
    Attempts suicide.
    Visits the wasteland where he has fantasised attacking women.

C
    Loses friends and avoids contact with females.
    Tormenting from new workmates.
    Pressure from parents to go out and socialise.
    Deterioration of relationships with parents.
    Reduced opportunities for feedback from other people.

Key learning
1. He is very different from others, unattractive, unlikeable and helpless.
2. Revenge fantasies can make him feel good.

and developing fantasies of a 'miracle cure' for his acne and of revenge on those who mocked and rejected him. The revenge fantasy included slashing the faces of other people so that they, too, would know the experience of feeling disfigured. Engagement in fantasy offered him both temporary relief and a feeling of power that was enhanced by journeys to the wasteland where he imagined making his attacks.

As can be seen from Table 1, these actions created a cycle of isolation and alienation but only intermittent relief from feelings associated with being teased. D thus found himself in a situation where there were virtually no people with whom he could share experiences and gain support. Without this he began to develop a further defensive strategy, convincing himself he was better than others, a more sensitive, charming and creative person.

Early adult and work experience

At the age of 19, in an attempt to evade the teasing of his workmates, he left his job as a printer and began work in a department store. This was an

---

TABLE 2: Stage 2 – early adult and work experience

A
 Sequences as in stage 1.
 Rejected by peers at printers.
 New salesman makes him aware of his isolation.

B/covert
 Experiences intense anxiety and expectations of rejection.
 Feeling of being able to control/play games with customers.
 Protective belief system maintained.

B/overt
 Changes job to go to retail clothes trade.
 Begins lying to workmates to present himself as a normal male but feels tense in case lies are seen through.
 Learns salesman identity and how to 'put up a front'. Successfully manipulates customers.
 Arranges date, misses it and attempts suicide.
 Maintains social isolation.

C
 Others are friendly but superficial.
 Admitted to hospital but discharged without follow-up.

Key learning
1. He is not helpless but can protect himself and manipulate others with 'salesman' techniques.
2. He will never succeed in relationships.
3. Can appear 'normal' only by lying, is vulnerable to discovery and could consequently re-experience rejection.

---

important move as his new job involved training in sales techniques. He was taught to play a role: if customers were unkind to him, then it would be the 'salesman' they were rejecting not the 'real' D. His new 'salesman' identity was very effective, and he reports that colleagues and customers now treated him in a friendly manner. He felt able to manipulate other people and devised a game of 'musical coat hangers' which involved the customer trying on as many clothes as possible. This 'success' confirmed his view of himself as superior but also compounded his frustration as it was the 'salesman' not the 'real' D achieving success and the customers still seemed more attractive and successful than he.

A chance remark from another salesman enquiring about holidays upset D's equilibrium. He feared that if his colleagues realised he had no one to go on holiday with they would also realise he was isolated and different. He had catastrophic thoughts that they would reject and torment him as his school friends had before. To prevent this he lied, making up friends and social activities to create an illusion of a normal life. This strategy offered only intermittent relief: the imaginary world of friends gave him a veneer of normality, but he could never relax for fear of being caught out.

Despite increased social success D felt unable to date women, especially those he worked with. He feared colleagues knowing if he was rejected or a sexual partner discovering the operation on his testicle and revealing he was 'not a whole man'. Instead he joined a dating agency and arranged a meeting. At the last minute he felt intense anxiety and, anticipating rejection and failure, attempted suicide and was admitted to hospital. He was discharged the following day without follow-up but with an enduring sense of pessimism about ever achieving a successful relationship. A further A:B:C sequence can thus be generated as shown in Table 2.

Fantasy development

The sequence of events which set the scene for D's offending occurred 4 years later when he was aged 29. It began when his plastic surgeon told him that nothing more could be done about his acne. This had a profound effect: D felt humiliated and angry that 18 years of hopes and dreams were squashed; he no longer had the excuse of waiting for treatment for not having a girlfriend, and thought that his colleagues must now realise he was 'sexually inadequate and not a real man' (see Table 3).

Shortly after the plastic surgeon's news, D's mother was diagnosed as having cancer and died within the year. Without the person he felt closest to, and unable to offer or receive support from his family he became preoccupied with death and the afterlife. Having felt alone throughout his life he dreaded the thought of being alone for eternity and began to comfort himself, as on previous occasions of stress, with fantasies. The new fantasy involved interesting companions he could be with and control after his death.

Six months later D moved to a council flat, but living alone, with even fewer opportunities for companionship, he felt increasingly isolated, anxious and depressed. The more he felt this way the more hostile he felt to his colleagues who all seemed successful, good-looking but rejecting. He felt particularly angry towards women whom he felt held the key to acceptance; a girlfriend could be the badge of normality that he craved. Thoughts of companions in the afterlife began to merge with his adolescent revenge fantasies to produce a fantasy of a massacre at the store. To enhance the feelings associated with the new fantasy he took a knife to work. Eventually his GP referred him to the local lay counselling service, completing the sequence shown in Table 4.

Psychiatric involvement

Despite establishing a good rapport with his counsellor, D was overwhelmed by the Christmas shopping rush. His feelings of anxiety became pervasive and his fantasies offered him little relief. He began to think that customers knew he was sexually inadequate and came to the shop just to look at him. He was even more avoidant of colleagues, preferring to eat lunch in his car rather

TABLE 3: Stage 3 – fantasy development 1

A
Sequences as in stage 2.
Plastic surgeon tells D he cannot be treated.
Mother dies.

B/covert
Feels angry and humiliated by plastic surgeon as dream of cure is suddenly 'squashed'.
Becomes preoccupied with death, fears being alone for eternity; fantasises about having companions.

B/overt
Increasingly avoidant of colleagues.

C
Relationship with father deteriorates.

Key learning
1. Flimsiness of unsupported fantasy.
2. Anxiety associated with death.

TABLE 4: Stage 4 – fantasy development 2

A
Sequences as in stage 3.
Offer of council flat.

B/covert
Increased sense of depression and anxiety.
Feels hostile towards colleagues.
Develops massacre fantasy.

B/overt
Moves into council flat.
Takes knife to work.
Complains of feelings of anxiety and depression.
Tells GP about taking knife to work.

C
Increasingly socially isolated.
Referred to lay counsellor.

Key learning
1. Anxiety and depression reinforced and more firmly associated with hostility.
2. Acting out elements of fantasy can enhance feelings associated with fantasy and thereby provide greater relief from negative affect.

than the canteen. Acquisition of a wooden dowling club, now part of his massacre fantasy, provided brief respite but his feelings showed no sign of easing in the new year. In desperation D told his GP his plan for a massacre. The GP was unable to arrange for D to be seen by a psychiatrist, so still

TABLE 5: Stage 5 – psychiatric involvement

A

    Sequences as in stage 4.
    Christmas shopping rush.

B/covert

    Increasingly anxious and panicky at work.
    Believes others are staring at him.

B/overt

    Avoids contact with colleagues/customers whenever possible.
    Acquires weapons in fantasy.
    Asks GP to admit him to hospital.
    Threatens to kill his counsellor and his family.
    Returns to GP having taken overdose.

C

    Admitted to local hospital for 5 weeks.
    Told that if he wants to have a massacre this cannot be prevented.
    Given 6 weeks sick leave.

Key learning
1. Others will not take responsibility for him.

TABLE 6: Stage 6 – fantasy try-outs

A

    Sequences as in stage 5.
    Michael Ryan perpetrates Hungerford massacre.

B/covert

    Makes decision to act out fantasies and beat Ryan's total.
    Experiences intense excitement while out prowling.
    Feels more confident at work.
    Habituates to excitement associated with nocturnal prowling and feels it's pointless if
    he's not going to act out the massacre fantasy.

B/overt

    Stops talking about fantasies.
    Starts prowling about neighbourhood at night.
    Plays tricks on potential victims.
    Is able to read private mail, etc.
    Acquires more weapons.

C

    Nearly gets caught.
    Relationship with therapist deteriorates.

Key learning
1. Acting out massacre fantasies and receiving recognition have been modelled.
2. Experiences intense thrill associated with nocturnal outings.

feeling desperate D went to his counsellor's home and told him that he and his family were victims in his fantasy. However, it was not until D returned to his GP the following week having taken an overdose that he was admitted to the local psychiatric hospital. This forms the basis of the sequence illustrated in Table 5.

During a 5-week period as an inpatient D was treated with antidepressants and felt more relaxed, perceiving that he was with people who did not judge by appearances. After a month D was discharged. He reports being told that there was nothing wrong with him and that if he wanted a massacre nobody could stop him. He returned to work 6 weeks later, during which time Michael Ryan perpetrated the Hungerford massacre.

Fantasy try-outs

The Hungerford massacre in some ways made D feel more inadequate, and this is an important antecedent for the A:B:C sequence described in Table 6. D felt reassured that there were other men like him, but compared himself unfavourably with those who did more than just dream. He decided to act out his fantasies, thinking it would 'be nice to beat Michael Ryan's total'. Killing 20 people, 'one for each year of his unhappiness', would achieve his aim.

From late summer he began to prowl his local area at night identifying two types of potential victim. The first were successful, rich, good-looking people that he called 'The Bourgeoisie' and on whom he could extract revenge for his failure. The second type would make interesting companions in the afterlife and he imagined controlling them with his superior personality. This prowling produced intense feelings of excitement: he felt confident about what he was doing. Also by observing potential victims through open curtains, opening their mail and so on he could learn intimate details about other people without having to know them personally or risk rejection. He was repeating the strategy, developed in childhood, of examining others' possessions to cope with feelings of alienation.

The nocturnal outings had the side-effect of making him feel confident at work, but as spring approached he found he had to take greater risks to obtain the same excitement. He began to play malicious tricks such as moving garden plant labels, vandalising cars, and throwing stones at courting couples. Despite the intense thrill of nearly being caught by the police with a knife in his car, he began to think that prowling without action was pointless. By late spring the frequency of the outings had reduced from 2–3 times a week to approximately once a week.

The offences and their triggers

The final A:B:C sequence illustrated in Table 7 contains the immediate antecedents to the attempted murders. Some of D's paintings had been

338   *Gresswell and Hollin*

TABLE 7: Stage 7 – the offences and their triggers

A
   Sequences as in stage 6.
   Woman attacked near to home. D interviewed by police as part of routine enquiries.
   Paintings entered for an exhibition are rejected.

B/covert
   Decides that if others can attack so can he.

B/overt
   Commits offence 1.
   Commits offence 2.

C
   'Fear in the eyes of first victim'.
   Caught by police.

Key learning
1. Banality of nocturnal outings without action.
2. He must increase risk to obtain previous excitement levels.

---

rejected from an exhibition. This failure was followed by a police interview in house-to-house enquiries relating to an assault on a local woman. Although the police did not suspect D, it was an important trigger: he thought, 'if someone else can do it, so can I'. He bought a crowbar to use as a weapon, went out prowling and committed minor acts of vandalism. He realised that it was a year since he had first disclosed his fantasies to his GP but that nothing had changed. He decided to act on the fantasies then and there or else give them up. He gained access to his elderly female victim's house using a rehearsed plan. Once inside he attacked his victim with a dowling club intending to beat her unconscious before killing her. Fortunately he had underestimated the force required to subdue her and fled when the club broke.

Although D had failed to kill his victim he felt that he had done well: he had seen 'fear in her eyes' and felt his victim was now like him and will 'never have peace of mind'. He retired to bed calm and unconcerned and slept well.

At his weekly counselling session, D discovered that the counsellor suspected him of committing the attack D did not in fact commit. He was extremely wary and refused to let D into his office, insisting instead that they walk, with D leading. That evening D went out intending to slash a victim's face so that the victim would be disfigured and know how D felt. Although he waited in a park for several hours no opportunity presented itself and he went home unsatisfied. The following evening he returned to the park with the same intention. Again no suitable victim appeared so he drove to town to select a victim from the people he had spied on. Arriving at the chosen victim's home and finding they were out, he parked his car, hid and waited. Upon arriving home the second victim, a man in late middle age, saw D and left his wife in his car to approach and challenge D. D stabbed him in the chest and drove away. The second victim and his wife managed to call the police and D was arrested.

DISCUSSION

Despite comparatively little research into multiple murder, a number of common background, cognitive and behavioural variables have been identified in the literature. These factors include histories of sexual and physical abuse, abandonment, failure to bond with parents, bedwetting, torturing animals, firesetting, a pervasive sense of isolation, alienation, use of sadistic sexual fantasy, compulsive masturbation, lack of acquired inhibitions against violence, depersonalisation of victims, and a belief that the use of violence against others is legitimate (McDonald, 1963; Brittain, 1967; MacCulloch, Snowden, Wood & Mills, 1983; Levin & Fox, 1985; Burgess et al., 1986; Holmes & De Burger, 1988; Ressler, Burgess & Douglas, 1988; Norris, 1990). However, these variables are not peculiar to multiple murderers (West, 1982) and are best viewed as relating to a 'set' or propensity for criminal behaviour that requires a specific trigger to be realised in a particular form.

The methodology developed in this paper offers a number of advantages for both research and clinical practice. First, it allows for a relatively coherent and concise summary of case material: in D's case this involved study of nearly 300 pages of depositions and reports and over 16 hours of interviews with D and other involved parties. Secondly, an understanding of the aetiology to an offence may help in setting clinical targets. The analysis of D's case, for example, emphasises that the massacre fantasies were not just for pleasure but were a means of coping with overwhelming despair aroused by minor social triggers. Training in alternative coping strategies may therefore be appropriate. Similarly it can be adduced that D's problems with relationships did not lie in the area of social skills or real rejection but in the intense feelings of anxiety and depressive cognitions that even fantasies of intimacy could elicit. Thirdly, this detailed knowledge allows for more precise identification of the types of environmental events that could provoke further episodes of violence, and may be linked with dangerousness. Finally, a steady accumulation of similar cases will allow comparisons to be made across offenders, thereby allowing theoretical issues of causality to be considered. As yet there is no means of assessing the universal importance of variables described in D's case in terms of their relationship to multiple murder. It is unwise to assume that multiple murderers are a homogeneous population, and we would argue that the basis for theory development may lie in the generation of testable hypotheses through in-depth qualitative analysis of single cases. For example, comparison of D's case with similar cases may further our understanding of 'successful' and 'unsuccessful' killers. Indeed, this methodology may provide an optimum means by which to devise a typology based on functional categories as well as topographical features.

The methodology we are proposing is not an absolute statement and material could be organised in different ways; as with any such study we may not have all the facts despite collecting information from many sources. Indeed, analysis of retrospective data faces a number of problems: the archival material may contain errors and the biases of those who made the recordings; the individual's own report is liable to error, both intentional and unintentional; and our own selection of information and interpretation is, of course, open to debate. However, as Hollin has noted:

> It is ironic that one of the many criticisms of behaviour analysis is that it is mechanical, rigid, and inflexible. The truth could not be more different: Making sense of a set of data, the product of the assessment, is a highly individual undertaking. As all practitioners have different learning histories, so their interpretations, hypotheses, and analyses will differ even within a common cognitive–behavioural framework. That there is no 'correct' or 'incorrect' behavioural analysis is a fact that many students are slow to grasp.
>
> (Hollin, 1990, p. 26)

In addition to the points made above, the methodology is time consuming, but does cover over 30 years' worth of material in detail with reasonable sophistication. Our future research will be directed at further refinements of the methodology to attempt to produce an even more parsimonious means of making sense of case material.

REFERENCES

ARCO, L. (1987). Researching functional relations in behaviour analysis and therapy. *Behaviour Change* **4**, 33–40.

BANDURA, A. (1977). *Social Learning Theory*. Englewood Cliffs, NJ: Prentice-Hall.

BARLOW, D.H. & HERSEN, M. (1984). *Single Case Experimental Designs: Strategies for Studying Behaviour Change*. New York: Pergamon.

BLACKMAN, D. (1980). Images of man in contemporary behaviourism. In: A.J. Chapman & D.M. Jones, Eds, *Models of Man*, pp. 99–113. Leicester: The British Psychological Society.

BLACKMAN, D. (1981). The experimental analysis of behaviour and its relevance to applied psychology. In: G. Davey, Ed., *Applications of Conditioning Theory*, pp. 1–28. London: Methuen.

BRITTAIN, R.P. (1967). The sadistic murderer. *Medicine, Science and the Law* **10**, 198–207.

BROMLEY, D.B. (1986). *The Case Study Method in Psychology and Related Disciplines*. Chichester: John Wiley.

BURGESS, A.W., HARTMAN, C.R., RESSLER, R.K., DOUGLAS, J.E. & McCORMACK, A. (1986). Sexual homicide: a motivational model. *Journal of Interpersonal Violence* **1**, 251–272.

HAYNES, S.N. & O'BRIEN, W.H. (1990). Functional analysis in behaviour therapy. *Clinical Psychology Review* **10**, 649–68.

HERBERT, M. (1978). *Conduct Disorders of Childhood and Adolescence: A Behavioural Approach to Assessment and Treatment*. New York: John Wiley.

HERBERT, M. (1981). *Behavioural Treatment of Problem Children: A Practice Manual*. London: Academic Press.

HOLLIN, C.R. (1990). *Cognitive–Behavioural Interventions with Young Offenders*. Elmsford, NY: Pergamon Press.

HOLMES, R.M. & DE BURGER, J. (1988). *Serial Murder*. Newbury Park, CA: Sage.

IWATA, B.A., DORSEY, M.F., SILFER, K.J., BAUMAN, K.E. & RICHMAN, G.S. (1982). Towards a functional analysis of self injury. *Analysis and Intervention in Developmental Disability* 2, 3–20.

JACKSON, H.F., GLASS, C. & HOPE, S. (1987). A functional analysis of recidivistic arson. *British Journal of Clinical Psychology* 26, 175–186.

JONES, R. (1983). Functional analysis: some cautionary notes. *Bulletin of the British Psychological Society* 36, 237–238.

JONES, R.S. & HESKIN, K.J. (1988). Towards a functional analysis of delinquent behaviour: a pilot study. *Counselling Psychology Quarterly* 1, 35–42.

LEVIN, J. & FOX, J.A. (1985). *Mass murder: America's Growing Menace*. New York: Plenum Press.

MacCULLOCH, M.J., SNOWDEN, P.R., WOOD, P.J.W. & MILLS, H.E. (1983). Sadistic fantasy, sadistic behaviour and offending. *British Journal of Psychiatry* 143, 20–29.

McDONALD, J.M. (1963). The threat to kill. *American Journal of Psychiatry* 120, 125–130.

NORRIS, J. (1990). *Serial Killers*. London: Arrow.

OWENS, R.G. & ASHCROFT, J.B. (1982). Functional analysis in applied psychology. *British Journal of Clinical Psychology* 21, 181–189.

RESSLER, R.K., BURGESS, A.W. & DOUGLAS, J.E. (1988). *Sexual Homicide: Patterns and Motives*. Lexington, MA: Lexington Books.

SKINNER, B.F. (1974). *About Behaviourism*. London: Jonathan Cape.

SLADE, P. (1982). Towards a functional analysis of anorexia nervosa and bulimia nervosa. *British Journal of Clinical Psychology* 21, 167–180.

WEST, D.J. (1982). *Delinquency: Its Roots, Careers and Prospects*. London: Heinemann.

Address correspondence to David M. Gresswell, Psychology Department, Rampton Hospital, Retford, Notts DN22 OPD, UK.

Part VI
Gender Issues

[23]

JACK THE RIPPER AND THE MYTH OF MALE VIOLENCE

JUDITH R. WALKOWITZ

> The hunt for Jack the Ripper—I remember that as well as I remember anything—I don't know if he was in my time or whether it was only talked about. But the boys—horrible little brutes they were — they used to say "Look out, here comes Jack the Ripper" if we were playing in the street some time—and we all used to run. Oh we were proper little cowards. They always pictured him with a big leather apron and a carving knife.
>
> (Mrs. Bartholemew, born 1892, in Poplar, East London. Interviewed by Anna Davin, June 1973.)

> The daily paper is carefully kept out of my way, and no hint of the Jack the Ripper murders reaches me at home. But the boys next door are well advised of them . . . [and] . . . have their story ready. "There's a man in a leather apron coming soon, to kill all the little girls in Tunbridge Wells. It's in the paper."
>
> He stands before me, vividly enough, that man with the leather apron and the uplifted, blood-stained knife. I have not forgotten the Bible story of King Herod's order to kill all the babies of Bethlehem. I scarcely ask myself if the boys are lying. It was true "in the days of Herod the king"—and what happened once can happen again. I delight the boys by running indoors screaming, begging Papa to take me away at once from Tunbridge Wells; nor is my confidence fully restored when Papa and Mamma both insist that the story is silly nonsense, made up to frighten me . . . Mamma and Papa, though generally right, can be mistaken. . . .
>
> (Helen Corke, *In Our Infancy: An Autobiography, Part 1, 1882-1912.* Cambridge: Cambridge University Press, 1975.)

Like Helen Corke and Mrs. Bartholemew, most of us have grown up in the shadow of Jack the Ripper. As the prototype of dozens of filmic and fictional treatments and as the inspiration for numerous real-life "heroes" of crime,[1] the Ripper has materially

Feminist Studies 8, no. 3 (Fall 1982). © 1982 by Judith R. Walkowitz.

contributed to women's sense of vulnerability in modern urban culture. Over the past hundred years, the Ripper murders have achieved the status of a modern myth of male violence against women, a story whose details have become vague and generaliz- ed, but whose "moral" message is clear: the city is a dangerous place for women, when they transgress the narrow boundaries of home and hearth and dare to enter public space.

This article seeks to exorcise that ghost from women's con- sciousness, by historicizing Jack the Ripper: by returning to the scene of the crimes and investigating how the story of Jack the Ripper was constructed out of the fissures and tensions of class, gender, and ethnic relations in 1888. To appreciate why the murders took on the significance that they did, let us assess the political moment when that "man-monster," "half-beast, half- man,"[2] stalked the streets of London in search of fallen women.[3]

The time was the autumn of 1888, when the respectable classes were obsessed with fears of class conflict and social disintegra- tion. Most of their anxieties focused on the East End of London, the scene of the Ripper murders, which symbolized social unrest born of urban degeneracy. A series of journalistic explorations in- to "Outcast London" published in the tabloid press in the 1880s had familiarized middle-class readers with the sordid and depress- ing living conditions of the East End poor and reminded them of the dangerous social proximity between vast numbers of casual laborers and a professional criminal class. Among concerned middle-class reformers, these exposes provoked a "consciousness of sin" — to quote Beatrice Webb — and stimulated a multitude of philanthropic activities in the East End, in the form of religious missions, college settlement houses, housing reform, and elaborate social surveys.[4] Class fear, however, rapidly over- shadowed middle-class guilt in the late 1880s when socialists began to organize demonstrations of the East End unemployed in the wealthy West End. In 1886, one of these demonstrations end- ed in some stoning of fashionable Pall Mall clubs and in sporadic looting and rioting in London's principal shopping district. For the next eighteen months, a real concern over public order ex- isted, and police forbade any further demonstrations. The tension peaked on November 18, 1887, "Bloody Sunday," when Lon- don's working classes tried to enter Trafalgar Square and were forcefully repressed by the police. To radicals and socialists, and to the poor themselves, the actions of the police showed con- tempt for the political rights of the poor and the state's exclusive interest in protecting the property of the rich. For the propertied classes, the menacing presence of the great "unwashed" in their part of town confirmed their worst fears of "Outcast London" as a vast unsupervised underclass that could be readily mobilized into the revolutionary ranks of the new socialist movement.[5] Coming so fast on the heels of the West End riots, the Jack the Ripper murders fed the flames of class hatred and distrust, on both sides.

The Ripper murders were the latest of a series of sexual scandals linking highlife and lowlife in London in the 1880s. In good part, feminists had helped to initiate this era of sexual scandals, through their political mobilization against state regulation of prostitution in the 1870s and 1880s and their active participation in the campaign against white slavery and child prostitution in London in 1885. Allied with radical working men and middle-class evangelicals, feminists had mounted a successful campaign against the Contagious Diseases Acts and secured their repeal in 1886. The feminist program coupled a libertarian defense of the constitutional rights of working-class women with an assault on the social and sexual prerogatives of men. A desire to liberate women from male sexual tyranny and brutality led to feminist demands for "no secrets" on sexual questions. By setting a "floodlight" on men's "doings,"[6] respectable women asserted themselves in the public discussion of sexuality for the first time, and they proceeded to uncover men's double lives, their sexual diseases, and their complicity in a system of vice that flourished in the undergrowth of respectable society.

In this spirit of sexual muckracking, Josephine Butler prevailed upon W.T. Stead, the editor of the *Pall Mall Gazette,* to expose the traffic in English girls in London. The result was the "Maiden Tribute of Modern Babylon," appearing in the summer of 1885, one of the most successful pieces of scandal journalism of the nineteenth century. Stead used sexual scandal to sell newspapers to a middle-class and working-class readership and ushered in a new era of tabloid sensationalism and cross-class prurience. "Maiden Tribute" documented in lurid detail how poor daughters of the people were trapped and drugged in padded cells and sold to upper-class rakes for the sum of five pounds. Stead's revelations forced the passage of the Criminal Law Amendment Act of 1885, which not only raised the age of consent for girls from thirteen to sixteen, but also gave police far greater power to prosecute streetwalkers and brothelkeepers. It also made "indecent" acts between consenting male adults illegal, forming the basis of legal proceedings against homosexuals until 1967. The excitement generated by the ''Maiden Tribute'' stimulated grass roots political activity: throughout Britain, social purity groups and vigilance committees were organized to oversee the local enforcement of the acts. Vigilance committees attacked music halls, theaters, and pornography as manifestations of ''male lust''; their signal triumph, however, was to force police crackdowns on solicitation and brothelkeeping in the metropolis and the major provincial cities. Thus, in the three years preceeding the Ripper murders, a massive political initiative against nonmarital, nonreproductive sexuality had been mobilized, whose initial victims were working-class prostitutes, precisely those women who had been the original objects of feminist pity and concern.[7]

Finally, one cannot emphasize too much the role of the popular press, itself a creature of the 1880s, in establishing Jack the Ripper as a media hero, in amplifying the terror of male violence, and in elaborating and interpreting the meaning of the Ripper murders to a ''mass'' audience. As other historians have noted, the tabloid press incorporated many of the forms and themes of popular culture, particularly those of sensationalist melodrama, the literary convention that shaped the Ripper narrative in all the London dailies, across the political spectrum.[8] Embedded in this convention was a titillating ''sexual script,'' based on the association of sex and violence, male dominance and female passivity, and the crossing of class boundaries in the male pursuit of the female object of desire.[9] But voyeurist interest in the Ripper murders can not be reduced solely to sexual titillation; when readers and actors in the Ripper drama immersed themselves in the details of the cases, they were equally compelled by the desire to extract meaning out of apparent disorder, to search out the clues to solve the mystery. In reviewing the events of autumn 1888, we should be aware of our own voyeuristic proclivities: to the extent that we are trying to derive meaning from the Ripper murders, we are engaged in an intellectual task similar to our Victorian predecessors.

THE FACTS OF THE CASE

What are the salient facts of the cases as they were presented in the London dailies? Within ten weeks (August 31 to November 9, 1888), five brutal murders of prostitutes took place, all but one within an "evil quarter of a mile" of Whitechapel, East London (the exception occurring just within the boundary of the City of London).[10] The murdered victims were Polly Nicholls, August 31; Annie Chapman, September 8; Catherine Eddowes and Elizabeth Stride (the "double event"), September 30; Mary Jane Kelly, November 9. The murders were performed at night, four in the open, with great daring and speed. All five took place in a densely populated area where the local residents kept a close watch on the movements of the inhabitants. Still, there were no witnesses to the crimes; the police could uncover no clues or apparent motives for the murders. Nor could they identify any serious suspects although hundreds of men were detained and interviewed all over London. The murderer was never caught.

The first element of the Ripper story, then, was its setting: Whitechapel, a notorious and poor locale, adjacent to the financial district (the City), and easily accessible from the West End by public transportation and private carriage. Part of London's declining inner industrial rim, Whitechapel stood at the edge of the vast East End, London's proletarian center, a "city" of nine hundred thousand. To middle-class observers, Whitechapel was an alien place, a center of cosmopolitan culture and entrepôt for foreign immigrants and refugees, whose latest wave consisted of poor Jews escaping the pogroms of Eastern Europe in the 1880s. Whitechapel was also notorious for its transient and homeless poor, living out of doors or in those "thief preserves,"[11] the common lodging houses.

By the 1880s, Whitechapel had come to epitomize the social ills of "Outcast London." Certainly, casual and seasonal employment, starvation wages, overcrowding at exploitative rents, an inhumane system of poor relief, declining traditional industries, and an increase in "sweated" labor were all marked features of living and working conditions there. But, as Jerry White has observed, the middle classes of London were far less concerned with the real problems of Whitechapel than with the symptoms they spawned: "street crime, prostitution, the threat of revolt, expensive pauperism, infectious disease spreading to respectable London—the whole panoply of shame of this 'boldest blotch on the face' of the capital of the civilized world."[12]

Whitechapel thus provided a stark and sensational backdrop for the Ripper murders: a moral landscape of light and darkness, a nether region of illicit sex and crime, both exciting and dangerous. "All sorts and conditions of men" could be met with on Whitechapel Road, the district's main thoroughfare, with its "flaunting shops," piles of glowing fruit, and "streaming naphtha lamps." A principal entertainment center for working-class London, Whitechapel Road also proved a magnet for rich young bloods from the West End who would tour the "toughest, roughest streets, taverns, and music halls" in search of new excitements.[13]

At night, the glittering brilliance of Whitechapel Road contrasted sharply with the dark mean streets just off the main thoroughfare. Turning into a side street, one was plunged into the "Cimmerian" darkness of "lower London." Here in the Flower and Dean street area, with its twenty-seven courts, alleys, and lanes, stood one of the last remaining rookeries of late-Victorian London. Here lay the "warrens of the poor," "all packed by a species that multiplies with astounding swiftness and with miserable results."[14] Here "it may be well to tuck out of view any bit of jewelry that may be glittering about." Even the police hesitated from entering the notorious Wentworth and Dorset streets alone. In the Flower and Dean street area it was useless for "them to follow when they happen to appear on the scene, as the houses communicate with one another, and a man pursued can run in and out."[15] In the same back slums and alleys, poor prostitutes, "fourpenny knee tremblers,"[16] lived and worked, often bringing their customers into some dark corner to avoid the price of a room. And here, during the "autumn of terror" of 1888, the bodies of four of the victims of Jack the Ripper were found.

Testimonies from the inquests also incorporated many of the more mundane elements of daily life into the Ripper narrative. Most of the bodies, for example, were found by people going to and from work: Robert Paul, a cabman on his way to Covent Garden market at 3:30 in the morning, found the crumpled body of Polly Nicholls in a doorway in Buck's Row; Louis Diemschutz, an "unlicensed hawker" and steward of the International Working Men's Educational Club on Berner Street, was returning home from work at 1:00 A.M. when he found Elizabeth Stride's body in a courtyard adjacent to the club, where he resided.[17] The same mean street that provided the setting for a murder also served as workplace and residence for poor inhabitants engaged in casual and sweated trades. In 39 Hanbury Street, "whose back premises" became the "scene" of Annie Chapman's murder, "no fewer than six separate families reside[d]." Its inhabitants included a packing case maker, two cabmen and their families, a pro-

Louis Diemschutz discovers the dead body of Elizabeth Stride, *Police Illustrated News*, 6 October 1888.

prietor of a cat meat shop (run on the premises), an old man and his "weak-minded" son, and an old lady kept "for charity" by the woman who "tenanted" the house.[18] Political and social institutions — the settlement house at Toynbee Hall, the Jewish socialist club at Berner Street, the Salvation Army mission, the London Hospital, the bastillelike board schools (state schools), the pubs and cheap music halls — all figured as part of the physical setting for the murders and the investigations, while the kitchens of the dosshouses (common lodging houses), the shed on Dorset Street where homeless women congregated, and the interior of the room where Mary Jane Kelly was killed were described in great detail in the press to evoke a sense of place.

Another compelling aspect of the Whitechapel murders was their mystery, the secrecy and impunity with which the murders were committed in public spaces, and the "mystery" as to "motives, clues, and methods." Unable to find historical precedents for the Whitechapel "horrors," commentators resorted to horrifying fictional analogues: "to the shadowy and wilful figures in Poe's and Stevenson's novels," or the "stealthy and cunning assassins in Gaboriau and du Boiscobey."[19] Indeed the events of autumn 1888 bore an "uncanny" resemblance to the literature of the fantastic: they incorporated the narrative themes and motifs of modern fantasy — social inversion, morbid psychological states, acts of violation and transgression, and descent into a social underworld — and gave utterance to "all that is not said, all that is unsayable through realism."[20] "London lies today under the spell of a great terror," declared the *Star.* "Some nameless reprobate, half-beast, half-man, is at large, who is daily gratifying his murderous instincts on the most miserable and defenceless class of the community."[21]

Besides the social setting and the mystery surrounding the murders, three additional features contributed to the grisly notoriety of the Whitechapel killings. All the murders were accompanied by acts of sexual mutilation, committed with some apparent skill and knowledge of the female body. Indeed the principal objective of the murderer seems to have been evisceration of the body after the victim had been strangled and had her throat cut. When the murderer had enough time, the uterus and other internal organs were removed, and the women's insides were often strewn about. Here is the description of the division surgeon, Dr. Phillips, when he arrived at the scene of Annie Chapman's murder.

The legs were brought up, the feet resting on the ground and knees turned outwards. The face was swollen and turned on the right side, the tongue protruding between the front teeth . . . . The small intestine and other portions of the stomach were lying on the right side of the ground above the right shoulder attached by a coil of the intestine to the rest of the stomach. There was a large quantity of blood, with a part of the stomach over the left shoulder . . . . The throat was deeply cut.[22]

In the midst of this saturnalia of destruction, the murderer had stopped to place Chapman's belongings in a neat pile at her feet, demonstrating uncannily cool deliberation. A young policeman was so affected by the spectacle that he could not eat meat for weeks. "My food sickened me. The sight of a butcher shop nauseated me."[23] "There was no doubt this time," recalled Dr. Halsted of the London Hospital, that the murderer "had removed certain parts of the body not normally mentioned in polite society and this perversion almost more than the murder itself excited the frenzy of the large crowd which gathered round the spot during the following day."[24]

The identification of the murderer with the sobriquet "Jack the Ripper" also gave notoriety to the event. At the time of the "double event" of September 30, an anonymous letter forecasting the murders and signed Jack the Ripper had been sent to the Central News Agency. A facsimile of the letter, and a postcard that followed from "Jack the Ripper," were republished in all the newspapers and posted at street corners. These first two letters set the tone for the rest (of which 350 have been collected in the files of Scotland yard).[25] Both were addressed "Dear Boss," both were jocular and teasing. They bragged of past and future exploits, and of how much the writer enjoyed his "work." "I am down on whores," declared the Ripper, "and I shan't quit ripping them up until I am buckled." I would tend to agree with police authorities who believed the initial letters were a "creation of an enterprising journalist";[26] in any case, they helped to establish the murders as a media event by focusing social anxieties and fantasies on a single, elusive, alienated figure, who communicated to a "mass" public through the newspaper. Anonymous yet polymorphous, the murderer was presumed to be, at various points in the discussion and by different constituencies, a Russian Jewish anarchist, a policeman, a local denizen of Whitechapel, an erotic maniac of the "upper classes" of society, a religious fanatic, a mad doctor, a scientific sociologist, and a woman.

However vague the identity of the murderer, the social profile of his victims that emerged from the evidence and testimonies of the inquests was remarkably detailed and precise. In the case of the first four victims, all were, according to the *Daily Telegraph*, "women of middle age, all were married and had lived apart from their husbands in consequence of intemperate habits, and were at the time of their death leading an irregular life, and eking out a miserable and precarious existence in common lodging houses."[27] These "drunken, vicious, miserable wretches whom it was almost a charity to relieve of the penalty of existence" were "not very particular about how they earned a living."[28] When they could, they worked as charwomen, marketwomen, or picked hops during the summer months in Kent. If they had to, they would resort to the streets as casual prostitutes. Economic need forced them to take to the streets on the nights they met their deaths. A short time before she was murdered, Polly Nicholls was seen staggering along Whitechapel Road by Emily Holland, her friend and neighbor. Holland offered to take her home, but Nicholls explained that she had no money for her lodging. "But I'll get my 'doss' money," she declared. "See what a jolly bonnet I've got now."[29] Annie Chapman voiced a similar intention, after she had been denied admission to her lodging house on Dorset Street because she did not have the fee of eight pence. "I haven't enough now, but keep my bed for me, I shan't be long."[30]

To middle-class readers of the *Times* and the *Morning Post*, the murders constituted a morality tale of stark proportions. These were economically desperate women, who violated their "womanhood" for the price of a night's lodging, and for whom the wages of sin were death. Outside of Whitechapel, the victims were viewed as unsympathetic objects of pity — by radicals and conservatives alike. Whatever guilt middle-class readers may have experienced over the "mangled ruins" of Annie Chapman, their compunctions were soon overwhelmed by feelings of fear and loathing towards the spectacle of the victims themselves. This paradoxical response to the "great social evil" was not unique; it was embedded in the literature of prostitution and earlier reformist efforts. But in earlier discussions of prostitution, reformers, including feminists, had sympathized with the history of young prostitutes, if not their present reality; and they adopted a protective and custodial attitude toward fallen women as "errant daughters." Both the older age of the Whitechapel victims and their apparent culpability in departing from the patriarchal home rendered this parent-child paradigm inapplicable.[31]

Judith R. Walkowitz   553

Polly Nicholls's last recorded words before she was murdered (Lodginghouse, Flower and Dean streets), *Police Illustrated News,* 12 October 1888.

The reality of these women's social experience, however, was not so easily abstracted into a simple tale of sin and retribution, nor were the women so isolated from a social community as respectable commentators presumed. On the contrary, testimonies at the inquests reveal a network of support and mutual aid among the poor, who understood much better than middle-class philanthropists the nature of casual employment and the hazards of poverty. Mary Jane Kelly seems to have remained on good terms with a number of her regular customers. On the night of her death, she encountered George Hutchinson, who had occasionally given her a few shillings in the past, and asked him if he had any money to give her. Most of the other murdered women had lovers with whom they lived and pooled their resources. These were practical relationships, but they often entailed strong emotional bonds. Catherine Eddowes and John Kelly paired off in the following way: "We got throwed together a good bit here in the lodging house," recounted Kelly, "and the result was we made a regular bargain."[32]

The murdered women were also part of an intense female network. Prostitutes as well as nonprostitutes inhabited a distinct female world where they gossiped, entertained each other, and participated in an intricate system of borrowing and lending. This female network supplemented women's heterosexual ties, but it occasionally challenged those male-female allegiances. When Catherine Picket, a flower seller and neighbor of Mary Jane Kelly, was attracted to Kelly's singing on the night of her murder, she arose from bed to go out and join her; at which point she was reprimanded by her husband, "You just leave the woman alone," and crawled back to bed.[33] Kelly herself was not as deferential to male authority; in fact, she had just separated from her lover, Joseph Barnett, after the two had quarreled over her taking in another "unfortuate" named Harvey "out of compassion."[34]

In sum, the social setting, the mysterious circumstances, the grisly mutilations, the ominous figure of Jack the Ripper, and the "deviant" lives of his victims turned the murders of five poor prostitutes into a national scandal.

RESPONSE TO THE MURDERS
Both on the streets of London and in the pages of the national press, diverse constituencies shaped their interpretation of the Ripper crisis according to their own political agendas. The first to

intervene and structure opinion on the subject were the police themselves, who followed up clues provided by local residents. Initially, the police treated the first murder of Polly Nicholls as one of many cases of unsolved assault; only later at the morgue was it discovered that the body had been severely mutilated. Police quickly ruled out robbery as a possible motive, given the extreme destitution of the victims. Acting on suggestions of local prostitutes and others they first investigated street gangs who preyed on prostitutes and extorted money from them. They looked for men in the local neighborhood who might have the tools or skills to perform the bloody mutilations — butchers and shoemakers. They eventually turned their attention to occupational groups, such as sailors on board cattleboats, whose presence in and out of London would explain the timing of the crisis and the mysterious disappearance of the murderer.[35]

The growing list of candidates reflected the local social economy of Whitechapel; it also mirrored the prejudice of the police and local residents. Whitechapel had a large, mobile, and rootless population of men who looked and acted in ways police found suspicious. They were obvious targets of police and popular suspicion.

Jews were targets of both. An endemic form of anti-Semitism existed in the East End, in part an expression of traditional xenophobia and in part a response to the unstable economy and shrinking material resources of the area. Whitechapel was experiencing a severe housing crisis due to the influx of Eastern European Jews and the conversion of housing stock into warehouses and commercial properties. Jews and gentiles, constituting, to a certain extent, two separate classes, had to coexist in the same small area and compete for resources.[36]

On the whole, the Jews were respectable and law-abiding (certainly in comparison with most of the local population), but they had their hoodlums. Suspicion fixed on one of these characters, a Jewish shoemaker named "Leather Apron," who extorted money from prostitutes. Leather Apron finally turned himself in to the police, in order to vindicate himself publicly and to escape the fury of the crowd.[37] The "Jacob the Ripper" theory[38] led to two developments: denunciation of Jews at the inquests as ritual murderers and widespread intimidation of Jews throughout the East End. On the streets popular anger precipitated anti-Jewish riots—one of three such outbreaks in late-nineteenth-century London—and false accusations against individual Jews, which in turn gave local youths license to rob and beat them.

In apprehending Jews as religious fanatics, police followed the lead of the local population. But in suspecting Jewish socialists and revolutionaries, they acted on their own suspicions and on instructions from above. However, police soon found that anti-Jewish feeling, which they had helped to foster, was getting out of hand. After Chapman's murder, hundreds of police were drafted into the East End to forestall a possible pogrom.[39]

By mid-September local police had their hands full. After Chapman's murder, a diabolical pattern seemed to emerge, and the impotence of the police to track down the culprit inspired a rising tide of public indignation. Something new was introduced into the public discussion. Suspicion shifted from the East End to the West End.

On September 12, the *Times* published a letter from Dr. Forbes Winslow, an expert in criminal insanity, hazarding the opinion that the murderer was not of the class of "Leather Apron," but was instead a "homicidal maniac" of the "upper class of society, as evidenced by the perverted cunning with which the killer had performed the mutilations and evaded justice."[40] Winslow based his "method of madness" theory on the assumption that only a cultivated intellect run amok could have committed such a sexually perverse act. His theory was picked up by the national dailies, discussed in medical journals, and prepared the way for the coroner's "bombshell" at the Chapman inquest on September 26. At that time, Mr. Wynne Baxter disclosed the fact that the murderer had removed the uterus from the body — it was missing — and that the mutilation demonstrated some anatomical skill. A possible motive for the murder, he suggested, was the sale of the organ to American medical schools — recalling the body-snatching crimes of the early nineteenth century.[41]

Fantasies ran wild in the correspondence pages of the national dailies, but the fantasies were never totally removed from social reality. The most significant and enduring cast of villains proposed by the press and by the experts were The Mad Doctor, The Religious Fanatic, The Upper-Class Erotic Maniac, The Scientific Sociologist. All these candidates were familiar protagonists in earlier sexual scandals such as "Maiden Tribute" and the campaign against the state regulation of prostitution. They were also representative of the types of men who were in fact stalking the streets of London in search of fallen women.[42]

Despite the theories about upper-class perverts and maniacal reformers, police still arrested the same motley collection of East End down-and-outers, including wandering lunatics, mad medical students, American cowboys, and Greek gypsies. They conducted a house-to-house search of Whitechapel, but not of the areas of London where the Ripper, if he were a "toff" (that is, a gentleman) would be lodging. Even when they apprehended respectable suspects in the act of harassing women, police did not follow through on the arrest—this despite the fact that the East End became a sideshow for West Enders fascinated by the murders, bent not only on observing but on hunting the Ripper, and in some cases, emulating his role as well.[43] "No less a personage than a director of the Bank of England," reported the *Echo*, "is so possessed by personal conviction that he has disguised himself as a day laborer, and is exploring the public houses, the common lodging houses, and other likely places to find the murderer."[44]

Amateur detectives supplemented "hundreds of police in uniform, in plain clothes and in all manner of disguise — some even dressed as women — who patrolled every end of every street in the 'danger zone' every few minutes." There were plenty of eccentric and disoriented men in Whitechapel to begin with, but the presence of amateur and professional sleuths, voyeurs, and cranks must have exacerbated the fears and anxieties of the local population.[45]

Respectable citizens of Whitechapel responded to the invasion of West Enders by organizing their own night patrols. Both the men of Toynbee Hall settlement house and Jewish community set up committees, and the socialist and radical working men's clubs formed the East London Trades and Labourer's Society Vigilance Committee.[46]

These activities were evidence of self-protection, but they also constituted surveillance of the unrespectable poor, and of lowlife women in particular. Social reformers at Toynbee Hall used the evidence collected by the night patrols to document the vicious state of the Flower and Dean street rookery and to agitate, as they had for years, for the closing down of those "nurseries of crimes,"[47] the common lodging houses. Beginning in late September, Canon Samuel Barnett, the rector of Toynbee Hall, and his supporters began a discussion in the pages of the *Times* and elsewhere on the meaning of the Whitechapel murders. The discussion focused not on the pathology of the criminal, but on the degraded conditions of the victims themselves.

By designating themselves vigilance committees, the male patrols in Whitechapel explicitly modeled themselves on similarly named social purity organizations already active in the area. Purity groups had closed down two hundred brothels in the East End in the year prior to the Ripper murders, rendering hundreds of women homeless, hence vulnerable to attack, and certainly making the lower stratum of prostitution — where the victims of the Ripper were situated — even more precarious as a means of subsistence. The message of social purity was mixed: it demanded that men control their own sexuality; but it effectively gave them more control over the sexuality of women, since it called upon them to protect their women and to repress brothels and streetwalkers. As Josephine Butler astutely observed, male purity reformers always found it more convenient to "let the pressure fall almost exclusively on women" as it "is more difficult, they say, to get at men." In Whitechapel, middle-class men, backed up by female moral reformers, spearheaded these efforts. Respectable working men, anxious to distance themselves from the "bestiality" of the residuum and to reinforce their male prerogatives inside and outside the family, were also recruited into the assault on vice.[48]

Excluded from the mobilization and press debate were the rough elements of Whitechapel, female or male. Their reaction to the murders sharply diverged from those of the organized working-class and middle-class philanthropists. To the Whitechapel poor, Annie Chapman and Mary Jane Kelly were not degraded outcasts, but members of their own class and community. At inquests, neighbors gave detailed accounts of the victims' lives. Sometimes they stressed the respectability of the women and occasionally refused to acknowledge that the victims drank or were prostitutes. Clearly the murdered women were well known in the neighborhood and many were well liked. Most popular of all was the last victim, Mary Jane Kelly, who was younger (twenty-four), prettier, and more tied to the life of prostitution than the earlier four victims. When men in a lodging house were asked by a reporter if they knew Kelly, they responded, "Did anyone not know her?" Kelly was respected in the neighborhood for being generous and gay-hearted, and "frequent in street brawls, sudden and quick in quarrels and—for a woman —handy with her fists."[49] During Kelly's funeral procession, the coffin was covered with wreaths from friends "using certain public houses in common with the murdered woman." As the

Mary Jane Kelly and her dark stranger, *Police Illustrated News*, 17 November 1888.

coffin passed, "ragged caps were doffed and slatternly looking women shed tears."[50] Dense crowds also lined the streets for the funeral cortege of Catherine Eddowes: "Manifestations of sympathy were everywhere visible," reported the *East London Observer*, "many among the crowd uncovering their heads as the hearse passed."[51]

The poor also expressed their anger at the Ripper murders by rioting. The West End press tended to depict crowd activity in the East End as both ominous and irrational.[52] But the victims of mob riot were not selected at random. The Whitechapel poor rioted against the Jews, against the police (for not solving the murders), and against doctors (they believed the mad doctor theory and popular antagonism toward regular doctors was intensified by the recent antivaccination movement. Anyone walking around with a little black bag was in trouble).[53] As press coverage of the murders increased, the poor began to act on information provided by the newpapers — particularly that the murders were committed by doctors and by "toffs." It was only after this idea was floated in the press that local residents provided police with a description of possible suspects who were "respectable in appearance" or who had the "appearance of a clerk."[54] The assumption that the Ripper was a "toff" also gave young working men license to accuse and intimidate their betters. During the Ripper manhunt, more than one amateur detective touring the Whitechapel area was accosted and had his gold watch nabbed. Another gentleman making his way along High Holborn in the City was pounced upon by a man of the "laboring class" yelling "Jack the Ripper."[55]

Response to the Ripper murders, then, reveals significant class divisions. It also exposes deep-seated sexual antagonisms, most frequently expressed by men towards women. This antagonism was aided and abetted by sensational newspaper coverage that blamed "women of evil life"[56] for bringing the murders on themselves, but elsewhere warned that "no woman is safe while this ghoul's abroad."[57] The popular press intensified terror among "pure" and "impure" women by juxtaposing reports on miscellaneous "attacks on women" to an account of the Whitechapel "horror"; by featuring an illustration of a "lady frightened to death" by a Ripper impersonator on the cover of the *Police Illustrated News*; and by proposing that the Ripper might change his venue to more respectable parts as Whitechapel became too dangerous for him.[58] Although the most popular theories and fantasies about the Ripper (such as the erotic maniac and the mad doctor) contained a coded discussion of the dangers of unrestrained male sexuality, misogynist fears of female sexuality and female automony also surfaced in speculations about a female Ripper. Most of these hostilities focused on prostitutes, who, in the words of one influential commentator, were so "unsexed" and depraved that they were capable of the most heinous crimes;[59] but suspicion also extended to midwives and medical women in as much as the "knowledge of surgery . . . has now been placed within female reach."[60] However different their social class and occupational mobility, prostitutes, midwives, and medical women shared two common characteristics: they possessed dangerous sexual knowledge and they asserted themselves in the public male domain.

Male reaction to the murders mirrored these misogynist attitudes and took a variety of forms, from a conscious imitation and impersonation of the Ripper to a more latent identification with the criminal and subtle exploitation of female terror.[61] In Whitechapel a series of gentlemen-sleuths used their amateur detective status as a cover to intimidate women. Here is a case in point:

On November 11, a woman named Humphries was passing George Yard and she met a man in the darkness. Trembling with agitation she asked him what he wanted. The man made no answer but laughed. He then made a hasty retreat. The women yelled "murder."[62]

She attracted the police who caught up with him, but "he referred the police to a well-known gentleman at the London Hospital and as a result he was set at liberty." Similar incidents occurred in the West End, involving respectable women; as soon as the assaulting gentleman could produce his business card and show a respectable address, both the lady and the police dropped the case. Laboring men were not immune from acting out the Ripper role themselves. Scores of men, some drunk, some mentally unbalanced, some claiming to be doctors and missing a black bag, gave themselves up to the police. In pubs across London, drunks bragged of their exploits as Jack the Ripper. Some Ripper impersonators harassed prostitutes and tried to extort money from them, with the threat that they would otherwise "Whitechapel" them. James Henderson, a tailor, was brought before the Dalston Magistrates for threatening Rosa Goldstein, an "unfortunate," with "ripping" her up if she did not go with him and for striking her several hard blows with his cane. Henderson was let off with

a fine of forty shillings, on the grounds that he had been drunk—
this, despite the fact that the severely injured Goldstein appeared
in court "with surgical bandages about her head" and "weak
from loss of blood."[63]

Besides these public acts of intimidation, a private reenactment
of the Ripper drama between husbands and wives was also staged
in various working-class areas of London. (I have no evidence of
middle-class cases.) In Lambeth, for example, magistrates received
many applications "with regard to threats used by husbands
against their wives, such as "I'll Whitechapel you" and "Look out
for Leather Apron." The *Daily News* reported the case of a man
who actually offered ten shillings for anyone who would rid him
of his wife by the "Whitechapel process."[64]

One case that reached the Old Bailey may provide some insight
into the circumstances that led up to the threat.[65] Sarah Brett of
Peckham was living out of wedlock with Thomas Onley. On October 3, three days after the "double event," her son arrived
home from sea with a friend. Brett permitted the friend, Frank
Hall, to board with them. On October 15, the common-law husband and the visitor went out and got drunk; when they returned, both abused and swore at her. Brett told the visitor not to in-
terfere; he smacked her and she returned the blow, knocking him
off his chair and ordering him to leave. This angered her man,
who then declared they were not even married and threatened to
do "a Whitechapel murder upon you." He was clearly too drunk
to carry out this undertaking and so retired upstairs to bed, leaving her with the visitor who then stabbed her, wounding her
severely.

What sense can we make out of this event? Typically, alcoholic
consumption helped to precipitate the conflict. Sarah Brett's role
was defensive but firm; she did not challenge the boundaries of
her "sphere," but she did exercise her prerogatives as manager of
household resources and amply demonstrated her own capacity
to defend herself. Although her common-law husband abused her
first, she only reprimanded the visitor. "It is quite sufficient for
Mr. Onley to commence upon me without you interfering." By
ordering the visitor out of the house, she nonetheless shamed
Onley. She threatened his masculinity; he responded by denying
the legitimacy of their relations — in sum, calling her a whore. He
then invoked the example of that most masterly of men, the
Whitechapel killer, leaving her with the young visitor who still
had the strength to carry out the husband's threat.

I am not trying to argue that the Ripper episode directly increased sexual violence; rather it covertly sanctioned male antagonism toward women and buttressed male authority over them. It established a common vocabulary and iconography of male violence that permeated the whole society, papering over class differences and obscuring the different material conditions that provoked sexual antagonism in different classes. [66] The Ripper drama invested male domination with a powerful mystique; it encouraged little boys in working-class Poplar and suburban Tunbridge Wells to intimidate and torment girls by playing at Jack the Ripper. "There's a man in a leather apron coming soon, to kill all the little girls in Tunbridge Wells. It's in the paper." "Look out, Here comes Jack the Ripper," was enough to send girls running from the street or from their own backyards into the safety of their homes.[67] Whatever their conscious ethos, male night patrols in Whitechapel had the same structural effect of enforcing the segregation of social space: women were relegated to the interior of a prayer meeting or their homes, behind locked doors; men were left to patrol the public spaces and the street. Male vigilantes also terrified women of the locale, who could not easily distinguish their molestors from their disguised protectors: "If the murderer be possessed . . . with the usual cunning of lunacy," one correspondent suggested in the *Saint James Gazette*, "I should think it probable that he was one of the first to enroll himself among the amateur detectives."[68]

Women's responses to the events surrounding the Ripper murders were as diverse as men's, yet overlaid by feelings of personal vulnerability. Women in Whitechapel were both fascinated and terrified by the murders: like their male counterparts, they bought up the latest editions of the half-penny evening newspapers; they gossiped about the gruesome details of the murders; and they crowded into the waxwork exhibits and peep shows where representations of the murdered victims were on display.[69] As we have seen, many also sympathized with the victims and came to the aid of prostitutes in their time of crisis. As one clergyman from Spitalfields remarked of the "fallen sisterhood": "these women are very good natured to each other. They are drawn together by a common danger and they will help each other all they can . . . ." Because the women clubbed together, and because common lodging housekeepers were generally "lenient" to regular customers, distress among prostitutes during the month of October was "not as great as one might expect," reported the *Daily News*.[70]

On the whole, respectable working women offered little collective resistance to public male intimidation. I found two exceptions among matchgirls and marketwomen who were part of an autonomous female work culture. On their own territory, marketwomen could organize *en masse*: a number of women "calling out 'Leather Apron,'" for instance, chased Henry Taylor when he threatened Mary Ann Perry with "ripping her up" in Claremarket; and similar incidents occurred in Spitalfields market, nearby the Ripper murders.[71] Marketwomen enjoyed an *esprit de corps* akin to the feisty, street-fighting matchgirls, who had just won a successful strike from the Bryant and May Match Factory, and who openly bragged about catching the Ripper.[72]

Neighborhood women, such as the Spitalfields marketwomen, participated in crowd activity during the day, but those who could, stayed inside at night behind locked doors. Women who earned their living on the streets at night — prostitutes — did not have that luxury. Some left Whitechapel, even the East End, for good. Others applied to the casual wards of the workhouse. Some slowly went back to the streets, first in groups of two or three, then occasionally alone. They armed themselves, and although they "joked" about encountering Jack—"I am the next for Jack," quipped one woman—they were obviously terrified at the prospect. Some even went to prayer meetings to avoid remaining home alone at night.[73]

Increased attendance at prayer meetings delighted female missionaries active in the Whitechapel area. "Of course we are taking advantage of the terror," explained one Salvation Army "lassie." Another woman who took advantage of the terror was Henrietta Barnett, wife of Samuel Barnett of Toynbee Hall. Distressed at hearing women gossiping about the murders, she got up a petition to the Queen and with the aid of board (state) schoolteachers and mission workers, obtained four thousand signatures of the "Women of Whitechapel." The petition begged the Queen to call upon "your servants in authority" to close down the lodging houses where the murdered victims resided.[74] Although not entirely absent from the Ripper mobilization, female moral reformers like Barnett occupied a subordinate role within it: they remained physically constrained within the female sphere and bent on keeping neighborhood women there as well, moving them inside into prayer meetings, out of earshot of salacious discussions of sex and violence, relinquishing public spaces and

Police Illustrated News, 22 September 1888.

sexual knowledge to men.

It is difficult to determine how much Barnett's petition truly represented the opinion of Whitechapel women. It probably reflected the views of Jewish women and female residents of model dwelling houses, if not the immediate neighbors of prostitutes. But the picture had another side. Although Jewish artisans' wives regarded the women of the lodging houses as "nogoodnicks, prostitutes, old bags and drunks,"[75] they still employed Catherine Eddowes and others like her to char and wash for them, to light their sabbath fires, sometimes even to mind their children. There was a tense and fragile social ecology between rough and respectable elements in Whitechapel, one that could be easily upset by outside intervention.[76] The murders threatened the safety of respectable women; they undoubtedly strained class relations in the neighborhood and intensified gender divisions. They effectively placed respectable women under "house arrest" and made them dependent on male protection.

Women outside of Whitechapel also took a keen interest in the murders, and some even tried their hand at armchair detecting. Queen Victoria for instance, repeatedly wrote into the Home Office and Scotland Yard with her pet theories, and actually forced Lord Salisbury to hold a cabinet meeting on Saturday to consider the question of a reward.[77] At least one woman gained some notoriety from the case: at Bradford Police Court on October 10, 1888, a "respectable young woman, named Maria Coroner, aged twenty-one, was charged with having written certain letters tending to cause a breach of the peace: they were signed 'Jack the Ripper.'"[78] Another woman believed that "respectable women like herself had nothing to fear from the Whitechapel murderer," as she thought it was true that he "respects and protects respectable females."[79] This was, of course, the line taken by police officials, who expressed amazement at the widespread female hysteria over the murders, since they were only perpetrated on prostitutes.

For many women, this was small comfort. Female vulnerability extended well beyond the boundaries of the "danger zone." Mary Hughes, a female professional who lived in the West End in 1888, recalled

how terrified and unbalanced we all were by the murders. It seemed to be round the corner, although it all happened in the East End, and we were in the West; but even so, I was afraid to got out after dark, if only to post a letter. Just

Judith R. Walkowitz   567

as dusk came on we used to hear down our quiet and ultra-respectable Edith Road the cries of newspaper boys in tones made as alarming as they could: "Another 'orrible murder . . . . Whitechapel! Disgustin' details . . . Murder!"[80]

What about the politicized edge of middle-class womanhood, the feminists? Did they mount any counterattack? Frances Power Cobbe enthusiastically entered into the fray and called for the use of female detectives whose "mother wit" would guide them to the murderer.[81] Josephine Butler and others expressed concern that the uproar over the murders would lead to the repression of brothels and subsequent homelessness of women. In so doing, they broke with more repressive purity advocates who were totally indifferent to the fate of the victims and to the rights of prostitutes. In the end, only the strict libertarians, female and male, came forward to defend prostitutes as human beings, with essential rights and liberties.[82]

The only piece of feminist anger to receive extensive coverage appeared in the pages of the *Daily News,* a liberal organ. The Whitechapel murders were not just homicides but "womenkilling," declared Florence Fenwick Miller, a noted London journalist, in her letter to the editor.[83] Researching the police columns, she concluded that attacks on prostitutes were not different from other violent assaults on women by men. They were not isolated events, but part of a "constant but ever increasing series of cruelties" perpetrated against women and treated leniently by judges.

Miller's letter generated a small flurry of responses supportive of her position and calling for women's economic and political emancipation. Kate Mitchell, a physician and feminist, applauded Miller's letter and cited the case, mentioned above, of James Henderson who was let off with a fine of forty shillings after severely beating a prostitute. Unless women were publicly emancipated, argued Mitchell, they would remain "ciphers" in the land and subject to male physical abuse.[84] The letters made an important association between public and domestic violence against women, but it would be a mistake to exaggerate their political impact. They remained isolated interventions in an overwhelmingly patriarchal debate; they were discounted or ignored by other dailies and failed to mobilize women over the issues.

The *Star,* a radical evening newspaper whose pages were open to socialists, disagreed with Miller. "It is the class question rather than the sex question that is at issue in this matter."[85] In their own journals, prominent socialists like William Morris and H.M.

Hyndman also refused to address the issue of sex antagonism; they tended to see sex oppression as a result of capitalist productive relations alone. For all their contempt of the proprietary press, the socialists' assessment of the murdered prostitutes as "unsexed" dehumanized "creatures" who had "violated their womanhood for the price of a night's lodging" was remarkably similar to that of the conservative and misogynist *Morning Post* and *Times*. To distinguish themselves from the bourgeois press, socialists would have had to overcome their ambivalence towards prostitutes and the unrespectable poor of Whitechapel and address the subject of male dominance.[86]

RESOLUTION

As we have seen, many discussions of class and gender were developed in relation to the events in Whitechapel, and were reflective of important cultural and social divisions within Victorian society. Nonetheless, the alternative perspectives — of feminists and libertarians, of the Whitechapel poor themselves — were ultimately subordinated to a dominant discussion in the media, shaped and articulated by those people in positions of power, namely, male professional experts. Within this dominant discourse, the discussion of class was more explicit and self-conscious than that of gender. In part, this fact relates to the precise moment of class antagonism when Jack the Ripper stalked the streets of London. The events in Whitechapel could be easily slotted into the "Outcast London" theme. They reinforced prevailing prejudices about the East End as a strange territory of savages, a social abyss, an inferno. The *Times* might well wring its hands about the responsibility of "our social organization" for spawning the crimes, but this momentary soul searching was readily domesticated into an attack on the symptoms, rather than on the causes, of urban poverty.[87]

Throughout the "autumn of terror," leader columns and correspondence pages were filled with conventional proposals to cure the social ills of Whitechapel: better lighting, improved paving, more biblewomen, more night refuges where poor women could sleep, and more laundries where they could work. Overshadowing these suggestions was one dominant theme — the necessity of slum clearance and the need to purge the lawless population of the common lodging houses from the neighborhood.[88] "Those of us who know Whitechapel know that the impulse that makes for murder is abroad in our streets every night," declared two Toynbee Hallers.[89] The "disorderly and depraved lives of the women," observed Canon Barnett, were more "appalling" than the actual murders.[90] Men like Barnett finally manipulated public opinion and consolidated it behind razing the common lodging houses of the Flower and Dean street area. Artisans' dwellings replaced them. The notoriety of the street impelled the respectable owners—the Henderson family— to sell their property as soon as the leases were up. The Rothschild Buildings (1892), for respectable Jewish artisans and their families, appeared over the site of the lodging houses where Catherine Eddowes and Elizabeth Stride once lived. Prostitutes and their fellow lodgers were thus rendered homeless and forced to migrate to the few remaining rough streets in the neighborhood. Through the surveillance of the vigilance committees and through this "urban renewal," the murders helped to intensify repressive activity already under way in the Whitechapel area.[91]

Such reform-minded responses coincided with a general dissipation of middle-class fears of "Outcast London." The disciplined and orderly 1889 dock strike persuaded many respectable observers that the East End poor were indeed salvageable because they could be organized into unions. Meanwhile, Charles Booth's massive survey of East London, also published in 1889, graphically demonstrated how small and unrepresentative the "criminal" population of the Flower and Dean street rookery actually was. When another Ripper-like murder occurred in July 1889 in Whitechapel, newspaper coverage was far less hysterical and obsessive. In class terms, the crisis had passed.[92]

Sexual fears and hostilities, on the other hand, were less satisfactorily allayed.[93] For the Ripper story has continued to provide a common vocabulary of male violence against women, a vocabulary now almost one hundred years old. Its persistence owes much to the mass media's exploitation of Ripper iconography — depictions of female mutilation in mainstream cinema, celebrations of the Ripper as a "hero" of crime — that intensify the dangers of male violence and convince women that they are helpless victims.

A few contemporary examples illustrate the deleterious effects of the Ripper legacy on women's lives and well-being. Between October 1977 and January 1981, women in the North of England were terrorized by a mass murderer, dubbed the "Yorkshire Ripper" by the newspapers, who principally preyed on prostitutes,

and who was believed — erroneously — to be the author of taped
messages sent to authorities. Newspaper discussion of the
murders and the trial (this recent Ripper was caught and convicted) reproduced the same categories that had earlier structured
press accounts of the Whitechapel "horrors": was the murderer
"mad" or "bad"; did the prostitutes bring the murders on
themselves; were all women at risk; did the murder setting of
"mean streets" explain or generate the crimes? But this time
around, the contemporary women's movement organized female
patrols against the threat, and a prostitutes' rights group protested
at the murder trial.[94]

At a more subtle level, traces of the Ripper's presence constantly intrude into urban women's consciousness. Walking down my
street in Manhattan recently, I came upon graffiti emblazoning the
Ripper's name on a side of a building. That same week the Lesbian
Herstory Archives forwarded to me a threatening letter from
"Jack the Ripper": "THE ORIGINAL JACK not a cheap imita-
tion/I've conquered death itself and am still on this earth waiting
to strike again."[95]

However pervasive, the Ripper image certainly does not tell us
all we need to know about male culture and male nature.
Feminists must probe behind the Ripper myth and analyze both
its simplified image and the complex reality it masks. By flatten-
ing history into myth, the Ripper story has rendered all men
suspect, vastly increasing female anxieties, and obscuring the
distinct material conditions that generate sexual antagonism and
male violence. Finally, the Ripper myth offers women no strategy
for resistance; on the contrary, it is about female passivity in the
face of male violence. Yet the current women's movement has
generated a range of responses that transcend that mythic fatality:
take-back-the-night marches, antirape hotlines, battered women's
shelters, antipornography demonstrations, and prostitutes' rights
coalitions offer diverse strategies against a false notion of universal female passivity. In the "real" world, neither male violence
nor female victimization has single-root causes or effects. Only
our cultural nightmares and media fantasies construct life this
way.

Judith R. Walkowitz   571

NOTES

This research was assisted by a grant from the American Council of Learned Societies, under a program funded by the National Endowment for the Humanities. Thanks also to the New York Institute for the Humanities for providing me with an office while I was on leave. I wish to thank the following individuals for their helpful advice and criticism: Dina Copelman, Anna Davin, Natalie Zemon Davis, Myra Jehlen, Temma Kaplan, Thomas Laqueur, Ruth Milkman, Judith Newton, Esther Newton, Rayna Rapp, Ellen Ross, Mary Ryan, Carroll Smith-Rosenberg, and Daniel Walkowitz.

The following abbreviations will be used for sources in this article (all periodicals were from London): *DC—Daily Chronicle, DN—Daily News, DT—Daily Telegraph, ELA—East London Advertiser, ELO—East London Observer, ES—Evening Standard,* HO—Home Office papers, *LWN—Lloyd's Weekly News,* Mepo.—Metropolitan Police papers, *MP—Morning Post, PMG—Pall Mall Gazette, RN—Reynolds' Newspaper, SJG—Saint James Gazette.*

[1]Noel Annan, quoted in Susan Brownmiller, *Against Our Will: Men, Women, and Rape* (New York: Bantam Books, 1976), p. 325.

[2]*DC,* 11 September 1888.

[3]Useful studies of the Ripper controversy include Donald Rumbelow, *The Complete Jack the Ripper* (New York: New American Library, 1975); Tom Cullen, *Autumn of Terror* (London: Bodley Head, 1965); Donald McCormick, *The Identity of Jack the Ripper* (London: Arrow Books, 1970); Alexander Kelly, *Jack the Ripper: A Bibliography and Review of the Literature* (London: A.A.L., 1973); Elwyn Jones, ed., *Ripper File* (London: Barker, 1975).

[4]Beatrice Webb, quoted in Gareth Stedman-Jones, *Outcast London: A Study in the Relationship between Classes in Victorian Society* (Oxford: Clarendon Press, 1971), p. 285.

[5]See Stedman-Jones, *Outcast London;* Victor Bailey, "The Dangerous Classes in Late-Victorian England: Some Reflections on the Social Foundations of Disturbance and Order with Special Reference to London in the 1880s" (Ph.D. dissertation, Warwick University, 1975). The resignation of Police Commissioner Warren, shortly after the murder of the fifth victim, Mary Jean Kelly, in November 1888, was one important political ramification of the Ripper episode.

[6]Josephine Butler, Royal Commission on the Contagious Diseases Acts, quoted in Glen Petrie, *A Singular Iniquity: The Campaigns of Josephine A. Butler* (New York: Viking Press, 1971), p. 114. On "sexual secrets" see William Leach, *True Love and Perfect Union: The Feminist Reform of Sex and Society* (New York: Basic Books, 1980).

[7]Judith R. Walkowitz, *Prostitution and Victorian Society: Women, Class, and the State* (New York: Cambridge University Press, 1980); Edward J. Bristow, *Vice and Vigilance: Purity Movements in Britain Since 1700* (MacMillan: Dublin, 1977).

[8]Peter Brooks, *The Melodramatic Imagination: Balzac, Henry James, Melodrama and the Mode of Excess* (New Haven: Yale University Press, 1976) chap. 1; Alan J. Lee, *The Origins of the Popular Press in England; 1855-1914* (London: Croom Helm, 1976), chap. 4; Louis James, *Fiction for the Working Man, 1830-1850: A Study of the Literature Produced for the Working Classes in Early Victorian Urban England* (London: Oxford University Press, 1963), pp. 108-18; chap. 9.

[9]Thanks to Mary P. Ryan for this observation.

[10]The number of murder victims credited to Jack the Ripper was contested at the

time and is still subject to dispute. During the "autumn of terror," two earlier murders of prostitutes were initially connected (in retrospect) with the five murders. Two subsequent murders in 1889 and 1891 were subsequently linked to the Ripper. However, two official reports, one by Police Commissioner McNaghton and another by a forensic specialist, Dr. Thomas Bond, asserted that only these five homicides bore the marks of a single killer. See, Mepo. 3/141, 10 November 1888; Sir Melville McNaghton letter, quoted in full in Rumbelow, *Complete Jack the Ripper,* pp. 132-36.

[11]Quoted in Jerry White, *Rothschild Buildings: Life in an East End Tenement Block, 1887-1920* (London: Routledge and Kegan Paul, 1980), p. 7.

[12]Ibid., p. 26

[13]"The East End Atrocities," *London City Mission Magazine,* 1 December 1888, 258-60; Chiam Bermant, *Point of Arrival: A Study of London's East End* (London: Methuen, 1975), p. 188.

[14]*ELO,* 27 July 1889.

[15]Quoted in White, *Rothschild Buildings,* p. 8.

[16]Arthur Harding, quoted in *East End Underworld: Chapters in the Life of Arthur Harding,* ed. Raphael Samuel (London: Routledge and Kegan Paul, 1981), p. 110.

[17]*Times,* 2 October 1888.

[18]*DC,* 19 September 1888.

[19]*LWN,* 7 October 1888.

[20]Rosemary Jackson, *Fantasy: The Literature of Subversion* (London and New York: Methuen, 1981), p. 25.

[21]*Star,* 8 September 1888.

[22]"A Reign of Terror in Whitechapel," *ELO,* 15 September 1888.

[23]Walter Dew, *I Caught Crippen* (London: Blackie & Son, 1938), p. 112.

[24]D.G. Halsted, *Doctor in the Nineties* (London: Christopher Johnson, 1959), p. 48.

[25]All the letters are collected in Mepo. 3/142.

[26]Sir Robert Anderson, *The Lighter Part of My Official Life* (London: Hodder and Stoughton, 1910), p. 138; HO 144 /A49301C/8a, 23 October 1888; Mepo. 3/142; Sir Melville McNaghton, *Days of My Years* (London: Edward Arnold, 1915), pp. 58,59.

[27]*DT,*24 September 1888.

[28]*PMG,* 10 September 1888.

[29]*DC,* 10 September 1888.

[30] *PMG,* 19 September 1888.

[31]*Commonweal,* 13 November 1888; Judith R. Walkowitz, "The Politics of Prostitution," *Signs* 6 (Autumn 1980): 124-27.

[32]Jones, *Ripper File,* p. 51.

[33]*DC,* 10 November 1888.

[34]*DT,* 10 November 1888.

[35]HO 144/220/A49301c/8a, 23 October 1888.

[36]Bermant, *Point of Arrival,* chap. 9; White, *Rothschild Buildings,* chap. 1; *Jewish Chronicle,* 5 October 1888.

[37]*ELO,* 15 September 1888; Dew, *I Caught Crippen,* pp. 108-11.

[38]Bermant, *Point of Arrival,* chap. 9; White, *Rothschild Buildings,* p. 25.

[39]HO 144/220/A49301C/8C and 15; A49301D/5. As Bermant *(Point of Arrival,* pp. 116-18) notes, the Police Commissioner, Sir Charles Warren, fearing a pogrom, wiped out a message scrawled on a wall near the double murder of Eddowes and Stride, "The Juwes are not the men that will be blamed for nothing." Elizabeth Stride's body had been found in front of the Working Men's International Club, a club for Jewish socialists.

Judith R. Walkowitz 573

[40]*Times,* 12 September 1888.

[41]Jones, *Ripper File,* pp. 24, 25.

[42]My book in progress on Jack the Ripper discusses the theories of the Ripper in some detail. These theories not only represent male fantasies of power, but also evidence a good deal of self-hatred.

[43]HO 144/220/A49301C/8a, 23 October 1888.

[44]*Echo,* 14 September 1888.

[45]Frederick Porter Wensley, *Detective Days* (London: Cassell & Co., 1931), p. 128; Halsted, *Doctor in the Nineties,* p. 45.

[46]*DC,* 15 September 1888; *DT,* 2, 4 October 1888; *DN,* 9 October 1888; Halsted, *Doctor in the Nineties,* p. 48.

[47]White, *Rothschild Buildings,* p. 9.

[48]Walkowitz, "Politics of Prostitution," pp. 129-30; Josephine Butler to Miss Priestman, 5 November 1896, Butler Collection, Fawcett Library, City of London Polytechnic, London; Henrietta Barnett, *Canon Barnett: His Life, Work, and Friends by his Wife,* 2 vols. (London: Murray, 1921), 2: 305-8.

[49]"The Terrible Crime," *Echo,* 10 November 1888.

[50]*DC,* 10 November 1888.

[51]"The Whitechapel Horrors," *ELO,* 13 October 1888.

[52]*Times,* 6 October 1888.

[53]Dew, *I Caught Crippen,* p. 107; *ELO,* 15 September 1888; Halsted, *Doctor in the Nineties,* pp. 54, 55; Mepo. 3/140. For popular antagonism against doctors, see R.M. McLeod, "Law, Medicine and Public Opinion: The Resistance to Compulsory Health Legislation, 1870-1901," *Public Law* (1967), 189-211; *The Threepenny Doctor: Doctor Jelley of Hackney* (London: Hackney Workers' Education Association, 1974).

[54]*ELO,* 13 October 1888.

[55]*DN,* 6, 15 October 1888; *Times,* 6 October 1888.

[56]*ES,* 9 November 1888.

[57]*Star,* 8 September 1888.

[58]*DC,* 18 September 1888; *Police Illustrated News,* 3 November; 1 December 1888; *Women's Penny Paper,* 6 November 1888.

[59]"G.S.O." to the *Times,* 22 September 1888.

[60]Letter to the Editor, *SJG,* 12 November 1888.

[61]It should be noted that male libertarians came to the defense of prostitutes in the pages of the *Personal Rights Journal* (November 1888), pp. 69, 76, 84.

[62]*Times,* 12 November 1888.

[63]Cullen, *Autumn of Terror,* p. 78; *Echo,* 1, 2, 3 October 1888; *ELO,* 6 October 1888; *MP,* 4 October 1888.

[64]*Times,* 1 October 1888; Cullen, *Autumn of Terror,* p. 79; *Echo,* 3 October 1888.

[65]Criminal Court London, 109 (1888-89), pp. 76-78. Thanks to Ellen Ross for this citation.

[66]Ellen Ross, "'Fierce Questions and Taunts': Married Life in Working-Class London, 1870-1914," this issue.

[67]Helen Corke, *In Our Infancy: An Autobiography, Part 1, 1882-1912* (Cambridge: Cambridge University Press, 1975), p. 25 (thanks to Dina Copelman for this citation); Mrs. Bartholemew, interview (thanks to Anna Davin for the transcript).

[68]Letter to the Editor, *SJG,* 16 November 1888.

[69]Montagu Williams, *Round London: Down East and Up West* (London: Macmillan & Co., 1892), p. 12; *PMG,* 18 October 1888.

[70]*DN,* 4 October 1888.

[71]*DT,* 4 October; 10 September 1888; *RN,* 9 September 1888.

[72]Mepo. 3/142, 5 October 1888.

[73]Dew, *I Caught Crippen,* p. 95; "Ready for the Whitechapel Fiend: Women Secretly Armed," *Police Illustrated News,* 22 September 1888; *DT,* 2 October 1888; *War Cry,* 1 December 1888.

[74]*War Cry,* 1 December 1888; Barnett, *Canon Barnett,* p. 306.

[75]Quoted in White, *Rothschild Buildings,* p. 125.

[76]Ibid., chap. 4.

[77]Rumbelow, *Complete Jack the Ripper,* p. 86.

[78]McCormick, *Identity,* p. 81.

[79]Rumbelow, *Complete Jack the Ripper,* p. 101.

[80]M.V. Hughes, *A London Family, 1870-1900* (London: Oxford University Press, 1957), p. 362.

[81]Frances Power Cobbe to the Editor, *Times,* 11 October 1888.

[82]*Dawn,* 1 November 1888; *Personal Rights Journal,* November 1888, pp. 69, 76, 84; *Sentinel,* December 1888, p. 145.

[83]*DN,* 2 October 1888.

[84]*DN,* 4, 6, 9, 11 October 1888.

[85]*Star,* 4 October 1888.

[86]See, for instance, *Justice,* 6 October 1888 and 17 November 1888; *Star,* 1 October 1888; Ben Tillett, quoted in William J. Fishman, *East End Jewish Radicals, 1875-1914* (London: Duckworth, 1975), p. 236.

[87]Peter Keating, "Fact and Fiction in the East End," in *The Victorian City,* ed. H.J. Dyos and M. Wolff, 2 vols. (London: Routledge & Kegan Paul, 1973), 1: 585-603; Bailey, "Dangerous Classes in Late-Victorian England"; *Times* leader, quoted in "Murder as an Advertisement," *PMG,* 19 September 1888.

[88]White, *Rothschild Buildings,* chap. 1. See, for example, *Times,* 22 September; 2, 11, 18, 26, 29, 30 October; 6, 16 November 1888. See the series of letters in the *Daily Telegraph* on the "Safe Four Percent," 21, 24, 26 September 1888.

[89]Thomas Hancock Nunn and Thomas Gardner to the Editor, *Times,* 6 October 1888. Both Nunn and Gardner were members of the National Vigilance Association, a repressive social purity group.

[90]*Times,* 16 November 1888.

[91]White, *Rothschild Buildings,* chap. 1.

[92]Jones, *Outcast London,* chap. 17; Keating, "Fact and Fiction," pp. 595, 596; *Star,* 20 July 1889.

[93]Medical doctors did try to allay fears by representing the Ripper as an individual erotic maniac whose activities were unconnected to the normal interactions between the sexes. See the letter from Dr. Thomas Bond, Mepo. 3/141, 10 November 1888; Richard Von Krafft-Ebing, *Psychopathia Sexualis: A Medico-Forensic Study,* trans. Harry E. Wedeck (New York: Putman, 1975), p. 119.

[94]Mandy Merck, "Looking at the Sutcliffe Case," *Spare Rib: A Women's Liberation Magazine* (July 1981); 16-18; Wendy Holliway, "I Just Wanted to Kill a Woman.' Why? The Ripper and Male Sexuality," *Feminist Review* 9 (Autumn 1981): 33-40.

[95]"Jack the Ripper" to Lesbian Herstory Archives, 5 October 1981, New York, New York.

[24]

Journal of Contemporary Criminal Justice
Vol. 7 • No. 4 • December 1991

Female Serial Murderesses:
Constructing Differentiating Typologies

Stephen T. Holmes
Eric Hickey
and
Ronald M. Holmes

Abstract

Despite the claims of several researchers in the examination of serial murder that there are no female serial killers,
the authors have researched the serial murders which
have occurred during the past fifty years and discovered
a large number of female serial murderesses. There is an
attempt to establish a typology of females who killed
serially in the same fashion which has been already
formed with male serial killers. With this typology
discussed, homicidal behavioral traits are also discussed.

Introduction

Serial murder is probably the most disturbing crime of the 1990s
(Holmes and DeBurger, 1988). Research on the subject appears both on an
academic level (Hickey, 1991; Holmes and DeBurger, 1985, 1988: Jenkins,
1987; Levin and Fox, 1985; Leyton, 1985; Ressler et al, 1988) and other
more narrative formats which tend to be deficient in documentation. Both
types of research and writings, however, indicate that the overwhelming
number of serial killers are men. For example, in a listing of forty-seven
serial killers by Holmes and DeBurger (22-23; 1988), only three were
females. Of the three female serialists, two killed family members and the
other murdered with her male lovers. Hickey (1991), in his study of 203
serial killers, identified 16 percent as female offenders. None is examined
by any of the previously cited researchers. Given the apparent scarcity of
females involved as multiple homicide offenders, sources are few which
address their incidence and etiology. By contrast, homicide is one of the
most carefully monitored crimes in American society.

Data on "Traditional" Homicide.

The rate of homicide decreased in the last decade. The Bureau of Justice Statistics reports:

"... the most recent decade of homicide data from the National Center for Health Statistics shows rates rising from 1976, peaking in 1980, and declining to levels below the 1976 rate" (15).

Studies now, however, indicate an increase in homicide rates, at least in many urbanized areas. Statistics in 1990, from more than a dozen large cities in America, report that homicides rates are higher now than ever. New York City, for example, recorded over 2,000 violent deaths by the end of 1990. The record number of homicides within the city limits of Washington, D.C. solidifies it's reputation as "Murder Capital of the United States." Throughout the 1980s the yearly toll of murder victims hovered near the 20,000 figure. In 1990 this figure rose to approximately 23,600. This represents not only a marked increase in the total number of murders but also a significant increase in the rate of killings (FBI, 1991).

The Uniform Crime Report, compiled by the FBI noted that most victims of homicide during the 1980s were killed by family, friends, and acquaintances. Most of these murders were a result of impulsive violence (Block, 1985) often fueled with alcohol or illegal drugs (Goodman et al., 1986). Increasingly, several large U.S. cities have seen persons die as a result of victim-offender disputes involving the sale, distribution, or use of illicit drugs (Zimring and Zuehl, 1986).

There are, however, few studies which empirically measure the number of those victimized by serial killers. Since most serial murders are considered to be "stranger to stranger" homicides, detection and apprehension is considerably more difficult. In turn, collecting accurate data becomes problematic. One source reported as many as 5,000 victims a year who fall prey to serial killers (Bernick and Spangler, 1985). Their data were gathered from interviewing "experts in the field." While there is no precise method to confirm this number, there is growing concern by law enforcement officials over the increase in the incidence of new cases each year. Similar to homicides in general, most of these serial killings are victims who fall prey to men.

Rationale for Serial Murder

Persons who murder serially kill for different reasons. Men kill typically for psychological gain and are intrinsically motivated. The anticipated gain is normally one which is psychological: sexual pleasure, the utlimate power

247   Female Serial Murderesses:
       Constructing Differentiating Typologies

over another human being, or aberrant hedonism (Holmes and DeBurger, 1985; Holmes, DeBurger and Holmes, 1988). Under normal conditions these types of offenders kill because of an inner need or compulsion to murder. There are indeed, some males who kill serially because of visions or voices but they are rare in comparison to most serial murderers (Holmes, 1988; Hickey, 1991).

By distinguishing the different types of men who murder serially and utilizing an analysis of motivation, victim selection, anticipated gain, methods of murder, and based upon an analysis of 400 cases, a taxonomy was developed of four different types of serial killers : Vision, Mission, Hedonistic and Power/Control (Holmes and DeBurger, 1985). But these classifications were based solely upon an examination of male offenders. Now, by expanding serial murder research, a similar typology is needed for consideration of female offenders.

The Female Serial Murderess

Despite the claim of Egger (1985) or Rule (Reynolds, 1990), there is clear evidence that some women are serial killers. One reason for the reluctance to accept women as serial killers, perhaps, has been an aversion to perceive women as being capable of fatal violence. Women tend not to kill for sexual reasons, nor does God or the devil typically impel them to homicide (Holmes, 1990; Hickey, 1991). Women have been stereotypically viewed as nuturing and vulnerable, not physically or psychologically capable of murder, unless provoked in an abusive situation. Such notions are being challenged as more research focuses upon women and their propensity for violent behavior.

The preponderance of women who kill do so because of ill-fated personal relationships. The typical female murderer not only kills someone she knows but often kills inside her own home. For example, sometimes in a marriage where physical violence is commonplace, the perceived manner in which to escape may be through fatal violence. In other cases, women having been spurned in love may kill as a perceived just response. In one highly publicized case, Jean Harris killed her lover, Dr. Townover, because of love gone awry. While these types of domestic homicides are common, serial murder involving females as offenders is relatively rare.

Hickey (1991) examined thirty-four female serial killers. He noted among his findings that 82% of the cases had occurred since 1900 and that almost one in two killers had a male accomplice. Perhaps one of the most interesting findings in Hickey's work was that more than one third of the women began their killing careers since 1970. He offered several explanations for this apparent occurrence: improved police investigation, population increase and increased media attention. The average woman killed for

9.2 years before her killing stopped, for whatever reason. Most were homemakers (32%), nurses (18%), or involved in other types of criminal careers (15%). One in five killers were found to have no occupational title whatsoever. Ninety-seven per cent were white and the average age was 33 when they began their killing careers.

Regarding women who stalked victims, Hickey found that in contrast to male serial offenders only one third of female serialists reported having killed strangers. And almost without exception, the females did not travel to more than one state in their quest for victims. Their motives and methods also differ from their male counterparts: these women tend to murder for material gain by using poisons or pills (Ibid., 107-118).

Some women who kill serially may do so because of their involvements in cults or "disciple" relationships. This type is illustrated by the women associated with the Charlie Manson family. Charlene Gallego, the common-law wife of serial killer, Gerald Gallego, willfully aided in the selection, abduction and murders of at least ten young people (van Hoffman, 1990).

There appear to be an increasing number of women who murder multiple victims. By simply using the parameters of three or more victims killed in a span of thirty days or more (Holmes and DeBurger, 1985), several cases involving female offenders can be identified. Belle Gunness murdered an estimated 14 to 49 husbands and suitors in LaPorte, Indiana. Nannie Doss murdered 11 husbands and family members in Tulsa. Martha Beck and her lover, Ray Fernandez, stalked and murdered as many as 20 women. In the early 1980s, Carol Bundy (no relation to Ted Bundy) became an excellent example of a lust serial murderess. Decapitating a former lover along with several other young female runaways, she and Douglas Clark are believed to have carried out numerous homicides in the Los Angeles area. She currently is serving time in prison for the murder of only one male victim while Douglas is on death row in California for the murders of 6 young women.

Often women serialists kill for purposes of comfort: money, insurance benefits or business interests. Dorothea Puente of Sacramento County, California was charged with 9 murders of elderly persons who rented rooms in her boarding home. She allegedly signed and cashed her victims' Social Security checks after their deaths. For some offenders, targeting the elderly may be financially attractive. Since 1975, there has been an apparent increase in multiple homicides involving the elderly (Hickey,1991).

There are, however, many female serialists who do not kill for comfort considerations. Sex, revenge, spurned love, all emerge as intrinsic motivations for homicide. The anticipated gains and loci of motivations may often vary from one female offender to another. Consequently, we will first examine some primary characteristics central to female serial killers

249   Female Serial Murderesses:
       Constructing Differentiating Typologies

including those of spatial mobility, gain, motivation, and method of murder.

Primary Characteristics and Typologies
of Female Serial Murderers

Utilizing the previously discussed parameters to identify female serial offenders: those who have killed more than three victims in a time span of at least thirty days, there emerges several ways in which to examine female serialists. Initially, distinctions alone were made between groups of female serial killers which included nurses, black widows and other categories (Hickey, 1986). However, further differences among categories may facilitate identification of definitive traits. Hopefully, these traits will aid law enforcement in the understanding and apprehension of these female offenders.

Spatial Mobility and Serial Murder

Initially, serial killers can be distinguished according to their geographic mobility. They tend to be either *geographically stable or geographically transient*. The first type are offenders who reside in one location and seek out their victims in that same or nearby area. Carol Bundy and Priscilla Ford are two examples. Carol lived in Los Angeles and selected victims usually from the Hollywood and Vine area. Priscilla Ford killed her victims in her hometown of Reno, Nevada. Her unfortunate victims were randomly selected pedestrians whom God commanded she kill.

Unlike the male serialist who appears to be almost equally divided between the stable and transient types, the female serial offender almost exclusively falls into the geographically stable category. This may occur as a result of traditional female roles which have centered most activities around the home and family. Additionally, women have not been as occupationally mobile as their male counterparts. Consequently, spatial mobility is limited, which in turn narrows the victim selection process.

The geographically transient are those few females who travel continually throughout their killing careers (Holmes and DeBurger, 1985: 30-31). Christine Gallego is an example. She and her common-law husband killed in California and Nevada. The geographically transient female serial killer presents problems similar to men of the same genre. Jurisdictional issues, lack of communication among law enforcement agencies, as well as the mobility of the killer, all add to the complexity of apprehending offenders.

In contrast, geographically stable female offenders, because of their lack of mobility, increase the likelihood of detection and apprehension. These offenders often maintain personal, occupational and social ties to the community. In addition, most of these cases involve only one law enforcement jurisdiction, which eliminates most interagency "turf" issues and facilitates communications. In Table 1., factors including spatial locations, method of killings, and victims were paired with the five types of serial murderesses identified in this paper.

Table 1
Homicidal Behavior Patterns of Female Serial Killers

Factors	Visionary	Comfort	Hedonistic	Disciple	Power
Victims					
Specific		X	X	X	X
Nonspecific	X				
Random	X		X		X
Non-random		X	X	X	X
Affiliative		X			
Strangers	X		X	X	X
Methods					
Act-focused	X		X	X	X
Processed		X	X	X	X
Planned		X	X	X	X
Spontaneous	X				
Organized		X	X	X	X
Disorganized	X				
Spatial Locations					
Concentrated		X	X	X	X
Nomadic	X		X		X

251   Female Serial Murderesses:
        Constructing Differentiating Typologies

The Visionary Serial Killer

Most serial killers are not considered to be psychotic and understand legally, if not morally, that murder is wrong (Hickey, 1991). They have no apparent feelings about the concern and welfare of others; most perhaps, could be classified as having character defects such as possessing antisocial personalities. By contrast, there are some who commit acts of homicides because they are extrinsically compelled to do so. A few see visions demanding that they kill everyone in the world or at least in their neighborhood. This was the case of Joseph Kallinger, profiled by Flora Schriebner in her book, The Shoemaker. "Charley", a floating head, periodically would speak to Kallinger with a command that he destroy all humans in the world, then kill his family and finally commit suicide. In a correctional hospital setting, Kallinger still admits that he sees Charley and would kill again if he were released from the secure facility where he presently is serving his sentence (Schriebner, 1984).

In this type of homicide, the perpetrator has a severe break with reality. This break can be demonstrated by the person's admission that he or she has spoken to God, an angel, a spirit or Satan himself. The motivation is extrinisic to the personality and comes from an apparition or an auditory hallucination. In such a case, the attack tends to be spontaneous, with the killer selecting a victim predicated upon a description given by the message-giver.

Priscilla Ford is an example of a visionary serial killer who heard the voice of God as she walked down the streets of Reno, Nevada. The voice demanded that she kill those she met on the street because they were "bad people" and deserved to die. The insanity defense was insufficient to keep her from Nevada's death row.

Another visionary serial murderess was Martha Wise. A forty year old widow living in Medina, Ohio, she killed her family members simply for revenge. She used arsenic to poison her mother after she had been ridiculed for being involved romantically with a man younger than herself. She later administered arsenic to her aunt and uncle but bungled an attempt in using the poison to kill the rest of her family. Wise claimed the devil had followed her everywhere and forced her to do the killings.

The Comfort Serial Killer

In contrast to the visionary type, the comfort serial killer is motivated to murder for material reasons, not for psychological gain. They tend to be the most prevalent of all female serialists. There are no voices or visions from God or the devil demanding that everyone must die. The offender will usually kill persons with whom she is acquainted. The material gain is typically money or the promise of money such as insurance benefits, acquisition of business interests or real estate.

In 1901, Amy Archer-Gilligan opened a rest home in Connecticut. During the next fourteen years she disposed of at least twenty-seven men and women by poisoning them. Of the men she nursed, she married five, insured each for substantial amounts of money and then poisoned each one. In other instances she killed elderly women after she helped them rewrite their wills. Similarly in Cincinnatti, Anna Hahn, self proclaimed "angel of mercy", provided "constant care" for several elderly men, only to see them each die suddenly.

During the mid 1970s, Janice Gibbs of Georgia, killed her husband, three sons and an infant grandson for $31,000 in insurance money. Mary Eleanor Smith trained her son in the "art of killing" to rob men and then dump the bodies in muriatic acid beneath their home in Montana. Dorethea Puente in Sacramento County, California was charged in 1988 with nine counts of murder after the authorities found bodies in the side yard of her rooming house. She alledgedly killed her roomers for their Social Security checks. Earlier in her criminal career, she had been convicted of forging checks belonging to her tenants. If guilty of the charges brought against her, she will join the ranks of geographically stable, comfort serial killers.

Hedonistic Serial Murder

 Perhaps the least understood and the least represented of all female serial killers is the hedonistic type. Hedonism is the striving for pleasure. In this sense, the hedonistic offender is one which has made a critical connection between fatal violence and personal, sexual gratification. Carol Bundy of California was alledgedly involved not only in the killing of a male victim but several young women who were runaways and prostitutes. She is believed to have helped her male accomplice, Douglas Clark, abduct and decapitate victims and then place the heads in her refrigerator. Later, the heads were retrieved and used in aberrant sex acts (Personal Interview, Douglas Clark). The motivation for the killing appears to be intrinisic to her personality: personal and sexual pleasure. To murder was pleasurable; Bundy did not rob the victims; no money, jewelry or personal articles were taken. The anticipated gain appears to be purely psychological. Bundy continues to maintain her innocence.

Power Seekers

Power is the ability to influence the behavior of others in accordance to one's own desires. Power may also be defined in this context as the ultimate domination of one person by another. For example, Jane Toppan, a nurse,

253   Female Serial Murderesses:
       Constructing Differentiating Typologies

is believed to have killed between seventy and one hundred victims. She proudly exclaimed that she had fooled the authorities,"...the stupid doctors and the ignorant relatives...This is my ambition-to have killed more people- more helpless people-than any man or woman has ever killed" (authors' files). Some killers will repeatedly poison their victims and then nurse them back to health. Finally, the patient is killed and the offender, usually a private nurse, moves on to another victim.

Genene Jones, a pediatric nurse in San Antonio was arrested for the murders of young children admitted to hospitals often for minor medical problems. Thought to be responsible for as many as sixteen deaths of infants (Elkind, 392), Jones felt a sense of importance working in a hospital setting as a primary medical caretaker. Recently, the Munchasen Syndrome by Proxy has been used to explain individuals who fabricate and induce medical problems in children under their care. Some individuals temporarily boost their feelings of low self esteem and worthlessness through involvement in life and death situations, such as those found in an emergency room, operating room or critical care unit. Jones was such a personality. Her behavior is akin "... to the volunteer fireman who sets a blaze, then appears first at the scene in hope of becoming a hero". Offenders usually receive some form of psychological satisfaction such as praise from superiors or gratitude from the patient and family.

Disciple Killer

Finally, some women kill when they are under the influence of a charaismatic leader. One of the most infamous cases involved the female followers of Charles Manson. Lynette Fromme, Leslie Van Hooten, and others willingly butchered victims at Manson's command. The gain is psychological; the personal acceptance of the woman by her "idol." Victim selection is usually decided upon by the male leader and reflects more of the leaders wants than those actually commiting the murders.

In 1982, Judy Neeley and her husband, Alvin, were involved in forgeries, burglaries and robberies. Eventually they began to seek greater thrill by abducting, abusing, raping and murdering their victims. Judy claimed that her husband forced her to commit tortures and murders because she was completely dominated by him. While in Alabama, they abducted a 13 year old girl and held her captive. Judy watched while Alvin repeatedly raped, tortured and abused the child. Finally, Judy injected liquid Drano into the girl's veins, but when that failed to kill, she shot her victim in the back and pushed her over a cliff. They later abducted a married couple, took them into a wooded area and shot them both. The man survived and later testified against the couple. The final number of their victims was never determined.

In another case, Charlene Gallego married her husband, Gerald, not knowing he was still legally married to another woman. She quickly accepted Gerald's lifestyle including his bizarre sexual fantasies. Involved in the killings of at least nine young women and one young man, Charlene eventually was apprehended and testified against her husband. She is presently in a Nevada prison serving two 16 year concurrent sentences.

Martha Beck and her lover Ray Fernandez advertised in lonely hearts magazines for female companionship. The approximately twenty women who answered these ads were strangled, battered, drowned, poisoned or shot to death. To demonstrate her loyalty for her lover, she eagerly drowned a two year old child who had accompanied their latest victim. Still holding the dead girl under water she gleefully exclaimed, "Oh, come and look what I've done, Sweetheart."

Personal relationships appear to facilitate violence in certain cases. Some individuals, in all likelihood, would never kill without the involvement of another person(s). Mutually shared fantasies involving violence and sexual experimentation appear to stimulate some relationships to actualize their fantasies. This observation has been documented among all sexual orientations.

This chemistry was particularly evident in the case of Alton Coleman and Debra Brown. She lived with an abusive and violent Coleman and violence became a part of their relationship. The propensity for violence became an integral part of their killing. On at least one occasion she followed Coleman's lead when she killed an elderly couple in Cincinnati beating them to death using a four foot wood candle stick, a crow bar, vice grip pliers and a knife. She is believed to have killed as many as eight persons in the company of Coleman. Even after the trial and her incarceration on death row, Brown remained loyal to Coleman and signed legal documents to become common law partners.

Conclusion

There are indications of an increasing number of women involved in serial murder. Priscilla Ford, Charlene Gallego, Thelma Barfield and others are examples of an emerging number of women serialists who pose a disturbing danger to our society. Though women represent a small percent of offender cases in serial murder, changing characteristics of the female offender may be impacting their representation. For example, Hickey offers two such changes:

Over the past few years, female offenders killed fewer family members (Comfort) while increasingly targeting strangers... (and) Those who had male partners were much more likely to use violence in killing their victims... (and) (1991; 127).

Although some research suggests many women kill for financial (ma-

255   Female Serial Murderesses:
        Constructing Differentiating Typologies

terial) gain, other more intrinsic and complex explanations need to be explored which address sociopathy and psychopathology. These differences, combined with public perception, have resulted in most of the research and literature being devoted to the male serialist.

About the Authors

Stephen T. Holmes is a Doctoral student in Criminal Justice at the University of Cincinnati. Mr. Holmes has been published in The Contemporary Journal of Criminal Justice, Knightbeat, and other professional and academic journals.

Dr. Eric Hickey is an associate professor at the University of California, Fresno. Dr. Hickey has recently authored Serial Killers and Their Victims, published by Brooks\Cole Publishing Co. Dr. Hickey has a national reputation in serial murder and has been published in the American Journal of Criminal Justice, The Journal of Contemporary Criminal Justice and other scholarly journals.

Ronald M. Holmes, Professor, University of Louisville. BA, Bellarmine College M.A.; University of Louisville; Ed.D. Indiana University. Probation Officer, State of Kentucky, Parole Office, Jefferson County, Kentucky. Author, Sex Crimes 1991, Profiling Violent Crimes 1990, Serial Murder 1988, as well as in Federal Probation, Police Chief, American Journal of Criminal Justice, and other professional and academic journals.

Bibliography

Bernick, B. and Spangler, J. 1985. Rovers kill up to 5,000 each year, experts say. Deseret News. September, Las Vegas.

Blackburn, D. 1990. Human harvest: The Sacramento murder story. New York: Knightsbridge Publishing Co.

Eckert, A. 1985. The Scarlet Mansion. New York: Bantam Books.

Elkin, P. 1989. The Death Shift. News York: Onyx Books.

Hickey, E. 1991. Serial killers and Their Victims. Pacific Groves, CA: Brooks/Cole Publishing Co.

Holmes, R. and DeBurger, J. 1985. Profiles in Terror: The Serial Murderer. Federal Probation. September. 29-34.

Holmes, R. and DeBurger, J. 1988. Serial Murder. Newbury Park, CA: Sage Publications.

Holmes, R., DeBurger, J. and Holmes, S. 1990. Inside the Mind of the Serial Murderer. American Journal of Criminal Justice. Vol. 13. No. 1. Fall. 1-9.

Levin, J. and Fox, J. 1985. Mass Murder: America's Growing Menace. New York: Plenum Press.

_____ Report to the Nation on Crime and Justice. 2nd Ed., Washing-
    ton, DC: Bureau of Justice Statistics
Ressler, R., Burgess, A. and Douglas, J. 1988. Sexual Homicides: Patterns
    and Motives. Lexington, MA: Lexington Books.
Reynolds, B. This is the beginning of the end for murderer. USA Today.
    August 30.
Schreiber, F. 1984. The Shoemaker: The Anatomy of a Psychotic. New
    York: Signet Books.
van Hoffman, E. 1990. A Venom in the Blood. New York: Donald I. Fine,
    Inc.

[25]

The purpose of this study was to investigate and describe the demographic, behavioral, and background characteristics of female serial murderers. A series of postulates about male serial murderers were developed after an extensive literature review. Data were collected from both primary and secondary sources on 14 female serial murderers in the United States. A preliminary profile of female serial murderers was then compared to the current knowledge of male serial murderers. Overall, there were generally more differences than similarities between male and female serial murderers. Results suggested differences in nine areas: victim damage, victim torture, weapon/method, stalking versus luring behaviors, crime scene organization, reasons for the murders, substance abuse history, psychiatric diagnosis, and household composition. Similarities appeared in five areas: broken homes, childhood abuse, race, educational level, and occupation.

Gender Differences in
Serial Murderers

A Preliminary Analysis

BELEA T. KEENEY
KATHLEEN M. HEIDE
University of South Florida

During the past two decades, serial murder has received increased attention from both law enforcement and the popular media. Recent research has suggested that female involvement in serial homicide was approximately the same as their representation in other types of murder in the United States (Hickey, 1991). This finding contradicted theorists who stated that serial murder was an almost exclusively male behavior (Egger, 1990; Leyton, 1986).

Research on this topic has been limited due to the rare occurrence of this phenomenon and the difficulty in obtaining access to these offenders. To date, no traditional, academic, empirical research has been attempted. This article reviews the participation of women in serial murder. After discussion of definitions of serial murder and female involvement in other types of murder, current knowledge of the phenomenon is examined. Analysis then focuses

Authors' Note: The authors acknowledge Christine Seller and James B. Halsted for their contributions to this study.

JOURNAL OF INTERPERSONAL VIOLENCE, Vol. 9 No. 3, September 1994 383-398
© 1994 Sage Publications, Inc.

384   JOURNAL OF INTERPERSONAL VIOLENCE / September 1994

on female serial murderers, and the variables that appear to affect their behavior are discussed.

Definitions of serial murder reported in the literature have lacked uniformity. In this study, serial murder is defined as "the premeditated murder of three or more victims committed over time, in separate incidents, in a civilian context, with the murder activity being chosen by the offender" (Keeney, 1992, p. 7). This definition excludes killing performed by military personnel as part of their job duties and assassinations by political terrorist groups. It does include health care workers who murder their patients, parents who murder their children, professional assassins who operate under the confines of organized crime syndicates, and persons who kill multiple spouses/lovers. The number of murder victims used in this definition coincided with the Federal Bureau of Investigation (FBI) designation.

FEMALE INVOLVEMENT IN MURDER

The United States has seen a fairly consistent rise in the reported murder rate during the past 26 years, from 5.1% in 1965 to 9.8% in 1991. However, perusal of FBI statistics showed that the proportion of total homicide arrests involving females has actually decreased from 17.6% in 1965 to 10.3% in 1991 (FBI, 1965-1991). Notwithstanding the proportionate decrease in female involvement in homicide, the actual number of women arrested for homicide showed a generally increasing trend, particularly for 1965 through 1983. During more recent years, the numbers of women arrested for homicide have tended to decrease. Interestingly, however, the number of women arrested for homicide in 1991 was still 36% greater than the number arrested in 1965.

FINDINGS ON MURDERERS

Two of the early historical studies on murder focused almost exclusively on male offenders (Guttmacher, 1960; Wolfgang, 1958). Subsequent studies of women who had been charged with and/or convicted of murders began to emerge during the late 1960s (Biggers, 1979; Blum & Fisher, 1978; Cole, Fisher, & Cole, 1968; Crump, 1986; Goetting, 1988; Ketner & Humphrey, 1980; McClain, 1981; Suval & Brisson, 1974; Weisheit, 1984; Wilbanks, 1980). Female murderers have shown more of a tendency to kill family members than have males (Biggers, 1979; Cole et al., 1968; Goetting, 1988;

McClain, 1981; Weisheit, 1984), to be somewhat older than men who murder (Biggers, 1979; Blum & Fisher, 1978; Suval & Brisson, 1974), and to have killed their victims in the home (Blum & Fisher, 1978; Goetting, 1988). They also have used guns and knives as their most common weapons of choice (Blum & Fisher, 1978; Cole et al., 1968; Goetting, 1988; McClain, 1981; Weisheit, 1984; Wilbanks, 1980). Female homicide offenders have tended to be from the lower socioeconomic classes, with an attendant lack of education and employment skills (Ketner & Humphrey, 1980; McClain, 1981; Suval & Brisson, 1974).

In contrast to the pattern of female murderers, the profile of males who murder has been studied more extensively. Early research (Guttmacher, 1960; Wolfgang & Ferracuti, 1967) concluded that they were typically young black males who killed in response to an argument or physical provocation. Males have tended to murder outside the home—in bars or streets—and to use guns and knives most commonly as weapons. Like the victims of women who kill, the victims of male murderers have usually been family members, friends, or acquaintances (Lester, 1991).

FINDINGS ON SERIAL MURDER

Of the 11 in-depth studies on serial murder reviewed for this research, only two acknowledged the role of women in this type of murder (Hickey, 1991; Holmes & DeBurger, 1988). From these studies, a series of findings per male serial murderers was generated pertaining to murder and postmurder behavior, social and psychological history, and demographics.

Murder and Postmurder Behavior

Male serial murderers have tended to inflict a great deal of victim damage in addition to causing death (Hickey, 1991; Leyton, 1986; Norris, 1988; Ressler, 1985) and to engage in the torture of their victims prior to death (Hickey, 1991; Levin & Fox, 1985; Norris, 1988; Ressler, 1985; Sears, 1991). Male serial murderers have also shown a tendency to use a "hands-on" approach in killing by using knives, blunt objects, and hands to kill their victims. The process of murdering and the power/domination effect have been cited as part of their motivation (Egger, 1985; Hickey, 1991; Holmes & DeBurger, 1988; Ressler, 1985; Rule, 1980).

Male serial murderers have shown a tendency toward "stalking" behaviors such as actively patroling for victims, aggressively pursuing victims, and/or

386   JOURNAL OF INTERPERSONAL VIOLENCE / September 1994

using physical force to procure victims (Hickey, 1991; Norris, 1988; Ressler, Burgess, & Douglas, 1988; Rule, 1980). They also have tended to commit either organized or disorganized types of murders when crime scenes have been compared (Ressler, 1985).

Male serial murderers have often attended their victims' funerals as a method of reliving the murder and as material for future fantasy experiences. They typically returned to their victims' graves, whether official or unofficial (Ressler et al., 1988). Male serial murderers have generally had affective goals, that is, murders committed for emotional or psychological reasons versus instrumental goals for practical reasons (Egger, 1990; Heide, 1986; Hickey, 1991; Holmes & DeBurger, 1988; Levin & Fox, 1985; Leyton, 1986; Linedecker, 1990; Norris, 1988; Ressler, 1992; Ritter, 1988; Rule, 1980).

Social and Psychological History

Several studies showed similar findings in the backgrounds of serial murderers. Male serial murderers have tended to be "first-born" children in their families of origin or the oldest children in their family units (Levin & Fox, 1985; Ressler et al., 1988). They have also tended to be raised in broken homes such as those of divorced parents, widows/widowers, single parents, or adopted families (Hickey, 1991; Leyton, 1986; Norris, 1988; Ressler, 1992).

Male serial murderers have often been victims of childhood abuse and/or neglect in their families of origin (Hickey, 1991; Holmes & DeBurger, 1988; Leyton, 1986; Norris, 1988; Ressler, 1992). Their parents have frequently been alcohol dependent or drug dependent (Heide, 1986; Norris, 1988; Ressler, 1992).

There has been no clear pattern in whether male serial murderers have had substance abuse problems themselves (Hickey, 1991; Norris, 1988). Available data have indicated that some serial murderers had symptoms of the "MacDonald Triad" (bed-wetting, fire-setting, and cruelty to animals) during childhood (Holmes & DeBurger, 1988; Levin & Fox, 1985; Norris, 1988) and some sustained head injuries (Norris, 1988; Sears, 1991).

No clear pattern is discernible regarding male serial murderers' encounters with law enforcement agencies as juveniles (Hickey, 1991; Leyton, 1986). Some research has reported that they have been institutionalized at some point in their lives (juvenile incarceration, foster homes, adult incarceration, etc.) prior to their arrests for murder (Leyton, 1986). Male serial murderers have tended to be psychiatrically diagnosed as antisocial personalities more often than schizophrenic or psychotic (Hickey, 1991; Holmes & DeBurger, 1988; Levin & Fox, 1985; Norris, 1988; Ressler, 1985).

Demographic Information

Male serial murderers have tended to be White (Hickey, 1991; Ressler, 1985; Rule, 1980) and to have had low to average levels of education, with a mean of a 10th-grade level (Hickey, 1991; Ressler et al., 1988). Their household composition (single, married, living alone, or other) at the time of the murders has been varied (Hickey, 1991). If working, male serial murderers have shown a tendency to be employed in low-level/blue-collar types of occupations (Hickey, 1991; Leyton, 1986; Ressler, 1985).

METHODOLOGY

The present study was designed to determine to what extent female serial murderers fit the current profile of male serial murderers. A series of both general and specific findings about the behavior, background, and demographic characteristics of male serial murderers based on the literature reviewed were generated and investigated with respect to female serial murderers. Previous research had not focused systematically on most of these variables and had been largely limited to profiles of male serial murderers.

Subjects

A total of 14 female serial murderers who acted alone were identified and selected through the use of several sources. First, newspaper indexes were examined to find women who were charged with multiple murders committed over time or charged with a single murder and strongly suspected by law enforcement of other murders. These indexes included the *New York Times* (1972-1992), *Los Angeles Times* (1972-1992), *Chicago Sun-Times* (1980-1992), *Atlanta Journal and Constitution* (1983-1989), and *St. Petersburg Times* (1975-1986). After perusal of the various indexes for identification purposes, the actual articles on microfilm were analyzed and used to gather information. Second, female serial murderers were identified by books, biographies, periodicals, and abstracts on murder.[1] Cases that occurred during the past 20 years were selected for examination because more recent cases tended to have more accurate information.

388   JOURNAL OF INTERPERSONAL VIOLENCE / September 1994

Data Collection Instrument

A 12-page instrument contained questions regarding basic demographic information and questions that were shaped from findings pertaining to male serial murderers. It provided a systematic framework with which to gather information from both primary and secondary sources. Of the 22 variables initially targeted for investigation, 14 had sufficient data for analysis. In some cases, due to the nature of the secondary data sources, information that had been available for male serial murderers was not available for their female counterparts. The variables omitted were funeral attendance, gravesite visits, birth order, chemical dependency of parents, MacDonald Triad, head injuries, juvenile encounters with law enforcement, and institutionalization.

Data Analysis Plan

Primary sources were used when possible. These included original documents (court transcripts, presentence investigation reports, psychological evaluations, correctional files) related to the cases. Secondary sources (mass media accounts, newspaper reports, biographies, electronic media reports) were also analyzed.

This study was exploratory and descriptive in nature. Given the lack of empirical data on female serial murderers, prediction of differences between male and female serial murderers at this stage seemed premature. Sources were examined to determine whether there was evidence or suggestion that might indicate the existence of the variables under study. Lack of reporting about a phenomenon was not treated as proof of its lack of existence. Because this research was conceived as a pilot study with a limited number of subjects, traditional statistical analysis was not appropriate. Statements were used as guidelines, rather than as hypotheses, to examine data available on female serial murderers.

FINDINGS

Results were based on the extent to which information was found. Due to the small number of subjects ($N = 14$), only raw numbers were reported. In samples of less than 50, percentages tend to be unstable and misleading. Variables for which data were available in at least 65% of the cases ($N = 9$) were included in this study with two exceptions. Because child abuse and chemical dependency were deemed such important variables, they were included in this analysis even though data were available in only 8 of the 14 cases.

Characteristics of the Sample

The mean age at arrest for this sample was 37.9 years, with a range of 40 years (19-59). The average age that the women began their murders was 32.9 years, with a range of 35 years (18-53). The 14 women were convicted of killing 27 victims; law enforcement agencies estimated that the women killed more than 88 people. None was charged with all of the murders for which she was allegedly responsible.

Of the 14 women, 13 were place-specific killers; that is, they operated in one small area such as a city, often in a hospital or their own homes. The remaining woman was a regional killer who operated in one state. Geographically, the state represented most often was Florida with four offenders; North Carolina and California each had two; Wisconsin, New York, Michigan, Texas, Georgia, and Alabama each had one offender in this sample. Nine offenders in the sample were from Southern states—the only pattern of regionality that was evident in this study.

The victim sample was taken only from confirmed victims, not those who were alleged or speculated. With regard to relationship to their victims ($N = 62$), victims who were in the custodial care of their murderers (patients, children with babysitters) were the largest category, comprising 43% of the sample. Family members (children, husbands, in-laws, fathers) were the second largest category with 37%. The remaining 20% consisted of strangers, acquaintances, and nonspousal lovers.

Murder and Postmurder Behaviors

Victim damage. Victim damage was measured by mutilation, dismemberment, and other evidence of "overkill" over and above what was required to cause death. Among the 62 victims, no sexual assault, mutilation, or dismemberment was evident.

Victim torture. Victim torture was measured by victim burns, evidence of multiple revivals and loss of consciousness, multiple stab wounds, and dismemberment while the victim was alive. Female serial murderers in this sample did not engage in torture of their victims prior to death. (It could be argued that a slow death by poison, spread over weeks and months, could be considered a form of torture.) There was no indication that females used their victims' suffering as a form of sexual release in the manner that some male serial murderers have done.

390   JOURNAL OF INTERPERSONAL VIOLENCE / September 1994

Weapon choice/method. The majority of female serial murderers used some form of poison to kill their victims. Overdoses of potassium, insulin, and prescribed medications, as well as arsenic and poison derivatives, were considered poisons for the purpose of this study. In the victim sample ($N =$ 62), 57% were killed with poison, 29% were smothered, 11% were killed by firearm, and 3% were killed by other methods (e.g., one instance of a victim deliberately being placed on his back under a medical condition that made this fatal, and one instance of drowning). There was little variation in these murderers' methods; only two of the women used more than one weapon choice/method to kill their multiple victims.

Stalking versus luring behaviors. None of the female serial murderers engaged in traditional stalking behaviors such as following the victim for a period of time, watching the victim from a distance, or engaging in Peeping Tom type of activities. Five murderers in this sample were aggressive in procuring victims in that they actively sought out boarding home tenants, insured and killed multiple lovers/husbands, or solicited prostitution clients apparently for the primary purpose of robbery.

Crime scene organization. The 14 female serial murderers left crime scenes that showed characteristics of both organized and disorganized offenders. According to FBI profilers, a planned offense, the personalization of the victim, the use of restraints, and the weapon/evidence absent from the scene are associated with organized offenders. Conversely, a spontaneous offense, a known victim and location, sudden violence, and the bodies left in view and at the death scene are associated with disorganized offenders. There was no definite demarcation in the female serial murderers in this study. Each offender's crime scene showed characteristics of both types of offenders. The typical crime scene involved a known victim who was helpless or powerless, and the weapon/cause of death was not immediately obvious. In addition, the typical crime scene involved a victim who was intimately known by the killer, with the body left in view and at the scene of death. Only one offender actually moved her victims from the death site and buried them.

Reasons for the murders. The sample was evenly divided between offenders who appeared to have had instrumental goals and those who appeared to have had affective goals. Seven apparently had instrumental goals, such as insurance benefits or other monetary gain upon the death of their victims. The other seven appeared to have had affective goals, that is, there was no apparent benefit except an emotional one upon the deaths of their victims.

One woman was reported to have experienced some tension release as a result of her murders.

Social and Psychological History

Broken homes. Of the 10 women for whom data were available, 4 were adopted by nonrelatives, 4 were raised in nontraditional homes composed of various relatives and nonrelatives, and 2 were raised in traditional homes with both biological parents until age 18. Nearly half ($n = 6$) were raised with siblings, ranging in number from one to six brothers and sisters.

Childhood abuse. Of the eight women for whom data were available, five reported overt sexual abuse such as being fondled, molested, or raped. Five reported physical abuse such as being beaten, slapped, or hit with objects. Four reported sexual assault/rape before age 18. Three reported physical neglect. Two reported exposure to violence/cruelty such as spouse abuse. Emotional neglect was reported by two women, and one was a victim of medical neglect. (Totals do not equal 14 due to the nonexclusiveness of categories.)

Chemical abuse history. Of the eight women for whom data were available, four showed social illegal drug use such as marijuana or cocaine. Three were social drinkers and three were alcoholics. The one subject who was chemically addicted or dependent on prescription drugs allegedly committed her murders under the influence. Two of the eight had sought treatment for alcohol or drug dependency. One was a teetotaler. (Totals do not equal 14 due to the nonexclusiveness of categories.)

Psychiatric diagnosis. Of the nine women for whom data were available, six were diagnosed with an "other pathology" after their arrests. The other pathologies category included histrionic, manic-depressive, borderline, and dissociative disorders. Three were diagnosed as antisocial personalities, and one was diagnosed as schizophrenic. One woman unsuccessfully used the insanity plea. One was adjudicated guilty but mentally ill.

Demographic Information

Race. Of the 11 women for whom data were available, all were White.

392   JOURNAL OF INTERPERSONAL VIOLENCE / September 1994

Educational level. Of the 10 women for whom data were available, 5 graduated from high school, 4 dropped out of high school with a mean educational level of 9.5 years, and 1 had received a GED. Four women had education beyond high school, typically a 1- or 2-year nursing degree. One woman had a high performance level in school with awards and scholarship, whereas two women had a poor performance level with a history of learning difficulties and truancy. (Totals do not equal 14 due to the nonexclusiveness of categories.)

Household composition. Of the 14 women in the sample for whom data were available, 13 were living with others at the time of the murders.

Occupation. Among the sample subjects, 11 were employed in one capacity or another at the time of the murders. Five were employed in traditional "pink-collar"-type jobs, including licensed practical nurses, housekeepers, or store clerks. Three were self-employed as a babysitter, prostitute, or shopkeeper. Four showed a history of menial employment, and four reported an unstable work history with periods of significant unemployment. Three had a stable work history with nearly continual employment throughout most of their adult lives (two of these were nurses and one was a secretary). One was a former blue-collar worker who had previously worked at a factory.

DISCUSSION

The findings suggested that there may be more differences than similarities between female serial murderers and their male counterparts. Of the 14 variables for which data were available and could be analyzed, 9 differences were found between female and male serial murderers with respect to behavior patterns, psychosocial history, and demographics. Differences between male and female serial murderers were evident in victim damage, victim torture, weapon/method, stalking versus luring behaviors, crime scene organization, reasons for the murders, substance abuse history, psychiatric diagnosis, and household composition. Similarities between the two groups were found with respect to broken homes, childhood abuse, race, education level, and occupation.

One major strength of this study was the focus on variables previously reported on male serial murderers. Hickey (1991) completed a thorough analysis of basic demographic information and victim findings for female serial murderers but without comparison to the variables found important by the FBI. In relation to previous research, the differences found between males and females in the present study regarding victim torture, victim damage, crime scene organization, weapon/method, and victim procurement were particularly significant. The similarities found, especially those of childhood abuse and broken homes, implied some background commonalities among serial murderers. In addition, the findings suggested new areas of exploration with regard to female serial murderers.

Of the variables that were eliminated due to lack of information, funeral attendance and gravesite visits are among those that warrant further attention. Because a large proportion of female serial murderers' victims were family members, it could be postulated that these two postmurder behaviors were actually quite high. (However, the meaning of this behavior in females is likely to be different from what it has been in males.) Additionally, the extent of juvenile encounters with law enforcement and institutionalization prior to the arrest for murder should also be reexamined. It was disappointing that the MacDonald Triad and head injuries were two variables that had to be omitted. Interviews of offenders and examination of medical and social service agency records would be a useful tool in uncovering the prevalence of these two variables among female serial murderers. The use of primary data, especially Department of Corrections files, would also be helpful.

The findings of this study were for the most part consistent with previous research regarding female serial murderers (Hickey, 1991; Holmes, 1994). Differences between the two groups in crime scene organization, psychiatric diagnosis, geographic distribution, body disposal, and mobility were substantive and merit further discussion.

The crime scenes of the women in this sample showed characteristics of both organized and disorganized murderers. Although the FBI does concede that some male serial murderers appear to be "mixed"-type offenders (Ressler, 1985; 1992), the use of such a category would not necessarily be useful to law enforcement investigations. A new set of criteria for female and custodial serial murderers seems to be in order.

One unusual finding of this study was the geographic distribution of these murderers. More than half of the women in this sample committed their crimes and were arrested in Southern states. In examining male serial murderers, Hickey (1991) found that the Pacific Northwest was the area in which most incarcerated male serial murderers had killed their victims. FBI statistics have shown that the murder rate has consistently been higher in the South than it has in other areas of the United States (FBI, 1965-1991).

Another fascinating finding was the almost complete lack of mobility of these offenders. Only Aileen Wuornos, a Florida prostitute, traveled at all during the commission of her murders; the rest of the sample remained in one place. Accordingly, "linkage blindness" (Egger, 1985, 1990) may not be a

394   JOURNAL OF INTERPERSONAL VIOLENCE / September 1994

problem in tracking these offenders. Rather, the problem appears to result from the failure of law enforcement and other professionals to recognize that a homicide has been committed and to respond appropriately. For female serial murderers who have killed their patients, for example, health care facilities appear to have been extremely reluctant to bring charges against an employee with the resultant possibility of a trial and media attention. One case in this sample was indicative of this type of administrative bungle. Genene Jones, a Texas nurse, was continually employed in a hospital long after numerous complaints and charges that she was injuring the children in her ward. In addition, family and friends may be unwilling to confront female killers with their suspicions regarding their behavior. The husband of Marybeth Tinning, the New York woman who murdered eight of her children, apparently did nothing to stop her behavior, suggest that she get therapy, or take steps to prevent further births.

The prevalence of childhood abuse has been well documented in many types of criminal offenders but specifically with murderers (Heide, 1992; Hickey, 1991; Holmes & DeBurger, 1988; Ressler et al., 1988). Various forms of abuse were reported by this sample. Abuse has different effects on different people. Experts agree that it often promotes future violence, breaks the human bond needed to empathize with others, and fosters angry, inadequate human beings (Magid & McKelvey, 1987). Research should focus on which types of abuse may have been experienced by these offenders.

Suggestions for Future Research

There were two major limitations of this study. First, the use of secondary data sources was, by its very nature, biased and incomplete. In addition, the accuracy of some data (e.g., the psychiatric diagnoses given) is of unknown reliability. Accordingly, the exclusive reliance on such sources cannot be recommended. As a preliminary study, however, this research can be used as a foundation for future work and exploration. Second, the lack of information about some variables was disappointing though expected, given the inherent limitation of secondary data sources. Future research should include more primary data sources, especially interviews with these offenders. Interviews with these offenders would provide a wider database, generate additional questions, and lead to new areas of concern.

Three areas warrant further investigation: the parenting received by these murderers, health care workers who murder their patients, and the fantasy life of female serial murderers. Two women in this sample were born to teenage mothers. Christine Falling, a Florida babysitter who killed several of her charges, was born to a 17-year-old girl. Wuornos's mother was 16 years old when she was born. The inherent disadvantage to children born of teenage mothers (lack of attachment, low birth weight, cycle of poverty) puts them at risk for future behavioral and criminal problems (Magid & McKelvey, 1987; Schorr, 1988). The patterns of parenting associated with serial murders may provide us with some answers for their behavior.

An additional question arises about health care workers who murder their patients. Several male nurses and nurses' aides have been convicted of killing their patients. An analysis of their backgrounds, crimes, and history might lend itself to a profile of male caregivers who murder. Further research into nurses who murder might uncover gender differences in that population group. For example, co-workers of nurse Brian Rosenfield of St. Petersburg, Florida, implied he may have experienced some sadistic satisfaction from torturing the patients he killed. By contrast, none of the female nurses in this sample was implicated in sadism.

Ressler (1985, 1992) emphasized the importance of a violent, sadistic fantasy life in his sample of male serial murderers. Perhaps females also have an active fantasy life, although it may be oriented in other directions. Genene Jones was said to have had grand ambitions about being a "super nurse." She administered select drugs to children that induced seizures and then attempted to save them by using the antidotal drugs that she knew would have a counteracting effect on the patients. These dynamics appear to be similar to those of the Munchausen syndrome by proxy (Manthei, 1988; Rosenberg, 1987).

Although serial murder is a statistically rare phenomenon, these findings and previous research indicate that it affects all age and demographic groups. Some female offenders have preyed solely on children whereas others have victimized middle-aged persons, the infirm, and the elderly in health care facilities. As our population ages and our family structure continues to change, families are experiencing more stressors that may cause them to harm their children, whether intentionally or not. Careful parenting may prove to be the most important factor in the prevention of future violent behavior.

Preliminary findings from this study suggest that important differences may exist between male and female serial murderers. Further research is needed to develop a reliable profile of female serial murderers. Perhaps factors could be found that might indicate to parents, educators, and others that some girls are at a higher risk than others of acting destructively.

In addition, research needs to proceed with respect to discovering the motivational dynamics that undergird serial murder. Although there may be genuine differences between male and female serial murderers, there may be

396   JOURNAL OF INTERPERSONAL VIOLENCE / September 1994

motivations to destroy other human beings that transcend gender. Fromm's theory of character holds promise in this regard. In *The Anatomy of Human Destructiveness*, Fromm (1973) distinguished between benign aggression and malignant aggression. Benign aggression is defensive in nature and is designed to promote life and preserve vital interests. Malignant aggression, by contrast, is destructive and unique to human beings. Men and women have existential needs such as needs for a frame of orientation and an object of devotion, for rootedness, for unity, and for a sense of effectiveness. Those who lack a sense of belonging and peace and who cannot achieve fulfillment in constructive ways (education, work, family, money) can affect society through acts of destructiveness. The serial murderers examined in this and previous research appear to be unhappy, unsuccessful individuals who choose to make their mark on society through violent means. Uncovering the neurophysiological, social, and psychological conditions that lead certain individuals to chart a destructive course appears essential if efforts at prevention are to be entertained seriously.

NOTE

1. For a complete listing of references used in this study, contact Belea T. Keeney, c/o Criminology Department, University of South Florida, 4202 E. Fowler Ave., SOC 107, Tampa, FL 33620-8100.

REFERENCES

Biggers, T. A. (1979). Death by murder: A study of women murderers. *Death Education, 3,* 1-9.

Blum, A., & Fisher, G. (1978). Women who kill. In I. L. Kutash, S. B. Kutash, & L. B. Schlesinger (Eds.), *Violence: Perspectives on murder and aggression* (pp. 187-197). San Francisco: Jossey-Bass.

Cole, K., Fisher, G., & Cole, S. (1968). Women who kill: A sociopsychological study. *Archives of General Psychiatry, 19,* 1-8.

Crump, A. (1986). Women and crime: A contemporary controversy. *International Journal of Offender Therapy and Comparative Criminology, 30,* 31-39.

Egger, S. (1985). Serial murder and the law enforcement response. *Dissertation Abstracts International, 47,* 1069A.

Egger, S. (1990). *Serial murder: An elusive phenomenon.* New York: Praeger.

Federal Bureau of Investigation. (1965-1991). Crime in the United States. In *Uniform Crime Reports.* Washington, DC: U.S. Department of Justice.

Fromm, E. (1973). *The anatomy of human destructiveness.* New York: Holt, Rinehart & Winston.

Goetting, A. (1988). Patterns of homicide among women. *Journal of Interpersonal Violence, 3,* 3-19.

Guttmacher, M. (1960). *The mind of the murderer.* New York: Grove Press.

Heide, K. M. (1986, May). Testimony during trial of serial murderer Bobby Joe Long. *State of Florida v. Robert J. Long.*

Heide, K. M. (1992). *Why kids kill parents.* Columbus: Ohio State University Press.

Hickey, E. (1991). *Serial murderers and their victims.* Belmont, CA: Wadsworth.

Holmes, R. (1994). *Murder in America.* Newbury Park, CA: Sage.

Holmes, R., & DeBurger, J. (1988). *Serial murder.* Newbury Park, CA: Sage.

Keeney, B. (1992). *Gender differences in serial murderers.* Unpublished masters thesis, University of South Florida, Tampa.

Ketner, L., & Humphrey, J. (1980). Homicide, sex role differences and role relationships. *Journal of Death and Dying, 20,* 379-386.

Lester, D. (1991). *Questions and answers about murder.* Philadelphia: Charles Press.

Levin, J., & Fox, J. (1985). *Mass murder: America's growing menace.* New York: Plenum.

Leyton, E. (1986). Compulsive killers: *The story of modern multiple murder.* New York: New York University Press.

Linedecker, C. (1990). *Serial thrill killers.* New York: Knightsbridge.

MacDonald, J. (1963). The threat to kill. *American Journal of Psychiatry, 120,* 125-130.

Magid, K., & McKelvey, C. (1987). *High risk.* Delta, CO: M & M.

Manthei, D. (1988). Munchausen syndrome by proxy: Covert child abuse. *Journal of Family Violence. 3,* 131-140.

McClain, P. (1981). Social and environmental characteristics of Black female homicide offenders. *Western Journal of Black Studies, 5,* 224-230.

Norris, J. (1988). *Serial killers: The growing menace.* New York: Doubleday.

Ressler, R. (1985). Crime scene and profile characteristics of organized and disorganized murders. *FBI Law Enforcement Bulletin, 54,* 18-25.

Ressler, R. (1992). *Whoever fights monsters.* New York: St. Martin's.

Ressler, R., Burgess, A., & Douglas, J. (1988). *Sexual homicide.* Lexington, MA: Lexington Books.

Ritter, B. (1988). Multiple murderers: The characteristics of the persons and the nature of their crimes. *Dissertation Abstracts International, 49,* 1971A.

Rosenberg, D. (1987). Web of deceit: A literature review of Munchausen syndrome by proxy. *Child Abuse & Neglect, 11,* 547-563.

Rule, A. (1980). *The stranger beside me.* New York: Norton.

Schorr, L. (1988). *Within our reach.* New York: Anchor Books.

Sears, D. (1991). *To kill again.* Wilmington, DE: Scholarly Resources.

Suval, E., & Brisson, R. (1974). Neither beauty nor beast: Female criminal homicide offenders. *Interpersonal Journal of Crime and Penology, 2,* 23-34.

Weisheit, R. (1984). Female homicide offenders: Trends over time in an institutionalized population. *Justice Quarterly, 1,* 471-489.

Wilbanks, W. (1980). Female homicide offenders in the U.S. *International Journal of Women's Studies, 6,* 302-310.

Wolfgang, M. E. (1958). *Patterns of criminal homicide.* Philadelphia: University of Pennsylvania Press.

Wolfgang, M. E., & Ferracuti, F. (1967). *The subculture of violence.* Beverly Hills, CA: Sage.

Belea T. Keeney received her bachelor's degree in interdisciplinary social science in 1990 and her masters degree in criminology in 1992 from the University of South Florida, Tampa. She has consulted with several Central Florida law enforcement agencies on

398   JOURNAL OF INTERPERSONAL VIOLENCE / September 1994

research projects concerning a variety of topics and is currently at work on a survey with the Hillsborough County sheriff's office. Her areas of interest include female criminality, serial murder, and the use of animal therapy in correctional settings.

Kathleen M. Heide is a professor of criminology at the University of South Florida, Tampa. She received her B.A. in psychology from Vassar College and her M.A. and Ph.D. in criminal justice from the State University of New York at Albany. She is an internationally recognized consultant on homicide and family violence and is the author of Why Kids Kill Parents: Child Abuse and Adolescent Homicide (Ohio State University Press, 1992). She is a licensed psychotherapist and a court-appointed expert in matters relating to homicide, sexual battery, and juveniles.

[26]

The Sexual Component of Serial Murder

Candice Skrapec

Eight-year-old Rose Ohliger was strangled before she was stabbed. Forensic reconstruction of the crime indicated that the murderer had stabbed the child in the chest while she was unconscious on the ground; there were no defence wounds on the hands. The close grouping of 13 knife blows to the left breast appear to have been delivered in rapid succession. There was evidence of trauma near the vaginal entry; the hymen was torn about one centimetre; traces of sperm were detected inside her underpants although they had not been removed. Ejaculation could not have occurred into the vagina. What appeared to have happened instead was that the perpetrator inserted a finger smeared with semen into the vagina; pelvic bruising suggested this was done with force. The clothing of the Ohliger child had been soaked in petroleum and set afire; that they were only charred owes largely to the damp chill of that February day in 1929. Six days earlier, a woman had been attacked from behind and stabbed 24 times; 18 of the wounds were directed to the head with those to her temple being particularly severe. The victim, who survived, reported that her attacker had dealt the stab wounds in quick succession. Both victims appeared to have been stabbed with a long, narrow-bladed knife, indicating a common assailant. Five days later, the body of a 45-year-old retired mechanic, Rudolf Scheer, was discovered in the same neighbourhood on the edge of Düsseldorf. He was last seen leaving a local pub in a drunken state late the previous night. It appeared he was approached from behind — again, there were no defence wounds — before being stabbed some 20 times. An autopsy revealed that a gash to his brain through the left temple, one in the neck and another in the back resulting in a pneumothorax caused his death. As with the earlier victims, no robbery took place. The choice of victim in Rose Ohliger and Frau Kühn, and the manner in which they were attacked, suggested that an "ordinary" kind of sex pervert was at work. This supposition of motive was dispelled, however, by the third victim. What the police knew was that there were three attacks, all taking place within ten days, at dusk, in isolated regions of the Flingern suburb. Each victim was stabbed in a manner that suggested rapid knife thrusts. One of the wounds was always in the temple. What was absent from the three crime scenes was apparent evidence of a common motive.

Two months later, a noose was thrown over the head of a 16-year-old girl from behind; the assailant attempted strangulation. Erna Penning's fierce resistance seemed to have caused the perpetrator to release her from the rope and flee. This occurred in the same neighbourhood as the earlier attacks. The following day a woman was also lassoed from behind, thrown to the ground and dragged a few yards whereupon she was suddenly released. Passersby, their curiosity aroused by the commotion, had begun making their way to it. Their description of the young man they saw running away led to the apprehension of a man who confessed to both murders as well as the three attempts. For police, his detailed accounts of the two most recent attacks left no doubt of his involvement in those crimes. By convincing police of his homicidal propensity in this way, the suspect's confession to the three earlier crimes was regarded as credible. The allegedly feeble-minded, illiterate, epileptic and homeless Strausberg was convicted. Considered a dangerous idiot, he was to be confined to a mental asylum for life.

But the attacks resumed. In late July a 35-year-old woman was strangled to death in a house of ill repute. A small amount of cash was apparently stolen. No public alarm sounded, however, as no knife was used and she was, *after all*, a prostitute.[1] On the night of August 21. three people were attacked within one hour while walking home. One woman sustained relatively minor stab wounds to her back; another suffered serious abdominal injury as the result of a violent thrust of a knife or knife-like implement. Then, in the same area, a man was stabbed in the back as, possibly in a drunken state, he tried to make his way up an embankment. The weapon, although seeming to be the same in these three cases, was different from the one used on Ohliger and Kuhn. Police suspected that a "Ripper" copycat may be at work. Three days later, the bodies of two adoptive sisters, one five the other 14 years of age, were found. Both had been strangled and then their throats cut with a Solingen dagger. The older child had also been stabbed in the back. There was no indication of sexual assault.[2] Less than 24 hours later, in a nearby village, a 26-year-old domestic servant was approached by a man who offered to escort her. After strolling through the marketplace she accompanied him to an isolated outskirt. When she refused and resisted his rough sexual advances he knifed her in the throat, head, shoulder, right side and right arm. A final thrust of the knife into her lower back was so violent that the end of it broke and lodged between two vertebrae. The attacker then desisted from further assault and made off with the victim's purse. Passersby responded to her cries and took her to the hospital. The knife tip enabled conclusive identification of the weapon as a Solingen dagger. Approximately one month later, the "Düsseldorf monster" struck again, killing Ida Reuter by bludgeoning her in the head with a heavy, blunt-edged instrument, leaving hammer-like impressions. The domestic servant had been vaginally raped, probably after she was already dead. The manner in which the body was left, clothing in disarray and legs parted to expose the genitals, was more typical of sexual outrage. The contents of her handbag as well as her underpants were missing. Within two weeks, Elisabeth Dörrier, an unemployed servant, was murdered in the same manner, apparently with the same blunt instrument. Vaginal injury suggested sexual assault. The perpetrator also took her handbag and underclothing.

Attacks continued into the autumn. One late October night, in separate incidents, two women were approached in the same Düsseldorf suburb as had been the site of previous assaults and hammered in the head. Both survived. Then, on the evening of November 7, a five-year-old girl was reported missing from the same district. Her body was found near a foot path two days later, face down, legs parted. Underneath her coat her clothing had been pushed up and her underpants torn. She had been strangled and then stabbed twice in the temples and 34 times in the breast. There was vaginal and anal injury. Sperm was found in her vagina. Forensic analysis indicated she was sexually violated while still alive but dying.

Police did not learn until November, when her body was found, that the domestic servant, Maria Hahn, who had not been seen since August 11, had been murdered. She had sustained three stab wounds to the left temple, a grouping of seven superficial wounds to the neck and ten in the breast area. The weapon used and pattern of stab wounds were like those in the Albermann case. The gaping anus of the decomposed body was consistent with anal penetration, also similar to the assault on the Albermann child.

The series of attacks in Düsseldorf ceased with the Albermann case. Police considered that there might be as many as four different murderers: a strangler, a stabber, a killer who used a hammer and possibly a deranged homosexual (or homophobe?) who targeted men. On the surface, investigators were presented with crimes suggesting different offenders. It became conceivable through subsequent evidence, particularly behavioural evidence, however, that, looking at the crimes on another level, what seemed to differ across crime scenes might instead be different facets of the same behaviour. This increasingly viable possibility forced the investigation onto a more productive although somehow less comprehensible level.

Violent and Sexual Behaviours

Serial murder, the killing of a number of people, at least three, over a period of time,[3] is interpersonal violence in extreme form. It is but one locus of violence. An informed approach to the study of serial murder will be mindful of the ways in which it is both like and unlike other forms of violent behaviour. We need to examine the phenomenon of serial murder in relation to established categories of violent and sexual behaviours.

Violence involving the taking of a life — one's own or another's — has been the focus of much research. A discrete literature treats the relationship between suicide and murder. There is, for example, the presentation by Wertham (1949) of the case of Robert Irwin, a triple murderer who exhibited a pattern of violence during times of personal crisis — what Wertham refers to as catathymic crisis. At such times, violence against self or others is experienced as the only escape from an unbearable emotional state. Wertham discusses the interchangeability in catathymic crisis of violence directed at oneself and that directed against others. Irwin claimed to be aware of his desire to end it all without killing himself but instead to kill someone else and, as he put it, "go to the chair for it" (Wertham, 1949: 133) Henry and Short (1954) present homicide and suicide as expressions of the same kind of aggressive impulse, the former involving direction of the impulse outward, the latter, inward. Lester and Lester (1975) elucidate a more complicated relationship. They suggest that homicides and suicides may have different meanings. motivations and consequences according to the cultural contexts in which they occur. In any case, it is generally agreed that an understanding of either homicide or suicide, both acts of violence, is furthered by study of the other.

To understand serial murder also requires study of the matrix of violence in which it lies. We must examine phenomenologically what serial murder is and what it is not. A review of the literature on the subject strikingly indicates that sexually offensive behaviours are commonly part of the violent history of male serial killers.[4] Should we understand serial murder that involves sexual violation to be an extreme degree of violence that manifestly, at least on its surface, is predominantly sexual? Is there a kind of continuum of violence along which some rapists progress towards serial murder? Case studies suggest that some do; many do not. For some, then, the sex appears to enhance what for them is the essential experience of violence. Or, does the sexual component in serial murder manifest instead something of an individual proclivity and preference for certain behaviour? Sexual violation is sought as an end in itself. Even if there does not exist an actual continuum on which serial murders involving sex should be placed in relation to, say, serial assaults involving sex, we must not dismiss in the study of serial murder what is learned about sexual assault generally. If, at the core of both crimes is the need/desire to violate others, and if this violation is to take the form of (or include) sexualized violence, then the literature on sex crimes must be accounted for in our study of serial murder.[5] This is not to say the driving motive of either serial murder involving sex or, for that matter, sexual assault per se, is primarily sexual. It is to say that we need to examine the role played by sexually assaultive behaviours in both types of offences. Whether serial murder represents an escalating progression of violence (through a series of rapes to murder) or is predilection (where the objective is murder in the absence of a history of rape behaviour), serial murder most often involves behaviours both sexual and violent.

The offensive behaviours may be instrumental to the perpetrator in obtaining what he wants because he is unable or unwilling to engage himself in conventional means of getting, for example, power, money or sex, or they may be the way he expresses his conflicts, frustration and rage. In the former case, the behaviours are readily comprehensible within their own context. From his study of sexual violence, Podolsky (1966) contends that in the rare instances when rapists murder, the killing is outwardly purposeful: to avoid detection by silencing the victim. No personal, subjective motive to kill appears, since subsequent attacks are generally limited to sexual assault. When the rapist does kill, it is out of a reactionary and circumscribed fear of apprehension. The murder is therefore instrumental, serving self-preservation. In other cases, crimes may be essentially emotive. Groth and Birnbaum (1979) view sex crimes as the means of expressing the aggressive emotions that they believe underlie sexual assaults. They focus on the hostility, control and dominance aspects of rapists' behaviours and recognize three main patterns of assault. The first involves minimal force where the objective is to secure power through sexual conquest or possession. Here the offender appears to need to subjugate his victim and uses sexual domination as his means of experiencing control. In a second type of assault, the rapist brutalizes his victim, seemingly needing to hurt the victim out of anger. Retribution takes form as aggressive and sexual bodily harm. This type of offender may be attempting to punish, and proceeds, this author proposes, from a position of self-conferred entitlement. Groth and Birnbaum speak of this as anger rape.

In the third instance, sadistic rape, victims are viciously assaulted, as evidenced by (often ritualistic) torture and mutilation. The sexual behaviour goes beyond domination to abomination. It is as though the offender needs to destroy the object of his sexual desires. Cameron and Frazer (1987) address this point directly, calling our attention to those aspects of masculine identity that are exposed through a lust to kill. That some men develop a taste for sexual murder is seen by Cameron and Frazer as a mere extension of normative aspects of male aggression. Sadistic behaviour, whereby the offender gains pleasure from acts of cruelty, suggests a profound disdain for (or fear of[6]) what the victim represents to the offender. It may be understood as a mediating factor linking aggression and sexuality, signalling an offensively defensive rage. Sex in this case is another weapon in an arsenal of degradation, which, at the same time, is immediately gratifying. Groth and Birnbaum maintain that rather than being an aggressive expression of sexuality, rape is a sexual expression of preexisting aggression. Sears likens serial murder to sexual sadism in terms of the intensity of both kinds of attacks and their predicating violent fantasies, but cautions that since "with many serial killers, sexual impulses do not seem to be a motivating force," serial murder cannot be said to be caused by sexual sadism (1991:69). In some cases where sexual violation of victims is evident, it may be that the killers are serial murderers who also happen to be sexual sadists. As Hazelwood, Dietz and Warren (1992) note, sexual sadism denotes a very broad category that includes individuals who fantasize sexually sadistic scenarios but do not enact them. On the other extreme are those whose violent fantasies become real-life scripts for torture and murder. A correlation between sadism, sexual or not, and murder should not surprise us as, arguably, the ultimate sadistic act is murder. This correlation is imperfect, however, leaving us to address questions about other possible kinds or levels of motive that are universally shared by serial murderers.

Psychosexual Imperatives

Much of the current literature on sexual assault echoes many of the interpretive themes of Groth and Birnbaum, specifically with regard to rape as it relates to control, anger and hatred as opposed to sex. Burgess, Hartman, Ressler, Douglas and McCormack describe sexual homicide as "result[ing] from one person killing another in the context of power, control, sexuality and aggressive brutality" (1986: 252). We should not be, however, too quick to dismiss the sexual component of the assaults as without critical importance or as somehow incidental to an underlying aggressive motivation. Sex in itself has a compelling quality to it. By and large, people repeatedly engage in sexual activity precisely because it is pleasurable. We should not lose sight of this in our discussion of sex-related offences, the research of Groth, among others, notwithstanding. Felson and Krohn (1990) contend that some rapists, especially younger ones, are essentially motivated by the need to seek sexual gratification from their victimizations rather than to harm their victims, which would be more suggestive of power/control motives. In their study drawing from the National Crime Victimization Survey data, rape victims were typically of the same age as would-be consensual partners of the offenders. This trend did not hold, however, for older rapists, who tended to harm victims more often. This apparent difference between younger and older rapists might be attributable to different stages of a criminal career in which the offender becomes increasingly violent, possibly in accordance with a rising threshold for violence-dependent arousal. Alternately, it may be that he becomes less focussed on sexual gratification over time. It is important to keep in view that most sexual offences do not involve murder. Both the manner of assaults as well as their underlying motives will evolve in accordance with the offender's continuing life experiences (which include the accumulating experience of his assaults over time).

Most sexual offences do not involve physical force or aggression and are non-violent. Examples include exhibitionism and voyeurism. Some offences are covertly sexual. Revitch and Schlesinger (1988) note that the commission of some break-and-enter offences, purse snatchings or other apparently non-sexual but violent crimes like choking, hitting or knifing victims may be sexually charged. Revitch (1978) describes some burglars as sexually motivated. In these cases, the offender will assault or kill females he encounters on the premises. These individuals have typically been identified as "opportunists." Given the research of Revitch, among others, however, leads this writer to question whether they are not, or do not perhaps become, predators. The implicit difference between the two portrayals derives from their respective motives. In either case, the offender is likely to recreate the crime in his mind afterward and incorporate the scenario into his repertoire of masturbatory fantasy. In their book on sexual homicide, Ressler, Burgess and Douglas (1988) refer to crime scenes in which conventional evidence of sexual assault is absent (or, this writer would add, obscured). Regardless of its behavioural manifestations, the sexual aspect has a more central role for some sex offenders than for others. Moreover, because sex tends to have such a reinforcing and indeed compelling quality, it is understandable how, for some individuals, it comes to dominate their consciousness to the point of relentless preoccupation.

The significance of women's vulnerability to sexual violence is inescapable. A feminist perspective might depict rape as a "normal" response to an abnormal environment in which the socialization of males to dominate is revered. Rape can be viewed also as the product of deviant life experience and individual psychopathology. These two views need not be mutually exclusive. It may be, for example, that the dysfunctional male overinterprets the prescriptive role for his gender by virtue of his individual pathology, which distorts the message. Both the male and his environment are implicated in this formulation, which seems a more reasoned position.

Brown notes that "[t]he idea of sexual murder providing intense relief from anxiety is remarkably similar to the function of a compulsion" (1991:17). Wertham (1949), on the other hand, asserts that compulsions play no role in criminal acts. In compulsions, in an effort to avert intolerable anxiety, individuals will engage in such outwardly harmless acts as avoiding stepping on cracks in pavement or wiping doorknobs with a handkerchief. Wertham argues against compulsion as an explanation of murder or suicide. In any case, it may be more useful to speak in terms of a compulsive aspect to the acts of serial murder rather than reducing the killings to compulsions and be bound by the trappings of clinical (or for that matter, legal) diagnosis. This approach allies itself with examining serial murders in terms of an addictive process rather than constituting an addiction per se.

 When the ability to function is impaired by a dependency on some external substance or agent, an individual may be said to have an addiction. In the case of Ted Bundy, a documentary video was produced entitled *Fatal Addiction*,[7] asserting that his years of murderous rampage were primarily the product of his self-proclaimed addiction to violent sexual pornography, which fuelled the violent fantasies he acted out. The literature provides numerous examples of serial killers who claim to have experienced mounting tension and irritability that could be dissipated only through an act of killing. One of the serial murderers the author interviewed at length for other research[8] found himself increasingly restless and agitated between his murders. Although not an alcoholic, he compared the tension to a "growing need for a drink." Once the murder is committed, the individual may describe feelings of release from the tension. Following the killing, the murderer is often able, for example, to relax into a sound sleep. This was indicated by serial murderers this author interviewed and is reported elsewhere in the literature (e.g., MacCulloch et al., 1983). For some time afterward, a feeling of calm pervades. While elements of what we recognize as addiction seem to be present, it is premature to identify serial murder as an addiction. It may be more useful, if not more correct, to examine those aspects of serial murder that suggest addiction as component processes in a system of interacting physiological, psychological and social elements. Similarly, the apparent compulsive quality of the series of killings should be entertained as part of a broader systems approach. It is a central argument of the present paper that we are likely to gain more from assuming a perspective of serial murder in terms of underlying processes than by attempting to view it as a discrete form of disorder. We risk being counterproductive if we reduce serial murder to an addiction or compulsion. This limitation of scope would exclude other equally if not more important factors that determine behaviour.

Serial Sexual Murder or Sexualized Serial Murder?

While the victims of most non-serial murderers are not violated sexually, the evidence from many serial murders suggests that a sexual component is involved. Why? Not all serial murders are primarily, if at all, sexual. With regard to male serial killers, however, certainly of the ones most familiar to us through law enforcement experience, academic study or the popular press, much of the violence is sexual. As an example, a victim may be raped or sodomized at some point or points before, during or after the killing. Sexualized behaviours would include binding a victim where the purpose of the restraints is not merely to confine the victim's movements but, another level entirely, because the offender is aroused by the victim's total vulnerability. Offenders have been known to be so involved with elaborating their means of restraint that this aspect of the crime assumes ritualistic proportion.

Abrahamsen equates the act of murder with acts of sex:

> The interaction between the violent murder act and the sexual act is striking. If we can think of the sexual act as an intensification of the equilibrium between tension and release, we can understand how murder, as it is experienced psychologically by the killer, can also be conceived as a vital expression of tension which explodes into release. (1973:40)

Moreover, he makes the case that sex can be substituted for violence and violence for sex. Certainly, there is a multidisciplinary literature on the subject of sex as a behavioural expression of aggression. In more specific terms, Meloy (1992: 76) cites Lunde and speaks of a temporal coupling of eroticism and violence that may occur within a classical conditioning paradigm. This assumes that, in the course of childhood, there is a merging of sexual and violent impulses. From what we know of human behaviour more generally, it seems likely that some type of neuroassociation occurs whereby sexual pleasure is linked to violence. From Bonime (1969), the linking of sexual arousal, aggressivity and specific imagery is understood as idiosyncratically shaped by the unique formative history of each individual. Starting from an initial reactive situation, the serial rapist, or the serial murderer, then evolves to become a proactive agent, stalking potential victims. The individual becomes increasingly active, seeking to gratify his impulses through violence. This predatory mien sustains his primitive aggressions. Concurrently, consciously or subconsciously, there may be retributive motive. The offence is sexually reinforced as the conditioned response, while providing the means to exact his revenge upon those who have hurt, angered or denied him. This latter component is consistent with Elliott Leyton's (1988) view of serial murder as a form of social protest.

Perhaps the most revealing question is whether the behaviour under discussion reflects serial sexual murder, implying sexual motive, or sexualized serial murder, wherein the modus operandi includes a sexual component. Serial sexual murder suggests that the killer engages in a series of murders for the main purpose of sexual gratification. He kills for an orgasm. In some instances, serial murder is paraphilic. Paraphilias are understood to reflect psychosexual disorder in which the preferred or exclusive means of sexual gratification is deviant. In contrast, sexualized serial murder posits different motive. In this case, the offender is driven by a desire or need to kill; that he will do so in a manner that is sexually gratifying is secondary. An imperative to kill suggests self-preservation motives. This latter formulation may find support in Leyton's examination of serial murder as a cultural phenomenon. Leyton's essential position on the sexual violation of victims is that it occurs as "more of an afterthought than a motivating force" (1988:136). The repetition of sexual violation throughout a series of murders, however, suggests to this author less an afterthought than at least concurrence. For some serial killers the acts of killing are primary and sexualized; for other serial killers the killings are secondary to sexual gratification. Sexual motivation is implicated in each case but on a different level.

Sexual orgasm is generally experienced as a pleasurable release of tension. As a motive, sex can be understood as a driving force with the offender intent upon sexual gratification. The sexual impulse,[9] where the impulse is "an incitement or stimulus to action arising from some state of mind or feeling,"[10] can provide the impetus to offend in a sexual manner. Acts of killing associated with the release of tensions may more readily embrace a sexual component. Where sexual arousal is critical to the individual's experience of a vital sense of self, and where the individual experiences a dreaded fear of "nothingness" in the Sartre[11] sense, or of death more directly, he may sexualize his murders to dispatch of an otherwise intolerable anxiety. Insightfully, Korn observes, "[t]he killer, for a moment, intoxicates himself with the illusion that he himself is beyond the fate of his victim" (1971:35). Sexual orgasm is the means to transcend a threatened or deadened existence. Sex as an equivalent of vitality becomes a means of reconstituting a sense of self; to restore the experience of being. Companion themes of control and possession become fundamental determinants of behaviour in such a scheme.

What were traditionally viewed as "nuisance" offences, peeping, indecent exposure and the like, are now being examined as part of a progression. More recent research suggests that there may be an escalation in offences from some of the so-called nuisance offences to rape and (lust)[12] murder. Reese (1979) and Holmes (1983), for example, discuss a number of nuisance sex crimes and note that while the acts themselves do not endanger others, some nuisance sex offenders go on to engage in more serious violent crimes. Some paraphiles follow a similar course. According to current clinical criteria, a diagnosis of paraphilia requires that an individual be distressed by or compelled to act out intense, unusual sexual fantasies.[13] Erotophonophilia, or paraphilic murder, according to Money (1990), is the erotic love of murder whereby anticipating the murder is arousing and committing the murder orgasmic. The particular method of killing necessary for gratification will vary according to idiosyncratic proclivities of the individual. Necrophilia, where the paraphilic attachment is to the corpse, differs from lust murder, which relies on the act of killing for sexual fulfillment. Money views lust murder as an addiction to lustful murder, whereas in paraphilic rape, the offender is seen as addicted to lustful violence (which can lead to murder).

In the Wisconsin trial of serial killer Jeffrey Dahmer, convicted for the murders of 17 young males, the defence offered that a paraphilia was the underlying basis for his sex murders and (unsuccessfully) advanced that he not be held culpable by virtue of an alleged "irresistible impulse" that followed from it. When the act of killing itself or aspects of the victimization are sexualized, it may reflect paraphilic process. There will likely be a history of precocious and deviant sexual behaviours. Through the course of his formative psychosexual development, the individual comes to be sexually gratified by deviant means. Concomittantly, he learns about empowerment through a progression of victims. He may begin with cruelty to animals. Sometimes he exhibits extreme cruelty to his peers. He learns about his capability to overpower. Coupled with an emerging pubescent sexuality, his already established need to control takes on an added dimension. Not only is there the personal satisfaction from taking control, there is a powerful sexual dimension. The exhilaration from empowerment becomes eroticized. By adulthood, he has been conditioned to experience optimal (or exclusive) arousal through violation. Whether the sexual behaviour is pre-, ante-, or postmortem depends on personal tastes as well as on his degree of comfort (relative ease versus unease) with a live victim. While the offender may experiment in an attempt to overcome boredom or diversify his repertoire (he may tire of a particular modus operandi), there are usually specific preferences that are evidenced in his preparatory and stalking behaviours, as well as certain things he does (and does not do) with his victims before, during and after the killings. If the offender is most gratified by the suffering of his victims, he is likely to violate them sexually before they are killed. Indeed, they may be dealt the actual "death blow" while being tortured. Postmortem sexual behaviour may suggest that the offender is able to relate sexually only to an unresisting, unrejecting — dead — person, or that his perversion includes necrophilic as well as premortem sexual acts. In all permutations, he exhibits a will to power. Myra Hindley, accomplice to serial killer Ian Brady, reported that Brady "enjoyed the perverse sense of power that his physical superiority over children gave him..." (Wilson and Seaman, 1990:19). The power and sex coalesce.

The alleged nature of a paraphilia is such that it emerges from an otherwise debilitating anxiety. To the extent that this is the case, the focus of our attention must not be limited to the sexuality of the behaviour but, rather, include consideration of unresolved conflict within the individual. This is not to say that the sexualization of aggression among male or, as in the much rarer case, female serial murderers is without meaning but, rather, that it is quite secondary to underlying anxiety. Ironically, however, with serial murder, like paraphilias in general, when the individual frees himself from personal and/or social taboos and engages in the perversion, the perverse acts become so compelling that he is, in effect, imprisoned by them.

Of particular importance is the level and nature of sexual functioning engaged in by the serial killer, alone during masturbatory activity, as well as with partners whom he does not kill. Exclusive and aberrant preferences imposed on sexual partners can signal the nature of his pathology. For example, an insistence to first engage in anal intercourse followed immediately by demands for fellatio may be taken to suggest a desire on his part to humiliate or degrade his partner. Or insistence that the sex partner take a cold shower immediately before intercourse with instructions not to move during the sex act might signal necrophilic leanings.

The way in which some series of murders play out are evidence of paraphilic disorder. They are the product of a profoundly deviant sexuality that demands destruction of the victim. According to Dietz (1986), sadism is the paraphilia most frequently associated with sex murders. In the extreme case, the paraphilia is the act of killing itself. Proal (1901) reports that French stranglers, including Verzeni and Vacher, claimed intense sexual excitement from killing women in this manner. In his classic work *Psychopathia Sexualis*, Krafft-Ebing (1978) details a number of similar cases.

The case of serial murderer Peter Kürten is particularly instructive regarding paraphilia. Departing from what has been our usual experience with serial killers, Kürten's victims were not selected on the basis of gender or age. Kürten explained to Karl Berg, through the course of the police psychiatrist's intensive and extended examination of Kürten, that it was not his purpose to kill his victims, although indeed many of them died. Instead, he would stab with a dagger or strike blows to the head with a hammer as many times as would be necessary to reach orgasm (Berg, 1954). The primary excitatory cue related to the flow of blood from the wounds he inflicted, regardless of the manner in which they were caused. Thus, the fact that he varied his weapon throughout his attacks, which led police to speculate different perpetrators were involved, was entirely consistent with his objective. That is, his modus operandi was essentially consistent, although on the surface it appeared to differ across crimes. If Kürten was gratified quickly, after only a few stabbings or blows, he had no need to incur further injury to the victim and would leave the scene. If it took longer, requiring more stabbings or blows, the victim was less likely to survive the attack. He thus killed not by design but circumstance. On days when he was unable to find a suitable victim, Kürten reported to Berg that he might return to the scene of an earlier attack — whether the victim had survived or been killed — and become sexually excited. Thus, the fact of the killings is incidental. Nonetheless, Kürten occupies a prominent position in the chronicles of serial murder. On the surface, Kürten looks like a serial murderer in, say, the "Ted Bundy" sense. The writer proposes, as discussed elsewhere,[14] that he is a serial murderer in a technical sense, in that he killed a number of people over a period of time. Yet, importantly, he differs from other serial killers in that his behaviour does not appear to be driven by a need to kill. This writer suspects that the Kürten case is not unique; that paraphilic motivation incidentally results in murder for a number of serial killers.

Conceiving the Problem: Clinical Disorder or Disordered Process

In his discussion of the psychopathology of sexual serial murderers, Brown (1991) concludes that most have been diagnosed as antisocial or sadistic personality disorders or as having a sexual disorder; a minority are considered psychotic and/or organically disordered. He suggests that serial sexual murderers may also suffer from a dissociative disorder. He is remiss in his statement that "[p]robably the only uninvestigated DSM-III-R[15] category which applies to these persons is multiple personality disorder." A series of articles appeared in the psychiatric literature regarding the Kenneth Bianchi (Hillside Strangler) case[16] and surrounding controversy about whether he had a multiple personality disorder. This apparent omission notwithstanding, Brown's reference to the behaviour based at least in part on a dissociative disorder is consistent with the views of other authors. Harold Vetter (1990) categorically applies dissociation and psychopathy to serial murderers in general. An assumption that seems to underlie Vetter's conception of antisocial personality disorder is that such individuals are skilled in rationalizing guilt. This assumes that the so-called psychopath has a conscience from which he needs to separate or dissociate his emotions from his reprehensible deeds. What, however, if the psychopath has no conscience? While this question challenges conventional wisdom regarding antisocial personality disorder, one need not invoke the psychoanalytic construct of superegos to appreciate the possibility that serial murderers fail to develop the capacity to experience guilt and remorse. If, as Vetter suggests, the serial murderer has a conscience, certainly dissociative processes are implicated in how the individual might continue to commit his antisocial acts as if he lacked one. This has not, however, been established. Alternate speculations might include, for example, the idea that the ability of the serial murderer to live with the fact of his murders is due to what might be likened to "holes" in his conscience — as suggested by psychiatric literature on so-called superego lacunae.[17] The main point to be made here is that the psychological mechanisms that give rise to, facilitate or otherwise compel serial murder behaviour are very complex and, as such, do not lend themselves to cursory analysis. A reading of Vetter's chapter gives little sense of the complexity or uncertainty of the psychological processes he proposes. Recent discoveries regarding neurotransmitters in the brain, for example, may prove to elucidate more precisely the mechanisms involved that render certain notably aggressive individuals more impulsive. While there is utility in clinical classifications, reliance upon categories of disorder may limit our level and degree of understanding of the behaviours we observe, particularly in light of the undoubted complexities involved. To try to understand the sexually violative behaviour among serial murderers in terms of psychopathy risks either becoming a tautological exercise or becomes a demand for the search for an additional disorder.

Vetter, as others before, appropriately distinguishes the "crazy" behaviours of serial murderers from "craziness" per se. While it is perhaps difficult for most people to separate the two, it is a critical distinction. To the extent that craziness implies psychosis — essentially a loss of grounding in reality — the majority of serial murderers are clinically sane. This does not, of course, suggest there is nothing wrong with them psychologically. It does suggest that the nature of what is wrong often does not coincide with what we know about psychotic episode or illness. Antisocial personality disorder (or one of its antecedent terms, psychopathy and sociopathy) is frequently mentioned in serial murderer case studies. Yet most psychopaths are not serial killers, and not all serial killers are psychopaths in the diagnostic sense. This category of mental disorder does not, therefore, adequately explain serial murder. Discussion on the level of processes (e.g., dissociation) may lead to better understanding the repeated killing behaviour with its inherent complexity. While Vetter's treatment of dissociative process tends to the superficial, he aptly calls for further study of serial murderers' capacity for dissociation. Also commendably, Meloy's treatise on psychopathy recognizes both processes and clinical disorder, without being undermined by the complexity it seeks to elucidate. He stresses, for example, the boredom experienced by the psychopath as "a restless, anhedonic feeling that is acted out through aggressive, hypomanic activity" (1992:107). For the psychopathic serial murderer, sexual aggression may come to be the antidote, albeit a temporary one, to the state Meloy describes. We need to identify the processes underlying serial murder behaviour, which may or may not speak to a diagnosable clinical disorder. The approach of Meloy is both necessary and exemplary in this regard.

We have learned that modus operandi — behaviour — can reveal the individual. It will reflect the degree of his criminal sophistication, it may be an index of his sociability and indicate probable level of intelligence or at least "street smarts." It may also clue underlying motivational dynamics. These aspects tend to become clearer as we follow the evolving sequence of a series of crimes, particularly as patterns of behaviour emerge.

By definition, modus operandi is individuated. The offender's methods of operation revolve around what works for him within his comfort zone of operation. That is, he will operate within a range of behaviours that do not arouse in him too much anxiety. He will conduct himself in a manner that he is both physically and psychologically comfortable with. He might, for example, choose victims from the neighbourhood in which he lives or works. Modus operandi is generally developed and refined so as to maximize payoffs while at the same time minimizing the probability of discomfort. Offenders tend to develop patterns of behaviour that most effectively serve these dual purposes. Often a ruse is employed to gain the confidence or compassion of the victim. Christopher Wilder was able to lure young women by presenting himself as a professional photographer with promises of a modelling career. Once the situation was manipulated into his control (his comfort zone), the successful businessman and convicted sex offender then sadistically killed his victims. Some serial killers stalk their victims. This predatory behaviour can be sexually arousing. The kind(s) of people the serial killer targets as victims, how he manoeuvres them into his comfort zone and establishes control over them (and maintains that control if he does not murder them immediately), how he kills them and then disposes of the bodies, are all part of his modus operandi. He is operating from a set of behaviours developed to meet his personal needs. Sometimes Peter Kürten robbed victims of their jewellery, sometimes he took their money, sometimes nothing. Sometimes he took items that he would use to bait later victims, reflecting a degree of criminal sophistication. In all cases he physically assaulted the body with a proximal weapon: his hands or an implement that afforded a continuity between his hands and the body (e.g., a hammer or knife). Such consistency in the manner of killing might be taken to suggest that Kürten sought an intimacy with his victims. The offender's behaviour, particularly when patterned, betrays his psychosexual, if not broader, psychological makeup.

Just as the sadistic rapist is excited by torture, some serial murderers are sexually gratified through a scenario of overkill. The killing of a victim is necessary but not sufficient. They are driven to go beyond the mechanics of murder to experience a powerful excitement that for them can come only from, say, the infliction of dozens of stab wounds or blows to the head, any one of which might be sufficient on its own to kill the victim. The frenzied scenario tends to be highly sexually charged.

The most revealing aspect of modus operandi is, arguably, victim choice. The earlier comment notwithstanding, it appears that the majority of male serial murderers choose victims who are either strangers or who bear only a slight acquaintanceship with them. In a figurative sense though, this writer questions whether the victim truly is a stranger to the killer. Indeed, he may objectify the victim in order to render him/her more knowable as one who represents that which he is so threatened by or so hates. The serial murderer can rationalize "knowing" his victims as those who would hurt or otherwise deprive (read deny) him.

At least some serial killers, it seems, are seeking omnipotence. They appear to be impressed by the "greatness" of what they have done. The author's current research is leading to an understanding that a sense of entitlement is a predominant and motivating factor. The case study literature is replete with examples of serial killers who were subjected to horrific abuse as children. Questions of the reliability of these reports notwithstanding, it does appear that serial murderers tend to experience themselves not as victimizers but victims. And, certainly, it is the child's — or for that matter, the adult's — experience of his world that is the singularly critical variable. For others to objectively evaluate the relative degree of traumatization is essentially meaningless in this regard. The perception of oneself as a victim may seek redress through the expression of self as the commander of one's own destiny and retribution through the expression of self as the commander of others' destinies. The killings may provide a needed experience of control. Sexual entitlement as a product of male socialization is a likely factor in a great proportion of serial homicides. The murders are attempts to take what has been withheld from them, what they feel is their due. The resentment for the deprivations expresses itself in the series of killings. Hatred is gratified through sexual debasement with its punishing overtones.

Fantasies: The Scripts of Violence

In Colin Wilson's (1978) insightful work *The Outsider*, we are directed to the Henri Barbusse novel *L'Enfer*. The hero is struck by the sight of women's skirts as they are lifted by gusts of wind. He is overcome by a need to know all women. As he walks a Paris street driven by this urge, he comes upon a woman who, after a brief exchange of words, takes him home. He seeks in her all women. The reality, of course, never matches the fantasy. He speaks of the sex with her as going "through the banal scene." Soon he is again, restlessly, trolling the pavement. The protagonist is angered by what he experiences as betrayal. He is deceived by a reality that fails to deliver. He is able to perceive, according to Wilson, that that which is counterfeit is truth. Yet the fantasy is so compelling that he continues the quest. And so it may be for serial killers.

It has been argued (e.g., Nettler, 1983) that there is a fundamental connection between eroticism and brutality. Normal sexuality is infused with themes of dominance and submission. Fantasies serve to both focus and intensify sexual experience. Masturbatory fantasies often evolve from pornography that combines images of brutality, domination and sex. Disturbed behaviour is the likely product of a consuming preoccupation with sexualized themes of debasement, mutilation and killing. Stoller conceives sex murder as a perversion like necrophilia, fetishism, or rape in that each includes overtly or not — but essential in the fantasy — hostility, revenge, triumph and a dehumanized object" (1975: 9). In 1986, the United States Attorney General's Commission on Pornography concluded that exposure to violent sexually explicit material is related to sexually violent behaviour.[18] Research by Donnerstein (1980) and Fishbach and Malamuth (1978), for example, demonstrates that men exposed to violent pornography are more likely to act aggressively towards women. While the relationship between prolonged and intensive exposure to violent sexual pornography and sexually assaultive behaviours has yet to be conclusively demonstrated, future research in this area will certainly inform our conceptions of serial murder.

Bonime acknowledges the normalcy of masturbation. He also points to masturbatory fantasy as providing optimal conditions for pathological gratification. Moreover, his research indicated that inherent in highly aggressive masturbatory fantasies was a depersonalization of others. He states, "*[t]he fantasy, physically augmented through pleasurable arousal and orgasm, is a symbolic and sexual charade expressing the optimum conditions for the (pathologically) most gratifying interpersonal success*" (1969: 33, original italics). In fantasy, unlike real-world relations, success is virtually ensured. With orgasm there is "a surge of power and triumph accompanied by a feeling of completeness and wholeness, a feeling only short-lived" (1969: 216). Like the quest of Barbusse's hero, however, fulfillment is elusive. For some, fantasy becomes their most reliable reality, however fleeting. This may help us to understand, in part, the viability of pornography; a market that provides a wide range of material to sustain and enhance the lives of our fantasies.

In pornographic genre, the current round of snuff films, in which one of the on-screen actors or actresses is actually murdered during the filming of a sex scene, is a frightening testament of modern appetites. The making of these motion pictures could, technically, be viewed as serial sexual homicides that are perpetrated for profit. The fact of their apparent market suggests an audience that is at least ready to entertain the arousal potential of the link between sex and murder. The role of pornography in both the developmental and criminal histories of sex murderers is likely to reveal important insights into the dynamics of their killing behaviour. The cumulative impact of pornographic images sets a standard of the worth(lessness) of women — as sex objects — in terms of which the individual learns how to relate to female bodies. In violent sexual pornography, intimacy is expressed as violence. Consistent with this is what we observe as an apparent preference among serial killers to use personal weapons like hands, fists or knives over more (physically and psychologically) distancing weapons such as guns.

Regardless of its course, fantasy is the first step in patterned and thus serial behaviours. The extreme cases are fantasy-inspired murders. Stream and Freeman recognize murder as enactment of fantasy when the killing is marked by ritualistic and deviant sexual behaviour. Meaningful discussion of violent and sexual behaviour will distinguish between thoughts and actions. We must at once appreciate that thoughts are not actions, and that actions generally follow from thoughts. Thus, many people entertain violent fantasies that merge sex and violence but never act upon them, presumably inhibited by those tensions around the moral prohibitions regarding acting them out. There may be some for whom the fantasy, and then, say, the rape no longer suffices, opening the door for sexual murder. For those who sexually violate others, the behaviour is most often the product of a highly developed cognitive map. They have obsessively rehearsed their crimes in their minds as elaborate fantasies before acting them out. Further, particularly for sadistic offenders, there is a penchant for keeping records of their exploits in the form of diaries, sketches, audio- and videotapes, still photographs, as well as newspaper clippings pertaining to their case, which are often used to augment later fantasies.

In reference to the Marquis de Sade, Wilson and Seaman speak of his years of incarceration as time spent with only his imagination — that agent of the human condition with the "curious power to *amplify* our desires" (1990: 6). Fantasies of floggings and the like evolved into daydreams of torture, mutilation and murder. Serial murderer Edmund Emil Kemper III (California's "Co-ed Killer") reports that early adolescence was a period marked by his most violent fantasies.[19] Many serial murderers develop a pronounced capacity for visualization, likely enhanced through their intensive and prolonged exposure to violent sexual pornography. This is evidenced by the extraordinary detail with which so many of them are able to recall their crimes. Such eidetic memory was evidenced by Kürten who, while detailing his crimes to officials, disclosed that the daydreams he had of his different crimes brought the same pleasure he had experienced when he had been visualizing or planning the attacks he had yet to commit. If one could speak in terms of an acuity of the mind's eye, many serial killers have a remarkable facility for perceiving and recalling a visual memory representation of their crime scenes.

Whereas modus operandi tends to be tailored to the individual offender's needs (i.e., whatever idiosyncratic means are needed to achieve his ends —

whatever it takes to reach an orgasm), motives are shared. That is, serial murders have an expressive function (e.g., the rage implied by overkill of victims) and/or are instrumental (e.g., for sexual pleasure or monetary gain). The method of operation can inform us of motive, but it is not coterminus with motive. Specifically, modus operandi is in the service of motive. To reiterate the earlier point, it is important to ascertain whether sex is the motive for the killings or an element of a killer's modus operandi. Thus, the serial killer targets prostitutes who are symbols of something that arouses tremendous hatred (or conflict) within him, and he is driven by a need to punish or destroy them. The killing is likely to be marked by much violence and degradation; he may humiliate the corpse. That he derives sexual pleasure from the killing is secondary to the compelling hatred he felt that led him to seek out his victims. He did, nonetheless, experience the arousal. This sexual component of the crime may be a major factor in his repeating the offence. Not only did the killing provide him with a way of acting out his hatred — a "righteous rage" in Jack Katz's (1988) sense — it was sexually gratifying.

Objectification of victims seems a standard aspect of the psychological modus operandi of serial murderers. How they come to render victims into objects is no doubt facilitated by the depersonalization of victims as rehearsed in fantasies. Because of the tendency for an offender to choose victims that have particular things in common (e.g., prostitute lifestyle, age, physical attributes) there is the suggestion that there is personal meaning to his choice of victims. One might argue that victim choice rests squarely on sexual appeal to the offender. Even if this is a pertinent factor, the assaultive behaviour goes beyond sex to murder, suggesting that the primary purpose of the attack is emotive rather than instrumental; that the perpetrator is seeking to impose his outrage or contempt for this victim who is important in terms of what she represents to him. She is experienced as a symbol, not an individual. This process of objectifying the victim attests to the power of the offender's emotions. What he apparently lacks, or where he is blocked, relates to a seeming inability to experience emotional empathy. Indeed, how can one put oneself in the emotional position of an object? The answer is that one cannot. Thus, the serial killer is psychologically (ergo, morally) immune to his murders.

Concluding Remarks

We need to know more: first of all, more about the incidence and prevalence of serial murder; more about what it is and is not. In other words, we need to continue to gather basic descriptive information about the phenomenon. It is the opinion of this author that too often specialists in the study of serial murderers are called upon to give the profile of serial killers and too often they provide one. This practice presupposes two things: that we have gathered enough information about serial murderers that such a generic profile is accurate and reliable, and that there is, indeed, such a type. An example may serve to illustrate doubts regarding these assumptions. Interviews conducted by this author with a number of serial murderers in Canada suggested that it may not be the case those whom serial murderers kill tend to be strangers to them. Of six convicted serial murderers interviewed during the summer of 1990, three knew their victims at least quite well. In fact, two of the killers had an ongoing intimate relationship with their victims. This observation is raised as a challenge to any who might take the position that we can claim a thorough descriptive grasp of the phenomenon of serial murder. Most of what has been written on male serial killers reports that they tend to kill people with whom they are not familiar; that is, strangers. Some researchers (e.g., Egger, 1990) view this lack of prior relationship as a defining characteristic of serial murder. Certainly, we can only describe what we know. It may be that there exists a greater range in the degrees of relationship between serial murderers and their victims than we have recognized. This writer suspects that we are unaware of the series of murders perpetrated by some offenders due to a tendency to relegate a murder involving intimates as domestic, and, therefore, a singular occurrence. While this is not to suggest that most serial murders are between intimate partners, it should alert us to broader possibilities. To the extent that this is the case, we have been talking about a phenomenon, serial murder, that we have still not yet adequately described.

This paper leaves unexamined those cases where the manner in which victims are killed is devoid of sexualized violation or association. A fuller understanding of serial murder involving sexual violation demands at once study of the similarities that sexual and non-sexual serial killings exhibit, as well as their apparent differences. In both cases, the extent of the serial murderer's violence towards his victims, before, during and after their deaths, is generally such that is incomprehensible to the ordinary person. It is perhaps what underlies this ability to abominate that enables him to murder repeatedly, and what also distinguishes him from other kinds of murderers, if not from the rest of humanity. Serial murder includes but is not limited to sexual murders. Exclusive focus on the sexual component of sexual killings is at the expense of a higher order of understanding of the murders themselves, as well as serial murder as a violent phenomenon.

Wilson and Seaman (1990) examine serial murder as a manifestation of violence from a psychological perspective. This author would underscore, however, the necessity of elucidating the role of biological and social factors, and their interactions with one another, in the aetiology of violent behaviour. Serial murderers come to their criminal careers along different paths. While some are likely more biologically and/or psychologically predisposed, others are impelled by circumstance. The behaviour is multiply determined by psychodynamic, sociocultural, biological and situational factors. It goes beyond the simplicity of personal choice or heredity.

Serial murder is an aberration, in statistical and behavioural terms. While many researchers and criminal justice professionals have a sense that the incidence of serial murder is increasing, so, too, are other forms of violent behaviour. The extraordinary publicity surrounding serial homicides suggests a society that is particularly fearful of these crimes, in spite of their relative rarity. It is incumbent upon those of us who have accepted the challenge of learning about serial murder to be ever-alert to its phenomenology. To understand what it is, we must also understand what it is not. Serial murder is the product of a number of complex processes rooted in specific biological, psychological and social aspects of the human condition. It is not, therefore, readily accessible by summary enquiry. The concern is that in our quest for a more fundamental understanding of serial murder we do not overshoot the mark. Attributions of power and control as motivating factors in serial murder have made a significant contribution to our academic enquiries. This writer cautions, however, against the total sublimation of sex to power and control motives. The reality is certainly more complex than this contention would allow. It is not only about sex any more than it is only about murder. Sexual violation of serial murder victims is a part, and an important one, of the picture that is serial murder. And serial murder, regardless of its form, brings into sharp relief the violent society in which it resides.

"Kürten is well known as a petty thief, but is otherwise harmless" (Wagner, 1993:107). This indictment, both limited and limiting, was offered by a man who had served time with Kürten and was asked if he thought Kürten was the "Düsseldorf Ripper." When Peter Kürten was arrested in May, 1930, his confession to the series murders and attacks unmasked "the monster of Düsseldorf." Remarkably, as the execution date approached, Kürten is reported to have asked if a severed head might hear the gushing of blood, perhaps intimating this would be, for him, the ultimate pleasure. Could there be a more paraphilic dénouement?

Endnotes

1.   This crime was never solved.

2.   As with other cases in which sexual assault of victims was not evidenced, one could surmise that the offender derived pleasure from the act of killing itself or that, in some manner (e.g., the unexpected arrival of someone else onto the scene) he was thwarted in his mission.

3.   The author uses this as an operational definition of serial murder while acknowledging there is no consensus regarding the necessary and sufficient criteria in the literature. Some definitions are very broad. For example, Sears considers serial murder as the killing of "many...at random and at will over a period of days, weeks, months, or even years, usually one at a time" (1991:ix). Other definitions specify particular motives, kinds of victims and modus operandi as categorical criteria. Such stipulations may be prematurely exclusionary.

4.   This paper proceeds as if sexual violation of homicide victims were the exclusive province of males. By and large, an evidenced sexual component is remarkably rare among the roughly 15 per cent of serial killers who are female. It does, however, exist. More generally, research by Jones and Barlow (1990) indicates that women have about as many sexual fantasies as do men. Kaplan (1991) studied women's sexual perversions and concluded psychiatry has largely missed the subtle emotional dynamics that are more integral to their perversions. Unlike sexual perversions among men, which tend to be more overtly sexual, women's perversions are manifestly more subtle, involving symbolic acts centred on emotional dramas of abandonment, separation and loss. For example, a woman who is extremely submissive to dominating lovers may be masochistic. Sexual submission becomes the way to momentarily triumph over fears of abandonment that are being re-enacted from childhood. The readily apparent differences between male and female serial killers present a tempting focus for study. As discussed elsewhere (Skrapec, in press), however, it is my contention that these differences serve to mask the more substantive underlying similarities between male and female multiple murderers.

5.   Another needed approach is to compare different kinds of offenders directly. For example, R. Langevin, M.H. Ben-Aron, P. Wright, V. Marchese and L. Handy compared 13 sex killers (some serial) with 13 non-sex killers (some serial) and 13 non-homicidal sexually aggressive men on a number of variables. See their 1988 article "The sex killer" in the *Annals of Sex Research, 1,* 263-301.

6.   Some males, rather than viewing sexual intercourse as a means of deriving power through penetration, may instead develop a hostility towards women owing to a profound fear of being "engulfed" during sexual intercourse.

7.   Stiles, Steven. (Producer and Director). (1989). *Fatal Addiction: Ted Bundy's Final Interview.* [Videotape]. Focus on the Family.

8.   Doctoral dissertation, in progress.

9.   See Colin Wilson (1963). *Origins of the Sexual Impulse.* New York: G. P. Putnam's Sons for an expansive discussion on sexual impulse.

10.   From *Oxford English Dictionary* (compact ed.). (1989). Oxford: Oxford University Press, p. 1394.

11.   See Jean-Paul Sartre. (1966). *Being and Nothingness.* New York: Pocket Books.

12   The term "lust murder" has been used in substantively different ways by different authors. The indiscriminate use of the term has served to obliterate its essence. The original German *lustmörder* described killings perpetrated for the enjoyment of killing. Podolsky describes lust murder as "a pathological equivalent of coitus" (1965: 178) "involving cutting or stabbing, particularly of the breasts or genitals; frequently with sucking or licking of the wounds, biting of the skin, sometimes a desire to drink the blood and eat the flesh of the victim...sometimes erection and ejaculation followed by violation of the victim; often there is no attempt at intercourse" (1965: 174). Hazelwood and Douglas characterize lust murder as "a mutilating attack or displacement of the breasts, rectum, or genitals." (1980: 18). Holmes uses the term synonymously with piquerism while noting that not all cases of piquerism result in the death of the victim, where an individual "can only be sexually excited when violence of a sexual/physical nature precedes or accompanies the sexual act. The violent, savage mutilation often serves as a psychological aphrodisiac to the murderer" (1983: 149). Brittain (1970) speaks of the sadistic murderer whose killings enact ritualized sadistic fantasy. Like Hazelwood and Douglas who stipulate that lust murders are premeditated in obsessive fantasies, Brittain cites the compelling role of fantasy. The popular media have typically portrayed so-called lust murders as sex murders, with little or no appreciation for the kinds of distinctions proposed by academic researchers and law enforcement practitioners.

13   American Psychiatric Association. (1987). *The Diagnostic and Statistical Manual of Mental Disorders* (3rd ed., rev.). Washington, D.C.: The American Psychiatric Association.

14   See C. Skrapec's Introduction to Berg, Karl. and Godwin, George. (1993). *The Sadist: An Account of the Crimes of a Serial Killer, Together with Peter Kürten: A Study in Sadism.* Montclair, N.J.: Patterson Smith.

15   See note 13 above.

16   For example, see Watkins, John G. (1984). The Bianchi (L.A. Hillside Strangler) case: Sociopath or multiple personality? *The International Journal of Clinical and Experimental Hypnosis.* *XXXII*(2), 67-101; and Orne, Martin T., Dinges, David F., and Orne, Emily Carota. (1984). On the differential diagnosis of multiple personality in the forensic context. *The International Journal of Clinical and Experimental Hypnosis, XXXII*(2), 118-169.

17   For example, see Johnson, A.M. and Szurek. (1952). The genesis of antisocial acting out in children and adults. *Psychoanalytic Quarterly, 21*(3), 323-343.

18   Department of Justice. (1986). *Attorney General's Commission on Pornography: Final Report.* Washington, D.C.: U.S. Government Printing Office.

19   Anderson, Bob (Producer and Director). (1978). *50 Weeks of Planned Killing.* [Television Documentary]. American Broadcasting Companies, Inc.

References

Abrahamsen, David. 1973. *The Murdering Mind*. New York: Harper and Row, Publishers.

Berg, Karl. 1954. *The Sadist* (O. Illner and G. Godwin, trans.). New York: Medical Press of New York. (Original work published 1932)

Bonime, Walter. 1969. "Masturbatory Fantasies and Personality Functioning." In J. H. Masserman (ed.), "Dynamics of Deviant Sexuality," *Science and Psychoanalysis, XV*. New York: Grune and Stratton.

Brittain, R. P. 1970. "The Sadistic Murderer." *Medical Science and the Law 10*: 198-207.

Brown, James S. 1991. "The Psychopathology of Serial Sexual Homicide: A Review of the Possibilities." *American Journal of Forensic Psychiatry 12*(1): 13-21.

Burgess, Ann W., Carol R. Hartman, Robert K. Ressler, John E. Douglas and Arlene McCormack. 1986. "Sexual Homicide: A Motivational Model." *Journal of Interpersonal Violence 1*(3): 251-272.

Cameron, Deborah and Elizabeth Frazer. 1987. *The Lust to Kill: A Feminist Investigation of Sexual Murder*. New York: New York University Press.

Dietz, Park Elliott. 1986. "Mass, Serial, and Sensational Homicides." *Bulletin of the New York Academy of Medicine 62*: 477-491.

Donnerstein, Edward. 1980. "Pornography and Violence Against Women." *Annals of the New York Academy of Science 347*: 277-288.

Egger, Steven A. 1990. *Serial Murder: An Elusive Phenomenon*. New York: Praeger.

Fishbach, Seymour and Neal Malamuth. 1978. "Sex and Aggression: Proving the Link." *Psychology Today 12*: 111-122.

Hazelwood, Robert R., Park Elliott Dietz and Janet Warren. 1992, Feb. "The Criminal Sexual Sadist." *FBI Law Enforcement Bulletin*, 12-20.

Hazelwood, Robert R. and John E. Douglas. 1980, Apr. "The Lust Murderer." *FBI Law Enforcement Bulletin*, 18-22.

Henry, A.F. and Short, J.F., Jr. 1954. *Suicide and Homicide*. New York: Free Press.

Holmes, Ronald M. 1983. *The Sex Offender and the Criminal Justice System*. Springfield, IL: Charles C. Thomas, Publisher.

Jones, Jennifer C. and David H. Barlow. 1990. "Self-reported Frequency of Sexual Urges, Fantasies, and Masturbatory Fantasies in Heterosexual Males and Females." *The Archives of Sexual Behavior 19*(3): 269-280.

Kaplan, Louise. 1991. *Female Perversions*. New York: Doubleday.

Katz, Jack. 1988. *Seductions of Crime: Moral and Sensual Attractions of Doing Evil*. New York: Basic Books.

Korn, Richard. 1971, Oct. "Of Crime, Criminal Justice and Corrections." *University of San Francisco Law Review VI*(1): 27-75.

Krafft-Ebing, Richard von. 1978. *Psychopathia Sexualis*. (F.S. Klaf, trans.). New York: First Scarborough Books. (Original work published 1886).

Lester, David and Gene Lester. 1975. *Crime of Passion: Murder and the Murderer*. Chicago: Nelson-Hall.

Leyton, Elliott. 1988. *Hunting Humans: Inside the Minds of Mass Murderers*. New York: Pocket Books.

MacCulloch, M. J., P. R. Snowden, P. J. W. Wood and H. E. Mills. 1983. "Sadistic Fantasy, Sadistic Behaviour and Offending." *British Journal of Psychiatry 143*: 20-29.

Meloy, J. Reid. 1992. *The Psychopathic Mind: Origins, Dynamics, and Treatment*. Northvale, NJ: Jason Aronson Inc.

Money, John. 1990. "Forensic Sexology: Paraphilic Serial Rape (Blastophilia) and Lust Murder (Erotophonophilia)." *American Journal of Psychotherapy XLIV*(1): 26-36.

Nettler, Gwynne. 1983. *Killing One Another*. Cincinnati, OH: Anderson Publishing Co.

Podolsky, Edward. 1966. "Sexual Violence." *Medical Digest 34*: 60-63.

Podolsky, Edward. 1965. "The Lust Murderer." *Medico-Legal Journal XXXIII*(IV): 174-178.

Proal, Louis. 1901. *Passion and Criminality in France: A Legal and Literary Study* (A.R. Allison, trans.). Paris: Charles Carrington.

Reese, James T. 1979, Aug. "Obsessive-Compulsive Behavior: The Nuisance Offender." *FBI Law Enforcement Bulletin*, 6-12.

Ressler, Robert K., Ann W. Burgess and John E. Douglas. 1988. *Sexual Homicide: Patterns and Motives*. Lexington, MA: Lexington Books.

Revitch, Eugene. 1978. "Sexually Motivated Burglaries." *The Bulletin of the American Academy of Psychiatry and the Law 6*: 277-283.

Revitch, Eugene and Louis B. Schlesinger. 1988. "Clinical Reflections on Sexual Aggression." In R. Prentky and V. Quinsey (eds.), *Human Sexual Aggression: Current Perspectives*, pp.59-61. *Annals of the New York Academy of Sciences 528*.

Sears, Donald J. 1991. *To Kill Again: The Motivation and Development of Serial Murder*. Wilmington, Delaware: Scholarly Resources, Inc.

Skrapec, Candice A. 1994. "Female Serial Murder: An Evolving Criminality." In H. Birch (ed.), *Moving Targets*. London: Virago Press.

Stoller, Robert J. 1975. *Perversion: The Erotic Form of Hatred*. New York: Pantheon Books.

Vetter, Harold. 1990. "Dissociation, Psychopathy, and the Serial Murderer." In S. Egger, *Serial Murder: An Elusive Phenomenon*, pp.73-92. New York: Praeger.

Wagner, Margaret Seaton. 1933. *The Monster of Düsseldorf: The Life and Trial of Peter Kürten*. New York: E.P. Dutton and Co., Inc.

Wertham, F. 1949. *The Show of Violence*. New York: Doubleday.

Wilson, C. 1978. *The Outsider*. London: W.H. Allen Publishing.

Wilson, Colin and Donald Seaman. 1990. *The Serial Killers: A Study in the Psychology of Violence*. London: W.H. Allen Publishing.

[27]

Feminist Perspectives
on Serial Murder

A Critical Analysis

JULIE CLUFF
ALLISON HUNTER
RONALD HINCH
The University of Guelph

This article offers a critical analysis of feminist perspectives on serial murder. It argues that feminist scholarship has been preoccupied with a particular type of serial murder and has, therefore, missed an opportunity to expand both its own and other analyses of serial murder. The article explores areas in which feminist scholarship can inform other analyses and suggests ways in which a feminist theory of serial murder can be improved by incorporating concerns expressed in mainstream criminological analysis.

The serial murder literature has produced a variety of theoretical explanations of its subject matter. Theories range from the micro to the macro level. Preceding most studies of serial murder is a cautionary warning that the small number of such killings and killers makes theorizing about serial murder difficult. It is, therefore, ironic that rather than examining all cases of serial murder, many analysts have excluded certain types of killings and certain types of killers. In doing so, the potential pool of research subjects is substantially reduced. For example, Leyton (1986) limited him-

AUTHORS' NOTE: We would like to express our appreciation to the reviewers and the editor for their comments on an earlier version of this article.

EDITOR'S NOTE: Reviewers were Ronald Holmes, Julie Goetz, and Candice Skrapec.

HOMICIDE STUDIES, Vol. 1 No. 3, August 1997 291-308

292   HOMICIDE STUDIES / August 1997

self to studying only those who kill for the sake of killing. He excluded professional hit men, agents of the state paid to torture and kill, and the Tylenol murderers. Egger (1984, 1990) and Holmes and DeBurger (1988) made similar exclusions.

Perhaps feminists make the most intriguing attempt to limit the study of serial murder, particularly radical feminists. They limit the study of serial murder to only those cases in which men engage in the sexually sadistic killing of women (Cameron & Frazer, 1987; Caputi, 1987; Chesler, 1993). They sometimes call it "sexual terrorism" (Cameron & Frazer, 1987) and portray it as an extreme form of "femicide" (Radford & Russell, 1992) or "gynocide" (Quindlen, 1993).

Our objective is to review feminist theorizing on serial murder. Although we will devote considerable attention to illustrating the weaknesses of feminist theorizing, we do not intend to vilify feminism. Our intent is to illustrate how feminist theorizing can contribute to a broader theory of serial murder. We begin by reviewing those aspects of feminist theorizing about serial murder that we find problematic and conclude by showing how feminist theory combined with other analyses can be helpful in developing a more comprehensive theory.

Although we disagree with some aspects of feminist theorizing, we concur with other aspects, especially the pursuit of a macro-level explanation. Some analysts (Dutton, 1994) have suggested that feminist theorizing about violence has been overly concerned with macro-level explanations. However, we argue that macro-level theorizing offers the opportunity to go beyond explanations of individual pathology to examine the role played by structural factors in shaping human behavior. We do not deny the utility of micro-level theorizing, recognizing that it has proven useful to police investigators. Several commentators have argued that it is vital to continue to develop micro-level analyses that may aid in the detection and apprehension of serial murderers (Egger, 1990; Jenkins, 1994). However, micro-level theorizing has become so dominant that the serial murder literature may be losing sight of the bigger picture. We need to know more about how social structure contributes to the creation of serial killers. Exclusive concentration on micro-level explanations is problematic—just as an exclusive concentration on macro-level explanations is problematic.

PROBLEMS WITH FEMINIST
THEORIZING ABOUT SERIAL MURDER

Several issues are relevant for the discussion of the feminist analysis of serial murder. These issues include the cavalier dismissal of the possibility that women can be serial killers, the issue of sensationalism, and the implication that feminist argument is ideological rather than analytical in nature.

Ignoring Female Serialists

Rather than study all forms of serial killing, feminists, especially radical feminists, have restricted their investigations to a narrow range of killings. They limit themselves to studying only male sexual predators and dismiss the possibility that women could be serial killers. Their main contention is that male serial killers are the product of patriarchal society. As Cameron and Frazer (1987) asserted, "Only men . . . are compulsive lone hunters, driven by the lust to kill—a sexual desire which finds its outlet in murder" (p. 1). The lust to kill is presented as an expression of patriarchal power. Some feminists have even argued against the use of gender-neutral terms when referring to serial murder. For example, Caputi (1990) claimed the use of gender-neutral terminology

> works to obscure what actually is going on out there, for the "people" who torture, kill, and mutilate in this way are men, while their victims are predominantly females, women and girls, and to a lesser extent, young men. As these hierarchial lines indicate, these are crimes of sexually political import, crimes rooted in a system of male supremacy in the same way that lynching is based in white supremacy. (p. 2)

As Jenkins (1994) observes, this is an extension of the feminist argument that every man is a potential rapist; every man is not only a potential rapist but also a potential serial killer.

By limiting the study of serial murder to male sexual predators, these feminists unnecessarily restrict the study of serial murder. If patriarchy is the only structural force generating serial murder, this reduces their analysis to a single-factor theory. The opportunity to extend the analysis to investigate other social-structural factors that might influence the creation of serial killers is lost. The

Serial Murder

influence of these other structural factors needs to be assessed. We need to know more about how such factors as class and race contribute to the patterns of serial killing found in particular societies.

Further, to restrict research to only those cases involving male sexual predators is to repeat the error that feminists claim unjustifiably limits mainstream criminology. They have frequently commented that mainstream criminology, preoccupied with male criminality, neglects or dismisses female criminality and presents a poor analysis of violent female criminality (Faith, 1993; Smart, 1976). For example, Faith (1993) stated that, to the extent that mainstream criminology has examined violent female offenders,

> academic . . . accounts of "women who kill" generally focus on women who can be readily demonized, sending out the conflicting messages that, on the one hand, only a complete psychopath or sociopath could commit these heinous crimes, and on the other hand, all women are potential killers and society (men) must control them. (p. 95)

However, although it appears that female serial killers could be easily demonized and dismissed as psychopaths, mainstream criminology has for the most part ignored them (Hickey, 1986, 1991; Holmes & Holmes, 1994; Scott, 1992). Ironically, feminist criminology also ignores female serialists.

If it is unacceptable for mainstream criminology to ignore or dismiss that women commit about 15% of all violent crime, then ignoring the study of female serial killers because they are only 15% (using Hickey's [1991] database of more than 200 serial killers) of known serial killers is equally problematic. The limited feminist commentary on specific cases of known female serial killers tends to dismiss these cases as exceptions or as something other than serial murder. For example, Cameron and Frazer (1987) recognized Myra Hindley as "the *only* serious *potential* counter-example to our proposition that sexual killers are men" (p. 144, emphasis added). Hindley was convicted along with Ian Brady for the sexually sadistic murders of two children, but Cameron and Frazer are uncertain if Hindley derived any sexual gratification from her participation in these killings. If she received sexual gratification, she could be classified as a serial murderer; if no sexual gratification was involved, then she would not be a serial killer.

In other cases, female perpetrators are excluded because they do not kill in a sexually sadistic fashion. Chesler (1993), for instance, argued that Aileen Wuornos is not a serial killer because she killed in response to her lifelong experience as a victim of abuse and neglect. At the age of 6 months, Wuornos and her brother had been abandoned by their mother. She was raised by her maternal grandmother and a physically abusive, alcoholic grandfather. By the age of 15, in 1971, she had given up a baby for adoption, run away from home several times, and dropped out of school. Her grandmother also died that same year, followed by her grandfather's suicide in 1976 and her brother's death in 1977 (Scott, 1992, p. 31). Wuornos married but subsequently left her abusive husband. She claims to have been raped several times during her lifetime and that her history as a rape victim was the impetus behind her killing spree. She had been working as a prostitute when the men she killed tried to rape her; therefore, she says, she was merely defending herself (Scott, 1992). Her claims of self-defense have resulted in Wuornos achieving heroine status among some feminists, for whom she symbolizes the struggle against oppressive male violence.

Similarly, Seagrave (1992) acknowledged the existence of female "multiple murderers" but refused to call them serial murderers because they are not sexually sadistic killers like male serial killers. Seagrave also dismissed female multiple murderers who kill for economic reasons (such as "black widows" who kill their husbands for financial gains) because they, too, lack the requisite sexual sadism.

Evidence shows that female serial killers exist, but this evidence has been systematically neglected in academic inquiry. This requires a more comprehensive examination of female serial killing. When serialists' patterns of victim selection and methods of killing (Hickey, 1986, 1991; Keeney & Heide, 1994; Scott, 1992) are compared with those found among conventional killers (Goetting, 1995; Jurik & Winn, 1990; Silverman & Kennedy, 1988; Wolfgang, 1958), men and women clearly kill in ways that are consistent with their gender roles. Among serial killers and conventional killers, males are more likely than females to kill strangers, whereas females are more likely than males to kill intimates, such as spouses or children. According to Hickey (1991, pp. 112, 139), 29% of female serialists killed strangers only, but 69% of male serialists killed only strangers. Further, whereas 50% of female serialists killed at least one family member, only 5% of male serialists killed at least one member of the family. When female serialists kill strangers, the tendency is either to kill people, such as nursing home patients, who are dependent on them or to act as accomplices to male serial killers.

As for methods of killing, men rely on brute force such as strangulation, beating, and shooting, whereas women use more subtle killing methods such as poison or suffocation. When disposing of their victims, male serialists leave them in public places, whereas female serialists are likely to conceal the disappearances of their victims. If they are unable to conceal the body, they rely on explanations that suggest other causes of death such as Sudden Infant Death Syndrome (SIDS). According to Hickey (1991, pp. 117, 149), the most frequent killing methods used by female serialists are some use of poison (52%), poison only (45%), some shooting (30%), and some bludgeoning (27%) but male serialists preferred mutilation (55%), firearms (45%), some bludgeoning (35%), and either strangulation of suffocation (33%).

The killing methods used by male and female serialists and the relationship with their victims also result in differential potential for detection. The brutality of male-perpetrated serial killing makes it easier to detect their crimes. Female serialists, however, are more difficult to detect. Female serialists avoid detection in part because their killing methods are less obvious and in part because there is reluctance by the community, including the police, to believe that these women are killers. Typically, the community feels pity for these women who have tragically lost someone close to them.

Consequently, female serialists can stay in one community for extended periods before arousing suspicion, whereas male serialists must frequently travel to other communities. If males do stay in one community, their killings are more likely to arouse suspicion and are detected sooner (Hickey, 1991; Scott, 1992).

Thus, the activity of female serialists often remains hidden. It is minimalized and normalized. It is not perceived to be murder, nor are they suspected to be killers. For example, Vera Renczi killed 33 lovers, 2 husbands, and her son before she was caught. No one thought these victims' disappearances were suspicious until the wife of one missing man insisted on a search of Renczi's house. It was not until the bodies were found in her basement that anyone thought she was a killer. According to Scott (1992), Renczi's image before the discovery was "as a tragic figure in the community who could not keep a husband or a lover" (p. 55).

A Mechanism to Control Women?

An important aspect of radical feminist theorizing on serial murder is the contention that serial murder is primarily aimed at the control of women. A close scrutiny of the literature reveals this to be a flawed argument. Certain types of male serial killers target women for the purpose of domination and/or control, but that does not mean that all serial killers have this purpose. Male serialists kill males almost as frequently as they kill females. Hickey (1991) pointed out that 36% of male serialists killed only females (i.e., 64% killed at least one male) and 21% killed only males. Further, as Jenkins (1994) and Hickey discussed, other target groups include racial/ethnic minorities and homosexuals. Serial killing, therefore, cannot be seen as uniquely motivated to serve as a mechanism by which to control women. There is a need to move beyond a focus on male sexual sadists who kill women if we are to have more comprehensive understanding of the motivating forces, both psychological and social, that generate serial murder.

Tendency Toward Sensationalism

Compounding these problems, according to Jenkins (1994), is the tendency for feminists to present sensationalistic and misleading statistics of serial murder rates. The most notorious examples are found in the work of Radford (1992a) and Caputi (1987). These authors inflate the number of events that can be attributed to serial murder and the number of events in which women are the victims. Both claim that nearly two thirds of the approximately 5,000[1] unsolved murders in the United States each year can be attributed to serial murder and that most victims are women.

These estimates are obviously in error. As Jenkins (1994) noted, if two thirds of the 5,000 unsolved murders each year are cases of male serial murderers killing women, then nearly 70% of all females murdered annually are killed by serialists. Quite simply, there is no evidence to support this contention. Jenkins saw a more realistic estimate of the annual total of all killings by serialists as 1% (around 200 victims) of known murders each year. Another commentator suggested that serial murderers may account for an even lower figure of only 100 killings annually (O'Reilly-Fleming, 1996).

Overestimating female victimization by serialists also undermines and trivializes the feminist analyses of domestic murder. More women are killed by husbands, former husbands, or lovers than are killed by serialists. The Bureau of Justice Statistics (1994) reported that approximately 22,000 murders are recorded each year in the United States. Of that total, close to 1,500 women were killed by intimates (including husbands, ex-husbands, boyfriends, and ex-boyfriends). Using Jenkins's (1994) estimate of the number of people killed by serialists each year, this means that for every woman killed by a serialist, seven are killed by intimate partners.

Misrepresenting the empirical basis on which any argument is predicated leaves advocates open to the criticism that the argument is simply dishonest. Rather than attempting a straightforward assessment of the problem, the advocate can be accused of deliberately misinforming the audience, thus raising questions concerning the credibility and veracity of the argument itself. The erroneous use of data also masks the potential for feminist arguments to make a more significant contribution to the study of serial murder. It is to this potential that we now turn.

POTENTIAL BENEFITS OF A FEMINIST
PERSPECTIVE ON SERIAL MURDER

Despite the problems discussed so far, feminist analyses of serial murder have provided some valuable insights. These insights come in two forms. First, their assessments of serial murder have revealed some weaknesses in other theories of violent crime. Second, an additional linkage has been provided from which to examine serial murder as the product of social-structural forces. Again, our intent is not to argue that micro-level explanations are not worthy pursuits. We wish instead to emphasize that macro-level perspectives must be incorporated to have a more comprehensive theory of the factors that lead to serial murder. Both of these areas of contribution deserve further elaboration.

Feminist Critique of Other Theories

Feminist scholarship regarding serial murder, and violent crime in general, has made significant contributions to developing explanations for societal violence. It has done so, in part, by showing how other theories do not offer clear, precise analyses. We will review these areas of feminist critique to show how they can be used to improve theorizing about serial murder.

Victim blaming. Feminists have long been concerned about the practice of victim blaming. They are highly critical of a societal tendency to deflect the blame away from the perpetrator toward the victim. They contend that victim blaming pervades the psychiatric profession, the media, and law enforcement practices (Clark & Lewis, 1977; Russell, 1984). With particular reference to serial murder, some feminists argue that victim blaming justifies law enforcement's tendency to disregard or downplay cases in which disreputable women, such as prostitutes or lower class individuals, are the victims of serial murder (Cameron & Frazer, 1987). Similarly, Cameron and Frazer (1987), as well as Caputi (1987), have been critical of the mother blaming and wife blaming that pervades much of the psychoanalytic literature on serial killers. According to Caputi, if these explanations are left unchallenged, "no one needs to look at social norms, institutions, and ideologies" (p. 199).

Feminists contend that these explanations serve to cloak the underlying social processes that are relevant in a discourse on serial murder. They are critical of the inclination toward reconstructing the victim's lifestyle and placing the victim's behavior on trial. Feminists demand that despite the victims' lifestyle or gender, the focus should be on the perpetrator. The dismissal of victim blaming centers the focus on the killer, aiding in the discovery of factors that generated the crime. This is not to argue that studying the victim/offender relationship should be ignored; rather, caution is urged to avoid the problem that frequently results from an overconcentration on the victim, the most frequent manifestation of which is victim blaming.

Rejecting biological/psychological reductionism. Moreover, feminists have advocated dismissal of theories that argue that serial murders can be explained via an exclusive concentration on the biological or psychological state of the perpetrator. Feminists contend that biological theories lack explanatory power: "Sex murder is not just a convenient label for a type of bodily act like 'shivering' or 'coughing', but a cultural category" (Cameron & Frazer, 1987, p. 81).

Psychological explanations also fall short because they mask responsibility for the killer behind a veil of psychopathology. Blaming the individual psychopath is easier than blaming the culture that normalizes expressions of violence against women (Caputi, 1989). In this regard, feminists have offered insightful criticisms of the way the media and some academics portray serial killers, like Jack the Ripper and Marc Lepine. The Ripper has been transformed into a "Mythic Hero" who functions to empower and inspire men to commit violent crimes against women (Caputi, 1989). Similarly, the "Montreal Massacre," an event in which Marc Lepine murdered 14 women, is often portrayed in the media as a senseless act of violence without reference to its political underpinnings.

The role of media images. Media images of the serial murderer as the monster, the beast, the psychopath, or the sociopath serve to deny that violence against women is normalized in patriarchal culture (Cameron & Frazer, 1987; Caputi, 1989; Radford, 1992b). Rather than concentrating on the larger meanings and motives of serial killing, the focus becomes the cause or drive of the individual killer. Caputi (1987) suggests that sexual violence and the depiction of violence has become normalized through the media. The sex criminal has become the epitome of masculinity, embodying the ideal of a patriarchal structure. In the process, women become objectified and marginalized. Ultimately, they lose their subjectivity, becoming objects of male fantasy, desire, and control (see Cameron & Frazer, 1987, for a similar argument).

To feminists, pornography is an extreme example of objectification. Serialist Ted Bundy's confession that he was a consumer of pornography is often used by feminists to verify the relationship between pornography and woman killing. *Gorenography* is a term used by some feminists to describe the kind of media that eroticize and sensationalize violence (Caputi & Russell, 1992), a form that can be found in ordinary products of pop culture. Although it may be true that some serialists have been consumers of pornography, the use of individualized accounts in which the serial murderer has an inordinate interest in pornography is not sufficient evidence to establish the linkage. Nonetheless, the contention that violence against women is rooted in components of social structure remains an important consideration.

Feminists, of course, are not the only theorists to suggest a connection between pornography and violence against women. Malamuth and Donnerstein (1984), Jenkins (1984), Leyton (1986), Levin and Fox (1985), McKenzie (1995), and Ressler, Burgess, and Douglas (1987) have made contributions in this area. They have tried to link pornography not only to violence against women but to more general patterns of violence. For example, Levin and Fox added that the "portrayal of violence is now often laced with either explicit sex or sexual innuendo, making aggression seem an intrinsic part of the erotic experience" (p. 26). They argue that the glorification of violence common to many popular forms of entertainment, movies, and television legitimizes violence and contributes to the creation of serial murderers of all types, not just women.

To repeat, the linkage between pornography (broadly defined) and violence is complex. From our viewpoint, it is important to study both pornography and violence in popular entertainment as a factor influencing some serialists. At the micro level, we need to understand how pornography might lead individual serialists to kill. But to fully understand the relationship, we need to know at the macro level how it is linked to patriarchal and other structural forces.

Linkages With Other Approaches

The feminist attempt to link serial killing of women to social-structural factors is an important development in the study of serial murder. We support the basic contention made by feminists that patriarchal social relations are a significant factor leading to the serial killing of women. However, we argue that, as a sole consideration, this places too narrow a focus on the study of serial murder. Expanding the scope of our analysis can lead to an understanding of the connection to other structural factors. Thus, we turn to a review of the contributions made by analysts who suggest linkages between serial murder and various components of the social structure.

Issues of class, patriarchy, and power. Leyton (1986) was one of the first researchers to hypothesize a connection between serial killing and components of the social structure. He says that with the onset of capitalism and the industrial era, two key themes emerged. The first, which he labeled as *petite bourgeoisie sensibilities*, refers to members of the upper class or middle class disciplining those who deviate from societally prescribed roles. This pattern, he argued, was more common in the 19th century. The second theme, which he labeled as *proletarian rebellion*, refers to people from the lower social echelons expressing their dissatisfaction with their marginal position in society. This form is the more common pattern found among contemporary multiple murderers. In essence, Leyton placed the murders in a social context, saying that serial murderers emerge out of a threatened class in times of class tension and struggle. Modern serial murderers are usually from the working classes or lower middle classes, and according to Leyton, "they are among the most class conscious people in America, obsessed with every nuance of status, class and power" (p. 30). In essence, these types of serial killers are frustrated and alienated, ultimately expressing their proletarian rebellion via acts of murder.

This thesis is similar to what mainstream criminology says about the typical conventional murderer. Known murderers are overwhelmingly from lower socioeconomic strata (Hagan, 1994; Luckenbill, 1984; Silverman & Kennedy, 1988; Wolfgang, 1958). They are typically the young, the poor, and the poorly educated. For example, regarding women who kill their children, Goetting (1995) observed that

> These are minority mothers who, for the most part, are living in loosely structured relationships with men, are poorly equipped to overcome the daily mundane struggles just to get by. They are drastically limited in the educational and occupational resources and in the social skills required to maintain a life of comfort and dignity. (p. 84)

When compared with similar studies of known serial killers, we find that killers of both sexes seem to share a sense of powerlessness derived from their socioeconomic situations (Hickey, 1991; Holmes & Holmes, 1994; Jenkins, 1994; Leyton, 1986; Scott, 1992).

Similarly, Scott (1992) linked the pattern of serial killing found among female serialists to both patriarchal and class struggles. She suggested that powerlessness, derived from female serialists' position in the class structure and their place in patriarchal society, are key factors leading some women to become serialists. For Scott, it is not surprising that these women chose to kill their intimates, the very people whom they feel have constrained them from fully participating in the public sphere. Hence, some women appear to kill for the same reasons males kill—as a vehicle for gaining a measure of power.

The notion that killing becomes a means of achieving power must also be assessed within the context of gender roles defined by patriarchal structures. Smart (1976), for example, argued that gender roles are socially constructed and are, therefore, dynamic. They reflect changing social patterns. To the extent that women's roles in contemporary society are changing, these changes are linked to increased economic opportunities and less rigid gender roles. Yet, these changes are not uniform. Not all women can take advantage of these role changes. Although women react to the differential access to changed circumstances in many different ways, it could be argued that women who become serialists react with deadly force. Just like Leyton's (1986) proletarian rebels who kill as an expression of their class consciousness, female serialists kill as an expression of their dislike of their role in patriarchal society.

There are ominous signs that the pattern of serial killing among female serialists may be changing. We noted previously that women target specific types of victims and use specific methods to do their killing. Hickey (1991), however, cautioned that female serialists have apparently begun to more frequently target strangers, especially when they kill with male accomplices. It is significant, of course, that women typically become serial killers of strangers, and/or employ torture and sexual violence, only when they have male accomplices. This may speak loudly about the importance of patriarchy and the gender roles it proscribes. Unfortunately, assessing whether the trend Hickey identified is real or an artifact of better detection is difficult because the data are incomplete. As Hickey noted, the reluctance of the police (and others) to accept that women can be serial killers may mean that many more female serialists than male serialists have escaped detection.

Linking social structure and victimology. Understanding the relation between social structure and victim selection also contributes to our comprehension of serial murder. If victimology tells us anything, it is that perpetrators choose their victims for a purpose. The work of Leyton (1986), Jenkins (1994), and Scott (1992) provides considerable insight into why serialists target certain victims. Leyton tells us that male serialists select victims who represent those forces or sectors of societies who are seen as blocking the perpetrator's upward social mobility. Killing these people is an act of resistance or rebellion against an entire class the killer believes to be holding him/her down. When serialists kill representatives of lower socioeconomic groups, the blow is intended as a symbolic strike against an insurgent group attempting to improve its social standing.

The targeting of specific racial or ethnic groups is a perfect illustration of this thesis. According to Jenkins (1994), some serialists may target ethnic groups because they seek to put these minorities in their place. Jenkins argued that within the United States, the targeting of Blacks by White serialists, the targeting of Whites by Black serialists, and, although rare, even the targeting of Blacks by Black serialists must be assessed within the context of American race relations.

As an extension of this argument, Scott (1992) argued that some female serialists kill those who are dependent on them (usually children, the elderly, or the infirm) to strike a blow against those social forces that limit these women's opportunities to take on more diverse social roles. Killing also gives these women a sense of power that is otherwise missing in their lives. For example, it could be argued that by killing her customers, Aileen Wuornos felt that she was taking control of situations in which she feared she had either lost control or was in danger of losing control.

Thus, the contention that some serialists kill to symbolically suppress racial or ethnic groups is similar to the radical feminist contention some serialists kill to symbolically subordinate women. Taken together, these observations broaden our understanding of the influence of social structure on the motivations of serial killers, both male and female. Serialists target specific groups as a means of fighting their own class, patriarchal, or power struggles.

CONCLUSION

Although feminists have pointed the analysis of serial murder in an important direction, ignoring issues of class and race has left their analyses incomplete. Thus, there is a need to broaden the feminist perspective on serial killing to enhance our understanding and to facilitate its potential reduction.

An excellent place to begin is to afford more attention to female serial murderers. Our point is not to advocate the simple acknowledgment that women can be serial killers; rather, we find that the feminist literature has missed several opportunities to develop a more comprehensive understanding of this issue.

One area that would allow for an expansion of feminist theory is to explore further the parallel ways in which women and other disadvantaged groups are treated as both victims and offenders. It appears that disadvantaged groups share a common fate: Their criminality and/or their victimization is ignored, dismissed, or otherwise treated as less significant than other forms of killing and/or victimization. Recognition of this point could lead to a much better understanding of serial murderers and their victims.

Feminist theorizing can provide a more powerful explanation for serial murder than it has done to date. It has illuminated the objectification of individuals as well as the glorification and normalization of violence within patriarchy. It has justifiably criticized the tendency toward victim blaming and found, particularly in certain psychological and biological theories, a tendency that works to obscure the full range of social mechanisms contributing to serial murder. Nevertheless, there are shortcomings in the feminist analysis of serial murder. Most notably, these include their narrow definitional criteria and an emphasis on ideology and sensationalism. These shortcomings demand an expansion and improvement of feminist analysis to account for the diversity in serial murderers and their differing modus operandi. Despite such shortcomings, we are convinced that when properly integrated with other analytical perspectives, feminist thought provides a unique opportunity to develop a more comprehensive theory of serial murder than has been offered to date.

NOTE

1. Radical feminists are not the only ones to have overestimated the rate of serial murder. Holmes and DeBurger (1988) also claimed that 3,000 to 5,000 serial murders were committed annually in the United States.

REFERENCES

Bureau of Justice Statistics. (1994). *Selected findings: Domestic violence, violence between intimates.* Washington, DC: U.S. Department of Justice.

Cameron, D., & Frazer, E. (1987). *The lust to kill: A feminist investigation of sexual murder.* New York: New York University Press.

Caputi, J. (1987). *The age of sex crime.* Bowling Green, OH: Bowling Green State University Popular Press.

Caputi, J. (1989). The sexual politics of murder. *Gender and Society, 3,* 437-456.

Caputi, J. (1990). The new founding fathers: The lore and lure of the serial killer in contemporary culture. *Journal of American Culture, 13,* 1-12.

Caputi, J., & Russell, D.E.H. (1992). Femicide: Sexist terrorism against women. In J. Radford & D.E.H. Russell (Eds.), *Femicide: The politics of woman killing* (pp. 13-21). New York: Maxwell MacMillan International.

Chesler, P. (1993). A woman's right to self-defence. *St. John's Law Review, 66,* 933-977.

Clark, L., & Lewis, D. (1977). *Rape: The price of coercive sexuality.* Toronto: Women's Press.

Dutton, D. G. (1994). Patriarchy and wife assault: The ecological fallacy. *Violence and Victims, 9,* 167-180.

Egger, S. A. (1984). A working definition of serial murder and the reduction of linkage blindness. *Journal of Police Science and Administration, 12,* 348-357.

Egger, S. A. (1990). Serial murder: A synthesis of literature and research. In S. A. Egger (Ed.), *Serial murder: An elusive phenomenon* (pp. 3-34). New York: Praeger.

Faith, K. (1993). *Unruly women: The politics of confinement and resistance.* Vancouver: Press Gang.

Goetting, A. (1995). *Homicide in families and other special populations.* New York: Springer.

Hagan, J. (1994). *Crime and disrepute.* Thousand Oaks, CA: Pine Forge.

Hickey, E. (1986). The female serial murderer. *Journal of Police and Criminal Psychology, 2,* 72-81.

Hickey, E. W. (1991). *Serial murders and their victims.* Belmont, CA: Wadsworth.

Holmes, R., & DeBurger, J. (1988). *Serial murder.* Newbury Park, CA: Sage.

Holmes, R., & Holmes, S. (1994). *Murder in America.* Thousand Oaks, CA: Sage.

Jenkins, P. (1994). *Using murder: The social construction of serial homicide.* New York: Aldine de Gruyter.

Jurik, N. C., & Winn, R. (1990). Gender and homicide: A comparison of men and women who kill. *Violence and Victims, 5,* 227-241.

Keeney, B. T., & Heide, K. M. (1994). Gender differences in serial murderers: A preliminary analysis. *Journal of Interpersonal Violence, 9,* 383-398.

Levin, J., & Fox, J. A. (1985). *Mass murder: America's growing menace.* New York: Plenum.

Leyton, E. (1986). *Hunting humans: The rise of multiple murder.* Toronto: McClelland and Stewart.

Luckenbill, D. F. (1984). Murder and assault. In R. F. Meier (Ed.), *Major forms of crime* (pp. 19-45). Beverly Hills, CA: Sage.

Malamuth, N. M., & Donnerstein, E. (Eds.). (1984). *Pornography and aggression.* Toronto: Academic Press.

McKenzie, C. (1995). A study of serial murder. *Journal of Offender Therapy and Comparative Criminology, 39,* 3-10.

O'Reilly-Fleming, T. (1996). The evolution of multiple murder in historical perspective. In T. O'Reilly-Fleming (Ed.), *Serial murder and mass murder: Theory, research and policy* (pp. 1-37). Toronto: Canadian Scholars.

Quindlen, A. (1993, March 10). Gynocide. *New York Times,* p. A19.

Radford, J. (1992a). Introduction. In J. Radford & D.E.H. Russell (Eds.), *Femicide: The politics of women killing* (pp. 5-12). New York: Maxwell MacMillan International.

Radford, J. (1992b). Where do we go from here? In J. Radford & D.E.H. Russell (Eds.), *Femicide: The politics of women killing* (pp. 5-12). New York: Maxwell MacMillan International.

Radford, J., & Russell, D.E.H. (Eds.). (1992). *Femicide: The politics of women killing.* New York: Maxwell MacMillan International.

Ressler, R., Burgess, A., & Douglas, J. (1987). *Sexual homicide: Patterns and motives.* Lexington, MA: Lexington.

Russell, D. (1984). *Sexual exploitation: Rape, child sexual abuse, and workplace harassment.* Beverly Hills, CA: Sage.

Scott, H. (1992). *Female serial killer: A well-kept secret of the gentler sex.* Unpublished master's thesis, University of Guelph, Ontario, Canada.

Seagrave, K. (1992). *Women serial and mass murderers: A worldwide reference, 1590 through 1990.* Jefferson, NC: McFarland.

Silverman, R. A., & Kennedy, L. W. (1988). Women who kill their children. *Violence and Victims, 3,* 113-126.

Smart, C. (1976). *Women, crime, and criminology: A feminist critique.* London: Routledge and Kegan Paul.

Wolfgang, M. (1958). *Patterns of criminal homicide.* Philadelphia: University of Pennsylvania Press.

Julie Cluff *received her B.A. in sociology from the University of Guelph in 1996. She begins postgraduate studies in the fall of 1997. Her interests are in legal studies, criminal justice, criminal behavior, and media images of crime.*

Allison Hunter *received her B.A. in sociology from the University of Guelph in 1997. She begins postgraduate studies in the fall of 1997. Her interests are in criminal justice, the sociology of law, law and social policy, and workfare and welfare reform.*

Ronald Hinch *is Associate Professor in the Department of Sociology and Anthropology at the University of Guelph. His research interests focus on issues related to the study of violence. He is the author of several articles assessing changes in Canadian sexual assault laws and, with Walter DeKeseredy, is the coauthor of* Woman Abuse: Sociological Perspectives *(Thompson Educational, 1991).*

Part VII
Policing Concerns

Crime Problems

The
Lust Murderer

By ROBERT R. HAZELWOOD
and JOHN E. DOUGLAS

Special Agents
Behavioral Science Unit
FBI Academy
Quantico, Va.

On August 29, 1975, the nude, mutilated body of a 25-year-old mother of two was found near Columbia, S.C. Both breasts had been removed, the reproductive system had been displaced, numerous cut and stab wounds were evidenced by the body, and there was indication of anthropophagy.[1]

This was the scene of a lust murder, one of the most heinous crimes committed by man. While not a common occurrence, it is one which frightens and arouses the public as does no other crime.

Of primary concern are those factors which differentiate the lust murder from the more common sadistic homicide, physical evidence present at the scene which may assist in determining the responsible individual(s), and possible personality characteristics of the murderer. It is not the authors' contention that the material presented is applicable to all such crimes or their perpetrators, but rather that the majority of the crimes and offenders involved will exhibit the characteristics set forth. The data presented here have not been quantified, but are based upon the authors' examination of case reports, interviews with investigative personnel, and a careful review of the literature. Minor variations of the terms used may occur, depending on the source of reference.

It is the authors' contention that the lust murder is unique and is distinguished from the sadistic homicide by the involvement of a mutilating attack or displacement of the breasts, rectum, or genitals. Further, while there are always exceptions, basically two types of individuals commit the lust murder. These individuals will be labeled as the Organized Nonsocial and the Disorganized Asocial personalities.

The Organized Nonsocial

The organized nonsocial (nonsocial) lust murderer exhibits complete indifference to the interests and welfare of society and displays an irresponsible and self-centered attitude. While disliking people in general, he does not avoid them. Instead, he is capable of displaying an amiable facade for as long as it takes to manipulate people toward his own personal goal. He is a methodical and cunning individual, as demonstrated in the perpetration of his crime. He is fully cognizant of the criminality of his act and its impact on society, and it is for this reason that he commits the crime. He generally lives some distance from the crime scene and will cruise, seeking a victim. Dr. Robert P. Brittain, author of "The Sadistic Murderer," has stated, "They (sadistic murderers) are excited by cruelty, whether in books or in films, in fact or fantasy."[2]

The Disorganized Asocial

The disorganized asocial (asocial) lust murderer exhibits primary characteristics of societal aversion. This individual prefers his own company to that of others and would be typified as a loner. He experiences difficulty in negotiating interpersonal relationships and consequently feels rejected and lonely. He lacks the cunning of the nonsocial type and commits the crime in a more frenzied and less methodical manner. The crime is likely to be committed in close proximity to his residence or place of employment, where he feels secure and more at ease.

The Crime

The lust murder is premeditated in the obsessive fantasies of the perpetrator. Yet, the killer may act on the "spur-of-the-moment" when the opportunity presents itself. That is to say, the murderer has precisely planned the crime in his fantasies, but has not consciously decided to act out those fantasies until the moment of the crime. Consequently, the victim is typically unknown to the killer, a fact borne out by the cases studied by the authors.

The location of the victim's body may be indicative of the type of murderer involved. Typically, the asocial type leaves the body at the scene of death, and while the location is not open to the casual observer, there has been no attempt to conceal the body. Conversely, the nonsocial type commits the crime in a secluded or isolated location and may later transport it to an area where it is likely to be found.

While there may be no conscious intent to be arrested, the nonsocial type wants the excitement derived from the publicity about the body's discovery and its impact on the victim's community.

The lust murder is committed in a brutally sadistic manner. While the victim may be either male or female, the crime is predominantly heterosexual and intraracial in nature. The victim's body exhibits gross mutilation and/or displacement of the breasts, rectum, or genitals and may have been subjected to excessive stabbing or slashing with a sharp instrument. The victim's death typically occurs shortly following abduction or attack, and the mutilation that takes place follows death. Dr. J. Paul de River notes in his book, *Crime and the Sexual Psychopath:*

> "The lust murderer, usually, after killing his victim, tortures, cuts, maims or slashes the victim in the regions on or about the genitalia, rectum, breast in the female, and about the neck, throat and buttocks, as usually these parts contain strong sexual significance to him, and serve as sexual stimulus." [3]

If, however, there is physical or medical evidence indicating the victim was subjected to torture or mutilation prior to death, this factor indicates that the perpetrator was the nonsocial rather than the asocial type.

Seldom will the lust murderer use a firearm to kill, for he experiences too little psychosexual gratification with such an impersonal weapon. Most frequently, death results from strangulation, blunt force, or the use of a pointed, sharp instrument. The asocial type is more prone to use a weapon of opportunity and may leave it at the scene, while the nonsocial type may carry the murder weapon with him and take it when departing the scene. Therefore, the murderer's choice of weapon and its proximity to the scene can be greatly significant to the investigation.

Dr. de River comments that the instrument itself may be symbolic to the murderer and he may place it in a position near the victim. This is a form of pride and exhibitionistic behavior and can be sexually gratifying to him. [4]

The investigator may find that the victim has been bitten on the breasts, buttocks, neck, abdomen, thighs, or genitals, as these body areas have sexual associations. Limb or breast amputation, or in some instances total dissection, may have taken place. Dis-

"The lust murder is premeditated in the obsessive fantasies of the perpetrator."

section of the victim's body, when committed by the nonsocial type, may be an attempt to hinder the identification of the victim. The asocial individual approaches his victim in much the same way as an inquisitive child with a new toy. He involves himself in an exploratory examination of the sexually significant parts of the body in an attempt to determine how they function and appear beneath the surface.

Occasionally, it will be noted that the murderer has smeared the victim's blood on himself, the victim, or the surface on which the body rests. This activity is more frequently associated with the asocial type and relates to the uncontrollable frenzy of the attack.

Penis penetration of the victim is not to be expected from the asocial individual, but is predominantly associated with the nonsocial type, even to the extent of "necrophilia." [5] These activities on the nonsocial's part reflect his desire to outrage society and call attention to his total disdain for societal acceptance. The asocial type more commonly inserts foreign objects into the body orifaces in a probing and curiosity-motivated, yet brutal, manner. Evidence of ejaculation may be found on or near the victim or her clothing.

Frequently, the murderer will take a "souvenir," normally an object or article of clothing belonging to the victim, but occasionally it may be a more personal reminder of the encounter—a

finger, a lock of hair, or a part of the body with sexual association. The souvenir is taken to enable the murderer to relive the scene in later fantasies. The killer here is acting out his fantasy, and complete possession of the victim is part of that fantasy. As previously mentioned, the perpetrator may commit an anthropophagic act and such an act is indicative of asocial involvement.

Finally, the scene itself will exhibit much less physical evidence when the murderer is the nonsocial type. As stated, the individual categorized as the nonsocial type is very cunning and more methodical than the asocial type, who commits a more frenzied assault. It is interesting to note, however, that both types may be compelled to return to the scene, albeit for different reasons. While the asocial type may return to engage in further mutilation or to relive the experience, the nonsocial type returns to determine if the body has been discovered and to check on the progress of the investigation. Instances have occurred when the nonsocial type changed the body's location to insure its discovery.

Of interest is the almost obsessive desire of the nonsocial type to assess the police investigation, even to the extent of frequenting police "hangouts" to eavesdrop on discussions of unsolved crimes, or in some manner, inserting himself into the investigation. In one case, the murderer returned to the scene after it had been examined by police laboratory technicians and deposited articles of clothing worn by the victim on the day she died. In both of two other cases, the killer visited the cemetery site of the victim and left articles belonging to the victim on her grave. It is as though he were involved in a "game" with the authorities. Such actions appear to further his "will to power" [6] or desire to control.

Portrait of the Lust Murderer

What set of circumstances create the individual who becomes the lust murderer? The authors do not possess the expertise to explain the multiple and complex casual factors associated with the psychological development of the individual who commits such a heinous crime. But, it is generally accepted that the foundation of the personality is formed within the first few years of life. While extreme stress, frequent narcotic use, or alcohol abuse can cause personality disorganization in later life, it is the early years that are critical to the personality structure and development.

Seldom does the lust murderer come from an environment of love and understanding. It is more likely that he was an abused or neglected child who experienced a great deal of conflict in his early life and was unable to develop and use adequate coping devices (i.e. defense mechanisms). Had he been able to do so, he would have withstood the stresses placed on him and developed normally in early childhood. It must be emphasized that many individuals are raised in environments not conducive to healthy psychological development, yet they become productive citizens. These stresses, frustrations, and subsequent anxieties, along with the inability to cope with them, may lead the individual to withdraw from the society which he perceives as hostile and threatening.

Through this internalization process, he becomes secluded and isolated from others and may eventually select suicide as an alternative to a life of loneliness and frustration. The authors have designated this reaction to life as disorganized asocial. This type possesses a poor self-image and secretly rejects the society which he feels rejects him. Family and associates would describe him a nice, quiet person who keeps to himself, but who never quite realized his potential. During adolescence, he may have engaged in voyeuristic activities or the theft of feminine clothing. Such activities serve as a substitute for his inability to approach women sexually in a mature and confident manner.

The individual designated by the authors as the organized nonsocial type harbors similar feelings of hostility, but elects not to withdraw and internalize his hostility. Rather, he overtly expresses it through aggressive and seemingly senseless acts against society. Typically, he begins to demonstrate his hostility as he passes through puberty and into adolescence. He would be described as a troublemaker and a manipulator of people, concerned only for himself. He experiences difficulties with family, friends,

"The lust murder is committed in a brutally sadistic manner."

and "authority figures" through antisocial acts which may include homicide. Thomas Strentz and Conrad Hassel, in the June 1978 issue of *Journal of Police Science and Administration,* wrote of a youth who had first murdered at the age of 15 and was committed to a mental institution. After his release, he murdered and dismembered eight women. [7] It is the nonsocial's aim to get even with society and inflict pain and punishment upon others.

The Role of Fantasy

As noted, the lust murder is premeditated in obsessive fantasies experienced by both the asocial and nonsocial murderers. Fantasy provides them an avenue of escape from a world of hate and rejection. Dr. James J. Reinhardt in his book, *Sex Perversions and Sex Crimes,* has written:

"A study of these cases almost invariably reveals a long struggle against what Reik calls the 'forward thrust.' By fantasy the murderer attempts to wall himself in against the fatal act, while at the same time gratifying the compulsive psychic demands in the development and use of *fantasy.*

These sadistic [fantasies] seem always to have preceded the brutal act of *lust* murder. These *fantasies* take all sorts of grotesque and cruel forms. The pervert, on this level of degeneracy, may resort to pornographic pictures, grotesque and cruel literary episodes, out of which he weaves fantasies. On these, his imagination dwells until he loses all contact with reality, only to find himself suddenly impelled to carry his fantasies into the world of actuality. This is done, apparently, by drawing human objects into the *fantasy.*" [8]

James Russell Odom, tried and convicted with James Clayton Lawson for the brutal lust murder described at the beginning of this article, stated that while he and Lawson were at a mental institution, they would express their fantasies about women:

"(Odom) raping them and Lawson mutilating them . . . (we had fantasized so much that at times I didn't know what was real." [9]

If he acts out the fantasy (commits the crime), his goal will be to destroy the victim and thereby become the sole possessor. James Lawson (mentioned above) is quoted as saying:

"Then I cut her throat so she would not scream. . . . at this time I wanted to cut her body so she would not look like a person and destroy her so she would not exist. I began to cut on her body. I remember cutting her breasts off. After this, all I remember is that I kept cutting on her body." [10]

The victim may represent something he desires sexually, but is unable to approach. Lawson speaks again, "I did not rape the girl. I only wanted to destroy her." [11]

Rarely encountered is the asocial type who is capable of normal heterosexual relationships. He may desire such relationships, but he also fears them. Dr. Reinhardt, on an interview with a famous lust murderer, wrote: ". . . he at first denied ever attempting any sex play with girls. Two days later with one of his rare shows of emotion he said, looking much ashamed, that twice, later correcting himself to eight times, he had touched girls 'on the breasts' and then pressed 'on the leg.' Always having done this, he would immediately burst into tears and 'be upset and unable to sleep'." [12]

The Psychological Profile

A psychological profile is an educated attempt to provide investigative agencies with specific information as to the type of individual who committed a certain crime. It must be clearly stated at the outset that what can be done in this area is limited, and prescribed investigative procedures should not be suspended, altered, or replaced by receipt of a profile. Rather, the material provided should be considered and employed as another investigative tool. The process is an art and not a science, and while it may be applicable to many types of investigations, its use is restricted primarily to crimes of violence or potential violence.

When prepared by the FBI, the profile may include the perpetrator's age, race, sex, socioeconomic and marital status, educational level, arrest history, location of residence in relation to the scene, and certain personality traits.

A profile is based on characteristic patterns or factors of uniqueness that distinguish certain individuals from the general population. In the case of lust murder, clues to those factors of uniqueness are found on the victim's body and at the scene and would include the amount and location of mutilation involved, type of weapon used, cause of death, and the position of the body. The profiler is searching for clues which indicate the probable personality configuration of the responsible individual.

"The location of the victim's body may be indicative of the type of murderer involved."

In preparing the profile, it is preferable to have access to the scene prior to its disturbance. In most instances, this is impossible. In lieu of being at the scene, the profiler must be provided investigative reports, autopsy protocols, detailed photographs of the body, scene, and surrounding area, as well as a map depicting the victim's last known location in relation to its present location and any known information pertaining to the victim and her activities.

There are violent crimes in which there is an absence of uniqueness; therefore, it is not possible to provide a profile. However, this is not likely to occur in the case of a lust murder.

Summary

While not a common occurrence, the lust murder frightens and arouses the public as does no other crime. The lust murder involves the death and subsequent mutilating attack of the breasts, rectum, and genital areas of the victim. The crime is typically heterosexual and intraracial in nature and is committed by one of two types of individuals: The disorganized asocial personality, or the organized nonsocial personality.

The organized nonsocial type feels rejection by and hatred for the society in which he lives. His hostile feelings are manifested overtly, and the lust murder is the final expression of the hatred he feels. The disorganized asocial type also feels rejection and hatred for his world, but withdraws and internalizes his feelings, living within a world of fantasy until he acts out that fantasy with his victim.

While commonalities exist in the commission of the lust murder, there are certain factors which may indicate the personality type involved. These factors include the location of the body, evidence of torture or mutilation having occurred prior to death, smearing of the victim's blood, evidence of penis penetration or anthropophagy, and the availability of physical evidence at the scene.

The crime is premeditated in the obsessive fantasies experienced by both the asocial and the nonsocial types, yet it is a crime of opportunity, one in which the victim is not usually known to the murderer.

The use of psychological profiling in such crimes may be of assistance in determining the personality type involved. It is a search for clues indicating the probable personality configuration of the responsible individual(s). It is a useful tool, but must not alter, suspend, or replace prescribed investigative procedures.   **FBI**

Footnotes
[1] Anthropophagy: Consuming the victim's flesh or blood.
[2] Robert P. Brittain, "The Sadistic Murderer," *Medical Science and the Law*, vol. IV (1970), p. 202.
[3] J. Paul de River, *Crime and the Sexual Psychopath* (Springfield, Ill.: Charles C. Thomas, 1950), p. 40.
[4] J. Paul de River, *The Sexual Criminal* (Springfield, Ill.: Charles C. Thomas, 1950), p. 233.
[5] Necrophilia: A desire for relations with the dead.
[6] Calvin S. Hall and Lindsey Gardner, *Theories of Personality*, 2d ed. (New York: John Wiley and Sons, Inc., 1970).
[7] Thomas Strentz and Conrad V. Hassel, "The Sociopath—A Criminal Enigma," *Journal of Police Science and Administration*, (June 1978).
[8] James J. Reinhardt, *Sex Perversions and Sex Crimes* (Springfield, Ill.: Charles C. Thomas, 1957), pp. 208–209.
[9] Statement of Odom as reported by *The Record* (newspaper) April 7, 1976, 1–A.
[10] Statement made to South Carolina law enforcement authorities by James Clayton Lawson on September 3, 1975.
[11] *Ibid.*
[12] Reinhardt, pp. 221–222.

[29]

Rape and Rape-Murder: One Offender and Twelve Victims

Robert K. Ressler, M.S., Ann Wolbert Burgess, D.N.Sc., and John E. Douglas, M.S.

This study analyzes data pertaining to 12 rapes and rape-murders committed by one male adolescent offender over a 4-year period. All offenses except the first were committed while the offender was under psychiatric and probationary supervision. The use or relinquishment of violence by the offender was found to be dependent on subtle interpersonal factors. The authors stress the importance of the use of crime scene data and interviews of patients who have committed sex crimes, the role of psychological profiles in apprehension of suspects, and the contribution of law enforcement as a data resource. (Am J Psychiatry 140:36–40, 1983)

Rape-murder, a crime of increasing concern in our society, results from one person killing another in the context of power, sexuality, and brutality. Although the literature is replete with reports on the murderer, it is relatively silent on the victim. This omission from the clinical literature significantly impedes our understanding of the possible variables in a rape assault and handicaps our progress in victimology. To contribute to the study of rape-murder, we report on 12 rapes committed by a male teenager over a 4-year period in which 5 of his victims were murdered following the rape.

PROFILE OF THE OFFENDER

The offender, born 24 years ago in the Midwest, was the youngest of 3 children and had an older adopted brother and natural sister. It is reported that he was an Rh baby and required a complete blood transfusion at birth. He has reportedly suffered no major health problems. The parents separated and divorced when he was age 7, and both parents remarried shortly thereafter. He continued to live with his mother even though her second marriage dissolved when he was 12. He completed age-level work until his senior year in

Received April 27, 1981; revised Oct. 13, 1981; accepted Nov. 4, 1981. From the Behavioral Science Unit, FBI Academy, Quantico, Va.; and Boston City Hospital, Boston, Mass. Address reprint requests to Mr. Ressler, FBI Academy, Quantico, VA 20135.

Supported in part by National Institute of Justice grant CX-0065.

Copyright © 1983 American Psychiatric Association 0002-953X/83/01/0036/05/$00.50.

high school, when he was involuntarily withdrawn from school due to excessive absenteeism and lack of progress.

He was of average intelligence and had aspired to attend college. He was athletically inclined and played league baseball. He was outgoing, often attended social events, and had a close circle of friends, both male and female. He saw himself as a leader, not a follower.

The offender's antisocial behavior was first recorded when he was age 9, when he and 3 other boys were caught by the school principal writing cusswords on the sidewalk. The boys were required to wash the sidewalk until the words were removed. His criminal record started when he was age 12 with assaultive and disruptive behavior involving breaking into an apartment and stealing property valued at $100. At age 13 he was charged with driving without an operator's license; at age 14 he was charged with burglary and rape and committed 2 minor acts of petty larceny as well as stealing a car. He readily admitted using alcohol and drugs of all types from his early teen years. He worked sporadically throughout his high school years as part of a program whereby he attended school in the morning and worked in the afternoon.

The offender was sent out of state to a psychiatric residential facility following the first felony of rape and burglary at age 14. During his 18-month stay he received individual insight-oriented psychotherapy, and the discharge recommendation was that he live at home, attend public school, and continue psychotherapy on a weekly outpatient basis, with his mother actively involved in his treatment. Three weeks after returning home from the residential facility he was charged with attempted armed robbery—an act intended to be rape. It took 1 year for him to come before a judge for sentencing on this charge, and in that time he had committed the first rape and murder but had not yet been charged for that offense. The disposition on the attempted armed robbery was probation and outpatient psychotherapy; he had served 8 months when he was apprehended for the 5 murders. His psychiatric diagnoses according to *DSM-II* have included adolescent adjustment reaction, character disorder without psychosis, and multiple personality. At the time of his arrest for the murders the young man was 19 years old, weighed 65 kg, and was 170 cm tall. He was given 5 life sentences for the 5 rape-murders. After 2 years of incarceration, he admitted to 6 additional rapes for which he was never charged.

PROFILE OF THE VICTIMS

All of the 12 victims were female, and they represented different ethnic groups. They ranged in age from 17 to 34 years and were older than the offender by 1 to 15 years. Several victims were taller and heavier than the offender. Nine of them were total strangers to him; he knew 3 by sight. Two of the 9 women who were strangers to him recognized him after his capture. Most of the victims were of middle-income status, and the majority lived in the apartment complex where the offender lived with his mother. All of the victims except 1 high school student were employed full-time and worked in such positions as teachers, postal supervisors, store buyers, airline stewardesses, and administrative assistants. Some of them also had part-time jobs and/or were continuing their college education. Most of the victims were not married; several were divorced. Two were known to have children. Five of the women were raped and murdered; 5 were raped only by the offender; and 2 were gang raped. One escaped from the offender before he could commit a sex crime. Most of the victims were approached at knife point as they entered the elevator in their apartment building. All rape-murder victims were abducted from the same location, killed in different areas, and found fully clothed. The time spent in locating their bodies ranged from 1 day to 6 weeks.

DATA COLLECTION

Data were collected in two ways: through interviews with the offender and completion of an interview guide and through the use of police reports, court evaluation records, photographs of crime scene investigations, and medical examiners' reports. An obvious limitation to the interviews was having to rely on the offender's memory and reconstruction of the crimes. This bias was countered with documentation from prison and court records. On the other hand, the offender's admission of 6 additional rapes adds to the data not available through official channels. Another methodological drawback was that the information on what victims said and did came from the offender.

FINDINGS

The analysis of the data suggests that the offender's criminal behavior changed in two major ways: The sexual aggression escalated from rape to rape and murder, and the offenses increased in frequency over time (see table 1). Of special note are the facts that 1) all rape and murder offenses except the first were committed while he was under psychiatric supervision and on probation, 2) the 6 rapes that were not charged to him were also committed while he was under psychiatric supervision and on probation, and 3) the 5

TABLE 1. Escalation of the Criminal Behavior of an Adolescent Boy

Boy's Age (years)	Offense	Victim's Age (years)	Disposition
12	Petty larceny		Probation
12	Disrupting school		Probation
13	Driving without an operator's license		Case continued until his 18th birthday
14	Burglary and rape	25	Sent to state psychiatric center
14	Petty larceny		Sent to state psychiatric center
14	Breaking and entering		Sent to state psychiatric center
16	Rape	25	Never charged
16	Rape	25	Never charged
16	Burglary and rape (codefendant)	17	Never charged
16	Rape (codefendant)	25	Never charged
17	Attempted armed robbery	22	Probation and outpatient therapy
18	Rape	25	Never charged
18	Rape and murder	24	Life imprisonment
19	Rape and murder	22	Life imprisonment
19	Rape and murder	34	Life imprisonment
19	Rape	25	Never charged
19	Rape and murder	27	Life imprisonment
19	Rape and murder	24	Life imprisonment

homicides were not linked to one offender and did not appear to include rape until he was apprehended and described the offenses.

Rape and Intended Rape: The First 7 Offenses

The first rape with which the offender was charged, when he was 14, occurred in the apartment next to where he lived with his mother. He had returned home from a party and had gone to bed but woke up fantasizing about the 25-year-old divorced neighbor woman who often employed him for small errands. He got up, went outside wearing a ski mask, scaled the apartment wall like a "cat burglar," and entered the woman's third-floor apartment through the balcony door. He raped the woman several times, left through the front door, returned to his own apartment, and went to sleep. He was apprehended 3 weeks later and was eventually convicted on the basis of evidence found in the apartment (i.e., fingerprints and clothing) rather than the victim's identification of him. A woman judge sentenced him to an out-of-state psychiatric residential facility.

The second rape (the first one with which he was never charged) occurred when he was 16 and home from the residential facility for Christmas vacation. The evening before he returned to the facility, he approached a woman in the elevator in the apartment complex and at knife point took her to another location and raped her. The second rape with which he was never charged (third in the sequence) occurred 3 months later when he approached a woman in the parking lot of a local school he attended while at the

RAPE-MURDER

residential facility. He forced the woman at knife point to drive to her apartment, where he raped her. The third and fourth rapes with which he was never charged included codefendants. While on a weekend pass, the offender and 2 other patients from the residential facility stole a car, traveled out of state, broke into a house, stole 2 guns and money, and each raped a 17-year-old girl who was in the house. The offender returned home; however, his mother immediately sent him back to the residential facility and he was counseled on his runaway behavior. Three months later he and another patient went to a local swimming pool. They broke into the women's locker room and raped a young woman, covering her head with a towel.

The sixth rape (the fifth for which he was never charged) occurred before the first rape-murder he committed and involved a woman he had seen in his own apartment building. He obtained an air pistol, captured her in the apartment elevator, took her to a storage room, and, covering her face with her jacket, raped her twice.

An attempted armed robbery (an act intended to be rape) occurred 3 weeks after his release from the residential treatment facility. He targeted a woman entering the elevator of the apartment complex, donned a ski mask, and held a knife to her. She was successful in escaping.

> She broke . . . pushed me out of the way and started going to the front of the elevator, pushed the button to open the door and started to run and she stumbled. I'd started to run after her and stumbled over her and at that point the knife fell and she was on the ground hollering and I was on the ground next to her, scared to death. My mind went blank. I ran out of the building. [He was subsequently arrested.]

Rape and Murder: The Last 6 Offenses

The offender selected the last 6 victims at random as he watched cars drive into the apartment complex where he lived. Once he targeted a victim, he would walk behind her, follow her into the apartment elevator, pull his knife, and tell her it was a holdup. Then they would leave the building, either for the victim's car or for an area near the apartment complex. In one case the pattern was reversed. The offender was hitchhiking and was given a ride by a woman who was going to a party in his apartment complex. She let him off at his building; he watched her park her car and then ran across the complex, entered the elevator with her, and captured her there. All abductions and murders occurred within his own territory. Thus, known territory was a distinct advantage for him. ("Going somewhere that I didn't know or where the cops patrolled might get me caught. I knew what time the cops came by in the morning because I'd be sitting there.") Indeed, he was right. One of the reasons he was not caught until after the fifth murder was that the police were looking for strangers—especially suspicious strangers—not a teenager living in the area.

The offender's use of either verbal or physical strategies to assert control over the victim depended on the victim's initial response. The victim who was compliant when he showed a weapon received no additional threats or orders. Victims who screamed received verbal threats, and those who refused to cooperate were physically struck.

Interaction Between Offender and Victim

Reconstruction of the victims' talk and actions as viewed from the offender's perspective revealed that conversation and behavior served to either neutralize or escalate his affective state.

Murder victim 1, rape victim 7. The woman's talk ("She asked which way I wanted it") raised the offender's suspicion of her life style. After the rape and while both were dressing, he had not decided on his next action. The woman's sudden attempt to escape triggered in him feelings of anger and frustration that resulted in increased aggression. He stated:

> She took off running down the ravine. That's when I grabbed her. I had her in an armlock. She was bigger than me. I started choking her . . . she stumbled . . . we rolled down the hill and into the water. I banged her head against the side of a rock and held her head under water.

Death was determined to be from strangulation.

Murder victim 2, rape victim 8. The woman's talk consisted of many questions ("She wanted to know why I wanted to do this; why I picked her; didn't I have a girl friend; what was my problem; what I was going to do"), which served to annoy him. The woman, talking while driving the car, suddenly stepped on the accelerator and attempted to counter his control by threatening to drive the car into a tree. He turned off the ignition and put his foot on the brake, and the car slid sideways. The car stopped, and the woman got out and ran across the road screaming for help. He said:

> I go into the woods after her. I see her run from behind a tree and that's when I go after her. From then on I knew I had to kill her. She trips over a log and that's when I catch up with her and I just start stabbing her.

The victim was stabbed 14 times in the chest.

Murder victim 3, rape victim 9. The offender claimed he had not decided whether he would kill this woman. He would not let her talk ("The more I got to know about the women the softer I got"). He ordered her to be quiet and turn on the radio. He described his thinking as follows:

> I was thinking . . . I've killed two. I might as well kill this one, too. . . . Something in me was wanting to kill. . . . I tied her up with her stockings and I started to walk away . . . then I heard her through the woods kind of rolling around and making muffled sounds. And I turned back and said, "No, I have to kill her. I've got to do this to preserve and protect myself."

The woman died from 21 stab wounds to the left side of the thorax and upper abdomen.

Rape victim 10. The offender had decided to kill this woman, but her talking saved her life ("She told me her father was dying of cancer"). Her talk evidently neutralized his aggression due to his identification with the situation ("I thought of my own brother who had cancer. I couldn't kill her. She had it bad already"). He threw her car keys out of the window and ran off into the woods.

Murder victim 4, rape victim 11. The offender had decided to kill this woman. Her resistance and attempt to escape triggered his violence.

> She scratched me across the face. I got mad; she started to run. I got up from falling down and chased her. She ran into a tree. I caught her. We wrestled, rolled over the embankment into the water. I landed with my face in the water. . . . That's where the idea to drown her came. . . . She was fighting and she was strong but I put her head under the water and just sat there with my hands on her neck.

The cause of death was drowning.

Murder victim 5, rape victim 12. This woman's talk led the offender to realize that she knew him. This knowledge escalated his fear of being apprehended and, in turn, led him to confess the 4 previous murders. The decision to kill was made quickly.

> We were walking along, through the culverts, underneath the highway. That's when I pulled out the knife and without even saying anything, I stabbed her . . . maybe 50–100 times.

He buried the victim's body in a shallow grave.

Behavior Following the Murders

Following each murder, the offender would usually take an item of jewelry from the woman's body for a souvenir, go back to the woman's car and search through her purse for money, drive her car for an extended period of time, park the car several blocks from his apartment, return to his apartment and go to bed, and watch television and newspapers for reports about the discovery of the body.

DISCUSSION

Psychodynamics of Rape-Murder

Some reports have suggested that rapists rarely murder (1) but that when they do, the motives are social rather than personal; that is, they murder to silence the victim and prevent detection (2). This motive differs from lust-murder, whereby sexuality and aggression fuse into a single psychological experience known as sadism (3). Rada (4) argued, and we agree, that rapists are capable of murder but for

different reasons than the lust-murderer. One reason, Rada suggested, is that in some rapists there appears to be a progressive increase in aggressive fantasies about women that over time may eventually lead to murder.

The case we have reported suggests that for some rapists there is a progression in the offender's *intent* or decision making toward killing. With the first 3 murders the offender made the decision to kill the women during the period he interacted with them, but in the last 2 murders, he decided ahead of time to kill them. This case also suggests an additional dimension to motive in rape-murder. The modern view of rape regards it as an act of violence expressing power as one motive (5). We suggest that the psychological motive of power expands for the rapist-murderer from a need for power over one person ("It was a real turn on to realize the victims weren't reporting or identifying me") to a need for power over a collective group ("I'm too slick for them") that included the police, judges, psychiatrists, and psychologists.

This case illustrates the influence of an individual's affective state when combined with various degrees of intent to commit murder. A review of the offender's last 6 offenses suggests that 2 affective states may influence the decision to kill: Escalating the anger motive in the rapist may trigger aggressive behavior aimed at establishing dominance and authority, and stimulating fear and decreasing the power motive in the rapist may trigger aggressive behavior aimed at self-preservation (5).

Interviewing Patients Charged with Crimes

The fact that the offender was under psychiatric supervision when he committed most of his criminal acts suggests that close attention be paid to psychiatric interviewing techniques. We offer the following two suggestions.

1. When interviewing a patient who has been charged with crimes, one should pay careful attention to the deviant behavior and focus on all dimensions of the interactional aspects of the crime. If possible, and if it is within agency policy, one should gather supplementary data regarding the crime scene, the victim's statements, police interviews, and official reports and talk with staff who have worked with the patient. These corroborating data will lend a perspective other than the patient's for assessment of and challenge to the patient. The interviewer should maintain a high index of suspicion when the patient denies committing or refuses to talk about the crime or deviant behavior and should consider the possibility that he or she is concealing other secretive and dangerous behavior. A parallel can be drawn between the dynamics of sex and secrecy (6) and incest and treatment.

2. Rape and attempted rape behavior should be viewed as serious and chronic and thus repetitive. The interviewer should not assume that a patient with a history of sexual assault has committed it only the number of times for which he or she is charged. When

RAPE-MURDER

the patient has been under stress and especially at times when he or she has been charged with other criminal acts (e.g., breaking and entering, stealing cars, larceny), the interviewer should inquire about concurrent assaultive behavior or rape fantasies. Our findings support those from Groth and associates' study (7) of convicted sex offenders recommended for treatment. Those authors reported that each offender had committed an average of 5 sexual assaults for which he was never apprehended.

Psychological Profiles

The fact that a psychiatrist wrote a psychological profile of the offender we have described suggests the need for further work in this area. The psychological profile is a critical technique in police work on unsolved crimes. In a comparison of the profile with the data obtained from the offender, two points can be made. First, no one speculated that the murder victims had been raped. The fact that they all were found fully clothed and without clinical evidence of sexual intercourse made the cases seem not sexually related. The offender admitted raping the victims several times. The possibility that he had a sexual dysfunction—retarded ejaculation—was never considered (8). Second, the profile report speculated that because he targeted women and used their underwear to bind them, he felt hostility toward his mother. Interview data suggested another authority figure in his life:

> That woman judge sent me to a diagnostic center. That's what started me off resenting authority. . . . Nobody could tell me what to do or when to do it or how to do it.

CONCLUSIONS

Gaps do exist in fully understanding a criminal act in general, and a sexual homicide in particular, because each of the various professionals and disciplines involved work with only one part of the picture. Cooperation through sharing information and collaborating on cases is often not practiced in the work setting. We undertook this study to address this gap in the transfer and sharing of criminal data. Frazier (9) encouraged the research step of developing descriptive patterns of murder as human action, with the caution to avoid simple, reductionistic conclusions about the causes of murder. We agree with this position and encourage studies across disciplines.

REFERENCES

1. Selkin J: Rape. Psychology Today, Jan 1975, pp 70–72, 74, 76
2. Podolsky E: Sexual violence. Medical Digest 34:60–63, 1966
3. Groth AN with Birnbaum HJ: Men Who Rape. New York, Plenum Press, 1979, p 44
4. Rada RT: Psychological factors in rapist behavior, in Clinical Aspects of the Rapist. Edited by Rada RT. New York, Grune & Stratton, 1978
5. Groth AN, Burgess AW, Holmstrom LL: Rape: power, anger, and sexuality. Am J Psychiatry 134:1239–1243, 1977
6. Burgess AW, Holmstrom LL: Sexual trauma of children and adolescents: pressure, sex and secrecy. Nurs Clin North Am 10:551–563, 1975
7. Groth AN, Longo R, McFadin B: Undetected recidivism among rapists and child molesters. Crime and Delinquency 28:450–458, 1982
8. Groth AN, Burgess AW: Sexual dysfunction during rape. N Engl J Med 297:764–766, 1977
9. Frazier SH: Murder—single and multiple. Aggression 52:304–312, 1974

[30]

The study of crime scene profiling efforts elicits two important patterns of sexual murders: organized and disorganized. These law enforcement categories have been derived from evidence and patterns of evidence at the site of sexual murders. The study then explores victim information and its relationship to the two categories. In particular, we explored victim response to the offender in terms of no resistance and active resistance to the assault. We found that regardless of type of resistance, active or passive, and category of offender, death ensued. When we examined nine victims who survived, the category of offender was not the predictor, rather, "chance happenings" preserved life.

Sexual Killers
and Their Victims

Identifying Patterns Through
Crime Scene Analysis

ROBERT K. RESSLER
FBI Academy

ANN W. BURGESS
University of Pennsylvania

JOHN E. DOUGLAS
FBI Academy

CAROL R. HARTMAN
Boston College

RALPH B. D'AGOSTINO
Boston University

Interpersonal violence spans a wide range of human behaviors of which murder represents one of the terminal disruptions in the equilibrium of a society. The tragedy of murder and its irrevocable effect on victims and families is often neglected in the focus on the mur-

Authors' Note: Preparation of this article was supported by Department of Justice grants: Office of Juvenile Justice and Delinquency Prevention (#84-JN-AX-K010) and

JOURNAL OF INTERPERSONAL VIOLENCE, Vol. 1 No. 3, September 1986 288-308
© 1986 Sage Publications, Inc.

derers. This interactional component between victim and murderer and its social impact needs to be addressed constantly if there is to be a balance in the understanding of such violence.

The voluminous scholarly and professional literature on murder traditionally has focused on the murderer and has presented a variety of ways to classify murderers (Lester, 1973; Wolfgang, 1958). Simon (1977) emphasizes that identifying personality profile types is crucial to the task of offender treatment and prediction of dangerousness for the prevention of murder. Wolfgang and Ferracuti (1967) identify two basic behaviors of murderers: (1) premeditated, intentional, felonious, planned, and rational murder; and (2) killing in the heat of passion or slaying as a result of intent to do harm, but without a specific intent to kill. They observe, "Many authors fail to distinguish between two basic types of murderers" and clarify that their concentration is on the second type, the "passionate" killer. In contrast, the type of killer frequently profiled by agents at the FBI's Behavioral Science Unit, who investigate unsolved murders at the request of local law enforcement officials, are those who not only plan their murders but who repeat their crimes.

The professional literature regarding murder victims has been relatively silent. When the interpersonal aspects of murder have been considered, victims are conceptualized in limited ways. One of the most pervasive ways of analyzing victims has been through the concept of victim precipitation and victim participation, a concept explored by sociologists and criminologists such as von Hentig (1940), Mendelsohn (1963), Wolfgang (1958), and Schafer (1968).

The victim is one of the causes of a crime, suggests Hans von Hentig. In 1948 he stated, "In a sense the victim shapes and molds the criminal. . . . To know one we must be acquainted with the complementary partner." Mendelsohn (1963, pp. 239-241), in writing of the biopsychosocial personality of the accused and of the victim, elaborated on the doctrine of victimology while preparing for the trial of a man who, had it not been for "the perversity of his former wife," would never have been found guilty of murdering her and her lover. Wolfgang (1958) has utilized the concept of victim precipitation in his well-known studies of criminal homicide, applying it to those cases in which the "role of the victim is characterized by his having

National Institute of Justice (#82-CX-0065). We wish to acknowledge gratefully Pierce Brooks and Marieanne L. Clark for contributions to earlier drafts of this article.

290 JOURNAL OF INTERPERSONAL VIOLENCE / September 1986

been the first in the homicide drama to use physical force directed against his subsequent slayer" (p. 252). An example is the husband who attacked his wife with a milk bottle, a brick, and a piece of concrete block while she was making breakfast. Having a butcher knife in her hand, she stabbed him. Wolfgang (1958) found victim-precipitated homicides represented 26% of a total of 588 homicides studied through police reports in Philadelphia. Adding to this concept, Schafer (1968, p. 152) concluded that "it is far from true that all crimes 'happen' to be committed; often the victim's negligence, precipitative action, or provocation contributes to the genesis or performance of a crime."

In contrast to this view, FBI profilers, in their work of analyzing crime scenes for clues leading to a suspect in an unsolved homicide, took a different approach. They did not find it helpful to perceive the victim as provoking the murder. Rather, the agents tried to be aware of how the offender thought and, subsequently, how he would respond to key characteristics of a victim. For example, a victim wearing a red dress and shoes was perceived by the offender as "asking for it." Such a victim can *not* communicate because the offender selects and interprets "communication cues" of which the victim is totally unaware. The agents understood the offender's habitual reasoning pattern that selects out characteristics of the victim, building a strong justification for violating her. The offender may retrospectively think he went "a bit too far," but will hold to his justifications. If a victim is passive, this is reason for attack; if the victim struggles, this is reason for the attack, and so it goes.

Thus the agents regarded all victim and crime scene information as critical data in their investigations. As a result of their insights into understanding the motivation of the offender, agents at the Behavioral Sciences Unit of the FBI Academy initiated a study of sexual homicide crime scenes and patterns of criminal behavior. Data obtained in the study were examined from the perspectives of crime scene analysis and of victim-murderer interaction.

STUDY

For several years, FBI agents, in profiling sexual murderers by analyzing crime scenes, have typed sexual murderers and the crime scene in terms of an organized/disorganized dichotomy. The premise for this dichotomy is that facets of the criminal's personality are evident in his offense. Like a fingerprint, the crime scene can be used to aid in identifying the murderer. An organized murderer is one who appears to plan his murders and who displays control (e.g., absence of clues) at the crime scene. The disorganized murderer is less apt to plan, and his crime scenes display haphazard (e.g., presence of clues at crime scene) behavior.

Our study was an exploratory one. Its major objectives were as follows: (1) to test, using statistical inferential procedures, if there are significant behavioral differences at the crime scenes between the crimes committed by organized offenders and those committed by disorganized murderers, and (2) to identify variables that may be useful in profiling murderers and on which the organized and disorganized murderers differ.

For the study to achieve its objectives, the agents first had to classify the 36 participating murderers into the organized/disorganized dichotomy. The dichotomy was as follows: 24 organized (with 97 victims); 12 disorganized (with 21 victims). The method for classification is published elsewhere (Ressler et al., 1985).

Data Set

The data set for the study comprised 36 convicted sexual murderers. Data were collected on 118 victims of these murderers. Of the victims, 9 survived the assaults; thus those 9 assaults were classified as attempted murders.

Each murderer who provided consent was interviewed extensively by FBI agents. The offender was asked questions regarding his background, his behavior at the crime scene, and his postoffense behavior. In addition, FBI agents reviewed criminal records of all participating offenders. The data set for each murderer consisted of the best available data compiled from these two sources.

Due to the complexities of obtaining these data and the confidentiality issues involved, there were "no response" answers to certain questions by some offenders. Although the missing data appear to have little effect on the univariate analysis, any interpretation of the results should consider this situation.

The data for this article were computerized and stored in separate files, which are described below.

(1) Background Information (on offender). This file contains 134 variables pertaining to the murderer. Variables within this file are

classified into eight categories: demographics, physical appearance, lifestyle, family structure, subject's early background history, family problems, subject's discipline/abuse, and subject's sexual history.

(2) Offense 1 (on offense). This file contains variables obtained from the offenses (e.g., the crime scenes). There are 119 variables in this file, which contains information for each separate crime. Variables in this file are classified into four categories: leading to the offense (such as frame of mind, premeditation of crime, and precipitating events); offender dress and residence variables relating to the offender at the time of offense; action during offense variables (such as conversation and behavior toward victim, weapons, and substance abuse); postoffense variables (such as keeping news clippings and visiting crime scene site and victim's grave).

(3) Victim 2 (on offense). This file contains 57 variables and is divided into two subsets: (1) victim characteristics (such as victim age, sex, height, weight, physique, race, complexion, attractiveness, marital status, residence, socioeconomic status, and actions during offense); and (2) offender's actions and behavior during the offense (such as victim mode of death, body position, sexual acts before and after death, postmortem acts, postmortem mutilation, and disposition of the body).

(4) Crime Scene (on offense). This file contains 47 variables and is divided into four categories: (1) vehicle variables relating to the mode of transportation of the offender and the description of his vehicle; (2) use of vehicle variable describing how a vehicle was used in the crime; (3) variables concerning physical evidence (weapon, fingerprints, and so on, left at the crime scene); and (4) distance variables measuring the distance from the crime scene to the victim's home, to the offender's home, and so on.

Data Analysis

Basically, the analysis was directed at testing for statistically significant differences between the organized and disorganized murderers. For variables in the Background Information data file, the unit of analysis was the murderer. The maximum sample sizes were 24 for the organized group of offenders and 12 for the disorganized group. For variables in the other data files, the maximum sample sizes were 97 victims for the organized and 21 victims for the disorganized offenders.

The major statistical analysis procedure employed for the variables was the two independent sample t test (D'Agostino, 1971, 1972; Lunney, 1970). For these variables, the F test for equality of variance was employed to aid in selecting the appropriate standard error for the denominator of the t test and the appropriate degrees of freedom. Variables significant at the .05 level of significance by the t test were identified. The full description of statistical tests employed is reported elsewhere (D'Agostino, 1985). The major findings of differences between crime scene variables and profile variables for organized and disorganized offenders are reported as follows. (See Table 1.)

Crime Scene Differences Between Organized and Disorganized Murderers

We first established that based on data available at the crime scene, there are significant differences between the organized and disorganized offender. However, there are no situations where the organized and disorganized offenders are mutually exclusive. That is, both types of murderers are capable of all types of behavior. For example, an organized murderer might not use a vehicle or a disorganized murderer might use restraints. Summary results are listed below. (See Table 2.)

Organized offenders are more apt to

- plan,
- use restraints,
- commit sexual acts with live victims,
- show or display control of victim (i.e., manipulative, threatening, want victim to show fear), and
- use a vehicle.

Disorganized offenders are more apt to

- leave weapon at the scene,
- position dead body,
- perform sexual acts on dead body,
- keep dead body,
- try to depersonalize the body, and
- not use a vehicle.

In meeting the study's first objective, we demonstrated that there are in fact consistencies and patterns in crime scenes that are objectively quantifiable and that distinguish organized from disorganized

TABLE 1

p Values for t-Test on Crime Scene and Profile Variables:
Organized and Disorganized Dichotomy

Crime Scene Variable	t-Test	Profile Variable	t-Test
strategy	.003	intell	.19
achvsex	.002	occup	.0001
restrain	.0001	prefocc	.081
weapnlft	.0001	birthord	.001
sexoff	.034	fathrsta	.053
sadism	.34	sexpref	.011
masochism	.0001	sexact1	.018
unusual2	.001	sexact2	.003
conv1	.002	sexconc1	.026
conv2	.010	sexconc5	.27
conv5	.0001	sexprob2	.007
conv6	.039	frame1	.0004
conv8	.045	frame4	.011
conv9	.0001	frame6	.012
react2	.006	frame7	.002
incraggr	.014	frame9	.0001
alcohol	.002	pstrss1	.009
position	.001	pstrss2	.0005
sb4death	.001	pstrss4	.0002
safdeath	.002	pstrss9	.026
pmact	.007	relat	.020
pmact7	.010	livewith	.013
pmact8	.022	distvres	.0001
torture	.0001	distwrk	.40
tort1	.003	trans	.023
tort4	.002	vecond	.044
tort5	.034	behav3	.026
tort9	.021	behav11	.004
keepbody	.090	behav12	.001
deperson	.050		
vehicle	.056		
ride	.0001		
assaults	.0001		
footps	.034		
weapon	.0001		

NOTE: See Tables 2 and 3 for definitions of terms.

TABLE 2

Crime Scene Variables Differentiating
Organized and Disorganized Sexual Murderers

		Percentage	
		Organized	*Disorganized*
ACTIONS DURING OFFENSE			
Offense 1 Data Set			
Strategy/	Planned versus Sudden; Organized more likely to have planned	86 (81)	44 (8)
Achvsex/	Violent act done to achieve sexual relations; Organized less likely	28 (68)	86 (7)
Restrain/	Restraints used; Organized more likely	49 (97)	10 (21)
Weaponlft/	Weapon left at scene of crime; Organized less likely	19 (67)	69 (16)
Sexoff/	Sexual acts committed; Organized more likely to commit sexual acts	76 (85)	46 (13)
Sadism/	Sadistic acts committed; Organized less likely	32 (97)	43 (21)
Masochsm/	Masochistic acts committed; Organized may, disorganized did not	15 (97)	0 (21)
Swallow semen/	Forced victim to do so; Organized may, disorganized did not	10 (97)	0 (21)

Organized shows more control (may be useful for cases in which victim lives)

Conversation with victim (aspects shown)			
Manipulative		51	14
Threatening		54	25
Inquisitive		45	10
Polite		43	19
Threatens family		4	0
Obtains name		41 (97)	0 (21)

Reactions desired by offender			
Fear/	Wants victim to show fear; Organized more likely	39 (69)	6 (16)
Lie still/	Wants victim to lie still; Organized more likely	29 (65)	0 (16)
Incraggr/	Things done to increase aggression; Organized more likely	62 (55)	20 (10)
Alcohol/	Alcohol use associated with offense; Organized have greater use	56 (97)	19 (21)

Victim 2 Data Set			
Position/	Victim's body positioned; Organized less apt to position body	22 (88)	55 (20)

(continued)

TABLE 2   Continued

		Percentage	
		Organized	*Disorganized*
SB4death/	Sexual acts before death (evidence at scene); Organized more likely	64 (87)	24 (21)
Safdeath/	Sexual acts after death (evidence at scene); Organized less likely	34 (73)	74 (19)

Victim 2 Data Set (continued)

Pmact/	Postmorten activity with body; Organized less likely	23 (88)	52 (21)
Pmact7/	Inserts foreign objects into victim's anus	0	29
Pmact8/	Inserts foreign objects into victim's vagina	10	38

VEHICLE IN CRIME
Crime Scene Data Set

Disorganized is less likely to do anything indicating planning or action with a vehicle.

Vehicle/	Vehicle involved in crime; Organized is more likely to use a car	85 (93)	62 (21)

Disorganized is unlikely to do the following:

   Offer victim a ride or give victim a ride
   Force victim into car
   Disable victim's car
   Bump victim's car
   Run victim's car off road
   Pretend to have an accident
   Expose himself from car
   Assault victim in car
   Park car and follow victim on foot
   Transport victim from encounter site to crime scene
     site or disposal site

Tort/	Postmortem mutilation Organized less likely to mutilate dead victim	27 (88)	76 (21)
Tort1/	Facial mutilation (disfigurement)	6	43
Tort2/	Genital mutilation	15	33
Tort3/	Breast mutilation	12	29
Tort4/	Disembowelment	2	43
Tort5/	Amputation	17	38
Tort9/	Vampirism (drink blood)	0	24
Keepbody/*	Offender keeps corpse; Organized less likely	14 (88)	33 (21)
Deperson/	Offender tries to depersonalize victim (blindfolding, eradication of features); Organized is less likely	8 (88)	32 (19)

VICTIM CHARACTERISTICS
Victim 2 Data Set

Agevic/**	Age of the victim; Organized has younger victims	$\overline{X} =$ 23 (93)	29 (20)

TABLE 2 Continued

			Percentage	
			Organized	*Disorganized*
Attract/	Physical attractiveness of the victim; Organized has more attractive victims (1 to 4 scale)	X =	1.6 (84)	2.0 (20)

EVIDENCE AT SCENE

Crime Scene Data Set

Footps/	Evidence of footprints; Organized less likely to leave footprints	5 (97)	29 (21)
Weapon/	Weapon left (can be used as evidence); Organized less likely to leave weapon for evidence	18 (97)	57 (21)

NOTE: n = numbers in parentheses.
*Level of significance is p = 0.09; not p = 0.05.
**Level of significance is p = 0.06; not p = 0.05.

sexual murderers. The labels "organized" and "disorganized" are not only convenient because of their visual connotations to the crime scene but also have an objectivity to them.

Profile Characteristic Differences Between Organized and Disorganized Murderers

After establishing crime scene differences we identified those characteristics that could be used in a criminal profile. By profile characteristics, we mean those characteristics that identify the subject as an individual. This contrasts with crime scene characteristics, the tangible clues left (or missing) at the crime scene where the body is found. Profile variables can be grouped into four areas: background variables; variables describing the situation of the criminal before the crime (precrime state); variables relating to residence, vehicle use, and distance to crime scene; and postoffense behavior variables.

Based on our analysis, there are different characteristics for the organized and disorganized murderers that may prove useful in developing criminal profiles. The statistically significant variables are summarized below. (See Table 3.)

Organized offenders are more

- intelligent,
- skilled in occupation,

TABLE 3
Profile Characteristics Differentiating
Organized and Disorganized Sexual Murderers

			Percentage	
			Organized	*Disorganized*
BACKGROUND				
Background Data Set				
Demographic				
Intell/	Intelligence;	$\overline{X}$ =	5.0	4.2
	Organized more intelligent		(22)	(12)
Lifestyle				
Occup/	Occupation;		50	0
	Organized more skilled		(24)	(11)
Prsfocc/	Preferred occupation is skilled work;		74	38
	Organized is more likely to want to do skilled work		(19)	(8)
Family Structure				
Birthord/	Birth order;	$\overline{X}$ =	2.7	1.3
	Organized have a higher birth order		(21)	(12)
Fathsta/	Father's work was unstable; % unstable =	12		45
	Organized more stable		(16)	(11)
Discipline/Abuse History				
Hostile/	Subject received hostile discipline as a child; Disorganized treated with more hostility			
Sex Acts/Preference				
Sexpref/	Sexual preference % heterosexual =	74		100
	(heterosexual versus other);			
	All disorganized were heterosexual		(23)	(11)
Disorganized is more inhibited and more likely to be a compulsive masturbator.				
Sexual Concerns				
Disorganized is more ignorant of sex and has more sexual aversions.				
Sexprob2/	Sexual problems;		12	62
	Disorganized is more likely to have had sexual problems		(17)	(8)
PRECRIME STATE (leading to offense)				
Offense 1 Data Set				
Frame1/	Angry frame of mind;	$\overline{X}$ =	2.0	3.3
	Organized more angry (1 to 5 scale: 1 = predominant; 5 = not at all)		(77)	(20)
Frame4/	Nervous;	$\overline{X}$ =	3.5	2.6
	Organized less nervous	X =	(73)	(20)
Frame6/	Organized less frightened	$\overline{X}$ =	4.1	3.0
Frame7/	Organized less confused	$\overline{X}$ =	4.4	3.0

TABLE 3   Continued

			Percentage
		Organized	*Disorganized*
Frame8/	Organized more depressed	$\overline{X} =$ 3.4	4.3
Frame9/	Organized calmer, more relaxed	$\overline{X} =$ 3.1	4.3

Precipitating Events/Precipitating Stress

Organized more likely to have events/stresses due to financial, marital, females, employment before the murder.

RESIDENCE/VEHICLE DISTANCE

Offense 1 Data Set

Relat/	Offender knows who victim is; % know	14	47
	Organized is less likely to know who victim is	(93)	(17)
Livewith/	Offender lives alone;	33	62
	Organized is less likely to live alone	(97)	(21)

Crime Scene Data Set

Distvres/	Distance crime scene to victim's house; Organized more apt to have scene farther away from victim's home than disorganized		
Distores/	Distance crime scene to offender's home; Disorganized lives nearer to crime scene than does organized		
Distowrk/	Distance crime scene to offender's work; Disorganized works nearer to crime scene than does organized		
Trans/	Usual transportation is by driving;	70	43
	Organized more apt to drive	(97)	(21)
Vecond/	Condition of the vehicle;		
	Organized more apt to have better conditioned vehicle	(62)	(11)

POSTOFFENSE BEHAVIOR

Offense 1 Data Set

Behav3/	Follows in media;	51	24
	Organized more likely to follow in media	(97)	(21)
Behav11/	Change jobs;	8	0
	Organized may change jobs, disorganized did not	(97)	(21)
Behav12/	Leave town;	11	0
	Organized may leave town, disorganized did not	(97)	(21)

NOTE: n = numbers in parentheses.

- likely to think out and plan the crime,
- likely to be angry and depressed at the time of the murder,
- likely to have a precipitating stress (financial, marital, female, job)
- likely to have a car in decent condition,
- likely to follow crime events in media, and
- likely to change jobs or leave town.

Disorganized offenders are more likely to

- be low birth order children,
- come from a home with unstable work for the father,
- have been treated with hostility as a child,
- be sexually inhibited and sexually ignorant, and to have sexual aversions,
- have parents with histories of sexual problems,
- have been frightened and confused at the time of the crime,
- know who the victim is,
- live alone, and
- have committed the crime closer to home/work.

The analysis established the existence of variables that may be useful in a criminal profile and for which the organized and disorganized sexual murderers differ and thus met the study's second objective.

VICTIMS OF ORGANIZED AND DISORGANIZED SEXUAL MURDERERS

The organized/disorganized dichotomy provided a new context for analyzing the victim-murderer interaction. Rather than using the traditional view of victim focused on the concept of precipitation and provocation as interpreted by criminologists from police reports of a murder, we examined our data of murdered victims from the perceptions of the offenders who had killed them. Thus our view is on victim response by type of offender analyzed through crime scene evidence.

Data were obtained for 118 victims, 9 of whom survived murder attempts. The majority of victims in the sample were white (93%), female (82%), and not married (80%). Ages for 113 victims ranged from 6 to 73 (ages were unavailable for 5 victims). Of the victims, 14, or 12%, were 14 years old or younger; 83, or 73%, were between 15 and 28 years old; and 16, or 14%, were 30 years or older. Thus the majority of victims (73%) were between ages 15 and 28, which matches the age range for rape victims in general.

The majority of victims (81% or 89) were strangers to the offender; 19%, or 21, were known to the murderer. Nearly half (47%) of the victims were closely related in age to the offender. Over one-third of the cases (37%) involved a younger victim than offender, and in 15% of the cases, the victim was older than the offender. More than half of the victims came from average or advantaged socioeconomic levels (62%), 30% had marginal incomes, and 9% had less than marginal incomes. In over one-third of the cases, the victim had a companion (i.e., was not alone) at the time of the assault; 63% were alone at the time of the murder.

Victim Response to Assailant

Any cause-effect determination in victim resistance reports needs to include the total series of interactions between a victim and assailant, including the dynamic sequencing of victim resistance and offender attack. Offenders were asked to report on their victims' resistance in terms of whether they tried to negotiate verbally, verbally refuse, scream, flee, or fight. The offender was then asked to report his own response to the victim's behavior. It is important to keep in mind that the data represent only the offender's perceptions of the victim-offender interaction.

In the 83 cases with victim response data, 23 victims (28%) acquiesced or offered no resistance as perceived by the offender. As one organized murderer said, "She was compliant. I showed her the gun. She dropped her purse and kind of wobbled a second and got her balance and said, 'All right; I'm not going to say anything. Just don't hurt me.'" A total of 26 (31%) victims tried verbal negotiation; 6 (7%) tried to refuse verbally; 8 (10%) screamed; 4 (5%) tried to escape; and 16 (19%) tried to fight the offender.

Offender reaction to the victim's resistance ranged from no reaction in 31 cases (34%) to violence in 24 (25%) cases. In 14 instances (15%), offenders threatened the victim verbally in response to victim resistance; in 23 cases (25%) offenders increased their aggression. Thus in two-thirds of the cases assailants countered victim resistance; often (50%) it was met with increased force and aggression. (In 9 cases the offender both verbally threatened the victim and increased his aggression.)

Our analysis of cases, in terms of an organized/disorganized dichotomy, found that of the 83 cases with data on victim response to assailant, the organized offenders had 67 victims and the disorganized had 16. Of the 16 victims of the disorganized offenders, 10 used nonforceful resistance (acquiescence or verbal resistance) and were killed. With the organized offender, 45 out of 67 victims used non-forceful resistance and died as well. In total, 55 out of 83 victims used nonforceful resistance. The data suggest that nonforceful resistance was not a deterrent with either of these offender types.

The interpretation of what is considered forceful resistance is important to clarify. We identified screaming and fleeing as physical (forceful) reactions because offenders specifically cited those victim responses as the reason for their use of increased aggression. With a majority of the offenders interviewed, both physical and verbal (or forceful and nonforceful) resistance played a part in triggering a reaction by the offenders.

An almost equal number of victims in our sample were said to have resisted physically (25) as were said to have made no attempt at resistance (23). Both types of victim actions resulted in death.

The FBI agents interviewed the murderers about deterrence to kill. This information was analyzed in terms of the organized/disorganized dichotomy. Organized murderers, who had a conscious intent based on motive to kill, said that factors such as witnesses and location did not matter because the murder fantasy was so well rehearsed that everything was controlled ("I always killed in my home, and there were no witnesses"). Or as one murderer said, "The victim did not have a choice. Killing was part of my fantasy." Also, the organized murderer with the detailed fantasy to kill either believed that he would never be caught or that he would have to be killed to be stopped. On the other hand, disorganized offenders, who were not consciously aware of their intent to kill, were able to identify factors that might deter their killing. They stated such deterrence factors as being in a populated location, having witnesses in the area, or coop-eration from the victim.

Surviving Victims

The surviving victims of murderers in the study provide insights about victim-murderer interactions in the context of the organized and disorganized classification. Victims who survived murder attempts of these killers used the following strategies: hiding from the assailant, jumping out of a car, feigning death, escaping the area, knocking the weapon out of the assailant's hand, and screaming for assistance. The following two cases illustrate victim-murderer dynamics as well as the crime scene and profile characteristics for each type of murderer.

Victim of an organized murderer. Driving home from work at 10:30 at night, a highway patrol officer passed a car pulled off the road. He noticed the car's dome light was on and the right front door was open; he then saw two people in a scuffle between the car and the woods. As he turned around to investigate, his headlights picked up a woman lying on the ground, fighting violently with a man on top of her. When the police officer approached them, the man dropped the gun he had been holding and held up his hands. The woman picked up the gun and ran to the officer screaming, "He's trying to kill me!" The assailant was handcuffed. He stated, "I just wanted to scare her. I just wanted to tie her up. I don't know if I would have raped her or not, but I might have. I just met her tonight."

The victim related that she worked part-time as a photographer's model and that she had been told by an agency that a man would take her to his studio to take photographs. As they were driving along the freeway, the man pulled over, saying he thought he had a flat tire. He then pulled a gun and said, "Do as I say and I won't hurt you." The victim reported,

> I said I would do what he said if he didn't hurt me. He told me to turn and put my hands behind my back, which I did, and he proceeded to tie my wrist. When he went to tie my hands together, I began to struggle because the gun was not in his hand. During the struggle the man began choking me and said, "I am losing my patience with you. With my record I would just as soon kill you and go the the gas chamber." He pulled the gun and pointed it at me. I grabbed at the gun, screamed, and beat on the window of the car, but no one would stop. We kept struggling, and the gun was discharged with the bullet going through my skirt and grazing my outer right leg. I decided if I got out of the car, someone would see me and stop. I got the door open and we fell out on the ground and we wrestled. Then the officer arrived.

This case example underscores the organized murderer's premeditated approach to the victim and his planned intent to kill. In this case, when the assailant tried to bargain with her by saying she would not be hurt if she cooperated, the victim did not believe him. Although the victim tried negotiating not to be harmed by the assailant, she

304   JOURNAL OF INTERPERSONAL VIOLENCE / September 1986

strategically waited for an opportunity when he did not have the gun (he had to drop the gun to tie her wrists) and fought at the point when her wrists were being tied. The gun was a straightforward death threat, yet being immobilized increased the woman's vulnerability. Thus she risked fighting despite the gun.

The assailant's preconceived strategies were based on his understanding of a victim's response to a violent death threat. This assailant had three prior victims whom he murdered. His first victim was contacted after he answered an ad in a lonely hearts column; in the second and third cases he posed as a photographer needing a model and went through an agency. He claimed to have raped all three women and then transported them to another location where he strangled them. The bodies were left in a desert; until the man was apprehended for the attempted murder, the bodies remained missing.

The murderer showed most of the characteristics of an organized sexual killer. The murders were carefully planned. The killer used ropes as restraints and raped the women prior to killing them. He also took photographs of his victims before he killed them; their faces showed great fear. The man's car was used to transport the victims to their deaths. The offender's IQ was in the superior range, and he had recently lost his job and moved from the Midwest to the West Coast. He followed newspaper accounts of his crimes.

However, in this case, this victim did not respond as his other victims. As a victim she did not acquiesce to his multiple threats and gun. She fought him. He continued his pursuit of dominance and intent to kill her. He shot her. From his view, the rules suddenly changed. He had a choice. He did not stop his action and say to himself, "This is not fitting in with my scheme," and leave the scene. Instead, he persisted in fitting her into his mode of escalation.

When apprehended by police, the assailant tried the same manipulative ploy with the officer. He claimed that he did not know if he would have raped the woman. The police officer disbelieved this statement (i.e., he believed the assailant had intended to kill) and the assailant was taken into custody.

Victim statement of disorganized murderer. According to the account of the surviving victim, a 21-year-old woman, she and some friends returned to a girlfriend's apartment after dining at a restaurant. After continued conversation and television viewing, everyone left except one of the men. The victim's girlfriend retired to her room as she had to work the next day; the victim stayed with the man, whom she knew, hoping he would "get the hint and leave." While they were watching television, she fell asleep lying on her side on the couch. When she awoke, she was "feeling funny" and lying on her back. A shadow or a figure at the edge of the couch was moving toward the bedroom. As the victim started to stand up, she saw her girlfriend standing between the bedroom and the living room with the man holding her by the wrist. Her friend was screaming. At about this time, the victim realized her pants were partly down around her thighs, and as she reached down to pull them up, she discovered she was covered with blood. Her face and abdomen had been slashed. The victim ran outside to a neighbor, holding her stomach as she ran. The neighbor let her in and called the police. After the victim was rushed to the hospital, she was found to have suffered multiple cuts and lacerations to her throat and face and extensive abdominal lacerations. The assailant had attempted to disembowel her. Her girlfriend was found lying nude in her bedroom with fatal multiple knife wounds in the abdomen, throat, and arms. A knife with a ten-inch blade (subsequently identified as the murder weapon) was lying near the victim.

The disorganized murderer often kills quickly to maintain control. In this case, control was achieved by the murderer's attack on sleeping women. The bodies were depersonalized through extensive cuttings and stab wounds and the weapon was left at the crime scene. The murderer knew his victims and had a history of masochistic behavior, as evidenced by autoerotic asphyxial practices as an adolescent and adult. The premeditated aspect of the crime was revealed by a letter, found in the murderer's car and dated five days before the murder, that stated that the killer intended to force one of the victims to eviscerate and emasculate him and that she was to be found innocent of the crimes.

One might speculate that the disorganization of the crime escalated when the offender's fantasy did not match the reality of the situation. In his evisceration fantasy, the assailant rehearsed the disembowelment both by assuming the role of victim and of victimizer. There is similarity in intent at the crime scene with the presence of two women. The assailant tries out the evisceration fantasy on the first victim and then attacks his fantasy object. We speculate that between the first and second victim he experienced tension relief from trying out of the fantasy and he escalates the murder behavior to a second target.

The accounts of surviving victims of an organized and a disorganized offender highlight their levels of awareness regarding the dangerousness of the offender. Both women acted independently in response to a situation they perceived as life threatening, and swift police and medical intervention combined with their efforts to save their lives. The killers were remarkable in their intent and assurance that they could successfully carry out their crimes. These men, at least in their own minds, had already rehearsed how they would kill and escape capture. The killing was an integral part of their fantasy. The murderers, in this sense, had consciously planned their murders— one, setting about to target a victim for his plan, and the other utilizing a chance encounter.

DISCUSSION

This article reports on a new typology of sexually oriented murderers based on crime scene evidence and victim resistance strategies and outcome in terms of this new classification. This new typology provides an opportunity to expand and advance the psychosocial framework for studying murderers that is sometimes criticized for its unproved theories, obscure interpretive level, and lack of attention to cultural factors (Wolfgang & Ferracuti, 1963) to include measurable, behavioral indicators from analysis of crime scene (e.g., presence or absence of a weapon; injury to victim). This law enforcement typology is based on discrete, verifiable concepts and behavior. It does not rest solely on controversial statements of motivation derived from a complex theory of subconscious motivation. Consequently, the typology has the potential for verifiable classification of acts and visual evidence, enhancing the investigation and study of murderers. For example, to hypothesize that a serial murderer killed a young woman to destroy his internal female identification with his sister is cumbersome and cannot be substantiated by analysis of crime scene evidence or other data available before his capture and evaluation. What is clear is the pattern of killing of young women of a certain age range in a repeated and particular systematic style. Analysis of these data from the crime scene may be useful in understanding the psychosocial nature of the murderer and lead (it is hoped) to his capture.

Additionally, we study victim response to the offender in terms of active versus passive response. We found that regardless of type of resistance (active or passive) or category of offender (organized versus disorganized), death ensued. When we examined 9 victims who survived, the category of offender was not the predictor, rather, "chance happenings" preserved life.

REFERENCES

Cox, D. R. (1970). *Analysis of binary data.* London: Methuen.

D'Agostino, R. B. (1971). A second look at analysis of variance on dichotomous data. *Journal of Ed. Meas., 8*, 327-333.

D'Agostino, R. B. (1972). Relation between the chi squared and ANOVA tests for testing the equality of k independent dichotomous populations. *American Statistician*, pp. 30-32.

D'Agostino, R. B. (1985). *Statistical inference procedures for crime scene patterns and profile characteristics of organized and disorganized offenders.* In Final Report to National Institute of Justice (#82-CX-0065), Washington, D.C.

Lester, D. (1973). Murder: A review. *Corrective and Social Psychiatry and Journal of Applied Behavior Therapy, 19* (4), 40-50.

Lunney, G. H. (1970). Using analysis of variance with a dichotomous dependent variable: An empirical study. *Journal of Ed. Meas., 4*, 263-269.

Mendelsohn, B. (1963). The origin of the doctrine of victimology. *Excerpta Criminologica, 3*, 239-244.

Ressler, R. K., et al. (1985). Violent crimes. *FBI Law Enforcement Bulletin, 54* (8), 1-33.

Schafer, S. (1968). *The victim and his criminal: A study in functional responsibility.* New York: Random House.

Simon, R. I. (1977). Type A, AB, B murderers: Their relationship to the victims and to the criminal justice system. *Bulletin of the American Academy of Psychiatry and the Law, 5* (3), 344-362.

von Hentig, H. (1940). Remarks on the interaction of perpetrator and victim. *Journal of Criminal Law and Criminology, 31*, 303-309.

von Hentig, H. (1948). *The criminal and his victim.* New Haven, CT: Yale University Press.

Wolfgang, M. E. (1958). *Patterns in criminal homicide.* Philadelphia: University of Pennsylvania.

Wolfgang, M. E., & Ferracuti, F. (1967). *The subculture of violence.* Great Britain: Tavistock.

Robert K. Ressler, M. S., is Supervisory Special Agent, Federal Bureau of Investigation, and Program Manager, Violent Criminal Apprehension Program, National Center for the Analysis of Violent Crime, FBI Academy, Quantico, VA.

Ann W. Burgess, R.N., D.N.Sc., is van Ameringen Professor of Psychiatric Mental Health Nursing, University of Pennsylvania, Philadelphia, and Associate Director of Nursing Research, Boston City Hospital, Boston.

John E. Douglas, M.S., is Supervisory Special Agent, Federal Bureau of Investigation, and Program Manager, Criminal Profiling and Crime Scene Assessment Program, National Center for the Analysis of Violent Crime, FBI Academy, Quantico, VA.

Carol R. Hartman, R.N., D.N.Sc., is Associate Professor and Coordinator of the Graduate Program in Psychiatric Mental Health Nursing, Boston College, Chestnut Hill, MA.

Ralph B. D'Agostino is Professor of Mathematics, Boston University, Boston.

[31]

The Presumptive Role of Fantasy in Serial Sexual Homicide

Robert Alan Prentky, Ph.D., Ann Wolbert Burgess, R.N., D.N.Sc.,
Frances Rokous, B.A., Austin Lee, Ph.D., Carol Hartman, R.N., D.N.Sc.,
Robert Ressler, M.S., and John Douglas, M.S.

The authors examined the role of fantasy as an internal drive mechanism for repetitive acts of sexual violence. A sample of 25 serial sexual murderers with three or more known victims each was compared with a sample of 17 single sexual murderers, with only one known victim each. The drive mechanism was hypothesized to be an intrusive fantasy life manifested in higher prevalences of paraphilias, documented or self-reported violent fantasies, and organized crime scenes in the serial murderers. All three hypotheses were supported.
(Am J Psychiatry 1989; 146:887–891)

Among the four violent Crime Index offenses of the Federal Bureau of Investigation (FBI), murder is the most infrequent, accounting for about 2% of the total violent crimes. And of those who murder once, only a small fraction murder again (1). Within the overall category of murder, homicides that appear to be sexually motivated are uncommon (2, 3), and serial sexual homicide is even more infrequent. Despite the proportionately few serial sexual murderers, the number of victims accounted for by each perpetrator is often very high. For instance, Ressler et al. (4) reported on the 118 known victims of 36 sexual murderers. The consequent impact of this small but very violent subgroup of offenders is indeed large.

Of even greater concern is that the frequency of these random, seemingly motiveless, murders appears to be increasing (5). Burgess et al. (5) noted that between 1976 and 1984 there was a 160% increase in murders with unknown motives. Motivated murders tend to have identifiable external precipitators; many of these murders are premeditated, intentional, rational acts or accidental killings committed in the heat of passion (6, 7). Sexual homicide, however, has typically been viewed as an anomalous event and has defied efforts to devise an explanatory model based on some theory-driven conceptualization of the behavior. In his classic paper on the subject, Brittain (8) disavowed any attempt at theoretical formulation and instead provided a descriptive profile of the sadistic murderer. Similarly, in his attempt to categorize sexual murderers, Revitch (9) described three cases (impulsive, compulsive, and catathymic or tension release) without positing any theory to explain the behavior.

MacCulloch et al. (10) provided a novel explanation of the motivation of 13 of the 16 sadistic patients they examined, whose crimes (not all homicide) appeared to be driven by "internal circumstances." MacCulloch et al. found a pattern of sadistic fantasies that, in repetition-compulsion fashion, were played out repeatedly—initially in fantasy only, later on in behavioral mock trials, and eventually in assaults. The more the fantasies were cognitively rehearsed, the more power they acquired.

The excellent descriptive case reports by Brittain (8), Revitch (9), MacCulloch et al. (10), and others have provided a rich source for hypothesis generation. In particular, MacCulloch et al. (10) underscored the critical importance of fantasy as a possible drive mechanism for extremely serious crimes that, until recently, were assigned to the wastebasket of "unknown motive." A number of plethysmography studies (11–13) provide support for the role of fantasy in perpetuating sexually assaultive behavior. As Abel and Blanchard noted, there is also abundant support in the psychoanalytic literature for the "high concordance between presence of deviant fantasies and occurrence of deviant behavior" (14, p. 468).

Burgess et al. (5) reported a fantasy-based motivational model for sexual homicide. The model, which has five interactive components (impaired development of attachments in early life; formative traumatic events; patterned responses that serve to generate fantasies; a private, internal world that is consumed with violent thoughts and leaves the person isolated and self-preoccupied; and a feedback filter that sustains repetitive thinking patterns), was tested on a sample of

Received April 25, 1988; revision received Dec. 15, 1988; accepted Feb. 2, 1989. From the Research Department, Massachusetts Treatment Center and Department of Psychiatry, Boston University School of Medicine; School of Nursing, University of Pennsylvania, Philadelphia; Department of Psychology, Yale University, New Haven, Conn.; Department of Mathematics, Boston University; School of Nursing, Boston College; and Behavioral Sciences Unit, Federal Bureau of Investigation, Quantico, Va. Address reprint requests to Dr. Prentky, Research Department, Massachusetts Treatment Center, Box 554, Bridgewater, MA 02324.

Supported by National Institute of Justice grant 82-IJ-CX-0058 and Office of Juvenile Justice and Delinquency Prevention grant 84-JW-AX-K010 from the U.S. Department of Justice, NIMH grant MH-32309, and the Commonwealth of Massachusetts.

Serial Murder

36 sexual murderers. In that initial study, Burgess et al. (5) found evidence for daydreaming and compulsive masturbation in over 80% of the sample in both childhood and adulthood.

Using the same sample, Ressler et al. (4) examined the role of the organized/disorganized dichotomy (15), which has proven to be a relatively powerful discriminator in two important areas, crime scene investigation and life history variables. Classification of a crime as organized or disorganized is made with data present at the scene of a murder and is based on the notion that highly repetitive, planned, well-thought-out offenses will be distinguishable from spontaneous, random, sloppy offenses. According to Ressler et al.'s prediction (4), the organized offender should be more characterized by a fantasy life that drives the offenses than is the disorganized offender. Ressler et al. found numerous differences between organized and disorganized offenders with respect to acts committed during their offenses, thus providing support for the validity of a typological discrimination that has theoretical roots in fantasy.

A critical, yet untested, question concerns putative differences between serial and single sexual murderers. The present study was intended to examine the presumptive role of fantasy as a drive mechanism for repetitive (i.e., serial) sexual murder. The working hypothesis was that serial sexual murderers are more likely to have underlying internal mechanisms that drive their assaultive behavior than single sexual murderers. This internal drive mechanism was hypothesized to take the form of an intrusive fantasy life that is manifested in 1) a higher prevalence of paraphilias, 2) a higher prevalence of organized crime scenes, and 3) a higher prevalence of violent fantasies.

METHOD

Subjects

The sample of serial sexual murderers consisted of 25 of the 36 murderers from an earlier study by the FBI (4, 5, 16). Only men who had committed three or more sexual homicides each were included in this study. The men were interviewed by special agents of the FBI in various U.S. prisons between 1979 and 1983. The data collected included information retrieved from official records, e.g., psychiatric and criminal records, pretrial records, court transcripts, interviews with correctional staff, and prison records. The information derived from these structured interviews and archival sources was coded with a questionnaire.

The sample of single sexual murderers consisted of seven offenders in the FBI sample and 10 men residing at the Massachusetts Treatment Center; each had murdered only once. The data for the Massachusetts Treatment Center subjects were archival. The clinical files of men committed to the center include past institution-

TABLE 1. Descriptive Characteristics of Serial and Single Sexual Murderers[a]

Characteristic	Serial (N=25)		Single (N=17)	
	N	%	N	%
Race				
Caucasian	24	96	14	82
Black	1	4	2	12
Marital status				
Married	5	21	3	20
Divorced or separated	7	29	5	27
Never married	12	50	9	53
IQ				
Above average (≥110)	14	58	4	29
Below average (≤90)	4	17	4	29
Age at time of first murder (years)				
<20	7	28	4	24
20–24	6	24	4	24
25–30	9	36	5	29
>30	3	12	4	24

[a]Some data were missing for some individuals, so percentages were based on varying total numbers of subjects.

alization records, school and employer records, parole summaries, probation records, and social service notes. Since the initial evaluation process includes clinical interviews, psychological testing, and review of final records from court-appointed examiners, this information is available as well. After evaluation, substantial information is added to the file during treatment, including psychiatric evaluations and progress reports on all aspects of the rehabilitation program. The clinical files were coded with a questionnaire similar to the one employed in the FBI study.

Some demographic characteristics of the two samples are provided in table 1. The serial group was almost exclusively Caucasian, while about one-fifth of the single group was either black or Hispanic. Marital status was almost identical for the two groups. Since the age of the offender at the onset of violent criminal activity could be a critical factor, we compared the two samples' ages at the time of their first sexual homicides. As shown in table 1, the samples were remarkably similar ($\chi^2=1.02$, df=3, p<0.80). The only noteworthy comparison concerned intelligence; 58% of the serial murderers but only 29% of the single murderers had higher than average IQs, although the difference was not statistically significant ($\chi^2=3.14$, df=2, p<0.21). This trend is entirely consistent with theoretical expectations and essentially parallels the difference between the groups in organization of the crime scene. That is, it has been hypothesized (15) that organized murderers have higher IQs than disorganized murderers. While intelligence seems to have little bearing on the quality or content of the fantasy, it does influence how well the fantasy is translated into behavior (i.e., how organized the crime is) and how successfully the offender eludes apprehension.

PRENTKY, BURGESS, ROKOUS, ET AL.

Procedure

Fantasy is a rather inclusive term that covers a wide range of cognitive processes. Our use of the term "fantasy" in this paper is based on an information processing model that interprets thoughts as derivations of incoming stimuli that have been processed and organized (17). Daydreaming has been defined as any cognitive activity representing a shift of attention away from a task (18). A fantasy, as it is defined in this study, is an elaborated set of cognitions (or thoughts) characterized by preoccupation (or rehearsal), anchored in emotion, and originating in daydreams. A fantasy is generally experienced as a collection of thoughts, although the individual may be aware of images, feelings, and internal dialogue. For present purposes a crime fantasy (involving rape, murder, or both) was positively coded if the interview or archival data indicated that the daydreaming content included intentional infliction of harm in a sadistic or sexually violent way.

In the case of a serial murderer, the crime scene of the first sexual homicide was examined. The homicide was classified as organized if the crime scene suggested that a semblance of order existed before, during, and after the offense and that this order was aimed at preventing detection (15). The homicide was classified as disorganized if the crime scene was characterized by great disarray, suggesting that the assault had been committed suddenly and with no apparent plan for preventing detection. The crime scene classifications were made by two special agents from the FBI, who used crime scene data only. These data consisted of physical evidence found at the crime scene that were hypothesized to reveal behavioral and personality traits of the murderer. The crime scene may have included the point of abduction, locations where the victim was held, the murder scene, and the final location of the body. Examples of such crime scene data are the use of restraints, manner of death, presence of a weapon, depersonalization of the victim (e.g., rendering the victim unidentifiable through disfigurement), evidence that the crime was staged, and physical evidence (e.g., personal artifacts of the victim or offender).

The planning variable was defined as premeditation. An offense was coded as planned when there was material evidence of a pre-existing strategy to carry out the crime, as reflected by the presence of crime-specific paraphernalia and/or weapons (as opposed to items or weapons of opportunity). Any evidence that the crime had been rehearsed before its execution (e.g., targeting a specific location) would also be considered planning.

The paraphilias were coded as present if there was clear, unambiguous evidence in the archives or from self-reports that the behavior was practiced and that it was not happenstance. The paraphilias were defined in concrete, behavioral terms and examples were provided—for the subject in the case of self-report and for the coders in the case of archival retrieval.

TABLE 2. Prevalence of Violent Fantasies, Paraphilias, and Organized Crime Scenes in Serial and Single Sexual Murderers[a]

Characteristic	Serial (N=25)		Single (N=17)		χ^2 (df=1)	p
	N	%	N	%		
Fantasies of rape, murder, or both	19	86	3	23	14.02	0.001
Paraphilias						
Compulsive masturbation	14	70	6	50	1.28	0.26
Indecent exposure	5	25	1	7	1.81	0.19[b]
Voyeurism	15	75	6	43	3.60	0.06
Fetishism	15	71	4	33	4.54	0.03
Cross-dressing	5	25	0	0	4.38	0.05[b]
Organized crime scene						
Organized	17	68	4	24	8.00	0.005
Planned	10	42	7	41	—	—

[a]Some data were missing for some individuals, so percentages were based on varying numbers of subjects.
[b]Derived from Fisher's exact test (one-tailed).

Eight variables were identified in the FBI data base and the Massachusetts Treatment Center data base that were conceptually identical and theoretically meaningful for testing a series of hypotheses regarding these two samples. The two sets of variables were merged to create a new set of dichotomous variables. The dichotomous variables were analyzed with the chi-square statistic. When the expected frequency for a cell was less than 5, the chi-square test was inappropriate and was replaced by Fisher's exact test (19). No subjects were omitted from the analyses because of missing data.

RESULTS

The results are shown in table 2. The a priori hypothesis regarding fantasy was strongly supported ($\chi^2=14.02$, df=1, p<0.001). Well over three-quarters of the serial group (86%), compared with less than one-quarter of the single group (23%), evidenced sufficiently obtrusive violent fantasies to be noted in the records.

Our hypothesis of a higher prevalence of paraphilias in the group of serial murderers was also supported. There were higher prevalences of all five paraphilias in the serial group than in the single group, and there were significant differences in fetishism ($\chi^2=4.54$, df=1, p<0.03) and cross-dressing ($\chi^2=4.38$, df=1, p<0.05).

Our a priori hypothesis regarding the organization or disorganization of the crime scene also was supported ($\chi^2=8.00$, df=1, p<0.005). Over two-thirds of the serial murderers' first sexual homicides were organized, while three-quarters of the sexual homicides committed by the single murderers were disorganized. There was no difference between groups with respect to the planning of the murder.

FANTASY AND SEXUAL HOMICIDE

DISCUSSION

Evidence from both clinical (10) and empirical (4) studies has underscored the importance of fantasy as a presumptive drive mechanism for sexual sadism and sexual homicide. This study provides support for that general conclusion and for greater specificity in the role of fantasy. That is, violent fantasy was present in 86% of the multiple (or serial) murderers and only 23% of the single murderers, suggesting a possible functional relationship between fantasy and repetitive assaultive behavior. While the precise function of consummated fantasy is speculative, we concur with Mac-Culloch et al. (10) that once the restraints inhibiting the acting out of the fantasy are no longer present, the individual is likely to engage in a series of progressively more accurate "trial runs" in an attempt to enact the fantasy as it is imagined. Since the trial runs can never precisely match the fantasy, the need to restage the fantasy with a new victim is established. MacCulloch et al. suggested that the shaping of the fantasy and the motivation for consummating the fantasy may be understood in terms of classical conditioning. Abel and Blanchard (14) discussed the role of fantasy in treatment, noting that "repeated pairing of . . . fantasized cues with orgasm results in their acquiring sexually arousing properties." Consistent with this notion is the finding (20) that at least three social learning variables may be important in linking sexual arousal to deviant fantasy: 1) parental modeling of deviant behavior in blatant or attenuated fashion, 2) repeated associations between the modeled deviant behavior and a strong positive affective response from the child, and 3) reinforcement of the child's deviant response. While it is unlikely that the translation of the fantasy into reality conforms precisely to a classical conditioning model, it does appear that the more the fantasy is rehearsed, the more power it acquires and the stronger the association between the fantasy content and sexual arousal. Indeed, the selective reinforcement of deviant fantasies through paired association with masturbation over a protracted period may help to explain not only the power of the fantasies but why they are so refractory to extinction (20).

Since it is commonly accepted that "normal" people often have sexually deviant fantasies (21), merely having a sadistic and/or homicidal fantasy does not mean that the fantasy will be acted out (22). In fact, fantasy may function as a substitute for behavior. Kaplan (23) has argued, for instance, that sadistic fantasies in healthy individuals may serve the purpose of discharging anger. According to Kaplan, sex and aggression are incompatible affects. The fantasy temporarily discharges the anger, thereby permitting the expression of sexual feelings. The critical question regarding the role of fantasy is What are the disinhibitory factors that encourage the translation of symbolic activity (e.g., the paraphilias) or cognitive activity (e.g., fantasies) into reality?

We found in this study that the serial murderers evidenced a higher frequency of paraphilias than the single murderers. This is entirely consistent with the greater prevalence of violent fantasy in the serial murderers. Not only does paraphilia suggest a preference for fantasy, but the paraphiliac may be seen as something of a fantasy-stimulus collector who seeks out secret experiences to add to his or her private, internal world of fantasy. Thus, acts such as peeping or exhibitionism serve to cultivate new secret experiences, which not only activate fantasy but provide the incentive (or motive) for playing out the fantasy. As Money (24) commented, "The paraphiliac's ideal is to be able to stage his/her erotic fantasy so as to perceive it as an actual experience."

It is interesting that of the five paraphilias we examined, the two with the largest intergroup differences—fetishism and cross-dressing—are also the ones that represent the enactment of some aspect of the fantasy life. Moreover, there is some evidence that fetishism and transvestism are more often associated with sexual aggression than other paraphilias. Wilson and Gosselin (25) studied a large number of fetishists, sadomasochists, transvestites/transsexuals, and normal control subjects and found that 88% of the fetishists also engaged in either sadomasochism or transvestism. More to the point is the study by Langevin et al. (26), who concluded that sadomasochistic fantasies in conjunction with a high degree of force may be premonitory signs of extreme dangerousness, including sexual murder. Langevin and his colleagues noted elsewhere (27) that not only is transvestism associated with other paraphilias but it "may go hand in hand with violent sexuality."

When the paraphilia is sexual homicide, the experience of the act—obtaining the victim, performing ritualistic acts, engaging the victim sexually either before or after death, killing the victim, disposing of the body, eluding detection, and following the police investigation in the media—provides a compelling motive for repetition (5). To the extent to which these components of the crime are contemplated and thought through beforehand, some element of fantasy must be involved. Indeed, evidence of forethought in the planning and/or execution of the crime is highly associated with degree of organization (15). Consistent with our prediction, the percentage of organized murders was almost three times as high in the group of serial murderers as in the single murderers.

On the other hand, the finding of no intergroup difference in planning is entirely inconsistent with our prediction. A scrutiny of the planning variable revealed several problems. The first was a failure to clearly distinguish between the planning of the offense in general and the planning of the actual murder. For the 10 single murderers who came from the Massachusetts Treatment Center, planning referred to the offense. Thus, for a number of single murderers the offense was coded as planned, but the murder itself appeared to have been unplanned (i.e., it resulted from an accident or lethal force used to subdue the victim). In addition, we were comparing the only murder committed by a single murderer with the first homicide committed by a serial murderer. In the cases of several serial murderers, the evidence for planning became clearer in subsequent homicides. Since those crimes were not considered, the cases were classified as "not planned."

These preliminary findings, based on a small sample of offenders, provide tentative support for the hypothesis that fantasy life may be importantly related to repeated acts of sexual violence. The potential utility of such a finding, if supported by follow-up studies with larger samples, lies primarily in the area of secondary intervention. Greater sensitivity to various behavioral manifestations of "high-risk fantasy" (e.g., certain paraphilias in conjunction with other critical factors, a history of explicit cruelty to animals, the playing out of sadistic fantasies in subviolent, presumably consenting relationships) may increase the accuracy of forecasting subsequent violence. In some cases of homicide investigation, recognizing the importance of fantasy in initiating and staging some murders has facilitated apprehension (15). Even greater than the potential benefits in crime scene investigation may be the contribution to the beleaguered efforts at clinical prediction of dangerousness. Since it is unlikely that violent behavior will decrease markedly, predictive neutrality is not a viable option. Thus, any assistance in identifying potentially homicidal people before they have murdered—or murder again—has enormous practical importance. One crucial task will be to answer the question of what leads an individual to translate a fantasy into reality. Of all those who harbor sadistic fantasies, only a small (unknown) fraction attempt to play out their fantasies. The presence of fantasy alone is a relatively poor harbinger of future conduct. Consequently, it is essential to scrutinize manifest behaviors that increase the probability of enacting fantasies.

REFERENCES

1. Busch KA, Cavanaugh JL: The study of multiple murder: preliminary examination of the interface between epistemology and methodology. J Interpersonal Violence 1986; 1:5–23
2. Revitch E: Sex murder and sex aggression. Med Soc New Jersey 1957; 54:519–523
3. Swigert VL, Farrell RA, Yoels WC: Sexual homicide: social, psychological, and legal aspects. Arch Sex Behav 1976; 5:391–401
4. Ressler RK, Burgess AW, Douglas JE, et al: Sexual killers and their victims: identifying patterns through crime scene analysis. J Interpersonal Violence 1986; 1:288–308
5. Burgess AW, Hartman CR, Ressler RK, et al: Sexual homicide: a motivational model. J Interpersonal Violence 1986; 1:251–272
6. Douglas JE, Ressler RK, Burgess AW, et al: Criminal profiling from crime scene analysis. Behavioral Sciences and the Law 1986; 41:401–421
7. Wolfgang ME, Ferracuti F: The Subculture of Violence. Beverly Hills, Calif, Sage Publications, 1967
8. Brittain RP: The sadistic murderer. Med Sci Law 1970; 10:198–207
9. Revitch E: Sex murder and the potential sex murderer. Dis Nerv Syst 1965; 26:640–648
10. MacCulloch MJ, Snowden PR, Wood PJW, et al: Sadistic fantasy, sadistic behaviour and offending. Br J Psychiatry 1983; 143:20–29
11. Abel GG, Barlow DH, Blanchard EB, et al: The components of rapists' sexual arousal. Arch Gen Psychiatry 1977; 34:895–903
12. Abel GG, Becker JV, Blanchard EB: Differentiating sexual aggressives with penile measures. Criminal Justice and Behavior 1978; 5:315–332
13. Quinsey VL, Chaplin TC: Penile responses to nonsexual violence among rapists. Criminal Justice and Behavior 1982; 9:372–381
14. Abel GG, Blanchard EB: The role of fantasy in the treatment of sexual deviation. Arch Gen Psychiatry 1974; 30:467–475
15. Ressler RK, Burgess AW: Violent crime. FBI Law Enforcement Bull 1985; 54:18–25
16. Ressler RK, Burgess AW, Douglas JE: Sexual Homicide: Patterns and Motives. Lexington, Mass, Lexington Books, 1988
17. Gardner H: The Mind's New Science. New York, Basic Books, 1985
18. Singer JL: Daydreaming. New York, Random House, 1966
19. Kendall M, Stuart A: The Advanced Theory of Statistics, vol 2. New York, Macmillan, 1979
20. Bandura A: Principles of Behavior Modification. New York, Holt, Rinehart & Winston, 1969
21. Crepault C, Couture M: Men's erotic fantasies. Arch Sex Behav 1980; 9:565–581
22. Schlesinger LB, Revitch E: Sexual Dynamics of Antisocial Behavior. Springfield, Ill, Charles C Thomas, 1983
23. Kaplan HS: Disorders of Sexual Desire. New York, Simon & Schuster, 1979
24. Money J: Love and Love Sickness. Baltimore, Johns Hopkins University Press, 1980
25. Wilson D, Gosselin C: Personality characteristics of fetishists, transvestites and sadomasochists. Personality and Individual Differences 1980; 1:289–295
26. Langevin R, Paitich D, Russon AE: Are rapists sexually anomalous, aggressive, or both? in Erotic Preference, Gender Identity, and Aggression in Men: New Research Studies. Edited by Langevin R. Hillsdale, NJ, Lawrence Erlbaum Associates, 1985
27. Steiner BW, Sanders RM, Langevin R: Crossdressing, erotic preference, and aggression: a comparison of male transvestites and transsexuals. Ibid

Name Index